*Essentials of*

# CHILDREN'S LITERATURE

*Essentials of*

# CHILDREN'S LITERATURE

Fourth Edition

## CARL M. TOMLINSON
*Northern Illinois University*

## CAROL LYNCH-BROWN
*Florida State University*

## ALLYN AND BACON

*Boston • London • Toronto • Sydney • Tokyo • Singapore*

Editor: *Aurora Martinez*
Editorial Assistant: *Beth Slater*
Marketing Manager: *Brad Parkins*
Manufacturing Buyer: *Megan Cochran*
Editorial–Production Services: *P. M. Gordon Associates, Inc.*
Production Administrator: *Deborah Brown*
Cover Administrator: *Linda Knowles*
Electronic Composition: *Omegatype Typography, Inc.*

Copyright © 2002, 1999, 1996, 1993 by Allyn & Bacon
A Pearson Education Company
75 Arlington Street
Boston, MA 02116

Internet: www.ablongman.com

LIBRARY OF CONGRESS CATALOGING-IN-PUBLICATION DATA

Tomlinson, Carl M.
    Essentials of children's literature / Carl M. Tomlinson, Carol Lynch-Brown.—4th ed.
      p.  cm.
    Rev. ed. of: Essentials of children's literature / Carol Lynch-Brown. 3rd. 1999.
    Includes bibliographical references and index.
    ISBN 0-205-33593-4
    1. Children's literature—Study and teaching (Higher)  2. Children's literature—History and criticism.  3. Children and literature.  4. Children's literature—Bibliography.  I. Lynch-Brown, Carol.  II. Lynch-Brown, Carol. Essentials of children's literature.  III. Title.
PN1009.A1 L96 2001
809'.89282'0711—dc21

2001033549

Printed in the United States of America
10  9  8  7  6  5  4  3  2  1     05  04  03  02  01

The cover illustration by Vera B. Williams, from the *Welcome to Your Library* poster, part of the The Children's Book Council's "Welcome to Your Library Poster Set," was reprinted by permission of the artist and The Children's Book Council, a nonprofit trade association encouraging the use and enjoyment of books and related literacy materials for young people. Information on the CBC and its programs, including National Children's Book Week materials, can be obtained from its web site: www.cbcbooks.org or through its headquarters: CBC, 12 West 37th Street, 2nd Floor, New York, NY 10018-7480, 212-966-1990.

*To June (C.M.T.)*
*To my grandson, Logan Brown (C.L.-B.)*

# Contents

PART TWO    CATEGORIES OF LITERATURE

## 4    Picture Books               72

## 5    Traditional Literature               97

# PREFACE

$E$ssentials of Children's Literature is a straightforward presentation on literature and sharing literature with children. This textbook is tailored to the beginning survey course in children's literature and is suitable as the literature text in an integrated language arts course. The full collaboration between the two authors has continued. We have shared in all decisions and revisions.

## OVERVIEW

### Part One: Children and Literature

The two chapters in Part One cover the introductory material students need in order to begin selecting, reading, and evaluating children's trade books. Chapter 1 defines children's literature, discusses its values, and provides research evidence supporting its use with children. Concepts about literature, elements of fiction, visual elements, and aspects of book format are treated extensively in Chapter 2. We mention well-known books as examples, when needed, but avoid lengthy reviews. We believe that instructors and their students can conduct in-depth booktalks within the context of their college courses. A facts-only approach is taken in all chapters.

### Part Two: Categories of Literature

Each of the eight chapters in Part Two defines and describes a specific category and discusses the types of books that fall within that category. Following the narrative is a list of notable authors (poets, illustrators, compilers, and so forth) in the category. Within each chapter are two lists: recommended read-aloud books within the category, and recommended books for students' use in selecting books to read within the category. These eight chapters include more than 2,000 recommended titles in end-of-chapter lists.

Chapter 3 presents the history and current status of poetry and plays; Chapter 4 focuses on picture books of all types and genres; Chapter 5 gives information about traditional fantasy from myths to folktales; and Chapter 6 deals with types of modern fantasy. Chapter 7 is devoted to realistic fiction; and since historical fiction is such an important subgenre of realistic fiction, it is treated separately in Chapter 8. Nonfiction and biography are explained in Chapter 9; and Chapter 10 treats the important topics of multicultural and international literature. It should be noted that multicultural and international books are included throughout this textbook. Some might argue that a separate chapter for multicultural literature reinforces the segregation that persists between cultures today. Our aim in providing a focus chapter for multicultural literature is to make this literature more visible (and easier to find and use) in a society where, until recently, it was all but nonexistent. Chapter 10 features the history and current status of multicultural and international literature in the children's book field and highlights notable writers and artists of this body of literature.

### Part Three: Literature in the School

The last two chapters focus on curriculum and teaching strategies. Step-by-step instructions are given for building and setting up a classroom library and library corner, producing a creative drama based on a book, conducting booktalks, and selecting and directing choral poetry. Also discussed are the "basalization" of literature, the literary canon, the efficacy of written book reports, students' First Amendment rights, and strategies for dealing with would-be censors.

### Appendices

Award lists, professional resources, children's magazines, short story collections, and transitional books can be found in the appendices. We indicate genre, type, or topic of the books in the Newbery and Caldecott Medal lists to assist students who may be seeking books of a particular type, topic, or genre for their free-choice readings or for their projects and term papers. Professional sources for the study of literature and pedagogy are included in Appendix B. Histories of children's literature that served as references for the development of the historical overview sections are also included in that appendix. Appendix C features magazines for children from preschool to middle grades. This important classroom resource is organized by content area and provides addresses for subscriptions. Short stories, a valuable, yet often neglected genre, are highlighted in Appendix D with recommended short story collections for reading aloud and for class study. Appendix E highlights transitional books, suitable for readers ages six through nine.

## P E D A G O G Y

We believe that the primary focus of a beginning survey course in children's literature should be reading children's trade books, not reading an exhaustive textbook about children's books. Students need direct experience with these trade books—reading them, reading them aloud to others, writing about them, comparing them, criticizing them, evaluating them, applying them to their own lives, and thinking about using them with their future students.

*Essentials of Children's Literature* provides a fuller treatment of literature than is typically found in language arts textbooks and can be an excellent choice for a second textbook. The book's relative brevity, its affordability, and its comprehensive coverage of content lend themselves to this use as a second textbook in a language arts or reading course.

One of our goals is to awaken students to the joy of reading. At the same time, the body of knowledge about literature and about teaching literature to children can be conveyed most efficiently through a textbook, freeing class time for involvement with literature. *Essentials of Children's Litera-*

*ture* presents this body of knowledge in a concise, direct narrative using brief lists, examples, figures, and tables in combination with prose.

## Notable Features of the Fourth Edition

- Expansion of Chapter 3 to include the important but often neglected genre of plays
- Addition of a new end-of-chapter book list, Bilingual Literature, in Chapter 10
- Discussion of the issue of censorship in the more positive terms of the First Amendment rights of children
- Author–title index of children's books (including award books in Appendix A)
- Suggested read-aloud list for each genre
- Updated and streamlined end-of-chapter book lists. Includes more than 2,000 recommended book titles for students, categorized by genres and subgenres with age levels noted
- Extensive coverage of children's book awards from the United States, Canada, Great Britain, Australia, and New Zealand
- Caldecott and Newbery books annotated for genre and age level to help students in selection
- Updated appendices and one new appendix on transitional books
- A thorough integration of multicultural and international children's literature as well as a separate chapter on these topics
- Introductory poems for each chapter to highlight the importance of introducing and sharing poetry throughout the school year
- Emphasis on the importance of cooperation between teachers and school and public librarians in fostering children's love of books

## ACKNOWLEDGMENTS

For their generous help, good advice, and valued opinions concerning this revision of *Essentials of Children's Literature*, we wish to express our appreciation to the following people:

Colleagues Donald Richgels, Chris Carger, and Rebecca Butler, Northern Illinois University, and Eliza Dresang, Marsha Gontarski, and Judith Irvin, Florida State University, for their wise counsel.

Our graduate students Victoria Van Cleave, Mary Costello, Judith Hughes, Lorayne Johansen, Laray Kelly, Carol Rine, and Christy Williams for their enthusiasm and innovations in teaching children's literature courses; our students Courtenay Bolger, Jonathon Damon, Dawn Lastinger, Robyn Maxey, and Rachel Quandt for their help in organizing and maintaining our children's literature collections; and Marie Sørensen for her assistance in reviewing books.

The librarians and children's literature consultants who helped us to locate information and books and were always willing to discuss books with us: Aimee Reist, Goldstein Library of Florida State University; Carole Fiore, State of Florida Library; Sharon Hartman, children's literature consultant, Tallahassee, Florida; Charles Larry, Founders Memorial Library of Northern Illinois University; and the children's librarians and staffs at the DeKalb Public Library, the Leon County Public Library, and the Bay County Public Library.

Maureen Grosvenor for her assistance in seeking permissions.

Merilee Miller, Publisher, Anchorage Press Plays; Lawrence Harbison, Editor, Samuel French, Inc.; Elisabeth Preston, Editor, *Plays, the Drama Magazine for Children;* Chris Angermann, Editor, Eldridge Publishing; Moses Goldberg, Producing Director, Stage One: Louisville's Children's Theatre; Liliane Heil, *Children's Book and Play Review;* Christy M. Taylor, Administrator, American Alliance for Theater and Education; Maureen Grosvenor, research assistant; and especially, Harold R. Oaks, Professor, Department of Theatre and Media Arts, Brigham Young University, for their assistance with information about the field of theatre for young audiences, publishers, and current plays.

The reviewers of the fourth edition: Joyce Hamon, University of Southern Indiana; Angela Place, University of Kansas; and Gail Yunk, Lorcas College.

The reviewers of the third edition: Rebecca S. Compton, East Central University; Gwendolyn Davis, University of Northern Colorado at Greensboro; Elizabeth A. Katos, University of Akron; and Geri Langman, Alverno College.

The reviewers of the second edition: Marilyn A. Greer, Mt. Vernon Nazarene College; and Margot C. Papworth, Cazenovia College–NY.

The reviewers of the first edition: Joanne E. Bernstein, Brookyn College; Carol J. Fox, Illinois State Library; M. Jean Greenlaw, University of North Texas; Judith Hakes, Angelo State University; John Hemphill, Greensboro College; Julie M. Jensen, University of Texas at Austin; Barbara Kiefer, Columbia University; Sam Perez, Western Washington University; Masha Rudman, University of Massachusetts at Amherst; Rosemary Salesi, University of Maine; and Donna Wiseman, Texas A & M University.

We are indebted to Vera B. Williams for the splendid cover for this edition of *Essentials of Children's Literature.* In her picture storybooks, Williams imbues her characters with all of the best traits we want to associate with children the world over—curiosity, joy, and the capacity to love and learn. The cover captures these traits and projects the overall message that reading and sharing good books is a joyous, rewarding enterprise.

A manual for this textbook is available to course instructors from the publisher by written request. Mail this request on letterhead to Allyn & Bacon, 75 Arlington Street, Boston, MA 02116.

## ABOUT THE AUTHORS

**Carl M. Tomlinson** is Professor of Language Arts and Children's Literature in the Department of Literacy Education at Northern Illinois University, where he has taught a variety of undergraduate and graduate courses for pre- and in-service teachers. After receiving a B.A. in Political Science, History, and Languages from Stetson University in DeLand, Florida, Dr. Tomlinson studied humanities and music in Lillehammer and Oslo, Norway, and taught for many years in the intermediate and middle grades before receiving his Ph.D. in Children's Literature and Reading from Florida State University.

Dr. Tomlinson was a founding member of Illinois's Rebecca Caudill Young Readers Book Award program and has served as a member of National Council of Teachers of English's Notable Books in the

Language Arts Committee and as treasurer of NCTE's Children's Literature Assembly. He was U.S. Associate Editor of *Bookbird: The Journal of International Children's Literature* from 1990 to 1995. He served as president of the United States Board of Books for Young People (USBBY) in 1999. He is editor of *Children's Books from Other Countries* (USBBY and Scarecrow Press, 1998), was a member of the Batchelder Award Committee in 2000, and has published articles in numberous journals including *The Reading Teacher, Middle School Journal, The New Advocate, The Journal of Children's Literature, Book Links,* and *Peabody Journal of Education.*

**Carol Lynch-Brown** is Professor of Reading and Language Arts and Elementary Education at Florida State University, where she teaches graduate and undergraduate courses in children's and young adult literature, reading, and language arts education. She received her B.A. degree in French Language and Literature and Elementary Education from the College of Saint Catherine in St. Paul, Minnesota, and received her M.A. degree in French from the University of Minnesota. She took additional graduate study at the Université de Caen and the Université de Nantes in France while teaching English in French public schools. She taught primary, intermediate, and middle grades for several years in the St. Paul and Minneapolis public schools before pursuing a Ph.D. in Early and Middle Childhood Education at The Ohio State University.

Dr. Lynch-Brown has been a board member of the Florida Reading Association (FRA), where she served as legislative chair and member of the FRA Book Award Committee. In 1997, she was a member of the Batchelder Award Committee of the American Library Association. She served as Southeast Regional Coordinator of the International Reading Association's Teachers' Choices Project and is past chair of IRA's Teachers' Choices Project. She co-authored the book *Enhancing Social Studies through Literacy Strategies,* published by the National Council for the Social Studies, and has published articles in numerous journals including *The Reading Teacher, Middle School Journal, The New Advocate,* and *Peabody Journal of Education.* She is currently serving as co-editor of *The Reading Teacher.*

# LEARNING *about* CHILDREN *and* THEIR LITERATURE

## BOOKS FALL OPEN

*Books fall open
you fall in,
delighted where
you've never been;
hear voices once
heard before,
reach world on world
through door on door;
find unexpected
keys to things
locked up beyond
imaginings.
What might you be,
perhaps become,*

*because one book
is somewhere? Some
wise delver into
wisdom, wit,
and wherewithal
has written it.
True books will venture,
dare you out,
whisper secrets,
maybe shout
across the glow
to you in need,
who hanker for
a book to read.*

—DAVID MCCORD

A child leans forward, head cupped in hands, eyes wide with anticipation, listening to a story: This is an image for all time. Whether that child is seated beside an open fire in the Stone Ages, on a rough bench in a medieval fairground, or in a modern-day classroom, the message of the image is the same: Children love a good story.

# DEFINITION OF CHILDREN'S LITERATURE

This book is written about literature for children from infancy to adolescence, for you who will be meeting and working with these children as teachers, librarians, and parents. In these roles, your opportunities to lead children to literature will be unparalleled, if you have the prerequisite knowledge.

*Children's literature* is good-quality trade books for children from birth to adolescence, covering topics of relevance and interest to children of those ages, through prose and poetry, fiction and nonfiction. This definition contains several key concepts that will be explained in the following sections. Understanding these concepts will help you find your way around the more than 180,000 children's titles currently in print (*Children's Books in Print,* 2000), the more than 8,000 new children's titles being published annually in the United States (*Bowker Annual: Library and Book Trade Almanac,* [Bogart, 2000]), as well as the additional thousands of children's books published worldwide each year in English.

## Content

Children's books are about the experiences of childhood, both good and bad. Whether these experiences are set in the past, present, or future, they should still be relevant to the child of today. Enjoying birthday parties, losing a tooth for the first time, anticipating adulthood, camping out and telling ghost stories, getting a new pet, enduring siblings, and dealing with family situations are experiences common to children today. The content of children's books also includes the amazingly diverse topics that are of interest to children, such as dinosaurs, Egyptian mummies, world records, and fighter planes.

The manner in which content is treated also helps to define children's books. Childhood stories told in a forthright, humorous, or suspenseful manner are appropriate for young readers; stories *about* childhood told in nostalgic or overly sentimental terms are inappropriate. Likewise, when stories show children as victims of natural and human-made disasters, the stories should emphasize the hope for a better future rather than the hopelessness and utter despair of the moment.

The subject matter of children's literature can be expressed in prose or poetry. If the literary work is prose, it must be presented as fiction (a product of the imagination, an invented story), nonfiction (factual), or a combination of the two.

Teachers and librarians distinguish between the terms *textbook* and *trade book.* A *textbook,* by design and content, is for the purpose of instruction. The basal reader used in many classrooms for reading instruction is an example of a textbook. In contrast, a *trade book,* by design and content, is primarily for the purposes of entertainment and information. Trade books are often referred to as *library books* and *storybooks.* The books that we will be discussing in this text will be trade books, not textbooks.

## Quality

Not all trade books aimed at young readers are worth attention. Books ranging in quality from excellent to poor are now readily available to parents, teachers, and children through bookstores and libraries. Look around and you will see racks of children's books in department stores, drugstores, and even grocery stores. But the question is: Are they *good* children's books?

*Quality in writing* is never easy to define, but it has to do with originality and importance of ideas, imaginative use of language, and beauty of literary and artistic style that enable a work to remain fresh, interesting, and meaningful for years and years. These books have permanent value.

This is not to say that books of good-but-not-great quality have no value. Children have enjoyed fast-moving, adventure-filled, easily predictable stories from the so-called chapbooks of the seventeenth and eighteenth centuries to the serial adventures of the Hardy Boys, Nancy Drew, the Babysitters Club, and the Animorphs of more recent times. These works have won no literary prizes, but many young readers enjoy them; and because books such as these encourage newly independent readers to read more, they have worth. However, you will probably not want to select books of this calibre to read aloud to your students. Why deprive them of the pleasure of reading such easy and enjoyable books independently? If children's entire literary experience were limited to serial adventures and other books of trendy but passing interest, they would miss much of the wonder of the natural world and the human experience. The best children's books offer readers enjoyment as well as memorable characters and situations and valuable insights into the human condition.

Many so-called children's books today are actually nothing more than advertisements for film and television characters and associated products, such as candy, clothing, and toys. These books represent the low end of the quality spectrum.

## THE PERSONAL VALUE OF LITERATURE TO CHILDREN

Literature for children leads to personal fulfillment and academic gains. Separating the values into personal and academic is an intellectual distinction, since both types benefit the child and are all proper parts of a child's schooling. The distinction is useful, however, since teachers and librarians must often justify the benefits of literature in the classroom and find the academic benefits the most convincing ones for administrators and parents.

### Enjoyment

The most important personal gain that good books offer to children is the most obvious one—enjoyment. Those of you who read widely as children will never forget the stories that were so funny that you laughed out loud, the poem that was so lilting that you never forgot it, or the mystery that was so scary that your heart thumped with apprehension. Such positive early experiences often lead to a lifetime of reading enjoyment.

### Imagination and Inspiration

By seeing the world around them in new ways and by considering ways of living other than their own, children increase their ability to think divergently. Stories often map the divergent paths that our ancestors might have taken or that our descendants might someday take. Through the vicarious experience of entering a different world from the present one, children develop their imaginations. In addition, stories about people, both real and imaginary, can inspire children to overcome obstacles, accept different perspectives, and formulate personal goals.

## *Vicarious Experience*

When a story is so convincingly written that readers feel as though they have lived through an experience or have actually been in the place and time where the story is set, the book has given them a *vicarious* experience. Experiences such as these are broadening for children because they, as readers, are taken to places and times that they could never actually visit—and might not want to! A vicarious experience can also be a good mental exercise for children, since they are asked to view situations from perspectives other than their own.

## *Understanding and Empathy*

Literature helps young people to gain an appreciation of the universality of human needs across history, which makes it possible for them to understand that all humans are, to some degree, alike. By introducing children to stories from many lands and cultures, teachers and librarians are building a solid foundation for multicultural and international understanding. Walking in someone else's shoes often helps children to develop a greater capacity to empathize with others. Children around the world can benefit from stories that explain what life is like for people who are restricted by disabilities, politics, or circumstance or whose lives are different from theirs because of culture or geography. Likewise, young readers of today can relate on a more personal level with the events and people of history.

## *Heritage*

Stories that are handed down from one generation to the next connect us to our past, to the roots of our specific cultures, national heritage, and general human condition. Stories are the repositories of culture. Knowing the tales, characters, expressions, and adages that are part of our cultural heritage is part of being culturally literate. In addition, stories based on actual events in the past help young people to gain a greater appreciation for what history is and for the people, both ordinary and extraordinary, who made history.

## *Moral Reasoning*

Often, story characters are placed in situations that require them to make moral decisions. Young readers naturally consider what they themselves would do in such a situation. As the story unfolds and the character's decision and the consequences of that choice are disclosed, readers discover whether their own decisions would have had positive outcomes. Regular experience with these types of stories can help young people to formulate their own concepts of right and wrong.

## *Literary and Artistic Preferences*

Another valuable result of children interacting with literature is that they quickly come to recognize the literary and artistic styles of many authors and illustrators. This is an important first step to literary awareness—that is, to recognize that the style of one writer or illustrator differs from another and that a piece of writing or an illustration has personal appeal. Children who read regularly from a wide variety of children's books soon develop their own personal preferences for types of books and select favorite authors and illustrators. Good teachers and librarians have long recognized that personal preference and interest as expressed through self-selection of reading materials are powerful reading motivators. They also know that the more children read and the greater the variety of literature they read, the more discerning readers they become.

The more children know about their world, the more they discover about themselves—who they are, what they value, and what they stand for. These personal insights alone are sufficient to warrant making good books an essential part of any child's home and school experiences. But literature is also valuable for its academic benefits, as will be discussed in the following section.

# THE ACADEMIC VALUE OF LITERATURE TO CHILDREN

In addition to the personal benefits of literature for young readers, there are several important academic benefits.

## Reading

Many of you already may have reached the common-sense deduction that reading ability, like any other skill, improves with practice. Many teachers and librarians believe that regular involvement with excellent and appropriate literature can foster language development in young children and can help them to learn to read and to value reading. This belief was supported in the landmark study *Becoming a Nation of Readers* (Anderson, Hiebert, Scott, & Wilkinson, 1985), which concludes, "The single most important activity for building the knowledge required for eventual success in reading is reading aloud to children" (p. 23). As educators, you should know some of the landmark research studies that have confirmed these beliefs and that have revealed other important findings about the worth of literature for children. Table 1.1 summarizes these studies and their findings.

Table 1.1 shows that in teaching children to read, two procedures seem especially important: reading excellent literature aloud to children and silent independent reading of free-choice material by children, both on a daily basis, if possible. To discover another truth, you must read between the lines of the table. Who makes the books available? Who decides to read aloud to the children? Who makes the first decisions about what to read aloud? Who makes a child's first experiences with literature enjoyable? Who makes the experiences interactive by asking thought-provoking questions? The truth is that there must first be someone, more than likely an adult, who has the knowledge, willingness, and patience to guide children to books. Who will this be? For some children, it will be their parents; for many others, it will be you—their teacher or librarian.

## Writing

Since people tend to assimilate or adopt what they like of what they read and hear, children may, by listening to and reading literature, begin to develop their own writing "voice," or unique, personal writing style. By listening to and reading excellent literature, children are exposed to rich vocabulary and excellent writing styles, which serve as good models for their own speaking and writing voices. The acquisition of a larger vocabulary through reading offers young writers a better word choice for their own stories. Devices found in books such as the use of dialect, dialogue, and precise description are often assimilated into students' own writing.

TABLE 1.1   Important Studies on Literature and Literacy

| Researcher(s) | Subjects | Findings |
| --- | --- | --- |
| *Reading* | | |
| Butler (1975) | Cushla, from ages 4 months to 3 years | Reading aloud from children's picture books to a severely disabled child from age 4 months enabled the child to learn to read. |
| Durkin (1966) | Children who learned to read before attending school | Children who learned to read before attending school were read to regularly from the age of 3. Early reading and early writing are often linked. |
| Cohen (1968) | 7-year-olds | Reading to children who have not been previously exposed to literature can help them learn to read. |
| Eldredge and Butterfield (1986) | 1,149 beginning readers in 50 classrooms | Use of children's literature to teach reading has a much greater positive effect on students' achievement and attitudes toward reading than does use of basals with traditional homogeneous grouping. |
| Anderson (1996) | Elementary-grade children | Even slight increases (10 minutes a day) in time spent reading independently lead to gains in reading achievement. Amount of free reading in early grades helps determine reading ability in grades 5 and 6. |
| Applebee (1978) | Children ages 2 to 17 | Children's sense of story grows as they mature. Literature has a positive effect on children's language development. |
| Carlsen and Sherrill (1988) | College students who were committed readers | Conditions that promote a love of reading include:<br>    Freedom of choice in reading material<br>    Availability of books and magazines<br>    Family members who read aloud<br>    Adults and peers who model reading<br>    Role models who value reading<br>    Sharing and discussing books<br>    Owning books<br>    Availability of libraries and librarians |
| *Writing* | | |
| McConaghy (1990) | First-graders in a literature-based reading and writing program | Children use in their own writing the literary conventions and forms they encounter in literature. |
| DeFord (1981) | First-graders in phonics-, skills-, and literature-based reading classes | Children in literature-based reading classrooms tend to produce a wider variety of written forms and better written stories than children in phonics or skills-based reading classes. |

TABLE 1.2    Major U.S., Canadian, and British Children's Book Awards

| Award/Country | Period | For/Year Established |
|---|---|---|
| Newbery Medal/United States | Annual | The most distinguished contribution to children's literature published in the previous year. Given to a U.S. author. Established 1922. |
| Caldecott Medal/United States | Annual | The most distinguished picture book for children published in the previous year. Given to a U.S. illustrator. Established 1938. |
| Laura Ingalls Wilder Award/ United States | Every 3 years | Lifetime work that has made a substantial and lasting contribution to children's literature. Given to a U.S. author or illustrator. Established 1954. |
| Mildred L. Batchelder Award/ United States | Annual | The most distinguished translated work for children published in the previous year. Given to a U.S. publisher. Established 1968. |
| Canadian Children's Book of the Year Award/Canada | Annual | The most distinguished contribution to children's literature by a Canadian published in the previous year. Established 1947. Also the most distinguished children's book published in French. Established 1954. |
| Amelia Frances Howard-Gibbon Medal/Canada | Annual | The most distinguished picture book for children published in the previous year. Given to a Canadian illustrator. Established 1971. |
| Carnegie Medal/Great Britain | Annual | The most distinguished contribution to children's literature first published in the United Kingdom in the previous year. Given to an author. Established 1936. |
| Kate Greenaway Medal/ Great Britain | Annual | The most distinguished picture book for children first published in the United Kingdom in the previous year. Given to an illustrator. Established 1956. |
| Hans Christian Andersen Award/ International | Every 2 years | Recognition of an entire body of work. Given to an author and an illustrator. Established 1956. |

In cooperation with various national teaching associations, The Children's Book Council (CBC) publishes annual, annotated lists of the best trade books to supplement content area subjects in grades K–8. Two excellent lists of this kind are Outstanding Science Trade Books for Children (published in cooperation with the National Science Teachers Association) and Notable Children's Trade Books in the Field of Social Studies (published in cooperation with the National Council for the Social Studies).

Extensive lists or bibliographies, often annotated, of both older and newer books are valuable aids in book selection. These are usually organized around subject headings and can be remarkably helpful and efficient when you are developing units of study and topical reading lists for students or when you are seeking read-aloud literature about a specific subject. Some of the most helpful bibliographic sources are the following:

*A to Zoo: Subject Access to Children's Picture Books,* 6th ed. (Lima & Lima, 2001)

*Adventuring with Books: A Booklist for Pre-K–Grade 6,* 12th ed. (Pierce, 2000)

*The Elementary School Library Collection: A Guide to Books and Other Media,* 22nd ed. (Homa, Schreck, & Hoebener, 2000)

*Selecting Books for the Elementary School Library Media Center: A Complete Guide* (Van Orden, 2000)

## LITERATURE FOR THE DEVELOPING CHILD

In this section we will discuss types of books and general topics most likely to be appreciated by children of different age levels. Children's physical, cognitive, language, and moral development are important considerations in book selection, as is their developing concept of story. By overlaying this general information with the specific interests of any child, you can recognize and make available literature that the children in your care will read with interest and enjoyment.

### Ages 0 to 2

Infants can enjoy and benefit from good literature. In choosing books for them, we must consider such practical aspects of physical development as how well they can see the illustrations and how long they will sit still for a book experience. For instance, books chosen for babies to hold and look at by themselves should feature clearly defined, brightly colored pictures, usually placed on a plain background. Most often, these books will be brief, plotless, idea books called *concept books,* and they will concern the everyday routines and familiar objects that fill the infants' lives. These books are often constructed of heavy, nontoxic cardboard and are called *board books.* Classic examples are *Dressing* by Helen Oxenbury (1981) and *What Is It?* by Tana Hoban (1985).

Since babies have a strong, positive reaction to any exaggerated patterns in sound or movement, the natural music created by strong rhymes and rhythms in *nursery rhymes,* as well as the brevity and humor of these verses, make them appropriate read-aloud material for children at this age level. For example, see *Here Comes Mother Goose* edited by Iona Opie and illustrated by Rosemary Wells (1999).

To take advantage of the primacy of the senses and muscular coordination in early learning, you will want to use *interactive books* with children from birth to age 2. In these books, participation (clapping, moving) or manipulation of the book (touching, opening little doors) is encouraged. Classic examples include *Pat the Bunny* by Dorothy Kunhardt (1962) and *Where's Spot?* by Eric Hill (1980).

All of the best baby books, whether wordless or with brief text, invite the reader or readers to "talk the book through." In this way the books promote oral language development, which is the child's first step toward literacy.

### Ages 2 to 4

Many aspects of the recommended books for babies apply as well to books for toddlers. Daily routines and objects familiar to the child remain good topics. For this audience, such topics can be incorporated into *picture storybooks* that feature simple plots, beautiful illustrations that tell part of the story, and interesting, humorous characters and situations. Story characters often exhibit the physical skills, such as running, buttoning and unbuttoning clothes, and locking and unlocking doors, that 2- to 4-year-olds take pride in having accomplished. These books are meant to be read aloud to the child. Shirley Hughes's *Alfie Gets in First* (1982) is a good example.

*Concept books* are excellent for children who are beginning to make sense of their world, and these concepts can now include numbers (*counting books*), letters (*ABC books*), and more complex concepts like opposites. The *illustrated dictionary* or *word book* is a type of concept book that promotes the naming and labeling of objects, actions, and people. Examples are *More, Fewer, Less* by Tana Hoban (1998) and *My First Word Book* by Angela Wilkes (1999).

Children aged 2 to 4 will enjoy nursery rhymes even more than they did as infants and will easily commit these verses to memory. *Folktales,* an important part of our literary heritage, work well with children at this age level, particularly the repetitive stories such as *Henny Penny* and *The Gingerbread Boy.* These stories and verses are also appropriate because their "good" and "bad" characters fit the 2- to 4-year-old's simplistic "right or wrong" sense of morality.

### Ages 4 to 7

Picture storybooks will still be the heart of the literature experience for children during these years. Most of these books are meant to be read aloud to children by a fluent reader, but it is common for children at this stage to choose a favorite picture storybook, memorize the text over repeated hearings, and enjoy the book on their own through "play-reading." Folktales are still a favorite for storytelling and read-aloud experiences, as are humorous poems with strong rhyme and rhythm.

During these years many children will acquire the fundamentals of reading: the notion that stories and the words within them carry meaning, the letter-sound relationship, left-to-right and top-to-bottom progression of print on the page, and a sight vocabulary (certain words that children can recognize and say on sight). *Easy-to-read books* (sometimes referred to as *books for beginning readers*) support children's enthusiasm for learning to read; these books make use of familiar words, word patterns, informative illustrations, and, in some cases, rhyme to make the text predictable. Examples are *No, David!* (1998) by David Shannon and *There Was an Old Lady Who Swallowed a Fly* by Simms Taback (1997). Physical growth and increasing independence are prominent topics in stories in which children interact with other children more than with adults, spend time away from home, and begin school. Examples are *Yo! Yes?* by Chris Raschka (1993) and *Chrysanthemum* by Kevin Henkes (1991).

Children at this age level exhibit great enthusiasm for finding out about the world and how it works. This interest can be fed and stimulated through *informational books* for the beginning reader. Examples include *A. Lincoln and Me,* written by Louise Borden and illustrated by Ted Lewin (1999), and *Red-Eyed Tree Frog* by Joy Cowley with photographs by Nic Bishop (1999).

Easy-to-read books are all heavily illustrated but vary widely in level of reading difficulty, as measured by the number and frequency of sight words, the predictability of words through pictorial or textual clues, the complexity of subject matter, and the relative importance of illustration and text on the page (Gunning, 1998). At the lower end are wordless picture books that tell straightforward stories and word or naming books in which the text is limited to brief captions. At the higher end are brief chapter books of about 250–300 words with illustrations on about every other page. It is especially important that books selected for beginning readers precisely match their interests and reading abilities, so as not to bore or dishearten them. A helpful guide to books of this type is *Beyond Picture Books: A Guide to First Readers* (Barstow & Riggle, 1995).

*Ages 7 to 9*

During these years most children who have had the benefit of a rich literature experience will become fluent and willing readers. This skill, combined with their increased flexibility in thinking, makes many new story types appropriate for these children. Now that they can understand and accept others' perspectives, they can enjoy reading about the lives of other children of the past, present, or future in *transitional readers* and later in *novels.*

Transitional readers are chapter books with simple, straightforward plots and writing styles for children who are ready to read slightly longer picture books and short chapter books, but not full-fledged novels. A helpful guide to transitional books is *Best Books for Building Literacy for Elementary School Children* (Gunning, 2000). Examples include the Ramona and Henry Huggins books by Beverly Cleary and the Julian books by Ann Cameron. At 8 or 9, children begin to assert their growing abilities to meet their own needs by doing such things as camping out in the backyard or biking to school alone. Fittingly, books for these children often center on the adventures of young characters within their neighborhoods and communities.

Chapter books with more sophisticated writing styles or more complicated plots can be greatly enjoyed as read-alouds in the classroom and as independent reading by the better readers. Also, many picture storybooks are appropriate for independent reading by children at this age level. For example, see *Hey, Al,* written by Arthur Yorinks and illustrated by Richard Egielski (1986), and *The Gardener,* written by Sarah Stewart and illustrated by David Small (1997). Story characters having both good and bad qualities and realistic problems mirror the 7- to 9-year-olds' maturing sense of morality as they begin to recognize that life and people do not fit into neat "good" and "bad" categories and that opinions different from their own may have validity. Lois Lowry's books about Sam, such as *See You Around, Sam!* (1996), are good examples.

A common phenomenon among children who are learning to read is the penchant for rereading the same book many times. Often misconstrued by adults as somehow wrong, the act of rereading the same text many times is, in fact, good reading practice made palatable to the child by the security of a familiar, or "friendly," text.

Although folktales continue to be popular with many 7-year-olds, studies have shown that interest in this genre generally peaks and falls off by age 8. Children then begin to show more interest in the here and now and begin to shift toward a preference for realism in their stories and poems.

*Ages 9 to 12*

With their rapidly developing physical and mental skills and abilities, 9- to 12-year-olds are ready for the great variety of literature that awaits them. Plots in novels can now be more complicated, including such devices as flashback and symbolism. Language devices such as speech patterns and dialects of earlier or different cultures can be managed. Both historical fiction and science fiction, which are set in the distant past and distant future, respectively, can be understood and enjoyed. Examples are *Shades of Gray* by Carolyn Reeder (1989) and *The Giver* by Lois Lowry (1993).

These children are particularly interested in reading about young people who, like themselves, are growing up, asserting and using their new-found skills, moving toward independence, and experiencing growth through meeting challenges. Survival stories, peer stories, and realistic animal stories intrigue these children. Moreover, stories that present alternative points of view, nontraditional characters, and moral dilemmas are well suited to young people whose moral development allows them to recognize the legitimacy of opinions, mores, and lifestyles different from their own. Examples include *Shiloh* by Phyllis Reynolds Naylor (1991), *The Great Gilly Hopkins* by Katherine Paterson (1978), *Nothing but the Truth* by Avi (1991), and *Wringer* by Jerry Spinelli (1997).

An interesting parallel to the 7- to 9-year-olds' tendency to reread books occurs at this age level. Many 9- to 12-year-olds discover series books, such as the Sweet Valley Twins or Matt Christopher's many sports-oriented series books, and read every book in the series, one after the other. This is rereading of a sort, since all books within such a series are written to a formula and vary only slightly one from the other. Since they are written to a formula, these series books are called *formula fiction* and appear as mysteries, fantasy and science fantasy adventures, and romances. Reading these books is beneficial to many children, simply because of the hours of reading practice they willingly gain. Two faults of the hugely successful romances such as The Babysitters Club, Sweet Valley Twins, Wild Fire, and Sweet Dreams, as pointed out by Elleman (1987), are their dependence on stereotyped female characters for whom success is too often defined in terms of popularity among boys and their almost exclusive reflection of white, middle-class, suburban life. The stereotyping of females in traditional roles is a debilitating message to convey to today's girls.

Although most 9- to 12-year-olds are competent readers, there is no valid reason for librarians or teachers to discontinue their read-aloud programs for these children. More challenging novels as well as sophisticated picture books for older children sometimes can be more fully appreciated by children when read aloud by an excellent reader. Examples include *Holes* by Louis Sachar (1998), *The Wretched Stone* by Chris Van Allsburg (1991), and *The Last Giants* by François Place (1993).

Teachers and librarians who are consistently successful in helping children find books they like rapidly narrow the field of choices by first considering general factors such as age level and types of books appropriate for children of that general age level. Then they consider more personal factors such as the child's current reading interests and reading ability to select specific titles. Knowing children's general reading preferences provides some guidance in book selection, but there is no substitute for knowing the child.

## CHILDREN'S READING PREFERENCES

A *reading preference* is a stated or implied choice between several reading options. For example, if in response to the question: Which would you rather read: a romance, a mystery, or a science fiction adventure? you choose the mystery option, you are stating a reading preference for mystery.

Many studies of children's reading preferences have been conducted. Differences in the choices offered to children and in the ways data were gathered from study to study make extensive generalization difficult, but a few patterns have emerged from these studies (Haynes, 1988):

- There are no significant differences between the preferences of boys and girls before age 9.
- The greatest differences in reading preferences of boys and girls occur between ages 10 and 13.
- Boys and girls in the middle grades (ages 10 to 13) share a pronounced preference for mystery and, to a lesser degree, humor, adventure, and animals.

- Preferences of boys in the middle grades include action and adventure stories and sports stories.
- Preferences of girls in the middle grades include fantasy stories, animal stories, and stories about people.

A teacher or librarian might use this information to make general predictions about what types of books boys or girls of a certain age might enjoy.

Reading preferences should not be the sole guide in making specific book recommendations to individuals. The reason for this should be clear when you consider the hypothetical question involving romance, mystery, and science fiction books posed earlier. Even though you had to choose one or the other of the options offered to you, it is quite possible that you rarely, if ever, read any of these types of books; mystery may have been just the least uninteresting to you of the three. Knowing this so-called preference would not benefit, and could possibly hinder, a teacher or librarian who was seeking to help you find a book that you would enjoy.

## CHILDREN'S READING INTERESTS

Reading interests and reading preferences are not the same. A *preference*, as noted above, implies a forced choice between options selected by someone other than oneself. An *interest*, on the other hand, comes from within oneself, can encompass whatever can be imagined, and implies freedom of choice. Knowledge of children's reading preferences provides information about children in general, but knowledge of children's reading interests is personal and individual. Since most teachers and school librarians work with particular groups of children over an extended time, they can learn the interests of each child within the group. In so doing, they gain powerful, effective knowledge to use in successfully matching children and books.

Common sense tells us that children will apply themselves more vigorously to read or learn something that they are interested in than they will to read or learn something that they find uninteresting or boring. Interest generates motivation, and good teachers and librarians put that motivation to work by guiding students to good books on topics that satisfy individual interests.

Learning your students' interests can be accomplished in several ways. The best way is to get to know your students by talking to them in whole-class sharing and in one-to-one conferences. All people like to talk about themselves and their interests; children are no different. One or more of the following questions might start a productive dialogue between you and a student:

1. What are your favorite things to do?
2. Are you very good at doing something? Tell me about it.
3. What would you like to learn more about?
4. What do you like to spend most of your free time doing?
5. Do you like fiction or nonfiction better?
6. What kinds of stories do you like to hear?
7. What kinds of books do you like to read?
8. Who is in your family? Tell me a little about each family member.

You can also learn about children's interests through their free-choice writing. Journal writing is particularly helpful in this regard. A perfectly valid and more direct approach is to ask children to list their interests. Many teachers keep such lists in their students' writing folders to use during individual conferences. Because children's interests change often, data of this sort must be updated regularly.

Yet another way for teachers and librarians to keep current on students' interests is to conduct their own interest inventories several times a year to assure that the reading selections available in their classrooms or school libraries reflect the general interests of their students. The following steps show one way to conduct a classroom interest inventory:

1.  Collect 30 to 40 appropriate books that are new to your students and that represent a wide variety of genres and topics.
2.  Number the books by inserting paper markers with numbers at the top.
3.  Note on a master list the number and genre of each book.
4.  Design a response form for students, such as the one shown in Figure 1.1.
5.  Hold each book up and tell your students the title, the type, and a one-sentence summary of the book. You might use the Library of Congress summary that is printed with the cataloging information on the copyright page of each book.
6.  Place the books in order on tables and shelves around the classroom or media center.
7.  Give the students 20 to 30 minutes to make the circuit, peruse the books, and mark their response forms.
8.  Collect and tally the students' responses and compare them with your master list to arrive at the types of books in which your students are currently most interested.

Classroom interest inventories not only provide teachers and librarians with helpful information about their students' current interests but also introduce children to new genres, topics, and titles. In this way, teachers and librarians can help accomplish their fundamental task of expanding students' fields of interest and knowledge bases.

Teachers and librarians are often surprised at how extensive and varied their students' interests are. Rockets and space travel? Lizards? Semitrailer trucks? When your students come to you with interests as diverse as these, expecting you to help them find books on these topics, you can, of course,

WOULD YOU LIKE TO READ THIS BOOK?

As you look at each book, answer this question by circling either YES or NO next to the appropriate book number. Be sure to match the book number and the item number before circling your answer.

| | | | | | |
|---|---|---|---|---|---|
| 1. | YES | NO | 16. | YES | NO |
| 2. | YES | NO | 17. | YES | NO |
| 3. | YES | NO | 18. | YES | NO |
| 4. | YES | NO | 19. | YES | NO |
| 5. | YES | NO | 20. | YES | NO |

Etc.

FIGURE 1.1   Sample Student Response Form for Interest Inventory send them to the card catalog or its computerized equivalent. In addition, however, you need to know about such general subject guide indexes as *Children's Catalog* (Price & Yaakov, 1996) and the annually updated *Subject Guide to Children's Books in Print,* which is a cross-referenced subject guide to all children's books listed in *Children's Books in Print.* (For more information on these resource books, see Appendix B.) There are few reference tools as helpful as a subject guide index for finding books on specific topics. On-line indexes, such as World Catalog, make searching for books by title and subject even easier.

## TRENDS IN CHILDREN'S LITERATURE

Looking at publishing and usage trends in the field of children's books over time helps to forecast future developments. Some of the following trends are heartening and deserve our support. Others are more questionable.

- A rapid increase in the publication of children's literature over the past thirty years (from 2,640 new titles in 1970 to approximately 8,300 new titles in 1999, as reported in the *Bowker Annual: Library and Book Trade Almanac* [Bogart, 2000]). A dramatic rise in the number of picture books, along with a significant increase in the number of heavily illustrated works of nonfiction and highly commercial television-related spin-offs account for much of this increase.

- Steadily increasing numbers of multicultural and international books. Our society's gradual acceptance of different voices and viewpoints, the increasing diversity of our school populations, and the rise in international co-publications (publishers in the United States and abroad sharing initial publishing costs), account for this trend.

- An increase in the amount and complexity of illustration in children's books. As illustration becomes a more dominant feature in children's books, text is becoming less dominant, particularly in picture storybooks, beginning readers, transitional books, and informational books. Readers are becoming more visually oriented as they spend more time watching television and playing video games and spend less time reading.

- Fewer full-length novels and more short, high-interest, low-reading-level novels being written for 10- to 14-year-olds; a steadily increasing market for the less challenging formula fiction series books (e.g., Goosebumps, Animorphs, The Babysitters Club, Sweet Valley Twins).

- Less variety and a lower level of literary excellence in books as established independent book publishers fall to corporate takeovers. Small-press publishers assume the task of publishing more challenging, original, "risky" books.

- Rapid growth of technology in all areas of publishing. As schools adopt computerized management reading programs such as Accelerated Reader, reading and books become less a means to enjoyment and discovering new information and more a matter of gaining points.

- Rapid increases in home schooling and charter schools that have created a need for more children's librarians in public libraries who can select good literature for purchase, advise readers effectively, and offer interesting programs for children of all ages.

- An increase in the publication of bilingual books, primarily English-Spanish, and Spanish-only books to accommodate the rapid increase in second language learner (SLL) students.

## REFERENCES

Anderson, R. C. (1996). Research foundations to support wide reading. In V. Greaney (Ed.), *Promoting reading: Views on making reading materials accessible to increase literacy levels* (pp. 55–77). Newark, DE: International Reading Association.

———, Hiebert, E. H., Scott, J. A., & Wilkinson, I. A. G. (1985). *Becoming a nation of readers: The report of the commission on reading.* Washington, DC: National Institute of Education.

Applebee, A. N. (1978). *The child's concept of story.* Chicago: University of Chicago.

Avi. (1991). *Nothing but the truth.* New York: Orchard.

Barstow, B., & Riggle, J. (1995). *Beyond picture books: A guide to first readers* (2nd ed.). New York: R. R. Bowker.

Bogart, D. (Ed.) (2000). *Bowker annual: Library and book trade almanac.* New Providence, NJ: R. R. Bowker.

Borden, L. (1999). *A. Lincoln and me.* Illustrated by T. Lewin. New York: Scholastic.

Butler, D. (1975). *Cushla and her books.* Boston: Horn Book.

Carlsen, G. R., & Sherrill, A. (1988). *Voices of readers: How we come to love books.* Urbana, IL: National Council of Teachers of English.

*Children's books in print.* (2000). New Providence, NJ: R. R. Bowker.

Cohen, D. (1968). The effect of literature on vocabulary and reading achievement. *Elementary English, 45,* 209–213, 217.

Cowley, J. (1999). *Red-eyed tree frog.* Illustrated by Nic Bishop. New York: Scholastic.

DeFord, D. (1981). Literacy, reading, writing, and other essentials. *Language Arts, 58*(6), 652–658.

Durkin, D. (1966). *Children who read early.* New York: Columbia Teachers College Press.

Eckhoff, B. (1983). How reading affects children's writing. *Language Arts, 60*(5), 607–616.

Eldredge, J. L., & Butterfield, D. (1986). Alternatives to traditional reading instruction. *The Reading Teacher, 40,* 32–37.

Elleman, B. (1987). Current trends in literature for children. *Library Trends, 35*(3), 413–426.

Gunning, T. G. (1998). *Best books for beginning readers.* Needham Heights, MA: Allyn and Bacon.

———. (2000). *Best books for building literacy for elementary school children.* Needham Heights, MA: Allyn and Bacon.

Haynes, C. (1988). Explanatory power of content for identifying children's literature preferences. *Dissertation Abstracts International, 49–12A,* p. 3617. (University Microfilms No. DEW8900468).

Henkes, K. (1991). *Chrysanthemum.* New York: Greenwillow.

Hill, E. (1980). *Where's Spot?* New York: Putnam.

Hoban, T. (1998). *More, fewer, less.* New York: Greenwillow.

———. (1985). *What is it?* New York: Greenwillow.

Homa, L., & Schreck, A., (Eds.). (2000). *The elementary school library collection: A guide to books and other media* (22nd ed.). Williamsport, PA: Brodart.

Hughes, S. (1982). *Alfie gets in first.* New York: Lothrop.

Kiefer, B. Z. (1994). *The potential of picturebooks: From visual literacy to aesthetic understanding.* Englewood Cliffs, NJ: Prentice Hall.

Kunhardt, D. (1962). *Pat the bunny.* New York: Golden.

Levstik, L. (1986). The relationship between historical response and narrative in a sixth-grade classroom. *Theory and Research in Social Education, 14,* 1–15.

Lima, C. W., & Lima, J. A. (2001). *A to zoo: Subject access to children's picture books* (6th ed.). New York: R. R. Bowker.

Lowry, L. (1993). *The giver.* New York: Houghton.

———. (1996). *See you around, Sam!* Illustrated by D. de Groat. New York: Houghton.

McConaghy, J. (1990). *Children learning through literature: A teacher researcher study.* Portsmouth, NH: Heinemann.

McCord, D. (1986). Books fall open. In *One at a Time.* Illustrated by Henry B. Kane. New York: Little, Brown.

Naylor, P. R. (1991). *Shiloh.* New York: Atheneum.

Opie, I. (Ed.). (1999). *Here comes Mother Goose.* Illustrated by Rosemary Wells. New York: Candlewick.

Oxenbury, H. (1981). *Dressing.* New York: Simon & Schuster.

Paterson, K. (1978). *The great Gilly Hopkins.* New York: Crowell.

Pierce, K. M. (Ed.). (2000). *Adventuring with books: A booklist for pre-K–grade 6* (12th ed.). Urbana, IL: National Council of Teachers of English.

Place, F. (1993). *The last giants.* New York: Godine.

Price, A., & Yaakov, J. (1996). *Children's catalog* (17th ed.). New York: H. W. Wilson.

Raschka, C. (1993). *Yo! Yes?* New York: Orchard.

Reeder, C. (1989). *Shades of gray.* New York: Macmillan.

Rosenblatt, L. (1978). *The reader, the text, the poem.* Carbondale, IL: Southern Illinois University.

Sachar, L. (1998). *Holes.* New York: Farrar.

Shannon, D. (1998). *No, David!* New York: Scholastic.

Spinelli, J. (1997). *Wringer.* New York: HarperCollins.

Stewart, S. (1997). *The gardener.* Illustrated by D. Small. New York: Farrar.

*Subject guide to children's books in print.* (2000). New York: R. R. Bowker.

Taback, S. (1997). *There was an old lady who swallowed a fly.* New York: Viking.

Van Allsburg, C. (1991). *The wretched stone.* Boston: Houghton.

Van Orden, P. (2000). *Selecting books for the elementary school library media center: A complete guide.* New York: Neal-Schuman.

Wilkes, A. (1999). *My first word book.* New York: DK.

World Catalog (available only through subscribing libraries). Dublin, OH: Online Computer Library Center, Inc.

Yorinks, A. (1986). *Hey, Al.* Illustrated by R. Egielski. New York: Farrar.

# 2

# LEARNING *about* BOOKS

## A BOOK

*I'm a strange contradiction; I'm new and I'm old,*
*I'm often in tatters, and oft deck'd in gold;*
*Though I never could read, yet letter'd I'm found;*
*Though blind, I enlighten; though loose, I am bound—*
*I am always in black, and I'm always in white;*
*I am grave and I'm gay, I am heavy and light.*
*In form too I differ—I'm thick and I'm thin,*
*I've no flesh, and no bones, yet I'm covered with skin;*
*I've more points than the compass, more stops than the flute—*
*I sing without voice, without speaking confute;*
*I'm English, I'm German, I'm French and I'm Dutch;*
*Some love me too fondly; some slight me too much;*
*I often die soon, though I sometimes live ages,*
*And no monarch alive has so many pages.*

—HANNAH MORE (1961)

In Chapter 1 we stated that reading is a fusion of text and reader and that each reading of a particular literary work results in a different transaction. Even rereadings by the same reader will result in a different experience. But if the transaction is different each time a book is read, how can general assessments of literary merit be made? Rosenblatt answers that although the notion of a single, correct reading of a literary work is rejected, "*given agreed-upon criteria,* it is possible to decide that some readings are more defensible than others" (1985, p. 36). Although each reading of a given literary work will be different, there are certain generally agreed-upon interpretations of that work by a community of educated readers. In this chapter, traditional literary elements are reviewed in order to heighten your awareness of literary criticism and to provide a more precise vocabulary for you to express your responses to children's books. Literary terms may also be considered as tools that your students can use to initiate and sustain conversations about literature. In using these terms in the classroom you can help children to acquire a literary vocabulary.

## ELEMENTS OF FICTION

Learning to evaluate children's books can best be accomplished by reading as many excellent books as possible. Gradually, your judgment on the merits of individual books will improve. Discussing your responses to these books with children, teachers, and other students and listening to their responses will also assist you in becoming a more appreciative critic. Understanding the different parts, or elements, of a piece of fiction and how they work together can help you to become more analytical about literary works; and this, too, can improve your judgment of literature. The elements of fiction are discussed separately in the following sections, but it is the unity of all these elements that produces the story.

### Plot

The events of the story and the sequence in which they are told constitute the plot of the story. In other words, the plot is what happens in the story. Plot is the most important element of fiction to the child reader. Often, adults believe that a story for children needs only to present familiar, everyday activities—the daily routines of life. Perhaps 2- and 3-year-olds will enjoy hearing narratives such as this, but by age 4, children want to find more excitement in books. A good plot produces conflict to build the excitement and suspense that are needed to keep the reader involved.

The nature of the *conflict* within the plot can arise from different sources. The basic conflict may be one that occurs within the main character, called *person-against-self.* In this type of story, the main character struggles against inner drives and personal tendencies to achieve some goal. Stories about adolescence will frequently have this conflict as the basis of the story problem. For example, in *Language of Goldfish* by Zibby Oneal, 13-year-old Carrie struggles to find herself and to accept herself and others. A conflict usually found in survival stories is the struggle the character has with the forces of nature. This conflict is called *person-against-nature.* Worthy examples are *Island of the Blue Dolphins* by Scott O'Dell and *Hatchet* by Gary Paulsen. In other children's stories, the source of the conflict is found between two characters. Conflicts with peers, problems with sibling rivalries, and stories of children rebelling against an adult are *person-against-person* conflicts. For example, the young badger, Frances, in *A Bargain for Frances* by Russell Hoban, struggles to get a fair deal from her friend, Thelma, who sells Frances a tea set. Occasionally, a story for children presents the main character in conflict with society. This conflict in children's stories is most often either about the environment being destroyed by new technology or changing times or about children caught up in a political upheaval such as war. The conflict is then called *person-against-society. My Brother Sam Is Dead* by James Lincoln

Collier and Christopher Collier and *Across Five Aprils* by Irene Hunt, both war stories, pose this type of conflict. In Jean Craighead George's *Julie of the Wolves,* protagonist Julie/Miyax struggles with the societal changes occurring in her native Alaskan community.

Plots are constructed in many different ways. The most usual plot structures found in children's stories are *chronological plots,* which cover a particular period of time and relate the events in order within the time period. For example, if a book relates the events of one week, then Monday's events will precede Tuesday's, and so on. An example of a story with a chronological plot is *Charlotte's Web* by E. B. White. There are two distinct types of chronological plots, progressive and episodic. In books with *progressive plots,* the first few chapters are the exposition, in which the characters, setting, and basic conflict are established. Following the expository chapters, the story builds through rising action to a climax. The climax occurs, a satisfactory conclusion (or denouement) is reached, and the story ends. Figure 2.1 suggests how a progressive, chronological, plot might be visualized.

An *episodic plot* ties together separate short stories or episodes, each an entity in itself with its own conflict and resolution. These episodes are typically unified by the same cast of characters and the same setting. Often, each episode comprises a chapter. Although the episodes are usually chronological, time relationships among the episodes may be nonexistent or loosely connected by "during that same year" or "later that month." An example of a short chapter book with an episodic plot structure is *Beezus and Ramona* by Beverly Cleary. Because episodic plots are less complex, they tend to be easier to read. Thus, the reader who is just making the transition from picture books to chapter books may find these plots particularly appealing. Many easy-to-read books for the beginning reader are also structured in this way. *Frog and Toad Are Friends* by Arnold Lobel is a good example of an episodic plot in an easy-to-read book. Figure 2.2 suggests how a chronological, episodic plot might be visualized.

Authors use a *flashback* to convey information about events that occurred earlier—for example, before the beginning of the first chapter. In this case, the chronology of events is disrupted, and the reader is taken back to an earlier time. Flashbacks can occur more than once and in different parts of a story. The use of a flashback permits authors to begin the story in the midst of the action but later fill in the background for full understanding of the present events. Flashbacks in children's books are mostly found in chapter books for older readers, since such plots can confuse children younger than age 8 or 9. Teachers can help students understand this plot structure by reading aloud good examples of this type of story, such as Jean Craighead George's *My Side of the Mountain.* Class discussion can then focus on the sequence of events and why the author may have chosen to relate the events in this

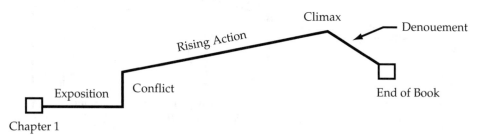

**FIGURE 2.1**   Diagram of a Progressive Plot

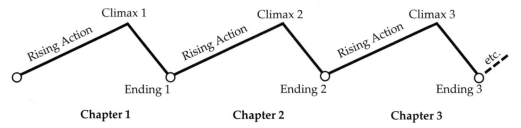

FIGURE 2.2   Diagram of an Episodic Plot

manner. Figure 2.3 illustrates the structure of a flashback in a book in which some events occurred before the beginning of the book.

A stylistic plot device that prepares readers for coming events in a story is *foreshadowing*. This device gives clues to a later event, possibly even the climax of the story. For example, in *Tuck Everlasting* by Natalie Babbitt the detailed description of the long yellow road in the first chapter foreshadows the long journey the Tuck family members must travel in their lives. You can alert young readers to one of the subtle ways authors prepare them for the outcomes of stories by discussing foreshadowing.

Plot is an important element to all readers, but especially to young readers, who enjoy fast-moving, exciting stories. A well-constructed plot contributes substantially to children's acceptance and enjoyment of stories.

### Characters

Memorable characters populate the world of children's literature. Ferdinand the bull, Charlotte the spider, Frances the badger, Little Toot the young tugboat, Karana the Native-American girl, and Peter, the African-American child with his dog Willie are all remembered fondly by generations of readers.

Characters, the "actors" in a story, are another element of fiction vital to the enjoyment of a story. A well-portrayed character can become a friend, a role model, or a temporary parent to a child reader.

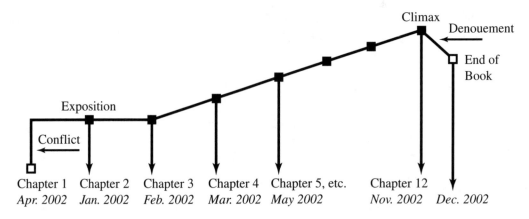

FIGURE 2.3   Diagram of a Flashback

Although young readers enjoy exciting events, the characters involved in those events must matter to the reader or the events no longer seem important. How characters are depicted and how they develop in the course of the story are important to the reader. Two aspects to consider in studying a character are characterization and character development.

*Characterization* refers to the way an author helps the reader to know a character. The most obvious way an author can do this is to describe the character's physical appearance and personality. Portraying the character's emotional and moral traits or revealing her relationships with other characters are more subtle and effective techniques. In the most convincing characterizations, we see the character through a combination of her own actions and dialogue, the responses of other characters to her, and the narrator's descriptions.

*Character development* refers to the changes, good or bad, the character undergoes during the course of events in the story. If a character experiences significant, life-altering events, we, as readers, expect that the character will somehow be different as a result of those events. For example, Matt, a boy of 11, who was left alone for months in the Maine territory to take care of his family's new cabin, becomes a stronger, more independent young man by the end of *The Sign of the Beaver* by Elizabeth George Speare.

In a work of fiction for children there are usually one or two main characters and some minor characters. Ideally, each main character, sometimes called the *protagonist,* will be a fully described, complex individual who possesses both good and bad traits, like a real person. Such a character is called a *round character.* For example, in the historical fiction novel *Catherine, Called Birdy* by Karen Cushman, Birdy, the protagonist whose father is seeking a suitable husband for her, is presented as a complex character with many strengths and weaknesses.

*Minor,* or *secondary, characters* may be described in a less complete or partial manner. The extent of description depends on what the reader needs to know about the character for a full understanding of the story. Some of the minor character's traits are described fully, whereas other facets of the character's personality may remain obscure. Because the purpose is to build the story and make it comprehensible, fragmentary knowledge of a minor character may suffice. In the novel *Under the Red-Blood Sun* by Graham Salisbury, Billy Wilson is portrayed as a loyal friend to Tomi, the protagonist, in this story about the treatment of Tomi's Japanese family in Hawaii during World War II. Occasionally, an author will insert a *flat character*—that is, a character described in a one-sided or underdeveloped manner. Although such people do not exist in real life, they may be justified within the story to propel the plot. Sometimes the character is shown as an all-evil or all-frivolous person; for instance, folktales present flat characters as symbols of good and evil. In some stories, a flat character plays the role of *character foil,* a person who is in direct juxtaposition to another character (usually the protagonist) and who serves to highlight the characteristics of the other individual. A character foil may occur as a flat or as a round character. For example, Hamilton Knapp, the mean boy who was willing to harm a dog to win, is portrayed as a flat character in *A View from Saturday* by E. L. Konigsburg. The character or force that is in direct opposition to the main character is called the *antagonist.* In Avi's *The True Confessions of Charlotte Doyle,* the ship's captain is a frightening antagonist to Charlotte.

The main characters in an excellent work of fiction for children are rounded, fully developed characters who undergo change in response to life-altering events. Because children generally prefer personified animals or children of their own age, or slightly older, as the main characters of their stories, authors of children's books often face a dilemma. Although in real life, children usually have restricted freedom of action and decision making within the confines of a family, the author can develop a more vivid and exciting story if the main characters are "on their own." Thus, in many children's stories, parents are absent, no longer living, or no longer functioning. Furthermore, by making up situations, authors are able to focus on just one aspect of life, thereby enabling young readers to see and understand this one facet of life more clearly.

## Setting

The time when the story occurs and the place(s) where it occurs constitute the setting of a story. The setting has a more or less important function depending on the story. For example, in historical fiction the authentic recreation of the period is essential to the comprehension of the story's events. In this situation, the setting, fully described both in time and place, is called an *integral setting*. The story could not be the same if placed in another setting. For example, in the historical novel *Bull Run* by Paul Fleischman, battle maps are included, and many of the sixteen characters whose points of view are presented discuss the battlegrounds.

By contrast, the setting in folktales is often vague and general. For example, "long ago in a cottage in the deep woods" is meant to convey a universal, timeless tale, one that could have happened anywhere and almost anytime except the present or very recent past. This type of setting is called a *backdrop setting*. It simply sets the stage and the mood.

## Theme

The literary theme of a story is its underlying meaning of significance. The term *theme* should not be confused with topic or theme as used in the sense of a thematic unit. Although we sometimes think of the literary *theme* as the message or moral of the story, it can just as likely be an aesthetic understanding, such as an appreciation for nature, or a viewpoint on a current societal issue. To identify the theme, you may ask yourself what the author's purpose was in writing the story, or what the author is saying through this story.

A theme is better expressed by means of a complete sentence than by a single word. For example, students often suggest that a theme found in *Charlotte's Web* by E. B. White is friendship. A better statement of the theme is "Friendship is one of the most satisfying things in the world," as Wilbur the pig tells us in the story. The single word *friendship* may be a topic found in the story, but it is not an expression of the theme.

Themes in children's books should be worthy of children's attention and should convey truth to them. Furthermore, the themes should be based on high moral and ethical standards. A theme must not overpower the plot and characters of the story, however; children read fiction for enjoyment, not for enlightenment. If the theme is expressed in a heavy-handed, obvious fashion, then the pleasure of the reading experience is diminished. Likewise, overly "teachy" or didactic themes detract from a reader's enjoyment of a story. Certainly a well-written book may convey a moral message, but it should also tell a good story from which the message evolves. In this way the theme is subtly conveyed to the reader. For example, in the picture book *Boundless Grace* by Mary Hoffman, Grace discovers that "families are what we make of them" in the course of a visit to the home of her father and stepmother.

Often, adults write stories not for children's pleasure but to teach morality lessons. Although we think of stories of this sort as the thinly disguised religious tracts found in the early history of children's literature, we must be alert to a tendency for some current authors to use children's literature as a platform to preach about drug abuse, animal rights, and other issues of contemporary interest. If the literary quality of these so-called problem novels is weakened, then the story and characters become secondary to the issue or problem. However, when moral values are embedded within the fabric of a powerful story, children can be led to develop a sense of right and wrong without feeling as if they are being indoctrinated.

## *Style*

Style is the way an author tells the story; it can be viewed as the writing itself, as opposed to the content of the book. However, the style must suit the content of the particular book; the two are intertwined.

Different aspects of style are considered in evaluating a work of fiction. Most obviously, you can look at the *words* chosen to tell the story. Are they long or short, common or uncommon, rhyming or melodic, boring and hackneyed or rich and challenging, unemotional or emotional, standard dialect or regional/minority dialect? The words should be appropriate to the story being told. As an evaluator of books for children, you will want to ask the following questions as you read: Why did the author choose these words? What effect was the author trying to achieve?

The *sentences* may also be considered. Do they read easily? Do they flow without the reader needing to reread to gain the meaning of the text? Sometimes an author chooses to limit the word choices to write a book that can be read by a beginning reader. Yet in the hands of a gifted writer, the sentences will remain no less melodic, varied in length and structure, and enjoyable to read and hear than sentences in the best books for the more advanced reader. A good example of a well-written book for beginning readers is Arnold Lobel's *Frog and Toad Are Friends*.

The *organization* of the book may be considered by noting the paragraphs and transitions, length of chapters, headings and chapter titles, preface, endnotes, prologue, epilogue, and length of the book. For the beginning reader it is important whether a story is divided into chapters. After years of looking at, listening to, and reading books without chapters, it is quite an accomplishment for a 6-year-old to move up to so-called chapter books, even if each chapter is only three pages long.

Chapter titles can provoke interest in what will follow, as well as provide the reader with clues to predict story events. Some books provide the readers with a prologue, an introductory statement telling events that precede the start of the story. Some authors include an epilogue, a concluding statement telling events that occur after the story has ended. Gary Paulsen, in speaking to readers about what they bring to the reading act in his prologue to *The Winter Room*, heightens sensitivity to the story that is to follow. In the epilogue of *Tuck Everlasting*, Natalie Babbitt allows the readers to revisit the scene of the story some years later and resolve at least one of the questions they inevitably have at the story's end. Occasionally, an author presents information on the sources or historical facts used in the story. In *Friedrich*, for example, Hans Peter Richter adds a chronology of historical events in the endnotes.

*Point of view* is another aspect of an author's style. If the story is told through the eyes and voice of a *third-person narrator* (the use of *he, she, it*), then the reader can know whatever the narrator knows about the events of the story. In many stories, the narrator is *omniscient* and can see into the minds of all characters and be at many places at the same time. The reader of E. B. White's *Charlotte's Web* can understand and interpret the story from many different perspectives because of White's use of the omniscient point of view.

Other stories are narrated from the perspective of only one character in the story. In this case, the story is still told in the third person, but the reader knows only what that particular character can see and understand. This latter technique is called *limited omniscient* point of view. In Mildred Taylor's *Roll of Thunder, Hear My Cry* the story is told by Cassie, the very astute 9-year-old protagonist.

Other times authors choose to tell the story through a *first-person narrator* (the use of *I*), generally the main character of the story. In such cases the reader gains a sense of closeness to the main character but is not privy to any information unavailable to this character. As you read, you will note that some authors have accomplished a first-person point of view by writing as though their main character were writing a diary or letters, as in *A Gathering of Days: A New England Girl's Journal, 1830–1832* by Joan Blos. Occasionally, a story is told in first person through the eyes of a minor character. For example, *Ben and Me,* by Robert Lawson, is the story of Benjamin Franklin told through the eyes of a mouse in his house. A *shifting point of view* permits the reader to see events from different characters' points of view. This technique is demanding on young readers' skill. When the point of view shifts, the author must carefully cue readers to the changing point of view, as Avi does in *Nothing but the Truth* by identifying sender, receiver, or discussants at the beginning of each letter, memorandum, telephone call, or face-to-face conversation.

*Symbolism* is an artistic invention that authors use to suggest invisible or intangible meanings by analogy to something else through association, resemblance, or convention. Often a symbol—a person, object, or situation—represents an abstract or figurative meaning in the story in addition to its literal meaning. Some symbols are universal and can be found repeatedly in literary works; others may be particular to the story. For example, a farm often stands for love and security in works of literature. Children often read only on a literal level, but they can be helped by teachers to note more obvious symbols existing in the books they are reading. If the symbolic feature recurs in the story, it is referred to as a *motif.* The number 3 is a common motif in folktales, for example.

A story for children must be more than a plot and a character study; a story integrates all the elements of fiction into a pleasing whole. In drawing together these elements, authors create new worlds for young readers.

## VISUAL ELEMENTS

In many children's books the story is told through both text and pictures. This is particularly true of picture books but is also true of other books for children in which pictures serve an important function. Many different purposes can be accomplished through book illustrations. They convey meaning and feeling by helping the reader to visualize the physical settings and the characters' appearance and actions. They also provide an aesthetic dimension to books by offering the readers additional pleasure and insights beyond the message within the text. Thus, the role of pictures in children's books is both to reflect the text and to extend and enrich it without contradicting its message.

When you read many illustrated books and carefully observe the illustrations and their relationships to the texts, you begin to increase your appreciation of this aspect of children's literature. You may consider the different parts of illustrations as one aspect of your evaluation of illustrations. In the picture book *The Picture That Mom Drew* by Kathy Mallat and Bruce McMillan, a visual and textual demonstration of the visual elements is presented. This book can be used to help students to become more observant of illustrations and their roles in books. These *visual elements* are line, color, shape, texture, and composition. They can help you to become more observant of illustrations so that you will learn to select well-illustrated books.

### Line

The stroke marks that form part of a picture and often define its outline are the lines. The line of a picture generally defines the objects within the picture. Artists may choose to use lines that are dark or pale, heavy or light, solid or broken, wide or thin, straight or curved, or have combinations of these elements. The lines may be mostly vertical, horizontal, or on a diagonal. In pictures of the ocean and open prairies, the lines are predominantly horizontal; the impression is one of calm and tranquility. If the ocean is stormy, then the lines are more likely diagonal and upward moving, suggesting action or emotion or both. Each of these choices results in a different visual effect and can help to set a different mood. In evaluating the element of line within a picture, you may ask yourself whether the lines of the picture help to create and convey both the meaning and the feeling of the story. John Steptoe's use of thick black outlines for the children in *Stevie* is successful in showing the resistance to friendship between the characters.

### Color

Color, another visual element of a book, may be observed for its hue, lightness, and saturation. Colors may be considered for the actual part of the color spectrum they represent or for their hue. The predominant colors may be from the cool end of the spectrum (the blues, greens, and gray-violets) or from the warm end of the color chart (the reds, oranges, and yellows). The colors may be intense or pale (that is, more or less saturated). The lightness of the colors may range from diaphanous to opaque. The colors used must first complement the text. For example, if the mood of the story is that of calm and contentment, the illustrator may choose soft, warm tones that strengthen the emotional warmth of the story. If the events and mood of the text change during the course of the story, then the colors will change to reflect and signal the shift occurring in the story. In Margaret Wise Brown's *Goodnight Moon*, the colors gradually darken from page to page, as the sun sets and night falls. Sometimes an illustrated book will be noteworthy for its lack of color, which can be very appropriate and effective, as in *Hildilid's Night* by Cheli Durán Ryan, illustrated by Arnold Lobel.

### Shape

Shape, or the spatial forms of a picture, is produced by areas of color and by lines joining and intersecting to suggest outlines of forms. Shapes can be evaluated for their simplicity or complexity, their definition or lack of definition, their rigidity (as in geometric shapes) or suppleness (as in organic shapes), and their size. It is easy to see how this visual element can help to create a mood or carry a message. In looking at shapes in a picture, the proportion of one object to another and the spaces surrounding the shapes are noteworthy for the nonverbal messages they carry (the bigger, the more important). The use of negative space or blank space may also be observed for its ability to highlight an object or to show isolation or loneliness. Chris Raschka effectively uses space on successive double-spreads to demonstrate a developing friendship between two boys in the Caldecott Honor book, *Yo! Yes?*

### Texture

The tactile surface characteristics of pictured objects comprise the texture of a picture. More simply, the impression of how a pictured object feels is its texture. Textures may be rough or slick, firm or spongy, hard or soft, jagged or smooth. Textural effects generally offer a greater sense of reality to a picture, as happens in Leo Lionni's *Frederick,* in which the torn edges of paper collage lend a convincing furriness to the little mice's bodies. Texture also permits the artist to provide contrasts within the picture.

### Composition

Composition includes the arrangement of the visual elements within a picture and the way in which these visual elements relate one to the other and combine to make the picture. Many artists arrange each illustration around a single focal point, which is often a key to understanding composition. The artist decides on proportion, balance, harmony, and disharmony within the various elements to produce the desired visual impact. The total effect should not overpower the story but rather extend and enrich the meaning and mood of the text.

Obviously, the details in the illustrations must not conflict with those in the text. Surprisingly, many examples can be cited in which the illustrator was not true to the text in all details. Children are keenly observant of these contradictions and find them distracting. Although children accept illustrations that are varied in all visual elements and artistic styles, they have little tolerance for inaccuracies.

## ARTISTIC STYLES

Children come to note the distinctive features that identify the work of their favorite illustrators. Although the style of a picture is individual to each artist, artwork in general can be grouped by style similarities. Five broad categories of artistic styles are realistic, impressionistic, expressionistic, abstract, and surrealistic. Although an artist's works seldom fit neatly into one single art style, facets of these styles may be merged into the artist's personal expression of the world.

*Realistic art* represents natural forms and provides accurate representations without idealization. Susan Jeffer's illustrations in *Black Beauty* by Anna Sewell are examples of realistic art, as is Christopher G. Knight's photographic rendering of the story *Sugaring Time* by Kathryn Lasky.

*Impressionistic art* depicts natural appearances of objects by rendering fleeting visual impressions with an emphasis on light. The illustrations in *Anno's Journey* by Mitsumasa Anno emphasize the play of light in nature.

*Expressionistic art* communicates an inner feeling or vision by distorting external reality. An example can be found in *A Chair for My Mother* by Vera B. Williams. Graphic art, used heavily in advertising and billboards, can be considered a form of expressionistic art. The intent of the artist is to draw attention to the central message by eliminating competing details. Donald Crews has successfully developed this art style into concept books for the very young child in *Truck* and *Freight Train.*

*Abstract art* emphasizes intrinsic form and surface qualities with little or no direct representation of objects but rather an emphasis on mood and feeling. The illustrations by Leo and Diane Dillon in *Why Mosquitoes Buzz in People's Ears* by Verna Aardema distort reality and thus convey the feelings evoked by the African tale.

In emphasizing the unconscious, *surrealistic art* often presents incongruous dream and fantasy images, sometimes juxtaposing unlikely objects. Molly Bang's illustrations in *The Grey Lady and the Strawberry Snatcher* present a semirealistic creature, the Grey Lady, in a nightmarish adventure. The unusual use of color and unlikely happenings reassure the reader that this wordless book is an imaginary story.

In addition, *primitive art* and *folk art* styles are seen in books about a particular era or culture. The style of art is reminiscent of the style prevalent at the time the story events occurred. In illustrating *Ox-Cart Man* by Donald Hall, Barbara Cooney uses features of Early American art in order to express the culture of early nineteenth-century New England. Folktales from tribal societies also present occasions for artists to choose a folk art style reminiscent of the art from earlier cultures.

Because *cartoons* are popular with children, some artists select this style for their children's books. In this type of art, exaggerated, rounded figures with little or no background are the focal point of the illustrations. Dr. Seuss's many books, such as *Horton Hatches the Egg* and *The Cat in the Hat,* as well as many of William Steig's popular stories, including *The Amazing Bone* and *Caleb and Kate,* have illustrations representative of the cartoon style.

## ARTISTIC MEDIA

The artistic media refer to the materials and technical means used by artists to create pictures. Although the variety of techniques and materials used by book illustrators is virtually unlimited, some of the more common media found in children's books are listed here.

*Drawing:* Pen and ink, colored pencils, pastels (colored chalk), charcoal pencils

The use of pastels combined with pen-and-ink drawings is found in the humorous illustrations of *Helen Oxenbury's A B C of Things.*

*Collage:* Real objects of assorted textures and designs such as lace, birchbark, buttons, torn paper, and cotton used to construct an illustration

Ezra Jack Keats used collage to illustrate his landmark picture book *The Snowy Day,* in which Peter, an African-American child, is first introduced.

*Print making:* Woodcuts, linoleum prints, block prints, lithography

Marcia Brown captures the flavor of an old folktale by using linocuts in *Dick Whittington and His Cat.*

*Photography:* Black and white, color

Tana Hoban draws on photography to illustrate her many concept books. She uses black and white photos, as in *Push Pull, Empty Full* as well as color photos, as in *Color Everywhere.*

*Painting:* Oils, acrylics, watercolors, gouache, tempera

In *The Rough-Face Girl* by Rafe Martin, illustrator David Shannon makes dramatic use of acrylics.

Of course, the tools with which the artist applies the paint will affect its look. Tools as varied as brushes, air brushes, and sponges are used for applying paint.

Artists will generally design a picture in one predominant medium, drawing from other media for special effects. Occasionally, an artist will choose to combine media more liberally to achieve the desired effect. Brief explanations of the artist's techniques and materials have recently begun to be included on the publishing history page of children's picture books; at other times they appear at the end of illustrated books.

## BOOK FORMAT

Children's books are more than text, or text and pictures combined. Other parts of a book contribute to the final product we call a book. The *dust jacket* is a removable paper cover wrapped around the book; it serves as protection against soiling. It also attracts purchasers and readers as well as informs them about the book, its author, and its illustrator. The *covers* of a book are usually made of two boards, which make the book more durable and allow it to stand on a shelf. When no dust jacket is on a book, the front cover provides the reader with a first impression of the story. The *title,* an important part of the text—usually first seen by the reader on the dust jacket or front cover—combines with the illustrations of the dust jacket or cover to communicate the nature of the story to young readers who choose books primarily by title and cover. Many titles suggest the topic of the story and can assist readers in deciding whether to read the book. Other titles and covers may not offer as much information about the story. In such cases, some explanation by a teacher or librarian in the form of a booktalk may prove invaluable to young readers seeking just such a book.

The *endpapers* are the pages glued to the inside front and back boards of the cover, and the *flyleaf* is the page facing each endpaper. In many fine, well-illustrated books, the endpaper and flyleaf are used to provoke curiosity in the reader for what follows, to set a mood, or to evoke an affective response in preparation for the story. Often, those first colors and first decorative touches are the visual introduction to the story. When readers turn the flyleaf, they are further prepared by the artist for the story by viewing the title page. The *title page* tells the book's full title and subtitle, if there is one; the names of the author(s) and illustrator(s); and the name and location of the publisher. Occasionally, a book will include a *frontispiece,* an illustration facing the title page, which is intended to establish the tone and to entice the reader to begin the story.

On the reverse side of the title page, often referred to as the *verso* of the title page, is the *publishing history* of the book. On this page is the copyright notice, a legal right giving only the holder permission to produce and sell the work. Others who wish to reproduce the work in any way must request permission of the copyright holder. The copyright is indicated by the international symbol ©. This symbol is followed by the name of the person(s) holding the copyright and the date it takes effect, which is the year the book is first published. Later publications are also listed. The country in which the book was printed, the number assigned to the book by the Library of Congress, the International Standard Book Number (ISBN), and the edition of the book are also included on this page. Many publishers now include on this page cataloguing information for libraries, a very brief annotation of the story, and a statement on the media and techniques used in the illustrations.

The title page typically presents the *typeface,* the style of print to be used throughout the book. The size and legibility of the typeface must be suited to the book's intended audience. In children's books this can be extremely important. Books for the young child who is just learning to read should have large, well-spaced print for easy eye scanning. The print style for an easy-to-read book should be a somewhat larger-than-average standard block print with easily distinguishable and recognizable uppercase and lowercase letters. Many children's trade books are now being produced in "big book" size for beginning reading activities with a whole class or group of children. In this case, the print needs to be large enough to be readily seen from a distance of 10 to 12 feet minimum. Legibility is diminished when background colors are used behind the text, leaving insufficient contrast for easy reading.

The size, shape, and darkness of the print type may vary from book to book. The lines may be heavy and strong or light and willowy. The choice of print type should enhance the overall visual message of the illustrations and fit with the illustrations in style and mood. Note also that the placement of the print on the pages in relation to the illustrations can subtly guide the reader and become a functional part of the story.

Unusual print styles are sometimes selected for a children's book. In a book with a diary format, the use of script print gives the impression of handwriting. In this case, the amount of script print is usually brief, and standard block print is used throughout most of the book for greater ease of reading. In place of print some illustrators choose to hand-letter the text. Classic examples of lettering as part of the illustrative component of a book are found in *Millions of Cats* by Wanda Gág and *The Story of Babar* by Jean de Brunhoff.

The *page layout* is also worth observing. You will notice that illustrations are variously placed one on a page, on facing pages, on alternating pages, or on parts of pages. When the picture extends across the two facing pages, it is called a *doublespread.* A doublespread gives the effect of motion, since the eye is drawn to the next page. It can also give a feeling of grandeur, openness, and expansiveness. Sometimes, a picture will begin on a right-hand page and spill over to the following page, the reverse side. This offers a strong sense of continuity from one part of the story to the next. Some pictures have a *frame.* Framing of a picture can work to distance the reader from the action, lend a sense of order to the story, or make the mood more formal. The frame itself may be anything from a simple line to a broad, ornately decorated ribbon of information. Decorations on a frame may repeat certain images or symbols to reinforce the meaning of the story.

*Pages* are another part of the book makeup. In evaluating the pages, you should ask yourself, What is the quality of the paper? Is it thick, high quality? Is it glossy or textured, white or colored? Are the pages square, rectangular, or shaped in the form of a concrete object? Are they in keeping with the rest of the book? Are unique or unusual page formats, such as half-pages, see-through pages, engineered pages, or partial pages, appropriate and logical?

The *size* of the book is also worth noting. Large picture books are well suited for reading aloud to a class. Smaller picture books are usually not satisfactory choices for read-alouds, unless, of course, you are reading to only one child or to a small group of children.

Next, consider the *book binding*. Books may be bound in hard cover, paperback, or in some special-purpose material. For example, books for babies are frequently bound in sturdy cardboard or vinyl to withstand the dual role of toy and book. When buying a hardcover book, determine whether the binding is glued or sewn. Look for the stitching. Sewn bindings last much longer than glued ones. Durability relative to cost is the usual trade-off you must weigh in selecting paper or hardcover bindings for classroom or school libraries. Generally speaking, the cost of hardcover books is justified when you expect fairly heavy use.

## BALANCE AND VARIETY IN BOOK SELECTIONS

In addition to evaluating the various textual and visual elements that are central to the issue of quality, the child's age and development and the balance and variety among books are also important considerations. In Chapter 1, the age and development of children relative to their reading materials were discussed. Because children in any elementary-grade class have a wide range of reading abilities and reading interests, you need to provide many different types of books, including picture books, easy-to-read books, short chapter books, longer books, and books of prose, poetry, fiction, and nonfiction. Selecting outstanding biographies for an entire year of reading aloud to a class would hardly offer students a range of literary experiences. Thus, balance among the *genres of literature* as well as *variety in topic* are essential. Classroom libraries are usually limited in scope; therefore, school libraries are necessary to provide adequate balance and variety of books for students' research needs and independent reading. Frequent visits to the library by the class and by individual students need to be arranged by the teacher and librarian.

A balance between *male and female main characters* over the course of a year is necessary if you are to meet the needs of children of both sexes and to help members of each sex understand more fully the perspectives, problems, and feelings of members of the opposite sex. Classroom and school library collections need to have a wide range of topics with a balance of male and female main characters.

In addition, understanding and empathy for people with disabilities can be gained through portrayals in books of children and adults with impairments. A positive image of people with disabilities needs to be conveyed in these books. Furthermore, children with disabilities need to see characters like themselves in books.

The representation of minorities as main characters is also essential if you are to present a realistic view of society and the world. Through well-written *multicultural literature,* children can see that someone from a different race, ethnic group, or religion has many of the same basic needs and feelings that they themselves have. Literature by and about people different from oneself can help to develop an understanding and appreciation for all peoples. Minority children will enjoy reading books in which children from backgrounds similar to their own play the leading, and sometimes, heroic roles. Characters with whom one can identify permit a deeper involvement in literature and at the same time help children to understand situations in their own lives.

*International literature*—that is, literature from other nations and regions of the world—needs to be included in read-aloud choices and in classroom and library collections in order to guide students toward global understanding. Through reading or listening to the favorite books of children from other nations, your children will experience cultural literacy on a worldwide basis.

## CATEGORIES OF LITERATURE

In Chapters 3 to 10 of this book, the various categories of children's books will be defined and explained, followed by book titles recommended for reading in each of the categories. Most of the chapters focus on the literary genres, as presented in Table 2.1.

However, Chapter 4 ("Picture Books") diverges from this pattern in that it discusses a book format, and Chapter 10 ("Multicultural and International Literature") presents books organized by topic. Although multicultural and international books have been placed in a separate chapter for special focus, many multicultural and international titles are also recommended in the genre chapters.

An overview of the genres and their relationships to one another is displayed in Table 2.1. These genres can be used in making balanced choices for library and classroom reading collections and for choosing books to read aloud. The number of the chapter in which each genre of literature is discussed is noted next to the genre.

**TABLE 2.1  Genres of Children's Literature**

| PROSE | | | | POETRY (3) | PLAYS (3) |
|---|---|---|---|---|---|
| *Fiction* | | | *Nonfiction (9)* | | |
| *Realistic (7)* | *Fantasy* | | | | |
| | *Traditional Literature (5)* | *Modern Fantasy (6)* | | | |
| Families | Myths | Modern folktales | Biographies | Nursery rhymes | Original plays |
| Peers | Epics | Animal fantasy | Biological science | Lyric poems | Adaptations |
| Mental, physical, and behavioral challenges | Legends/tall tales | Personified toys and objects | Physical science | Narrative poems | |
| Cultural diversity | Folktales | Unusual characters/ situations | Social science | | |
| Animals | Fables | | Applied science | | |
| Sports | Religious stories | Worlds of little people | Humanities | | |
| Mysteries | | Supernatural events/mystery | | | |
| Romance and sexuality | | Historical fantasy | | | |
| Rites of passage | | Quest stories | | | |
| Adventure and survival | | Science fiction/ fantasy | | | |
| *Historical (8)* | | | | | |

## R E F E R E N C E S

More, H. (1961). A book. In W. Cole (Ed.), *Poems for seasons and celebrations.* Cleveland: World Publishing.

Rosenblatt, L. M. (1985). The transactional theory of the literary work: Implications for research. In C. R. Cooper (Ed.), *Researching response to literature and the teaching of literature: Points of departure* (pp. 33–53). Norwood, NJ: Ablex.

# 3

# POETRY *and* PLAYS

*What is Poetry? Who knows?*
*Not a rose, but the scent of the rose;*
*Not the sky, but the light in the sky;*
*Not the fly, but the gleam of the fly;*
*Not the sea, but the sound of the sea;*
*Not myself, but what makes me*
*See, hear, and feel something that prose*
*Cannot: and what it is, who knows?*

— ELEANOR FARJEON

This chapter is presented in two sections. The first section focuses on poetry, information about poetry, and its uses in the classroom. The second section focuses on plays, information about plays, and their importance in a good language arts curriculum.

Poetry and plays represent two of the three major components of literature: prose, poetry, and plays. While poetry is an accepted, albeit underused, genre in the elementary classroom, the genre of plays is truly neglected. Because of their underuse and neglect we have chosen to discuss poetry and plays before other types of literature. We hope you will read and reread favorite poems to your students each day and bring plays and the theatre into your classroom on a regular basis.

## SECTION ONE: *Poetry*

Poetry, in the form of nursery rhymes, is a natural beginning to literature for young children and an enjoyable literary form for all ages. In their earliest years, children acquire language and knowledge of the world around them through listening and observing. Poetry, primarily an oral form of literature that draws heavily on the auditory perceptions of the listeners, is ideally suited to children at this stage. Then, throughout the elementary and middle school years, poetry that relates to any and every subject can be found and shared orally during the school day, providing a flash of humor or a new perspective on the subject.

## DEFINITION AND DESCRIPTION

*P*oetry is the expression of ideas and feelings through a rhythmical composition of imaginative and beautiful words selected for their sonorous effects. In its origin, poetry was oral, and as various minstrels traversed the countryside, they recited poetry and sang songs to groups of listeners of all ages. The musicality of poetry makes it an especially suitable literary form for teachers to read aloud and, at times, to put to music.

Children often believe that rhyme is an essential ingredient of poetry; yet some types of poetry do not rhyme. What, then, distinguishes poetry from prose? The concentration of thought and feeling expressed in succinct, exact, and beautiful language, as well as an underlying pulse or rhythm are the traits that most strongly set poetry apart from prose.

Not all rhyming, rhythmical language merits the label of poetry. *Verse* is a language form in which simple thoughts or stories are told in rhyme with a distinct beat or meter. Mother Goose and nursery rhymes are good examples of well-known, simple verses for children. And, of course, we are all too aware of the *jingle,* a catchy repetition of sounds heard so often in commercials. The most important feature of verses and jingles is their strong rhyme and rhythm. Content is light or even silly. Although verses and jingles can be enjoyable and have a place in the classroom, poetry can enrich children's lives by giving them new insights and fresh views on life's experiences and by bringing forth strong emotional responses.

The term *poetry* is used in this chapter both to refer to a higher quality of language—a form of language that can evoke great depth of feeling and provoke new insights through imaginative and beautiful language—and to refer to favorite verses of childhood.

## TYPES OF POETRY BOOKS

*P*oetry touches our minds and hearts through drawing on our five senses. Children, too, are reached by poetry, even though the subjects that move them may differ from those that move adults. A wide variety of poetry books is available today for use by students and teachers. Selecting books of poetry for use in the classroom as bridges between classroom activities, as materials for reading, and as literature for enjoyment will require teachers to review and evaluate the many types of poetry books: anthologies, Mother Goose and nursery rhyme books, nursery and folk songbooks, books of poems on special topics and by favorite poets, and single illustrated poems in picture book formats.

## Mother Goose and Nursery Rhyme Books

*Mother Goose and nursery rhyme books* are heavily illustrated collections of traditional verse. *Tomie dePaola's Mother Goose,* collected and illustrated by Tomie dePaola, is a good example. Often, a familiar illustration is all a child needs to get her or him to recite one of these well-loved verses. Collected nursery rhymes first appeared in editions of Charles Perrault's *Tales of Mother Goose* in France in the early eighteenth century. These verses are now part of our children's literary heritage. Also, they have proven to be a wonderful introduction to the world of literature for young children. In societies in which countless allusions are made every day to the characters and situations found in nursery rhymes, knowledge of this literature is a mark of being culturally literate.

Because so many of these verses exist, the better collections include large numbers of them thoughtfully organized around themes or topics; they are indexed by titles or first lines. A favorite book of this kind is *The Book of Nursery and Mother Goose Rhymes,* collected and illustrated by Marguerite de Angeli. Some lesser-known traditional verses were collected and illustrated by Arnold Lobel in *The Random House Book of Mother Goose.*

## Nursery and Folk Songbooks

*Nursery and folk songbooks* are heavily illustrated collections of both traditional and modern verses and their musical notation. *Songs from Mother Goose,* compiled by Nancy Larrick and illustrated by Robin Spowart, is a good example. Melody further emphasizes the innate musicality of these verses and turns some verses into games ("Ring around the Roses") and others into lullabies ("Rock-a-bye Baby"). In choosing a songbook, teachers, librarians, and parents should ascertain that there is a good selection of songs and that the music is well arranged for young voices and playable. Those who plan to work with preschoolers and first- and second-graders will be wise to make these songs part of their repertoire.

## Anthologies of Poetry

A large, comprehensive *anthology* of poetry for children is a must in every classroom. Anthologies should be organized by subjects for easy retrieval of poems appropriate for almost any occasion. In addition, indices of poets and titles, or first lines, are usually provided in these texts. Works by contemporary and traditional poets can be found in most of these anthologies; they appeal to a wide age range, providing nursery rhymes for toddlers as well as longer, narrative poems for the middle-grade student. An example is *A New Treasury of Children's Poetry: Old Favorites and New Discoveries,* selected by Joanna Cole.

## Specialized Poetry Books

*Specialized poetry books* are also readily available in which the poems are all by one poet, on one topic, for one age group, or of one poetic form. These specialized collections become necessary adjuncts for a teacher and class who come to love certain kinds of poetry or specific poets. Beautifully illustrated collections are also available and seem to be especially enjoyed by children for independent reading of poetry. Examples include *Words with Wrinkled Knees: Animal Poems* by Barbara Juster Esbensen and *Doodle Soup* by John Ciardi.

### Single Illustrated Poems

Single narrative poems of medium length are presented more frequently in picture book formats. These editions make poetry more appealing and accessible to many children, but in some cases the illustrations may remove the opportunity for children to form their own mental images from the language created by poets. The poetry section of your school library is worth perusing for interesting poetry books to use in the classroom.

## ELEMENTS OF POETRY

Just as with a work of fiction, the elements of a poem should be considered if the reader is to understand and evaluate the poem. Each of these parts—meaning, rhythm, sound patterns, figurative language, and sense imagery—is discussed in the following list.

- *Meaning.* Meaning is the underlying idea, feeling, or mood expressed through the poem. As with other literary forms, poetry is a form of communication; it is the way a poet chooses to express emotions and thoughts. Thus, the meaning of the poem is the expressed or implied message the poet conveys.
- *Rhythm.* Rhythm is the beat or regular cadence of the poem. Poetry, usually an oral form of literature, relies on rhythm to help communicate meaning. A fast rhythm is effected through short lines, clipped syllables, sharp, high vowel sounds, such as the sounds represented by the letters *a, e,* and *i,* and abrupt consonant sounds, such as the sounds represented by the letters *k, t, w,* and *p.* A fast rhythm can provide the listener with a feeling of happiness, excitement, drama, and even tension and suspense. A slow rhythm is effected by longer lines, multisyllabic words, full or low vowel sounds such as the sounds represented by the letters *o* and *u,* and resonating consonant sounds such as the sounds represented by the letters *m, n,* and *r.* A slow rhythm can evoke languor, tranquility, inevitability, and harmony, among other feelings. A change in rhythm during a poem signals the listener to a change in meaning.

In the poems that follow, "Song for a Blue Roadster" exhibits a fast rhythm that evokes the rapid speed of an automobile; "Slowly" proceeds more slowly in communicating the calm and quiet of summer.

### SONG FOR A BLUE ROADSTER

*Fly, roadster, fly!*
*The sun is high,*
*Gold are the fields*
*We hurry by,*
*Green are the woods*
*As we slide through*
*Past harbor and headland,*
*Blue on blue.*

*Fly, Roadster, fly!*
*The hay smells sweet,*
*And the flowers are fringing*
*Each village street,*

*Where carts are blue*
*And barns are red,*
*And the road unwinds*
*Like a twist of thread.*

*Fly, Roadster, fly!*
*Leave Time behind;*
*Out of sight*
*Shall be out of mind.*
*Shine and shadow*
*Blue sea, green bough,*
*Nothing is real*
*But Here and Now.*

— R A C H E L   F I E L D

*S L O W L Y*

*Slowly the tide creeps up the sand,*
*Slowly the shadows cross the land.*
*Slowly the cart-horse pulls his mile,*
*Slowly the old man mounts the stile.*

*Slowly the hands move round the clock,*
*Slowly the dew dries on the dock.*
*Slow is the snail—but slowest of all*
*The green moss spreads on the old brick wall.*

— J A M E S   R E E V E S

- *Sound Patterns.* Sound patterns are made by repeated sounds and combinations of sounds in the words. Words, phrases, or lines are sometimes repeated in their entirety. Also, parts of words may be repeated, as with rhyme, the sound device that children most recognize and enjoy. *Rhyme* occurs when the ends of words (the last vowel sound and any consonant sound that may follow it) have the same sounds. Examples of rhyming words are *vat, rat, that, brat,* and *flat,* as well as *hay, they, flay, stray,* and *obey. Assonance* is another pattern poets use for effects. In this case, the same vowel sound is heard repeatedly within a line or a few lines of poetry. Assonance is exemplified in these words: *hoop, gloom, moon, moot,* and *boots. Alliteration* is a pattern in which initial consonant sounds are heard frequently within a few lines of poetry. Examples are *ship, shy,* and *shape. Consonance* is similar to alliteration but usually refers to a close juxtaposition of similar final consonant sounds, as in fla*ck*, chu*ck*, and stro*ke*. *Onomatopoeia* is the device in which the sound of the word imitates the real-world sound. Examples are *buzz* for the sound of a bee and *hiss* for the sound a snake makes.
- *Figurative Language.* Figurative language takes many different forms, but it involves comparing or contrasting one object, idea, or feeling with another one. A *simile* is a direct comparison, typically using *like* or *as* to point out the similarities. A *metaphor* is an implied comparison without a signal word to evoke the similarities. *Personification* is the attribution of human qualities to animate, nonhuman beings or to inanimate objects for the purpose of drawing a comparison between

the animal or object and human beings. *Hyperbole* is an exaggeration to highlight reality or to point out ridiculousness. Children often delight in hyperbole because it appeals to their strong sense of the absurd.

- *Sense Imagery*. A poet will play on one or more of the five senses in descriptive and narrative language. *Sight* may be awakened through the depiction of beauty; *hearing* may be evoked by the sounds of a city street; *smell* and *taste* may be recalled through the description of a fish left too long in the sun; and finally, *touch* can be sensitized through describing the gritty discomfort of a wet swimsuit caked with sand from the beach. After listening to a poem, children can be asked to think about which of the senses the poet is appealing to.

These elements of poetry may be considered to select varied types of poems and to group them for presentation. However, little is gained by teaching each of these elements as a separate item to be memorized and/or analyzed. Poetic analysis has caused many students to dislike poetry. On the other hand, students whose teachers love poetry, select it wisely, read it aloud well, and provide students with many opportunities to enjoy it will come to appreciate poetry.

# E V A L U A T I O N   A N D   S E L E C T I O N   O F   P O E T R Y

The criteria to keep in mind in evaluating a poem for use with children are as follows:

- The ideas and feelings expressed are worthy, fresh, and imaginative.
- The expression of the ideas and feelings is unique, often causing the reader to perceive ordinary things in new ways.
- The poem is appropriate to the experiences of children and does not preach to them.
- The poem presents the world through a child's perspective and focuses on children's lives and activities as well as on activities to which people of all ages can relate.
- A poem that panders to children's base instincts is probably best avoided and replaced by other enjoyable, worthy choices.
- Poetry collections should be judged on the quality of the poetry choices. If you decide that the poetry is well selected, consider the illustrations and the appearance of the book. Beautiful illustrations do not ensure a good collection of poems within the covers.
- Children report a preference for narrative poems. You will want to include some narrative poems along with other types of poetry.
- Although certain poets may be favored by your students, they will also enjoy the poetry of many other writers. Thus, be sure to share with your students poems by a variety of authors.

In selecting poems to read to students, the list of notable poets at the end of this chapter, the Golden Age poets listed on page 45, and the list of poets who have won the National Council of Teachers of English (NCTE) Award are good starting points. The NCTE Award was established in 1977 in the United States to honor living U.S. poets whose poetry has contributed substantially to the lives of children. This award is given to a poet for the entire body of writing for children ages 3 through 13 and is now given every three years.

NCTE EXCELLENCE IN POETRY FOR CHILDREN AWARD WINNERS

1977    David McCord
1978    Aileen Fisher
1979    Karla Kuskin
1980    Myra Cohn Livingston
1981    Eve Merriam
1982    John Ciardi
1985    Lilian Moore
1988    Arnold Adoff
1991    Valerie Worth
1994    Barbara Juster Esbensen
1997    Eloise Greenfield
2000    X. J. Kennedy

Although more poetry for children is being written and published and many teachers and their students are enjoying this genre of literature, some teachers report that they do not share poetry because of their uncertainty about selecting poems for their students. By learning about students' preferences in poetry and some of the best-loved poems and most respected poets, a teacher can become more skillful at selecting good and enjoyable poems for students. The next section will review research on children's preferences in poetry.

## Children's Poetry Preferences

The findings from two surveys of children's poetry preferences can be helpful to teachers in selecting poems for a new group of students. Fisher and Natarella (1982) surveyed primary-grade children and their teachers, and Terry (1974) studied intermediate-grade children. The two age groups were similar, although not identical, in their preferences.

- Both age groups preferred narrative poems over lyric poems.
- Limericks were the favored poetic form of both age groups.
- Free verse and haiku were not well liked by either age group.
- Children of both age groups preferred poems that had pronounced sound patterns of all kinds, but especially enjoyed poems that rhymed.
- Rhythm was also an important element to students of both age groups; they preferred poems with regular, distinctive beats.
- Imagery and figurative language were not as well received by students of both age groups; students reported that they did not always understand poems with considerable figurative language.
- Children of both age groups liked humorous poems, poems about animals, and poems about enjoyable familiar experiences.
- The subjects most preferred by primary-grade children were strange and fantastic events, animals, and other children; the older children preferred the realistic contents of humor, enjoyable familiar experiences, and animals.

A study by Kutiper and Wilson (1993) was conducted to determine whether an examination of school library circulation records would confirm the findings of the earlier poetry preference studies. The findings of this library circulation study indicated that the humorous contemporary poetry of Shel Silverstein and Jack Prelutsky dominated the students' choices. The collections of poetry written by the NCTE award winners did not circulate widely; nor were they widely available in the school libraries studied, even though these poets reflect a higher quality of language and usage than is found in the light verse so popular with students. Kutiper and Wilson stated that real interest in poetry must go beyond Prelutsky and Silverstein. This interest needs to be developed by teachers who provide an array of poetry that builds on students' natural interests.

Children's appreciation of poetry can be broadened and deepened by a good teacher, but you may be wise to proceed with caution on less-liked aspects of poetry until your students become fans of poetry. Thus, a good selection of rhyming, narrative poems with distinct rhythms about humorous events, well-liked familiar experiences, and animals is a good starting point for students who have little experience with poetry.

## HISTORICAL OVERVIEW OF POETRY

Poetry for children began centuries ago in the form of nursery rhymes that were recited to babies and toddlers by caregivers. These verses were passed along via the oral tradition. The earliest published collection of nursery rhymes that survives today is *Tommy Thumb's Pretty Song Book* (1744), which is housed in the British Museum (Gillespie, 1970). This songbook contains familiar rhymes such as "Hickory Dickory Dock" and "Mary Mary Quite Contrary." These rhymes and others like them came to be called *Mother Goose rhymes,* but the term *Mother Goose* was first used in France by Charles Perrault in his *Stories and Tales of Past Times with Morals; or, Tales of Mother Goose* (1697) to refer to his collection of fairy tales. Later editions contained nursery rhymes, which became so popular that Mother Goose became a general name for nursery rhymes. The rhymes are light, rhythmical, and often nonsensical verses shared with young children. The rhymes are recited by parents, and children soon become familiar with them and join in the fun. For many, nursery rhymes and other poems were the first forms of literature experienced; these poems symbolize the reassuring sounds of childhood.

Another early type of poetry was quite different from nursery rhymes and was intended for a somewhat older audience of children. Poems of a moral and religious bent were shared with obvious didactic intent, reflecting the strict attitude toward the rearing of children that held sway in the Western world from the Middle Ages to the late nineteenth century. Fear of death and punishment was instilled as a means of gaining obedience to authority. Ann and Jane Taylor's *Original Poems, for Infant Minds, by Several Young Persons* (1804) provided verse of this kind. Some titles of poems from this early collection are "The Idle Boy," "Greedy Richard," "Meddlesome Matty," and "The Church-Yard." A few purely descriptive, nondidactic poems from this same collection are still remembered today, especially "Twinkle, Twinkle Little Star." Clement Moore's "Visit from St. Nicholas" (1823), another nondidactic, narrative poem, is still enjoyed and known today as " 'Twas the Night Before Christmas."

Poetry for children flourished from the middle of the nineteenth century through the 1920s, a period that can be considered the Golden Age of Poetry for Children. Page 45 lists the poets, countries, landmark works and dates, and characteristics. The Golden Age of Poetry moved away from moralistic

# MILESTONES

## *in POETRY during the GOLDEN AGE*

| DATE | POET | LANDMARK WORK | COUNTRY | CHARACTERISTIC |
|------|------|---------------|---------|----------------|
| 1846 | Edward Lear | *A Book of Nonsense* | England | Father of nonsense poetry, limericks |
| 1864 | Lewis Carroll | "Jabberwocky" | England | Nonsense verses, such as those in *Alice's Adventures in Wonderland* |
| 1872 | Christina Rossetti | *Sing Song* | England | Poems on children and the small things around them |
| 1885 | Robert Louis Stevenson | *A Child's Garden of Verses* | England | Descriptive poems of childhood memories |
| 1888 | Ernest Thayer | "Casey at the Bat" | U.S.A. | Famous ballad on baseball |
| 1890 | Laura E. Richards | *In My Nursery* | U.S.A. | Poems with hilarious situations, wordplay, and strong rhythm |
| 1896 | Eugene Field | *Poems of Childhood* | U.S.A. | Poems reflecting on children and child life |
| 1902 | Walter de la Mare | *Songs of Childhood* | England | Musical and imaginative poetry |
| 1920 | Rose Fyleman | *Fairies and Chimneys* | England | Imaginative poems about fairies |
| 1922 | A. A. Milne | *When We Were Very Young* | England | Poems of fun in which the child's world is observed |
| 1926 | Rachel Field | *Taxis and Toadstools* | U.S.A. | Poems about city and country through the child's eyes |

poetry and instead provided children with poems describing the beauty of life and nature, with poems of humor, nonsense, and word fun, and with imaginative poems that interpreted life from the child's perspective. Much of the Golden Age poetry retains its appeal for today's children; for example, *A Child's Garden of Verses* (1885) by Robert Louis Stevenson remains a favorite collection of poems among parents and children. This positive shift in poetry for children set the standard for poetry for the remainder of the twentieth century.

In the 1960s and 1970s, the general trend toward realism in children's literature was also reflected in poetry. More topics considered suitable for the child audience resulted in protest poetry, poems about girls in nontraditional roles, and irreverent poems. For example, parents, teachers, and other adults became fair game for ridicule and mockery. Minority poets were more frequently published, and their poetry gained in popularity. Most of the early poetry for children before the 1950s was by English poets, but during the last half of the century, many U.S., Canadian, and Australian poets have gained favor with children. Poems by John Ciardi, Myra Cohn Livingston, Jack Prelutsky, Shel Silverstein, Dennis Lee, and Max Fatchen have engendered popular interest in this genre. As mentioned in the previous section, the National Council of Teachers of English Award for Excellence in Poetry for Children was established in 1977 and has conferred a new importance on poetry for children.

Popularity of poetry in the classroom began in the 1980s and continues into this decade. Developments in the publishing industry attest to this popularity. For example, Boyds Mills Press has a division devoted to children's poetry, called Windsong. Publishers continue to present both single poems and collections of poems in beautifully illustrated book formats. In the 1980s, Nancy Willard's *A Visit to William Blake's Inn: Poems for Innocent and Experienced Travelers* and Paul Fleischman's *Joyful Noise: Poems for Two Voices* received Newbery Medals, indicating greater recognition of poetry for young people in the United States. In 1994, the Japanese poet Michio Mado was awarded the international Hans Christian Andersen Medal, an honor seldom bestowed on a poet. An increase in the publication of anthologies of poems by and about minorities, such as *Pass It On*, edited by Wade Hudson, has also been noted in the 1990s. This increased publication has also resulted in greater attention to earlier African American poets, such as Paul Laurence Dunbar, Countee Cullen, and Langston Hughes.

## POETRY  TYPES  AND  FORMS

Poetry can be classified in many ways; one way is to consider two main types that generally differ in purpose: lyric and narrative poetry. *Lyric poetry* captures a moment, a feeling, or a scene, and is descriptive in nature, whereas *narrative poetry* tells a story or includes a sequence of events. From this definition, you will recognize the following selection to be a lyric poem.

*G I R A F F E S*

*Stilted creatures,*
*Features fashioned as a joke,*
*Boned and buckled,*
*Finger painted,*
*They stand in the field*
*On long-pronged legs*
*As if thrust there.*
*They airily feed,*
*Slightly swaying,*
*Like hammer-headed flowers.*

*Bizarre they are,*
*Built silent and high,*
*Ornaments against the sky.*
*Ears like leaves*
*To hear the silken*
*Brushing of the clouds.*

— S y   K a h n

The next selection is an example of a narrative poem:

*THE  BROKEN-LEGG'D  MAN*

*I saw the other day when I went shopping in the store*
*A man I hadn't ever ever seen in there before,*
*A man whose leg was broken and who leaned upon a crutch—*
*I asked him very kindly if it hurt him very much.*
*"Not at all!" said the broken-legg'd man.*

*I ran around behind him for I thought that I would see*
*The broken leg all bandaged up and bent back at the knee;*
*But I didn't see the leg at all, there wasn't any there,*
*So I asked him very kindly if he had it hid somewhere.*
*"Not at all!" said the broken-legg'd man.*

*"Then where," I asked him, "is it? Did a tiger bite it off?*
*Or did you get your foot wet when you had a nasty cough?*
*Did someone jump down on your leg when it was very new?*
*Or did you simply cut it off because you wanted to?"*
*"Not at all!" said the broken-legg'd man.*

*"What was it then?" I asked the man, and this is what he said:*
*"I crossed a busy crossing when the traffic light was red;*
*A big black car came whizzing by and knocked me off my feet."*
*"Of course you looked both ways," I said, "before you crossed the street."*
*"Not at all!" said the broken-legg'd man.*

*"They rushed me to a hospital right quickly," he went on,*
*"And when I woke in nice white sheets I saw my leg was gone;*
*That's why you see me walking now on nothing but a crutch."*
*"I'm glad," said I, "you told me, and I thank you very much!"*
*"Not at all!" said the broken-legg'd man.*

— J O H N  M A C K E Y  S H A W

Poetry can also be categorized by its *poetic form,* which refers to the way the poem is structured or put together. *Couplets, tercets, quatrains,* and *cinquains* refer to the number (two, three, four, and five) of lines of poetry in a stanza—a set of lines of poetry grouped together. Couplets, tercets, quatrains, and cinquains usually rhyme, though the rhyme scheme may vary; these poetic forms may constitute an entire poem, or a poem may be comprised of a few stanzas of couplets, tercets, and so on.

Other specific poetic forms frequently found in children's poetry are limericks, ballads, haiku, free verse, and concrete poetry.

A limerick is a humorous, one-stanza, five-line verse form (usually a narrative), in which lines 1, 2, and 5 rhyme and are of the same length and lines 3 and 4 rhyme and are of the same length but shorter than the other lines. The following is an example of a limerick by Edward Lear, the poet who popularized this poetic form in the nineteenth century.

*T H E R E   W A S   A N   O L D   P E R S O N   W H O S E   H A B I T S*

*There was an old person whose habits*
*Induced him to feed upon rabbits;*
*When he'd eaten eighteen,*
*He turned perfectly green,*
*Upon which he relinquished those habits.*

—  E D W A R D   L E A R

A *ballad* is a fairly long narrative poem of popular origin, usually adapted to singing. These traditional story poems are often romantic or heroic. "The Outlandish Knight," a thirteen-stanza ballad, tells the tale of the clever young woman who tricks the man who deceived her.

*T H E   O U T L A N D I S H   K N I G H T*

*An outlandish knight came out of the North,*
  *To woo a maiden fair;*
*He promised to take her to the North lands,*
  *Her father's only heir.*

*"Come, fetch me some of your father's gold,*
  *And some of your mother's fee;*
*And two of the best nags out of the stable,*
  *Where they stand thirty and three."*

*She fetched him some of her father's gold*
  *And some of her mother's fee;*
*And two of the best nags out of the stable,*
  *Where they stood thirty and three.*

*He mounted her on her milk-white steed,*
  *He on the dapple grey;*
*They rode till they came unto the sea-side,*
  *Three hours before it was day.*

*"Light off, light off thy milk-white steed,*
  *And deliver it unto me;*
*Six pretty maids have I drowned here,*
  *And thou the seventh shall be."*

*"Pull off, pull off thy silken gown,*
  *And deliver it unto me;*
*Methinks it looks too rich and too gay*
  *To rot in the salt sea."*

*"Pull off, pull off thy silken stays,*
  *And deliver them unto me;*
*Methinks they are too fine and gay*
  *To rot in the salt sea."*

*"Pull off, pull off the Holland smock*
  *And deliver it unto me;*
*Methinks it looks too rich and gay*
  *To rot in the salt sea."*

*"If I must pull off my Holland smock,*
   *Pray turn thy back unto me,*
*For it is not fitting that such a ruffian*
   *A woman unclad should see."*

*He turned his back towards her,*
   *And viewed the leaves so green;*
*She catch'd him round the middle so small,*
   *And tumbled him into the stream.*

*He dropped high, and he dropped low,*
   *Until he came to the tide—*
*"Catch hold of my hand, my pretty maiden,*
   *And I will make you my bride."*

*"Lie there, lie there, you false-hearted man,*
   *Lie there instead of me;*
*Six pretty maidens have you drowned here,*
   *And the seventh has drowned thee."*

*She mounted on her milk-white steed,*
   *And led the dapple grey.*
*She rode til she came to her father's hall,*
   *Three hours before it was day.*

—TRADITIONAL

*Haiku* is a lyric, unrhymed poem of Japanese origin with seventeen syllables, arranged on three lines with a syllable count of five, seven, and five. Haiku is highly evocative poetry that frequently espouses harmony with and appreciation of nature. Here is an example.

*Small bird, forgive me.*
*I'll hear the end of your song*
   *in some other world.*

—ANONYMOUS (TRANSLATED BY HARRY BEHN)

*Free verse* is unrhymed poetry with little or light rhythm. Sometimes words within a line will rhyme. The subjects of free verse are often abstract and philosophical; they are always reflective.

*LAST DAY OF SCHOOL*

*Look out!*
*If you aren't careful*
*it will happen like this: Someone*
*will say the word*
*and that*
*word*
*will catapult you    down*
*the halls   out*
*the doors  and into*
*a serious collision*
*with*
*SUMMER!*

—BARBARA JUSTER ESBENSEN

Concrete poetry is written and printed in a shape that signifies the subject of the poem. Concrete poems are a form of poetry that must be seen as well as heard to be fully appreciated. These poems do not usually have rhyme or definite rhythm; they rely mostly on the words, their meanings and shapes, and the way the words are arranged on the page to evoke images. In "Concrete Cat" you will note through the position of the word that the mouse appears to have met with an accident.

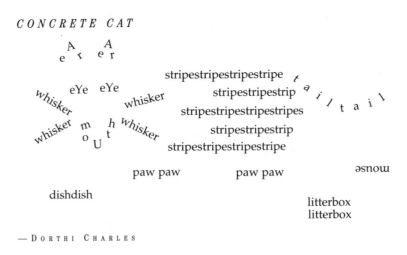

*CONCRETE CAT*

— Dorthi Charles

## POETRY IN THE CLASSROOM

Poetry is enjoyable for students of all ages. It enhances students' development of literacy. Teachers and librarians can entice students into a lifelong love for poetry through making available a well-balanced collection of poetry books and through providing many experiences with poetry.

### Students' Listening to and Saying Poems

Teachers and librarians can begin by providing even very young students with many opportunities to hear and say poems. Later, when students have developed a love of poetry and an affinity for the language play in poems, students can read poetry by fine poets and poems by their classmates and can begin to write poems themselves. In other words, poetry needs to be shared in both oral and written forms.

Poetry should be introduced first and often to children in an oral form. As discussed earlier, poetry was in its origins an oral form of literature; it still relies heavily on the auditory perceptions of listeners. Moreover, children's oral language is the basis for their later acquisition of literacy. These two facts combine nicely to make listening to poems and saying poems a natural early introduction to literature for children. Some teachers report that they do not share poetry with their students because of their uncertainty about how to read it aloud. By practicing the poems ahead of time and by reading poetry frequently, a teacher can overcome this reluctance. The rewards to both students and teachers are worth the effort. The next section offers suggestions to help you become an effective reader of poetry.

**READING POETRY ALOUD TO CHILDREN**    Poetry should be read aloud to students on a daily basis. Brief, positive encounters with one to three poems at a time are best. Too many poems in one sitting may overwhelm students or make the reading tedious. Introduce the poem to the class before reading it aloud, either by tying the poem in with something else or by briefly telling why you chose to read this poem aloud. Then state the title of the poem and begin to read. After reading the poem, be sure to announce the name of the poet so that students discover the writers they especially enjoy. In addition, the following points will help you to read poetry well:

- The most important rule to keep in mind is that poetry should be read for its meaning. Stress the meaning elements of the poem just as you do when reading prose. Often, the words in poetry are phrased in such a way that you must continue past the end of the line to the next line before pausing. In other words, the breaks must be determined by the meaning units of the poem, not by the lines.

- A corollary of the first rule is that a reader should not overemphasize the beat of the poem. Doing so results in an annoying singsong effect. The natural rhythm of the poem will be felt in a more interesting way if you avoid an unnatural, meaningless reading and let the poetic language provide the rhythm.

- Poetry should be enunciated clearly. Each sound and each syllable of a poem are important and must be heard to be appreciated. This often means that you will need to slow down your normal reading pace to give full value to each sound.

- Poetry needs to be performed and dramatized. Take some chances and try out different effects (using different voices, elongating words, singing, shouting, whispering, pausing dramatically, and so on) as you read poems aloud. Your voice is a powerful tool: You may change it from louder to softer to only a whisper; you may start at a deep, low pitch and rise to a medium and eventually high pitch; you may speak very quickly in a clipped fashion and then slow down and drawl out the words.

- Poems may need to be read aloud a number of times because their many meanings may be perceived only after the literal sense is known. Also, favorite poems can be enjoyed again and again, as teachers and students savor one more reading. Another way to provide students with opportunities to listen to poems is by recording audiotapes of poems for the listening center and making them available along with the poem in print, on a chart or in a book, for the student to listen to and read. Commercially made tapes with popular poets reading their works, accompanied by music, are available and are quite popular with children. Some teachers have asked parents to peruse a poetry anthology, select a favorite poem, and then read the poem on tape for use in the listening center.

- After reading a poem aloud, some form of response is usually enjoyed. Sometimes the response students have to a poem is simply the desire to hear it again. Other times, students need just a few moments to reflect silently on the poem. Some poems warrant discussion, and students can take the opportunity to tell how the poem made them feel or what it made them think about.

*CHORAL POETRY*    A time-honored technique for providing opportunities to say and hear poems over and over again is given by choral poetry. *Choral poetry* consists of interpreting and saying a poem together as a group activity. These poems may either be practiced and recited aloud or rehearsed and read aloud. Students enjoy this way of experiencing poetry because they have a participatory role in the activity. Most poetry, intended to be listened to, is suitable for choral presentation. The following sections explain how to select choral poems and teach them to students.

1. *Selection.*

At first, select a short poem (from one to four stanzas) until your students develop some skill in memorizing, reciting, and performing poems. Humorous narrative poems are good first choices. Later, you will want to experiment with longer poems.

2. *Memorization.*

For most choral presentations, the first step is for the teacher to select and read aloud a poem that is well liked by the students. Then each line or pair of lines is said by the teacher and repeated by the students until they know them. It is preferable for the students to repeat the lines after the teacher and for the teacher to avoid reciting with the class, so that the students will commit the poem to memory instead of waiting for the teacher's voice. Once the entire poem is learned in this way, variations can be added for performing the poem. Although students need to rehearse a poem to intone it similarly, some longer poems with older students who read well will not be memorized but will be practiced and read together as a group.

3. *Arrangements.*

Options for reading a poem chorally include unison, two- or three-part, solo voices, cumulative buildup, and simultaneous voices, as is now explained.

- In unison choral speaking, the students learn the poem and recite it together as a group. Two-part or three-part choral poetry is usually based on arranging students into voice types (for example, high, medium, and low) to achieve different effects and by selecting lines of the poem for each group to recite or read.

- Solo voices can be added to either of these presentations and are sometimes used for asking a question or making an exclamation.

- Some poems lend themselves to cumulative buildup presentations. A cumulative buildup is effected by having, for example, only two voices say the first line, then two more join in on the second, and then two more, gradually building to a crescendo until the entire class says the last line or stanza.

- Poems can be presented by simultaneous recitation, which forms a presentation similar to a musical round. In this case, group one begins the poem and recites it all the way through. When group one begins the third line, for example, then group two starts the first line, and the two groups recite simultaneously until the end. Other groups can, of course, be added.

- Poetry selected and arranged for dramatic choral readings on a particular theme infuses an interesting variation into choral poetry. Paul Fleischman's *Joyful Noise: Poems for Two Voices* (1988) and *I Am Phoenix: Poems for Two Voices* (1985) are collections of poetry on a single theme for older children. These poems are written in a manner that is already suitable for choral reading. The poems in *Joyful Noise* describe different insects; *I Am Phoenix* contains poems about birds. The poems in each of these collections were written to be read aloud by two readers at once, one reading the left half of the page and one reading the right half. At times, the readers read certain lines simultaneously. Pairs of students may each take a different poem from the collection for presentation.

Many other variations can be developed for use in choral presentations. Let imagination be your guide. Words and lines can be spun into ghostly moans, or barked, or sung, or repeated. Choreography adds visual impact, as do simple props. As soon as children learn that poems do not have to be read sedately through exactly as written, they will begin to find excitement and deeper meaning in poetry.

4. *Performance.*

Incorporating action, gestures, body movements, and finger plays can produce more interesting and enjoyable presentations. Occasionally performing a well-honed choral poem for an audience can bring pride to young performers. Remember, the best audiences are close by—the class next door, the principal, the librarian, the custodian, or a visiting parent. Students truly enjoy this nonthreatening way of sharing poetry. Stimulate creativity by reading different poems and allowing various interpretations to reveal the imagination and insight of your students.

In addition to the group activity of performing choral poetry, teachers can encourage an individual student to learn a poem by heart, voluntarily, and then to recite the poem in a small group or as part of a group performance, perhaps around a theme. For example, a small group of interested students might each select a poem about weather as part of their study about weather in science. Jane Yolen's collection of weather poems, *Weather Report,* could be a resource for this activity.

## Students' Reading and Writing Poems

*LEARNING TO READ POETRY*   Children enjoy reading poetry silently and aloud to others. The classroom library corner should have one or two comprehensive poetry anthologies for students to browse through for general purposes. In addition, two or three specialized collections by a single poet, such as *Garbage Delight* (1978) by Dennis Lee, and another two or three books of poems on a single topic, such as *Cats Are Cats* (1988) by Nancy Larrick, compiler, are needed as well. Students can be encouraged to make copies of their favorite poems from these various collections to develop personal, individual anthologies. Many students choose to illustrate these and arrange the poems in new and inventive ways. Rotating the poetry books occasionally over the course of the school year will spark renewed interest in reading poetry.

Other activities to encourage the reading of poetry by students follow:

- Place students in pairs to take turns reading favorite poems to one another. Make videotapes or audiotapes of these readings and permit students to listen to or watch their own and other students' readings of poetry. Teachers have found that when students listen to their own reading of poetry they begin to note singsong readings and learn to avoid them.

- Ask each student to select three poems by one poet (for example, a Golden Age poet, or an NCTE poet) and find something out about the poet; then place students in small groups of five or six to tell briefly about the poet and read the three poems aloud. Paul B. Janeczko's *The Place My Words Are Looking For: What Poets Say about and through Their Work* (1990) is an excellent resource for this purpose. Comments on the work of more than forty poets and examples of their poetry can assist students in this activity.

- Have students find three poems on the same topic, such as trees, mice, or friendship; then read them aloud in small groups.

- Students may also find poems that are of the same poetic form—cinquains, limericks, and so forth; or that exhibit similar poetic elements—rhyme, alliteration, or onomatopoeia; or that have fast or slow rhythms. These poems can then comprise the poems for reading aloud that day or week.

*LEARNING TO WRITE POETRY*    A rich poetry environment stimulates children's interest in writing their own poems. Children need to be very familiar with poetry of many kinds and by many poets before they should be expected to compose poems. The collection of poems *Inner Chimes: Poems on Poetry* (1992) may be a natural starting place for helping students to think about poetry and what it is. Poems by various renowned children's poets writing about creating poetry have been selected by Bobbye S. Goldstein for this volume. Other books that provide suggestions on how to include poetry in the classroom are *Sunrises and Songs: Reading and Writing Poetry in an Elementary Classroom* (1990) by Amy McClure, Peggy Harrison, and Sheryl Reed and *How to Write a Poem* (1996) by Margaret Ryan.

Teachers often start the writing of poetry as a collaborative effort. The class brainstorms for ideas, then composes the poem orally as the teacher writes it on the board or on chart paper. As students become comfortable with writing group poetry, they can branch off and begin composing poems in pairs or their own individual poems.

Children should be reminded that poetry is a form of communication and that they should think of an idea, feeling, or event to write about in their poems. They should be reminded that poetry does not have to rhyme and that they may write about something of interest to them. Children's poetry follows no absolute rules; perfection of form should not be a goal. Other suggestions to foster poetry writing include the following:

- Have students compile personal and class anthologies of their own poems or their favorite poems.
- Design bulletin boards with poetry displays of students' own poems as well as copies of poems by favorite poets.
- Let students rework a narrative poem into a different genre, such as a newspaper article or a letter. In turn, students may attempt the reverse—taking a newspaper article and putting it to verse.
- Suggest to students that they design posters, individually or in groups, to illustrate a favorite poem. Posters are then displayed around the school for a few weeks.
- Encourage students to model the works of professional poets by attempting imitation of a whole poem or of specific techniques.
- Read aloud many poems of one poetic form; then analyze the form with the students to reveal the characteristics of its structure. Quatrains, cinquains, haiku, concrete poems, and limericks can all be used as models with students once they have an appreciation for poetry and for the specific poetic form.

Some poets have suggested other models and patterns for students to follow in writing poetry. Kenneth Koch's *Rose, Where Did You Get That Red?* (1990) and *Wishes, Lies, and Dreams* (1999); M. K. Glover's *A Garden of Poets: Poetry Writing in the Elementary Classroom (1999); Lee Bennett Hopkins's Pass the Poetry, Please!* (1987); David McCord's *One at a Time* (1977); Myra Cohn Livingston's *Poem Making: Ways to Begin Writing Poetry* (1991); Paul Janeczko's *How to Write Poetry* (1999); and Paul Janeczko's *Poetry from A to Z: A Guide for Young Writers* (1994) are useful resources for teachers who want to encourage students to compose poems. Finally, there is a list of Do's and Don'ts for teaching poetry.

| Do | Don't |
| --- | --- |
| Read poetry aloud every day | Limit poetry choices to one or two poets or types of poems |
| Practice reading a poem before reading it aloud for the first time to students | Choose all poems from one anthology |
| Choose poetry the students will like | Have poetry marathon days or weeks to make up for not sharing poetry regularly |
| Intersperse classic poems/poets and new poems/poets with more popular poems/poets | Read poems in a singsong style |
| Make a variety of excellent poetry anthologies and specialized poetry books available in the classroom | Make the analysis of poetry the focus of poetry study |
| Inspire students to enjoy poetry by reciting poems from memory and by sharing poems you have written | Force students to memorize and recite poems |
| Encourage students to recite and write poems | Forget to display students' original poems |
| Direct choral poetry presentations | Have students copy poems for handwriting practice |
| Feature a notable poet each month | Make the main emphasis of poetry be the writing of formula poems |
| Begin and end each day with a poem | Forget poetry |

## SECTION TWO: *Plays*

Plays should be included in a well-balanced literary curriculum for children. Children when allowed to play freely often dramatize their daily lives and fantasies. In playacting, children can act out in ways not normally allowed, giving expression to hidden feelings. Children's linguistic abilities can improve if they become actively engaged in the literature of the theatre by reading plays, performing plays, and watching others perform plays. And, of course, children delight in plays and playacting.

The use of the same word, *play,* for the main, natural activity of childhood is not a coincidence. The development and use of the imagination in the child's creation of play and in the creation of theatre are similar. The same human needs are met. In a play and in a child's own play, imagination transforms reality and endows ordinary objects with fantastic qualities. Imagination also helps the actor create a character for the enjoyment of the audience (Davis, 1981). The persons who long ago performed plays for the enjoyment of audiences were called players long before they were called actors.

Plays provide many of the same personal benefits to young readers as prose. Students enjoy reading plays and are able to experience a story vicariously quite readily through the play form. Plays can also help students develop their imaginations and ability to empathize with others (Smolkin, 1995). In addition, reading plays aloud and performing plays are natural ways to develop and demonstrate a child's oral reading fluency—the ability to read smoothly without hesitation and with good comprehension—a reading goal many teachers have for their students. McKean (2000–2001) offers practical acting tips for teachers and students to develop excellent oral reading interpretations. Plays provide a natural reason to develop these traits and put oral reading to use in a purposeful way.

## D E F I N I T I O N   A N D   D E S C R I P T I O N

*Plays,* as a literary genre, refers to written, dramatic compositions or scripts intended to be acted. A play may be divided into parts called *acts;* in turn, each act may be divided into *scenes.* The script usually has set, costume, and stage directions noted, as well as dialogue provided for each actor. Plays are usually published in *playbooks* or *acting editions,* 4 × 8 paperback books, by publishers who specialize in plays. These playbooks are quite inexpensive and can be purchased directly from the publishers or ordered through bookstores. A teacher or school may purchase a set of playbooks for children's use in group reading situations. Generally, if the plays are for classroom use, no royalty need be paid. If they are being used in a school but for an audience beyond the classroom, there is usually a moderate royalty fee as indicated in the publisher's catalog.

In addition to published plays for young audiences, some other terms worth clarifying are *readers' theatre, creative drama* (sometimes referred to as creative dramatics or informal drama), *recreational drama,* and *children's theatre. Readers' theatre* is the oral presentation of literature by actors, and usually a narrator, reading from a script; it is a form of play reading, a dramatic reading that depends largely on voice and gestures to convey additional meaning. Generally no stage sets, costumes, or stage movements are involved in readers' theatre. *Creative drama* is informal drama that lends itself to the reenactment of story experiences. This form of drama is spontaneously generated by the participants who compose and act out their parts as the drama progresses. Generally no scripts are developed or lines read or memorized. Creative drama is a process-centered form of drama performed for the benefit of the participants. *Recreational drama* is a formal theatrical presentation where the development and experience of the performers is as important as the enjoyment by the audience. School and camp plays are examples of recreational drama. *Children's theatre,* sometimes referred to as theatre for young audiences, is a formal theatrical experience in which a play is presented for an audience of children. Usually the performers are skilled actors, and the production is overseen by trained directors (Goldberg, 1974).

In this chapter we address published plays found in books and magazines as a literary genre—that is, as material to be read by children, either independently or in small groups. Some of these same plays also may be performed in children's theatres. We recommend that teachers and librarians emphasize the informal reading of plays by children during the elementary school years. Recreational plays and formal play productions are better left to middle school or older students. The dramatic processes of creative drama and readers' theatre, discussed in Chapter 12, are also suitable for elementary grade students.

## EVALUATION AND SELECTION OF PLAYS

A good play has a subject that appeals to children, an interesting character or two, and a problem that thickens or worsens, but gets resolved satisfactorily in the end. Humor always appeals to children, and conflict between characters is needed for interest and drama. Dialogue must be natural and reflect the personality of the character speaking. One or more of the characters in the play must have child appeal; typically such a character is a child or a childlike figure; a personified animal, doll, or other creature; or an adult with magical traits. Many published plays are planned for more elaborate productions than time will permit in the classroom. Such details can be interesting for children to read about, even if they are not likely to be able to produce the play as suggested.

Children's plays in the United States have been viewed as the stepchild both in the field of theatre and in the field of children's literature. Although some writers have given substantial attention to the development of play scripts for children, their work has not always been as highly valued by theatre producers and critics as that of playwrights who write for adults. Children's literature specialists have viewed drama primarily from a process perspective with scant attention given to the writing and publication of plays. Few plays have been published purely for reading enjoyment, and few have been included in the literary canon for children. For these reasons, locating and selecting plays can be a challenge.

Published children's plays have relied heavily on adaptations of narrative children's literature. Original plays can be found, but are not numerous. *Children's Book and Play Review,* a professional journal that appears five times a year, provides reviews of ten or twelve children's plays in each issue and has feature articles occasionally about the publication status of children's plays. (See Appendix B for subscription information.) Other review journals, such as *School Library Journal, Booklist,* and *Horn Book* Magazine, occasionally review published plays as well. The International Association of Theatre for Children and Young People periodically publishes international bibliographies of plays organized by country and provides a synopsis of each play, as well as its length, type, number of characters, languages in which it is available, and source for ordering (Oaks, 1996).

At the present time eighteen to twenty publishing houses handle children's plays. Eleven publishers have specialized in plays for children and deserve special mention here:

Anchorage Press Plays, P.O. Box 2901, Louisville, KY 40201–2901, formerly Children's Theatre Press, one of the oldest publishing houses for children's plays, remains a major publisher of children's plays with a backlist of approximately 290 plays for children.

Baker's Plays, P.O. Box 699222, Quincy, MA 02269, is a general play publisher with a specialization in children's plays with both a backlist and recent titles. The current list has approximately 110 plays.

Contemporary Drama Service, 885 Elkton Drive, Colorado Springs, CO 80907, publishes plays for middle school and high school students, has approximately 500 plays, and publishes 25 new plays each year.

Dramatic Publishing Company, 311 Washington Street, Woodstock, IL 60098, has a large list of approximately 180 children's and young adult plays.

Eldredge Publishing, P.O. Box 1595, Venice, FL 34284, is one of the oldest children's play publishers with a large list of approximately 600 plays and publishes 30 or more new plays each year.

I. E. Clark, Inc., Box 246, Schulenberg, TX 78956, is a general publisher with over 60 children's plays including some bilingual plays.

Kalmbach Publishing Company (now includes Plays, Inc., Publishers), 21027 Crossroads Circle, Waukesha, WI 53187, is a general publisher that publishes 50–60 royalty-free new plays for children each year in the moderately priced magazine, *Plays, the Drama Magazine for Young People.* Anthologies drawn from these plays are also available.

New Plays, Inc., New Plays for Children, P.O. Box 5074, Charlottesville, VA 22905, is a publisher that specializes in children's plays with 100 titles available, many for the middle school level.

Pioneer Drama Service, P.O. Box 4267, Englewood, CO 80155, is a general publisher of plays with more than 130 plays for children.

Samuel French, Inc., 45 W. 25th St. New York, NY 10010, is a large general publisher of plays with a large backlist of children's plays, but is publishing few new children's plays currently.

Smith and Kraus, Inc. c/o IDS, 300 Bedford Street, Building B, Suite 213, Manchester, NH 03101, is a publisher of plays and play anthologies for children.

The American Alliance of Theatre and Education (AATE) gives two awards that are useful in identifying notable children's plays and playwrights. The Distinguished Play Award, established in 1983, is given annually to honor the playwright and publisher of the works voted as the best original plays for young people published during the preceding year in category A, for upper and secondary school age audiences, and category B, for elementary and middle school age audiences. Beginning in 1997 category C was added for the best adaptation. (See Appendix A for the complete list of winners.) The Charlotte B. Chorpenning Playwright Award, first conferred in 1967, honors a body of work by a children's playwright. The award is given annually, if merited.

### CHARLOTTE B. CHORPENNING PLAYWRIGHT AWARD WINNERS

| | |
|---|---|
| 1967 | Aurand Harris |
| 1968 | Martha Bennett King |
| 1969 | Marian Johnson |
| 1970 | Madge Miller |
| 1971 | Joanna Halpert Kraus |
| 1972 | Ed Graczxk |
| 1973 | Alan Cullen |
| 1974 | Rosemary Musil |
| 1975 | Helen P. Avery |
| 1976 | Joseph Robinette |
| 1977 | Flora B. Atkin |
| 1978 | Suzan L. Zeder |
| 1979 | Jonathan Levy |
| 1980 | Moses Goldberg |
| 1981–84 | No award |
| 1985 | Aurand Harris |

| 1986 | Virginia Glasgow Koste |
| 1987–88 | No award |
| 1989 | Brian Kral |
| 1990–93 | No award |
| 1994 | James Still |
| 1995 | Max Bush |
| 1996–98 | No award |
| 1999 | Sandra Fenichel Asher |
| 2000 | No award |

Anthologies are a good source of plays for children's reading enjoyment. One publisher, Smith and Kraus, Inc., has many play anthologies available on a variety of topics, such as holidays, cultural diversity, and mythology. Some recent anthologies from Smith and Kraus have been included in the Recommended Books of Plays at the end of this chapter. An index of 500 plays for young actors has recently been made available from this same publisher (Slaight & Esty, 1997).

## HISTORICAL OVERVIEW OF PLAYS

Plays were seldom written exclusively for children prior to the twentieth century, yet for centuries plays were written and performed for a general audience that included children. Church dramas also have a long tradition that can be traced back to the Middle Ages when the Catholic Church used such plays as a means of educating. Examples of plays appealing to children but intended for a general audience are *Gulliver's Travels, Huckleberry Finn,* and Shaw's *Androcles and the Lion,* among others. J. M. Barrie's *Peter Pan,* the most widely acknowledged classic of the genre of plays for children, has had great appeal to children during its long history of production beginning in 1904.

The main stimulus for writing plays has been the development and existence of children's theatres and theatre groups that have a need for material. Children's theatre in the United States has generally been independent of the adult professional theatre, is community based with substantial contributions by amateurs, has suffered from limited budgets, and yet has tenaciously survived. Programs by theatres specializing in productions for young people began in the early twentieth century when the influential, though short-lived, Children's Educational Theatre was founded in 1903 in New York.

Following the establishment of theatres for children, a small number of plays and collections of plays for children began to be written and published. In 1910 the Drama League of America was founded in Evanston, Illinois, to encourage the appreciation of dramatic literature and to establish community playhouses. The League compiled and distributed a small but growing list of plays for children to encourage more children's theatre across the country. Small children's theatres gradually arose in many communities.

With the spread of children's theatre groups there was an increase in the number of published scripts; for example, as early as 1921, *A Treasury of Plays for Children* by Montrose J. Moses appeared. An early children's playwright of exceptional note was Charlotte B. Chorpenning (1872–1955), who published with Anchorage Press Plays. She was artistic director of the Goodman Children's Theatre of the Art Institute of Chicago from 1931 until her death and wrote many plays for its use. Her contributions to juvenile dramatic literature were outstanding both for the quality and quantity of her work. Her observations of children's interests at each age level are still useful to playwrights (McCaslin, 1971).

During the 1960s and 1970s professional theatre companies for young audiences began to appear. They encountered an extremely limited body of children's plays suitable to their needs. This lack was the major stimulus for a rapid increase in children's play publishing (Oaks, 1997). An outstanding children's playwright who wrote during this period was Aurand Harris, a playwright of children's plays from 1945 to the time of his death in 1996. He left behind a rich legacy of published plays that include original works as well as adaptations of folktales and modern literature. He is particularly noted for exploring different styles for children's theatre, including a vaudevillian show (*The Toby Show*), a melodrama (*Rags to Riches*), and even a serious drama that treats the topic of death (*The Arkansaw Bear*). He remained for many years the most produced children's playwright in the United States. He was the first winner of the Charlotte B. Chorpenning Award and the only playwright to win it twice, in 1967 and in 1985. Other children's playwrights who have been honored for a number of their children's plays include James Still, Edward Mast, and Suzan L. Zeder.

## TYPES OF PLAYS

Traditionally plays are categorized within types such as drama, comedy, farce, melodrama, and tragedy. Dramas and comedies are the most common play types found in children's plays. Some children's theatres produce *participation plays,* sometimes referred to as interactive theatre. A participation play is the presentation of a drama with an established story line constructed to involve structured opportunities for active involvement by the audience.

In children's plays the distinction between adaptations and original plays is important. Many adaptations of traditional literature, generally folktales, fables, and Bible stories, have been made and are readily available from most of the children's play publishers. Adaptations of modern children's literature, such as Mary Hoffman's *Amazing Grace* and Maurice Sendak's *Where the Wild Things Are,* are being published with increasing frequency.

Original plays, that is, stories originating in play form, are scarce. They represent fewer than one third of the new plays published annually. This fact is unfortunate because children enjoy new stories in play form even more than recreations of well-known folktales or story books. According to Sather (1976) children indicate a preference for plays with stories never heard before. Original plays on all topics for children and adaptations of contemporary children's literature are needed for all age levels. The publication of children's plays is growing rapidly. It has increased substantially from ten or twelve a year in the early 1960s to more than 200 a year at the beginning of the twenty-first century.

The natural play of children and the theatre are "manifestations of the same human need to make concrete the intangible, to make explicable the inexplicable, to make accessible the incomprehensible, and to make memorable the significant" (Davis, 1981, p. 14). Plays help children come to terms with the unknown and the threatening and help to heighten their appreciation of the actual and the enjoyment of the human comedy. Make plays a vital part of your literary curriculum.

# REFERENCES

Charles, D. (1982). Concrete cat. In X. J. Kennedy & D. M. Kennedy (Eds.), *Knock at a star.* Illustrated by K. A. Weinhaus. Boston: Little, Brown.

Davis, D. (1981). *Theater for young people.* New York: Beaufort.

Esbensen, B. J. (1984). Last day of school. In B. J. Esbensen, *Cold stars and fireflies: Poems of the four seasons.* Illustrated by S. Bonners. New York: Crowell.

Farjeon, Eleanor. (1983). Poetry. In J. Prelutsky, *The Random House Book of Poetry for Children.* Illustrated by Arnold Lobel. New York: Random House.

Field, Rachel. (1957). Song for a Blue Roadster. In H. Ferris, *Favorite Poems, Old and New.* Illustrated by Leonard Weisgard. New York: Doubleday.

Fisher, C. J., & Natarella, M. A. (1982). Young children's preferences in poetry: A national survey of first, second and third graders. *Research in the Teaching of English, 16*(4), 339–354.

Gillespie, M. C. (1970). *Literature for children: History and trends.* Dubuque, IA: Wm. C. Brown.

Glover, M. K. (1999). *A garden of poets: Poetry writing in the elementary classroom.* Urbana, IL: National Council of Teachers of English.

Goldberg, M. (1974). *Children's theatre: A philosophy and a method.* Englewood Cliffs, NJ: Prentice-Hall.

Hopkins, L. B. (1987). *Pass the poetry please!* New York: Harper & Row.

Janeczko, P. B., Selector. (1990) *The place my words are looking for: What poets say about and through their work.* New York: Bradbury.

Janeczko, P. B. (1994). *Poetry from a to z: A guide for young writers.* New York: Bradbury.

———. (1999). *How to write poetry.* New York: Scholastic.

Kahn, S. (1967). Giraffes. In S. Dunning, E. Lueders, & H. Smith, *Reflections on a gift of watermelon pickle.* New York: Lothrop, Lee and Shepard.

Koch, K. (1990). *Rose, where did you get that red?* New York: Random.

———. (1999). (1970). *Wishes, lies and dreams: Teaching children to write poetry.* New York: Random.

Kutiper, K., and P. Wilson. (1993). Updating poetry preferences: A look at the poetry children really like. *The Reading Teacher, 47*(1), 28–35.

Lear, E. (1946). *The complete nonsense book.* New York: Dodd, Mead.

Livingston, M. C. (1991). *Poem making: Ways to begin writing poetry.* New York: HarperCollins.

McCaslin, N. (1971). *Theatre for children in the United States.* Norman: University of Oklahoma Press.

McClure, A., P. Harrison, & S. Reed. (1990). *Sunrises and songs: Reading and writing poetry in an elementary classroom.* Portsmouth, NH: Heinemann.

McKean, B. (2000–2001). Speak the speech, I pray you! Preparing to read aloud dramatically. *The Reading Teacher, 54*(4), 358–360.

Moses, M. J. (Ed.). (1921). *Treasury of plays for children.* Boston: Little, Brown.

Oaks, H. (Ed.). (1996). *Outstanding plays for young audiences: International bibliography,* vol. 5. Seattle, WA: United States Center for the International Association of Theatre for Children and Young People.

Oaks, H. (1997). Collections of plays for young audiences. *Children's Book and Play Review, 17*(4), 1–3.

Reeves, J. (1963). Slowly. In E. Blishen (Ed.), *Oxford book of poetry for children.* Illustrated by B. Wildsmith. Oxford: Oxford University Press.

Ryan, M. (1996). *How to write a poem.* New York: Watts.

Sather, S. P. (1976). A critical assessment of children's plays. *Children's Theatre Review, 25*(1), 2–5.

Shaw, J. M. (1967). The broken-legg'd man. In J. M. Shaw, *The things I want: Poems for two children.* Tallahassee, FL: Florida State University Library.

Slaight, C., & Esty, J. (Ed.). (1997). *The Smith and Kraus play index for young actors.* North Stratford, NH: Smith and Kraus.

Small bird. (1971). In H. Behn (Ed. and Trans.), *More cricket songs.* San Diego: Harcourt.

Smolkin, L. B. (1995). The literature of the theatre and aesthetic response: Welcoming plays into the world of children's literature. *The New Advocate, 8*(2), 109–123.

Terry, A. C. (1974). *Children's poetry preferences: A national survey of upper elementary grades.* Urbana, IL: National Council of Teachers of English.

## NOTABLE POETS AND PLAYWRIGHTS

**Arnold Adoff,** recipient of the National Council of Teachers of English (NCTE) Award for Excellence in Poetry for Children. Many poems about relating to people across racial groups. *All the Colors of the Race.*

**Sandra Fenichel Asher,** a playwright whose plays focus on the real life struggles of young adults. *Things Are Seldom What They Seem; A Woman Called Truth.*

**Laurie Brooks,** a playwright noted for her unique approach with an arena theatre setting and audience questions for older students. *The Wrestling Match.*

**John Ciardi,** an NCTE award-winning poet known for his humor and, at times, satire in poems for children. *The Man Who Sang the Sillies.*

**Walter de la Mare,** British poet who gave new importance to early childhood experiences. *Songs of Childhood.*

**Eleanor Farjeon,** first recipient of the Hans Christian Andersen Award in 1956. British poet known for well-written poems. *Poems for Children.*

**Max Fatchen,** Australian poet noted for his poems about children's thoughts and activities. *The Country Mail Is Coming: Poems from Down Under.*

**Aileen Fisher,** an NCTE award-winning poet whose poems express a closeness to nature and all its inhabitants. *Going Barefoot.*

**Paul Fleischman,** winner of the Newbery Medal for his *Joyful Noise: Poems for Two Voices* in which the poems are composed and printed for two readers to read lines in unison and solo.

**Nikki Giovanni,** an African-American poet known for her free verse (using mostly lowercase letters) about growing up African-American. *Spin a Soft Black Song: Poems for Children.*

**Moses Goldberg,** playwright noted for his participation plays for very young audiences. *Puss in Boots: A Participation Play; Aladdin: A Participation Play.*

**Eloise Greenfield,** 1997 recipient of the NCTE Award for Excellence in Poetry and an African-American poet noted for poems of courage and love. *Under the Sunday Tree.*

**Aurand Harris,** prolific children's playwright and author of *Androcles and the Lion,* a play performed more than 9,000 times. *The Arkansaw Bear; The Prince and the Pauper; Rags to Riches.*

**Langston Hughes,** African-American poet whose protest poems speak of racial pride. *Selected Poems of Langston Hughes.*

**X. J. Kennedy,** a favorite creator of nonsense and humorous verse about contemporary themes. *One Wonderful Night in August and Other Nonsense Jingles.*

**Karla Kuskin,** an NCTE award-winning poet known for sometimes serious, sometimes funny poems, including many narrative poems. *Dogs & Dragons, Trees & Dreams: A Collection of Poems.*

**Dennis Lee,** popular Canadian poet known for humorous poetry. *Alligator Pie.*

**Myra Cohn Livingston,** an NCTE award-winning poet and an anthologist whose poetry exhibits a balance of perspective and form. *Whispers and Other Poems.*

**David McCord,** the first winner of the NCTE Award for Excellence in Poetry for Children, known for regular rhythms, agile language, and the use of shape in his poems. *One at a Time.*

**Eve Merriam,** an NCTE award-winning poet whose poems, often humorous, and sometimes controversial, display an inventive use of language. *A Poem for a Pickle: Funnybone Verses.*

**A. A. Milne,** English poet whose two collections of poems from the 1920s, *When We Were Very Young* and *Now We Are Six,* remain enjoyable today.

**Naomi Shihab Nye,** a Palestine-American poet and anthologist whose meditative poems offer global perspectives and whose edited collections include Mexican, Native American, and Middle Eastern poetry. *Come with Me: Poems for a Journey; This Same Sky: A Collection of Poems from Around the World.*

**Jack Prelutsky,** a popular contemporary poet known for his nonsense poems and poems with humorous characters. *Nightmares: Poems to Trouble Your Sleep.*

**Robert Service,** classic Canadian poet of well-loved narrative poems. *The Cremation of Sam McGee.*

**Shel Silverstein,** popular contemporary children's poet who creates nonsense and humorous poetry. *Where the Sidewalk Ends.*

**Robert Louis Stevenson,** Golden Age poet whose *A Child's Garden of Verses* remains a classic.

**James Still,** award-winning playwright noted for his highly original fantasy play, *In the Suicide Mountains,* and for cross-generational plays. *And Then They Came for Me: Remembering the World of Anne Frank; Amber Waves.*

**David Wood,** noted British playwright for children who has developed screenplays and musical plays from children's literature. *Babe, the Sheep-Pig; The Gingerbread Man.*

**Suzan L. Zelder,** experimental playwright who has written contemporary plays and musicals for a multigenerational audience. *Step on a Crack; Mother HIcks; The Taste of Sunrise.*

## RECOMMENDED POETRY BOOKS

*Because poetry is usually of interest to a broad age group, entries of poetry books indicate age only for books mainly suitable for young adults. These books are marked YA.*

### Mother Goose and Nursery Rhyme Books

Arenson, Roberta. *One, Two, Skip a Few! First Number Rhymes.* Illustrated. Barefoot, 1998.

Arnold, Ted. *Mother Goose's Words of Wisdom: A Book of Months.* Dial, 1990.

Cook, Scott. *Mother Goose.* Knopf, 1994.

Cousins, Lucy, illustrator. *The Little Dog Laughed and Other Nursery Rhymes.* Dutton, 1990.

de Angeli, Marguerite. *Marguerite de Angeli's Book of Nursery and Mother Goose Rhymes.* Doubleday, 1954.

dePaola, Tomie, compiler. *Tomie dePaola's Mother Goose.* Putnam, 1985.

Emerson, Sally, selector. *The Nursery Treasury: A Collection of Baby Games, Rhymes and Lullabies.* Illustrated by Moira and Colin MacLean. Doubleday, 1988.

Greenaway, Kate. *Mother Goose, or The Old Nursery Rhymes.* Warne, 1881.

Griego, Margot C., Betsy L. Bucks, Sharon S. Gilbert, and Laurel H. Kimball. *Tortillitas para Mama.* Illustrated by Barbara Cooney. Holt, 1981.

Hale, Sarah Josepha. *Mary Had a Little Lamb.* Photographs by Bruce McMillan. Scholastic, 1990.

Lobel, Arnold, selector. *The Random House Book of Mother Goose.* Random, 1986.

———. *Whiskers and Rhymes.* Greenwillow, 1985.

Opie, Iona, editor. *Here Comes Mother Goose.* Illustrated by Rosemary Wells. Candlewick, 1999.

Opie, Peter, and Iona Opie, compilers. *Tail Feathers from Mother Goose: The Opie Rhyme Book.* Little, Brown, 1988.

Petersham, Maud, and Miska Petersham. *The Rooster Crows: A Book of American Rhymes and Jingles.* Macmillan, 1945.

Rojankovsky, Feodor. *The Tall Book of Mother Goose.* Harper, 1942.

Sutherland, Zena. *The Orchard Book of Nursery Rhymes.* Illustrated by Faith Jaques. Orchard, 1990.

Wright, Blanche Fisher. *The Real Mother Goose.* Rand McNally, 1916.

### Nursery and Folk Songbooks

Brett, Jan, illustrator. *The Twelve Days of Christmas.* Dodd, 1986.

dePaola, Tomie. *Tomie dePaola's Book of Christmas Carols.* Putnam, 1987.

Durell, Ann, selector. *The Diane Goode Book of American Folk Tales and Songs.* Illustrated by Diane Goode. Dutton, 1989.

Eddleman, David, editor. *The Great Children's Songbook.* Illustrated by Andrew J. Dowty. Carl Fischer, 1998.

Fox, Dan, editor. *Go In and Out the Window: An Illustrated Songbook for Young People.* Holt/Metropolitan Museum of Art, 1987.

Guthrie, Woody. *This Land Is Your Land.* Illustrated by Kathy Jakobsen. Little, 1998.

Hart, Jane. *Singing Bee: A Collection of Favorite Children's Songs.* Illustrated by Anita Lobel. Lothrop, 1989 (1982).

Higgensen, Vy, selector. *This Is My Song!: A Collection of Gospel Music for the Family.* Illustrated by Brenda Joysmith. Crown, 1995.

Krull, Kathleen, editor. *Gonna Sing My Head Off! American Folk Songs for Children.* Illustrated by Allen Garns. Knopf, 1992.

Langstaff, John, editor. *What a Morning! The Christmas Story in Black Spirituals.* Illustrated by Ashley Bryan, arrangements for singing and piano by John Andrew Ross. Macmillan, 1987.

Larrick, Nancy, compiler. *Songs from Mother Goose: With the Traditional Melody for Each.* Illustrated by Robin Spowart. Harper, 1989.

Orozco, José-Luis. *De Colores and Other Latin-American Folk Songs for Children.* Illustrated by Elisa Kleven. Dutton, 1994.

Raffi. *Raffi's Christmas Treasury.* Illustrated by Nadine Bernard Westcott. Crown, 1988.

Staines, Bill. *All God's Critters Got a Place in the Choir.* Illustrated by Margot Zemach. Dutton, 1989.

Titherington, Jeanne. *Baby's Boat.* Greenwillow, 1992.

Yolen, Jane, editor. *The Lullaby Songbook.* Musical arrangements by Adam Stemple. Illustrated by Charles Mikolaycak. Harcourt, 1986.

## Anthologies of Poetry

Booth, David, editor. *'Til All the Stars Have Fallen.* Illustrated by Kady Denton. Viking, 1989.

Cole, Joanna, compiler. *A New Treasury of Children's Poetry; Old Favorites and New Discoveries.* Illustrated by Judith Gwyn Brown. Doubleday, 1984.

de Regniers, Beatrice Schenk, Eva Moore, Mary Michaels White, and Jean Carr. *Sing a Song of Popcorn: Every Child's Book of Poems.* Scholastic, 1988.

Downie, Mary, and Barbara Robertson, compilers. *The New Wind Has Wings.* Oxford/Merrimack, 1985.

Elledge, Scott, editor. *Wider than the Sky: Poems to Grow Up with.* HarperCollins, 1990.

Ferris, Helen, compiler. *Favorite Poems Old and New.* Illustrated by Leonard Weisgard. Doubleday, 1957.

Hall, Donald, editor. *The Oxford Illustrated Book of American Children's Poems.* Oxford University, 1999.

Harrison, Michael, and Christopher Stuart-Clark, editors. *The Oxford Treasury of Children's Poems.* Oxford, 1988.

———. *The Oxford Treasury of Classic Poems.* Oxford 1996. Ages 11–YA.

Hopkins, Lee Bennett, editor. *Climb into My Lap: First Poems to Read Together.* Illustrated by Kathryn Brown. Simon & Schuster, 2000.

———. *My America: A Poetry Atlas of the United States.* Simon & Schuster, 2000.

Janeczko, Paul, editor. *Preposterous: Poems of Youth.* Watts, 1991.

Kennedy, X. J., and Dorothy Kennedy, editors. *Knock at a Star: A Child's Introduction to Poetry,* Rev. Ed. Illustrated by Karen Lee Baher. Little, Brown, 1999.

Larrick, Nancy. *Piping Down the Valleys Wild.* Illustrated by Ellen Raskin. Delacorte, 1985 (1968).

Nye, Naomi Shihab, editor. *What Have You Lost?* Illustrated. Greenwillow, 1999.

Opie, Iona, and Peter Opie. *I Saw Esau: The Schoolchild's Pocket Book.* Illustrated by Maurice Sendak. Candlewick, 1992.

Philip, Neil, editor. *A New Treasury of Poetry.* Illustrated by John Lawrence. Stewart, Tabori & Chang, 1990.

Prelutsky, Jack, editor. *The Random House Book of Poetry for Children.* Illustrated by Arnold Lobel. Random House, 1983.

———, editor. *Read-Aloud Rhymes for the Very Young.* Illustrated by Marc Brown. Knopf, 1986.

———, editor. *The 20th Century Children's Poetry Treasury.* Illustrated by Meilo So. Knopf, 1999.

Rosen, Michael, editor. *Poems for the Very Young.* Illustrated by Bob Graham. Kingfisher, 1993.

Rosenberg, Liz, editor. *The Invisible Ladder: An Anthology of Contemporary American Poems for Young Readers.* Holt, 1996. Ages 11–YA.

———. *Earth-Shattering Poems.* Holt, 1997. Both books with commentary by poets and ideas for writing.

Wilner, Isabel. *The Poetry Troupe: An Anthology of Poems to Read Aloud.* Scribner's, 1977.

## Specialized Poetry Books

Adoff, Arnold. *All the Colors of the Race.* Illustrated by John Steptoe. Lothrop, 1982.

———. *Chocolate Dreams.* Illustrated by Turi Mac-Combie. Lothrop, 1989.

———. *In for Winter, Out for Spring.* Illustrated by Jerry Pinkney. Harcourt, 1991.

———. *Sports Pages.* Illustrated by Steve Kuzma. Lippincott, 1986.

———. *Touch the Poem.* Illustrated by Lisa Desimini. Scholastic, 2000.

Alarcon, Francisco X. *From the Bellybutton of the Moon and Other Summer Poems: Del ombligo de la luna y otros poemas de verano.* Illustrated by Maya Christina Gonzalez. Children's Book Press, 1998.

———. *Laughing Tomatoes: And Other Spring Poems.* Illustrated by Maya Christina Gonzalez. Children's Book Press, 1997. Bilingual, Spanish-English.

Bierhorst, John, editor. *The Sacred Path: Spells, Prayers & Power Songs of the American Indians.* Morrow, 1983.

Booth, David, editor. *Voices on the Wind: Poems for All Seasons.* Illustrated by Michèle Lemieux. Morrow, 1990.

Brooks, Gwendolyn. *Bronzeville Boys and Girls.* Illustrated by Ronni Solbert. Harper, 1956.

Brown, Margaret Wise. *Under the Sun and the Moon and Other Poems.* Illustrated by Tom Leonard. Hyperion, 1993.

Carlson, Lori M., editor. *Cool Salsa: Bilingual Poems on Growing Up Latino in the United States.* Holt, 1994. Ages: YA.

Carter, Anne, compiler. *Birds, Beasts, and Fishes: A Selection of Animal Poems.* Illustrated by Reg Cartwright. Macmillan, 1991.

Cassedy, Sylvia. *Roomrimes: Poems.* Illustrated by Michele Chessare. Crowell, 1987.

———. *Zoomrimes: Poems about Things That Go.* Illustrated by Michele Chessare. HarperCollins, 1993.

———, and Kunihiro Suetake, editors. *Red Dragonfly on My Shoulder.* Illustrated by Molly Bang. Translated from Japanese by editors. HarperCollins, 1992.

Ciardi, John. *Doodle Soup.* Illustrated by Merle Nacht. Houghton, 1985.

———. *The Hopeful Trout and Other Limericks.* Illustrated by Susan Meddaugh. Houghton, 1989.

———. *The Man Who Sang the Sillies.* Illustrated by Edward Gorey. Lippincott, 1961.

———. *You Read to Me, I'll Read to You.* Illustrated by Edward Gorey. Lippincott, 1962.

Clinton, Catherine, editor. *I, Too, Sing America: Three Centuries of African-American Poetry.* Illustrated by Stephen Alcorn. Houghton, 1998.

Cole, Joanna. *Anna Banana: 101 Jump-Rope Rhymes.* Illustrated by Alan Tiegreen. Morrow, 1989.

Cole, William, editor. *A Zooful of Animals.* Illustrated by Lynn Munsinger. Houghton, 1992.

Cullen, Countee. *The Lost Zoo.* Illustrated by Brian Pinkney. Silver Burdett, 1991 (1969).

Cullinan, Bernice E., editor. *A Jar of Tiny Stars: Poems by NCTE Award-Winning Poets.* Boyds Mills, 1995.

Demi, editor-illustrator. *In the Eyes of the Cat: Japanese Poetry for All Seasons.* Translated by Tze-si Hvang. Holt, 1992.

dePaola, Tomie. *Tomie dePaola's Book of Poems.* Putnam, 1988.

Dunbar, Paul Laurence. *Jump Back, Honey: The Poems of Paul Laurence Dunbar.* Hyperion, 1999.

Esbensen, Barbara Juster. *Who Shrank My Grandmother's House: Poems of Discovery.* Illustrated by Eric Beddows. HarperCollins, 1992.

———. *Words with Wrinkled Knees: Animal Poems.* Illustrated by John Stadler. Crowell, 1986.

Fatchen, Max. *The Country Mail Is Coming: Poems from Down Under.* Little, Brown, 1990.

Feelings, Tom, editor-illustrator. *Soul Looks Back in Wonder.* Dial, 1993.

Fields, Julia. *The Green Lion of Zion Street.* Illustrated by Jerry Pinkney. Macmillan, 1988.

Fisher, Aileen. *Out in the Dark and the Daylight.* Harper, 1980.

Fleischman, Paul. *Big Talk: Poems for Four Voices.* Illustrated by Beppe Giacobbe. Candlewick, 2000. Ages 9–14.

————. *I Am Phoenix: Poems for Two Voices.* Illustrated by Eric Beddows. Harper, 1985.

————. *Joyful Noise: Poems for Two Voices.* Illustrated by Eric Beddows. Harper, 1988.

Florian, Douglas. *Bing Bang Boing.* Harcourt, 1994.

————. *Mammalabilia.* Illustrated. Harcourt, 2000.

————. *Winter Eyes.* Illustrated. Greenwillow, 1999.

Frank, Josette, selector. *Snow Toward Evening: A Year in a River Valley/Nature Poems.* Illustrated by Thomas Locker. Dial, 1990.

George, Kristine O'Connell. *The Great Frog Race and Other Poems.* Illustrated by Kate Kiesler. Clarion, 1997.

————. *Little Dog Poems.* Illustrated by June Otani. Clarion, 1999.

————. *Old Elm Speaks: Tree Poems.* Illustrated by Kate Kiesler. Clarion, 1998.

Giovanni, Nikki. *Spin a Soft Black Song: Poems for Children.* Illustrated by George Martins. Hill & Wang, 1985 (1971).

————, editor. *Grand Mothers: Poems, Reminiscences, and Short Stories about the Keepers of Our Traditions.* Holt, 1994. Ages: YA.

Glaser, Isabel Joshlin, editor. *Dreams of Glory: Poems Starring Girls.* Simon & Schuster, 1995.

Goldstein, Bobbye S., editor. *Inner Chimes: Poems on Poetry.* Illustrated by Jane Breskin Zalben. Wordsong/Boyds Mills, 1992.

Gordon, Ruth, editor. *Peeling the Onion.* HarperCollins, 1993. Ages: YA.

————, editor. *Pierced by a Ray of Sun: Poems about the Times We Feel Alone.* HarperCollins, 1995. Ages 12–YA.

————, compiler. *Time Is the Longest Distance: An Anthology of Poems.* HarperCollins, 1991.

Greenfield, Eloise. *Honey, I Love, and Other Love Poems.* Illustrated by Diane and Leo Dillon. Crowell, 1978.

————. *Under the Sunday Tree.* Illustrated by Amos Ferguson. Harper, 1988.

Grimes, Nikki. *It's Raining Laughter.* Photos by Myles C. Pinkney. Dial, 1997.

————. *Meet Danitra Brown.* Illustrated by Floyd Cooper. Morrow, 1994.

————. *My Man Blue.* Illustrated by Jerome Lagarrigue. Dial, 1999.

Harrison, David L. *Somebody Catch My Homework.* Illustrated by Betsy Lewin. Boyds Mills, 1993.

Hoberman, Mary Ann. *Fathers, Mothers, Sisters, Brothers: A Collection of Family Poems.* Illustrated by Marylin Hafner. Little, 1991.

————, editor. *My Song Is Beautiful: Poems and Pictures in Many Voices.* Little, 1994.

Holman, Felice, compiler. *Side by Side: Poems to Read Together.* Illustrated by Hilary Knight. Simon & Schuster, 1988.

————. *The Song in My Head.* Illustrated by Jim Spanfeller. Scribner's, 1985.

Hopkins, Lee Bennett, editor. *April Bubbles Chocolate: An ABC of Poetry.* Illustrated by Barry Root. Simon & Schuster, 1994.

————, editor. *Dinosaurs.* Illustrated by Murray Tinkelman. Harcourt, 1987.

————, compiler. *Hand in Hand: An American History through Poetry.* Illustrated by Peter M. Fiore. Simon & Schuster, 1994.

————, selector. *Opening Days: Sports Poems.* Illustrated by Scott Medlock. Harcourt, 1996.

Huck, Charlotte, editor. *Secret Places.* Illustrated by Lindsay Barrett George. Greenwillow, 1993.

Hudson, Wade, editor. *Pass It On: African American Poetry for Children.* Illustrated by Floyd Cooper. Scholastic, 1993.

Hughes, Langston. *The Dream Keeper and Other Poems.* Illustrated by Brian Pinkney. Knopf, 1994 (1932).

*In Daddy's Arms I Am Tall: African Americans Celebrating Fathers.* Illustrated by Javaka Steptoe. Lee & Low, 1997.

James, Simon, editor. *Days Like This: A Collection of Small Poems.* Illustrated. Candlewick, 2000.

Janeczko, Paul B., editor. *Looking for Your Name: A Collection of Contemporary Poems.* Orchard, 1993. Ages: YA.

————, editor. *The Music of What Happens: Poems That Tell Stories.* Watts, 1988.

————. *Poetry from A to Z: A Guide for Young Writers.* Bradbury, 1994.

Katz, Bobbi. *We, the People.* Illustrated by Nina Crews. Greenwillow, 2000. First-person poems focused on U.S. history; could be used as dramatic monologues.

Kennedy, X. J. *Brats.* Illustrated by James Watts. Atheneum, 1986.

————. *The Forgetful Wishing Well: Poems for Young People.* Illustrated by Monica Incisa. Atheneum, 1985.

————. *Fresh Brats.* Illustrated by James Watts. Macmillan, 1990.

Knudson, R. R., and May Swenson, editors. *American Sports Poems.* Watts, 1988.

Kurtz, Jane. *River Friendly, River Wild.* Illustrated by Neil Brennan. Simon & Schuster, 2000.

Kuskin, Karla. *Dogs & Dragons, Trees & Dreams: A Collection of Poems.* Harper, 1980.

Larrick, Nancy, compiler. *Cats Are Cats.* Illustrated by Ed Young. Philomel, 1988.

————, compiler. *Mice Are Nice.* Illustrated by Ed Young. Philomel, 1990.

————. *To the Moon and Back: A Collection of Poems.* Illustrated by Catharine O'Neill. Delacorte, 1991.

————, compiler. *When the Dark Comes Dancing: A Bedtime Poetry Book.* Illustrated by John Wallner. Philomel, 1983.

Lear, Edward. *The Complete Nonsense Book.* Dodd, 1946.

Lee, Dennis. *Garbage Delight.* Illustrated by Frank Newfeld. Houghton, 1978.

Lenski, Lois. *Sing a Song of People.* Illustrated by Giles Laroche. Little, Brown, 1987.

Levy, Constance. *A Tree Place and Other Poems.* Illustrated by Robert Subuda. Macmillan, 1994.

Lewis, J. Patrick. *Doodle Dandies: Poems That Take Shape.* Illustrated by Lisa Desimini. Simon & Schuster, 1998.

————. *Freedom Like Sunlight: Praisesongs for Black Americans.* Creative Editions, 2000.

Lillegard, Dee. *Wake up House! Rooms Full of Poems.* Illustrated by Don Carter. Knopf, 2000.

Livingston, Myra Cohn. *A Circle of Seasons.* Illustrated by Leonard Everett Fisher. Holiday, 1982.

————. *Roll Along: Poems on Wheels.* Macmillan, 1993.

————, editor. *Thanksgiving Poems.* Illustrated by Stephen Gammell. Holiday, 1985.

Mado, Michio. *The Magic Pocket.* Illustrated by Mitsumasa Anno. Translated from Japanese by The Empress Michiko of Japan. Simon & Schuster, 1998.

McCord, David. *One at a Time: Collected Poems for the Young.* Illustrated by Henry B. Kane. Little, 1977.

McNaughton, Colin. *Making Friends with Frankenstein: A Book of Monstrous Poems and Pictures.* Candlewick, 1994.

Merriam, Eve. *Blackberry Ink.* Illustrated by Hans Wilhelm. Morrow, 1985.

————. *Halloween ABC.* Illustrated by Lane Smith. Macmillan, 1987.

————. *The Inner City Mother Goose.* Illustrated by David Diaz. Simon & Schuster, 1996 (1969). Ages 14–YA.

————. *You Be Good & I'll Be Night: Jump-on-the-Bed Poems.* Illustrated by Karen Lee Schmidt. Morrow, 1988.

Milne, A. A. *The World of Christopher Robin.* Illustrated by Ernest Shepard. Dutton, 1958.

Moore, Lilian. *Something New Begins: New and Selected Poems.* Illustrated by Mary Jane Dunton. Atheneum, 1982.

Morrison, Lillian, compiler. *At the Crack of the Bat: Baseball Poems.* Illustrated by Steve Cieslawsky. Hyperion, 1992.

————, compiler. *Rhythm Road: Poems to Move to.* Lothrop, 1988.

Myers, Walter Dean. *Brown Angels: An Album of Pictures and Verse.* HarperCollins, 1993.

————. *Harlem.* Illustrated by Christopher Myers. Scholastic, 1997. Ages 11–YA.

Nash, Ogden. *Custard and Company: Poems by Ogden Nash.* Illustrated by Quentin Blake. Little, 1980.

Nye, Naomi Shihab. *Come with Me: Poems for a Journey.* Illustrated by Dan Yaccarino. Greenwillow, 2000.

————, editor. *The Space Between Our Footsteps: Poems and Paintings from the Middle East.* Simon & Schuster, 1998.

————, editor. *This Same Sky: A Collection of Poems from around the World.* Four Winds, 1992. Ages: YA.

Nye, Naomi, and Paul B. Janeczko, editors. *I Feel a Little Jumpy around You: A Book of Her Poems and His Poems Collected in Pairs.* Simon & Schuster, 1996. Ages 12–YA.

O'Neill, Mary. *Hailstones and Halibut Bones: Adventures in Color.* Illustrated by Leonard Weisgard. Doubleday, 1989 (1961).

Otten, Charlotte F. *January Rides the Wind: A Book of Months.* Illustrated by Todd L. W. Doney. Lothrop, 1997.

Panzer, Nora, editor. *Celebrate America: In Poetry and Art.* Hyperion, 1994. Ages 12–YA.

Pomerantz, Charlotte. *If I Had a Paka: Poems in Eleven Languages.* Illustrated by Nancy Tafuri. Greenwillow, 1982.

Pooley, Sarah, selector. *A Day of Rhymes.* Knopf, 1988.

Prelutsky, Jack. *The Dragons Are Singing Tonight.* Illustrated by Peter Sis. Greenwillow, 1993.

————, editor. *For Laughing out Loud: Poems to Tickle Your Funnybone.* Illustrated by Marjorie Priceman. Knopf, 1991.

————. *The New Kid on the Block.* Illustrated by James Stevenson. Greenwillow, 1984.

————. *A Pizza the Size of the Sun.* Illustrated by James Stevenson. Greenwillow, 1996.

————. *Something Big Has Been Here.* Illustrated by James Stevenson. Greenwillow, 1990.

Richardson, Polly, editor. *Animal Poems.* Illustrated by Meg Rutherford. Barrons, 1992.

Rochelle, Belinda. *Words with Wings: A Treasury of African-American Poetry and Art.* HarperCollins/Amistad, 2001.

Schmidt, Annie M. G. *Pink Lemonade.* Illustrated by Timothy Foley. Translated by Henrietta Ten Harmsel. Eerdmans, 1992 (1981).

Schwartz, Alvin. *And the Green Grass Grew All Around.* Illustrated by Sue Truesdell. HarperCollins, 1992.

Seabrooke, Brenda. *Judy Scuppernong.* Dutton, 1990. Ages 9–12.

Silverstein, Shel. *A Light in the Attic.* Illustrated by author. Harper, 1981.

————. *Where the Sidewalk Ends: The Poems and Drawings of Shel Silverstein.* Harper, 1974.

Singer, Marilyn. *Turtle in July.* Illustrated by Jerry Pinkney. Macmillan, 1989.

Sneve, Virginia Driving Hawk, selector. *Dancing Teepees: Poems of American Indian Youth.* Illustrated by Stephen Gammell. Holiday, 1989.

Soto, Gary. *A Fire in My Hands.* Scholastic, 1990. Ages 12–YA.

————. *Neighborhood Odes.* Illustrated by David Diaz. Harcourt, 1992.

Stevenson, James. *Sweet Corn: Poems.* Greenwillow, 1995.

————. *Popcorn.* Greenwillow, 1998.

Stevenson, Robert Louis. *A Child's Garden of Verses.* Chronicle, 1989 (1885).

Strickland, Dorothy S., and Michael R., editors. *Families: Poems Celebrating the African American Experience.* Illustrated by John Ward. Wordsong/Boyds Mills, 1994.

Swann, Brian. *A Basket Full of White Eggs: Riddle Poems.* Illustrated by Ponder Goembel. Orchard, 1988.

Thomas, Joyce Carol. *Brown Honey in Broomwheat Tea.* Illustrated by Floyd Cooper. HarperCollins, 1993.

Updike, John. *A Child's Calendar.* Illustrated by Trina Schart Hyman. Holiday, 1999.

Viorst, Judith. *If I Were in Charge of the World and Other Worries: Poems for Children and Their Parents.* Illustrated by Lynne Cherry. Atheneum, 1982.

Wallace, Daisy, editor. *Fairy Poems.* Illustrated by Trina Schart Hyman. Holiday, 1980.

Westcott, Nadine Bernard, editor. *Never Take a Pig to Lunch: And Other Poems about the Fun of Eating.* Illustrated by Nadine Bernard Wescott. Orchard, 1994.

Whipple, Laura, editor. *Celebrating America: A Collection of Poems and Images of the American Spirit.* Putnam/Philomel, 1994. Ages: YA.

————, compiler. *Eric Carle's Animals Animals.* Illustrated by Eric Carle. Philomel, 1989.

————, compiler. *Eric Carle's Dragons and Other Creatures That Never Were.* Illustrated by Eric Carle. Philomel, 1991.

Wilbur, Richard. *The Disappearing Alphabet.* Illustrated by David Diaz. Harcourt, 1998.

Willard, Nancy. *A Visit to William Blake's Inn: Poems for Innocent and Experienced Travelers.* Illustrated by Alice and Martin Provensen. Harcourt, 1981.

Woolger, David, editor. *Who Do You Think You Are? Poems about People.* Oxford, 1990.

Worth, Valerie. *More Small Poems.* Illustrated by Natalie Babbitt. Farrar, 1976.

Yolen, Jane. *Best Witches: Poems for Halloween.* Illustrated by Elise Primavera. Putnam, 1988.

————. *Bird Watch: A Book of Poetry.* Illustrated by Ted Lewin. Philomel, 1990.

————, editor. *Sleep Rhymes around the World.* Illustrated by 17 international artists. Wordsong/Boyds Mills, 1994.

————, editor. *Weather Report.* Illustrated by Anne Gusman. Wordsong/Boyds Mills, 1993.

## Single Illustrated Poems

*Note the distinction between* poems *and stories told in verse. Heavily illustrated poems are listed here. Illustrated stories told in verse are included under the heading of Picture Storybooks in Chapter 4.*

Browning, Robert. *The Pied Piper of Hamelin.* Illustrated by Kate Greenaway. Warne, 1888.

Bryan, Ashley. *Turtle Knows Your Name.* Atheneum, 1989.

Burleigh, Robert. *Hoops.* Illustrated by Stephen T. Johnson. Harcourt, 1997.

cummings, e.e. *hist whist.* Illustrated by Deborah Kogan Ray. Crown, 1989.

————. *little tree.* Illustrated by Deborah Kogan Ray. Crown, 1987.

Fisher, Aileen. *Listen Rabbit.* Illustrated by Symeon Shimin. Crowell, 1964.

Frost, Robert. *Stopping by Woods on a Snowy Evening.* Illustrated by Susan Jeffers. Dutton, 1978.

Johnson, James Weldon. *The Creation.* Illustrated by James Ransome. Holiday, 1994.

Lear, Edward. *The Jumblies.* Illustrated by Ted Rand. Putnam, 1989.

————. *The Owl and the Pussycat.* Illustrated by Jan Brett. Putnam, 1991.

————. *The Scroobious Pip.* Completed by Ogden Nash. Illustrated by Nancy Ekholm Burkert. Harper, 1968.

Lewis, J. Patrick. *A Hippopotamusn't and Other Animal Verses.* Illustrated by Victoria Chess. Dial, 1990.

Little, Lessie Jones. *Children of Long Ago.* Illustrated by Jan Spivey Gilchrist. Putnam, 1988.

Longfellow, Henry Wadsworth. *Paul Revere's Ride.* Illustrated by Ted Rand. Dutton, 1990.

Moore, Clement Clarke. *The Night before Christmas.* Illustrated by Tomie dePaola. Holiday House, 1980.

Ryder, Joanne. *Earthdance.* Illustrated by Norman Gorbaty. Holt, 1996.

Rylant, Cynthia. *Waiting to Waltz: A Childhood.* Illustrated by Stephen Gammell. Bradbury, 1984.

Service, Robert W. *The Cremation of Sam McGee.* Illustrated by Ted Harrison. Greenwillow, 1987.

————. *The Shooting of Dan McGrew.* Illustrated by Ted Harrison. Godine, 1988.

Siebert, Diane. *Heartland.* Illustrated by Wendell Minor. HarperCollins, 1989.

————. *Sierra.* Illustrated by Wendell Minor. HarperCollins, 1991.

Steig, Jeanne. *Consider the Lemming.* Illustrated by William Steig. Farrar, 1988.

Taylor, Jane. *Twinkle, Twinkle, Little Star.* Illustrated by Michael Hague. Morrow, 1992.

Thayer, Ernest Lawrence. *Casey at the Bat.* Illustrated by Patricia Polacco. Putnam, 1992 (1888).

Thomas, Joyce Carol. *Cherish Me!* Illustrated by Nneka Bennett. HarperFestival, 1998.

Treece, Henry. *The Magic Wood.* Illustrated by Barry Moser. HarperCollins, 1992 (1945).

Willard, Nancy. *The Tale I Told Sasha.* Illustrated by David Christiana. Little, Brown, 1999.

Young, Ruth. *Golden Bear.* Illustrated by Rachel Isadora. Viking, 1992.

## RECOMMENDED BOOKS OF PLAYS

### Anthologies of Plays

Bedard, R. L., editor. *Dramatic Literature for Children: A Century in Review.* Anchorage, 1984. Ages 9–YA.

Bruchac, Joseph. *Pushing Up the Sky: Seven Native American Plays for Children.* Dial, 2000. Ages 7–11.

Bush, Max. *Plays for Young Audiences.* Edited by Roger Ellis. Meriwether, 1995. Ages 9–YA. Ten full-length plays by award-winning playwrights.

Carlson, Lori Marie, selector. *You're On! Seven Plays in English and Spanish.* Morrow, 1999. Ages 9–15.

Ellis, Roger, editor. *Audition Monologues for Student Actors: Selections from Contemporary Plays.* Meriwether, 1999. Ages 13–YA.

Ellis, Roger, and Ted Zapel, editors. *Multicultural Theatre II: Contemporary Hispanic, Asian, and African American Plays.* Meriwether, 1998. Ages 12–YA.

Gallo, D. R. *Center Stage: One Act Plays for Teenage Readers and Actors.* Harper, 1990. Ages 12–YA.

Gerke, Pamela. *Multicultural Plays for Children, vol. 1: Grades K–3.* Smith and Kraus, 1996. Ages 5–8.

———. *Multicultural Plays for Children, vol. 2: Grades 4–6.* Smith and Kraus, 1996. Ages 9–12.

Gilfond, Henry. *Holiday Plays for Reading.* Walker, 1985. Ages 7–11.

Harris, Aurand, editor. *Short Plays of Theatre Classics.* Anchorage, 1991. Ages 9–YA. An international selection.

Jennings, Coleman A., editor. *Eight Plays for Children: The New Generation Play Project.* University of Texas Press, 1999. Ages 10–YA.

———, editor. *Theatre for Young Audiences.* St. Martin's Press, 1998. Ages 9–12. Mostly recent short plays.

Jennings, Coleman A., and Aurand Harris, editors. *Plays Children Love, vol. 2: A Treasury of Contemporary and Classic Plays for Children.* St. Martin's Press, 1988. Ages 7–12. Contains 20 plays.

Kamerman, Sylvia E. *Thirty Plays from Favorite Stories.* Plays, Inc., 1998. Ages 7–12.

Mamet, David. *Three Children's Plays.* Grove Press, 1986. Ages 7–11.

McCullough, L. E. *Plays from Fairy Tales: Grades K–3.* Also, *Plays from Mythology: Grades 4–6.* Smith and Kraus, 1998. Ages 5–8.

Schneider, Wolfgang. *Theatre for Children: Nine Contemporary Plays.* Verlag der Autoren, 1996. Ages 10–YA. Brief history of theatre for children in Germany followed by nine plays, many in English for the first time.

Sierra, J. *Fantastic Theater: Puppets and Plays for Young Performers and Audiences.* H. W. Wilson, 1991. Ages 7–10.

Slaight, C., and J. Sharrar. *Multicultural Monologues for Young Actors.* Smith and Kraus, 1995. Ages 11–14.

Stevens, Chambers. *Magnificent Monologues for Kids.* Sandcastle, 1999. Ages 6–11. Includes 51 brief monologues.

Surface, Mary Hall. *Most Valuable Player: And Four Other All-Star Plays for Young Audiences.* Smith and Kraus, 1999. Ages 13–YA.

———. *Short Scenes and Monologues for Middle School Actors.* Smith and Kraus, 2000. Ages 11–14. Includes monologues and scenes for two actors.

Swortzell, Lowell, editor. *Theatre for Young Audiences: Around the World in 21 Plays.* Applause Theatre Book Publishers, 1997. Ages 13–YA.

———. *Cinderella: The World's Favorite Fairy Tale.* New Plays, 1992. Ages 7–10. Three plays of Cinderella from China, Russia, and the United States/ Native American.

Thistle, Louise. *Dramatizing Aesop's Fables: Grades K–6.* Smith and Kraus, 1997. Ages 5–12.

———. *Dramatizing Mother Goose: Introducing Students to Classic Literature through Drama.* Smith and Kraus, 1998. Ages 5–12.

Williams, Marcia, adapter. *Tales from Shakespeare: Seven Plays.* Illustrated. Candlewick, 1998. Ages 7–11.

Winther, Barbara. *Plays from Hispanic Tales: One Act, Royalty-Free Dramatizations for Young People from Hispanic Stories and Folktales.* Plays, Inc., 1998. Ages 10–YA.

## Single Plays

Asher, Sandra Fenichel. *The Wolf and Its Shadow.* Anchorage, 2000. Ages 6–9.

———. *A Woman Called Truth.* Dramatic Publishing, 1993. Ages 10–YA.

Brooks, Laurie. *The Wrestling Season.* Dramatic Publishing, 2000. Ages 12–YA. Unique approach, play performed on an arena wrestling mat with actors answering audience questions at the end.

Bush, Max. *Ghost of the Riverhouse.* Anchorage, 1997. Ages 9–12.

———. *Sarah.* Dramatic Publishing, 2000. Ages 12–YA.

Butterfield, Moira. *Hansel and Gretel.* Playtales Series. Heinemann, 1997. Also, *Sleeping Beauty.* Ages 7–10.

DeVita, James. *Bambi, a Life in the Woods.* Anchorage, 1995. Ages 9–12.

———. *Excavating Mom.* Dramatic Publishing, 1998. Ages 12–14.

Goldberg, Moses. *Puss in Boots* (a participation play). Anchorage, 1992. His plays are especially appealing for children in early childhood, ages 3–8.

Harris, Aurand. *Androcles and the Lion* (a musical). Anchorage, 1964. Ages 4–8.

———. *The Arkansaw Bear.* Anchorage,1980. Ages 4–8.

———. *A Toby Show.* Anchorage, 1978. Ages 4–8.

Mast, Edward. *Jungalbook.* Anchorage, 1991. Ages 6–10.

———. *Wolf Child: The Correction of Joseph.* Anchorage, 1999. Ages 6–10.

Myers, Walter Dean. *Monster.* HarperCollins, 1998. Ages 13–YA. A novel written as a television script.

Soto, Gary. *Nerdlandia: A Play.* Penguin, 1999. Ages 13–YA. Some Spanish dialogue.

Still, James. *And Then They Came for Me: Remembering the World of Anne Frank.* Dramatic Publishing, 1999. Ages 12–YA.

Surface, Mary Hall. *The Sorcerer's Apprentice* (playscript). Anchorage, 1994. Ages 8–12.

Wood, David, adapter. *Babe, the Sheep-Pig: A Play.* Samuel French, 1997. Ages 6–10.

York, Y., adapter. *Afternoon of the Elves.* Dramatic Publishing, 2000. Ages 9–12.

———, adapter. *The Garden of Rikki Tikki Tavi.* Dramatic Publishing, 1999. Ages 8–12.

Zeder, Suzan L. *Doors.* Anchorage, 1985. Ages 6–10.

———. *Mother Hicks, Playscript.* Anchorage, 1986. Ages 5–8.

———. *Step on a Crack.* Anchorage, 1976. Ages 6–12.

———. *The Taste of Sunrise* (prequel to *Mother Hicks*). Anchorage, 1999. Ages 5–9.

# 4

# PICTURE BOOKS

MY BOOK!

*I did it!*
*I did it!*
*Come and look*
*At what I've done!*
*I read a book!*
*When someone wrote it*
*Long ago*
*For me to read,*
*How did he know*
*That this was the book*
*I'd take from the shelf*
*And lie on the floor*
*And read by myself?*
*I really read it!*
*Just like that!*
*Word by word,*
*From first to last!*
*I'm sleeping with*
*This book in bed,*
*This is the FIRST book*
*I've ever read!*

—DAVID L. HARRISON

In an era when picture books abound and provide many children with a delightful introduction to the world of books, it is difficult to imagine a time when books had no illustrations. Nonetheless, the picture book as we know it is a product of the twentieth century. The development of different types of picture books over the last half century can be seen as a response to our developing awareness of the importance of early learning.

## DEFINITION AND DESCRIPTION

*Picture books* are profusely illustrated books in which the illustrations are, to varying degrees, essential to the enjoyment and understanding of the story. For this reason, illustrations in picture books are said to be integral to the story. The illustrations in picture books provide actual plot or concept information as well as clues to character traits, settings, and moods. Without the illustrations, therefore, these books would be diminished, and in some cases the story would make no sense or would be nonexistent.

Many children's books have illustrations but are not picture books. For example, novels and anthologies often have a few scattered illustrations that depict what has already been described in the text or that serve to decorate the text. These illustrations are said to be *incidental* to the story. When well done, illustrations of this kind are appreciated and enjoyed by readers, but they are not necessary for a complete understanding of the story.

## EVALUATION AND SELECTION OF PICTURE BOOKS

Children's first experiences with books must be enjoyable or they will soon not want to be involved with books. Negative experiences could mean that they may never learn to read or to enjoy reading. Over a period of time, evaluation and selection of picture books become a matter of achieving a good balance between what children naturally enjoy and what you want to lead them to enjoy.

The following criteria will help you to identify the best of the picture books:

- The ideas in picture books should be original or presented in an original way. Picture books on topics that children enjoy and find interesting are preferable to books about childhood, in the sense of nostalgia for or reminiscence of childhood. Books of the latter sort are for adults, not children.
- Picture books should avoid racial, ethnic, or sexual stereotyping in text and illustrations. Forms of stereotyping include implying that all members of a group possess the same characteristics and failing to portray members of a certain group as participating in selected roles.
- Language and writing style should be rich and varied but not so complicated as to be incomprehensible to the child. It is desirable to feature new or unusual vocabulary within the context of interesting situations and complementary illustrations. Avoid overly sentimental and trite language, as well as writing characterized by short, choppy sentences and lifeless vocabulary.
- Illustrations should be appropriate in complexity to the age of the intended audience. In picture books for infants, look for relatively uncomplicated pages showing outlined figures against a plain background. Elements of perspective or unusual page design in which only parts of a figure are shown may not be readily understood or appreciated by very young children.
- Children prefer color in illustrations, but color is not essential if illustrations are to work well in picture books. The more important point to consider is whether color or black and white is right for the story.
- Text and illustrations must be well integrated. This means more than that the illustrations on a certain page "go along with" the accompanying text. It means that the illustrations complement or add to the text either by presenting added information about plot, characters, or setting or by

projecting the mood of the story through color and line. Good integration of text and illustrations demands a balance; one must not overwhelm the other.

- When a book is to be shared with a large group, the illustrations must be large enough to be seen from a distance.

- Books selected for infants and toddlers must be durable and safe. Durability is determined by type of cover, type of binding, and paper quality, as discussed in Chapter 2. Safety is ensured by rounded corners, nontoxic materials, washable pages, and no loose attachments.

---

## E X C E L L E N T   P I C T U R E   B O O K S   T O   R E A D   A L O U D

*(Books for each level vary in difficulty and should be selected with the students' literary backgrounds in mind.)*

### P R I M A R Y   L E V E L          A G E S   5 – 8

Alborough, Jez. *Where's My Teddy?* Candlewick, 1992.

Falconer, Ian. *Olivia.* Atheneum, 2000.

Graham, Bob. *Benny, an Adventure Story.* Candlewick, 1999.

Heide, Florence P., and Gilliland, Judith H. *The Day of Ahmed's Secret.* Illustrated by Ted Lewin. Lothrop, 1990.

Henkes, Kevin. *Chrysanthemum.* Greenwillow, 1991.

Hoban, Russell. *A Bargain for Frances.* Illustrated by Lillian Hoban. Harper, 1970.

Hoffman, Mary. *Amazing Grace.* Illustrated by Caroline Binch. Dial, 1991.

Rathman, Peggy. *Officer Buckle and Gloria.* Putnam, 1995.

Waddell, Martin. *Farmer Duck.* Illustrated by Helen Oxenbury. Candlewick, 1992.

### I N T E R M E D I A T E   L E V E L        A G E S   8 – 1 1

Agee, Jon. *The Incredible Painting of Felix Clousseau.* Farrar, 1988.

Baker, Olaf. *Where the Buffaloes Begin.* Illustrated by Stephen Gammell. Warne, 1981.

Browne, Anthony. *Willy the Dreamer.* Candlewick, 1998.

Dorros, Arthur. *Abuela.* Illustrated by Elisa Kleven. Dutton, 1991.

Gerstein, Mordicai. *The Mountains of Tibet.* Harper, 1987.

Offen, Hilda. *Nice Work, Little Wolf.* Dutton, 1992.

Steig, William. *The Amazing Bone.* Farrar, 1976.

Van Allsburg, Chris. *The Wretched Stone.* Houghton, 1991.

Yorinks, Arthur. *Hey, Al.* Illustrated by Richard Egielski. Farrar, 1986.

### A D V A N C E D   L E V E L        A G E S   1 1 – 1 4

Browne, Anthony. *Zoo.* Knopf, 1993.

Collington, Peter. *The Coming of the Surfman.* Knopf, 1994.

Foreman, Michael. *War Game.* Arcade, 1994.

Gallaz, Christophe, and Innocenti, Roberto. *Rose Blanche.* Illustrated by Roberto Innocenti. Creative, 1985.

Hooks, William H. *The Ballad of Belle Dorcas.* Illustrated by Brian Pinkney. Knopf, 1990.

Polacco, Patricia. *Pink and Say.* Philomel, 1994.

- The amount of text on the pages of a picture book determines how long it will take to read the book aloud or for a child to read the book to herself or himself. Generally, the longer the text, the older the intended audience. Note that children's willingness to listen to stories grows with experience, which may result in a younger child who has been read to regularly having a much longer attention span than an older child with no story experience.

Adults sometimes have difficulty perceiving the contributions that illustrations make to picture books. The following general guidelines may improve your ability to "read" illustrations.

- Note characters and actions that are *not* mentioned in the text. Illustrations can contribute to plot.
- Note how characters' physical characteristics are conveyed through the illustrations. Illustrations can contribute to characterization.
- Note how details such as clothing, architecture, and modes of transportation establish and depict place and era of the story. Illustrations can contribute to setting.
- Note whether and how the story's message and mood are conveyed by or underscored in the illustrations. Illustrations can contribute to theme and mood.

Teachers and librarians often rely on the professional judgment of committees that choose what they consider to be the most outstanding picture books published each year in this country and abroad. The most prestigious picture book award in the United States is the Caldecott Medal. The equivalent award in Great Britain is the Kate Greenaway Medal, and in Canada the Amelia Frances Howard-Gibbon Medal. (See Appendix A for lists of award winners.) Another reliable source of information about good quality picture books is "The New York Times Best Illustrated Children's Books of the Year," published in early November as a part of *The New York Times Book Review Supplement.*

## HISTORICAL OVERVIEW OF PICTURE BOOKS

*O*rbis Pictus (The World in Pictures), an ABC book written and illustrated by John Amos Comenius in Moravia and published in 1657, is considered to be the first children's picture book. Comenius's emphasis on using pictures to explain and expand the meaning of the text in books for young people was an important first. But since early books were rare and prohibitively expensive, they were seen by very few children. Moreover, until well into the nineteenth century, Europeans and Americans believed that books were for the serious business of educating and soul saving, not for enjoyment! Today's full-color, extravagantly illustrated, highly amusing picture book is the product of the following important developments.

- Technological advances in color printing. Improved four-color printing presses and printing techniques made high-quality illustrations in books more affordable. These advances were a direct result of the Industrial Revolution.
- A more understanding attitude toward childhood. As late as the eighteenth century, the Western world thought of children as miniature adults and expected them to behave and work accordingly. During the nineteenth century, society began to accept the notion of childhood as a time for playing and learning. At the same time, the general economy began to be able to afford the average child the leisure time these activities require.

- Higher standards of excellence in picture book illustrations. The first great children's book illustrators lived in the 1800s. The beauty, charm, and humor of the illustrations of Randolph Caldecott, Kate Greenaway, and Walter Crane brought children's book art to the attention of the general public. The establishment of national awards for excellence in children's book illustration in the twentieth century had the same effect and encouraged more artists to enter the children's book field.
- A greater demand for books. Growth of public school systems and public and school library systems accounted for much of this increase in the number of books for children. In addition, reading came to be recognized as one of the child's best tools for learning and for gaining a worthy source of entertainment.

As a result of these developments, an economic, social, and political infrastructure that would support the widespread publishing of children's books was in place in most of the Western world by the early twentieth century. With its superb children's book illustrators and color printers of the time, England led the world in publishing picture books from the 1860s until the 1930s. Milestones in the development of picture books are highlighted on page 77.

Today, the picture book genre is well established. Current trends in the field are toward an ever-widening audience, more multicultural themes, and realistic themes, as is demonstrated by the controversial picture book, *Daddy's Roommate* by Michael Willhoite (1990), about a two-father family. Other current trends include greater diversity in formats and more illustrated retellings of folktales. An interesting trend of the 1990s is to publish picture books with high levels of conceptual difficulty and artistic sophistication, intended for middle grade and junior high school students. Other trends are toward more bilingual (especially English-Spanish) picture books and toward greater and more effective use of illustration in informational books. Microchip technology has made it possible to produce books that emit sounds or talk when certain pages are opened. More and more books are available on CD-ROM and are reader-interactive.

## TYPES OF PICTURE BOOKS

The first picture books were meant to be read aloud to children. The latter half of the twentieth century, in response to new educational theories and new markets, saw the development of new types of picture books to be read and enjoyed independently by a wider range of children than just kindergartners and first-graders. Thus, today's picture books differ in intended audience, purpose, format, and relative amount of text and illustration. These differences are not absolute, however; quite often one will find a picture book having characteristics of several specific types. With the understanding that overlap between types is inevitable, you will want to learn to recognize the following kinds of picture books (organized by the intended age of the primary audience from youngest to oldest). Informational picture books are covered in Chapter 9.

### Baby Books

Baby books are simply designed, brightly illustrated, durable picture books that are intended for use with children aged 0 to 2. An example is *Dressing* by Helen Oxenbury. Baby books gained popularity in

# MILESTONES

*in the Development of the PICTURE BOOK*

| DATE | EVENT | SIGNIFICANCE |
|---|---|---|
| 1484 | Publication of *Aesop's Fables,* illustrated by William Caxton. | One of the first known illustrated books enjoyed by children. |
| 1657 | Publication of *Orbis Pictus,* written and illustrated by John Amos Comenius. | Considered to be the first picture book for children. |
| 1860–1900 | Golden Age of children's book illustration in Great Britain, led by Randolph Caldecott, Walter Crane, and Kate Greenaway. | Increased awareness, stature, popularity, and appreciation of children's picture books. |
| 1902 | Publication of *The Tale of Peter Rabbit* by Beatrix Potter. | Early important modern picture storybook in English. |
| 1928 | Publication of *Millions of Cats* by Wanda Gág. | Early important modern American picture storybook. |
| 1938 | Establishment of the Caldecott Award for illustration in children's books in the United States. | Promoted excellence in illustrating for children and encouraged talented artists to illustrate children's books. |
| 1940 | Publication of *Pat the Bunny* by Dorothy Kunhardt. | One of the first books for babies. Began the move to supply different types of picture books for different child audiences. |
| 1957 | Publication of *The Cat in the Hat,* written and illustrated by Dr. Seuss, and *Little Bear,* written by Else Minarik and illustrated by Maurice Sendak. | Introduced the easy-to-read genre of picture books. |
| 1962 | Publication of *A Snowy Day,* written and illustrated by Ezra Jack Keats. | One of the first picture books with a minority character as the protagonist to win the Caldecott Medal. |
| 1967 | Publication of *A Boy, a Dog, and a Frog,* illustrated by Mercer Mayer. | Popularized the wordless book genre. |
| 1972 | Publication of *Push Pull, Empty Full* by Tana Hoban. | Signaled the growing popularity of the concept picture book. |
| 1974 | Publication of *Arrow to the Sun: A Pueblo Indian Tale* by Gerald McDermott. | Signaled the emergence of picture books for older readers as a distinct type of picture book. |
| 1981 | Publication of "The Baby Board Books" by Helen Oxenbury. | Baby books were established as a distinct and important type of picture book. |
| 1990 | *Color Zoo* by Lois Ehlert wins a Caldecott Honor Award. | Recognition of the engineered book genre. |
| 1991 | *Black and White* by David Macaulay wins Caldecott Medal. | Denoted acceptance of nontraditional picture book formats. |
| 2000 | *Joseph Had a Little Overcoat* by Simms Taback wins Caldecott Medal. | First engineered book to win the Caldecott Medal. |

the 1980s in response to the growing evidence of the remarkable learning capacity of very young children. The types of baby books actually denote the material used in their construction. *Board books* are constructed of heavy, laminated cardboard and are either bound as a book with pages or made to fold out in an accordion fashion. *Vinyl books* and *cloth books* are also types of baby books. These books have little or no text. Their content, which deals with the objects and routines that are familiar to the infant and toddler, is presented mainly by the illustrations. The best baby books, such as those produced by Helen Oxenbury and Jan Ormerod, are intelligently designed to emphasize patterns and associations to promote dialogue between the caregiver and the young child, who will often look at these books together.

## Interactive Books

Interactive books are picture books that stimulate a child's verbal or physical participation as the book is read. These books ask the child direct questions, invite unison recitation of chants or repeated lines, encourage clapping or moving to the rhythm of the words, or require the child to touch or manipulate the book or find objects in the illustrations. *Each Peach Pear Plum,* Janet and Allan Ahlberg's "I Spy" book featuring well-known nursery rhyme characters, is a good example. The intended audience is usually children aged 2 to 6, and the books are seen as an extension of their world of play. One classic example of this type of book that is still greatly enjoyed by toddlers today is Dorothy Kunhardt's *Pat the Bunny* (1940).

## Toy Books

Sometimes called *engineered* or *mechanical books,* toy books use paper that has been engineered (i.e., cut, folded, constructed) to provide pop-up, see-through, movable, changeable, or three-dimensional illustrations. Toy books can be found for all ages, but only those that have the simpler types of engineering, such as pages of varying widths or drilled holes for see-through effects (as in Eric Carle's *The Very Hungry Caterpillar*), would be appropriate for most young children. Toy books with fragile or elaborate pop-up features would not last in the hands of a very young child.

## Wordless Books

The wordless book depends entirely on carefully sequenced illustrations to present the story. There is no text, or the text is limited to one or two pages in the book, so the illustrations must be highly narrative. *A Small Miracle* by Peter Collington is a good example of this category. Wordless books are generally intended for prereaders, usually children aged 4 to 6. When children "read" these illustrations in their own words, they benefit from the book's visual story structure in several ways:

- They develop a concept of story as a cohesive narrative with a beginning and an end.
- They use language inventively, which promotes language development.
- They learn the front-to-back, left-to-right page progression in reading.
- They begin to understand that stories can be found not only in books but in themselves.

Publishers began to produce wordless picture books in noticeable quantities in the 1960s. Mercer Mayer, with his wordless book series about a boy, a dog, and a frog, helped to popularize this type of picture book. More sophisticated wordless books for older readers, such as David Weisner's *Sector 7,* are also available.

## Alphabet Books

The alphabet, or ABC, book presents the alphabet letter by letter to acquaint young children with the shapes, names, and, in some cases, the sounds of the twenty-six letters. For example, see *Wildflower ABC: An Alphabet of Potato Prints* by Diana Pomeroy. Almost all ABC book authors and illustrators choose a theme (animals, elves, fruit, etc.) or device (finding the many objects in the accompanying illustration beginning with the featured letter) to give their books cohesion. Literally hundreds of ABC picture books have been published during the last twenty years, and naturally some are better than others. In choosing an ABC book, consider the appropriateness of the theme or device for students, whether both uppercase and lowercase letters are displayed, and the use of a simple, easy-to-read style of print.

Most ABC books are intended for the nonreader or beginning reader. Some authors and illustrators use the alphabet itself as a device for presenting information or wordplay. In these cases, the intended audience already knows the alphabet. In *Tomorrow's Alphabet,* written by George Shannon and illustrated by Donald Crews, each letter is presented as a puzzle to solve on two pages.

## Counting Books

The counting book presents numbers, usually 1 through 10, to acquaint young children with the numerals and their shapes (1, 2, 3, . . . ), the number names (one, two, three, . . . ), the sense of what quantity each numeral represents, and the counting sequence. *Let's Count* by Tana Hoban is a good example of this type of book. As with alphabet books, authors and illustrators of counting books employ themes or devices to make them more cohesive and interesting. Specific considerations in evaluating a counting book include the appeal to children of the theme and objects chosen to illustrate the number concepts, and the clarity with which the illustrator presents the concept of number.

Illustrators often fill their alphabet and counting books with unusual and intriguing objects for children to name and count, such as aardvarks, barracudas, and chameleons. Children pick up a great deal of interesting information and vocabulary in this way. You will be in the best position to decide whether the novelty of these objects will be motivating or confusing to your students.

## Concept Books

A concept book is a picture book that explores or explains an idea or concept (e.g., opposites), an object (e.g., a train), or an activity (e.g., working) rather than telling a story. Many concept books have no plot but use repeated elements in the illustrations and text to tie the book together. A good example is *Trucks, Trucks, Trucks* by Peter Sís. Limited text and clearly understood illustrations in the best concept books stimulate children's exploratory talk about the concepts, objects, and activities presented.

Alphabet and counting books are considered types of concept books. Another variety of the concept book that is popular with 2- to 4-year-olds is the naming book, which presents simple, labeled pictures of people, animals, and objects for young children to identify. *My First Word Book* by Angela Wilkes is an example of a naming book.

### Pattern Books

Easy-to-read books that strongly emphasize word patterns are called *pattern books*. They are also some-times referred to as *predictable books* because of the predictability of the text due to rhyme, repetition, and illustration clues, or *decodable texts* because of the language regularities in which certain phono-logical patterns are repeated. Word patterns in these books are achieved mainly by repetition of lines or parts of lines, such as "There was an old lady who swallowed a . . . " in Simms Taback's *There Was an Old Lady Who Swallowed a Fly*. In evaluating these books, one looks for natural-sounding, familiar lan-guage patterns. Generally, these books resemble the picture storybook in format.

### Picture Storybooks

The picture storybook is a picture book in which both illustrations and text are equally responsible for telling the story. Text and illustration occur with equal frequency in these books, and on most double spreads, both are in view. A good example is *Officer Buckle and Gloria* by Peggy Rathmann. *The Tale of Peter Rabbit*, written and illustrated by Beatrix Potter and published in England in 1902, has been called the first modern picture book. The first modern American picture storybook, *Millions of Cats*, written and illustrated by Wanda Gág, was published in 1928. The picture storybook is the most com-mon type of picture book.

The text of most picture storybooks is meant to be read aloud to the intended audience of 4- to 7-year-olds, at least for the first time or two, and often includes challenging vocabulary. Many of the best picture storybooks are also read and enjoyed independently by children 8 years old and up.

### Easy-to-Read Books

Easy-to-read books are created to help the beginning reader read independently with success. These books have limited text on each page, large print, double spacing, and short sentences. There is usually an illustration on about every other page. Language is often, but not always, controlled, and words are short and familiar. For example, see *Good Night, Good Knight* by Shelley M. Thomas, illustrated by Jen-nifer Plecas. Easy-to-read picture books were first developed in the 1950s by such authors as Dr. Seuss (*The Cat in the Hat, Fox in Sox*) and Else Holmelund Minarik, who, along with illustrator Maurice Sendak, created the Little Bear series. Easy-to-read books can be used with children whenever they want to learn to read, but the audience for this type of book is usually the 5- to 7-year-old.

The easy-to-read book differs in appearance from the picture storybook in several obvious ways. Because they are intended for independent reading, they do not have to be seen from a distance and may be smaller; the text takes up a greater proportion of each page; and the text is often divided into short chapters.

### Picture Books for Older Readers

Anyone, regardless of age, can enjoy beautiful and interesting illustrations, but, more often than not, picture books are not found in classrooms above grade three. This curious lack of picture books in the intermediate, middle, and junior high school grades may be due, in part, to resistance among adults who influence children in their book choices to include picture books after the primary grades, as Gontarski (1994) found. A wiser approach would be to promote both textual and visual literacy by making appropriate picture books an option in any reading situation. Picture books for older readers are generally more sophisticated, abstract, or complex in themes, stories, and illustrations and are suitable for children aged 10 and older. A good example is *The Watertower* by Gary Crew, illustrated by Steven Woolman. This type of picture book began to appear in the 1970s, and now artists such as David Macaulay, Anthony Browne, and Jörg Steiner are known for their picture books for older readers. The most common types of picture books for older readers are picture storybooks, wordless books, toy books, and informational picture books.

## Transitional Books

Transitional books are a special type of book for the child who can read but has not yet become a fluent reader. These books, which are less profusely illustrated and have lengthier text than the other types of books discussed in this chapter, are not picture books. They lie somewhere between picture books and full-length novels. A good example of a transitional book is *Not My Dog* by Colby Rodowsky, illustrated by Thomas Yezerski.

Characteristics of transitional books are an uncomplicated writing style and vocabulary, an illustration on about every third page, division of text into chapters, slightly enlarged print, and a length of approximately 50–80 pages. Children who read these books are typically between the ages of 8 and 11. Often, books for the transitional reader occur in series, such as Donald Sobol's Encyclopedia Brown books, Ann Cameron's Julian books, and Robert Newton Peck's Soup books. See Appendix E for a list of good transitional books.

With easy-to-read and transitional books in mind, it is wise to remember that children by the age of 5 or 6 have become accustomed to hearing wonderful, richly descriptive stories read and told to them. They are fluent and often sophisticated users of oral language. For children to find themselves suddenly limited to simplistic, boring stories while learning to read would be disheartening, to say the least. To write well for the beginning reader is a real challenge, since these stories must treat interesting topics in vivid language while remaining relatively easy to read. Finding the best of these books for the beginning and transitional readers in your charge will be time well spent.

During the twentieth century the picture book was begun and developed as a genre, diversified to meet the demands of an ever-expanding audience and market, and improved as a result of new and refined printing technology. As researchers came to realize the connections between positive early experiences with good literature, early learning, and future school success, new types of picture books were developed to serve both younger and older audiences. Today, high-quality picture books on nearly every imaginable topic can enrich the lives and imaginations of young children and the classrooms and libraries where they learn.

## REFERENCES

Gontarski, M. (1994). Visual literacy as it relates to picture book use by selected fifth grade students. Unpublished doctoral dissertation, The Florida State University, Tallahassee, FL.

Harrison, David L. (1993). My book! In D. L. Harrison, *Somebody catch my homework*. Illustrated by Betsy Lewin. Honesdale, PA: Boyds Mills.

## NOTABLE AUTHORS AND ILLUSTRATORS OF PICTURE BOOKS

**Molly Bang,** author/illustrator. Wordless and concept books illustrated in a variety of styles and media. *The Grey Lady and the Strawberry Snatcher; Ten, Nine, Eight.*

**Ludwig Bemelmans,** author/illustrator. Creator of the Madeline series of picture storybooks. *Madeline; Madeline's Rescue.*

**Marcia Brown,** author/illustrator. Reteller and illustrator of folktales from foreign lands. Three Caldecott Medals, six Caldecott Honor Book Awards. *Once a Mouse . . . ; Stone Soup.*

**Anthony Browne,** author/illustrator. British. Surreal illustrations in picture books for older readers. *Gorilla; The Tunnel.*

**Eric Carle,** author/illustrator. Unusually formatted picture storybooks and concept books about insects and animals. *The Grouchy Ladybug; The Very Busy Spider.*

**Barbara Cooney,** author/illustrator. Picture storybooks reflect values of New England. *Miss Rumphius.*

**Floyd Cooper,** illustrator. Uses watercolor and erasers to create characters from many cultures. *The Girl Who Loved Caterpillars.*

**Donald Crews,** author/illustrator. Noted for use of expressionist art style in concept books. *Tomorrow's Alphabet* (by George Shannon).

**Tomie dePaola,** author/illustrator. Droll characters like Strega Nona and Big Anthony; uses formal, balanced artistic style. *The Legend of the Bluebonnet; Strega Nona: An Old Tale.*

**Leo and Diane Dillon,** illustrators. Illustrators of stories from Black Africa and picture books for older readers. *Ashanti to Zulu.*

**Lois Ehlert,** author/illustrator. Bold color, geometric shapes, and engineered pages characterize her informational books. *Color Zoo.*

**Denise Fleming,** author/illustrator. Creates pattern books of handmade paper. *In the Small, Small Pond; Mama Cat Has Three Kittens.*

**Stephen Gammell,** illustrator. Uses colored pencil in an informal, airy style. *The Relatives Came* (by Cynthia Rylant).

**Kevin Henkes,** author/illustrator. Creator of family situation animal fantasies featuring mice. *Chrysanthemum; Julius, the Baby of the World; Owen.*

**Eric Hill,** author/illustrator. Features Spot, the dog, in toy and board books. *Where's Spot?*

**Russell Hoban,** author. Creator of Frances, the badger, in easy-to-read books. *Bedtime for Frances.*

**Tana Hoban,** author/illustrator. Using photographs, created some of the first and best concept books. *Push Pull, Empty Full; Is It Rough? Is It Smooth? Is It Shiny?*

**Shirley Hughes,** author/illustrator. British. Picture storybooks about family life. *Alfie Gets in First.*

**Pat Hutchins,** author/illustrator. British. Pattern books for beginning readers. *Rosie's Walk; Tidy Titch.*

**Trina Schart Hyman,** illustrator. Illustrator of retold folktales. *Little Red Riding Hood; Hershel and the Hanukkah Goblins.*

**Ezra Jack Keats,** author/illustrator. One of the first to portray ethnic minorities in the United States as major characters in picture books. *A Snowy Day; Peter's Chair.*

**Steven Kellogg,** author/illustrator. Uses animals as characters in picture storybooks. *Island of the Skog.*

**Leo Lionni,** author/illustrator. Uses collage technique to illustrate modern fables. *Swimmy; Frederick.*

**Arnold Lobel,** author/illustrator. Creator of "Frog and Toad" easy-to-read series. *Days with Frog and Toad; Fables.*

**David Macaulay,** author/illustrator. Creator of informational picture books and picture books with unusual formats for older readers. *Black and White; Cathedral.*

**James Marshall,** author/illustrator. Humorously retold and illustrated folktales. *Goldilocks and the Three Bears.*

**Bill Martin, Jr.,** author. Pattern and rhyming stories for the beginning reader. *Brown Bear, Brown Bear, What Do You See?* (illustrated by Eric Carle).

**Patricia McKissack,** author. Picture storybooks with African-American characters and themes. *Nettie Jo's Friends* (illustrated by Scott Cook).

**Else Holmelund Minarik,** author. Her "Little Bear" books were some of the first easy-to-read books. *Little Bear's Visit* (illustrated by Maurice Sendak).

**Helen Oxenbury,** author/illustrator. British. Board books for babies. *Dressing; Say Goodnight.*

**Brian Pinkney,** illustrator. Uses distinctive scratch-board technique in folktales and biographies featuring African Americans. *Duke Ellington: The Piano Prince and His Orchestra* (by Andrea Davis Pinkney).

**Jerry Pinkney,** illustrator. Represents the African-American experience in realistic, watercolor illustrations. *Mirandy and Brother Wind* (by Patricia McKissack).

**Patricia Polacco,** author/illustrator. Stories feature homespun characters from varied ethnic backgrounds, particularly Russia. *Babushka's Doll; Chicken Sunday.*

**Allen Say,** author/illustrator. Realistic watercolors depict stories of the Japanese-American experience. *Grandfather's Journey.*

**Maurice Sendak,** author/illustrator. Explores the dreams and imagination of children in complex picture storybooks. *Where the Wild Things Are; Outside Over There.*

**Dr. Seuss** (pseudonym of Theodor Geisel), author/illustrator. One of the first to develop the easy-to-read genre. *The Cat in the Hat.*

**Peter Sís,** author/illustrator. Noted for abstract style and complex subjects in picture books for older readers. *Starry Messenger.*

**William Steig,** author/illustrator. Animal fantasy picture storybooks. *Doctor De Soto.*

**Chris Van Allsburg,** author/illustrator. Uses shadow and unusual perspectives to create mysterious moods in picture storybooks for intermediate-grade readers. *Jumanji; The Garden of Abdul Gasazi.*

**Simms Taback,** author/illustrator. Noted for folk art style and effective use of paper engineering in engaging interpretations of poems. *Joseph Had a Little Overcoat.*

**Rosemary Wells,** author/illustrator. Creator of excellent board books and pattern books. *Hooray for Max; Noisy Nora.*

**David Wiesner,** author/illustrator. Creator of wordless fantasy stories. *Tuesday; Free Fall.*

**Vera B. Williams,** author/illustrator. Expressive artistic style used to depict nontraditional families in picture storybooks. *A Chair for My Mother; Three Days on a River in a Red Canoe.*

**David Wisniewski,** author/illustrator. Uses intricate cut paper and layering technique to illustrate ancient stories and legends. *Golem; Rain Player.*

**Ed Young,** author/illustrator. Chinese-American illustrator of folktales who uses varied media to create mood and textures. *Lon Po Po: A Red-Riding Hood Story from China; Seven Blind Mice.*

**Paul O. Zelinsky,** illustrator. Illustrates folktales with richly colored oil paintings. *Rumpelstiltskin* (adapted by illustrator).

## RECOMMENDED PICTURE BOOKS

*Ages refer to approximate interest levels.*
*YA = young adult.*

### Baby Books

*These books are generally suitable for ages 0 to 3.*

Hoban, Tana. *What Is It?* Greenwillow, 1985.

Kunhardt, Dorothy. *Pat the Bunny.* Golden, 1940.

Ormerod, Jan. *Bend and Stretch.* Lothrop, 1987. (Others in this series: *Making Friends; Mom's Home; This Little Nose.*)

————. *To Baby with Love.* Lothrop, 1994.

Oxenbury, Helen. "Out and About Books." *The Birthday Party.* Dutton, 1983. (Others in this series: *The Car Trip; The Checkup; The Dancing Class; Eating Out; First Day of School; Grandma and Grandpa; Our Dog.*)

————. *I Can.* (Baby Board Book) Random, 1986. (Others in this series: *I Hear; I See; I Touch.*)

————. "The Baby Board Books." *Dressing.* Simon & Schuster, 1981. (Others in this series: *Family; Friends; Playing; Working.*)

————. "Very First Books." *Mother's Helper.* Dial, 1982. (Others in this series: *Shopping Trip; Beach Day; Good Night, Good Morning; Monkey See, Monkey Do.*)

Ricklen, Neil. *Baby's Clothes.* Simon & Schuster, 1994. (Others in this series of 24: *Baby's Friends; Baby's Home; Baby's Toys.*)

————. *My Clothes/Mi Ropa.* Macmillan, 1994. (Others in this bilingual English/Spanish series: *My Numbers/Mis Números.*)

Uff, Caroline. *Lulu's Busy Day.* Walker, 2000. (See also *Happy Birthday, Lulu.*)

Wells, Rosemary. "Very First Books." *Max's Bath.* Dial, 1985. (Others in this series: *Max's Bedtime; Max's Birthday; Max's Breakfast; Max's First Word; Max's New Suit; Max's Ride; Max's Toys.*)

## Interactive Books

Ahlberg, Janet, and Allen Ahlberg. *Each Peach Pear Plum: An I-Spy Story.* Viking, 1978. Ages 2–4.

————. *Peek-a Boo!* Viking, 1981. Ages 3–5.

Carlstrom, Nancy White. *Jesse Bear, What Will You Wear?* Illustrated by Bruce Degan. Macmillan, 1986. Ages 2–4. (Others in this series: *Tra-la Tub; Tum-Tum Tickle; Yum-Yum Crumble.*)

Cook, Trish. *So Much.* Illustrated by Helen Oxenbury. Candlewick, 1994. Ages 3–5.

Hill, Eric. *Where's Spot?* Putnam, 1980. (Others in this series: *Spot's First Walk; Spot's Birthday Party; Spot's First Christmas.*) Ages 3–5.

Knight, Hilary. *Where's Wallace?* Simon & Schuster, 2000 (1964). Ages 4–7.

Kunhardt, Dorothy. *Pat the Bunny.* Golden, 1999 (1962). Ages 2–4.

Marzollo, Jean. *I Spy Fantasy: A Book of Picture Riddles.* Illustrated by Walter Wick. Scholastic, 1994. Ages 5–9. (Others in this series: *I Spy Mystery.*)

Rose, Dorothy. *Follow Me!* Illustrated by Ann Bogart. Simon & Schuster, 1993. Ages 2–5. (Others in this series: *Peek-a-Boo!; What Do Lambs Say?; Where's Your Nose?*)

Shapiro, Arnold. *Who Says That?* Illustrated by Monica Wellington. Dutton, 1991. Ages 3–5.

Spires, Elizabeth. *With One White Wing: Puzzles in Poems and Pictures.* Illustrated by Eric Blegvad. Simon & Schuster, 1995. Ages 7–10.

Tafuri, Nancy. *Have You Seen My Duckling?* Greenwillow, 1984. Ages 3–5.

Watanabe, Shigeo. "I Can Do It All by Myself." *How Do I Put It On?* Illustrated by Yasou Ohtomo. Philomel, 1980. (Also in this series: *What a Good Lunch!; Get Set Go!; I'm King of the Castle; Where's My Daddy?; I Can Ride It!*) Ages 4–6.

Wilkes, Angela. *My First Activity Book.* Knopf, 1990. Ages 3–5.

Williams, Vera B. *"More More More," Said the Baby.* Greenwillow, 1990. Ages 2–4.

## Toy Books

Baum, L. Frank. *The Wonderful World of Oz: A Commemorative Pop-Up.* Illustrated by Robert Sabuda. Simon & Schuster, 2000. Ages 6–9.

Carle, Eric. *The Honeybee and the Robber: A Moving/Picture Book.* Philomel, 1995 (1981). Ages 5–7.

————. *The Very Hungry Caterpillar.* World, 1968. Ages 4–6.

————. *The Very Lonely Firefly.* Putnam, 1995. Ages 2–6.

————. *The Very Quiet Cricket.* Putnam, 1990. Ages 2–6.

Carter, David A., and James Diaz. *Elements of Pop-Up.* Simon & Schuster, 1999. Ages 12–Adult.

Hellen, Nancy. *The Bus Stop.* Orchard, 1988. Ages 5–7.

————. *Old MacDonald Had a Farm.* Orchard, 1990. Ages 5–7.

Hill, Eric. *Where's Spot?* Putnam, 1980. Ages 3–5.

Jonas, Ann. *Where Can It Be?* Greenwillow, 1986. Ages 5–7.

Reasoner, Charles. *Whose Mommy Is This?* Price, 1994. Ages 3–6.

Taback, Simms. *There Was an Old Lady Who Swallowed a Fly.* Viking, 1997. Ages 5–7. (See also Pattern Books.)

Young, Ed. *Mouse Match: A Chinese Folktale.* Harcourt, 1997. Ages 4–7.

## Wordless Books

*These books are generally suitable for ages 3 to 6. Ages will be provided only for those books intended for an older audience.*

Anno, Mitsumasa. *Anno's Journey.* Collins, 1978. Ages 8–10.

Baker, Jeannie. *Window.* Greenwillow, 1991. Ages 7–12.

Briggs, Raymond. *The Snowman.* Random, 1978.

Carle, Eric. *Do You Want to Be My Friend?* Harper, 1971.

Collington, Peter. *A Small Miracle.* Knopf, 1997. Ages 4–7.

Day, Alexandra. *Carl Goes Shopping.* Farrar, 1989. (See others in the series.)

Feelings, Tom. *The Middle Passage: White Ships/Black Cargo.* Dial, 1995. Ages 9–14.

Hutchins, Pat. *Changes, Changes.* Macmillan, 1971.

Martin, Rafe. *Will's Mammoth.* Illustrated by Stephen Gammell. Putnam, 1989.

Mayer, Mercer. *A Boy, a Dog, and a Frog.* Dial, 1967. (Others in this series: *Frog, Where Are You?; A Boy, a Dog, and a Friend; Frog on His Own; Frog Goes to Dinner; One Frog Too Many,* with Marianna Mayer.)

McCully, Emily Arnold. *The Christmas Gift.* Harper, 1988.

———. *School.* Harper, 1987.

Popov, Nikolai. *Why?* North-South, 1996. Ages 8–12. (See also Picture Books for Older Readers.)

Prater, John. *The Gift.* Viking, 1986. Ages 6–8.

Spier, Peter. *Noah's Ark.* Doubleday, 1977. Ages 6–8.

———. *Oh, Were They Ever Happy!* Doubleday, 1978. Ages 6–8.

———. *Peter Spier's Rain.* Doubleday, 1982.

Vincent, Gabrielle. *a day, a dog.* Front Street, 1999. Ages 6–8.

Wiesner, David. *Free Fall.* Lothrop, 1988. Ages 6–10.

———. *Tuesday.* Clarion, 1991. Ages 6–10.

———. *Sector 7.* Clarion, 1999. Ages 6–10.

## Alphabet Books

*These books are generally suitable for ages 3 to 6. Ages will be provided only for those books intended for an older audience.*

Aylesworth, Jim. *Old Black Fly.* Illustrated by Stephen Gammell. Holt, 1992.

Azarian, Mary. *A Farmer's Alphabet.* Godine, 1981.

Bunting, J. *My First ABC Book.* Dorling Kindersley, 1993.

Dodson, Peter. *An Alphabet of Dinosaurs.* Illustrated by Wayne D. Barlowe. Scholastic, 1995. Ages 4–9.

Ehlert, Lois. *Eating the Alphabet: Fruits and Vegetables from A to Z.* Harcourt, 1989.

Ellis, Veronica Freeman. *Afro-Bets First Book about Africa.* Illustrated by George Ford. Just Us Books, 1990.

Fain, Kathleen. *Handsigns: A Sign Language Alphabet.* Chronicle, 1993. Ages 5–8.

Feelings, Muriel. *Jambo Means Hello: Swahili Alphabet Book.* Illustrated by Tom Feelings. Dial, 1974. Ages 6–8.

Greenaway, Kate. *A—Apple Pie.* Warne, 1886.

Hepworth, Cathi. *ANTics! An Alphabetical Anthology.* Putnam, 1992. Ages 7–9.

Hoban, Tana. *A, B, See!* Greenwillow, 1982.

Holtz, Lara Tankel. *DK Alphabet Book.* Illustrated by Dave King. DK, 1997. Ages 5–8.

Johnson, Stephen T. *Alphabet City.* Viking, 1995. Ages 6–9.

Jonas, Ann. *Aardvarks, Disembark!* Greenwillow, 1990.

Kitchen, Bert. *Animal Alphabet.* Dial, 1984.

Lobel, Anita. *Alison's Zinnia.* Greenwillow, 1990.

Lobel, Arnold. *On Market Street.* Illustrated by Anita Lobel. Greenwillow, 1981.

MacDonald, Suse. *Alphabatics.* Bradbury, 1986.

Martin, Bill, Jr., and John Archambault. *Chicka Chicka Boom Boom.* Illustrated by Lois Ehlert. Simon & Schuster, 1989.

Mullins, Patricia. *V for Vanishing: An Alphabet of Endangered Animals.* HarperCollins, 1993. Ages 6–8.

Musgrove, Margaret. *Ashanti to Zulu: African Traditions.* Illustrated by Leo and Diane Dillon. Dial, 1976. Ages 8–12.

Nathan, Cheryl. *Bugs and Beasties ABC.* Cool Kids Press, 1995. Ages 4–6.

Neumeier, Marty, and Byron Glaser. *Action Alphabet.* Greenwillow, 1985.

Pelletier, David. *The Graphic Alphabet.* Orchard, 1996. Ages 9–12.

Pomeroy, Diana. *Wildflower ABC: An Alphabet of Potato Prints.* Harcourt, 1997. Ages 3–6.

Provensen, Alice, and Martin Provensen. *A Peaceable Kingdom: The Shaker ABCEDARIUS.* Viking, 1978. Ages 6–8.

Rankin, Laura. *The Handmade Alphabet.* Dial, 1991. Ages 6–11.

Shannon, George. *Tomorrow's Alphabet.* Illustrated by Donald Crews. Greenwillow, 1996. Ages 6–8.

Shaw, Eve. *Grandmother's Alphabet.* Pfeifer-Hamilton, 1997. Ages 5–8.

Tapahonso, Luci, and Eleanor Schick. *Navajo ABC: A Dine Alphabet Book.* Illustrated by Eleanor Schick. Simon & Schuster, 1995. Ages 5–8.

Van Allsburg, Chris. *The Z Was Zapped.* Houghton Mifflin, 1987. Ages 6–10.

## Counting Books

*These books are generally suitable for ages 4 to 7. Ages will be provided only for those books intended for an older audience.*

Aker, Susan. *What Comes in 2's, 3's & 4's?* Illustrated by Bernie Karlin. Simon & Schuster, 1990.

Alda, Arlene. *Arlene Alda's 1 2 3: What Do You See?* Tricycle, 1998. Ages 3–7.

Anno, Mitsumasa. *Anno's Counting Book.* Crowell, 1977. Ages 7–9.

Bang, Molly. *Ten, Nine, Eight.* Greenwillow, 1983.

Fleming, Denise. *Count!* Holt, 1992.

Giganti, Paul. *Each Orange Had Eight Slices.* Illustrated by Donald Crews. Greenwillow, 1992.

Hoban, Tana. *1, 2, 3.* Greenwillow, 1985.

———. *26 Letters and 99 Cents.* Greenwillow, 1987.

———. *Let's Count.* Greenwillow, 1999.

Jonas, Ann. *Splash!* Morrow, 1995.

Kitchen, Bert. *Animal Numbers.* Dial, 1987.

*Lifesize Animal Counting Book, The.* Dorling Kindersley, 1994.

Moss, Lloyd. *Zin! Zin! Zin! A Violin.* Illustrated by Marjorie Priceman. Simon & Schuster, 1995. Ages 4–7.

Sturges, Philemon. *Ten Flashing Fireflies.* Illustrated by Anna Vojtech. North-South, 1995. Ages 4–6.

Tafuri, Nancy. *Who's Counting?* Greenwillow, 1986.

Testa, Fulvio. *If You Take a Pencil.* Dial, 1982.

Walsh, Ellen S. *Mouse Count.* Harcourt, 1991.

## Concept Books

*These books are generally suitable for ages 3 to 5. Ages will be provided only for those books intended for an older audience.*

Bang, Molly. *When Sophie Gets Angry—Really, Really Angry . . . .* Scholastic, 1999. Ages 3–6.

Barton, Byron. *Dinosaurs, Dinosaurs.* Crowell, 1989.

———. *Machines at Work.* Crowell, 1987.

Brown, Craig. *Tractor.* Greenwillow, 1995. Ages 4–6.

Cabrera, Jane. *Cat's Colors.* Dial, 1997. Ages 1–4.

Crews, Donald. *Freight Train.* Greenwillow, 1978.

———. *Truck.* Greenwillow, 1980.

Ehlert, Lois. *Growing Vegetable Soup.* Harcourt, 1987.

———. *Red Leaf, Yellow Leaf.* Harcourt, 1991. Ages 5–7.

Hoban, Tana. *Color Everywhere.* Morrow, 1995.

———. *Is It Red? Is It Yellow? Is It Blue?* Greenwillow, 1978.

———. *Look Again!* Macmillan, 1971.

———. *Over, Under, and Through and Other Spatial Concepts.* Macmillan, 1973.

———. *Push Pull, Empty Full: A Book of Opposites.* Macmillan, 1972.

Hughes, Shirley. *Alfie Gets in First.* Lothrop, 1982.

———. *Alfie Gives a Hand.* Lothrop, 1984.

———. *Angel Mae.* Lothrop, 1989.

———. "Nursery Collection." *Bathwater's Hot.* Lothrop, 1985. (Others in this series: *Noisy; When We Went to the Park.*)

Isadora, Rachel. *I Hear.* Greenwillow, 1985. (Also in this series: *I Touch; I See.*)

Krauss, Ruth. *A Hole Is to Dig.* Illustrated by Maurice Sendak. Harper, 1952.

Lesser, Carolyn. *What a Wonderful Day to Be a Cow.* Illustrated by Melissa B. Mathis. Knopf, 1995. Ages 5–7.

Levey, Judith S., editor. *Macmillan Picture Wordbook.* Macmillan, 1990.

London, Jonathon. *Like Butter on Pancakes.* Illustrated by G. Brian Karas. Viking, 1995. Ages 4–6.

Lyon, George Ella. *Who Came Down That Road?* Illustrated by Peter Catalanotto. Orchard, 1992. Ages 4–7.

Martin, Bill, Jr., and John Archambault. *Listen to the Rain.* Illustrated by James Endicott. Holt, 1988.

McCloskey, Robert. *Time of Wonder.* Viking, 1957.

McDonald, Golden. (pseudonym of Margaret Wise Brown). *The Little Island.* Illustrated by Leonard Weisgard. Doubleday, 1946.

McMillan, Bruce. *Super Super Superwords.* Lothrop, 1989.

———. *Time To. . . .* Lothrop, 1989.

Miller, Margaret. *Now I'm Big.* Greenwillow, 1996. Ages 4–6.

———. *Whose Shoe?* Greenwillow, 1991.

*My Little Color Library* (six books, six colors). Dorling Kindersley, 1993.

Rogers, Fred. *Making Friends.* Photographs by Jim Judkis. Putnam, 1987.

———. *Moving.* Photographs by Jim Judkis. Putnam, 1987.

Rotner, Shelley. *Wheels Around.* Houghton, 1995. Ages 4–7.

Scarry, Richard. *My First Word Book.* Random House, 1986.

———. *Richard Scarry's Biggest Word Book Ever!* Random House, 1985.

Schwartz, David M. *If You Made a Million.* Illustrated by Steven Kellogg. Photographs by George Ancona. Lothrop, 1989.

Serfozo, Mary. *What's What: A Guessing Game.* Illustrated by Keiko Narahashi. McElderry, 1996. Ages 2–5.

———. *Who Said Red?* Illustrated by Keiko Narahashi. Macmillan, 1988.

Sís, Peter. *Fire Truck.* Greenwillow, 1998. Ages 1–3. (Also a counting book.)

———. *Trucks, Trucks, Trucks.* Greenwillow, 1999. Ages 1–3.

Walsh, Ellen Stoll. *Mouse Paint.* Harcourt, 1989.

Wilkes, Angela. *My First Word Book.* DK, 1999.

Winthrop, Elizabeth. *Shoes.* Illustrated by William Joyce. Harper, 1986.

## Pattern Books

Asch, Frank. *Monkey Face.* Parents' Magazine Press, 1977.

Charlip, Remy. *Fortunately.* Aladdin, 1993 (originally published by Parents' Magazine Press, 1964).

Cuyler, Margery. *That's Good, That's Bad.* Illustrated by David Catrow. Holt, 1991.

Emberley, Barbara. *Drummer Hoff.* Illustrated by Ed Emberley. Prentice-Hall, 1967.

Fleming, Denise. *In the Small, Small Pond.* Holt, 1993. Ages 4–6.

———. *In the Tall, Tall Grass.* Holt, 1991. Ages 4–6.

———. *Mama Cat Has Three Kittens.* Holt, 1998. Ages 2–5.

Guarino, Deborah. *Is Your Mama a Llama?* Illustrated by Stephen Kellogg. Scholastic, 1989.

Hellen, Nancy. *The Bus Stop.* Orchard, 1988.

Hogrogian, Nonny. *One Fine Day.* Macmillan, 1971.

Joslin, Sesyle. *What Do You Say, Dear?* Illustrated by Maurice Sendak. HarperCollins, 1987. (Originally published by Addison-Wesley, 1958. See also *What Do You Do, Dear?*)

Martin, Bill, Jr. *Brown Bear, Brown Bear, What Do You See?* Illustrated by Eric Carle. Holt, 1983.

———. *Polar Bear, Polar Bear, What Do You Hear?* Illustrated by Eric Carle. Holt, 1991.

McDonald, Megan. *Is This a House for Hermit Crab?* Illustrated by S. D. Schindler. Orchard, 1990.

Rosen, Michael, reteller. *We're Going on a Bear Hunt.* Illustrated by Helen Oxenbury. Macmillan, 1989.

Shannon, David. *No, David!* Scholastic, 1998. Ages 2–5.

Taback, Simms. *Joseph Had a Little Overcoat.* Viking, 1999. Ages 3–6.

———. *There Was an Old Lady Who Swallowed a Fly.* Viking, 1997. Ages 5–7. (See also Toy Books.)

Weiss, Nikki. *Where Does the Brown Bear Go?* Greenwillow, 1989.

Williams, Sue. *I Went Walking.* Illustrated by Julie Vivas. Harcourt, 1990.

## Picture Storybooks

Ackerman, Karen. *Song and Dance Man.* Illustrated by Stephen Gammell. Knopf, 1988. Ages 6–8.

Alarcón, Karen B. *Louella Mae, She's Run Away.* Illustrated by Roseann Litzinger. Holt, 1997. Ages 3–5.

Alexander, Lloyd. *The Fortune-Tellers.* Illustrated by Trina Schart Hyman. Dutton, 1992. Ages 6–8.

Alexander, Martha. *Nobody Asked Me If I Wanted a Baby Sister.* Dial, 1971. Ages 5–7.

Allard, Harry. *Miss Nelson Is Missing.* Illustrated by James Marshall, Houghton, 1977. Ages 6–8.

———. *The Stupids Have a Ball.* Illustrated by James Marshall. Houghton, 1977. Ages 6–8.

———, and James Marshall. *Miss Nelson Has a Field Day.* Illustrated by James Marshall. Houghton, 1985. Ages 6–8.

Aruego, Jose. *Look What I Can Do.* Scribner's, 1971. Ages 5–7.

Babbitt, Natalie. *The Devil's Other Storybook.* Farrar, 1987. Ages 6–8.

———. *Nellie: A Cat on Her Own.* Farrar, 1989. Ages 6–8.

Baker, Jeannie. *Where the Forest Meets the Sea.* Greenwillow, 1988. Ages 8–10.

Baker, Olaf. *Where the Buffaloes Begin.* Illustrated by Stephen Gammell. Warne, 1981. Ages 8–10.

Bang, Molly. *The Paper Crane.* Greenwillow, 1985. Ages 8–10.

Banks, Kate. *And If the Moon Could Talk.* Illustrated by George Hallensleben. Farrar, 1998.

———. *Baboon.* Illustrated by George Hallensleben. Farrar, 1997. Ages 3–5.

Baylor, Byrd. *The Best Town in the World.* Illustrated by Ronald Himler. Scribner's, 1983. Ages 7–9.

———. *Hawk, I'm Your Brother.* Illustrated by Peter Parnall. Scribner's, 1976. Ages 7–9.

———. *The Table Where Rich People Sit.* Illustrated by Peter Parnall. Scribner's, 1994. Ages 7–10.

Bemelmans, Ludwig. *Madeline.* Viking, 1939. Ages 5–7.

———. *Madeline's Rescue.* Viking, 1953. Ages 5–7.

Best, Cari. *Three Cheers for Catherine the Great!* Illustrated by Giselle Potter. DK Ink, 1999. Ages 6–9.

Blos, Joan W. *Old Henry.* Illustrated by Stephen Gammell. Morrow, 1987. Ages 7–9.

Bottner, Barbara. *Bootsie Barker Bites.* Illustrated by Peggy Rathman. Putnam, 1992. Ages 4–7.

Bradby, Marie. *More Than Anything Else.* Illustrated by Chris K. Soentpiet. Orchard, 1995. Ages 4–8.

Brett, Jan. *The Wild Christmas Reindeer.* Putnam, 1990. Ages 6–8.

Bröger, Achim. *The Santa Clauses.* Illustrated by Ute Krause. Dial, 1986. Ages 6–8.

Brown, Marc. *Arthur's Baby.* Little, Brown, 1987. Ages 5–7.

———. *D. W. the Picky Eater.* Little, Brown, 1995. Ages 5–8.

Brown, Margaret Wise. *Goodnight Moon.* Illustrated by Clement Hurd. Harper, 1947. Ages 4–6.

Browne, Anthony. *Gorilla.* Knopf, 1985. Ages 7–9.

———. *Voices in the Park.* DK Ink, 1998. Ages 6–10.

Bunting, Eve. *Ghost's Hour, Spook's Hour.* Illustrated by Donald Carrick. Clarion, 1987. Ages 7–9.

———. *Train to Somewhere.* Illustrated by Ronald Himler. Clarion, 1996. Ages 7–10.

———. *The Wall.* Illustrated by Ronald Himler. Clarion, 1990. Ages 7–9.

———. *The Wednesday Surprise.* Illustrated by Donald Carrick. Clarion, 1989. Ages 6–10.

Burningham, John. *Grandpa.* Crown, 1985. Ages 5–7.

———. *Mr. Gumpy's Motor Car.* Harper, 1976.

———. *Time to Get Out of the Bath, Shirley.* Crowell, 1978.

Burton, Virginia Lee. *The Little House.* Houghton, 1942. Ages 5–7.

———. *Mike Mulligan and His Steam Shovel.* Houghton, 1939. Ages 5–7.

Carle, Eric. *The Grouchy Ladybug.* Crowell, 1971. Ages 5–7.

———. *The Mixed-Up Chameleon.* Crowell, 1975. Ages 6–8.

———. *The Very Busy Spider.* Philomel, 1984. Ages 5–7.

Carrick, Carol. *What Happened to Patrick's Dinosaurs?* Illustrated by Donald Carrick. Clarion, 1986. Ages 6–8.

Catalanotto, Peter. *The Painter.* Orchard, 1995. Ages 4–7.

Caudill, Rebecca. *A Pocketful of Cricket.* Illustrated by Evaline Ness. Holt, 1964. Ages 6–8.

Cazet, Denys. *Never Spit on Your Shoes.* Orchard, 1990. Ages 6–10.

Cherry, Lynne. *The Great Kapok Tree: A Tale of the Amazon Rainforest.* Harcourt, 1990. Ages 6–10.

Chetwin, Grace. *Box and Cox.* Illustrated by David Small. Bradbury, 1990. Ages 7–9.

Cole, Brock. *Buttons.* Farrar, 2000. Ages 6–8.

Cooney, Barbara. *Island Boy.* Viking, 1988. Ages 6–10.

———. *Miss Rumphius.* Viking, 1982. Ages 6–10.

Coy, John. *Night Driving.* Illustrated by Peter McCarty. Holt, 1996. Ages 4–6.

Crews, Donald. *Bigmama's.* Greenwillow, 1991. Ages 4–7.

———. *Shortcut.* Greenwillow, 1992. Ages 4–7.

Cronin, Doreen. *Click, Clack, Moo: Cows That Type.* Illustrated by Betsy Lewin. Simon & Schuster, 2000. Ages 4–7.

Daly, Niki. *Not So Fast Songololo.* Atheneum, 1986. Ages 6–8.

Day, Alexandra. *Frank and Ernest.* Scholastic, 1988. Ages 6–10.

———. *Frank and Ernest Play Ball.* Scholastic, 1990. Ages 6–10.

de Brunhoff, Jean. *The Story of Babar.* Random House, 1933. Ages 6–8.

dePaola, Tomie. *The Art Lesson.* Putnam, 1989. Ages 6–8.

———. *Nana Upstairs, Nana Downstairs.* Putnam, 1973. Ages 6–8.

———. *Strega Nona.* Prentice Hall, 1975. Ages 5–7.

Dorros, Arthur. *Abuela.* Illustrated by Elisa Kleven. Dutton, 1991. Ages 5–7.

Duvoisin, Roger. *Petunia.* Knopf, 1950. Ages 6–8.

Egan, Tim. *Metropolitan Cow.* Houghton, 1996. Ages 4–7.

Erdrich, Louise. *Grandmother's Pigeon.* Illustrated by Jim LaMarche. Hyperion, 1996. Ages 5–8.

Ets, Marie Hall, and Aurora Labastida. *Nine Days to Christmas.* Illustrated by Marie Hall Ets. Viking, 1959. Ages 7–9.

Falconer, Ian. *Olivia..* Atheneum, 2000. Ages 4–7.

Feelings, Tom, selector and illustrator. *Soul Looks Back in Wonder.* Dial, 1993. Ages 8–12.

Feiffer, Jules. *Bark, George.* HarperCollins, 1999. Ages 3–5.

———. *I Lost My Bear.* Morrow, 1998. Ages 3–7.

Flack, Marjorie. *The Story about Ping.* Illustrated by Kurt Wiese. Viking, 1933. Ages 7–9.

Ford, Miela. *Sunflower.* Greenwillow, 1995. Ages 5–7.

Fox, Mem. *Hattie and the Fox.* Illustrated by Patricia Mullins. Bradbury, 1987. Ages 6–8.

———. *Night Noises.* Illustrated by Terry Denton. Gulliver, 1989. Ages 6–8.

———. *Shoes from Grandpa.* Illustrated by Patricia Mullins. Orchard, 1990. Ages 6–8.

———. *Wilfrid Gordon McDonald Partridge.* Illustrated by Julie Vivas. Kane/Miller, 1985. Ages 6–8.

Freeman, Don. *Corduroy.* Viking, 1968. Ages 3–5.

———. *A Pocket for Corduroy.* Viking, 1978. Ages 3–5.

Friedman, Ina. *How My Parents Learned to Eat.* Illustrated by Allen Say. Houghton, 1984. Ages 7–9.

Gág, Wanda. *Millions of Cats.* Coward-McCann, 1928. Ages 4–6.

Galbraith, Kathryn. *Laura Charlotte.* Illustrated by Floyd Cooper. Philomel, 1990. Ages 6–8.

Gerstein, Mordicai. *The Mountains of Tibet.* Harper, 1987. Ages 7–9. (Modern folktale)

Goode, Diane. *I Hear a Noise.* Dutton, 1988. Ages 5–7.

Graham, Bob. *Benny, An Adventure Story.* Candlewick, 1999. Ages 5–8.

———. *Max.* Candlewick, 2000. Ages 4–7.

Gray, Nigel. *A Country Far Away.* Illustrated by Philippe Dupasquier. Orchard, 1989. Ages 7–9.

Greenfield, Eloise. *Nathaniel Talking.* Illustrated by Jan Spivey Gilchrist. Writers and Readers, 1989. Ages 6–8.

———. *She Come Bringing Me That Little Baby Girl.* Illustrated by John Steptoe. Lippincott, 1974. Ages 6–8.

Grifalconi, Ann. *The Village of Round and Square Houses.* Little, Brown, 1986. Ages 6–8.

Griffith, Helen. *Grandaddy's Stars.* Illustrated by James Stevenson. Morrow, 1995. Ages 6–8.

Grossman, Bill. *Tommy at the Grocery Store.* Illustrated by Victoria Chess. Harper, 1989. Ages 6–10.

Hader, Berta, and Elmer Hader. *The Big Snow.* Macmillan, 1948. Ages 6–8.

Hall, Donald. *Ox-Cart Man.* Illustrated by Barbara Cooney. Viking, 1979. Ages 7–9.

Heide, Florence Parry, and Judith Heide Gilliland. *The Day of Ahmed's Secret.* Illustrated by Ted Lewin. Lothrop, 1990. Ages 6–10.

Hendershot, Judith. *In Coal Country.* Illustrated by Thomas B. Allen. Knopf, 1987. Ages 7–9.

Henkes, Kevin. *Chrysanthemum.* Greenwillow, 1991. Ages 5–7.

———. *Julius, the Baby of the World.* Greenwillow, 1990. Ages 5–7.

———. *Lily's Purple Plastic Purse.* Greenwillow, 1996. Ages 5–7.

———. *Owen.* Greenwillow, 1993. Ages 2–4.

———. *Sheila Rae the Brave.* Greenwillow, 1987. Ages 5–7.

———. *Wemberley Worried.* Greenwillow, 2000. Ages 5–8.

Hest, Amy. *In the Rain with Baby Duck.* Candlewick, 1995. Ages 3–6.

———. *The Midnight Eaters.* Illustrated by Karen Gundersheimer. Four Winds, 1989. Ages 6–8.

Hissey, Jane. *Little Bear's Trousers.* Putnam, 1987. Ages 4–6.

———. *Old Bear.* Putnam, 1986. Ages 4–6.

Ho, Minfong. *Hush!: A Thai Lullaby.* Illustrated by Holly Meade. Orchard, 1996. Ages 4–6.

Hoban, Russell. *A Baby Sister for Frances.* Illustrated by Lillian Hoban. Harper, 1964. (Others in this series: *Bedtime for Frances,* illustrated by Garth Williams, 1969; *Best Friends for Frances,* illustrated by Lillian Hoban, 1969; *A Bargain for Frances,* illustrated by Lillian Hoban. Harper, 1970.) Ages 4–6.

Hoberman, Mary Ann. *One of Each.* Illustrated by Marjorie Priceman. Little, Brown, 1997. Ages 3–7.

Hoffman, Mary. *Amazing Grace.* Illustrated by Caroline Binch. Dial, 1991. Ages 5–7.

Hort, Lenny. *The Seals on the Bus.* Illustrated by G. Brian Karas. Holt, 2000. Ages 4–7.

Houston, Gloria. *My Great-Aunt Arizona.* Illustrated by Susan C. Lamb. Harper, 1992. Ages 7–9.

———. *The Year of the Perfect Christmas Tree: An Appalachian Story.* Illustrated by Barbara Cooney. Dial, 1988. Ages 7–9.

Howard, Elizabeth Fitzgerald. *Chita's Christmas Tree.* Illustrated by James Ransome. Bradbury, 1989. Ages 6–8.

———. *Aunt Flossie's Hats (and Crab Cakes Later).* Illustrated by Floyd Cooper. Clarion, 1991. Ages 6–9.

Howe, James. *There's a Monster under My Bed.* Illustrated by David Rose. Atheneum, 1986. Ages 5–7.

Hughes, Shirley. *An Evening at Alfie's.* Lothrop, 1985. Ages 5–7.

Ichikawa, Satomi. *Nora's Castle.* Putnam, 1986. Ages 5–7.

Isaacs, Anne. *Swamp Angel.* Illustrated by Paul O. Zelinsky. Dutton, 1994.

Isadora, Rachel. *Ben's Trumpet.* Greenwillow, 1979. Ages 6–10.

Johnson, Angela. *Tell Me a Story, Mama.* Illustrated by David Soman. Orchard, 1989. Ages 6–8.

Johnson, Crockett. *Harold and the Purple Crayon.* Harper, 1955. Ages 5–7.

Jonas, Ann. *The Quilt.* Greenwillow, 1984. Ages 7–9.

Jonell, Lynne. *Mommy Go Away!* Illustrated by Petra Mathers. Putnam, 1997. Ages 4–6.

Joose, Barbara M. *Snow Day!* Illustrated by Jennifer Plecas. Clarion, 1995. Ages 5–7.

Joyce, William. *Bently and Egg.* HarperCollins, 1992. Ages 4–8.

———. *Santa Calls.* HarperCollins, 1993. Ages 5–8.

Jukes, Mavis. *Like Jake and Me.* Illustrated by Lloyd Bloom. Knopf, 1984. Ages 6–8.

Keats, Ezra Jack. *Goggles.* Macmillan, 1969. Ages 5–7.

———. *Peter's Chair.* Harper, 1967. Ages 4–6.

———. *The Snowy Day.* Viking, 1962. Ages 4–6.

———. *Whistle for Willie.* Viking, 1964. Ages 5–7.

Kellogg, Steven. *Pinkerton, Behave!* Dial, 1979. Ages 6–8.

Kesey, Ken. *Little Tricker the Squirrel Meets Big Double the Bear.* Illustrated by Barry Moser. Viking, 1990. Ages 8–11.

Kleven, Elisa. *The Puddle Pail.* Dutton, 1997. Ages 5–8.

Komaiko, Leah. *Annie Bananie.* Illustrated by Laura Cornell. Harper, 1987. Ages 6–8.

Krensky, Stephen. *How Santa Got His Job.* Illustrated by S. D. Schindler. Simon & Schuster, 1998. Ages 5–8.

Krudop, Walter L. *Something Is Growing.* Atheneum, 1995. Ages 5–7.

Kuskin, Karla. *The Philharmonic Gets Dressed.* Illustrated by Marc Simont. Harper, 1982. Ages 6–10.

Kvasnosky, Laura McGee. *Zelda and Ivy.* Candlewick, 1998. Ages 6–8.

———. *Zelda and Ivy One Christmas.* Candlewick, 2000. Ages 6–8.

Lasker, Joe. *A Tournament of Knights.* Crowell, 1986. Ages 8–10.

Lattimore, Deborah Nourse. *The Lady with the Ship on Her Head.* Harcourt, 1990. Ages 8–10.

Leaf, Munro. *The Story of Ferdinand.* Illustrated by Robert Lawson. Viking, 1936. Ages 7–9.

Legge, David. *Bamboozled.* Scholastic, 1995. Ages 5–8.

Lester, Helen. *Hooway for Wodney Wat.* Illustrated by Lynn Munsinger. Houghton, 1999. Ages 4–7.

Lester, Julius. *Sam and the Tigers: A New Telling of Little Black Sambo.* Illustrated by Jerry Pinkney. Dial, 1996. Ages 3–8.

Levinson, Riki. *Watch the Stars Come Out.* Illustrated by Diane Goode. Dutton, 1985. Ages 7–9.

Lewis, Kim. *My Friend Harry.* Candlewick, 1995. Ages 3–5.

Lincoln, Abraham. *The Gettysburg Address.* Illustrated by Michael McCurdy. Houghton, 1995. Ages 5–YA.

Lionni, Leo. *Alexander and the Wind-up Mouse.* Pantheon 1967. Ages 6–8.

———. *The Biggest House in the World.* Pantheon, 1968. Ages 5–7.

———. *Inch by Inch.* Astor-Honor, 1960. Ages 5–7.

———. *Swimmy.* Pantheon, 1963. Ages 6–8.

Locker, Thomas. *Where the River Begins.* Dial, 1984. Ages 6–8.

Lum, Kate. *What? Cried Granny: An Almost Bedtime Story.* Illustrated by Adrian Johnson. Dial, 1999. Ages 5–8.

Lyon, George Ella. *Come a Tide.* Illustrated by Stephen Gammell. Orchard, 1990. Ages 6–8.

MacLachlan, Patricia. *Mama One, Mama Two.* Illustrated by Ruth Lercher Bornstein. Harper, 1982. Ages 8–10.

Mahy, Margaret. *The Great White Man-Eating Shark: A Cautionary Tale.* Illustrated by Jonathan Allen. Dial, 1990. Ages 8–10.

———. *17 Kings and 42 Elephants.* Illustrated by Patricia McCarthy. Dial, 1987. Ages 6–10.

Markum, Patricia. *The Little Painter of Sabana Grande.* Macmillan, 1993. Ages 7–9.

Marshall, James. *George and Martha.* Houghton, 1972. Ages 6–8.

———. *George and Martha Round and Round.* Houghton, 1988. Ages 6–8.

Martin, Bill, Jr., and John Archambault. *Knots on a Counting Rope.* Illustrated by Ted Rand. Holt, 1987. Ages 6–8.

Mayer, Mercer. *There's a Nightmare in My Closet.* Dial, 1968. Ages 5–7.

McCloskey, Robert. *Blueberries for Sal.* Viking, 1948. Ages 5–7.

———. *Make Way for Ducklings.* Viking, 1941. Ages 5–7.

———. *One Morning in Maine.* Viking, 1952. Ages 7–9.

McCully, Emily A. *The Pirate Queen.* Putnam, 1995. Ages 7–10.

McDonald, Megan. *Insects Are My Life.* Illustrated by Paul B. Johnson. Orchard, 1995. Ages 5–8.

McKissack, Patricia C., and Fredrick L. *Christmas in the Big House, Christmas in the Quarters.* Illustrated by John Thompson. Scholastic, 1994. Ages 8–12.

———. *Flossie and the Fox.* Illustrated by Rachel Isadora. Dial, 1986. Ages 7–9.

McNaughton, Colin. *Suddenly!* Harcourt, 1995. Ages 4–6.

Meddaugh, Susan. *Martha Blah Blah.* Houghton, 1996. Ages 5–7.

———. *Martha Speaks.* Houghton, 1992. Ages 4–8.

Melmed, Laura K. *The Rainbabies.* Illustrated by Jim LaMarche. Lothrop, 1992. Ages 7–9.

Merrill, Jean, adapter. *The Girl Who Loved Caterpillars.* Illustrated by Floyd Cooper. Philomel, 1992. Ages 7–12.

Mochizuki, Ken. *Baseball Saved Us.* Illustrated by Dom Lee. Lee & Low, 1993. Ages 7–9.

Mollel, Tololwa. *The Orphan Boy.* Illustrated by Paul Morin. Clarion, 1991. Ages 7–9.

Mosel, Arlene, adapter. *The Funny Little Woman.* Illustrated by Blair Lent. Dutton, 1972. Ages 6–8.

Ness, Evaline. *Sam, Bangs and Moonshine.* Holt, 1966. Ages 6–8.

Olaleye, Isaac. *Bitter Bananas.* Illustrated by Ed Young. Boyds Mills, 1994.

Peet, Bill. *Cyrus the Unsinkable Sea Serpent.* Houghton, 1975. Ages 5–7.

———. *Merle the High Flying Squirrel.* Houghton, 1974. Ages 5–7.

Peters, Lisa Westberg. *Cold Little Duck, Duck, Duck.* Illustrated by Sam Williams. Greenwillow, 2000. Ages 1–4.

Pilkey, Dav. *The Hallo-Weiner.* Scholastic, 1995. Ages 5–8.

———. *The Paperboy.* Orchard, 1996. Ages 6–9.

Polacco, Patricia. *Babushka's Doll.* Simon & Schuster, 1990. Ages 6–8.

———. *Chicken Sunday.* Putnam, 1992. Ages 4–9.

———. *The Keeping Quilt.* Simon & Schuster, 1988. Ages 6–8.

———. *Pink and Say.* Philomel, 1994. Ages 8–11.

———. *Thunder Cake.* Putnam, 1990. Ages 6–8.

Politi, Leo. *Song of the Swallows.* Scribner's, 1949. Ages 6–8.

Pomerantz, Charlotte. *The Chalk Doll.* Illustrated by Frané Lessac. Harper, 1989. Ages 7–9.

Potter, Beatrix. *The Tale of Peter Rabbit.* Warne, 1902. (See 20 other titles in the series.) Ages 5–7.

Priceman, Marjorie. *How to Make an Apple Pie and See the World.* Knopf, 1994. Ages 6–8.

Provensen, Alice, and Martin Provensen. *The Glorious Flight: Across the Channel with Louis Blériot.* Viking: 1983. Ages 8–10.

———. *Shaker Lane.* Viking, 1987. Ages 7–9.

Ransome, Arthur. *The Fool of the World and the Flying Ship.* Illustrated by Uri Shulevitz. Farrar, 1968. Ages 6–8.

Raschka, Chris. *Can't Sleep.* Orchard, 1995. Ages 3–5.

———. *Mysterious Thelonious.* Orchard, 1997. Ages 5–8.

Rathman, Peggy. *10 Minutes Till Bedtime.* Putnam, 1998. Ages 3–6.

———. *Officer Buckle and Gloria.* Putnam, 1995. Ages 6–8.

Rey, Hans A. *Curious George.* Houghton, 1941. (See others in the Curious George series.) Ages 5–7.

Riley, Linnea. *Mouse Mess.* Scholastic, 1997. Ages 4–6.

Ringgold, Faith. *Aunt Harriet's Underground Railroad in the Sky.* Crown, 1992. Ages 6–9.

———. *Tar Beach.* Crown, 1991. Ages 8–10.

Rounds, Glen. *Once We Had a Horse.* Holiday, 1996. Ages 5–8.

Ryan, Cheli Duran. *Hildilid's Night.* Illustrated by Arnold Lobel. Macmillan, 1971. Ages 6–8.

Rylant, Cynthia. *The Relatives Came.* Illustrated by Stephen Gammell. Bradbury, 1985. Ages 6–10.

———. *When I Was Young in the Mountains.* Illustrated by Diane Goode. Dutton, 1982. Ages 7–9.

Sanfield, Steve. *Bit by Bit.* Illustrated by Susan Gaber. Philomel, 1995. Ages 5–8.

Say, Allen. *Grandfather's Journey.* Houghton, 1993. Ages 8–10.

———. *Tree of Cranes.* Houghton, 1991. Ages 7–9.

Schertle, Alice. *William and Grandpa.* Illustrated by Lydia Dabcovich. Lothrop, 1989. Ages 6–8.

Schwartz, Amy. *Annabelle Swift, Kindergartner.* Orchard, 1988. Ages 5–7.

Scieszka, Jon. *Math Curse.* Illustrated by Lane Smith. Viking, 1995. Ages 8–10.

———. *The Stinky Cheese Man and Other Fairly Stupid Tales.* Illustrated by Lane Smith. Viking, 1992. Ages 7–10.

Scott, Ann Herbert. *Sam.* Illustrated by Symeon Shimin. McGraw-Hill, 1967. Ages 7–9.

Sendak, Maurice. *In the Night Kitchen.* Harper, 1970. Ages 7–9.

———. *Where the Wild Things Are.* Harper, 1963. Ages 5–7.

Seuss, Dr. (pseudonym of Theodor S. Geisel). *And to Think That I Saw It on Mulberry Street.* Vanguard, 1937. Ages 5–7.

———. *The 500 Hats of Bartholomew Cubbins.* Vanguard, 1938. Ages 5–7.

———. *Horton Hatches the Egg.* Random, 1940. Ages 6–8.

———. *Oh, the Places You'll Go!* Random, 1990. Ages 6–8.

———. *Thidwick the Big-Hearted Moose.* Random, 1948. Ages 6–8.

Shelby, Anne. *Homeplace.* Illustrated by Wendy A. Halperin. Orchard, 1995. Ages 4–7.

Shulevitz, Uri. *Snow.* Farrar, 1998. Ages 3–6.

Silverman, Erica. *Don't Fidget a Feather.* Illustrated by S. D. Schindler. Macmillan, 1994. Ages 4–6.

Simont, Marc. *The Goose That Almost Got Cooked.* Scholastic, 1997. Ages 4–7.

Sís, Peter. *Komodo!* Greenwillow, 1993. Ages 4–7.

———. *Madlenka.* Farrar, 2000. Ages 5–8.

Slobodkina, Esphyr, *Caps for Sale.* Addison-Wesley, 1947. Ages 4–6.

Small, David. *George Washington's Cows.* Farrar, 1994. Ages 5–8.

———. *Imogene's Antlers.* Crown, 1985. Ages 6–8.

Soto, Gary. *Chato's Kitchen.* Illustrated by Susan Guevara. Putnam, 1995.

———. *Too Many Tamales.* Illustrated by Ed Martinez. Putnam, 1993.

Stanley, Diane. *Saving Sweetness.* Illustrated by G. Brian Karas. Putnam, 1996. Ages 4–7.

Steig, William. *The Amazing Bone.* Farrar, 1976. Ages 7–9.

———. *Doctor De Soto.* Farrar, 1982. Ages 7–9.

———. *Pete's a Pizza.* HarperCollins, 1998. Ages 2–5.

———. *Sylvester and the Magic Pebble.* Simon & Schuster, 1969. Ages 7–9.

———. *The Toy Brother.* HarperCollins, 1996. Ages 6–9.

Steptoe, John. *Stevie.* Harper, 1969. Ages 5–7.

Stevens, Janet. *From Pictures to Words: A Book about Making a Book.* Holiday, 1995. Ages 5–8.

Stevenson, James. *All Aboard!* Greenwillow, 1995. Ages 6–8.

Stewart, Sarah. *The Gardener.* Illustrated by David Small. Farrar, 1997. Ages 4–7.

Stock, Catherine. *Where Are You Going, Manyoni?* Morrow, 1993.

Stuve-Bodeen, Stephanie. *Elizabeti's Doll.* Illustrated by Christy Hale. Lee & Low, 1998. Ages 3–7.

Swope, Sam. *The Araboolies of Liberty Street.* Illustrated by Barry Root. Clarkson N. Potter, 1989. Ages 6–8.

Tejima. *Fox's Dream.* Translated from Japanese by Susan Matsui. Philomel, 1987. Ages 6–8.

Tompert, Ann. *Grandfather Tang's Story.* Illustrated by Robert Andrew Parker. Crown, 1990. Ages 7–9.

Tresselt, Alvin. *White Snow, Bright Snow.* Illustrated by Roger Duvoisin. Lothrop, 1947. Ages 4–6.

Udry, Janice May. *The Moon Jumpers.* Illustrated by Maurice Sendak. Harper, 1959. Ages 5–7.

Ungerer, Tomi. *The Beast of Monsieur Racine.* Farrar, 1971. Ages 6–8.

Van Allsburg, Chris. *Jumanji.* Houghton, 1981. Ages 6–10.

———. *The Sweetest Fig.* Houghton, 1993. Ages 8–11.

———. *Two Bad Ants.* Houghton, 1988.

———. *The Wretched Stone.* Houghton, 1991. Ages 8–11.

Van Laan, Nancy. *Possum Come a-Knockin'.* Illustrated by George Booth. Knopf, 1990. Ages 7–9.

Vincent, Gabrielle. *Where Are You, Ernest and Celestine?* Greenwillow, 1986. Ages 6–8.

Viorst, Judith. *Alexander and the Terrible, Horrible, No Good, Very Bad Day.* Illustrated by Ray Cruz. Atheneum, 1972. Ages 5–7.

———. *Alexander, Who's Not (Do You Hear Me? I Mean It!) Going to Move.* Illustrated by Robin Glasser. Atheneum, 1995. Ages 4–8.

———. *Alexander Who Used to Be Rich Last Sunday.* Illustrated by Ray Cruz. Atheneum, 1978. Ages 6–8.

———. *I'll Fix Anthony.* Illustrated by Arnold Lobel. Harper, 1969. Ages 4–6.

Waber, Bernard. *Do You See a Mouse?* Houghton, 1995. Ages 5–9.

———. *Ira Says Goodbye.* Houghton, 1988. Ages 6–8.

———. *Ira Sleeps Over.* Houghton, 1972. Ages 6–8.

Waddell, Martin. *Can't You Sleep, Little Bear?* Illustrated by Barbara Firth. Candlewick, 1992. Ages 2–4.

———. *Farmer Duck.* Illustrated by Helen Oxenbury. Candlewick, 1992. Ages 4–6.

———. *When the Teddy Bears Came.* Illustrated by Penny Dale. Candlewick, 1995. Ages 3–5.

Walter, Mildred Pitts. *My Mama Needs Me.* Illustrated by Pat Cummings. Lothrop, 1983. Ages 5–7.

Wells, Rosemary. *Bunny Cakes.* Dial, 1997. Ages 2–6.

———. *Shy Charles.* Dial, 1988. Ages 4–6.

Wiesner, David. *June 29, 1999.* Clarion, 1992. Ages 6–9.

Wild, Margaret. *The Very Best of Friends.* Illustrated by Julie Vivas. Harcourt, 1990. Ages 6–8.

Willhoit, Michael. *Daddy's Roommate.* Alyson, 1990.

Williams, Karen L. *Galimoto.* Illustrated by Catherine Stock. Lothrop, 1990. Ages 7–9.

Williams, Margery. *The Velveteen Rabbit.* Illustrated by William Nicholson. Doubleday, 1922. Ages 6–8.

Williams, Sherley Anne. *Working Cotton.* Illustrated by Carole Byard. Harcourt, 1992. Ages 5–7.

Williams, Vera B. *A Chair for My Mother.* Greenwillow, 1982. Ages 6–8.

———. *Scooter.* Greenwillow, 1993. Ages 8–10.

———. *Stringbean's Trip to the Shining Sea.* Illustrated by author and Jennifer Williams. Greenwillow, 1988. Ages 7–9.

Wong, Janet S. *Buzz.* Harcourt, 2000. Ages 3–5.

Wood, Audrey. *Heckedy Peg.* Illustrated by Don Wood. Harcourt, 1987. Ages 6–8.

Xiong, Blia, reteller. *Nine-in-One Grr! Grr!.* Adapted by Cathy Spagnoli. Illustrated by Nancy Hom. Children's Book Press, 1990. Ages 6–8.

Yaccarino, Dan. *Deep in the Jungle.* Atheneum, 2000. Ages 5–9.

Yashima, Taro. (pseudonym of Jun Iwamatsu). *Crow Boy.* Viking, 1955. Ages 7–9.

Yolen, Jane. *Owl Moon.* Illustrated by John Schoenherr. Putnam, 1987. Ages 6–8.

Yorinks, Arthur. *Company's Coming.* Illustrated by David Small. Crown, 1988. Ages 7–9.

———. *Hey, Al.* Illustrated by Richard Egielski. Farrar, 1986. Ages 7–9.

Young, Ed. *Seven Blind Mice.* Philomel, 1992. Ages 6–10. (Modern folktale)

Ziefert, Harriet. *A New Coat for Anna.* Illustrated by Anita Lobel. Knopf, 1986. Ages 6–8.

Zion, Gene. *Harry, the Dirty Dog.* Illustrated by Margaret B. Graham. HarperTrophy, 1976 (1956). Ages 4–6.

Zolotow, Charlotte. *If It Weren't for You.* Illustrated by Ben Shecter. Harper, 1966. Ages 6–8.

———. *Mr. Rabbit and the Lovely Present.* Illustrated by Maurice Sendak. Harper, 1962. Ages 5–7.

———. *Say It!* Illustrated by James Stevenson. Greenwillow, 1980. Ages 6–8.

———. *When the Wind Stops* (revised edition). Illustrated by Stefano Vitale. HarperCollins, 1995. Ages 3–5.

———. *William's Doll.* Illustrated by William Pène du Bois. Harper, 1972. Ages 6–8.

### Easy-to-Read Books

*These books are generally suitable for ages 4 to 8.*

Barrett, Judi. *Animals Should Definitely Not Act Like People.* Atheneum, 1980.

———. *Animals Should Definitely Not Wear Clothing.* Atheneum, 1977.

Barton, Byron. *The Wee Little Woman.* HarperCollins, 1995. Ages 4–6.

Brown, Margaret Wise. *Four Fur Feet.* Illustrated by Woodleigh M. Hubbard. Hyperion, 1994. Ages 3–6.

———. *Goodnight Moon.* Harper, 1947.

———. *The Runaway Bunny.* Illustrated by Clement Hurd. Harper, 1991 (1942). Ages 2–5.

Bulla, Clyde Robert. *The Christmas Coat.* Illustrated by Sylvie Wickstrom. Knopf, 1990.

Byars, Betsy, *Ant Plays Bear.* Illustrated by Marc Simont. Viking, 1997. Ages 6–8.

———. *My Brother, Ant.* Illustrated by Marc Simont. Viking, 1996. Ages 6–8.

Coerr, Eleanor. *The Josefina Story Quilt.* Illustrated by Bruce Degen. Harper, 1986.

Cole, Joanna, and Stephanie Calmenson. *The Gator Girls.* Illustrated by Lynn Munsinger. Morrow, 1995. Ages 7–8.

———, compilers. *Ready . . . Set . . . Read!: The Beginning Reader's Treasury.* Illustrated by Anne Burgess and Chris Demarest. Doubleday, 1990.

dePaola, Tomie. *The Comic Adventures of Old Mother Hubbard and Her Dog.* Harcourt, 1981.

de Regniers, Beatrice Schenk. *May I Bring a Friend?* Illustrated by Beni Montresor. Atheneum, 1964.

Emberley, Barbara. *One Wide River to Cross.* Prentice-Hall, 1966.

Fox, Mem. *Shoes from Grandpa.* Orchard, 1990.

Gág, Wanda. *Millions of Cats.* Coward-McCann, 1928.

George, William. *Fishing at Long Pond.* Illustrated by Lindsay B. George. Greenwillow, 1991.

Guest, Elissa Haden. *Iris and Walter.* Illustrated by Christine Davenier. Harcourt/Gulliver, 2000. Ages 6–8.

Hoban, Lillian. *Arthur's Great Big Valentine.* Harper, 1989.

Hutchins, Pat. *The Doorbell Rang.* Greenwillow, 1986.

———. *Rosie's Walk.* Macmillan, 1968.

———. *Tidy Titch.* Greenwillow, 1991.

———. *Titch.* Macmillan, 1971.

———. *The Wind Blew.* Macmillan, 1974.

Johnson, Crockett. *A Picture for Harold's Room.* Harper, 1960.

Kraus, Robert. *Leo the Late Bloomer.* Illustrated by José Aruego. Dutton, 1971.

Little, Jean. *Emma's Magic Winter.* Illustrated by Jennifer Plecas. HarperCollins, 1998. Ages 6–8.

Lobel, Arnold. *Mouse Soup.* Harper, 1977.

———. "Frog and Toad Series." *Frog and Toad Are Friends.* Harper, 1970. (Others in this series: *Frog and Toad Together,* 1972; *Frog and Toad All Year,* 1976; *Days with Frog and Toad,* 1979.)

Lyon, George Ella. *Who Came Down That Road?* Illustrated by Peter Catalanotto. Orchard, 1992.

Minarik, Else Holmelund. *Little Bear.* Illustrated by Maurice Sendak. Harper, 1957. (Others in the Little Bear series: *Father Bear Comes Home,* 1959; *Little Bear's Friend,* 1960; *Little Bear's Visit,* 1961; *A Kiss for Little Bear,* 1968.)

Monjo, F. N. *The Drinking Gourd.* Illustrated by Fred Brenner. Harper, 1970.

Moore, Lilian. *I'll Meet You at the Cucumbers.* Illustrated by Sharon Wooding. Atheneum, 1988.

Numeroff, Laura Joffe. *If You Give a Mouse a Cookie.* Harper, 1985.

Raschka, Chris. *Yo! Yes?* Orchard, 1993. (See also *Ring! Yo?*)

Rodda, Emily. *Power and Glory.* Illustrated by Geoff Kelly. Greenwillow, 1996. Ages 5–7.

Rylant, Cynthia. *Henry and Mudge.* Illustrated by Suçie Stevenson. Bradbury, 1987. (See others in this series.)

Seuss, Dr. (pseudonym of Theodor S. Geisel). *The Cat in the Hat.* Random, 1957.

———. *The Cat in the Hat Comes Back.* Random, 1958.

———. *Fox in Sox.* Random, 1965.

Thomas, Shelley Moore. *Good Night, Good Knight.* Illustrated by Jennifer Plecas. Dutton, 2000. Ages 5–8.

Titherington, Jeanne. *Pumpkin Pumpkin.* Greenwillow, 1986.

Van Leeuwen, Jean. *Amanda Pig, Schoolgirl.* Illustrated by Ann Schweninger. Dial, 1997. Ages 5–6.

Waber, Bernard. *Bearsie Bear and the Surprise Sleepover Party.* Houghton, 1997. Ages 4–7.

Welch, Willy. *Playing Right Field.* Illustrated by Marc Simont. Scholastic, 1995. Ages 5–8.

Wells, Rosemary. *Noisy Nora.* Dial, 1973.

Winter, Jeanette. *Follow the Drinking Gourd.* Knopf, 1988.

Wood, Audrey. *The Napping House.* Illustrated by Don Wood. Harcourt, 1984.

Zolotow, Charlotte. *Do You Know What I'll Do?* Illustrated by Garth Williams. Harper, 1958.

———. *If It Weren't for You.* Harper, 1966.

### Picture Books for Older Readers

Bang, Molly. *Goose.* Scholastic, 1996. Ages 8–10.

———. *The Paper Crane.* Greenwillow, 1985. Ages 8–10.

Briggs, Raymond. *The Man.* Random House, 1995. Ages 9–14.

Browne, Anthony. *Piggybook.* Knopf, 1986. Ages 9–YA.

———. *The Tunnel.* Knopf, 1990. Ages 8–12.

———. *Zoo.* Knopf, 1993. Ages 8–YA.

Burkert, Nancy Ekholm. *Valentine and Orson.* Farrar, 1989. Ages 9–YA.

Capote, Truman. *A Christmas Memory.* Illustrated by Beth Peck. Knopf, 1989. Ages 8–10.

Cendrars, Blaise. *Shadow.* Illustrated by Marcia Brown. Scribner's, 1982. Ages 8–10.

Collington, Peter. *The Coming of the Surfman.* Knopf, 1994. Ages 8–14.

Crew, Gary. *The Watertower.* Illustrated by Steven Woolman. Kane/Miller, 1995. Ages 10–14.

Diaz, Jorge. *The Rebellious Alphabet.* Illustrated by Øivind S. Jorfald. Translated by Geoffrey Fox. Holt, 1993. Ages 9–12.

Ekoomiak, Normee. *Arctic Memories.* Holt, 1990. Ages 9–12.

Foreman, Michael. *War Game.* Arcade, 1993. Ages 10–14.

Gallaz, Christophe, and Roberto Innocenti. *Rose Blanche.* Illustrated by Roberto Innocenti. Creative Education, 1985. Ages 9–YA.

Hamanaka, Sheila. *The Journey: Japanese Americans, Racism, and Renewal.* Orchard, 1990. Ages 9–YA.

Hastings, Selina. *Sir Gawain and the Loathly Lady.* Illustrated by Juan Wijngaard. Lothrop, 1985. Ages 9–12.

Heide, Florence P. *The Shrinking of Treehorn.* Illustrated by Edward Gorey. Holiday, 1971. See also *Treehorn Times Three* (Dell, 1992), a collection which includes *The Shrinking of Treehorn.* Ages 8–11.

Hodges, Margaret. *Saint George and the Dragon.* Illustrated by Trina Schart Hyman. Little, Brown, 1984. Ages 8–10.

Hooks, William H. *The Ballad of Belle Dorcas.* Illustrated by Brian Pinkney. Knopf, 1990. Ages 10–12.

Lattimore, Deborah Nourse. *The Flame of Peace: A Tale of the Aztecs.* Harper, 1987. Ages 8–10.

———. *The Lady With the Ship on Her Head.* Harcourt, 1990. Ages 9–12.

Macaulay, David. *Motel of the Mysteries.* Houghton, 1979. Ages 11–14.

———. *Shortcut.* Houghton, 1995. Ages 9–12.

Martin, Jacqueline, M. *Grandmother Bryant's Pocket.* Illustrated by Petra Mathers. Houghton, 1996. Ages 8–11.

Maruki, Toshi. *Hiroshima No Pika.* Lothrop, 1980. Ages 9–YA.

McDermott, Gerald. *Arrow to the Sun: A Pueblo Indian Tale.* Viking, 1974. Ages 8–10.

Müller, Jörg. *The Changing City.* Atheneum, 1977. Ages 9–YA. (See also *The Changing Countryside.*)

Musgrove, Margaret. *Ashanti to Zulu.* Illustrated by Leo and Diane Dillon. Dial, 1976. Ages 8–10.

Paterson, Katherine. *The Tale of the Mandarin Ducks.* Illustrated by Leo and Diane Dillon. Dutton, 1990. Ages 8–10.

Popov, Nikolai. *Why?* North-South, 1996. Ages 8–12. (Wordless)

Schwartz, David M. *G Is for Googol: A Math Alphabet Book.* Illustrated by Marissa Moss. Tricycle, 1998. Ages 10–YA.

Scieszka, Jon. *The True Story of the Three Little Pigs! By A. Wolf.* Illustrated by Lane Smith. Viking, 1989. Ages 8–11.

Sendak, Maurice. *Outside over There.* Harper, 1981. Ages 9–YA.

Sís, Peter. *Starry Messenger.* Farrar, 1996.

———. *Tibet through the Red Box.* Farrar, 1998.

Steiner, Jörg. *The Animals' Rebellion.* Illustrated by Jörg Müller. Translated by Susan Leubuscher and Tadzio Koelb. Atomium, 1990. Ages 8–12.

———. *The Bear Who Wanted to Be a Bear.* Illustrated by Jörg Müller. Atheneum, 1977. Ages 8–12.

———. *Rabbit Island.* Illustrated by Jörg Müller. Harcourt, 1978. Ages 8–12.

Turner, Ann. *Dakota Dugout.* Illustrated by Ronald Himler. Macmillan, 1985. Ages 9–11.

Van Allsburg, Chris. *The Mysteries of Harris Burdick.* Houghton, 1984. Ages 8–10.

———. *The Wreck of the Zephyr.* Houghton, 1983. Ages 8–10.

Ward, Lynd. *The Biggest Bear.* Houghton, 1952. Ages 7–9.

Wick, Walter. *Walter Wick's Optical Tricks.* Scholastic, 1998. Ages 9–YA.

Willard, Nancy. *Pish, Posh, Said Hieronymous Bosch.* Illustrated by Leo and Diane and Lee Dillon. Harcourt, 1991. Ages 9–YA.

Wisniewski, David. *Elfwyn's Saga.* Lothrop, 1990. Ages 8–10.

———. *Rain Player.* Houghton, 1991. Ages 8–10.

## Illustrated Books of Poetry

*See Chapter 3 recommended books list.*

## Illustrated Nursery Rhymes and Folk Songbooks

*See Chapter 3 recommended books list.*

## Illustrated Traditional and Modern Folktales

*See Chapter 5 recommended books list.*

# TRADITIONAL LITERATURE

## LISTEN!

*Quiet your faces; be crossed every thumb;*
*Fix on me deep your eyes . . .*
*And out of my mind a story shall come—*
*Old, and lovely, and wise.*

—WALTER DE LA MARE

Visual narratives told by ancient cave paintings in Europe, Asia, and Australia show us that prehistoric humans had stories to tell long before they had a written language. For thousands of years before writing was discovered, the best of these stories were preserved through the art of storytelling from one generation to the next. Surely these stories survived because people enjoyed hearing them. Even today, their entertainment value cannot be denied. In folk literature we have our most ancient stories and a priceless literary heritage that links us to our beginnings as thinking beings.

## DEFINITION AND DESCRIPTION

*Traditional literature* is the body of ancient stories and poems that grew out of the human quest to understand the natural and spiritual worlds and that was preserved through time by the oral tradition of storytelling before being eventually written down. Having no known or identifiable authors, these stories and poems are attributed to entire groups of people or cultures. Although in ancient times some traditional stories may have been told as truths or may have been thought to contain elements of truth, today we consider them to be mostly or wholly fantasy.

Traditional literature includes several different types of stories, but because they were all shared orally for so long, they have many features in common. For example, plots are generally shorter than in other genres of literature because all but the essential details were omitted during countless retellings. Action, in turn, is concentrated, which kept audiences alert and interested. Characters in traditional literature tend to have only one outstanding quality, which made them easy to identify. In these stories the audience has no doubt about who is good and who is bad. Settings are unimportant and are described and referred to in the vaguest of terms, such as "In the beginning . . ." or "Long ago in a land far away. . . ." The language, though full of rhythm and melody, is sparse, since lengthy explanations and descriptions were also pared down or eliminated by countless retellings. Style is characterized by stock beginnings and endings ("Once upon a time" and "They lived happily ever after"), motifs or recurring features (use of the number 3, as in three sisters, three wishes), and repetition of refrains or chants ("Mirror, mirror, on the wall . . ."). Themes that are most common in these stories are good versus evil, the power of perseverance, and explanations for the ways of the world. One feature that makes these stories particular favorites of young children is that they almost always have a happy ending.

Folklore is still being created, particularly in some of the developing countries where the oral tradition remains the chief means of communication. In the United States, urban legends, jokes, and jump-rope rhymes are all part of the constantly evolving body of folklore. These stories and rhymes are of unknown origin, but because they are certainly not ancient, they will not be treated in this chapter.

## EVALUATION AND SELECTION OF TRADITIONAL LITERATURE

For thousands of years, people of all ages were the intended audience for traditional stories. In our scientifically enlightened times, these stories have come to be seen as childlike in their use of the supernatural and magic but nonetheless charming and entertaining. The following list of evaluation criteria was developed with a general child audience in mind.

- A traditional tale, even though written down, should preserve the narrative, or storytelling, style and should sound as though it is being told.
- Retold versions of traditional tales must preserve the essential content that made the stories vital to people for thousands of years and that makes them relevant to children today.
- A traditional tale should preserve the flavor of the culture or country of its origin through the use of colloquialisms, unusual speech patterns, a few easily understood foreign terms, or proper names that are common to the culture.

- In illustrated versions of traditional literature, text and illustrations must be of high quality, and illustrations must match the tone of the text and help to capture the essence of the culture of origin. There are instances when it would be tempting to base one's evaluation and selection mainly on illustrations. Not all illustrators are skillful as writers, however.
- Though simple in other respects, traditional tales employ a rich literary style. Even very young children are fascinated by the chants, stylistic flourishes, and colorful vocabulary that are characteristic of masterful storytelling.
- In evaluating collections of traditional literature, it is important to consider all of the criteria listed above, as well as the number and variety of tales in the collection and the quality of reference aids, such as tables of contents and indexes.

Some adults raise concerns that the gruesome violence that is sometimes found in traditional stories harms or traumatizes children. In recent times, many traditional stories have been rewritten to omit the violence, as in the Disney versions of folktales. In a "softened" version of "Snow White," the evil stepmother is either forgiven by the heroine or banished from the kingdom. More authentic versions of the tale end like this:

> Then she [the stepmother] railed and cursed, and was beside herself with disappointment and anger. First she thought she would not go to the wedding; but then she felt she should have no peace until she went and saw the bride. And when she saw her she knew her for Snow-white, and could not stir from the place for anger and terror. For they had ready red-hot iron shoes, in which she had to dance until she fell down dead. (From Jakob Grimm and Wilhelm Grimm, *Household Stories*, translated by Lucy Crane [Macmillan, 1886].)

Critics of the softened versions of traditional tales claim that altering the stories robs them of their power, their appeal, and their psychological benefit to children, who, in the original versions, are reassured that the evil force is gone forever and cannot come back to hurt them. We believe that young children who have heard "softened" versions of folktales have a right to know the earlier, unaltered versions when they are old enough to cope with the violence or harsh justice they contain. Likewise, as children enter the upper intermediate and middle grades, they should be made aware of the male chauvinism and poor feminine role models, from ever-sinister stepmothers to ever-helpless princesses, rampant in folktales.

# HISTORICAL OVERVIEW OF TRADITIONAL LITERATURE

Perhaps the world's first stories grew out of the dreams, wishes, ritual chants, or retellings of the notable exploits of our primitive ancestors. No one knows. Little can be said about the early history of this genre except that these stories existed only in oral form for thousands of years.

Folklorists are intrigued by the startling similarity of traditional tales around the world. Cinderella-like tales, for example, can be found in every culture. One explanation for this is that the first humans

## E X C E L L E N T   T R A D I T I O N A L   L I T E R A T U R E
## T O   R E A D   A L O U D

*(Books for each level vary in difficulty and should be selected with students' literary backgrounds in mind.)*

P R I M A R Y   L E V E L                    A G E S   5 – 8

Babbitt, Natalie. *Ouch! A Tale from Grimm.* Illustrated by Fred Marcellino. HarperCollins, 1998.

Brown, Marcia. *Stone Soup.* Scribner's, 1975 (1947).

dePaola, Tomie. *Strega Nona.* Prentice Hall, 1975.

Marshall, James. *The Three Little Pigs.* Dial, 1989.

San Souci, Robert D., reteller. *Cendrillon: A Caribbean Cinderella.* Illustrated by Brian Pinkney. Simon & Schuster, 1998.

————. *The Talking Eggs: A Folktale from the American South.* Illustrated by Jerry Pinkney. Dial, 1989.

Stamm, Claus. *Three Strong Women: A Tall Tale from Japan.* Illustrated by Jean and Mou-sien Tseng. Viking, 1990 (1962).

Stevens, Janet. *Tops & Bottoms.* Harcourt, 1995.

I N T E R M E D I A T E   L E V E L        A G E S   8 – 1 1

*Aesop's Fables.* Illustrated by Jerry Pinkney. North-South/Sea Star, 2000.

dePaola, Tomie. *The Legend of the Bluebonnet.* Putnam, 1983.

Hodges, Margaret. *The Hero of Bremen.* Illustrated by Charles Mikolaycak. Holiday, 1993.

Lester, Julius. *The Tales of Uncle Remus: The Adventures of Brer Rabbit.* Illustrated by Jerry Pinkney. Dial, 1987.

Lunge-Larsen, Lise, reteller. *The Troll with No Heart in His Body: And Other Tales of Trolls from Norway.* Illustrated by Betsy Bowen. Houghton, 1999.

McKissack, Patricia C. *The Dark-Thirty: Southern Tales of the Supernatural.* Illustrated by Brian Pinkney. Knopf, 1992.

Osborne, Mary Pope. *American Tall Tales.* Illustrated by Michael McCurdy. Knopf, 1991.

Van Laan, Nancy. *With a Whoop and a Holler: A Bushel of Lore from Way Down South.* Illustrated by Scott Cook. Atheneum, 1998.

A D V A N C E D   L E V E L                A G E S   1 1 – 1 4

Aliki. *The Gods and Goddesses of Olympus.* HarperCollins, 1994.

Grimm, Jakob and Wilhelm. *Hansel and Gretel.* Illustrated by Anthony Browne. Knopf, 1988 (1981).

Hamilton, Virginia. *In the Beginning: Creation Stories from Around the World.* Illustrated by Barry Moser. Harcourt, 1988.

Lester, Julius. *When the Beginning Began: Stories about God, the Creatures, and Us.* Illustrated by Emily Lisker. Harcourt, 1999.

San Souci, Robert D. *The Faithful Friend.* Illustrated by Brian Pinkney. Simon & Schuster, 1995.

Tchana, Katrina, reteller. *The Serpent Slayer: And Other Stories of Strong Women.* Illustrated by Trina Schart Hyman. Little, 2000. Ages 9–YA.

created these stories and took them along as they populated the globe. We call this theory *monogenesis,* or "single origin." Another theory credits the fundamental psychological similarity of humans for the similarity of their stories. *Polygenesis,* or "many origins," holds that early humans had similar urges and motives; asked similar, fundamental questions about themselves and the world around them; and, logically, created similar stories in response. Both theories have merit; and since the answer lies hidden in ancient prehistory, neither theory has prevailed over the other.

The first known English publication of any traditional literature was that of *Aesop's Fables* in 1484 by William Caxton, the printer. Although this work was instantly popular, further collections of traditional stories in print were slow to come, owing mainly to the Puritans, who disapproved of any and all popular literature. During the Puritan Movement, which lasted roughly from 1500 to 1700, traditional literature retained its popularity with the common people through the *chapbook,* named after the chapmen, or peddlers, who sold them. These inexpensive little books contained stories of adventure and humor that were loosely based on the epics, legends, and folk heroes of traditional literature.

As the Romantic Movement gradually replaced the Puritan Movement in Europe in the eighteenth century, traditional literature was accepted by all levels of society once more. The first evidence of this change in attitude was the publication by Charles Perrault in 1697 in France of eight "courtly" tales under the title *Tales of Mother Goose.* Included in this collection were "Cinderella," "The Sleeping Beauty," "Little Red Riding Hood," and "Puss in Boots." The popularity of this publication is evidenced by its many editions in both France and England, but it was another hundred years before the next collection of traditional literature appeared.

The publication in 1812 of Jakob and Wilhelm Grimm's *Nursery and Household Tales,* which included such tales as "Rumpelstiltskin," "Snow White and the Seven Dwarfs," and "Hansel and Gretel," gave the world some of its best-loved stories. As the nineteenth century progressed, other important collections of traditional literature appeared in Europe and England for the first time. In Norway, Peter Christian Asbjörnsen and Jörgen Moe collected such folktales as "The Three Billy Goats Gruff," "East o' the Sun and West o' the Moon," "Henny Penny," and "Pancake"; these were published in 1851 in book form under the title *The Norwegian Folktales.* In England, Joseph Jacobs compiled from already printed sources his *English Fairy Tales* (1894), which included "The Three Bears," "The Three Little Pigs," and "The Little Red Hen." Jacobs's adaptations of many tales for a child audience is an important part of his contribution. By the time the Scot, Andrew Lang, published his valuable four-volume collection of folktales from around the world (*The Blue, Red, Green,* and *Yellow Fairy Books,* 1889–1894), the value and importance of traditional literature had been generally accepted. Milestones in the development of traditional literature are highlighted on page 102.

The popularity of traditional literature with children has continued to grow in the twenty-first century, owing in part to a renewed interest in storytelling. Other trends contributing to the popularity of this genre are the publication of single illustrated retellings of works of traditional literature, publication of cultural variants of traditional tales from around the world, and publication of newly discovered ethnic folk literature of many Canadian and U.S. minorities in collections and single illustrated works. Surely, these trends indicate both a healthy respect for the importance of our folk literary heritage and a general recognition of the worth of all traditional literature.

# M I L E S T O N E S

*in the Development of* TRADITIONAL  LITERATURE

| DATE | EVENT | SIGNIFICANCE |
|---|---|---|
| Prehistory–1500s | Oral storytelling | Kept ancient stories alive and provided literature to common people |
| 500 B.C. | Aesop, a supposed Greek slave, wrote classic fables | Established the fable as a type of traditional literature |
| 1484 | *Aesop's Fables* published by William Caxton in England | First known publication of traditional literature |
| 1500–1700 | Puritan Movement | Prevented the publication of traditional literature by the legitimate press |
| | Chapbooks emerge | Helped keep interest in traditional heroes alive during Puritan Movement |
| Late 1600s | Jean de La Fontaine of France adapted earlier fables in verse form | Popularized the fable |
| 1697 | *Tales of Mother Goose* published by Charles Perrault in France | First written version of folktales |
| 1700s | Romantic Movement | Traditional fantasy promoted and embraced in Europe |
| 1812 | Wilhelm and Jakob Grimm collected and published *Nursery and Household Tales* in Germany | Helped to popularize folk literature |
| 1851 | Asbjörnsen and Moe collected and published *The Norwegian Folktales* in Norway | Helped to popularize folk literature |
| 1894 | Joseph Jacobs collected and published *English Fairy Tales* in England; adapted many tales for a child audience | Helped to popularize folk literature |
| 1889–1894 | Andrew Lang collected and published four volumes of folktales from around the world | Growing popularity and knowledge of folktales worldwide helped to popularize folk literature |

# TYPES  OF  TRADITIONAL  LITERATURE

For the beginning student of traditional literature, classification of stories can be confusing. For instance, not everyone uses the same terms when referring to certain types of traditional stories. Also, we have a large body of modern stories that were written by known authors in the style of the traditional ones but are not of ancient and unknown origin and therefore are not "traditional" in the strict sense.

We have chosen the term *traditional literature* to refer to the entire body of stories passed down from ancient times by the oral tradition. The term *folktale* is sometimes used in the same way. The term *retold tale* refers to a version of a tale that is obviously based upon an earlier, well-known tale but in which the language and bits of the plot have been altered to modernize or further dramatize the story. Nowadays, retold tales are often accompanied by completely new and original illustrations that sometimes give remarkable insights into the deeper meaning or relevance of these tales. *Variant,* a term often used in reference to folktales, refers to a story that shares fundamental elements of plot or character with other stories, and therefore is said to be in the same story family. There are hundreds of variants of "Cinderella," for example, from all over the world. All of the following types of traditional literature occur in variant and retold tale versions.

## Myths

Myths are stories that recount and explain the origins of the world and the phenomena of nature. They are sometimes referred to as *creation stories.* Myths may have originated in ancient religious rituals. The characters in these stories are mainly gods and goddesses, with occasional mention of humans, and the setting is high above earth in the home of the gods. Though often violent, myths nonetheless mirror human nature and the essence of our sometimes primitive emotions, instincts, and desires. Some folklorists believe that myths are the foundation of all other ancient stories. The best-known mythologies are of Greek, Roman, and Norse origin.

Many excellent collections of myths are currently available for children (see the list at the end of this chapter). In addition, single myths are often published in picture book format (see the list at the end of Chapter 4). The complexity and symbolism often found in myths make them appropriate for an older audience (9 years and up) than is usual with traditional literature. Some myths have been simplified for a younger audience, but oversimplification robs these stories of their power and appeal.

## Epics

Epics are long stories of human adventure and heroism recounted in many episodes. Some epics are told in verse. Epics are grounded in mythology, and their characters can be both human and divine. However, the hero is always human or, in some cases, superhuman, as was Ulysses in the *Odyssey,* Beowulf in the epic of that name, and Roland in *The Song of Roland.* The setting is earthly but not always realistic. Because of their length and complexity, epics are perhaps more suitable for students in high school or college, but on the strength of their compelling characters and events, some epics have been adapted and shortened for younger audiences. *Dragonslayer,* an adaptation of *Beowulf* by Rosemary Sutcliff, is a good example.

## Legends and Tall Tales

Legends are stories based on either real or supposedly real individuals and their marvelous deeds. Legendary characters such as King Arthur, Lancelot, and Merlin, and legendary settings such as Camelot, are a tantalizing mix of realism and fantasy. Although the feats of the heroes of legend defy belief today, in ancient times these stories were considered factual.

Tall tales are highly exaggerated accounts of the exploits of persons, both real and imagined, so they may be considered a subcategory of legends, albeit of much more recent origin. In the evolution of the tall tale, however, as each teller embroidered upon the hero's abilities or deeds, the tales became outlandishly exaggerated and were valued more for their humor and braggadocio than for their factual content. Legends, in contrast, are more austere in tone. Well-known North American tall-tale heroes are Pecos Bill, Paul Bunyan, John Henry, and Johnny Appleseed. Lesser known but equally amazing are such tall-tale heroines as Annie Christmas and Sally Ann Thunder Ann Whirlwind Crockett. Legends, because of their length, seriousness, and complexity, are often suitable for middle-graders; the shorter and more humorous tall tales can be enjoyed by children aged 7 and up.

## Folktales

Folktales are stories that grew out of the lives and imaginations of the people, or folk. Folktales have always been children's favorite type of traditional literature and are enjoyed by children from about age 3 and up. One of the most interesting and important characteristics of these tales is their universality. No theories adequately explain this phenomenon, but the folktales of all cultures, regardless of geography or other surface cultural differences, are remarkably similar.

Folktales vary in content as to their original intended audiences. Long ago, the nobility and their courtiers heard stories of the heroism, valor, and benevolence of people like themselves—the ruling classes. In contrast, the stories heard by the common people portrayed the ruling classes as unjust or hard taskmasters whose riches were fair game for those common folk who were quick-witted or strong enough to acquire them. These class-conscious tales are sometimes referred to as *castle* and *cottage* tales, respectively.

Some people use the terms *folktale* and *fairy tale* interchangeably. In fact, the majority of these stories have no fairies or magic characters in them, so to use one term in place of the other can be confusing and erroneous. We categorize fairy tales under *magic tales,* a kind of folktale having magic characters such as fairies.

The following is a list of the most prevalent kinds of folktales. Note that some folktales have characteristics of two or more folktale categories.

*CUMULATIVE*   The cumulative tale uses repetition, accumulation, and rhythm to make an entertaining story out of the barest of plots. Because of its simplicity, rhythm, and humor, the cumulative tale has special appeal to 3- to 5-year-olds. "The Gingerbread Boy," with its runaway cookie and his growing host of pursuers, is a good example of this kind of tale.

*HUMOROUS*   The humorous tale revolves around a character's incredibly stupid and funny mistakes. These tales are also known as noodleheads, sillies, drolls, and numbskulls. They have endured, no doubt, for their comic appeal and the guaranteed laughter they evoke. Some famous noodleheads are the Norwegian husband who kept house (and nearly demolished it) and Clever Elsie, who was so addle-brained that she got herself confused with someone else and was never heard from again.

*BEAST*   Beast tales feature talking animals and overstated action. Human characters sometimes occur. Young children accept and enjoy these talking animals, and older children can appreciate the fact that the animals symbolize humans. "Goldilocks and the Three Bears," perhaps the best-loved folktale of all, is a good example of a beast tale.

*MAGIC*  Magic tales, also known as wonder tales or fairy tales, contain elements of magic or enchantment in characters, plots, or settings. Fairies, elves, pixies, brownies, witches, magicians, genies, and fairy godparents are pivotal characters in these stories, and they use magic objects or words to weave their enchantments. Talking mirrors, hundred-year naps, glass palaces, enchanted forests, thumb-sized heroines, and magic kisses are the stuff of magic tales. "Aladdin and the Wonderful Lamp" is a well-loved magic tale.

*POURQUOI*  Pourquoi tales explain phenomena of nature. The word *pourquoi* is French for *why*, and these tales can be understood as primitive explanations for the many "why" questions early humans asked. The strong connection between these tales and myths is obvious, which is why some folklorists identify pourquoi tales as the simplest myths. Note, however, that deities play no role in pourquoi tales as they do in myths. Moreover, the setting in pourquoi tales is earthly, while the setting in myths is the realm of the gods. An example of a pourquoi tale is "Why the Sun and the Moon Live in the Sky."

*REALISTIC*  Realistic tales are those whose characters, plot, and setting could conceivably have occurred. There is no magic in these tales, and any exaggeration is limited to the possible. Only a few realistic tales exist. "The Hero of Bremen" is a good example.

## Fables

The fable is a simple story that incorporates characters—typically animals—whose actions teach a moral lesson or universal truth. Often, the moral is stated at the end of the story. Throughout history, fables have appealed to adults as well as to children, for the best of these stories are both simple and wise. Moreover, their use of animals as symbols for human behavior have made them safe, yet effective, political tools. Perhaps because of their adult appeal, fables were put into print far earlier than other forms of traditional literature.

Aesop's fables compose the best-known collection of fables in the Western world, but other collections deserve our notice. From Persia, there are the *Panchatantra Tales;* from India, the *Jataka Tales;* and from France, the collected fables of Jean de La Fontaine.

## Religious Stories

Stories based on religious writings or taken intact from religious manuscripts are considered to be religious stories. These stories may recount milestones in the development of a religion and its leadership, or they may present a piece of religious doctrine in narrative form. Stories of the latter sort are usually called *parables*.

Scholars of religion, language, and mythology have found a definite thread of continuity from myth and folk narrative to early religious thinking and writing. Many of the stories, figures, and rituals described in the sacred scriptures of Christianity, Hinduism, and Buddhism, among other religions, have their roots in ancient mythology.

Regardless of whether one considers the religious stories to be fact or fiction, the important point is that these wonderful stories should be shared with children. Because religion in the classroom is potentially controversial, however, many teachers and librarians do not feel comfortable sharing stories with any religious connection. This is unfortunate, since many wonderful stories and some superlative literature, as well as characters, sayings, and situations essential to the culturally literate person, are therefore missed.

Traditional literature, the wealth of ancient stories accumulated over the course of human existence, is one of the treasures of our species. We listen to these endlessly fascinating stories, we reflect on them, and they help to tell us who we are. Good companions of our childhood, they easily become part of us and stay with us throughout our lives. Every child deserves access to this wonderful literary heritage.

## R E F E R E N C E S

de la Mare, Walter. (1930). Listen! In W. de la Mare, *Poems for children.* New York: Holt.

Grimm, J., & Grimm, W. (1886). *Household stories.* Translated by L. Crane. New York: Macmillan.

## N O T A B L E   R E T E L L E R S   A N D   I L L U S T R A T O R S   O F   T R A D I T I O N A L   L I T E R A T U R E

**Verna Aardema,** reteller of African folktales. *When the Rains Came to Kapiti Plain; Why Mosquitoes Buzz in People's Ears.*

**Marcia Brown,** author and illustrator; seven of her nine Caldecott Medals or Honor Book Awards are for illustrating folktales. *Cinderella; Once a Mouse.*

**Nancy Ekholm Burkert,** author and illustrator whose meticulously detailed, authentic illustrations bring depth to folktales. *Snow White and the Seven Dwarfs* (translated by Randall Jarrell).

**Tomie dePaola,** reteller, illustrator, and collector of Italian folktales and Bible stories. *Strega Nona.*

**Walt Disney,** animated film producer whose greatly sentimentalized versions of folktales popularized the genre. "Snow White and the Seven Dwarfs."

**Leonard Everett Fisher,** reteller and illustrator of Greek and Mexican mythology. *Theseus and the Minotaur.*

**Paul Galdone,** illustrator of numerous classic folktales. *The Gingerbread Boy; Androcles and the Lion.*

**Paul Goble,** author and illustrator. Reteller and illustrator of folktales and legends of the North American Indian. *Beyond the Ridge.*

**Margaret Hodges,** reteller of folktales for older children. *Saint George and the Dragon* (illustrated by Trina Schart Hyman).

**Trina Schart Hyman,** reteller and illustrator of classic folktales. *Little Red Riding Hood; The Sleeping Beauty.*

**Eric A. Kimmel,** reteller of folktales from around the world; particularly known for his Yiddish stories. *Hershel and the Hanukkah Goblins; The Spotted Pony: A Collection of Hanukkah Stories.*

**Julius Lester,** reteller of African-American folktales and creation stories. *When the Beginning Began: Stories about God, the Creatures, and Us; John Henry.*

**James Marshall,** reteller and illustrator of humorously irreverent versions of classic folktales. *Goldilocks and the Three Bears.*

**Gerald McDermott,** reteller and illustrator of Native American myths and folktales. *Raven: A Trickster Tale from the Pacific Northwest.*

**Robert D. San Souci,** adaptor of obscure or almost-forgotten stories from many different places and ethnic groups. *The Faithful Friend; The Talking Eggs.*

**Janet Stevens,** reteller and illustrator of humorous beast tales from around the world. *Tops & Bottoms; various Anansi* tales from Africa.

**Ed Young,** Chinese-American illustrator of Chinese folktale variants. *Lon Po Po: A Red Riding Hood Story from China; Seven Blind Mice.*

**Paul O. Zelinsky,** illustrator whose realistic oil paintings provide insights into the meaning of folktales. *Hansel and Gretel; Rumpelstiltskin.*

## RECOMMENDED TRADITIONAL LITERATURE

*Ages refer to approximate interest levels. YA = young adult.*

### *Myths*

Aliki, reteller. *The Gods and Goddesses of Olympus.* HarperCollins, 1994. Ages 8–12.

Asimov, Isaac. *Words from the Myths.* Illustrated by William Barss. Houghton, 1961. Ages 9–YA.

Bierhorst, John. *The Woman Who Fell from the Sky: The Iroquois Story of Creation.* Illustrated by Robert A. Parker. Morrow, 1993. Ages 7–10.

Climo, Shirley, reteller. *Atalanta's Race: A Greek Myth.* Illustrated by Alexander Koshkin. Clarion, 1995. Ages 8–13.

d'Aulaire, Ingri, and Edgar Parin d'Aulaire. *Book of Greek Myths.* Doubleday, 1962. Ages 8–10.

————. *Norse Gods and Giants.* Doubleday, 1967. Ages 8–10.

Fisher, Leonard Everett. *The Olympians: Great Gods and Goddesses of Ancient Greece.* Holiday, 1984. Ages 9–12.

Hamilton, Virginia, reteller. *In the Beginning: Creation Stories from Around the World.* Illustrated by Barry Moser. Harcourt, 1988. Ages 9–12.

Low, Alice. *The Macmillan Book of Greek Gods and Heroes.* Illustrated by Arvis Stewart. Macmillan, 1985. Ages 9–12.

McCaughrean, Geraldine. *The Golden Hoard: Myths and Legends of the World.* Illustrated by Bee Willey. McElderry, 1996. Ages 8–12.

Sutcliff, Rosemary. *The Wanderings of Odysseus: The Story of the Odyssey.* Illustrated by Alan Lee. Delacorte, 1996. Ages 10–13.

### *Epics*

Fisher, Leonard Everett. *Cyclops.* Holiday, 1991. Ages 8–10.

————. *Jason and the Golden Fleece.* Holiday, 1990. Ages 9–12.

————. *The Olympians.* Holiday, 1984. Ages 8–10.

————. *Theseus and the Minotaur.* Holiday, 1988. Ages 9–12.

Hutton, Warwick, reteller. *Theseus and the Minotaur.* Macmillan, 1989. Ages 8–10.

Sutcliff, Rosemary. *Black Ships before Troy: The Story of the Iliad.* Illustrated by Alan Lee. Delacorte, 1993. Ages 11–14.

————. *Dragonslayer: The Story of Beowulf.* Puffin, 1986 (1966).

### *Legends and Tall Tales*

Blair, Walter. *Tall Tale America: A Legendary History of Our Humorous Heroes.* Illustrated by Glen Rounds. Coward-McCann, 1944. Ages 7–9.

dePaola, Tomie. *The Legend of the Bluebonnet.* Putnam, 1983. Ages 8–11.

————, reteller. *The Legend of the Indian Paintbrush.* Putnam, 1988. Ages 6–8.

————. *The Legend of the Poinsettia.* Putnam, 1994. Ages 6–8.

Dewey, Ariane. *The Narrow Escapes of Davy Crockett.* Greenwillow, 1990. Ages 8–10.

Dixon, Ann, reteller. *The Sleeping Lady.* Illustrated by Elizabeth Johns. Alaska Northwest Books, 1994. Ages 8–14.

Goble, Paul. *The Girl Who Loved Wild Horses.* Bradbury, 1978. Ages 7–9.

Greene, Ellin. *The Legend of the Christmas Rose.* Illustrated by Charles Mikolaycak. Holiday, 1990. Ages 6–8.

Hastings, Selina. *Sir Gawain and the Green Knight.* Illustrated by Juan Wijngaard. Lothrop, 1981. Ages 9–12.

————. *Sir Gawain and the Loathly Lady.* Illustrated by Juan Wijngaard. Lothrop, 1985. Ages 9–12.

Hodges, Margaret. *Saint George and the Dragon.* Illustrated by Trina Schart Hyman. Little, Brown, 1984. Ages 8–10.

Kellogg, Steven, reteller. *Paul Bunyan.* Morrow, 1984. Ages 6–8.

————, reteller. *Pecos Bill.* Morrow, 1986. Ages 6–8.

Kimmel, Eric A., reteller. *Gershon's Monster: A Story for the Jewish New Year.* Illustrated by Jon J. Muth. Scholastic, 2000. Ages 6–11.

Lester, Julius. *John Henry.* Illustrated by Jerry Pinkney. Dial, 1994. Ages 8–10.

Lister, Robin. *The Legend of King Arthur.* Illustrated by Alan Baker. Doubleday, 1990.

McCully, Emily Arnold. *Beautiful Warrior: The Legend of the Nun's Kung Fu.* Scholastic, 1998. Ages 5–9.

Osborn, Mary Pope. *American Tall Tales.* Illustrated by Michael McCurdy. Knopf, 1991. Ages 8–11.

Pyle, Howard. *The Merry Adventures of Robin Hood.* Scribner's, 1946 (1883). Ages 9–12.

————. *The Story of King Arthur and His Knights.* Scribner's, 1984 (1883). Ages 9–12.

Rounds, Glen. *Washday on Noah's Ark: A Story of Noah's Ark According to Glen Rounds.* Holiday, 1985. Ages 6–8.

San Souci, Robert D. *Cut from the Same Cloth: American Women of Myth, Legend, and Tall Tale.* Illustrated by Brian Pinkney. Philomel, 1993. Ages 8–12.

————. *Young Merlin.* Illustrated by Daniel Horne. Doubleday, 1990. Ages 9–12.

Stamm, Claus. *Three Strong Women: A Tall Tale from Japan.* Illustrated by Jean and Mou-sien Tseng. Viking, 1990 (1962). Ages 6–8.

Thomassie, Tynia. *Feliciana Feydra LeRoux: A Cajun Tall Tale.* Illustrated by Cat Bowman Smith. Little, Brown, 1995. Ages 6–9.

## Folktales

*(Note country, continent, or culture of origin after each entry.)*

Aardema, Verna, reteller. *Borreguita and the Coyote.* Illustrated by Petra Mathers. Knopf, 1991. Ages 5–8. (Mexico)

————, reteller. *Traveling to Tondo: A Tale of the Nkundo of Zaire.* Illustrated by Will Hillenbrand. Knopf, 1990. Ages 7–9. (Zaire)

————, reteller. *Why Mosquitoes Buzz in People's Ears.* Illustrated by Leo and Diane Dillon. Dial, 1975. Ages 5–7. (Kenya)

Asbjörnsen, Peter Christian, and Jörgen E. Moe. *The Three Billy Goats Gruff.* Illustrated by Marcia Brown. Harcourt, 1957. Ages 6–8. (Norway)

Babbitt, Natalie. *Ouch! A Tale from Grimm.* Illustrated by Fred Marcellino. HarperCollins, 1998. Ages 4–7. (Germany)

Bierhorst, John, editor. *The Dancing Fox: Arctic Folktales.* Illustrated by Mary K. Okheena. Morrow, 1997. Ages 9–13. (Inuit)

Brett, Jan. *Beauty and the Beast.* Clarion, 1989. Ages 6–8. (France)

————. *The Mitten.* Putnam, 1989. Ages 5–7. (Ukraine)

Brown, Marcia. *Dick Whittington and His Cat.* Scribner's, 1950. Ages 6–8. (England)

————. *Once a Mouse.* Scribner's, 1961. Ages 7–9. (India)

————. *Stone Soup.* Scribner's, 1975 (1947). Ages 6–8. (France)

Bruchac, Joseph. *The First Strawberries: A Cherokee Story.* Illustrated by Anna Vojtech. Dial, 1993. Ages 7–9. (Native-American)

Casanova, Mary, reteller. *The Hunter: A Chinese Folktale.* Illustrated by Ed Young. Atheneum, 2000. Ages 5–8. (China)

Cecil, Laura, reteller. *The Frog Princess.* Illustrated by Emma C. Clark. Greenwillow, 1995. Ages 4–8. (United Kingdom)

Chaucer, Geoffrey. *Canterbury Tales.* Adapted by Barbara Cohen. Illustrated by Trina Schart Hyman. Lothrop, 1988. Ages 8–10. (England)

Climo, Shirley. *The Egyptian Cinderella.* Illustrated by Ruth Heller. Crowell, 1989. Ages 7–9. (Egypt)

————. *The Korean Cinderella.* Illustrated by Ruth Heller. HarperCollins, 1993. Ages 7–9. (Korea)

Cohn, Amy L., editor. *From Sea to Shining Sea: A Treasury of American Folklore and Folk Songs.* Scholastic, 1993. Ages 4–10. (United States)

Cooney, Barbara. *Chanticleer and the Fox.* Crowell, 1958. Ages 6–8. (England)

Cooper, Susan, reteller. *The Selkie Girl.* Illustrated by Warwick Hutton. McElderry, 1986. Ages 7–9. (Scotland)

————, reteller. *The Silver Cow.* Illustrated by Warwick Hutton. Atheneum, 1983. Ages 8–10. (Wales)

————. *Tam Lin.* Illustrated by Warwick Hutton. McElderry, 1991. Ages 8–10. (Scotland)

Corrin, Sara and Stephen, retellers. *The Pied Piper of Hamelin.* Illustrated by Errol Le Cain. Harcourt, 1989. Ages 7–9. (Germany)

d'Aulaire, Ingri, and Edgar Parin d'Aulaire, editors and illustrators. *East of the Sun and West of the Moon.* Viking, 1969 (1938). Ages 7–9. (Norway)

Day, Nancy R. *The Lion's Whiskers: An Ethiopian Folktale.* Illustrated by Ann Grifalconi. Scholastic, 1995. Ages 8–14. (Ethiopia)

Demi. *One Grain of Rice.* Scholastic, 1997. Ages 8–11. (India)

dePaola, Tomie. *Strega Nona.* Prentice Hall, 1975. Ages 6–8. (Italy)

————. *Tomie dePaola's Favorite Nursery Tales.* Putnam, 1986. Ages 4–6.

Ehlert, Lois. *Cuckoo/Cucu.* Harcourt, 1997. Ages 4–7. (Hispanic)

————. *Moon Rope: A Peruvian Folktale.* Harcourt, 1992. Ages 4–8. (Peru)

Emberley, Rebecca, reteller. *Three Cool Kids.* Little, Brown, 1995. Ages 4–7. (Norway)

Esbensen, Barbara Juster, reteller. *The Star Maiden: An Ojibway Tale.* Illustrated by Helen K. Davie. Little, Brown, 1988. Ages 7–9. (Native-American)

Galdone, Paul. *The Gingerbread Boy.* Clarion, 1975. Ages 4–6. (England)

————. *Henny Penny.* Seabury, 1968. Ages 5–7. (England)

————. *The Little Red Hen.* Seabury, 1973. Ages 5–7. (England)

————. *Old Mother Hubbard and Her Dog.* McGraw-Hill, 1960. Ages 5–7. (England)

————. *The Three Billy Goats Gruff.* Seabury, 1973. Ages 5–7. (Norway)

Galloway, Priscilla. *Truly Grim Tales.* Delacorte, 1995. Ages 9–12.

Geras, Adèle. *My Grandmother's Stories: A Collection of Jewish Folk Tales.* Illustrated by Jael Jordan. Knopf, 1990. Ages 8–10. (Jewish)

Geringer, Laura, adapter. *The Seven Ravens.* Illustrated by E. S. Gazsi. HarperCollins, 1994. Ages 7–10. (Germany)

Glass, Andrew, reteller. *Folks Call Me Appleseed John.* Doubleday, 1995. Ages 7–10. (United States)

Goble, Paul. *Beyond the Ridge.* Bradbury, 1989. Ages 8–10. (Native-American)

————. *Buffalo Woman.* Bradbury, 1984. Ages 7–9. (Native-American)

————. *The Girl Who Loved Wild Horses.* Bradbury, 1978. Ages 7–9. (Native-American)

————, reteller. *Iktomi and the Berries: A Plains Indian Story.* Orchard, 1989. Ages 7–9. (Native-American)

————, reteller. *Iktomi and the Boulder: A Plains Indian Story.* Orchard, 1988. Ages 7–9. (Native-American)

Grimm, Jakob, and Wilhelm Grimm. *The Bremen Town Musicians.* Illustrated by Joseph Palecek. Translated by Anthea Bell. Picture Book Studio, 1988. Ages 6–8. (Germany)

————. *Favorite Tales from Grimm.* Retold by Nancy Garden. Illustrated by Mercer Mayer. Four Winds, 1982. Ages 6–8. (Germany)

————. *Hansel and Gretel.* Illustrated by Anthony Browne. Knopf, 1998 (1981). Ages 8–14. (Germany)

————. *Hansel and Gretel.* Translated by Elizabeth D. Crawford. Illustrated by Lisbeth Zwerger. Morrow, 1979. Ages 6–8. (Germany)

————. *Hansel and Gretel.* Retold by Rika Lesser. Illustrated by Paul O. Zelinsky. Dodd Mead, 1984. Ages 7–9. (Germany)

————. *Little Red Riding Hood.* Illustrated by Trina Schart Hyman. Holiday, 1982. Ages 6–8. (Germany)

————. *Rumpelstiltskin.* Retold and illustrated by Paul O. Zelinsky. Dutton, 1986. Ages 7–9. (Germany)

————. *Snow-White and the Seven Dwarfs.* Translated by Randall Jarrell. Illustrated by Nancy Ekholm Burkert. Farrar, 1972. Ages 8–10. (Germany)

Hadithi, Mwenye. *Crafty Chameleon.* Illustrated by Adrienne Kennaway. Little, Brown, 1987. Ages 6–8. (Africa)

————. *Hot Hippo.* Illustrated by Adrienne Kennaway. Little, Brown, 1986. Ages 6–8. (Africa)

————. *Lazy Lion.* Illustrated by Adrienne Kennaway. Little, Brown, 1990. Ages 6–8. (Africa)

Haley, Gail E. *Jack and the Bean Tree.* Crown, 1986. Ages 6–8. (United States, Appalachia)

————. *A Story, A Story.* Atheneum, 1970. Ages 6–8. (Africa)

Hamilton, Virginia. *Her Stories: African American Folktales, Fairy Tales, and True Tales.* Illustrated by Leo and Diane Dillon. Scholastic, 1995. Ages 9-YA. (United States)

————. *The People Could Fly: American Black Folktales.* Illustrated by Leo and Diane Dillon. Knopf, 1985. Ages 8–10. (African-American)

————. *When Birds Could Talk and Bats Could Sing: The Adventures of Bruh Sparrow, Sis Wren, and Their Friends.* Scholastic, 1996. Illustrated by Barry Moser. Ages 9–12. (United States, South)

Han, Suzanne C. *The Rabbit's Escape.* Illustrated by Yumi Heo. Holt, 1995. Ages 5–8. (Korea)

Haviland, Virginia. *Favorite Fairy Tales Told in India.* Illustrated by Blair Lent. Little, Brown, 1973. Ages 7–9. (India)

————. *Favorite Fairy Tales Told in Italy.* Illustrated by Evaline Ness. Little, Brown, 1965. Ages 7–9. (Italy)

————. *Favorite Fairy Tales Told in Norway.* Illustrated by Leonard Weisgard. Little, Brown, 1961. Ages 7–9. (Norway)

Heo, Yumi, reteller. *The Green Frogs: A Korean Folktale.* Houghton, 1996. Ages 4–7. (Korea)

Hodges, Margaret. *The Hero of Bremen.* Illustrated by Charles Mikolaycak. Holiday, 1993. Ages 8–11. (Germany)

Hogrogian, Nonny. *One Fine Day.* Macmillan, 1971. Ages 4–6. (Armenia)

Hong, Lily Toy, reteller. *Two of Everything: A Chinese Folktale.* Albert Whitman, 1993. Ages 5–8. (China)

Hooks, William H. *The Ballad of Belle Dorcas.* Illustrated by Brian Pinkney. Knopf, 1990. Ages 8–10. (United States)

————. *Freedom's Fruit.* Illustrated by James Ransome. Random House, 1995. Ages 8–11. (United States, Carolinas)

————, reteller. *Moss Gown.* Illustrated by Donald Carrick. Clarion, 1987. Ages 7–9. (United States; a Cinderella variant)

Huck, Charlotte. *Princess Furball.* Illustrated by Anita Lobel. Greenwillow, 1989. Ages 6–8. (Germany; a Cinderella variant)

Hutton, Warwick. *Beauty and the Beast.* Atheneum, 1975. Ages 7–9. (France)

————, reteller. *The Trojan Horse.* Macmillan/McElderry, 1992. Ages 6–10. (Greece)

Ishii, Momoko, reteller. *The Tongue-Cut Sparrow.* Translated from Japanese by Katherine Paterson. Illustrated by Suekichi Akaba. Lodestar, 1987. Ages 7–9. (Japan)

Ivimey, John W. *The Complete Story of the Three Blind Mice.* Illustrated by Paul Galdone. Clarion, 1987. Ages 6–8. (England; expanded)

————. *Three Blind Mice.* Illustrated by Victoria Chess. Little, Brown, 1990. Ages 7–9. (England)

Joseph, Lynn. *A Wave in Her Pocket: Stories from Trinidad.* Illustrated by Brian Pinkney. Clarion, 1991. Ages 7–9. (Trinidad)

Kajikawa, Kimiko, adaptor. *Yoshi's Feast.* Illustrated by Yumi Heo. DK Ink, 2000. Ages 5–9. (Japan)

Karlin, Barbara, reteller. *Cinderella.* Illustrated by James Marshall. Little, Brown, 1989. Ages 6–8. (France)

Kellogg, Steven. *Chicken Little.* Morrow, 1985. Ages 4–6. (United States; modern folktale)

————, reteller. *Johnny Appleseed.* Morrow, 1988. Ages 6–8. (United States)

————. *Paul Bunyan.* Morrow, 1984. Ages 6–8. (United States)

————. *Pecos Bill.* Morrow, 1986. Ages 6–8. (United States)

Kimmel, Eric. *Anansi and the Talking Melon.* Illustrated by Janet Stevens. Holiday, 1994. Ages 5–7. (Africa)

————. *Anansi Goes Fishing.* Illustrated by Janet Stevens. Holiday, 1993. Ages 5–7. (Africa)

————. *Baba Yaga: A Russian Folktale.* Illustrated by Megan Lloyd. Holiday, 1991. Ages 7–9. (Russia)

————. *Coyote Steals the Blanket: A Ute Tale.* Illustrated by Janet Stevens. Holiday, 1993. Ages 5–7. (Native American: Ute)

————. *The Gingerbread Man.* Illustrated by Megan Lloyd. Holiday, 1993. Ages 5–7. (England)

————. *Iron John.* Illustrated by Trina Schart Hyman. Holiday, 1994. Ages 8–10. (Germany)

Kurtz, Jane. *Fire on the Mountain.* Illustrated by E. B. Lewis. Simon & Schuster, 1994. Ages 7–9. (Ethiopia)

Langstaff, John, and Feodor Rojankovsky. *Frog Went A-Courtin'.* Illustrated by Feodor Rojankovsky. Harcourt, 1955. Ages 6–8. (England)

Lester, Julius. *How Many Spots Does a Leopard Have? and Other Tales.* Illustrated by David Shannon. Scholastic, 1989. Ages 7–9. (African-American)

————, reteller. *The Tales of Uncle Remus: The Adventures of Brer Rabbit.* Illustrated by Jerry Pinkney. Dial, 1987. (See also: *More Tales of Uncle Remus: Further Adventures of Brer Rabbit, His Friends, Enemies, and Others.* Dial, 1988.) Ages 7–9. (African-American)

Lindbergh, Reeve. *Johnny Appleseed.* Illustrated by Kathy Jakobsen. Little, Brown, 1990. Ages 6–8. (United States)

Lottridge, Celia Barker. *The Name of the Tree: A Bantu Folktale.* Illustrated by Ian Wallace. Macmillan, 1990. Ages 6–8. (Africa)

Louie, Ai-Ling. *Yeh-Shen: A Cinderella Story from China.* Illustrated by Ed Young. Philomel, 1982. Ages 7–9. (China)

Lunge-Larsen, Lise, reteller. *The Troll with No Heart in His Body: And Other Tales of Trolls from Norway.* Illustrated by Betsy Bowen. Houghton, 1999. Ages 7–11. (Norway)

MacGill-Callahan, Sheila. *The Children of Lir.* Illustrated by Gennady Spirin. Dial, 1993. Ages 5–8. (Wales)

Mahy, Margaret. *The Seven Chinese Brothers.* Illustrated by Jean and Mou-sien Tseng. Scholastic, 1990. Ages 6–8. (China)

Marshall, James. *Goldilocks and the Three Bears.* Dial, 1988. Ages 5–7. (England)

————. *Red Riding Hood.* Dial, 1987. Ages 6–8. (Germany)

————. *The Three Little Pigs.* Dial, 1989. Ages 5–7. (England)

Martin, Rafe, reteller. *Foolish Rabbit's Big Mistake.* Illustrated by Ed Young. Putnam, 1985. Ages 6–8. (India)

————. *Mysterious Tales of Japan.* Illustrated by Tatsuro Kiuchi. Putnam, 1996. Ages 8–13. (Japan)

————. *The Rough-Face Girl.* Illustrated by David Shannon. Putnam, 1992. Ages 8–10. (Native-American)

Mayer, Mercer. *East of the Sun and West of the Moon.* Four Winds, 1980. Ages 7–9. (Norway)

McDermott, Gerald. *Anansi the Spider.* Holt, 1972. Ages 6–8. (Africa)

————. *Arrow to the Sun.* Viking, 1974. Ages 8–10. (Native-American)

————. *Raven: A Trickster Tale from the Pacific Northwest.* Harcourt, 1993. Ages 5–9. (Native-American)

McKissack, Patricia C. *The Dark-Thirty: Southern Tales of the Supernatural.* Illustrated by Brian Pinkney. Knopf, 1992. Ages 8–11. (United States, South)

McVitty, Walter, reteller. *Ali Baba and the Forty Thieves.* Illustrated by Margaret Early. Abrams, 1989. Ages 6–8. (Middle East)

Merrill, Jean. *The Girl Who Loved Caterpillars: A Twelfth-Century Tale from Japan.* Illustrated by Floyd Cooper. Putnam, 1992. Ages 5–8. (Japan)

Mollel, Tololwa M. *The Orphan Boy.* Illustrated by Paul Morin. Clarion, 1990. Ages 7–9. (Tanzania)

Montresor, Beni, adapter. *Little Red Riding Hood.* Doubleday, 1991. Ages 8–10. (Germany)

Morimoto, Junko. *The Two Bullies.* Translated from Japanese by Isao Morimoto. Crown, 1999. Ages 5–7. (Japan)

Mosel, Arlene. *The Funny Little Woman.* Illustrated by Blair Lent. Dutton, 1972. Ages 6–8. (Japan)

————. *Tikki Tikki Tembo.* Illustrated by Blair Lent. Holt, 1968. Ages 6–8. (China)

Newton, Pam. *The Stonecutter: An Indian Folktale.* Putnam, 1990. Ages 7–9. (India)

Parks, Van Dyke, and Malcolm Jones, adaptors and retellers. (Original story by Joel Chandler Harris.) *Jump!: The Adventures of Brer Rabbit.* Illustrated by Barry Moser. Harcourt, 1986. (See also: *Jump Again!: More Adventures of Brer Rabbit,* 1987; *Jump on Over!: The Adventures of Brer Rabbit and His Family,* 1989.) Ages 7–9. (African-American)

Paterson, Katherine. *The Tale of the Mandarin Ducks.* Illustrated by Leo and Diane Dillon. Lodestar, 1990. Ages 7–9. (Japan)

Perrault, Charles. *Cinderella.* Illustrated by Marcia Brown. Scribner's, 1954. Ages 6–8. (France)

———. *Puss in Boots.* Illustrated by Fred Marcellino. Farrar, 1990. Ages 6–8. (France)

Polacco, Patricia. *Babushka Baba Yaga.* Philomel, 1993. Ages 7–9. (Russia)

Ransome, Arthur. *The Fool of the World and the Flying Ship.* Illustrated by Uri Shulevitz. Farrar, 1968. Ages 6–8. (Russia)

Richard, Françoise. *On Cat Mountain.* Illustrated by Anne Buguet. Translated by Arthur A. Levine. Putnam, 1993. Ages 8–12. (Japan)

Rounds, Glen, reteller. *Old MacDonald Had a Farm.* Holiday, 1989. Ages 4–6. (England)

San Souci, Robert D., reteller. *Cendrillon: A Caribbean Cinderella.* Illustrated by Brian Pinkney. Simon & Schuster, 1998. Ages 5–7. (The Caribbean)

———. *The Faithful Friend.* Illustrated by Brian Pinkney. Simon & Schuster, 1995. Ages 11–14. (Martinique)

———. *Sootface: An Ojibwa Cinderella Story.* Illustrated by Daniel San Souci. Doubleday, 1994. Ages 5–8. (Native-American)

———. *The Talking Eggs: A Folktale from the American South.* Illustrated by Jerry Pinkney. Dial, 1989. Ages 7–9. (African-American)

Schwartz, Alvin. *Witcracks: Jokes and Jests from American Folklore.* Illustrated by Glen Rounds. Lippincott, 1973. Ages 6–12. (United States)

Shannon, George. *More Stories to Solve: Fifteen Folktales from Around the World.* Illustrated by Peter Sís. Greenwillow, 1990. Ages 7–10.

Sierra, Judy, reteller. *Nursery Tales around the World.* Illustrated by Stefano Vitale. Clarion, 1996. Ages 3–7.

———. *Tasty Baby Belly Buttons: A Japanese Folktale.* Illustrated by Meilo So. Knopf, 1999. Ages 4–7. (Japan)

———, reteller. *Wiley and the Hairy Man.* Illustrated by Brian Pinkney. Lodestar, 1996. Ages 5–8. (United States, Alabama)

Singer, Isaac Bashevis. *The Golem.* Illustrated by Uri Shulevitz. Farrar, 1982. Ages 8–10. (Jewish)

———. *When Shlemiel Went to Warsaw and Other Stories.* Translated by the author and Elizabeth Shub. Illustrated by Margot Zemach. Farrar, 1968. Ages 8–10. (Jewish)

Snyder, Diane. *The Boy of the Three-Year Nap.* Illustrated by Allen Say. Houghton, 1988. Ages 7–9. (Japan)

Souhami, Jessica. *The Leopard's Drum. An Asante Tale from West Africa.* Little, Brown, 1996. Ages 4–8. (Africa)

Steptoe, John, reteller. *Mufaro's Beautiful Daughters: An African Tale.* Lothrop, 1987. Ages 6–8. (Africa)

———. *The Story of Jumping Mouse.* Lothrop, 1984. Ages 7–9. (Native-American)

Stevens, Janet, adaptor. *How the Manx Cat Lost Its Tail.* Harcourt, 1990. Ages 6–8. (England; Isle of Man)

———. *Tops & Bottoms.* Harcourt, 1995. Ages 5–8. (Europe and American South)

Taylor, C. J. *How We Saw the World: Nine Native Stories of the Way Things Began.* Tundra, 1993. Ages 8–10. (Native-American)

Tchana, Katrina, reteller. *The Serpent Slayer: And Other Stories of Strong Women.* Illustrated by Trina Schart Hyman. Little, 2000. Ages 9–YA.

Tejima. *Ho-Limlim: A Rabbit Tale from Japan.* Philomel, 1990. Ages 6–8. (Japan)

Tompert, Ann. *Bamboo Hats and a Rice Cake.* Illustrated by Demi. Crown, 1993. Ages 7–9. (Japan)

Trivizas, Eugene. *The Three Little Wolves and the Big Bad Pig.* Illustrated by Helen Oxenbury. Macmillan/McElderry, 1993. Ages 5–9. (England; a Three Little Pigs variant)

Uchida, Yoshiko, reteller. *The Wise Old Woman.* Illustrated by Martin Springett. McElderry, 1994. Ages 7–9. (Japan)

Van Laan, Nancy. *So Say the Little Monkeys.* Illustrated by Yumi Heo. Atheneum, 1998. Ages 2–5. (Brazil)

———. *With a Whoop and a Holler: A Bushel of Lore from Way Down South.* Illustrated by Scott Cook. Atheneum, 1998. Ages 9–12. (American South)

Wells, Ruth, reteller. *The Farmer and the Poor God: A Folktale from Japan.* Illustrated by Yoshi. Simon & Schuster, 1996. Ages 5–11. (Japan)

Winthrop, Elizabeth. *Vasilissa the Beautiful.* Illustrated by Alexander Koshkin. HarperCollins, 1991. Ages 7–9. (Russia)

Wisniewski, David. *Elfwyn's Saga.* Lothrop, 1990. Ages 8–10. (Iceland)

Yolen, Jane. *Tam Lin.* Illustrated by Charles Mikolaycak. Harcourt, 1990. Ages 7–9. (Scotland)

Young, Ed. *Lon Po Po: A Red Riding-Hood Story from China.* Philomel, 1989. Ages 7–9. (China)

Zelinsky, Paul O., reteller. *Rapunzel.* Dutton, 1997. Ages 5–8. (Germany)

———, reteller. *Rumpelstiltskin.* Dutton, 1986. Ages 6–8. (Germany)

Zemach, Harve. *Duffy and the Devil.* Illustrated by Margot Zemach. Farrar, 1973. Ages 6–8. (England)

Zemach, Margot. *It Could Always Be Worse.* Farrar, 1977. Ages 6–8. (Jewish)

## Fables

*Aesop's Fables.* Illustrated by Jerry Pinkney. North-South/Sea Star, 2000. Ages 5–9.

Brett, Jan. *Town Mouse, Country Mouse.* Putnam, 1994. Ages 6–8.

Brown, Marcia. *Once a Mouse.* Scribner's, 1961. Ages 6–8.

Clark, Margaret, reteller. *The Best of Aesop's Fables.* Illustrated by Charlotte Voake. Little, Brown, 1990. Ages 7–9.

De Roin, Nancy. *Jataka Tales: Fables from the Buddha.* Illustrated by Ellen Lanyon. Houghton, 1975. Ages 7–9.

Gatti, Anne. *Aesop's Fables.* Illustrated by Safaya Salter. Harcourt, 1992. Ages 7–10.

Lobel, Arnold. *Fables.* Harper, 1980. Ages 6–8.

Paxton, Tom, reteller. *Belling the Cat and Other Aesop's Fables.* Illustrated by Robert Rayevsky. Morrow, 1990. Ages 7–9.

Stevens, Janet. *The Town Mouse and the Country Mouse: An Aesop Fable.* Holiday, 1987. Ages 6–8.

Ward, Helen, adapter. *The Hare and the Tortoise: A Fable from Aesop.* Millbrook, 1999. Ages 4–8.

## Religious Stories

Bach, Alice, and J. Cheryl Exum. *Moses' Ark: Stories from the Bible.* Illustrated by Leo and Diane Dillon. Delacorte, 1989. Ages 6–8.

Bible, New Testament. *Christmas: The King James Version.* Illustrated by Jan Pieńkowski. Knopf, 1984. Ages 6–10.

———. *Easter: The King James Version.* Illustrated by Jan Pieńkowski. Knopf, 1989. Ages 6–8

Bierhorst, John, translator. *Spirit Child: A Story of the Nativity.* Illustrated by Barbara Cooney. Morrow, 1984. Ages 7–9.

Chaikin, Miriam, adaptor. *Exodus.* Illustrated by Charles Mikolaycak. Holiday, 1987. Ages 6–8.

Demi. *Buddha.* Holt, 1996. Ages 8–12.

———. *Buddha Stories* (Jataka tales). Holt, 1997. Ages 7–10.

dePaola, Tomie. *Tomie dePaola's Book of Bible Stories.* Putnam, 1990. Ages 6–10.

Geisert, Arthur. *The Ark.* Houghton, 1988. Ages 6–8.

Goldin, Barbara Diamond. *Journeys with Elijah: Eight Tales of the Prophet.* Illustrated by Jerry Pinkney. Harcourt, 1999. Ages 7–YA.

Goodhart, Pippa. *Noah Makes a Boat.* Illustrated by Bernard Lodge. Houghton, 1997. Ages 4–6.

Hutton, Warwick. *Jonah and the Great Fish.* Atheneum, 1983. Ages 6–8.

———, adaptor. *Adam and Eve: The Bible Story.* Macmillan, 1987. Ages 6–8.

———, reteller. *Moses in the Bulrushes.* Atheneum, 1986. Ages 6–8.

Johnson, James Weldon. *The Creation.* Illustrated by James E. Ransome. Holiday, 1994.

Kimmel, Eric A., reteller. *The Spotted Pony: A Collection of Hanukkah Stories.* Illustrated by Leonard Everett Fisher. Holiday, 1992.

Lester, Julius. *When the Beginning Began: Stories about God, the Creatures, and Us.* Illustrated by Emily Lisker. Harcourt, 1999. Ages 11–14.

Spier, Peter. *Noah's Ark.* Doubleday, 1977. Ages 6–8.

Vivas, Julie. *The Nativity.* Harcourt, 1988. Ages 6–10.

Wisniewski, David. *Golem.* Clarion, 1996. Ages 6–12.

# 6

# Modern Fantasy

*Do you know*
*If you try*
*You really can*
*Touch the sky?*

*Lean a ladder*
*Against the moon*
*And climb, climb high*
*Talk to the stars*
*And leave your handprints*
*All across the sky*

*Jump on a cloud*
*And spend the day*
*Trampoline-jumping*
*Through the air*
*Climb a rainbow*
*And watch the world*
*From way up there*
*Then ride that rainbow slide*
*Back home.*

— S H E R E E   F I T C H

Modern fantasy has its roots in traditional fantasy from which motifs, characters, stylistic elements, and, at times, themes have been drawn. Many of the most revered works of children's literature fall into the genre of modern fantasy. *The Adventures of Pinocchio, Alice's Adventures in Wonderland, The Wizard of Oz, The Wind in the Willows, Winnie-the-Pooh, Pippi Longstocking,* and *Charlotte's Web* immediately come to mind. The creation of stories that are highly imaginative—yet believable—is the hallmark of this genre.

114

# DEFINITION AND DESCRIPTION

*Modern fantasy* refers to the body of literature in which the events, the settings, or the characters are outside the realm of possibility. A fantasy is a story that cannot happen in the real world, and for this reason this genre has been called the literature of the fanciful impossible. In these stories, animals talk, inanimate objects come to life, people are giants or thumb-sized, imaginary worlds are inhabited, and future worlds are explored, just to name a few of the possibilities. Modern fantasies are written by known authors, and this distinguishes the genre from traditional literature, in which the tales are handed down through the oral tradition and have no known author. Although the events could not happen in real life, modern fantasies often contain truths that help the reader to understand today's world.

The *cycle format,* in which one book is linked to another through characters, settings, or both, is especially prevalent in modern fantasy. Elleman (1987) states, "Events in [fantasy] cycle books are often strung out over three or four volumes. Authors attempt to make each novel self-contained, with varying degrees of success, but usually readers need the entire series for full impact" (p. 418). The cycle format appeals to readers who become attached to certain characters and then delight in reading the next book in the series. An example of the cycle format can be found in the chronicles of the creatures of Redwall Abbey, a series of animal fantasies by Brian Jacques.

# EVALUATION AND SELECTION OF MODERN FANTASY

The usual standards for fine fiction must also be met by authors of modern fantasy. Believable and well-rounded characters who develop and change, well-constructed plots, well-described settings with internal consistency, a style appropriate to the story, and worthy themes are elements to be expected in all fiction. In addition, the following criteria apply specifically to modern fantasy:

- Authors of modern fantasy have the challenge of persuading readers to open themselves up to believing that which is contrary to reality, strange, whimsical, or magical yet has an internal logic and consistency. Sometimes, authors will accomplish this through beginning the story in a familiar and ordinary setting with typical, contemporary human beings as characters. A transition is then made from this realistic world to the fantasy world. An example of this literary device is found in C. S. Lewis's *The Lion, the Witch, and the Wardrobe,* in which the children in the story enter a wardrobe in an old house only to discover that the back of the wardrobe leads into the land of Narnia, a fantasy world with unusual characters. Other fantasies begin in the imagined world but manage, through well-described settings and consistent well-rounded characters, to make this new reality believable. Either way, the plot, characters, and setting must be so well developed that the child reader is able to suspend disbelief and to accept the impossible as real.

- For a modern fantasy to be truly imaginative, the author must provide a unique setting. In some stories, the setting may move beyond the realistic in both time (moving to the past, future, or holding time still) and place (imagined worlds); in other stories only one of these elements (place or time) will go beyond reality. Moreover, a modern fantasy author's creation must be original, a fresh vision from a mind with special insight.

---

# EXCELLENT MODERN FANTASY TO READ ALOUD

*(Books for each level vary in difficulty and should be selected with the students' literary backgrounds in mind.)*

### PRIMARY LEVEL                    AGES 5 – 8

Ahlberg, Allan. *The Giant Baby.* Illustrated by Fritz Wegner. Viking, 1995.

Andersen, Hans Christian. *The Ugly Duckling.* Illustrated by Alan Marks. Translated by Anthea Bell. Picture Book Studio, 1989.

Dickinson, Peter. *Chuck and Danielle.* Delacorte, 1996.

King-Smith, Dick. *Ace: The Very Important Pig.* Illustrated by Lynette Hemmant. Crown, 1990.

Labatt, Mary. *Aliens in Woodford.* Kids Can Press, 2000.

Mahy, Margaret. *The Five Sisters.* Illustrated by Patricia MacCarthy. Viking, 1997.

Milne, A. A. *Winnie-the-Pooh.* Illustrated by Ernest Shepard. Dutton, 1926.

Yolen, Jane. *Sleeping Ugly.* Illustrated by Diane Stanley. Coward, 1981.

### INTERMEDIATE LEVEL          AGES 8 – 11

Avi. *Poppy.* Illustrated by Brian Floca. Orchard, 1995.

Babbitt, Natalie. *Tuck Everlasting.* Farrar, 1975.

Dahl, Roald. *James and the Giant Peach.* Illustrated by Nancy E. Burkert. Knopf, 1961.

Isaacs, Anne. *Swamp Angel.* Illustrated by Paul Zelinsky. Dutton, 1994.

Jacques, Brian. *Redwall.* Illustrated by Gary Chalk. Philomel, 1987.

Levine, Gail Carson. *Ella Enchanted.* HarperCollins, 1997.

Lewis, Clive Staples. *The Lion, the Witch, and the Wardrobe.* Illustrated by Pauline Baynes. Macmillan, 1950.

McKay, Hillary. *The Amber Cat.* Simon & Schuster, 1997.

O'Brien, Robert C. *Mrs. Frisby and the Rats of NIMH.* Illustrated by Zena Bernstein. Atheneum, 1971.

Pullman, Phillip. *I Was a Rat.* Illustrated by Kevin Hawkes. Knopf, 2000.

Rowling, J. K. *Harry Potter and the Sorcerer's Stone.* Scholastic, 1998.

### ADVANCED LEVEL                AGES 11 – 14

Billingsley, Franny. *The Folk Keeper.* Simon & Schuster, 1999.

Clement-Davies, David. *Fire Bringer.* Dutton, 2000.

Conrad, Pam. *Stonewords: A Ghost Story.* Harper, 1990.

Hamilton, Virginia. *The Magical Adventures of Pretty Pearl.* Harper, 1983.

Ibbotson, Eva. *The Secret of Platform 13.* Dutton, 1998.

Lowry, Lois. *Gathering Blue.* Houghton, 2000.

McGraw, Eloise. *The Moorchild.* Simon & Schuster, 1996.

Waugh, Sylvia. *Space Race.* Delacorte, 2000.

---

# HISTORICAL OVERVIEW OF MODERN FANTASY

Imaginative literature did not appear until the eighteenth century. These stories were not intended primarily for children but were political satires that came to be enjoyed by children as well as adults. *Gulliver's Travels* (1726) by the Irish clergyman Jonathan Swift is the most noteworthy of such books. In this adult satire ridiculing the antics of the English court and its politics, the hero, Gulliver, travels to strange, imaginary places—one inhabited by six-inch Lilliputians, another inhabited by giants. These imaginary worlds are described in fascinating detail and with sufficient humor to appeal to a child audience.

Charles Kingsley's *The Water Babies* (1863) took a contemporary child and set him in another world. Kingsley's unique tale was marred by heavy didactic passages; however, it paved the way for the classic masterpiece of fantasy. In England in 1865, Charles Lutwidge Dodgson, an Oxford don who used the pen name Lewis Carroll, wrote *Alice's Adventures in Wonderland,* which tells of a fantastic journey Alice takes to an imaginary world. The total absence of didacticism—replaced by humor and fantasy— resulted in the book's lasting appeal and world fame. Other fantasies that originated in England shortly after the appearance of *Alice* include *The Light Princess* (1867) and *At the Back of the North Wind* (1871) by George MacDonald, *The Magic Fishbone* (1868) by Charles Dickens, and *Just So Stories* (1902) by Rudyard Kipling. This early development of modern fantasy for children in England was un-rivaled by any other country and established the standard for the genre worldwide.

Modern fantasy has continued to thrive in England into the twenty-first century. Noteworthy con-tributions from England include Beatrix Potter's *The Tale of Peter Rabbit* (1902), *The Wind in the Wil-lows* (1908) by Kenneth Grahame, *The Velveteen Rabbit* (1922) by Margery Williams, *Winnie-the-Pooh* (1926) by A. A. Milne, *Mary Poppins* (1934) by Pamela Travers, *The Hobbit* (1937) by J. R. R. Tolkien, *The Lion, the Witch, and the Wardrobe* (1950) by C. S. Lewis, *The Borrowers* (1953) by Mary Norton, and *The Children of Green Knowe* (1955) by Lucy M. Boston.

Early books of modern fantasy from other countries include *The Adventures of Pinocchio* (1881) by Carlo Collodi (Carlo Lorenzini) from Italy and *Journey to the Center of the Earth* (1864), *Twenty Thousand Leagues under the Sea* (1869), and *Around the World in Eighty Days* (1872) by the Frenchman Jules Verne. Verne's works are considered the first science fiction novels and remain pop-ular today with adults and children. Later in France, Jean de Brunhoff wrote an internationally popu-lar series of animal fantasies about a family of elephants. The first of these was *The Story of Babar* (1937).

Some works of fantasy from Scandinavia also deserve recognition. Hans Christian Andersen, a Dane, published many modern folktales, stories that were very similar in literary elements to the tra-ditional tales. However, Andersen was the originator of most of his tales, for which his own life experi-ences were the inspiration. "The Ugly Duckling," "The Emperor's New Clothes," and "Thumbelina" are three of the most loved of Andersen's stories. His tales were published in 1835 and are considered the first modern fairy tales. In 1907, Selma Lagerlöf produced *The Wonderful Adventures of Nils,* a geo-graphic sortie around Sweden by a small boy-turned-elf who flies on the back of a goose. Almost half a century later, another Swedish author, Astrid Lindgren, produced *Pippi Longstocking* (1945). Pippi, a lively, rambunctious, and very strong heroine who throws caution to the wind, lives an independent life of escapades that are envied by children the world over. From Finland in 1964 came *The Tales of Moom-invalley* by Tove Jansson, the first of a series of books focusing on small imaginary creatures called Moomins, who hibernate in the winter and frolic and adventure in the summer.

The United States also produced some outstanding early modern fantasies, beginning with *The Wonderful Wizard of Oz* (1900) by L. Frank Baum, which is considered to be the first classic U.S. mod-ern fantasy for children. Other landmark U.S. works of modern fantasy are the memorable animal fan-tasy *Rabbit Hill* (1944) by Robert Lawson; *Charlotte's Web* (1952) by E. B. White, the best-known and best-loved U.S. work of fantasy; *The Book of Three* (1964), the first of the Prydain Chronicles by Lloyd Alexander; and *A Wrinkle in Time* (1962) by Madeleine L'Engle, which is considered a modern classic in science fiction for children.

Science fiction, the most recent development in modern fantasy, is said to owe its birth to the nineteenth-century novels of Jules Verne (*Journey to the Center of the Earth*, 1864; *20,000 Leagues under the Sea*, 1869) and H. G. Wells (*Time Machine*, 1895). Adults, not children, were the primary audience for these novels, however. It was not until the twentieth century that science fiction began to be aimed specifically at children. The Tom Swift series by Victor Appleton (collective pseudonym for the Stratemeyer Syndicate), although stilted in style and devoid of female characters, can be considered the first science fiction for children. The first Tom Swift book appeared in 1910 (*Tom Swift and His Airship*), with additional titles of the series appearing in rapid succession.

Then, in 1963, Madeleine L'Engle's novel *A Wrinkle in Time* was awarded the Newbery Medal. From this point forward, many science fiction novels for children began to appear. In the late 1960s and 1970s, the theme of mind control was popular. John Christopher's Tripods trilogy and William Sleator's *House of Stairs* are good examples. Space travel and future worlds were frequent science fiction topics in the 1980s. Examples are H. M. Hoover's *The Shepherd Moon* (1984) and Pamela Sargent's *Earthseed* (1983). Milestones in the development of modern fantasy are highlighted on page 119.

Modern fantasy is a genre for children that remains strong, especially in Great Britain and other English-speaking countries. Although personified toys and animals remain popular and prevalent in children's books, growth in this genre appears to be in stories in which fantasy is interwoven into other genres—science fiction, science fantasy, and historical fantasy. Fractured folktales, a form of modern folktales, began a new trend with the popularity of Jon Scieszka's *The True Story of 3 Little Pigs by A. Wolf*, illustrated by Lane Smith and published in 1989. *Fractured Folktales* are traditional folktales with a contemporary twist or a tale told from a new perspective. This blurring of traditional genres can also be seen in the interesting mixture of the logic of realistic mystery stories with supernatural elements, as in the popular mysteries of John Bellairs and Mary Downing Hahn. Modern fantasy is likely to continue to be a popular genre with children and authors, as evidenced by the extraordinary popularity of the best-selling Harry Potter quest series by J. K. Rowling, whose first novel in the series was published in 1998. The rich literary works of modern fantasy will continue to challenge children's imaginations and enhance their lives.

## TYPES OF MODERN FANTASY

In modern fantasy, as in other genres, the distinctions between types are not totally discrete. The types of modern fantasy in the sections that follow are a starting point for thinking about the variety of fantastic stories, motifs, themes, and characters that gifted authors have created. Additional categories could be listed, and you will find that some stories may fit appropriately in more than one category. For example, *The Root Cellar* by Janet Lunn has been discussed as an historical fantasy because of its authentic historical setting, but its inclusion of spirits from the past also categorizes this story under the label of Supernatural Events and Mystery Fantasy.

# M I L E S T O N E S

*in the Development of MODERN FANTASY*

| DATE | EVENT | SIGNIFICANCE |
|------|-------|--------------|
| 1726 | *Gulliver's Travels* by Jonathan Swift (England) | An adult novel prototype for children's fantasy adventures |
| 1835 | *Fairy Tales* by Hans Christian Andersen (Denmark) | First modern folktales |
| 1864 | *Journey to the Center of the Earth* by Jules Verne (France) | First science fiction novel (for adults) |
| 1865 | *Alice's Adventures in Wonderland* by Lewis Carroll (England) | First children's masterpiece of modern fantasy |
| 1881 | *The Adventures of Pinocchio* by Carlo Collodi (Italy) | Early classic personified toy story |
| 1900 | *The Wonderful Wizard of Oz* by L. Frank Baum (United States) | First classic U.S. modern fantasy for children |
| 1908 | *The Wind in the Willows* by Kenneth Grahame (England) | Early classic animal fantasy |
| 1910 | *Tom Swift and His Airship* by Victor Appleton (United States) | First science fiction novel for children |
| 1926 | *Winnie-the-Pooh* by A. A. Milne (England) | Early classic personified toy story |
| 1926 | *Amazing Stories*, science fiction magazine, begun (United States) | Formal recognition of science fiction as a literary genre |
| 1937 | *The Hobbit* by J. R. R. Tolkien (England) | Early quest adventure with a cult following |
| 1945 | *Pippi Longstocking*, by Astrid Lindgren (Sweden) | Classic unusual-character fantasy |
| 1947 | *Rocket Ship Galileo* by Robert Heinlein (United States) | Science fiction novel for children about a journey to the moon |
| 1950 | *The Lion, the Witch, and the Wardrobe* by C. S. Lewis (England) | Early classic quest adventure for children; first of the Narnia series |
| 1952 | *Charlotte's Web* by E. B. White (United States) | Classic U.S. animal fantasy |
| 1953 | *The Borrowers* by Mary Norton (England) | Classic little people fantasy |
| 1962 | *A Wrinkle in Time* by Madeleine L'Engle (United States) | Classic U.S. science fiction novel for children |
| 1964 | *The Book of Three* by Lloyd Alexander (United States) | First book in classic quest series, the Prydain Chronicles |
| 1987 | *Redwall* by Brian Jacques (England) | First book of exciting animal fantasy series |
| 1993 | *The Giver* by Lois Lowry (United States) | Popular futuristic fiction novel; Newbery Medal winner |
| 1998 | *Harry Potter and the Sorcerer's Stone* by J. K. Rowling (England) | First book in the best-selling quest fantasy series |

## Modern Folktales

Modern folktales, or *literary folktales* as they are also called, are tales told in a form similar to that of a traditional tale with the accompanying typical elements: little character description; strong conflict; fast-moving plot with a sudden resolution; vague setting; and, in some cases, magical elements. But these modern tales have a known, identifiable author who has written the tale in this form. In other words, the tales do not spring from the cultural heritage of a group of people through the oral tradition but rather from the mind of one creator. However, this distinction does not matter at all to children, who delight in these tales as much as they do in the old folktales. Fractured folktaales are a recent addition to the modern folktale genre.

The tales of Hans Christian Andersen are the earliest and best known of these modern tales. More recently, other authors, including Anne Isaacs (*Swamp Angel*) and Robin McKinley (*Beauty* and *Spindle's End*), have become known for their modern folktales.

Modern folktales are an important counterbalance to traditional tales. As was noted in Chapter 5, many of the traditional tales present an old-fashioned, stereotypic view of male and female characters. Many of the modern tales present more assertive female characters who are clearly in charge of their own destinies. An example is *The Practical Princess* by Jay Williams.

## Animal Fantasy

Animal fantasies are stories in which animals behave as human beings in that they experience emotions, talk, and have the ability to reason. Usually, the animals in fantasies will (and should) retain many of their animal characteristics. In the best of these animal fantasies, the author will interpret the animal for the reader in human terms without destroying the animal's integrity or removing it from membership in the animal world. For example, a rabbit character in an animal fantasy will retain her natural abilities of speed and camouflage to outsmart her adversaries. At the same time, however, the author will permit the reader to see human qualities such as caring and love by having the rabbit carry on conversations with family members.

Animal fantasies can be read to very young children who enjoy the exciting but reassuring adventures in books. Examples are *The Tale of Peter Rabbit* by Beatrix Potter and *The Runaway Bunny* by Margaret Wise Brown. Books for children in primary grades include somewhat longer stories, often in a humorous vein, such as Beverly Cleary's mouse stories, *Runaway Ralph* and *The Mouse and the Motorcycle;* Deborah and James Howe's humor-filled books, *Bunnicula* and *Howliday Inn;* and Michael Bond's *Paddington Bear.* Enjoyable animal fantasies for the young reader often have easy-to-follow, episodic plots.

Fully developed novels of modern fantasy with subtle and complex characterizations and a progressive plot are especially suitable for reading aloud to children in their elementary school years. *Charlotte's Web* by E. B. White remains a favorite read-aloud book; *The Cricket in Times Square* by George Selden is also popular. A beautifully written book with richly drawn characterizations is *The Wind in the Willows* by Kenneth Grahame, who describes in artistic detail the life of animal friends along a riverbank. This book features an episodic plot structure but has a challenging style that is appropriate to intermediate-grade students. *The Lemming Condition* by Alan Arkin, a short novel with a progressive plot, is also appreciated by intermediate-grade students who enjoy discussing the risks of being a follower. Although the interest in animal fantasy peaks at age 8 or 9, many children and adults continue to enjoy well-written animal fantasies. In animal fantasies for older readers, an entire animal world is usually created, with all of the relationships among its members that might be found in a novel portraying human behavior. *Mrs. Frisby and the Rats of NIMH* by Robert C. O'Brien, *Watership Down* by Richard Adams, and *Redwall* by Brian Jacques are examples of complex, fully developed animal fantasy novels for readers in fifth grade through adulthood.

## Personified Toys and Objects

Stories in which admired objects or beloved toys are brought to life and believed in by a child or adult character in the story are the focus of this type of fantasy. An early classic example of these stories is *The Adventures of Pinocchio* by Carlo Collodi (Carlo Lorenzini), in which a mischievous puppet comes to life, runs away from his maker, and has many exciting and dangerous escapades. In these stories, the object, toy, or doll becomes real to the human protagonist and, in turn, becomes real to the child reader (who has perhaps also imagined a toy coming to life). An example of a personified machine story can be found in Virginia Lee Burton's *Mike Mulligan and His Steam Shovel,* in which a close relationship exists between a steam shovel and its human operator. The responsibilities of parenthood are often assumed by the child protagonist who must nourish, protect, assist, and extricate the toy-come-to-life from various predicaments. This motif of responsibility is found in the recent story, *The Castle in the Attic,* by Elizabeth Winthrop. Personified toy and object stories appeal to children from preschool through upper elementary grades.

## Unusual Characters and Strange Situations

Some authors approach fantasy through reality but take it beyond reality to the ridiculous or exaggerated. Generally, those stories can be best described as having unusual characters or strange situations. Without doubt, *Alice's Adventures in Wonderland* by Lewis Carroll is the best known of this type of modern fantasy. More recent writers of modern fantasy have described such strange situations as a boy sailing across the Atlantic Ocean in a giant peach (*James and the Giant Peach* by Roald Dahl) and such unusual characters as a perfect, factory-made boy (*Konrad* by Christine Nöstlinger).

Modern fantasy appeals to readers of all ages. Florence Parry Heide's *The Shrinking of Treehorn* portrays a young boy who, one day, starts to shrink, but no one notices. The story is fascinating to middle-school students. Jean Merrill's *The Pushcart War* also is enjoyed by somewhat older students. This preposterous and amusing satire tells of a struggle between pushcart peddlers and truck drivers in New York City. In *Tuck Everlasting,* Natalie Babbitt explores the theme of immortality and its consequences, a provocative theme for children and adults.

## Worlds of Little People

Some authors have written about worlds inhabited by miniature people who have developed a culture of their own in this world or who live in another world. In Mary Norton's *The Borrowers,* small people live in our world but take our discards to create their own world. It is, of course, eventually human beings who threaten their existence and cause them to seek safety elsewhere. Carol Kendall described the Land Between the Mountains where the Minnipins live in *The Gammage Cup,* a story about little people struggling against the pressure to conform. A recent version of *Gulliver's Travels* can be found in *The Minpins* (1991) by Roald Dahl. Stories of little people delight children because they can identify with the indignities foisted upon little and powerless people and because the big people in these stories are invariably outdone by the more ingenious little people.

## Supernatural Events and Mystery Fantasy

Many recent fantasies evoke the supernatural. One common form of supernatural literature found in children's books is the ghost story. Some ghost stories intrigue younger children, especially when the topic is treated humorously and reassuringly, as in *The Ghosts of Hungryhouse Lane* by Sam McBratney. In this story, children find out about three ghosts in their new home but unearth ways to satisfy the needs of the ghosts. Ghosts in children's books can be fearful threats or helpful protectors. The ghost of the priest in John Bellairs's *The Curse of the Blue Figurine* is the very soul of evil, whereas *Whispers from the Dead* by Joan Lowery Nixon features a ghost who prevents a murder.

Many authors write mysteries for children in which the solution is partially supernatural or arrived at with supernatural assistance. One author who is well known for many such fantasy mysteries is John Bellairs.

Witchcraft and other aspects of the occult sometimes play a role in children's fantasy books. Witches are often portrayed as the broom-wielding villains of both traditional and modern tales, such as the Russian stories of Baba Yaga. Halloween and its traditions are also frequently presented in children's stories. Witchcraft has recently been the focus of criticism because of an upsurge of sects whose members refer to themselves as witches. Also, some parents' groups have attempted to censor children's books featuring witches, Halloween, and other elements of the occult. Chapter 11 has a full discussion on censorship and schools' responsibilities in these situations.

## Historical Fantasy

Historical fantasy, sometimes called *time-warp fantasy,* is a story in which a present-day protagonist goes back in time to a different era. A contrast between the two time periods is shown to readers through the modern-day protagonist's discoveries of and astonishment with earlier customs. Historical fantasies must fully and authentically develop the historical setting, both time and place, just as in a book of historical fiction. Canadian Janet Lunn, in *The Root Cellar,* succeeds in producing this type of mixed-genre story. David Wiseman, in *Jeremy Visick,* also presents an interesting historical fantasy that will appeal to intermediate-grade students and older.

## Quest Stories

Quest stories are adventure stories with a search motif. The quest may be pursuit for a lofty purpose, such as justice or love, or for a rich reward, such as a magical power or a hidden treasure. Quest stories that are serious in tone are called *high fantasy.* Many of these novels are set in medieval times and are reminiscent of the search for the holy grail. In these high fantasies, an imaginary otherworld fully portrays the society, its history, family trees, geographic location, population, religion, customs, and traditions. The conflict in these tales usually centers on the struggle between good and evil. Often, characters are drawn from myth and legend. The protagonist is engaged in a struggle against external forces of evil and internal temptations of weakness. Thus, the quest usually represents a journey of self-discovery and personal growth for the protagonist, in addition to the search for the reward. *The Hobbit,* written by J. R. R. Tolkien in 1937, is one of the first of these high fantasies; it retains a cult of followers even today. Because of the greater complexity of these novels, their allure is for children in fifth grade and higher, including adults, of course. Good examples are C. S. Lewis's Narnia series starting with *The Lion, the Witch, and the Wardrobe,* Lloyd Alexander's Prydain series starting with *The Book of Three,* and Susan Cooper's Arthurian quest series starting with *Over Sea, under Stone.*

## Science Fiction and Science Fantasy

Science fiction is a form of imaginative literature that provides a picture of something that could happen based on real scientific facts and principles. Therefore, story elements in science fiction must have the appearance of scientific plausibility or technical possibility. Hypotheses about the future of humankind and the universe presented in science fiction appear plausible and possible to the reader because settings and events are built on extensions of known technologies and scientific concepts.

In novels of science fiction, such topics as mind control, genetic engineering, space technologies and travel, visitors from outer space, and future political and social systems all seem possible to the readers. These novels especially fascinate many young people because they feature characters who must learn to adjust to change and to become new people, two aspects of living that adolescents also experience. In addition, science fiction stories may portray the world, or one very much like it, that young people will one day inhabit; for this reason, science fiction has sometimes been called *futuristic fiction.*

Science fiction is a type of fiction that you will want to know about because of its growing popularity among children and adolescents. If you are reluctant to read science fiction or have never read it, you may want to start with some books by William Sleator (*Interstellar Pig; The Duplicate*), H. M. Hoover (*Children of Morrow; This Time of Darkness*), or John Christopher (*The White Mountains*).

The distinction between science fiction and science fantasy is not clearly defined or universally accepted. *Science fantasy* is a popularized type of science fiction in which a scientific explanation, though not necessarily plausible, is offered for imaginative leaps into the unknown. Science fantasy presents a world that often mixes elements of mythology and traditional fantasy with scientific or technological concepts, resulting in a setting that has some scientific basis but never has existed or never could exist. A worthy example is *Collidescope* by Grace Chetwin. These novels, which usually appear in series, appeal to adolescents and young adults and, like many series, are sometimes formulaic and of mixed quality.

The *science fantasy gamebook* is a trend in science fantasy that appeals to a wide age range of young people, particularly boys, from age 8 to upper teen years. Gamebooks involve fantasies developed in numbered segments so that the reader may choose from alternatives in determining the outcome of the story. These science fantasies, book adaptations of the computer games programmed for participation and decision making, usually contain violent scenes and characters. Marshall (1988) points out that because of the violent nature of these gamebooks, some adults tend to be concerned, whereas others "see the popularity of the books as a change from the well-documented findings that interest in reading declines fast, in teenage boys" (p. 44). For example, see *Talisman of Death* by Steve Jackson and Ian Livingstone.

Modern fantasy has appeal for persons with nonliteral minds, for people who go beyond the letter of a story to its spirit. Children, with their lively imaginations, are especially open to reading fantasies. The many types and topics within this genre—animal fantasies, little people stories, tales of personified toys, mystery fantasies, stories of unusual people and situations, quest tales, science fiction, and so on—offer children a breadth of inspiring and delightful entertainment. Since the level of conceptual difficulty varies considerably in this genre, modern fantasy offers many excellent stories for children, from the youngest to the oldest.

## R E F E R E N C E S

Elleman, B. (1987). Current trends in literature for children. *Library Trends, 35*(3): 413–426.

Fitch, S. (1998). Ladder to the sky. In J. Prelutsky (Ed.), *Imagine that!* Illustrated by Kevin Hawkes. New York: Knopf.

Marshall, M. R. (1988). *An introduction to the world of children's books* (2nd ed.). Brookfield, VT: Gower.

## N O T A B L E　A U T H O R S　O F　M O D E R N　F A N T A S Y

**Lloyd Alexander,** author of high fantasy based on Welsh mythology, noted for the Prydain series with *The Book of Three* and four other titles.

**Hans Christian Andersen,** nineteenth-century Dane, father of modern folktales. Author of such literary folktales as *The Ugly Duckling* and *The Little Mermaid.*

**Natalie Babbitt,** author of *Tuck Everlasting,* a book about immortality.

**John Bellairs,** author of mysteries containing supernatural elements. The *House with a Clock in Its Walls* is the first book of a trilogy.

**John Christopher,** British science fiction author who created the Tripods series set in the twenty-first century. *The White Mountains; City of Gold and Lead.*

**Susan Cooper,** author of high fantasies based on Arthurian legends. *Over Sea, under Stone* is the first in a five-book series.

**Roald Dahl,** British author of many popular fantasies known for humor and exaggerated characters. *James and the Giant Peach; Charlie and the Chocolate Factory.*

**Peter Dickinson,** British author of modern fantasies including science fiction novels. *Eva; Heartsease.*

**Mary Downing Hahn,** author of popular mystery novels. *Wait Till Helen Comes: A Ghost Story; The Doll in the Garden: A Ghost Story.*

**Virginia Hamilton,** African-American author of stories with supernatural elements. *Sweet Whispers, Brother Rush; Justice and Her Brothers.*

**Brian Jacques,** author of the Redwall Abbey animal fantasy series. *The Bellmaker; Mossflower.*

**Dick King-Smith,** British author of animal fantasies. *Pigs Might Fly; Babe: The Gallant Pig.*

**Robert Lawson,** author of animal fantasies and biographical fiction. *Rabbit Hill; Ben and Me.*

**Madeleine L'Engle,** noted for a popular science fiction milestone book, *A Wrinkle in Time,* and its sequels.

**C. S. Lewis,** British creator of the Chronicles of Narnia, a series of adventure quest stories. *The Lion, the Witch, and the Wardrobe.*

**Lois Lowry,** winner of the 1994 Newbery Medal for *The Giver,* a popular work of science fiction.

**Anne McCaffrey,** science fiction author who writes of Menolly, a young woman with special musical talents, in *Dragonsong.*

**Robin McKinley,** author of quest tales with a female protagonist and a mythical setting. *The Blue Sword; The Hero and the Crown.*

**A. A. Milne,** British author of the whimsical classic *Winnie-the-Pooh.*

**Mary Norton,** British author of *The Borrowers,* a series of little people stories.

**Philip Pullman,** British creator of *His Dark Materials* fantasies, a trilogy comprised of *The Golden Compass, The Subtle Knife,* and *The Amber Spyglass.*

**J. K. Rowling,** British author of the popular, best-selling series about Harry Potter, a child wizard. *Harry Potter and the Sorcerer's Stone.*

**William Sleator,** author of science fiction novels. *Interstellar Pig; The Duplicate.*

**Sylvia Waugh,** British author of the Mennyms series about a family of life-sized rag dolls. *The Mennyms Alive.*

**E. B. White,** author of the classic animal fantasy *Charlotte's Web.*

**Betty Ren Wright,** author of popular mystery novels. *The Dollhouse Murders; The Ghost Witch.*

## RECOMMENDED MODERN FANTASY BOOKS

*Ages refer to approximate interest levels*
*YA = young adult readers.*

### Modern Folktales

Andersen, Hans Christian. *The Emperor's New Clothes.* Illustrated by Angela Barrett. Translated by Naomi Lewis. Candlewick, 1997. Ages 7–9.

———. *The Snow Queen.* Illustrated by Susan Jeffers. Dial, 1982. Ages 8–10.

———. *Thumbelina.* Illustrated by Lisbeth Zwerger. Translated by Anthea Bell. Picture Book Studio, 1985. Ages 6–9.

———. *The Ugly Duckling.* Illustrated by Jerry Pinkney. Morrow, 1989. Ages 6–9.

Brooke, William J. *Teller of Tales.* Illustrated by Eric Beddows. HarperCollins, 1994. Ages 10–YA.

———. *A Telling of the Tales: Five Stories.* Illustrated by Richard Egielski. Harper, 1991. Ages 10–YA.

Fleishman, Sid. *McBroom and the Beanstalk.* Illustrated by Walter Lorraine. Little, Brown, 1978. Ages 6–8. Others in the McBroom series: *McBroom Tells a Lie; McBroom and the Great Race; McBroom's Ghost; McBroom's Zoo; McBroom's Ear; McBroom and the Big Wind; McBroom and the Big Almanac.*

French, Fiona. *Snow White in New York.* Oxford, 1986. Ages 7–10.

Hamilton, Virginia. *The Magical Adventures of Pretty Pearl.* Harper, 1983. Ages 10–YA.

Isaacs, Anne. *Swamp Angel.* Illustrated by Paul Zelinsky. Dutton, 1994. Ages 7–10.

Levine, Gail Carson. *Ella Enchanted.* HarperCollins, 1997. Ages 10–13.

McKinley, Robin. *Beauty: A Retelling of the Beauty and the Beast.* Harper, 1978. Ages 10–YA.

———. *Rose Daughter.* Greenwillow, 1997. Ages 11–YA.

———. *Spindle's End.* Putnam, 2000. Ages 12–YA.

Napoli, Donna Jo. *Crazy Jack.* Delacorte, 1999. Ages 11–YA.

———. *Zel.* Dutton, 1996. Ages 13–YA.

Nolen, Jerdine. *Harvey Potter's Balloon Farm.* Illustrated by Mark Buehner. Lothrop, 1994. Ages 5–9.

Osborne, Mary Pope. *Kate and the Beanstalk.* Illustrated by Giselle Potter. Schwartz/Atheneum, 2000. Ages 5–8.

Pyle, Howard. *Bearskin.* Illustrated by Trina Schart Hyman. Morrow, 1997. Ages 7–9.

Sandburg, Carl. *The Huckabuck Family: And How They Raised Popcorn in Nebraska and Quit and Came Back.* Illustrated by David Small. Farrar, 1999. Ages 5–8.

Scieszka, Jon. *The True Story of the 3 Little Pigs by A. Wolf.* Illustrated by Lane Smith. Viking, 1989. Ages 7–12.

Stanley, Diane. *Rumpelstiltskin's Daughter.* Morrow, 1997. Ages 5–9.

Thurber, James. *The Great Quillow.* Harcourt, 1994. Ages 8–10.

Willard, Nancy. *Beauty and the Beast.* Illustrated by Barry Moser. Harcourt, 1992. Ages 8–11.

Williams, Jay. *The Practical Princess and Other Liberating Fairy Tales.* Parents' Magazine, 1978. Ages 6–9.

Yolen, Jane. *Sleeping Ugly.* Illustrated by Diane Stanley. Coward, 1981. Ages 7–10.

## Animal Fantasies

Adams, Richard. *Watership Down.* Macmillan, 1974. Ages 12–YA.

Arkin, Alan. *Cassie Loves Beethoven.* Hyperion, 2000. Ages 9–12. Humorous.

———. *The Lemming Condition.* Illustrated by Joan Sandin. Harper, 1976. Ages 10–YA.

Atwater, Richard, and Florence Atwater. *Mr. Popper's Penguins.* Illustrated by Robert Lawson. Little, 1938. Ages 8–11.

Avi. *Poppy.* Illustrated by Brian Floca. Orchard, 1995. Ages 8–11.

Cleary, Beverly. *The Mouse and the Motorcycle.* Illustrated by Louis Darling. Morrow, 1965. Ages 7–11.

———. *Ralph S. Mouse.* Illustrated by Paul O. Zelinsky. Morrow, 1982. Ages 7–11.

———. *Runaway Ralph.* Illustrated by Louis Darling. Morrow, 1970. Ages 7–11.

Clement-Davies, David. *Fire Bringer.* Dutton, 2000. Ages 12–YA.

Dickinson, Peter. *Chuck and Danielle.* Delacorte, 1996. Ages 8–11.

Grahame, Kenneth. *The Wind in the Willows.* Illustrated by E. H. Shepard. Scribner's, 1908. Ages 8–12.

Howe, Deborah, and James Howe. *Bunnicula: A Rabbit-Tale of Mystery.* Illustrated by Alan Daniel. Atheneum, 1979. Ages 8–11.

Howe, James. *Howliday Inn.* Atheneum, 1982. Ages 8–11.

Jacques, Brian. *Lord Brocktree.* (Redwall series.) Philomel, 2000. Ages 9–12.

———. *Redwall.* Illustrated by Gary Chalk. Philomel, 1987. Ages 11–YA. Others in the Redwall series are *Mossflower, Mattimeo, Mariel of Redwall, Salamandastron, The Bellmaker.*

King-Smith, Dick. *Ace: The Very Important Pig.* Illustrated by Lynette Hemmant. Crown, 1990. Ages 7–11.

———. *Babe: The Gallant Pig.* Illustrated by Mary Rayner. Crown, 1985. Ages 7–11.

———. *Harriet's Hare.* Crown, 1995. Ages 7–9.

———. *Pigs Might Fly.* Illustrated by Mary Rayner. Viking, 1982. Ages 8–11.

Kipling, Rudyard. *Just So Stories.* Doubleday, 1902. Ages 6–10.

Labatt, Mary. *Aliens in Woodford.* Kids Can Press, 2000. Ages 7–10. Humorous.

Lawson, Robert. *Rabbit Hill.* Viking, 1944. Ages 8–11.

Lisle, Janet Taylor. *Forest.* Watts, 1993. Ages 9–12.

Marshall, James. *Rats on the Range and Other Stories.* Dial, 1993. Ages 5–8.

———. *Rats on the Roof and Other Stories.* Dial, 1991. Ages 6–9.

Michels, Tilde. *Rabbit Spring.* Harcourt, 1988. Ages 7–10.

Pinkwater, Daniel. *Mush, A Dog from Space.* Simon & Schuster, 1995. Ages 7–9.

Seidler, Tor. *Mean Margaret.* Illustrated by Jon Agee. HarperCollins, 1997. Ages 8–11.

Selden, George. *The Cricket in Times Square.* Illustrated by Garth Williams. Farrar, 1960. Ages 8–11.

Steig, William. *Abel's Island.* Farrar, 1976. Ages 8–11.

———. *Dominic.* Farrar, 1972. Ages 8–11.

White, E. B. *Charlotte's Web.* Illustrated by Garth Williams. Harper, 1952. Ages 8–11.

———. *Stuart Little.* Illustrated by Garth Williams. Harper, 1945. Ages 8–11.

## Personified Toys and Objects

Bailey, Carolyn. *Miss Hickory.* Illustrated by Ruth Gannett. Viking, 1968. Ages 8–11.

Bond, Michael. *A Bear Called Paddington.* Illustrated by Peggy Fortnum. Houghton, 1960. Ages 7–10.

Cassedy, Sylvia. *Behind the Attic Wall.* Crowell, 1983. Ages 10–13.

Collodi, Carlo (pseudonym of Carlo Lorenzini). *The Adventures of Pinocchio.* Illustrated by Attilio Mussino. Translated by Carol Della Chiesa. Macmillan, 1881. Ages 8–10.

Fleming, Ian. *Chitty-Chitty-Bang-Bang: The Magical Car.* Illustrated by John Burningham. Random, 1964. Ages 8–11.

Mahy, Margaret. *The Five Sisters.* Illustrated by Patricia MacCarthy. Viking, 1997. Ages 7–10.

Martin, Ann M., and Laura Godwin. *The Doll People.* Illustrated by Brian Selznick. Hyperion, 2000. Ages 8–12.

Milne, A. A. *The House at Pooh Corner.* Illustrated by Ernest Shepard. Dutton, 1928. Ages 6–9.

————. *Winnie-the-Pooh.* Illustrated by Ernest Shepard. Dutton, 1926. Ages 6–9.

Waugh, Sylvia. *The Mennyms.* Morrow, 1994. Ages 8–12.

————. *Mennyms in the Wilderness.* Greenwillow, 1995. Ages 8–11.

Winthrop, Elizabeth. *The Battle for the Castle.* Holiday, 1993. Ages 8–12.

————. *The Castle in the Attic.* Holiday, 1985. Ages 8–12.

## Unusual Characters and Strange Situations

Ahlberg, Allan. *The Giant Baby.* Illustrated by Fritz Wegner. Viking, 1995. Ages 7–11.

Aiken, Joan. *Cold Shoulder Road.* Delacorte, 1996. Ages 10–13.

————. *Is Underground.* Delacorte, 1993. Ages 10–13.

Babbitt, Natalie. *The Search for Delicious.* Farrar, 1969. Ages 9–12.

————. *Tuck Everlasting.* Farrar, 1975. Ages 10–YA.

Barrie, Sir James. *Peter Pan.* Illustrated by Nora Unwin. Scribner's, 1911. Ages 8–11.

Baum, L. Frank. *The Wonderful Wizard of Oz.* Illustrated by Lisbeth Zwerger. North-South, 1996 (1900). Ages 8–11.

Billingsley, Franny. *The Folk Keeper.* Simon & Schuster, 1999. Ages 10–13.

————. *Well Wished.* Simon & Schuster, 1997. Ages 10–12.

Boston, Lucy M. *The Children of Green Knowe.* Illustrated by Peter Boston. Harcourt, 1955. Ages 8–11. The first of a series of fantasies set in an English manor house. Others include *Enemy at Green Knowe, River at Green Knowe, Stranger at Green Knowe,* and *Treasure of Green Knowe.*

Butterworth, Oliver. *The Enormous Egg.* Illustrated by Louis Darling. Little, Brown, 1956. Ages 8–11.

Carroll, Lewis (pseud. for Charles Lutwidge Dodgson). *Alice's Adventures in Wonderland* and *Through the Looking Glass.* First published in 1865. A recent edition is illustrated by Anthony Browne. Knopf, 1988. Ages 9–13.

Dahl, Roald. *Charlie and the Chocolate Factory.* Illustrated by Joseph Schindelman. Knopf, 1964. Ages 8–11.

————. *James and the Giant Peach.* Illustrated by Nancy E. Burkert. Knopf, 1961. Ages 8–11.

————. *Matilda.* Illustrated by Quentin Blake. Viking, 1988. Ages 8–11.

Farmer, Nancy. *The Ear, the Eye and the Arm.* Orchard, 1994. Ages 11–14. Humorous.

Heide, Florence Parry. *The Shrinking of Treehorn.* Illustrated by Edward Gorey. Holiday, 1971. Ages 7–10. See also *Treehorn Times Three* (Dell, 1992).

Jones, Diana Wynne. *Castle in the Air.* Greenwillow, 1991. Ages 11–YA.

Juster, Norton. *The Phantom Tollbooth.* Illustrated by Jules Feiffer. Random, 1961. Ages 10–13.

Lindgren, Astrid. *Pippi Longstocking.* Translated by Florence Lamborn. Viking, 1950. Ages 8–11.

Mayne, William. *Earthfasts.* Dutton, 1967. Ages 12–YA.

McGraw, Eloise. *The Moorchild.* Simon & Schuster, 1996. Ages 9–12.

Merrill, Jean. *The Pushcart War.* Illustrated by Ronni Solbert. Harper, 1964. Ages 10–YA.

Nöstlinger, Christine. *Konrad.* Watts, 1977. Ages 8–11.

Pullman, Philip. *I Was a Rat!* Illustrated by Kevin Hawkes. Knopf, 2000. Ages 8–12.

Travers, P. L. *Mary Poppins.* Illustrated by Mary Shepard. Harcourt, 1934. Ages 9–12.

## Worlds of Little People

Dahl, Roald. *The Minpins.* Illustrated by Patrick Benson. Viking, 1991. Ages 5–8.

Kendall, Carol. *The Firelings.* Atheneum, 1982. Ages 9–12.

————. *The Gammage Cup.* Illustrated by Erik Blegvad. Harcourt, 1959. Ages 8–12.

————. *The Whisper of Glocken.* Harcourt, 1965. Ages 8–12.

Norton, Mary. *The Borrowers.* Illustrated by Beth and Joe Krush. Harcourt, 1953. Ages 8–11. This is the first of a series of little people fantasies, including *The Borrowers Afield, The Borrowers Afloat, The Borrowers Aloft,* and *The Borrowers Avenged.*

Swift, Jonathan. *Gulliver in Lilliput.* Retold by Margaret Hodges. Illustrated by Kimberly Bulcken Root. Holiday, 1995. Ages 8–11. Nine-chapter, illustrated retelling.

## Supernatural Events and Mystery Fantasy

Alcock, Vivien. *Singer to the Sea God.* Delacorte, 1993. Ages 12–YA.

Almond, David. *Skellig.* Delacorte, 1999. Ages 10–YA.

Babbitt, Natalie. *The Devil's Other Storybook.* Farrar, 1987. Ages 8–11.

———. *Kneeknock Rise.* Farrar, 1970. Ages 9–12.

Bauer, Marion Dane. *A Taste of Smoke.* Houghton, 1993. Ages 8–12.

Bellairs, John. *The Curse of the Blue Figurine.* Dial, 1983. Ages 10–YA.

Bond, Nancy. *Another Shore.* McElderry, 1988. Ages 11–YA.

Brittain, Bill. *Dr. Dredd's Wagon of Wonders.* Illustrated by Andrew Glass. Harper, 1987. Ages 8–12.

———. *The Wish Giver.* Illustrated by Andrew Glass. Harper, 1983. Ages 9–12.

Charbonneau, Eileen. *The Ghosts of Stony Clove.* Orchard, 1988. Ages 10–YA.

Conrad, Pam. *Stonewords: A Ghost Story.* Harper, 1990. Ages 8–12.

Cooper, Susan. *The Boggart.* McElderry, 1993. Ages 9–12.

Coville, Bruce. *The Skull of Truth.* Illustrated by Gary A. Lippincott. Harcourt, 1997. Ages 9–12.

DeFelice, Cynthia. *The Ghost of Fossil Glen.* Farrar, 1998. Ages 9–12.

Duncan, Lois. *Locked in Time.* Little, Brown, 1985. Ages 9–12.

———. *Third Eye.* Little, Brown, 1984. Ages 9–12.

Fleischman, Sid. *The Midnight Horse.* Illustrated by Peter Sís. Greenwillow, 1990. Ages 8–11.

Garfield, Leon. *The Empty Sleeve.* Delacorte, 1988. Ages 10–YA.

Hahn, Mary Downing. *The Doll in the Garden: A Ghost Story.* Clarion, 1989. Ages 9–12.

———. *Wait Till Helen Comes: A Ghost Story.* Clarion, 1986. Ages 9–13.

Hamilton, Virginia. *Sweet Whispers, Brother Rush.* Philomel, 1982. Ages 11–YA.

Ibbotson, Eva. *Island of the Aunts.* Illustrated by Kevin Hawkes. Dutton, 2000. Ages 9–12.

Jones, Diana Wynne. *Dark Lord of Derkholm.* Greenwillow, 1998. (Also its sequel, *Year of the Griffin.* Greenwillow, 2000.) Ages 12–YA.

Key, Alexander. *Escape to Witch Mountain.* Illustrated by Leon B. Wisdom, Jr. Westminster, 1968. Ages 10–12.

Lively, Penelope. *The Ghost of Thomas Kempe.* Illustrated by Anthony Maitland. Dutton, 1973. Ages 9–12.

Mahy, Margaret. *Dangerous Spaces.* Viking, 1991. Ages 8–12.

———. *Memory.* McElderry, 1988. Ages 11–YA.

McBratney, Sam. *The Ghosts of Hungryhouse Lane.* Holt, 1989. Ages 7–10.

McKissack, Patricia C. *The Dark-Thirty: Southern Tales of the Supernatural.* Illustrated by Brian Pinkney. Knopf, 1992. Ages 9–12.

Nixon, Joan Lowery. *Whispers from the Dead.* Delacorte, 1989. Ages 10–YA.

Pearce, Philippa. *Tom's Midnight Garden.* Lippincott, 1959. Ages 9–12.

Pierce, Meredith Ann. *The Darkangel.* Little, Brown, 1982. Ages 11–14. Others in Darkangel trilogy: *A Gathering of Gargoyles* and *The Pearl of the Soul of the World.*

Price, Susan. *The Ghost Drum: A Cat's Tale.* Farrar, 1987. Ages 8–12.

———. *Ghost Song.* Farrar, 1992. Ages 9–12.

Pullman, Philip. *Clockwork.* Illustrated by Leonid Gore. Scholastic, 1998. Ages 9–13.

Sherman, Josepha. *Child of Faerie, Child of Earth.* Walker, 1992. Ages 11–YA.

Smith, Sherwood. *Wren's Quest.* Harcourt, 1993. Ages 10–YA.

Westall, Robert. *Ghost Abbey.* Scholastic, 1989. Ages 10–YA.

Wright, Betty Ren. *The Dollhouse Murders.* Holiday, 1983. Ages 9–12.

———. *The Ghost Witch.* Illustrated by Ellen Eagle. Holiday, 1993. Ages 8–11.

Wrightson, Patricia. *The Nargun and the Stars.* Atheneum, 1974. Ages 10–13.

## Historical Fantasy

Alphin, Elaine M. *The Ghost Cadet.* Holt, 1991. Ages 9–12.

Bellairs, John. *The Ghost in the Mirrors.* Dial, 1993. Ages 10–14.

Branford, Henrietta. *Fire, Bed, and Bone.* Candlewick, 1998. Ages 10–13. Set in late fourteenth-century England; told from a hunting hound's point of view.

Chetwin, Grace. *Friends in Time.* Bradbury, 1992. Ages 9–12.

Cooney, Caroline B. *Both Sides of Time.* Delacorte, 1995. Ages 12–YA.

Cooper, Susan. *King of Shadows.* Simon & Schuster, 1999. Ages 10–13.

Cresswell, Helen. *Moondial.* Macmillan, 1987. Ages 10–YA.

Dickinson, Peter. *A Bone from a Dry Sea.* Delacorte, 1993. Ages 12–YA.

Lawson, Robert. *Ben and Me.* Little, 1939. Ages 9–12.

Lunn, Janet. *The Root Cellar.* Scribner's, 1983. Ages 10–13.

McKay, Hillary. *The Amber Cat.* Simon & Schuster, 1997. Ages 9–12.

Park, Ruth. *Playing Beatie Bow.* Atheneum, 1982. Ages 10–YA.

Slepian, Jan. *Back to Before.* Philomel, 1993. Ages 10–13.

Voigt, Cynthia. *Building Blocks.* Atheneum, 1984. Ages 9–11.

Wiseman, David. *Jeremy Visick.* Houghton, 1981. Ages 10–13.

Yolen, Jane. *The Devil's Arithmetic.* Viking, 1988. Ages 10–13.

## Quest Stories

Alexander, Lloyd. *The Book of Three.* Holt, 1964. Ages 10–YA. The first of the Prydain Chronicles, a series of five quest fantasies, including *The Black Cauldron, The Castle of Llyr, The High King,* and *Taran Wanderer.*

———. *The Remarkable Journey of Prince Jen.* Dutton, 1991. Ages 10–YA.

Cooper, Susan. *Over Sea, under Stone.* Illustrated by Margery Gill. Harcourt, 1965. Ages 10–YA. This is the first of a five-book Arthurian quest series, including *The Dark Is Rising, Greenwitch, The Grey King,* and *Silver on the Tree.*

Ibbotson, Eva. *The Secret of Platform 13.* Dutton, 1998. Ages 9–13.

———. *Which Witch?* Dutton, 1999. Ages 10–14.

Kelleher, Victor. *The Red King.* Dial, 1990. Ages 12–YA.

Le Guin, Ursula K. *A Wizard of Earthsea.* Parnassus, 1968. Ages 11–YA. Other books in this series are *The Farthest Shore, The Tombs of Atuan,* and *Tehanu: The Last Book of Earthsea.*

Lewis, Clive Staples. *The Lion, the Witch, and the Wardrobe.* Illustrated by Pauline Baynes. Macmillan, 1950. Ages 9–12. The first in a series of quest fantasies, including *The Horse and His Boy, The Last Battle, The Magician's Nephew, Prince Caspian, The Silver Chair,* and *The Voyage of the Dawn Treader.*

McGowen, Tom. *The Magical Fellowship.* Dutton, 1991. Ages 9–13.

———. *The Magician's Apprentice.* Dutton, 1987. Ages 9–13.

McKinley, Robin. *The Blue Sword.* Greenwillow, 1982. Ages 11–YA.

———. *The Hero and the Crown.* Greenwillow, 1984. Ages 11–YA.

Paterson, Katherine. *Parzival: The Quest of the Grail Knight.* Lodestar, 1998. Ages 10–YA.

Pullman, Philip. *The Golden Compass.* Knopf, 1996. Ages 12–YA. First of His Dark Materials trilogy. Also *The Subtle Knife,* Knopf, 1998, and *The Amber Spyglass,* Knopf, 1999.

Rowling, J. K. *Harry Potter and the Sorcerer's Stone.* Scholastic, 1998. Ages 9–13. The first in a series of quest fantasies, including *Harry Potter and the Chamber of Secrets,* 1999; *Harry Potter and the Prisoner of Azkabar,* 1999; and *Harry Potter and the Goblet of Fire,* 2000.

Sutcliff, Rosemary. *The Light Beyond the Forest.* Dutton, 1980. Ages 12–YA.

———. *The Road to Camlaan: The Death of King Arthur.* Dutton, 1982. Ages 12–YA.

Tolkien, J. R. R. *The Hobbit.* Houghton, 1938. Ages 10–YA.

Turner, Megan Whelan. *The Thief.* Greenwillow, 1996. Ages 11–YA.

Wrede, Patricia C. *Calling on Dragons.* Harcourt, 1993. Ages 9–12.

———. *Dealing with Dragons.* Harcourt, 1990. Ages 9–12.

Yolen, Jane. *Dragon's Blood.* Delacorte, 1982. Ages 10–13.

## Science Fiction and Science Fantasy

Alcock, Vivien. *The Monster Garden.* Delacorte, 1988. Ages 10–14.

Bechard, Margaret. *Star Hatchling.* Viking, 1995. Ages 9–12.

Brittain, Bill. *Shape-Changer.* HarperCollins, 1994. Ages 8–12.

Cameron, Eleanor. *The Wonderful Flight to the Mushroom Planet.* Illustrated by Robert Henneberger. Little, 1954. Ages 7–9.

Chetwin, Grace. *Collidescope.* Bradbury, 1990. Ages 11–YA.

Christopher, John. *The City of Gold and Lead.* Macmillan, 1967. Ages 11–YA.

———. *The Pool of Fire.* Macmillan, 1968. Ages 11–YA.

———. *The White Mountains.* Macmillan, 1967. Ages 11–YA.

Conly, Jane Leslie. *Racso and Rats of NIMH.* Illustrated by Leonard Lubin. Harper, 1986. Ages 9–12.

———. *R. T., Margaret, and the Rats of NIMH.* HarperCollins, 1990. Ages 9–12.

Dickinson, Peter. *Eva.* Delacorte, 1989. Ages 12–YA.

du Bois, William Pène. *The Twenty-One Balloons.* Viking, 1947. Ages 8–12.

Engdahl, Sylvia. *Enchantress from the Stars.* Atheneum, 1970. Ages 11–YA.

———. *The Far Side of Evil.* Atheneum, 1971. Ages 11–YA.

———. *This Star Shall Abide.* Atheneum, 1972. Ages 11–YA.

Hoover, H. M. *Away Is a Strange Place to Be.* Dutton, 1989. Ages 9–12.

———. *Children of Morrow.* Four Winds, 1973. Ages 11–YA.

———. *Orvis.* Viking, 1987. Ages 10–YA.

———. *The Shepherd Moon.* Viking, 1984. Ages 11–YA.

———. *This Time of Darkness.* Viking, 1980. Ages 11–YA.

Hughes, Monica. *Invitation to the Game.* Simon & Schuster, 1990. Ages 12–YA.

———. *The Keeper of the Isis Light.* Atheneum, 1984. Ages 9–YA.

Key, Alexander. *The Forgotten Door.* Westminster, 1965. Ages 10–12.

Klause, Annette Curtis. *Alien Secrets.* Delacorte, 1993. Ages 10–13.

L'Engle, Madeleine. *A Swiftly Tilting Planet.* Farrar, 1978. Ages 11–YA.

———. *A Wind in the Door.* Farrar, 1973. Ages 11–YA.

———. *A Wrinkle in Time.* Farrar, 1962. Ages 11–YA.

Lowry, Lois. *Gathering Blue.* Houghton, 2000. Ages 10–YA.

———. *The Giver.* Houghton, 1993. Ages 11–YA.

McCaffrey, Anne. *Dragonsinger.* Atheneum, 1977. Ages 11–YA.

———. *Dragonsong.* Atheneum, 1976. Ages 11–YA.

Nix, Garth. *Shade's Children.* HarperCollins, 1997. Ages 12–YA.

O'Brien, Robert C. *Mrs. Frisby and the Rats of NIMH.* Illustrated by Zena Bernstein. Atheneum, 1971. Ages 9–12. (See sequels by Conly.)

———. *Z for Zachariah.* Atheneum, 1975. Ages 11–YA.

Paton Walsh, Jill. *The Green Book.* Illustrated by Lloyd Bloom. Farrar, 1982. Ages 8–11.

Pinkwater, Daniel Manus. *Fat Men from Space.* Dodd, 1977. Ages 8–11.

Rubinstein, Gillian. *Beyond the Labyrinth.* Watts, 1990. Ages 12–YA.

———. *Galax–Arena.* Simon & Schuster, 1995. Ages 12–A.

Sleator, William. *The Boy Who Reversed Himself.* Dutton, 1986. Ages 10–YA.

———. *The Duplicate.* Dutton, 1988. Ages 11–YA.

———. *House of Stairs.* Dutton, 1974. Ages 11–YA.

———. *Interstellar Pig.* Dutton, 1984. Ages 11–YA.

Waugh, Sylvia. *Space Race.* Delacorte, 2000. Ages 9–12.

# REALISTIC FICTION

*standing in the hall against the*
*wall with my little brother, blown*
*like leaves against the wall by their*
*voices, my head like a pingpong ball*
*between the paddles of their anger:*
*I knew what it meant*
*to tremble like a leaf.*

*Cold with their wrath, I heard*
*the claws of the rain*
*pounce. Floods*
*poured through the city,*
*skies clapped over me,*
*and I was shaken, shaken*
*like a mouse*
*between their jaws.*

—RUTH WHITMAN

Children's lives are sometimes sad and harsh. Realistic stories of today openly address these situations as well as the happy and humorous situations of life. Children of all ages appreciate stories about people who seem like themselves or who are involved in familiar activities. These realistic fiction stories have appealed to children for many years and continue to do so today.

# DEFINITION AND DESCRIPTION

*Realistic fiction* refers to stories that could indeed happen to people and animals; that is, it is within the realm of possibility that such events could occur or could have occurred. The protagonists of these stories are fictitious characters created by the author, but their actions and reactions are quite like those of real people or real animals. Sometimes events in these stories are exaggerated or outlandish— hardly probable but definitely possible. These stories, too, fit under the definition of realistic fiction.

Realism in literature is a complex, multifaceted concept. Marshall (1988) considers various components of realism in literature, including factual, situational, emotional, and social. *Factual realism* is provided by the description of actual people, places, and events in a book. When this occurs, the facts need to be recorded accurately. For example, usually in historical fiction and occasionally in realistic fiction, the names and locations of actual places are included in the story, with accurate and complete descriptions. *Situational realism* is provided by a situation that is not only possible but also quite likely, often in an identifiable location with characters of an identifiable age and social class, making the whole treatment believable. The survival story, which often hinges on a life-threatening situation, is an example of a story built on situational realism. *Emotional realism* is provided by the appearance of believable feelings and relationships among characters. Rite-of-passage or growing-up stories often employ emotional realism. *Social realism* is provided by an honest portrayal of society and its conditions of the moment, including both healthy and adverse conditions. In almost all good realistic stories, several of these components of realism occur, with varying degrees of emphasis.

*Contemporary realism* is a term used to describe stories that take place in the present time and portray attitudes and mores of the present culture. Unlike realistic books of several decades ago that depicted only happy families and were never controversial, today's contemporary realism often focuses on current societal issues, such as alcoholism, racism, poverty, and homelessness. These contemporary books still tell of the happy, funny times in children's lives, but they also include the harsh, unpleasant times that are, sadly, a part of many children's lives. Child abuse and neglect, peer problems, the effects of divorce on children, drug abuse, physical and mental disabilities, disillusionment, and alienation from the mainstream of society are all topics that are included in the contemporary realistic novel.

Authors of contemporary realistic fiction set their stories in the present or recent past. But, in time, features of these stories, such as dialogue and allusions to popular culture, customs, and dress become dated and the stories are therefore no longer contemporary, though they may still be realistic. Older stories that obviously no longer describe today's world, though they may have once been contemporary realistic fiction, are now simply realistic fiction.

The *problem novel* is a contemporary realistic story in which the conflict overwhelms the plot and characterization. The problem novel is written to provide the author with a soapbox from which to lecture or as a vehicle for capitalizing on whichever societal problem is currently at the forefront. Generally, these stories lack depth, have weak character development and consist of little, if any, plot. Problem novels remind us that it is always necessary to read literature carefully to find books worthy of children's attention.

Topics for realistic fiction are drawn from all aspects of life—stories of humorous, everyday escapades of well-adjusted children in happy families and stories about animals portrayed realistically. Other common topics of realistic fiction are mysteries, adventures, romances, sports stories, and stories about children from other countries.

# EVALUATION AND SELECTION
# OF REALISTIC FICTION

The criteria for evaluating realistic fiction are the same as those for any work of fiction. Well-developed characters who manifest change as a result of significant life events, a well-structured plot with sufficient conflict and suspense to hold the reader's interest, a time and place suitable to the storyline, and a worthy theme are basic literary elements expected of any work of fiction, including works of realistic fiction.

- Some realistic novels portray adverse and discouraging social situations, such as homelessness and poverty; yet it remains important that the stories permit some cause for optimism. Children need to trust that this world can be a good place in which to live and that it can be made a better place through the efforts of individuals. Children also need to understand that problems can be overcome or ameliorated.

- Themes in realistic stories often convey moral values, such as the rewards of kindness and generosity to others. However, these moral values must spring naturally from the story, as a by-product of the story itself, not as the main reason for the story. At times, adults write books for children with the sole intent of teaching or preaching, and the story itself is nothing more than a thin disguise for a heavy-handed moral lesson. This may have been acceptable in the past, but today a good story must be the *raison d'être* of a children's book. The moral must not overwhelm the story but may be its logical outcome.

- A novel of realistic fiction must be believable, even though all aspects may not be probable. Some adults and children have a tendency to criticize a story when the events are not probable. An example is *Homecoming* by Cynthia Voigt, in which four children manage to travel hundreds of miles alone with almost no money to reach their grandmother's house. Admittedly, this storyline may be improbable, yet it is certainly possible. Other aspects of *Homecoming* are more ordinarily realistic; for example, the characters are well developed and the relationships among the characters seem quite ordinary. Sometimes, an author goes closer to the edge of the believable range to produce a more exciting, suspense-filled story. In fiction, the story is of paramount importance, and the sacrifice of some probability for a good story does not usually interfere with the pleasure children gain from a book. It may instead help to create interest in the story.

- Much of the controversy involving children's books centers on topics that are often found in realistic fiction novels, such as premarital sex, pregnancy, homosexuality, and the use of profanity. Many of these controversial books fall within the types of realism labeled "Moral Choices" and "Romance and Sexuality" in the recommended reading list at the end of this chapter. Chapter 11 provides a full discussion of issues surrounding controversial books and censorship.

- An aspect of writing style that students greatly appreciate is humor. Although humor may be found in stories of any genre, it is more often found in realistic fiction. Humorous stories feature characters caught up in silly situations or involved in funny escapades. Children often are amused by the incongruities presented in these predicament stories. Other humorous stories draw on word play for their humor. *Bagthorpes Unlimited* by Helen Cresswell is a good example of a humorous story. In the list of recommended books at the end of this chapter, humorous books are indicated.

# EXCELLENT REALISTIC FICTION TO READ ALOUD

*(Books for each level vary in difficulty and should be selected with the students' literary backgrounds in mind.)*

### PRIMARY LEVEL                AGES 5–8

Cameron, Ann. *More Stories Julian Tells.* Illustrated by Ann Strugnell. Knopf, 1986.
Cleary, Beverly. *Ramona Quimby, Age 8.* Illustrated by Alan Tiegreen. Morrow, 1981. Humorous.
Fleming, Virginia. *Be Good to Eddie Lee.* Illustrated by Floyd Cooper. Philomel, 1993.
Gardiner, John Reynolds. *Stone Fox.* Illustrated by Marcia Sewall. Crowell, 1980.
Henry, Marguerite. *Misty of Chincoteague.* Illustrated by Wesley Dennis. Rand, 1947.
Lord, Bette Bao. *In the Year of the Boar and Jackie Robinson.* Illustrated by Marc Simont. Harper, 1984.
Lowry, Lois. *See You Around, Sam!* Illustrated by Diane de Groat. Houghton, 1996.

### INTERMEDIATE LEVEL       AGES 8–11

DiCamillo, Kate. *Because of Winn-Dixie.* Candlewick, 2000.
Gantos, Jack. *Joey Pigza Swallowed the Key.* Farrar, 1998.
Horvath, Polly. *Trolls.* Farrar, 1999.
Lowry, Lois. *Anastasia at Your Service.* Illustrated by Diane de Groat. Houghton, 1982. Humorous.
McKay, Hillary. *Dog Friday.* Simon & Schuster, 1995.
Myers, Walter Dean. *Scorpions.* Harper, 1988.
Naidoo, Beverley. *Journey to Jo'burg: A South African Story.* Illustrated by Eric Velasquez. Lippincott, 1986.
Naylor, Phyllis Reynolds. *Shiloh.* Atheneum, 1991.
Park, Barbara. *Skinnybones.* Knopf, 1982. Humorous.
Sachar, Louis. *Holes.* Farrar, 1998.
Slote, Alfred. *The Trading Game.* Lippincott, 1990.
Spinelli, Jerry. *Wringer.* HarperCollins, 1997.
Yumoto, Kazumi. *The Friends.* Translated by Cathy Hirano. Farrar, 1996.

### ADVANCED LEVEL              AGES 11–14

Avi. *Nothing but the Truth.* Orchard, 1991.
Creech, Sharon. *Walk Two Moons.* HarperCollins, 1994.
Crew, Gary. *Angel's Gate.* Simon & Schuster, 1995.
Doherty, Berlie. *Dear Nobody.* Orchard, 1992.
Fine, Anne. *The Tulip Touch.* Little, Brown, 1997.
Fogelin, Adrian. *Crossing Jordan.* Peachtree, 2000.
George, Jean Craighead. *Julie.* HarperCollins, 1994.
Koertge, Ron. *The Harmony Arms.* Little, 1992. Humorous.
Konigsburg, E. L. *Silent to the Bone.* Simon & Schuster, 2000.
Myers, Walter Dean. *Monster.* HarperCollins, 1999. TV script.
Paulsen, Gary. *Hatchet.* Bradbury, 1987.
Rawls, Wilson. *Summer of the Monkeys.* Doubleday, 1976. Humorous.
Staples, Suzanne Fisher. *Shabanu: Daughter of the Wind.* Knopf, 1989.
White, Ruth. *Belle Prater's Boy.* Farrar, 1996.

Selection of realistic fiction for classroom and library collections and for read-alouds should be balanced among the different types of realistic stories. A steady diet of humorous read-alouds does not offer the richness of experience to children that they deserve, nor does it provide for the varied reading interests of a group of children. It is extremely important to read aloud some books with females as main characters, some with males as main characters, some with members of minorities as main characters. The Edgar Allan Poe Award for Juvenile Mystery Novels can be helpful to you in selecting good mysteries—the most popular story type of all for intermediate-grade students. This award was established in 1961 by the Mystery Writers of America and is awarded annually in order to honor U.S. authors of mysteries for children. The list of winners is included in Appendix A.

Realistic fiction stories are easy for children to relate to and enjoy. Children can often see their own lives, or lives much like their own, in these stories. Intermediate-grade children report on reading interest surveys that realistic fiction is their favorite genre. Of course, some children may prefer other categories, but realistic fiction does hold high appeal for many children at all grade levels.

## HISTORICAL OVERVIEW OF REALISTIC FICTION

The earliest realistic stories were didactic ones that were intended to teach morality and manners to young readers. The characters of the children's stories of the 1700s were usually wooden, lifeless boys and girls whose lives were spent in good works; however, in England during this period, two significant events affecting the future of children's literature occurred. *Robinson Crusoe* by Daniel Defoe was published in 1719 for adults but became a popular book among children. This forerunner of the adventure-survival story for children recounts the tale of a shipwrecked sailor who struggles against the forces of nature for survival on an island. Then in 1744, John Newbery began to publish, expressly for a child audience, books of realistic fiction intended to entertain as well as to educate. These two events laid the groundwork for establishing children's literature as a separate branch of literature. Milestones in the development of realistic fiction are highlighted on page 136.

The first type of realistic fiction for children that avoided the heavy didactic persuasion was the adventure story. Imitators of *Robinson Crusoe* were many, including the very popular *Swiss Family Robinson* by Johann Wyss of Switzerland in 1812. Later adventure stories of renown from England were *Treasure Island* (1883) and *Kidnapped* (1886) by Robert Louis Stevenson; and from the United States, *The Adventures of Tom Sawyer* (1876) and *The Adventures of Huckleberry Finn* (1884) by Mark Twain (pseudonym of Samuel Clemens). Clemens, through the addition of sharp humor and characters who were in many ways less than admirable but nonetheless appealing, took an important step toward increased realism in stories.

Realistic family stories also came on the scene during the 1800s with *Little Women* (1868) by Louisa May Alcott and *Five Little Peppers and How They Grew* (1880), the first of a series of family stories by Harriet M. Lothrop (pseudonym of Margaret Sydney). The family story remains a favorite in the twentieth century, with early memorable books such as *Rebecca of Sunnybrook Farm* (1903) by Kate Douglas Wiggins, the series *Anne of Green Gables* (1908) by Canadian Lucy Maud Montgomery, and *The Secret Garden* (1910) by Frances Hodgson Burnett. Since Anne of *Anne of Green Gables* and Mary of

# M I L E S T O N E S

*in the Development of* REALISTIC FICTION

| DATE | EVENT | SIGNIFICANCE |
|------|-------|--------------|
| 1719 | *Robinson Crusoe* by Daniel Defoe (England) | Early survival/adventure on a desert island; many imitators |
| 1812 | *Swiss Family Robinson* by Johann Wyss (Switzerland) | Most successful imitation of *Robinson Crusoe* |
| 1865 | *Hans Brinker, or The Silver Skates* by Mary Mapes Dodge (United States) | An early story set in another land (Holland) |
| 1868 | *Little Women* by Louisa May Alcott (United States) | An early family story of great popularity |
| 1876 | *The Adventures of Tom Sawyer* by Mark Twain (United States) | Classic adventure story set along the Mississippi |
| 1877 | *Black Beauty* by Anna Sewell (England) | Early horse story deploring inhumane treatment of animals |
| 1880 | *Heidi* by Johanna Spyri (Switzerland) | An early international story popular in the United States |
| 1883 | *Treasure Island* by Robert Louis Stevenson (England) | Classic adventure story with pirates |
| 1894 | *Beautiful Joe* by Margaret M. Saunders (Canada) | Early dog story, popular and sentimental |
| 1908 | *Anne of Green Gables* by Lucy Maud Montgomery (Canada) | Early family story about an orphan and her new family |
| 1910 | *The Secret Garden* by Frances Hodgson Burnett (United States) | A classic sentimental novel of two children adjusting to life |
| 1934 | *The Good Master* by Kate Seredy (United States) | Newbery winner set in Hungary |
| 1938 | *The Yearling* by Marjorie Kinnan Rawlings (United States) | Classic animal story and coming-of-age story |
| 1941 | *In My Mother's House* by Ann Nolan Clark (United States) | Early story featuring Native Americans |
| 1945 | *Strawberry Girl* by Lois Lenski (United States) | Regional story set in Florida |
| 1964 | *Harriet the Spy* by Louise Fitzhugh (United States) | The beginning of the new realism movement |
| 1970 | *Are You There, God? It's Me, Margaret* by Judy Blume (United States) | Early book with frank treatment of sex |
| 1971 | *The Planet of Junior Brown* by Virginia Hamilton (United States) | Realistic novel featuring minority main characters by an African-American author |
| 1986 | *A Fine White Dust* by Cynthia Rylant (United States) and *On My Honor* by Marion Dane Bauer (United States) | Newbery Honor books that feature clear moral dilemmas |
| 1990 | *Maniac Magee* by Jerry Spinelli (United States) | Newbery Medal winner presenting the importance of family |
| 1991 | *Nothing but the Truth* by Avi (United States) | Newbery Honor book, documentary novel |
| 2000 | *Monster* by Walter Dean Myers (United States) | First winner of the Michael L. Printz Award for Excellence in Literature for Young Adults |

*The Secret Garden* were orphans, the books by Burnett and Montgomery can be considered precursors of adjustment stories that addressed the special needs of children with problems. Stories of happy and often large families continued to thrive and peaked in the 1940s and 1950s in family story series about the Moffat family by Eleanor Estes and about the Melendy family by Elizabeth Enright. Beverly Cleary's Henry Huggins stories and Sydney Taylor's All-of-a-Kind Family series continued this tradition into the 1950s and 1960s. These stories are often referred to as the *happy family* stories, and, compared with much of today's contemporary realism for children, these stories do seem almost lighthearted.

Children from other lands is another theme that can be found in many realistic stories for children. *Hans Brinker, or The Silver Skates* (1865) by Mary Mapes Dodge and *Heidi* (1880) by Johanna Spyri of Switzerland are set in Holland and Switzerland, respectively, and were two of the earliest *other lands* books. In the United States, Kate Seredy was awarded a Newbery Medal for *The Good Master* (1934), which was set in Hungary. One of the purposes of these early stories was to provide children with an understanding and appreciation of foreign cultures. This theme continues to be seen in recent books published both by U.S. authors and by authors from other countries whose works are later published in the United States.

Realistic animal stories for children began to appear in the latter half of the nineteenth century. *Black Beauty* (1877) by Anna Sewell was a plea for humane treatment of animals and, though quite sentimental in places and completely personified (i.e., the animal is given human qualities), is still appreciated by some readers. *Beautiful Joe* (1894) by Margaret Marshall Saunders of Canada was a sentimental but well-loved dog story from this era. In 1894, Rudyard Kipling's *The Jungle Books*—exciting animal stories set in India—appeared, and these stories continue to hold the attention of readers today. Animal stories showing the maturing of the young human protagonist who assists the animal in the story remained popular throughout the twentieth century. Canadian authors, such as Sheila Burnford, have been especially recognized for their contributions to this type of story.

Regional stories and stories about children of minority groups began to appear with more frequency in the 1940s. *Strawberry Girl* (1945), by Lois Lenski, featured rural Florida and was one of the first regional stories. *In My Mother's House* (1941), by Ann Nolan Clark, featured Pueblo Indians; *Bright April* (1946) by Marguerite de Angeli discussed prejudice toward African Americans. However, it was only in the 1960s and 1970s that books written by minorities began to achieve national recognition. *Zeely* (1967) by Virginia Hamilton and *Stevie* (1969) by John Steptoe portray African-American childhood experiences and are two of the earliest and most noteworthy books representing this trend toward increased minority authorship—a trend that continues today.

A new era in realistic fiction for children was ushered in with the publication of *Harriet the Spy* by Louise Fitzhugh in 1964. This story of an unhappy and, at times, unpleasant girl depicted Harriet, her parents, and her classmates as anything but ideal or sympathetic human beings. This trend toward a more graphic and explicitly truthful portrayal of life and the inclusion of many topics that were previously considered taboo continued in children's books in the 1970s and 1980s and still prevails today. For example, Judy Blume's books are especially frank about sexual development and the emotional reactions to that development. Other controversial topics such as death, divorce, drugs, pacifism, alcoholism, and handicaps, which have always been a part of childhood, became permissible topics in children's books. Parents and other adults began to be shown, at times, as less than perfect, and families began to be portrayed as they truly are, not as one might believe they should be. This newer, franker brand of realism, sometimes referred to as the *new realism,* changed the world of children's books. The rosy cheer and avoidance of unpleasantness of earlier times were replaced by head-on discussion of all topics reflective of contemporary experience. The new realism books may be less lighthearted than their predecessors, but they are also more truthful and more real. At the present time, censorship of materials for children, including children's trade books, is rampant, in part, because of a trend toward more conservative family values.

# TYPES OF REALISTIC FICTION

The subject matter of realistic fiction includes the child's whole world of relationships with self and others: the joys, sorrows, challenges, adjustments, anxieties, and satisfactions of human life. Realistic books will often treat more than one aspect of human life; thus, some realistic fiction books can be categorized by more than one of the following topics.

## *Families*

Stories about the *nuclear family*—children and their relationships with parents and siblings—are a natural subject of books for children. Childhood for most children is spent in close contact with family members. Family stories for younger children often portray a happy child with loving parents. In these stories the everyday activities are shown—from brushing teeth to cooking dinner. Easy chapter books appealing to newly independent readers can be found within this type. These stories often show the child at play and sometimes explore sibling relationships as well. *Anastasia Krupnik* by Lois Lowry and *Ramona Quimby, Age 8* by Beverly Cleary are good examples of this type of book.

   *Extended families* can also be found in children's books. Aunts, uncles, grandparents, and cousins are important in the real lives of many children and may also be enjoyed in stories written for children. Sometimes a book will tell of a child being raised by a member of the extended family; other times a relative is portrayed as a supportive family member. See *Arthur for the Very First Time* by Patricia MacLachlan and *The Unmaking of Rabbit* by Constance C. Greene.

   The *alternative family* of today's world is also depicted in family stories. Not all family stories present the safe and secure world of healthy, intact families. Separation, divorce, single-parent families, and reconstructed families of stepparents and stepchildren are often the backdrop of stories today. For example, see *The Night Daddy* by Maria Gripe, and *Mom, the Wolfman and Me* by Norma Klein. The difficulty children and adults encounter in adjusting to these new family situations becomes the primary conflict in some stories. Temporary family situations, such as foster care for children, are also described in books about family life. It is important for children to see families other than the typical mother, father, and two children portrayed positively in books.

## *Peers*

In addition to adapting to one's family situation, children must also learn to cope with their peers. Many realistic stories show children struggling for *acceptance by peers* in a group situation. School settings are common in these stories. Examples include *Blubber* by Judy Blume and *Skinnybones* by Barbara Park. Neighborhoods, clubhouses, and summer camps are other common settings. For instance, see *The*

*Goats* by Brock Cole and *Jennifer, Hecate, MacBeth, William McKinley, and Me, Elizabeth* by E. L. Konigsburg.

Developing *close friendships* is another focus of stories about peer relationships. Friends may be of the same sex or the opposite sex, of the same age or a very different age, or of the same culture or a different culture. A concern for friendship and how to be a good friend to someone are shared traits of these stories. *Bridge to Terabithia* by Katherine Paterson and *Onion John* by Joseph Krumgold are good examples of this type of book.

## Mental, Physical, and Behavioral Challenges

Many children must deal with difficult challenges in their lives. Some children have disabilities; others have a family member or a friend with a disability. These disabilities may be physical, such as scoliosis; emotional, such as bipolar disorder; mental, such as mental retardation or learning disabilities; behavioral, such as hyperactivity; or multiple. Yet children do not like to appear different or strange to others. Authors of children's books are becoming increasingly sensitive to the need for positive portrayals of individuals with special challenges. Well-written, honest stories of such individuals in children's books can help other children to gain an understanding of disabilities and to empathize with people who have disabilities. Some children's books include a minor character with a disability, often a parent or a sibling of the protagonist; this type of story can be valuable in helping to develop among family members and classmates a greater sensitivity to individuals with disabilities. As inclusion of special education students into regular classrooms becomes a more common practice, this trend in children's literature can be an important educational resource. As an example, Jane Leslie Conly's Newbery Honor Book winner, *Crazy Lady!,* deals with physical disabilities and mental retardation.

## Cultural Diversity

Part of growing up involves the discovery that not all people are the same; part of becoming a healthy and humane adult is accepting the differences in oneself and in others. Today's children are growing up in a multicultural society in which an understanding and appreciation of cultural and linguistic differences among peoples are essential for societal harmony and cooperation. *Multicultural books* are those in which the main characters are from a racial, language, religious, or ethnic minority such as African Americans, Asian Americans, Hispanic Americans, Jewish Americans, or Native Americans. These books can be instrumental in developing in all children new understanding and appreciation for others as well as providing characters with whom minority children themselves may more readily identify. *Yellow Bird and Me* by Joyce Hansen is a good example. Each year, more authors and illustrators from minority groups are recognized for their contributions to children's literature.

As our earth hastens toward becoming an international community, children will be members of an international community. Books set in *foreign countries* may be written by U.S. authors about life in another culture or by a foreign author about his own country. These books can help children develop an awareness of people from other countries and an appreciation for children whose lives differ from their own. Examples include *Buster's World* by Bjarne Reuter and *Shabanu: Daughter of the Wind* by Suzanne Fisher Staples. For further discussion of multicultural and international children's literature of a variety of genres, see Chapter 10.

### Animals

Animal stories remain an ever-popular genre with children, dog and horse stories being the most popular. In realistic animal stories the animal protagonist behaves like an animal and is not personified. Usually, a child is also a protagonist in these stories. Examples are *The Black Stallion* by Walter Farley and *The Incredible Journey* by Sheila Burnford.

### Sports

Sports stories often present a story in which a child protagonist struggles to become accepted as a member of a team and does eventually succeed through determination and hard work. *Undercover Tailback* by Matt Christopher is a good example of a sports story. Although traditionally written with boys as the main characters, some sports stories are now available that feature girls as protagonists.

### Mysteries

Mysteries, popular with boys and girls, range from simple "whodunits" to complex character stories. The element of suspense is a strong part of the appeal of these stories. Mysteries have won more state children's choice awards than any other type of story, a fact that suggests that mysteries are truly favorites of many children. See *Encyclopedia Brown* by Donald J. Sobol and *The Dollhouse Murders* by Betty Ren Wright.

### Moral Choices

Characters in many realistic fiction novels face moments of crisis, situations of great difficulty, or events in which a decision may change someone's life. These situations are often similar to those children will face in their lives. Through these stories children can understand the difficult decisions the character is faced with and can discuss the consequences that may result from the choice made. Teachers often select these books for class study with intermediate and middle grade students. Using a book in which a character is faced with a difficult moral choice can stimulate lively discussions. An example is Marion Dane Bauer's *On My Honor,* in which the main character must face the devastating consequences of his choice.

### Romance and Sexuality

Romance stories are popular with preteens and teens, especially girls. Some stories depict boy-girl friendships, as in *The Grooming of Alice* by Phyllis Reynolds Naylor. Other novels portray physical attraction as in Iain Lawrence's *Ghost Boy.* Since the 1990s more stories of characters dealing with pregnancy and teenage parenting have appeared; some realistic examples are Virginia Euwer Wolff's *Make Lemonade* and Berlie Doherty's *Dear Nobody.*

Children become aware of their *growing sexuality* during preteen and teen years as they begin to mature. Some stories for older teens show attraction between members of the opposite sex as well as members of the same sex, with the beginning of sexual activity sometimes depicted in relationships. Stories that portray the struggle of young people coming to terms with a homosexual or lesbian sexual orientation are seen more frequently than they were in the past; other stories show the cruelty of society toward young homosexuals or lesbians. See *Deliver Us from Evie* by M. E. Kerr and *Then Again, Maybe I Won't* by Judy Blume.

## Rites of Passage

From birth to age 10, most children's lives revolve around family, friends, and classmates, but during the preteen and teen years a shift toward self-discovery and independence occurs. Rapid growth and change are seen in the physical, emotional, moral, and intellectual domains of life. These changes are reflected in books for adolescents. Sometimes books that deal with the trials and tribulations encountered during growth from childhood to adulthood are called *rite of passage* books. A *rite of passage* refers to an event in one's life that marks a change in one's status. Examples of rite of passage books are *A Fine White Dust* by Cynthia Rylant and *The 18th Emergency* by Betsy Byars.

## Adventure and Survival

Facing physical danger, an external force, also contributes to the maturing process. Stories of *survival and adventure* are ones in which the young protagonist must rely on will and ingenuity to survive a life-threatening situation. Although most survival stories are set in isolated places, a growing number are being set in cities where gangs, drug wars, and abandonment are indeed life threatening. Adventure stories may be set in any environment where the protagonist has freedom of action. *Hatchet* by Gary Paulsen and *Scorpions* by Walther Dean Myers are examples of this type of book.

Stories in the realistic fiction genre present familiar situations with which children can readily identify, often reflect contemporary life, and portray settings not so different from the homes, schools, towns, and cities known to today's children. The protagonists of these stories are frequently testing themselves as they grow toward adulthood; young readers can therefore empathize and gain insight into their own predicaments. Your challenge will be to stay abreast of good realistic stories in order to provide a wide range of books that will entertain, encourage, and inspire your students.

## REFERENCES

Marshall, M. R. (1988). *An introduction to the world of children's books* (2nd ed.). Brookfield, VT: Gower.

Whitman, R. (1968). Listening to grownups quarreling. In R. Whitman, *The marriage wig and other stories*. Orlando, FL: Harcourt.

## NOTABLE AUTHORS OF REALISTIC FICTION

**Judy Blume,** author of popular, sometimes controversial, novels focusing on problems of preteens and teens. *Are You There God? It's Me, Margaret; Tales of a Fourth Grade Nothing.*

**Betsy Byars,** author of stories about children who face and overcome family and personal problems. *The Pinballs; The Summer of the Swans.*

**Matt Christopher,** author of many sports stories. *Dirt Bike Racer.*

**Beverly Cleary,** author of humorous family stories about everyday happenings. *Ramona Quimby, Age 8; Dear Mr. Henshaw.*

**Vera and Bill Cleaver,** authors of Appalachian-based realistic fiction. *Where the Lilies Bloom.*

**Brock Cole,** author of realistic novels about adolescents and their relationships with peers and family. *The Goats; Celine; Nothing but the Facts.*

**Sharon Creech,** author of novels about girls seeking their families to find themselves. *Walk Two Moons; Chasing Redbird.*

**Berlie Doherty,** British Carnegie Medal winner for her realistic novels about family relationships. *Granny Was a Buffer Girl; The Snake-Stone.*

**Anne Fine,** British author of realistic peer stories and Carnegie Medal winning author. *Flour Babies; The Tulip Touch.*

**Jean Craighead George,** author of ecological fiction and survival in nature stories. *Julie of the Wolves; My Side of the Mountain.*

**Virginia Hamilton,** author of stories about the African-American experience. *Zeely; The Planet of Junior Brown.*

**Marguerite Henry,** author of many horse stories. *King of the Wind; Misty of Chincoteague.*

**Elaine L. Konigsburg,** author of sensitive and humorous stories of preteens and teens. *From the Mixed-Up Files of Mrs. Basil E. Frankweiler; (George).*

**Jean Little,** Canadian author who writes family-adjustment stories. *Mine for Keeps; Mama's Going to Buy You a Mockingbird.*

**Walter Dean Myers,** author of novels about African-American adolescents in city settings. *Scorpions; Fast Sam, Cool Clyde, and Stuff.*

**Phyllis Reynolds Naylor,** author of eight books about Alice and her family, including *Alice the Brave.* Also noted for Newbery Medal winner *Shiloh* and its sequels.

**Katherine Paterson,** author of stories featuring relationships with peers and family. *The Great Gilly Hopkins; Bridge to Terabithia.*

**Gary Paulsen,** author of nature survival adventures often set in northern United States or Canada. *Hatchet; Dogsong.*

**Cynthia Rylant,** author of introspective realistic stories often set in Appalachia. *Every Living Thing; Missing May.*

**Louis Sachar,** author of *Holes,* warm and humorous novel that intertwines past and present events to solve a mystery. (Also, *Wayside School Is Falling Down,* a light, humorous modern fantasy series.)

**Alfred Slote,** author of sports stories. *The Trading Game; Hang Tough, Paul Mather.*

**Zilpha Keatley Snyder,** author of mystery stories. *The Famous Stanley Kidnapping Case; The Egypt Game.*

**Donald Sobol,** author of a mystery series for transitional readers. Encyclopedia Brown series.

**Jerry Spinelli,** author of realistic novels of peers and their escapades, including Newbery Medal winner *Maniac Magee* and Newbery Honor book *Wringer.*

**Suzanne Fisher Staples,** author of the Newbery Honor books *Shabanu* and its sequel *Haveli,* set in the Cholistan Desert of Pakistan. Her stories present conflicts within and between diverse cultures.

**Cynthia Voigt,** author of stories about the Tillerman family of four children and their friends. *Dicey's Song; A Solitary Blue.*

**Jacqueline Woodson,** African-American author whose novels often treat sensitive issues of sexuality, abuse, and race. *I Hadn't Meant to Tell You This; From the Notebooks of Melanin Sun.*

**Laurence Yep,** author of novels about the Asian-American experience. *Child of the Owl; Dragonwings.*

## R E C O M M E N D E D   R E A L I S T I C   F I C T I O N   B O O K S

*Ages refer to approximate interest levels.*
*YA = young adult readers.*

### *Families*

Alcock, Vivien. *A Kind of Thief.* Delacorte, 1992. Ages 10–14.

Bauer, Marion Dane. *A Question of Trust.* Scholastic, 1994. Ages 10–13.

Bawden, Nina. *Humbug.* Clarion, 1992. Ages 9–12.

———. *Kept in the Dark.* Lothrop, 1982. Ages 10–YA.

———. *The Outside Child.* Lothrop, 1989. Ages 10–YA.

Brooks, Bruce. *Everywhere.* HarperCollins, 1990. Ages 11–YA.

———. *What Hearts.* HarperCollins, 1992. Ages 11–YA.

Byars, Betsy C. *After the Goat Man.* Illustrated by Ronald Himler. Viking, 1974. Ages 9–12.

Cameron, Ann. *More Stories Julian Tells.* Illustrated by Ann Strugnell. Knopf, 1986. Ages 7–11.

Cleary, Beverly. *Dear Mr. Henshaw.* Illustrated by Paul Zelinsky. Morrow, 1983. Ages 9–12.

———. *Ramona and Her Father.* Illustrated by Alan Tiegreen. Morrow, 1977. Ages 7–10. Humorous.

————. *Ramona Quimby, Age 8.* Illustrated by Alan Tiegreen. Morrow, 1981. Ages 7–10. Humorous.

————. *Ramona the Pest.* Illustrated by Louis Darling. Morrow, 1968. Ages 5–8. Humorous.

Cleaver, Vera and Bill. *Where the Lilies Bloom.* Illustrated by Jim Spanfeller. Lippincott, 1969. Ages 11–YA.

Coman, Carolyn. *Many Stones.* Front Street, 2000. Ages 11–YA.

————. *Tell Me Everything.* Farrar, 1993. Ages 11–YA.

Conly, Jane Leslie. *While No One Was Watching.* Holt, 1998. Ages 11–YA.

Corcoran, Barbara. *Annie's Monster.* Atheneum, 1990. Ages 10–YA.

Creech, Sharon. *Chasing Redbird.* HarperCollins, 1997. Ages 10–13.

————. *Walk Two Moons.* HarperCollins, 1994. Ages 10–13.

Cresswell, Helen. *Bagthorpes Liberated: Being the Seventh Part of the Bagthorpe Saga.* Macmillan, 1989. Ages 8–12. Humorous.

————. *Bagthorpes Unlimited.* Penguin, 1978. Ages 10–12. Humorous.

————. *Ordinary Jack.* Macmillan, 1977. Ages 8–12. Humorous.

Cutler, Jane. *No Dogs Allowed.* Illustrated by Tracey Campbell Pearson. Farrar, 1992. Ages 8–11.

Danziger, Paula. *Amber Brown Goes Fourth.* HarperCollins, 1995. Ages 7–10.

————. *Forever Amber Brown.* Illustrated by Tony Ross. Putnam, 1996. Ages 7–10.

Doherty, Berlie. *The Snake-Stone.* Orchard, 1996. Ages 12–YA.

Ellis, Sarah. *A Family Project.* Macmillan, 1988. Ages 10–14.

————. *Next-Door Neighbors.* Macmillan, 1990. Ages 9–13.

Feiffer, Jules. *The Man in the Ceiling.* HarperCollins, 1993. Ages 9–12.

Fine, Anne. *Step by Wicked Step.* Little, Brown, 1996. Ages 9–12.

Fox, Paula. *How Many Miles to Babylon?* Illustrated by Paul Giovanipoulos. White, 1967. Ages 11–YA.

————. *Monkey Island.* Watts, 1991. Ages 9–12.

————. *One-Eyed Cat.* Bradbury, 1984. Ages 9–12.

————. *The Village by the Sea.* Watts, 1988. Ages 10–13.

————. *Western Wind.* Orchard, 1993. Ages 9–12.

Greene, Constance C. *Al(exandra) the Great.* Viking, 1982. Ages 8–12.

Griffin, Adele. *The Other Shepards.* Hyperion, 1998. Ages 11–YA.

————. *The Unmaking of Rabbit.* Viking, 1972. Ages 9–11.

Gripe, Maria. *The Night Daddy.* Illustrated by Harald Gripe. Translated from the Swedish by Gerry Bothmer. Delacorte, 1971. Ages 9–11.

Hamilton, Virginia. *Cousins.* Putnam, 1990. Ages 9–13.

Henkes, Kevin. *Sun and Spoon.* Greenwillow, 1997. Ages 8–11.

Hermes, Patricia. *Mama, Let's Dance.* Little, 1991. Ages 10–YA.

Horvath, Polly. *Trolls.* Farrar, 1999. Ages 8–12. Humorous.

Johnson, Angela. *Toning the Sweep.* Orchard, 1993. Ages 11–YA.

Klein, Norma. *Mom, the Wolf Man, and Me.* Pantheon, 1972. Ages 11–YA.

Koertge, Ron. *The Harmony Arms.* Little, 1992. Ages 11–YA. Humorous.

Konigsburg, E. L. *From the Mixed-Up Files of Mrs. Basil E. Frankweiler.* Atheneum, 1967. Ages 9–12.

Koss, Amy Goldman. *The Ashwater Experiment.* Dial, 1999. Ages 9–13.

Little, Jean. *Mama's Going to Buy You a Mockingbird.* Viking, 1985. Ages 10–13.

Lowry, Lois. *All About Sam.* Illustrated by Diane de Groat. Houghton, 1988. Ages 8–12. Humorous.

————. *Anastasia at Your Service.* Illustrated by Diane de Groat. Houghton, 1982. Ages 8–12. Humorous.

————. *Anastasia Krupnik.* Houghton, 1985. Ages 8–12. Humorous.

————. *Attaboy, Sam!* Illustrated by Diane de Groat. Houghton, 1992. Ages 7–11. Humorous.

————. *Rabble Starkey.* Houghton, 1987. Ages 10–13.

————. *See You Around, Sam!* Illustrated by Diane de Groat. Houghton, 1996. Ages 7–11.

————. *A Summer to Die.* Houghton, 1977. Ages 10–13.

MacLachlan, Patricia. *Arthur for the Very First Time.* Illustrated by Lloyd Bloom. HarperCollins, 1980. Ages 8–11.

————. *Baby.* Delacorte, 1993. Ages 10–YA.

————. *Journey.* Illustrated by Barry Moser. Delacorte, 1991. Ages 10–14.

Mathis, Sharon Bell. *The Hundred Penny Box.* Illustrated by Leo and Diane Dillon. Viking, 1975. Ages 7–10.

McEwan, Ian. *The Daydreamer.* HarperCollins, 1994. Ages 10–YA.

McKay, Hilary. *The Exiles.* Macmillan, 1992. Ages 9–12. Humorous.

————. *The Exiles at Home.* Macmillan, 1994. Ages 9–12.

————. *The Exiles in Love.* Simon & Schuster, 1998. Ages 9–12.

Morganstern, Susie. *Secret Letters from 0–10.* Translated from French by Gill Rosner. Viking, 1998. Ages 10–13.

Naylor, Phyllis Reynolds. *Alice in April.* Atheneum, 1993. Ages 9–13. Humorous.

————. *Reluctantly Alice.* Atheneum, 1991. Ages 8–11.

Nolan, Han. *Dancing on the Edge.* Harcourt, 1997. Ages 12–YA.

Park, Barbara. *Mick Harte Was Here.* Knopf, 1995. Ages 9–12.

Paterson, Katherine. *The Great Gilly Hopkins.* Crowell, 1978. Ages 9–12.

————. *Park's Quest.* Dutton, 1988. Ages 13–YA.

Procházková, Iva. *The Season of Secret Wishes.* Translated by Elizabeth D. Crawford. Lothrop, 1989. Ages 9–12.

Rylant, Cynthia. *A Blue-Eyed Daisy.* Bradbury, 1985. Ages 9–12.

————. *Missing May.* Orchard, 1992. Ages 10–YA.

Sachs, Marilyn. *The Bears' House.* Illustrated by Louis Glanzman. Doubleday, 1971. Ages 9–12.

Slepian, Jan. *The Broccoli Tapes.* Philomel, 1989. Ages 10–13.

Smith, Doris Buchanan. *The Pennywhistle Tree.* Putnam, 1991. Ages 9–12.

Stolz, Mary. *The Bully of Barkham Street.* Illustrated by Leonard Shortall. Harper, 1963. Ages 8–11.

————. *A Dog on Barkham Street.* Harper, 1960. Ages 8–11.

————. *Stealing Home.* HarperCollins, 1992. Ages 8–12.

Voigt, Cynthia. *Homecoming.* Atheneum, 1981. Ages 9–12.

————. *A Solitary Blue.* Atheneum, 1983. Ages 10–YA.

————. *Sons from Afar.* Atheneum, 1987. Ages 10–YA.

Walter, Mildred Pitts. *Justin and the Best Biscuits in the World.* Illustrated by Catherine Stock. Lothrop, 1986. Ages 8–11.

White, Ruth. *Belle Prater's Boy.* Farrar, 1996. Ages 10–13.

Williams, Vera B. *Scooter.* Morrow, 1993. Ages 8–12.

## Peers

Blume, Judy. *Blubber.* Bradbury, 1974. Ages 9–12.

————. *Tales of a Fourth Grade Nothing.* Illustrated by Roy Doty. Dutton, 1972. Ages 8–12. Humorous.

Byars, Betsy C. *Bingo Brown, Gypsy Lover.* Viking, 1990. Ages 11-YA.

————. *The Burning Questions of Bingo Brown.* Viking, 1988. Ages 9–12.

Clements, Andrew. *Frindle.* Illustrated by Brian Selznick. Simon & Schuster, 1996. Ages 8–12. Humorous.

Cole, Brock. *The Goats.* Farrar, 1987. Ages 11–YA.

Crutcher, Chris. *Staying Fat for Sarah Byrnes.* Greenwillow, 1993. Ages 13–YA.

Estes, Eleanor. *The Hundred Dresses.* Illustrated by Louis Slobodkin. Harcourt, 1944. Ages 8–11.

Fine, Anne. *Alias Madame Doubtfire.* Little, Brown, 1988. Ages 9–12.

————. *The Tulip Touch.* Little, Brown, 1997. Ages 10–YA.

Fitzhugh, Louise. *Harriet the Spy.* Harper, 1964. Ages 9–12.

Gantos, Jack. *Heads or Tails: Stories from the Sixth Grade.* Farrar, 1994. Ages 10–14.

Gilson, Jamie. *Sticks and Stones and Skeleton Bones.* Illustrated by Dee deRosa. Lothrop, 1991. Ages 8–11.

Greene, Bette. *Philip Hall Likes Me, I Reckon Maybe.* Illustrated by Charles Lilly. Dial, 1974. Ages 9–12.

Grove, Vicki. *Reaching Dustin.* Putnam, 1998. Ages 10–13.

Haas, Jessie. *Skipping School.* Greenwillow, 1992. Ages 12–YA.

Hamilton, Virginia. *The Planet of Junior Brown.* Macmillan, 1971. Ages 12–YA.

Henkes, Kevin. *Words of Stone.* Greenwillow, 1992. Ages 8–12.

Hesse, Karen. *Phoenix Rising.* Holt, 1994. Ages 12–YA.

Hurwitz, Johanna. *Class Clown.* Illustrated by Sheila Hamanaka. Morrow, 1987. Ages 6–9.

———. *Russell and Elisa.* Morrow, 1989. Ages 6–9.

Klein, Robin. *Enemies.* Illustrated by Noela Young. Dutton, 1989. Ages 9–12.

Kline, Suzy. *Herbie Jones and the Class Gift.* Illustrated by Richard Williams. Putnam, 1987. Ages 8–11.

———. *What's the Matter with Herbie Jones?* Illustrated by Richard Williams. Putnam, 1986. Ages 8–11.

Konigsburg, E. L. *Jennifer, Hecate, MacBeth, William McKinley, and Me, Elizabeth.* Atheneum, 1967. Ages 8–12.

Krumgold, Joseph. *Onion John.* Illustrated by Symeon Shimin. HarperCollins, 1959. Ages 9–12.

Lisle, Janet Taylor. *Afternoon of the Elves.* Watts, 1989. Ages 9–12.

MacLachlan, Patricia. *The Facts and Fictions of Minna Pratt.* Harper, 1988. Ages 7–11.

Mark, Jan. *Handles.* Atheneum, 1985. Ages 11–YA.

———. *Thunder and Lightnings.* Crowell, 1979. Ages 11–YA.

Marsden, John. *Letters from the Inside* Houghton, 1994. Ages 12–YA.

———. *So Much to Tell You.* Joy Street, 1989. Ages 12–YA.

Park, Barbara. *Almost Starring Skinnybones.* Knopf, 1988. Ages 9–12. Humorous.

———. *Skinnybones.* Knopf, 1982. Ages 9–12. Humorous.

Paterson, Katherine. *Bridge to Terabithia.* Illustrated by Donna Diamond. Crowell, 1977. Ages 9–13.

Perkins, Lynne Rae. *All Alone in the Universe.* Greenwillow, 1999. Ages 10–14.

Phipson, Joan. *Hit and Run.* Atheneum, 1985. Ages 10–YA.

Rapp, Adam. *The Buffalo Tree.* Front Street, 1997. Ages 12–YA.

Shreve, Susan. *The Gift of the Girl Who Couldn't Hear.* Morrow, 1991. Ages 10–13.

Skinner, David. *The Wrecker.* Simon & Schuster, 1995. Ages 10–14.

Smith, Doris Buchanan. *A Taste of Blackberries.* Illustrated by Charles Robinson. Crowell, 1973. Ages 9–12.

Spinelli, Jerry. *Maniac Magee.* Little, Brown, 1990. Ages 9–12.

———. *Wringer.* HarperCollins, 1997. Ages 9–12.

Thesman, Jean. *The Rain Catchers.* Houghton, 1991. Ages 12–YA.

Tolan, Stephanie S. *Save Halloween!* Morrow, 1993. Ages 9–12.

Voigt, Cynthia. *Bad Girls.* Scholastic, 1996. Ages 8–12. See also sequel: *Bad, Badder, Baddest.* 1997.

Williams, Vera B. *Scooter.* Greenwillow, 1993. Ages 9–12.

Yarbrough, Camille. *The Shimmershine Queens.* Putnam, 1988. Ages 9–12.

## Mental, Physical, and Behavioral Challenges

Anderson, Rachel. *The Bus People.* Holt, 1992. Ages 10–14. Character portrayals, different disabilities.

Bawden, Nina. *The Witch's Daughter.* Clarion, 1991 (1966). Ages 9–12. Visual impairment.

Blume, Judy. *Deenie.* Bradbury, 1973. Ages 12–YA. Scoliosis.

Byars, Betsy. *The Summer of the Swans.* Illustrated by Ted CoConis. Viking, 1970. Ages 10–14. Mental retardation.

Carrick, Carol. *Stay Away from Simon.* Illustrated by Donald Carrick. Clarion, 1985. Ages 7–9. Mental retardation. Picture book.

Clifton, Lucille. *My Friend Jacob.* Illustrated by Thomas DiGrazia. Dutton, 1980. Ages 5–8. Mental retardation. Picture book.

Conly, Jane Leslie. *Crazy Lady!* HarperCollins, 1993. Ages 10–YA. Mental retardation.

Cowen-Fletcher, Jane. *Mama Zooms.* Scholastic, 1993. Ages 5–8. Physical disability. Picture book.

Fleming, Virginia. *Be Good to Eddie Lee.* Illustrated by Floyd Cooper. Philomel, 1993. Ages 6–8. Down syndrome. Picture book.

Gantos, Jack. *Joey Pigza Loses Control.* Farrar, 2000. Ages 9–13. Attention deficit/hyperactivity.

———. *Joey Pigza Swallowed the Key.* Farrar, 1998. Ages 9–13. AD/HD.

Garrigue, Sheila. *Between Friends.* Scholastic, 1986. Ages 10–13. Down syndrome.

Hamilton, Virginia. *Plain City.* Scholastic, 1993. Ages 10–YA.

Hines, Anna Grossnickle. *Gramma's Walk.* Greenwillow, 1993. Ages 5–8. Physical disability. Picture book.

Howard, Ellen. *Edith Herself.* Illustrated by Ronald Hinter. Atheneum, 1987. Ages 7–11. Epilepsy.

Johnston, Julie. *Hero of Lesser Causes.* Little, 1993. Ages 11–YA. Poliomyelitis.

Klein, Robin. *Boss of the Pool.* Penguin, 1986. Ages 8–11. Down syndrome.

Konigsburg, E. L. *(George).* Atheneum, 1970. Ages 12–YA. Emotional disability.

———. *Silent to the Bone.* Simon & Schuster, 2000. Ages 11–YA. Mutism.

Laird, Elizabeth. *Loving Ben.* Delacorte, 1988. Ages 10–YA. Hydrocephalic infant.

Lasker, Joe. *He's My Brother.* Illustrated by the author. Whitman, 1974. Ages 7–10. Learning disability.

Levin, Betty. *Fire in the Wind.* Greenwillow, 1995. Ages 11–YA. Mental disability.

Little, Jean. *From Anna.* Illustrated by Joan Sandin. Harper & Row, 1972. Ages 9–12. Visual impairment.

———. *Listen for the Singing.* HarperCollins, 1991. Ages 10–13. Visual impairment.

———. *Mine for Keeps.* Illustrated by Lewis Parker. Little, 1962. Ages 9–12. Cerebral palsy.

———. *Take Wing.* Little, Brown, 1968. Ages 9–12. Mental retardation.

Madsen, Jane M., and Bockoras, Diane. *Please Don't Tease Me. . . .* Illustrated by Kathleen T. Brinko. Judson, 1983. Ages 11–14. Physical disability.

Mazer, Harry. *The Wild Kid.* Simon & Schuster, 1998. Ages 9–13. Down syndrome.

McCormick, Patricia. *Cut.* Front Street, 2000. Ages 13–YA. Mental health.

Mikaelsen, Ben. *Petey.* Hyperion, 1998. Ages 12–YA. Cerebral palsy.

Oneal, Zibby. *The Language of Goldfish.* Viking, 1980. Ages 12–YA. Emotional disability.

Osofsley, Audrey. *My Buddy.* Illustrated by Ted Rand. Holt, 1994. Ages 6–8. Muscular dystrophy.

Paulsen, Gary. *The Monument.* Delacorte, 1991. Ages 11–YA. Physical disability.

Philbrick, Rodman. *Freak the Mighty.* Blue Sky, 1993. Ages 12–YA. Learning disability.

Rubin, Susan Goldman. *Emily Good as Gold.* Harcourt, 1993. Ages 12–YA. Mental retardation.

Slepian, Jan. *The Alfred Summer.* Macmillan, 1980. Ages 11–14. Cerebral palsy.

———. *Lester's Turn.* Macmillan, 1981. Ages 11–14. Cerebral palsy.

———. *Risk n' Roses.* Putnam, 1990. Ages 11–YA. Mental retardation.

Taylor, Theodore. *Tuck Triumphant.* Doubleday, 1991. Ages 10–YA. Hearing impairment.

Thesman, Jean. *When the Road Ends.* Houghton, 1992. Ages 10–YA. Physical disability.

Trueman, Terry. *Stuck in Neutral.* HarperCollins, 2000. Ages 11–YA. Cerebral palsy.

Voigt, Cynthia. *Dicey's Song.* Atheneum, 1983. Ages 10–YA. Mental illness.

Wilson, Nancy Hope. *The Reason for Janey.* Macmillan, 1994. Ages 10–13. Mental retardation.

Wolff, Virginia Euwer. *Probably Still Nick Swanson.* Holt, 1988. Ages 12–YA. Learning disability.

## Cultural Diversity

*See also Chapter 10, "Multicultural and International Literature."*

Abelove, Joan. *Go and Come Back.* DK Ink, 1998. Ages 12–YA.

Beake, Lesley. *The Song of Be.* Holt, 1993. Ages 12–YA.

Berry, James. *The Future-Telling Lady and Other Stories.* HarperCollins, 1993. Ages 10-YA.

Casey, Maude. *Over the Water.* Holt, 1994. Ages 12–YA.

Dorris, Michael. *The Window.* Hyperion, 1997. Ages 11–14.

Fogelin, Adrian. *Crossing Jordan.* Peachtree, 2000. Ages 11–13.

Gordon, Sheila. *Waiting for the Rain: A Novel of South Africa.* Watts, 1987. Ages 11–YA.

Hansen, Joyce. *Yellow Bird and Me.* Clarion, 1986. Ages 9–12.

Hill, Anthony. *The Burnt Stick.* Houghton, 1995. Ages 8–11.

Ho, Minfong. *The Clay Marble.* Farrar, 1991. Ages 11–14.

Kurtz, Jane. *The Storyteller's Beads.* Harcourt, 1998. Ages 10–13.

Lord, Bette Bao. *In the Year of the Boar and Jackie Robinson.* Illustrated by Marc Simont. Harper, 1984. Ages 7–10.

Maartens, Maretha. *Paper Bird: A Novel of South Africa.* Translated by Madeleine van Biljon. Clarion, 1991. Ages 10–YA.

Martinez, Victor. *Parrot in the Oven: Mi Vida.* Harper-Collins, 1996. Ages 12–YA.

Myers, Walter Dean. *The Mouse Rap.* Harper, 1990. Ages 11–YA.

Naidoo, Beverley. *Chain of Fire.* Illustrated by Eric Velasquez. Lippincott, 1990. Ages 11–YA.

———. *Journey to Jo'burg: A South African Story.* Illustrated by Eric Velasquez. Lippincott, 1986. Ages 8–12.

———. *No Turning Back: A Novel of South Africa.* HarperCollins, 1997. Ages 10–13.

Namioka, Lensey. *Yang the Youngest and His Terrible Ear.* Little, 1992. Ages 9–12.

Nye, Naomi Shihab. *Habibi.* Simon & Schuster, 1997. Ages 12–YA.

Reuter, Bjarne. *Buster's World.* Translated from the Danish by Anthea Bell. Dutton, 1989. Ages 9–12.

———. *The Sheik of Hope Street.* Translated from the Danish by Anthea Bell. Dutton, 1991. Ages 9–12.

Staples, Suzanne Fisher. *Haveli: A Young Woman's Courageous Struggle for Freedom in Present-day Pakistan.* Knopf, 1993. Ages 12–YA.

———. *Shabanu: Daughter of the Wind.* Knopf, 1989. Ages 12–YA.

———. *Shiva's Fire.* Farrar, 2000. Ages 12–YA.

Temple, Frances. *Grab Hands and Run.* Orchard, 1993. Ages 12–YA.

———. *Taste of Salt: A Story of Modern Haiti.* Watts, 1992. Ages 12–YA.

———. *Tonight, by Sea.* Orchard, 1995. Ages 12–YA.

Walter, Mildred Pitts. *Have a Happy———.* Illustrated by Carole Byard. Lothrop, 1989. Ages 9–12.

Whelan, Gloria. *Homeless Bird.* HarperCollins, 2000. Ages 10–13.

Woodson, Jacqueline. *I Hadn't Meant to Tell You This.* Delacorte, 1994. Ages 12–YA.

Yep, Laurence. *Thief of Hearts.* HarperCollins, 1995. Ages 10–13.

Yumoto, Kazumi. *The Friends.* Translated by Cathy Hirano. Farrar, 1996. Ages 8–12.

## Animals

Burnford, Sheila. *The Incredible Journey.* Illustrated by Carl Burger. Little, 1961. Ages 8–11.

Cutler, Jane. *No Dogs Allowed.* Illustrated by Tracey Campbell Pearson. Farrar, 1992. Ages 8–11.

DiCamillo, Kate. *Because of Winn-Dixie.* Candlewick, 2000. Ages 9–12.

Eckert, Allan W. *Incident at Hawk's Hill.* Illustrated by John Schoenherr. Little, Brown, 1971. Ages 10–YA.

Farley, Steven. *The Black Stallion's Shadow.* Random, 1996. Ages 9–12.

Farley, Walter. *The Black Stallion.* Illustrated by Keith Ward. Random House, 1941. Ages 8–11.

Fleischman, Sid. *Jim Ugly.* Illustrated by Jos. A. Smith. Greenwillow, 1992. Ages 9–12.

Gardiner, John Reynolds. *Stone Fox.* Illustrated by Marcia Sewall. Crowell, 1980. Ages 7–11.

George, Jean Craighead. *The Cry of the Crow.* Harper, 1980. Ages 10–13.

Gipson, Fred. *Old Yeller.* Illustrated by Carl Burger. Harper, 1956. Ages 10–YA.

Haas, Jessie. *A Blue for Beware.* Illustrated by Joseph A. Smith. Greenwillow, 1995. Ages 8–11.

———. *The Sixth Sense: And Other Stories.* Greenwillow, 1991. Ages 11–YA.

Henry, Marguerite. *King of the Wind.* Illustrated by Wesley Dennis. Rand, 1948. Ages 7–11.

———. *Misty of Chincoteague.* Illustrated by Wesley Dennis. Rand, 1947. Ages 7–11.

Hesse, Karen. *Sable.* Holt, 1994. Ages 8–11.

Kjelgaard, Jim. *Big Red.* Illustrated by Bob Kuhn. Holiday, 1945. Ages 9–12.

Little, Jean. *Different Dragons.* Illustrated by Laura Fernandez. Viking, 1987. Ages 8–12.

McKay, Hilary. *Dog Friday.* Simon & Schuster, 1995. Ages 9–11.

Mowat, Farley. *Owls in the Family.* Illustrated by Robert Frankenberg. Little, 1962. Ages 9–12.

Rawls, Wilson. *Summer of the Monkeys.* Doubleday, 1976. Ages 9–11. Humorous.

———. *Where the Red Fern Grows.* Doubleday, 1961. Ages 9–11.

Reaver, Chap. *Bill.* Delacorte, 1994. Ages 11–YA.

Rylant, Cynthia. *Every Living Thing.* Illustrated by S. D. Schindler. Bradbury, 1985. Ages 11–YA.

Savage, Deborah. *Under a Different Sky.* Houghton, 1997. Ages 12–YA.

Sewell, Anna. *Black Beauty.* Illustrated by John Speirs. Simon & Schuster, 1982. Ages 9–11.

Taylor, Theodore. *The Trouble with Tuck.* Doubleday, 1981. Ages 7–10.

## Sports

Christopher, Matt. *Centerfield Ballhawk.* Illustrated by Ellen Beier. Brown/Springboard, 1992. Ages 7–9.

———. *Return of the Home Run Kid.* Illustrated by Paul Casale. Little, 1992. Ages 9–12.

———. *Undercover Tailback.* Illustrated by Paul Casale. Little, 1992. Ages 8–11.

Cohen, Barbara. *Thank You, Jackie Robinson.* Illustrated by Richard Cuffari. Lothrop, 1974. Ages 8–11.

Crutcher, Chris. *Athletic Shorts: Six Short Stories.* Greenwillow, 1991. Ages 13–YA.

———. *Ironman.* Greenwillow, 1995. Ages 12–YA.

Hughes, Dean. *Team Picture.* Simon & Schuster, 1996. Ages 11–14.

Lynch, Chris. *Iceman.* HarperCollins, 1994. Ages 14–YA.

———. *Shadow Boxer.* HarperCollins, 1993. Ages 12–YA.

Myers, Walter Dean. *Slam!* Scholastic, 1996. Ages 12–YA.

Slote, Alfred. *Hang Tough, Paul Mather.* Lippincott, 1973. Ages 9–12.

———. *The Trading Game.* Lippincott, 1990. Ages 9–12.

Smith, Robert Kimmel. *Bobby Baseball.* Illustrated by Alan Tiegreen. Delacorte, 1989. Ages 8–11.

## Mysteries

Avi. *The Man Who Was Poe.* Orchard, 1989. Ages 10–YA.

Bunting, Eve. *Coffin on a Case.* HarperCollins, 1992. Ages 9–12.

Crew, Gary. *Angel's Gate.* Simon & Schuster, 1995. Ages 11-YA.

Cross, Gillian. *A Map to Nowhere.* Holiday, 1989. Ages 10–13.

———. *Wolf.* Holiday, 1991. Ages 10–13.

DeFelice, Cynthia. *Death at Devil's Track.* Farrar, 2000. Ages 10–13. Also, moral issue and adventure.

Fitzgerald, John D. *The Great Brain Is Back.* Dial, 1995. Ages 8–11.

Garfield, Leon. *The December Rose.* Viking, 1987. Ages 10–YA.

Nixon, Joan Lowery. *The Name of the Game Was Murder.* Delacorte, 1993. Ages 11–14.

Pearce, Philippa. *The Way to Sattin Shore.* Illustrated by Charlotte Voake. Greenwillow, 1984. Ages 10–13.

Prather, Ray. *Fish & Bones.* HarperCollins, 1992. Ages 11–YA.

Raskin, Ellen. *Figgs & Phantoms.* Dutton, 1989. Ages 9–12.

———. *The Westing Game.* Dutton, 1978. Ages 9–12.

Sachar, Louis. *Holes.* Farrar, 1998. Ages 10–14.

Sobol, Donald J. *Encyclopedia Brown.* Lodestar/Dutton, 1963. Ages 8–10.

———. *Encyclopedia Brown and the Case of Pablo's Nose.* Illustrated by Eric Velasquez. Delacorte, 1996. Ages 8–11.

Van Draanen, Wendelin. *Sammy Keyes & the Hotel Thief.* Knopf, 1998. Another in this series with a female protagonist is *Sammy Keyes & the Sisters of Mercy.* Knopf, 1999. Ages 9–12.

Wallace, Barbara Brooks. *Peppermints in the Parlor.* Atheneum, 1980. Ages 9–12.

———. *The Twin in the Tavern.* Atheneum, 1993. Ages 9–12.

Wright, Betty Ren. *The Dollhouse Murders.* Holiday House, 1983. Ages 9–12.

## Moral Choices

Avi. *Nothing but the Truth.* Orchard, 1991. Ages 11–YA.

Bauer, Marion Dane. *On My Honor.* Clarion, 1986. Ages 8–12.

Cole, Brock. *The Goats.* Farrar, 1987. Ages 11–YA.

Cooney, Caroline. *Driver's Ed.* Delacorte, 1994. Ages 13–YA.

Cormier, Robert. *The Chocolate War.* Pantheon, 1974. Ages 12–YA.

Fleischman, Paul. *Whirligig.* Holt, 1998. Ages 12–YA.

Hinton, S. E. *The Outsiders.* Viking, 1967. Ages 13–YA.

———. *That Was Then, This Is Now.* Viking, 1967. Ages 13–YA.

Lynch, Chris. *Slot Machine.* HarperCollins, 1995. Ages 12–YA.

Myers, Walter Dean. *Monster.* HarperCollins, 1999. Ages 13–YA.

———. *Somewhere in the Darkness.* Scholastic, 1992. Ages 12–YA.

Naylor, Phyllis Reynolds. *Saving Shiloh.* Simon & Schuster, 1997. Ages 8–11.

———. *Shiloh.* Atheneum,1991. Ages 8–11.

———. *Shiloh Season.* Simon & Schuster, 1996. Ages 8–11.

Soto, Gary. *Baseball in April and Other Stories.* Harcourt, 1991. Ages 10–YA.

Spinelli, Jerry. *Maniac Magee.* HarperCollins, 1990. Ages 9–12.

Walter, Virginia. *Making Up Megaboy.* Illustrated by Katrina Roecklein. DK Ink, 1998. Ages 11–13.

Yolen, Jane, and Bruce Coville. *Armageddon Summer.* Harcourt, 1998. Ages 11–13. Chapters alternate between boy and girl protagonists.

## Romance and Sexuality

Bauer, Marion Dane, Editor. *Am I Blue? Coming Out from the Silence.* HarperCollins, 1994. Ages 14–YA.

Blume, Judy. *It's Not the End of the World.* Bradbury, 1972. Ages 11–YA.

———. *Then Again, Maybe I Won't.* Bradbury, 1971. Ages 10–YA.

Clements, Bruce. *Tom Loves Anna Loves Tom.* Farrar, 1990. Ages 12–YA.

Cole, Brock. *Celine.* Farrar, 1989. Ages 12–YA.

Doherty, Berlie. *Dear Nobody.* Orchard, 1992. Ages 12–YA.

Fox, Paula. *The Eagle Kite.* Orchard, 1995. Ages 12–YA.

Kerr, M. E. *Deliver Us from Evie.* HarperCollins, 1994. Ages 13–YA.

Lawrence, Iain. *Ghost Boy.* Delacorte, 2000. Ages 12–YA.

Naylor, Phyllis Reynolds. *The Grooming of Alice.* Simon & Schuster, 2000. Ages 11–13.

Nelson, Theresa. *Earthshine.* Watts, 1994. Ages 11–YA.

Paterson, Katherine. *Jacob Have I Loved.* Crowell, 1980. Ages 12–YA.

Plummer, Louise. *My Name Is Sus5an Smith. The 5 Is Silent.* Delacorte, 1991. Ages 13–YA.

Williams-Garcia, Rita. *Like Sisters on the Homefront.* Lodestar, 1995. Ages 12–YA.

Winick, Judd. *Pedro and Me: Friendship, Loss, and What I Learned.* Holt, 2000. Ages YA. (Graphic novel)

Wolff, Virginia Euwer. *Make Lemonade.* Holt, 1993. Ages 12–YA.

———. *True Believer.* Atheneum, 2001. Ages 12–YA.

Woodson, Jacqueline. *From the Notebooks of Melanin Sun.* Scholastic, 1995. Ages 12–YA.

———. *The House You Pass on the Way.* Delacorte, 1997. Ages 12–YA.

## Rites of Passage

Bauer, Joan. *Squashed.* Delacorte, 1992. Ages 11–14. Humorous.

Blume, Judy. *Are You There, God? It's Me, Margaret.* Bradbury, 1970. Ages 10–YA.

Byars, Betsy. *The 18th Emergency.* Viking, 1973. Ages 9–12.

Ehrlich, Amy. *Where It Stops, Nobody Knows.* Dial, 1988. Ages 12–YA.

Fine, Anne. *Flour Babies.* Little, Brown, 1994. Ages 10–14.

————. *My War with Goggle-Eyes.* Little, Brown, 1989. Ages 11–14.

Lawrence, Iain. *Ghost Boy.* Delacorte, 2000. Ages 12–YA.

Peck, Robert Newton. *A Day No Pigs Would Die.* Knopf, 1973. Ages 11–YA.

Rylant, Cynthia. *A Fine White Dust.* Bradbury, 1986. Ages 9–12.

Salisbury, Graham. *Blue Skin of the Sea.* Delacorte, 1992. Ages 12–YA.

## Adventure and Survival

Buss, Fran Leeper, and Daisy Cubias. *Journey of the Sparrows.* Dutton, 1991. Ages 12–YA.

Carter, Alden R. *Between a Rock and a Hard Place.* Scholastic, 1995. Ages 11–YA.

Coleman, Michael. *Weirdo's War.* Orchard, 1998. Ages 9–13.

Creech, Sharon. *The Wanderer.* HarperCollins, 2000. Ages 11–YA.

Cross, Gillian. *The Great American Elephant Chase.* Holiday, 1993. Ages 9–12.

Farmer, Nancy. *A Girl Named Disaster.* Orchard, 1996. Ages 11–YA.

George, Jean Craighead. *Julie.* HarperCollins, 1994. Ages 11–YA.

————. *Julie of the Wolves.* Illustrated by John Schoenherr. Harper, 1972. Ages 11–YA.

————. *The Missing Gator of Gumbo Limbo: An Ecological Mystery.* HarperCollins, 1992. Ages 10–12.

————. *My Side of the Mountain.* Dutton, 1959. Ages 9–12.

Mahy, Margaret. *Underrunners.* Viking, 1992. Ages 12–YA.

Mikaelson, Ben. *Stranded.* Hyperion, 1995. Ages 11–YA.

Myers, Walter Dean. *Scorpions.* Harper, 1988. Ages 10–YA.

Naylor, Phyllis Reynolds. *The Fear Place.* Atheneum, 1994. Ages 11–YA.

Paulsen, Gary. *Hatchet.* Bradbury, 1987. Ages 9–12.

————. *The Haymeadow.* Illustrated by Ruth Wright Paulsen. Delacorte, 1992. Ages 12–YA.

————. *The River.* Delacorte, 1991. Ages 11–YA.

————. *The Voyage of the Frog.* Bradbury, 1989. Ages 12–YA.

Pullman, Philip. *The Ruby in the Smoke.* Knopf, 1987. Ages 14–YA. London, 1800s.

Ross, Ramon Royal. *Harper & Moon.* Atheneum, 1993. Ages 10–YA.

Thiele, Colin. *Shadow Shark.* Harper, 1988. Ages 10–13.

# 8

# HISTORICAL FICTION

*On the wind-beaten plains*
*once lived my ancestors.*
*In the days of peaceful moods,*
*they wandered and hunted.*
*In days of need or greed,*
*they warred and loafed.*
*Beneath the lazy sun, kind winds above,*
*they laughed and feasted.*
*Through the starlit night, under the moon,*
*they dreamed and loved.*
*Now, from the wind-beaten plains,*
*only their dust rises.*

— GREY COHOE

Historical fiction brings history to life by placing appealing child characters in accurately described historical settings. By telling the stories of these characters' everyday lives as well as presenting their triumphs and failures, authors of historical fiction provide young readers with the human side of history, making it more real and more memorable.

## DEFINITION AND DESCRIPTION

*Historical fiction* is realistic fiction set in a time remote enough from the present to be considered history. That is, although the story is imaginary, it is within the realm of possibility that such events could have occurred. In these stories, historical facts blend with imaginary characters and plot. The facts are actual historical events, authentic period settings, and real historical figures. An imaginary story is constructed around these facts. In the *Reference Guide to Historical Fiction for Children and Young Adults,* Adamson (1987) states:

> Historical fiction recreates a particular historical period with or without historical figures as incidental characters. It is generally written about a time period in which the author has not lived or no more recently than one generation before its composition. For example, fiction written in 1987 must be set, at the latest, in 1967, to be considered historical. Fiction written in 1930 but set in 1925 does not fulfill this criterion for legitimate historical fiction. (p. ix)

In the most common form of historical fiction, the main characters of the story are imaginary, but some secondary characters may be actual historical figures. An example of this type of historical fiction is the 1944 Newbery Medal winner, *Johnny Tremain* by Esther Forbes. Set in the U.S. Revolutionary War period, this story tells of Johnny, a fictitious character, who is apprenticed to a silversmith. In the course of the story, Samuel Adams, John Hancock, and Paul Revere are introduced as minor characters.

In another form of historical fiction, the past is described complete with the social traditions, customs, morals, and values of the period but with no mention of an actual historical event nor actual historical figures as characters. The physical location is also accurately reconstructed for the readers. An example of this story type is *The Witch of Blackbird Pond* by Elizabeth George Speare. The Puritan way of life in Connecticut in the 1600s is depicted in this story about young Kit from Barbados who becomes involved in a witchcraft trial. The locales and traditions are accurate reconstructions of Puritan life of that era, whereas the characters, dialogue, day-to-day events, and details are fictitious. Both these forms of historical stories qualify as historical fiction under the definition of this genre.

A third type of historical story is one in which elements of fantasy are found, and therefore the story does not qualify as historical fiction. For example, time warps and other supernatural features may be found in Canadian Janet Lunn's *The Root Cellar* and in Jane Yolen's *The Devil's Arithmetic.* These stories are *historical fantasy* and are included in Chapter 6, "Modern Fantasy." Picture books in the historical fiction genre are discussed in Chapter 4, "Picture Books."

## EVALUATION AND SELECTION OF HISTORICAL FICTION

Historical fiction must first be evaluated for its story strength. It must tell an engaging story. The author must develop rounded, complex characters with whom children can identify. The author should also develop a universal theme that is worthy and thought provoking without being didactic. In addition, the author of historical fiction must present historical facts with as much accuracy and objectivity as books of history. This means that a setting must be described in sufficient detail as to provide an authentic sense of that time and that place without overwhelming the story. Details such as hair and clothing styles, home architecture and furnishings, foods and food preparation, and modes of transportation must be subtly woven into the story to provide a convincing, authentic period setting. The characters must act within the traditions and norms of their times.

Expressing the language or dialect of the period presents a particular challenge to the author of historical stories. Dialogue that occurs within the text often becomes problematic for the writer. If the speech of the period is greatly different from that of today, then the author faces a decision: Remain true to the language of the time but cause readers difficulties in comprehending, or present the language in today's dialect but lose the flavor and authenticity of the language of the period. In any case, it seems important that the language not jar the reader by its obvious inappropriateness or lose the reader by its extreme difficulty. Most children's authors strive to attain the middle ground—some flavor of a language difference but modified to be understandable to the child reader. Young listeners adapt easily to dialects when they are modeled well by their teachers and may even find occasion to use the dialect to lend flavor to their subsequent writing.

Many educators are convinced of the benefits students gain through integrataing history and literature as part of the social studies curriculum. Smith, Monson, and Dobson (1992) found in their study that the students in fifth grade classrooms in which historical novels were used along with standard instructional materials recalled more historical facts and indicated greater enjoyment in their social studies classes than the students in classrooms that had a similar curriculum without the addition of historical novels.

Many adults today are unaware that the history they learned as children may have been biased or one-sided. Some authors attempt to include more modern interpretations of historical events in historical fiction by setting the record straight or adding a minority presence to the story. However, as was previously mentioned, care must be taken that the characters behave in a historically accurate fashion.

In summary, the criteria for evaluating historical fiction are as follows:

- An engrossing story with well-developed characters
- An interesting plot
- Worthy but subtle themes
- An authentic, well-described setting that informs the reader but does not overwhelm the story
- Historical accuracy in describing places, events and facts, morals, manners, customs, and behaviors of the people

The Scott O'Dell Award, an award established in 1981 by the author Scott O'Dell and administered by Zena Sutherland, honors what is judged to be the most outstanding work of children's historical fiction published in the previous year. The work must be written by a U.S. citizen and be set in the New World. The list of the Scott O'Dell Award winners found in Appendix A can be a source for selecting outstanding historical fiction for use with students. The National Council of Social Studies publishes a list of the most notable trade books in the field of social studies from the preceding year in the April/May issue of its journal, *Social Education*. This list includes many works of historical fiction, as well as nonfiction works, and is a useful source to locate recent books of this genre.

# EARLY  BOOKS  AND  TRENDS
# IN  HISTORICAL  FICTION

Although historical stories were written for children as early as the 1800s, few titles remain of interest from those early years. The early books placed an emphasis on exciting events and idealized real-life characters—much in the style of heroic legends. Howard Pyle's works were an exception to this pattern. Two of his historical novels, *Otto of the Silver Hand* (1888) and *Men of Iron* (1891), set in the Middle Ages, approach in quality many of the more recent works. However, few other stories written before World War I had memorable characters presented as well-rounded, complex individuals. Most of these stories seem unconvincing today.

Between World War I and World War II, historical stories appeared in which well-developed characters involved in realistic events were portrayed in authentic period settings. In 1929, Eric Kelly won the Newbery Medal for *The Trumpeter of Krakow,* set in Poland in the Middle Ages. This exciting adventure features two children who outwit the Tartars who have captured one of their fathers. From the 1930s, a few truly remarkable books remain popular with children today. *Calico Bush* (1931) by Rachel Field tells the story of Marguerite Ledoux, a French servant girl who settles in Maine in 1743. Between 1932 and 1943, the first eight books of the Little House series by Laura Ingalls Wilder were published. These stories have continued to grow in popularity, partially as a result of the long-lasting television series based on the books. *Johnny Tremain* by Esther Forbes was awarded the Newbery Medal in 1944. This Revolutionary era novel is considered a children's classic.

The period after World War II saw a flowering of historical fiction for children in both English and American literature. Many outstanding books were published in the fifteen years following the war. Examples are *The Door in the Wall* by Marguerite de Angeli, published in 1949; *The Buffalo Knife* by William O. Steele, published in 1952; *The Courage of Sarah Noble* by Alice Dalgliesh, published in 1954; *The Sword in the Tree* by Clyde Robert Bulla, published in 1956; *Calico Captive,* by Elizabeth George Speare, published in 1957; the best-selling Newbery Medal–winning book *The Witch of Blackbird Pond* by Elizabeth George Speare, published in 1958; *The Cabin Faced West* by Jean Fritz, published in 1958; and *The Lantern Bearers* by Rosemary Sutcliff, published in 1959. In 1954, the Laura Ingalls Wilder Award was awarded to (and named for) Laura Ingalls Wilder, an author of historical fiction. This award, the "Hall of Fame" of children's authors and illustrators, honors an author or illustrator whose books, published in the United States, have made a substantial and lasting contribution to children's literature. By 1960, the genre of historical fiction was well established as a fine resource for children's enjoyment and enrichment. Milestones in the development of historical fiction are highlighted on page 156.

Historical fiction continues to flourish today. Some older historical fiction novels have been criticized for portraying some cultural groups in an extremely negative light. For example, two Newbery Medal winners, *Caddie Woodlawn* by Carol Ryrie Brink and *The Matchlock Gun* by Walter D. Edmonds, have been faulted for their negative portrayals of Native Americans. However, minority authors have written a number of excellent works based on the early experiences of their cultural groups in North America; for example, see *Song of the Trees* and its sequels by Mildred Taylor and *Journey to Topaz* and its sequel by Yoshiko Uchida. Of special note are also many outstanding, recently published books set during the years leading up to and including World War II. The establishment in 1981 of the Scott O'Dell

EXCELLENT HISTORICAL FICTION TO READ ALOUD

*(Books for each level vary in difficulty and should be selected with the students' literary backgrounds in mind.)*

PRIMARY LEVEL    AGES 5-8

Bunting, Eve. *Train to Somewhere.* Illustrated by Ronald Himler. Clarion, 1996.

MacLachlan, Patricia. *Sarah, Plain and Tall.* Harper, 1985.

Turner, Ann. *Mississippi Mud: Three Prairie Journals.* Illustrated by Robert J. Clark. HarperCollins, 1997.

Wilder, Laura Ingalls. *Little House in the Big Woods.* Harper, 1932.

INTERMEDIATE LEVEL    AGES 8-11

Anderson, Rachel. *Black Water.* Holt, 1995.

Curtis, Christopher Paul. *The Watsons Go to Birmingham—1963.* Delacorte, 1995.

Dorris, Michael. *Sees behind Trees.* Hyperion, 1996.

Fleischman, Sid. *Bandit's Moon.* Illustrated by Joseph A. Smith. Greenwillow, 1998.

Giff, Patricia Reilly. *Lily's Crossing.* Delacorte, 1997.

Lowry, Lois. *Number the Stars.* Houghton, 1989.

Orlev, Uri. *The Island on Bird Street.* Translated from the Hebrew by Hillel Halkin. Houghton, 1983.

Polacco, Patricia. *Pink and Say.* Philomel, 1994.

Reeder, Carolyn. *Shades of Gray.* Macmillan, 1989.

Skurzynski, Gloria. *What Happened in Hamelin.* Four Winds, 1979.

Speare, Elizabeth George. *The Sign of the Beaver.* Houghton, 1983.

ADVANCED LEVEL    AGES 11-14

Berry, James. *Ajeemah and His Son.* HarperCollins, 1992.

Cushman, Karen. *Catherine, Called Birdy.* Clarion, 1994.

Fleischman, Paul. *Bull Run.* HarperCollins, 1993.

Hesse, Karen. *Stowaway.* Simon & Schuster, 2000.

Holt, Kimberly Willis. *When Zachary Beaver Came to Town.* Holt, 1999.

Lyons, Mary E. *Dear Ellen Bee: A Civil War Scrapbook of Two Union Spies.* Simon & Schuster, 2000.

Paterson, Katherine. *Jip, His Story.* Dutton, 1996.

Temple, Frances. *The Ramsay Scallop.* Orchard, 1994.

Wolff, Virginia Euwer. *Bat 6.* Scholastic, 1998.

Award for Historical Fiction has begun to offer additional recognition for authors of this genre. In 1989, Elizabeth George Speare was selected to receive the Laura Ingalls Wilder Award for the entire body of her work, which comprises four outstanding works of historical fiction for children.

## TOPICS IN HISTORICAL FICTION

Two ways of considering the topics treated in historical fiction novels are by the universal themes presented in the books and by the historical periods in which the books are set. First, some *common themes* that can be found within historical fiction novels for children are suggested with titles of

# M I L E S T O N E S

*in the Development of* H I S T O R I C A L   F I C T I O N

| 1888 | *Otto of the Silver Hand* by Howard Pyle | Early recognized work of historical fiction |
| 1929 | The Newbery Medal given to *The Trumpeter of Krakow* by Eric Kelly | National recognition for an early work of historical fiction |
| 1932–1943 | Publication of the first eight books of *Little House* series by Laura Ingalls Wilder | Classic historical fiction |
| 1944 | *Johnny Tremain* by Esther Forbes given the Newbery Medal | Classic historical adventure set during the American Revolution era |
| 1949–1960 | Many historical novels published, including *The Door in the Wall,* by Marguerite de Angeli, *The Witch of Blackbird Pond* by Elizabeth George Speare, *The Lantern Bearers* by Rosemary Sutcliff | Dramatic increase in the quality and quantity of historical novels for children |
| 1954 | Establishment of the Laura Ingalls Wilder Award, first awarded to Wilder | Recognition of an historical fiction author for the entire body of her work |
| 1961 | Scott O'Dell's *Island of the Blue Dolphins* awarded the Newbery Medal | Landmark book of historical fiction with a strong female protagonist from a minority culture |
| 1971 | *Journey to Topaz* by Yoshiko Uchida | Early historical work about and by a minority (Japanese American) |
| 1972 | Scott O'Dell awarded the Hans Christian Andersen Award | International recognition of a U.S. author of historical novels |
| 1975 | *The Song of the Trees* by Mildred Taylor | First in a series of books about an African-American family's struggle starting in the Depression era |
| 1984 | Establishment of the Scott O'Dell Award | Award given for outstanding historical novel set in North America brings recognition to the genre |
| 1989 | Elizabeth George Speare awarded the Laura Ingalls Wilder Award | Recognition of an author of historical fiction for her substantial contribution to children's literature |
| 1989 | *Number the Stars* by Lois Lowry | Newbery Medal book about the Holocaust set in World War II Denmark |
| 1993 | *Bull Run* by Paul Fleischman | Novel set during the U.S. Civil War and told through personal episodes |
| 1994 | *Catherine, Called Birdy* by Karen Cushman | Novel set in medieval England and told through a girl's journal |
| 1999 | *When Zachary Beaver Came to Town* by Kimberly Willis Holt. | Winner of the National Book Award for Young People's Literature, features a physically challenged boy. |
| 2000 | *Fever 1793* by Laurie Halse Anderson | Novel set in Philadelphia during the yellow fever epidemic |

books in which the theme is developed. Next, six *historical periods* in which historical fiction novels can be found are reviewed in capsule form.

## Themes in Historical Fiction

Common themes that extend across time and place in historical stories can be an approach for presenting historical fiction to children. For example, a theme, such as seeking new frontiers, is explored through a small group of books set in different times and places. Some possible themes for development in this manner are listed below with suggestions of books that might be selected for the study of the theme. Other themes may be discovered when you read historical fiction novels and consider the commonalities to be found among them.

### SEEKING NEW FRONTIERS
*The Cabin Faced West* by Jean Fritz
*Little House in the Big Woods* by Laura Ingalls Wilder
*Wagon Wheels* by Barbara Brenner
*Beyond the Divide* by Kathryn Lasky
*On to Oregon* by Honoré Morrow
*The Ballad of Lucy Whipple* by Karen Cushman

### SEARCH FOR FREEDOM FROM PERSECUTION
*Jump Ship to Freedom* by James Lincoln Collier and Christopher Collier
*The Island on Bird Street* by Uri Orlev
*The Upstairs Room* by Johanna Reiss
*Sing Down the Moon* by Scott O'Dell
*The Endless Steppe* by Esther Hautzig
*The Witch of Blackbird Pond* by Elizabeth George Speare
*The Butterfly* by Patricia Polacco

### EFFECTS OF WAR
*My Brother Sam Is Dead* by James Lincoln Collier and Christopher Collier
*Across Five Aprils* by Irene Hunt
*Shades of Gray* by Carolyn Reeder
*Pink and Say* by Patricia Polacco
*Bat 6* by Virginia Euwer Wolff
*Caged Eagles* by Eric Walters
*Solider's Heart* by Gary Paulsen

### FAMILY CLOSENESS IN TIMES OF ADVERSITY
*Journey Home* by Yoshiko Uchida
*Journey to America* by Sonia Levitin
*Roll of Thunder, Hear My Cry* by Mildred Taylor
*Upon the Head of the Goat* by Aranka Siegal
*Fever 1793* by Laurie Halse Anderson
*Nory Ryan's Song* by Patricia Reilly Giff

## Periods of History in Fiction

The natural relationship of historical fiction stories to the study of history and geography suggests building whole units of study around periods of both world and U.S. history in which good stories for children are set. The following capsule statements about seven historical periods will give you an idea of how these units might be organized. At the end of the chapter (under Recommended Books), you will find works of historical fiction organized by these seven historical periods.

*BEGINNINGS OF CIVILIZATION UP TO 3000 B.C.*    This period represents prehistoric cultures and civilizations. Early peoples (Java, Neanderthals, Cro-Magnons) and early civilizations in the Middle East and Asia are included. Egyptians, Syrians, and Phoenicians developed civilizations; and Hebrews produced a religious faith, Judaism, that resulted in the Old Testament. The subcontinent of India was the site of Aryan civilizations. Chinese dynasties were responsible for excellent works of art and agricultural systems of irrigation. An example of an historical novel set in this time period is A. Linevski's *An Old Tale Carved Out of Stone.*

*CIVILIZATIONS OF THE ANCIENT WORLD, 3000 B.C. TO A.D. 600*    The era of the Greek city-states was followed by a period of Roman rule in western Europe. Christianity was founded in Jerusalem and spread throughout Europe. Ancient Asia was the site of enduring civilizations that bred two remarkable men born about 560 B.C.: the Indian religious leader Buddha and the Chinese philosopher Confucius. Both have had a lasting influence on their civilizations. One novel set in this time period retells the story of Moses leading his people from Egypt to the promised land in Sonia Levitin's *Escape from Egypt.*

*CIVILIZATIONS OF THE MEDIEVAL WORLD, 600 TO 1500*    The eastern part of the Roman Empire maintained its stability and preserved the civilization from the capital of Constantinople. This civilization, the Byzantine Empire, created a distinct culture and branch of the Christian Church—the Orthodox Church—which influenced Russia to adopt both the religion and the culture. Following the fall of the Roman Empire, western Europe dissolved into isolated separate regions without strong governments. Many of the responsibilities of government were carried out by the Christian Church. The Church dominated the economic, political, cultural, and educational life of the Middle Ages in western Europe. These feudal societies eventually gave rise to the separate nations of modern Europe. During this era, early African and American civilizations arose independently. The great civilizations of China and Japan continued to flourish throughout these centuries. As examples, Marguerite de Angeli's *The Door in the Wall* and Karen Cushman's *Catherine, Called Birdy* portray medieval life in England.

*THE EMERGENCE OF MODERN NATIONS, 1500 TO 1800*    The Renaissance, a literary and artistic movement, swept western Europe. Many important developments of this period included the invention of the printing press, a new emphasis on reason, a reformation of the Christian Church, and advances in science. During this same period, central governments throughout Europe increased their power. Spain, and then France, dominated Europe in the 1500s and 1600s. In the 1700s, Russia, Austria, and Prussia rose to power. This was also a time when Europeans explored and settled in Africa, India, and the Americas. The Portuguese and Spanish took the lead in explorations and acquired many foreign colonies. England, the Netherlands, France, and Russia also colonized and influenced East Asia, India, Africa, and the Americas.

Revolutions created new governments and new nations. The American Revolution (1776–1781) created a new nation; the French Revolution in 1789 affected the direction of governments toward democracy in all of Europe. Napoleon built an empire across Europe, resulting in the uniting of European nations to defeat Napoleon. The nations of Latin America also began to gain their independence. China expanded gradually under the Ming and Ch'ing dynasties. Japan prospered under the Tokugawa shogunate. The United States and Canada were the sites of rapid population increases due to immigration; the settlements in North America were predominantly along the eastern coasts. Some westward expansion was beginning in the United States and Canada. For example, a story relating the challenges of settling the Maine frontier in the 1700s is Elizabeth George Speare's *The Sign of the Beaver.*

*THE DEVELOPMENT OF INDUSTRIAL SOCIETY, 1800 TO 1914*   The 1800s were marked by a rapid shift from agricultural societies to industrial societies. Great Britain was an early site for this change. The factory system developed and prospered, while working and living conditions deteriorated for the worker. Two stories about life as a millworker in this period are Katherine Paterson's *Lyddie* and James Lincoln Collier and Christopher Collier's *The Clock*. New technology—railroad trains, steamboats, the telegraph and telephone—affected transportation and communications. Advances in science and medicine helped to explain the nature of life and improved the quality of life. Education developed into an important institution in western Europe and North America. Europe underwent revolutions that readjusted boundaries and eventually led to the unification of new nations.

The westward movement was fully realized as pioneers settled across the United States and Canada. The building of railroads hastened the establishment of new settlements. Native Americans struggled for survival in the face of these massive population shifts. Black slavery had existed in the American colonies from earliest days, but in the 1800s, slavery became a social and economic issue resulting in the Civil War (1861–1865). Slavery was abolished and the Union was preserved at the cost of 600,000 lives and a major rift between the North and the South. Carolyn Reeder's *Shades of Gray* portrays a family torn apart by this war.

The United States grew in economic and political strength. An age of imperialism resulted in firm control of large areas of the world by other world powers such as England, France, and Belgium. Great Britain dominated India and parts of Africa and continued its influence over Canada, Australia, and New Zealand, while Japan became a powerful force in east Asia.

*WORLD WARS IN THE TWENTIETH CENTURY, 1914 TO 1945*   This era includes World War I (1914–1918) in Europe, in which the United States and Canada joined and fought with the Allies (Great Britain, France, Russia, Greece, and Rumania); the between-wars period that included the Great Depression; Hitler's rise to power in 1933; and World War II (1939–1945) in Europe and Asia, in which Canada and the United States joined forces with England, France, and Russia to battle Germany, Italy, and Japan. In 1917, the Bolshevik Revolution established a Communist government in Russia. In 1931, Great Britain recognized Canada, Australia, New Zealand, and South Africa as completely independent. However, each nation declared its loyalty to the British monarch and continued its cultural ties with Great Britain. The Holocaust during World War II—the persecution and killing of Jewish and other people by the Nazi regime—stands out as one of the most atrocious periods in modern history. Hans Peter Richter's *Friedrich* tells of the horrors of the Holocaust as it affected a Jewish boy's life. World War II ended shortly after the United States dropped nuclear devices on Hiroshima and Nagasaki, Japan.

*POST–WORLD WAR II ERA, 1945 TO 1980s*    During this era, the United States and western European nations were involved in a struggle for world influence against the communist nations, particularly the Soviet Union and China. A massive arms buildup, including nuclear weapons, was undertaken by the major nations of both sides. The Korean War (1950–1953) and the Vietnam War (1965–1973) were major conflicts in which the United States fought to contain Communist expansion. The Korean War, combined with the postwar economic recovery of Japan, drew attention to the growing importance of East Asia in world affairs. A novel for children, *The Purple Heart* by Marc Talbert, describes the Vietnam War era. The Soviet Union launched a series of satellites beginning with Sputnik I on October 4, 1957, inaugurating the space age. An explosion of scientific knowledge occurred as a result of increased spending for weapons development and space exploration. The 1950s and 1960s have been described as the Cold War decades because of the increasing hostility between the Soviet Union and the United States. In the 1970s, public pressure mounted in the United States to reduce the nation's external military commitments.

During the 1960s a strong civil rights movement, led by Martin Luther King, Jr., and other prominent figures of the era, fought for equal treatment of African-Americans. The movement led to desegregation of schools, restaurants, transportation, and housing. Equal rights for women were also sought during the feminist movement in the 1970s. An example of a book set in the 1960s is Trudy Krisher's *Spite Fences,* a story of race relations in Georgia.

Many fine works of historical fiction for children can now be found. Children have an opportunity to live vicariously the lives of people from long ago—people from different cultures and from different parts of the world.

## REFERENCES

Adamson, L. G. (1987). *A reference guide to historical fiction for children and young adults.* Westport, CT: Greenwood Press.

Cohoe, G. (1972). Ancestors. In T. Allen (Ed.), *The whispering wind: Poetry by young American Indians.* New York: Doubleday.

Smith, J. A., Monson, J. A., & Dobson, D. (1992). A case study on integrating history and reading instruction through literature. *Social Education, 56,* 370–375.

## NOTABLE  AUTHORS  OF  HISTORICAL  FICTION

**James Lincoln Collier and Christopher Collier,** authors of novels set in U.S. Revolutionary War era. *My Brother Sam Is Dead.*

**Christopher Paul Curtis,** African-American author of two historical novels: the Newbery Medal book, *Bud, Not Buddy,* a Depression era novel, and Newbery Honor book, *The Watsons Go to Birmingham—1963.*

**Karen Cushman,** author of two Newbery acclaimed historical novels set in the Middle Ages. *Catherine, Called Birdy; The Midwife's Apprentice.*

**Karen Hesse,** author of 1998 Newbery Medal winner, *Out of the Dust,* set in Oklahoma in the 1930s. Also noted for historical novel *Letters from Rifka.*

**Kimberly Willis Holt,** author of novels about characters with disabilities and set in small towns of the American South. *My Louisiana Sky: When Zachary Beaver Came to Town.*

**Lois Lowry,** author of the historical fiction novel *Number the Stars,* Newbery Medal winner in 1990. Also noted for realistic fiction and modern fantasy novels.

Patricia MacLachlan, Newbery Medal–winning author noted for a wide range of literature for children, including works of historical fiction. *Sarah, Plain and Tall; Skylark.*

Scott O'Dell, author of many stories based on Native American and Mexican-American cultures. *Island of the Blue Dolphins.*

Uri Orlev, noted Israeli author of historical fiction novels treating the Holocaust and its aftermath. *The Island on Bird Street; Lydia, Queen of Palestine.*

Carolyn Reeder, author of two historical novels set in the U.S. Civil War era. *Across the Lines; Shades of Gray.*

Elizabeth George Speare, winner of Scott O'Dell, Newbery, and Laura Ingalls Wilder Awards for her works of historical fiction. *The Sign of the Beaver.*

Mildred Taylor, author of seven stories of an African-American land-owning family, beginning in the 1930s and set in rural Mississippi. *Roll of Thunder, Hear My Cry.*

Laura Ingalls Wilder, author of the Little House series based on the Ingalls family's experiences as pioneers in the Midwest.

Laurence Yep, author of historical fiction about Chinese Americans and their adjustments to life in the United States. *Dragonwings.*

## RECOMMENDED HISTORICAL FICTION BOOKS

*Ages refer to approximate interest levels. YA = young adult readers. Locales and dates of settings are noted. Historical biographies are arranged by these same eras and placed at the end of Chapter 9.*

### Beginnings of Civilization up to 3000 B.C.

Behn, Harry. *The Faraway Lurs.* World, 1963. Ages 12–15. Northern Europe, 3500 B.C.

Linevski, A. *An Old Tale Carved Out of Stone.* Translated by Maria Polushkin. Crown, 1973. Ages 10–14. Early Siberia.

Osborne, Chester. *The Memory String.* Atheneum, 1984. Ages 8–12. Siberian Peninsula, 25,000 B.C.

Steele, William O. *The Magic Amulet.* Harcourt, 1979. Ages 10–14. North America, 10,000 B.C.

Treece, Henry. *The Dream-Time.* Meredith, 1968. Ages 11–14. British Isles, 11,000 B.C.

Wibberley, Leonard. *Attar of the Ice Valley.* Farrar, 1968. Ages 11–YA. Europe, 50,000 B.C.

### Civilizations of the Ancient World, 3000 B.C. to A.D. 600

Hunter, Mollie. *The Stronghold.* Harper, 1974. Ages 9–12. British Isles, 100 B.C.

Levitin, Sonia. *Escape from Egypt.* Little, Brown, 1994. Ages 14–YA. Jews, 1200 B.C.

McGraw, Eloise Jarvis. *Mara, Daughter of the Nile.* Penguin, 1953. Ages 11–YA. Ancient Egypt, 1550 B.C.

Paton Walsh, Jill. *Children of the Fox.* Farrar, 1978. Ages 10–14. Ancient Persia, 400 B.C.

Speare, Elizabeth George. *The Bronze Bow.* Houghton, 1961. Ages 10–14. Jerusalem, A.D. 30.

Sutcliff, Rosemary. *Song for a Dark Queen.* Crowell, 1978. Ages 10–14. British Isles, A.D. 50.

———. *Sun Horse, Moon Horse.* Dutton, 1978. Ages 10–14. British Isles, 100 B.C.

### Civilizations of the Medieval World, 600 to 1500

Alder, Elizabeth. *The King's Shadow.* Farrar, 1995. Ages 12–YA. England, end of Saxon era, pre-1066.

Bulla, Clyde Robert. *Viking Adventure.* Crowell, 1963. Ages 7–10. Norway, 900s.

Cushman, Karen. *Catherine, Called Birdy.* Clarion, 1994. Ages 11–YA. England, manor life, 1290s.

———. *Matilda Bone.* Clarion, 2000. Ages 11–YA. Medieval England, medical practitioner.

———. *The Midwife's Apprentice.* Clarion, 1995. Ages 12–YA. England, Middle Ages.

de Angeli, Marguerite. *The Door in the Wall.* Doubleday, 1949. Ages 9–12. England, 1300s.

Dorris, Michael. *Morning Girl.* Hyperion, 1992. Ages 9–12. Taino Indians, 1490s.

Fleischman, Sid. *The Whipping Boy.* Greenwillow, 1986. Ages 9–11. England, Middle Ages.

Haugaard, Erik Christian. *Hakon of Rogen's Saga.* Houghton, 1963. Ages 9–12. Vikings, 900s.

Newth, Mette. *The Transformation.* Translated by Faith Ingwarsen. Farrar, 2000. Ages YA. Greenland, Inuit girl, 1400s.

Skurzynski, Gloria. *Manwolf.* Houghton, 1981. Ages 10–14. Poland, 1380s.

———. *Spider's Voice.* Simon & Schuster, 1999. Ages 13–YA. France, twelfth century, medieval lovers Abélard and Héloïse.

———. *What Happened in Hamelin.* Four Winds, 1979. Ages 10–14. Germany, 1200s.

Temple, Frances. *The Ramsay Scallop.* Orchard, 1994. Ages 12–YA. England, 1299.

## *The Emergence of Modern Nations, 1500 to 1800*

Anderson, Laurie Halse. *Fever 1793.* Simon & Schuster, 2000. Ages 11–YA. Philadelphia, yellow fever epidemic, freed slaves' role, 1793.

Avi. *The Fighting Ground.* Lippincott, 1984. Ages 10–14. U.S. Revolutionary War era, 1770s.

Bosse, Malcolm. *The Examination.* Farrar, 1994. Ages 11–YA. China, sixteenth-century Ming Dynasty.

Bowen, Gary. *Stranded at Plimoth Plantation 1626.* Illustrated by Gary Bowen. HarperCollins, 1994. Ages 9–12. Jamestown, settler life, 1620s.

Bruchac, Joseph. *The Arrow over the Door.* Dial, 1998. Ages 9–12. Quaker boy and Abenaki Indian boy in 1777.

Caudill, Rebecca. *Tree of Freedom.* Illustrated by Dorothy Bayley. Viking, 1949. Ages 10–12. Kentucky, U.S. Revolutionary War era.

Clapp, Patricia. *Constance: A Story of Early Plymouth.* Lothrop, 1968. Ages 10–14. U.S. colonial era, 1620s.

———. *I'm Deborah Sampson: A Soldier in the War of the Revolution.* Lothrop, 1977. Ages 9–12. U.S. Revolutionary War era, 1770s.

———. *Witches' Children: A Story of Salem.* Lothrop, 1982. Ages 10–YA. U.S. colonial era, 1690s.

Collier, James Lincoln, and Christopher Collier. *Jump Ship to Freedom.* Delacorte, 1981. Ages 9–12. U.S. slavery, 1780s.

———. *My Brother Sam Is Dead.* Four Winds, 1974. Ages 10–14. U.S. Revolutionary War era, 1770s.

———. *War Comes to Willy Freeman.* Delacorte, 1983. Ages 9–12. U.S. Revolutionary War era, U.S. slavery, 1780s.

Dalgliesh, Alice. *The Courage of Sarah Noble.* Scribner's, 1954. Ages 7–9. U.S. pioneers, early 1700s.

Dorris, Michael. *Guests.* Hyperion, 1994. Ages 8–12. First Thanksgiving feast, Native-American boy.

———. *Sees behind Trees.* Hyperion, 1996. Ages 8–12. Sixteenth century, pre-Colonial America, partially sighted, Native-American boy.

Forbes, Esther. *Johnny Tremain.* Houghton, 1943. Ages 10–13. U.S. Revolutionary War era, 1770s.

Fritz, Jean. *The Cabin Faced West.* Coward, 1958. Ages 7–10. U.S. pioneers, 1700s.

Gauch, Patricia. *This Time, Tempe Wick?* Coward, 1974. Ages 7–10. U.S. Revolutionary War era, 1780s.

Haugaard, Erik Christian. *The Boy and the Samurai.* Houghton Mifflin, 1991. Ages 10–13. Sixteenth-century Japan.

———. *A Messenger for Parliament.* Houghton, 1976. Ages 10–14. England, 1640s.

Hesse, Karen. *Stowaway.* Simon & Schuster, 2000. Ages 10–YA. British sailing ship, Captain Cook's voyage, 1768.

Lasky, Kathryn. *Beyond the Burning Time.* Scholastic, 1994. Ages 11–YA. U.S. colonial era, Salem witch trials, 1690s.

Lawrence, Iain. *The Wreckers.* Delacorte, 1998. Ages 10–14. Cornwall, England in 1799, a survival mystery.

Namioka, Lensey. *The Coming of the Bear.* HarperCollins, 1992. Ages 10–YA. Japan, 1600s.

O'Dell, Scott. *The Captive.* Houghton, 1979. Ages 10–14. Mexico, 1500s.

Rinaldi, Ann. *A Break with Charity: A Story about the Salem Witch Trials.* Harcourt, 1992. Ages 12–YA. Salem witch trials, 1692.

———. *The Fifth of March: A Story of the Boston Massacre.* Harcourt, 1993. Ages 11–YA. Boston, indentured servant, 1770s.

———. *A Stitch in Time.* Scholastic, 1994. Ages 12–YA. Salem, Massachusetts, family saga, 1788–1791.

Speare, Elizabeth George. *The Sign of the Beaver.* Houghton, 1983. Ages 8–12. Maine frontier, 1700s.

————. *The Witch of Blackbird Pond.* Houghton, 1958. Ages 10–14. U.S. colonial era, 1680s.

Sutcliff, Rosemary. *Bonnie Dundee.* Dutton, 1984. Ages 10–14. Scotland, 1600s.

Van Leeuwen, Jean. *Going West.* Illustrated by Thomas B. Allen. Doubleday/Dial, 1992. Ages 5–8. Wagon train, picture book.

## The Development of Industrial Society, 1800 to 1914

Aiken, Joan. *The Teeth of the Gale.* Harper, 1988. Ages 9–YA. Spain, 1820s.

Anderson, Rachel. *Black Water.* Holt, 1995. Ages 9–12. Late nineteenth-century England, boy with epilepsy.

Angell, Judie. *One-Way to Ansonia.* Bradbury, 1985. Ages 10–YA. U.S. immigrants, 1890s.

Armstrong, Jennifer. *Black-Eyed Susan.* Illustrated by Emily Martindale. Crown, 1995. Ages 8–12. Dakota Territory, pioneer life.

Armstrong, William H. *Sounder.* Harper, 1969. Ages 9–12. U.S. South, African Americans, early 1900s.

Avi. *Beyond the Western Sea: The Escape from Home.* Orchard, 1996. Ages 11–14. Ireland, 1851.

————. *The True Confessions of Charlotte Doyle.* Orchard, 1990. Ages 8–12. England, United States, 1830s.

Beatty, Patricia. *Charley Skedaddle.* Morrow, 1987. Ages 11–14. U.S. Civil War, 1860s.

————. *Jayhawker.* Morrow, 1991. Ages 10–14. Kansas, slavery, underground railroad, 1800s.

————. *Turn Homeward, Hannalee.* Morrow, 1984. Ages 10–14. U.S. Civil War, 1860s.

Belpré, Pura. *Firefly Summer.* Piñata, 1996. Ages 10–13. Puerto Rico, about 1900.

Berry, James. *Ajeemah and His Son.* HarperCollins, 1992. Ages 12–YA. Slavery, United States, 1807.

Blos, Joan. *A Gathering of Days: A New England Girl's Journal, 1830–32.* Scribner's, 1979. Ages 8–11. New England, 1830s.

Brenner, Barbara. *Wagon Wheels.* Harper, 1978. Ages 7–9. U.S. pioneers, African Americans, 1870s.

Bunting, Eve. *Train to Somewhere.* Illustrated by Ronald Himler. Clarion, 1996. Ages 7–10. Orphan train from New York to the Midwest in 1878. Picture book.

Clark, Clara Gillow. *Nellie Bishop.* Boyds Mills, 1996. Ages 12–YA. Pennsylvania canal town, 1880s.

Collier, James Lincoln, and Christopher Collier. *The Clock.* Delacorte, 1992. Ages 9–12. Connecticut mill life, early 1800s.

————. *With Every Drop of Blood.* Delacorte, 1994. Ages 10–14. Virginia, race relations, slavery, Civil War era.

Conlon-McKenna, Marita. *Fields of Home.* Illustrated by Donald Teskey. Holiday, 1997. Ages 9–12. Ireland, mid-1800s.

————. *Under the Hawthorn Tree.* Illustrated by Donald Teskey. Holiday, 1990. Ages 10–12. Ireland, mid-1800s.

Conrad, Pam. *Prairie Songs.* Harper, 1985. Ages 10–14. Nebraska, late 1800s.

Crew, Gary. *Bright Star.* Illustrated by Anne Spudvillas. Kane/Miller, 1997. Ages 9–12. Australia, 1861, dairy farm. Picture book.

Cushman, Karen. *The Ballad of Lucy Whipple.* Clarion, 1996. Ages 10–13. Massachusetts to California, Gold Rush.

De Felice, Cynthia. *Weasel.* Macmillan, 1990. Ages 9–12. Ohio frontier, 1830s.

DeVries, David. *Home at Last.* Dell, 1992. Ages 10–13. Orphan train, New York to Nebraska, 1800s.

Fleischman, Paul. *Bull Run.* HarperCollins, 1993. Ages 10–YA. U.S. Civil War era, 1860s.

————. *Coming-and-Going Men: Four Tales.* Illustrated by Randy Gaul. Harper, 1985. Ages 11–YA. Vermont, 1800.

Fleischman, Sid. *Bandit's Moon.* Illustrated by Joseph A. Smith. Greenwillow, 1998. Ages 8–12. California Gold Rush era, Mexican bandit Joaquin Murieta.

Fox, Paula. *The Slave Dancer.* Bradbury, 1973. Ages 11–YA. U.S. slave trade, 1840s.

Fritz, Jean. *Brady.* Coward, 1960. Ages 9–12. Pennsylvania, underground railroad, 1830s.

Garner, Alan. *The Stone Book Quartet.* Dell, 1988. Ages 10–12. Four generations of a family in Cheshire, England, beginning in the late 1800s.

Giff, Patricia Reilly. *Nory Ryan's Song.* Delacorte, 2000. Ages 9–13. Ireland, potato famine, 1845.

Hansen, Joyce. *The Captive.* Scholastic, 1994. Ages 11–YA. U.S. slave trade, Civil War era.

————. *Which Way Freedom?* Walker, 1986. Ages 11–YA. United States, slavery, Civil War era.

Harvey, Brett. *Cassie's Journey: Going West in the 1860's.* Illustrated by Deborah Kogan Ray. Holiday, 1988. Ages 7–9. U.S. frontier, 1860s.

Highwater, Jamake. *Legend Days.* Harper, 1984. Ages 10–YA. United States, Northern Plains Indians, 1800s.

Holland, Isabelle. *Behind the Lines.* Scholastic, 1994. Ages 11–YA. U.S. Civil War.

Holman, Felice. *The Wild Children.* Scribner's, 1983. Ages 9–12. Russia, early 1900s.

Hudson, Jan. *Sweetgrass.* Philomel, 1989. Ages 11–YA. Canada, Dakota Indians, 1830s.

Hunt, Irene. *Across Five Aprils.* Follett, 1964. Ages 10–YA. U.S. Civil War era, 1860s.

Irwin, Hadley. *Jim-Dandy.* Macmillan, 1994. Ages 11–YA. General Custer, horse story, 1870s.

Kudlinsky, Kathleen V. *Night Bird: A Story of the Seminole Indians.* Viking, 1993. Ages 8–11. Florida, Seminole Indians, 1850s.

Lasky, Kathryn. *Beyond the Divide.* Macmillan, 1983. Ages 12–YA. Westward expansion, 1849.

————. *The Bone Wars.* Morrow, 1988. Ages 11–YA. U.S. frontier, mid-1800s.

Lawlor, Laurie. *George on His Own.* Whitman, 1993. Ages 9–12. Frontier life, homesteading in South Dakota, early 1900s.

Lunn, Janet. *Shadow in Hawthorn Bay.* Scribner's, 1986/Dennys, 1986. Ages 12–YA. Canada frontier, early 1800s.

Lyons, Mary E. *Dear Ellen Bee: A Civil War Scrapbook of Two Union Spies.* Simon & Schuster, 2000. Ages 10–13. Richmond, Virginia, Civil War era.

————. *Letters from a Slave Girl: The Story of Harriet Jacobs.* Scribner's, 1992. Ages 10–YA. North Carolina, slavery, early 1800s.

MacLachlan, Patricia. *Sarah, Plain and Tall.* Harper, 1985. Ages 7–10. U.S. frontier, 1850s.

————. *Skylark.* HarperCollins, 1994. Ages 8–11. Sequel to *Sarah, Plain and Tall.*

Moeri, Louise. *Save Queen of Sheba.* Dutton, 1981. Ages 9–12. U.S. frontier, 1800s.

Morrow, Honoré. *On to Oregon!* Morrow, 1954. Ages 9–12. U.S. frontier, 1840s.

Nixon, Joan Lowery. *A Family Apart.* Bantam, 1987. Ages 10–13. New York City, Orphan Train, 1860s.

O'Dell, Scott. *Island of the Blue Dolphins.* Houghton, 1960. Ages 10–14. Pacific island, Native Americans, mid-1800s.

————. *Sing Down the Moon.* Houghton, 1970. Ages 12–YA. United States, Navajo Indians, 1860s.

————, and Elizabeth Hall. *Thunder Rolling in the Mountains.* Houghton, 1992. Ages 10–14. Native-American removal to reservations, 1870s.

Paterson, Katherine. *Jip, His Story.* Dutton, 1996. Ages 10–14. Vermont poor farm, 1850s.

————. *Lyddie.* Dutton, 1991. Ages 12–YA. Massachusetts, mill life, mid-1800s.

————. *Preacher's Boy.* Clarion. 1999. Ages 10–13. Vermont, turn of the century.

Paulsen, Gary. *Nightjohn.* Delacorte, 1993. Ages 11–YA. U.S. slavery.

————. *Sarny: A Life Remembered.* Delacorte, 1997. Ages 11–YA. New Orleans, freed slaves, 1860s.

————. *Soldier's Heart.* Delacorte, 1998. Ages 10–13. Minnesota, Civil War.

Polacco, Patricia. *Pink and Say.* Philomel, 1994. Ages 8–11. U.S. Civil War, race relations. Picture book.

Reeder, Carolyn. *Across the Lines.* Simon & Schuster, 1997. Ages 9–12. Race relations, 1864–1965.

————. *Shades of Gray.* Macmillan, 1989. Ages 9–12. U.S. Civil War era, 1860s.

Rinaldi, Ann. *An Acquaintance with Darkness.* Harcourt, 1997. Ages 12–YA. Washington, D.C., Lincoln assassination.

————. *In My Father's House.* Scholastic, 1993. Ages 12–YA. U.S. Civil War era, 1860s.

Robinet, Harriette Gillem. *Forty Acres and Maybe a Mule.* Atheneum, 1998. Ages 8–12. Reconstruction era treatment of former slave families in 1865; set in South Carolina and Georgia.

Savage, Deborah. *To Race a Dream.* Houghton, 1994. Small Minnesota town, horse story, early 1900s.

Snyder, Zilpha Keatley. *Gib Rides Home.* Delacorte, 1998. Ages 9–12. Taken from an orphanage to work on a farm, early 1900s. Also, *Gib and the Gray Ghost.* Delacorte, 2000.

Taylor, Mildred D. *The Well.* Dial, 1995. Ages 9–11. Mississippi, 1910 drought, Logan family.

Turner, Ann. *Grasshopper Summer.* Macmillan, 1989. Ages 9–12. United States, Kentucky to Dakota Territory, 1870s.

———. *Mississippi Mud: Three Prairie Journals.* Illustrated by Robert J. Clark. HarperCollins, 1997. Ages 7–11. Kentucky to Oregon, pioneers, in verse. Picture book.

Weitzman, David. *Thrashin' Time: Harvest Days in the Dakotas.* Godine, 1991. Ages 10–13. U.S. western settlements, 1912.

Wilder, Laura Ingalls. *Little House in the Big Woods.* Harper, 1932. Ages 7–10. Wisconsin frontier, 1800s.

Wisler, G. Clifton. *Jericho's Journey.* Dutton, 1993. Ages 9–12. Move from Tennessee to Texas, pioneer life.

Yee, Paul. *Tales from Gold Mountain: Stories of the Chinese in the New World.* Illustrated by Simon Ng. Macmillan, 1990. Ages 10–14. United States and Canada, 1800s.

Yep, Laurence. *Dragon's Gate.* HarperCollins, 1993. Ages 9–12. Sierra Nevada, transcontinental railroad, 1867.

———. *Dragonwings.* Harper, 1979. Ages 9–12. California, early 1900s.

———. *The Serpent's Children.* Harper, 1984. Ages 9–12. China, 1830s.

## World Wars in the Twentieth Century, 1914 to 1945

Anderson, Rachel. *Paper Faces.* Holt, 1993. Ages 12–YA. England, World War II.

Avi. *Who Was That Masked Man, Anyway?* Orchard, 1992. Ages 9–12. United States, World War II.

Bat-Ami, Miriam. *Two Suns in the Sky.* Front Street, 1999. Ages 13–YA. World War II in New York state, relations among European refugees and U.S. citizens.

Chang, Margaret, and Raymond Chang. *In the Eye of the War.* Macmillan, 1990. Ages 10–12. China, World War II.

Coerr, Eleanor. *Mieko and the Fifth Treasure.* Putnam, 1993. Ages 9–12. World War II, Nagasaki bombardment, Japan, 1945.

Cormier, Robert. *Frenchtown Summer.* Delacorte, 1999. Monument, Massachusetts, post–World War I. Ages 11–14.

Curtis, Christopher Paul. *Bud, Not Buddy.* Delacorte, 1999. Ages 9–13. Michigan, Depression era.

DeJong, Meindert. *The House of Sixty Fathers.* Harper, 1956. Ages 8–12. China, World War II.

Doucet, Sharon Arms. *Fiddle Fever.* Clarion, 2000. Ages 9–13. Cajun life in southern Louisiana, World War I.

Dowell, Frances O'Roark. *Davey Coe.* Atheneum, 2000. Ages 9–13. North Carolina, 1928 murder trial.

Garrigue, Sheila. *The Eternal Spring of Mr. Ito.* Bradbury, 1985. Ages 8–11. Canada, Japanese-Canadian internment, World War II.

Gee, Maurice. *The Fat Man.* Simon & Schuster, 1997. Ages 13–YA. Depression, New Zealand, haunting psychological thriller.

———. *The Fire-Raiser.* Houghton, 1992. Ages 11–YA. New Zealand, World War I era.

Giff, Patricia Reilly. *Lily's Crossing.* Delacorte, 1997. Ages 9–12. United States, World War II.

Greene, Bette. *Summer of My German Soldier.* Dial, 1973. Ages 9–12. United States, World War II.

Hahn, Mary Downing. *Following My Footsteps.* Clarion, 1996. Ages 10–13. North Carolina, physical disability, polio, World War II.

Hautzig, Esther. *The Endless Steppe.* Harper, 1968. Ages 10–14. Russia, Jews, World War II.

Hesse, Karen. *Letters from Rifka.* Holt, 1992. Ages 9–12. Russian immigration to the United States, 1919.

———. *Out of the Dust.* Scholastic, 1997. Ages 11–YA. Oklahoma, 1930s.

Heuck, Sigrid. *The Hideout.* Translated from the German by Rika Lesser. Dutton, 1988. Ages 9–12. Germany, Jews, World War II.

Hoestlandt, Jo. *Star of Fear, Star of Hope.* Illustrated by Johanna Kang. Translated by Mark Polizzotti. Walker, 1995. Ages 9–12. Northern France, 1942, German occupation, persecution of Jews. Picture book.

Hooks, William H. *Circle of Fire.* Atheneum, 1982. Ages 9–12. Rural North Carolina, Ku Klux Klan, 1930s.

Kogawa, Joy. *Naomi's Road.* Oxford, 1986. Ages 9–12. Canada, British Columbia, Japanese-Canadian internment, World War II.

Koller, Jackie. *Nothing to Fear.* Harcourt, 1991. Ages 10–13. Irish immigrant family in New York City, 1929.

Levitin, Sonia. *Anne's Promise.* Atheneum, 1993. Ages 10–14. German immigration to United States, World War II era.

———. *Journey to America.* Atheneum, 1970. Ages 10–14. Germany, Jews, World War II era.

Lisle, Janet Taylor. *The Art of Keeping Cool.* Simon & Schuster, 2000. Ages 10–13. United States and Canada, World War II.

Lowry, Lois. *Number the Stars.* Houghton, 1989. Ages 8–12. Denmark, World War II.

Lyon, George Ella. *Borrowed Children.* Watts, 1988. Ages 10–14. Kentucky, Depression era, 1930s.

Magorian, Michelle. *Good Night, Mr. Tom.* Harper, 1982. Ages 11–14. England, World War II.

Matas, Carol. *Lisa's War.* Scribner's, 1989. Ages 10–13. Denmark, Jews, World War II.

Morpurgo, Michael. *Waiting for Anya.* Viking, 1991. Ages 10–14. Southern France, Jews, World War II.

Myers, Anna. *Fire in the Hills.* Walker, 1996. Ages 11–YA. Rural Oklahoma, World War I, German immigrant family, conscientious objector.

Napoli, Donna Jo. *Stones in Water.* Dutton, 1997. Ages 9–13. Italy, work camps, World War II.

Orlev, Uri. *The Island on Bird Street.* Translated from the Hebrew by Hillel Halkin. Houghton, 1983. Ages 9–13. Poland, Jews, World War II.

———. *Lydia, Queen of Palestine.* Translated from the Hebrew by Hillel Halkin. Houghton, 1993. Ages 8–12. Escape to Palestine from Romania, World War II era.

———. *The Man from the Other Side.* Translated from the Hebrew by Hillel Halkin. Houghton, 1991. Ages 12–YA. Poland, Jews, World War II.

Pearson, Kit. *Looking at the Moon.* Viking, 1992. Ages 10–YA. Toronto, World War II, 1943.

Peck, Richard. *A Long Way from Chicago.* Dial, 1998. Ages 9–12. Southern Illinois, 1930s. Humorous.

———. *A Year Down Yonder.* Dial, 2000. Ages 10–YA. Southern Illinois, Recession era, 1937. Humorous.

Pelgrom, Els. *The Winter When Time Was Frozen.* Translated from the Dutch by Maryka and Rafael Rudnik. Morrow, 1980. Ages 9–12. Holland, World War II.

Polacco, Patricia. *The Butterfly.* Philomel, 2000. Ages 10–YA. Picture book. French Resistance, Jewish persecution, World War II.

Reiss, Johanna. *The Upstairs Room.* Crowell, 1972. Ages 10–14. Holland, Jews, World War II.

Reuter, Bjarne. *The Boys from St. Petri.* Translated from Danish by Anthea Bell. Dutton, 1994. Ages 12–YA. Denmark, World War II.

Richter, Hans Peter. *Friedrich.* Translated from the German by Edite Kroll. Holt, 1970. Ages 10–14. Germany, Jews, World War II.

Ryan, Pam Muñoz. *Esperanza Rising.* Scholastic, 2000. Ages 9–13. Mexico and United States, Depression era.

Salisbury, Graham. *Under the Blood-Red Sun.* Delacorte, 1994. Ages 10–YA. Japanese residents of Hawaii, World War II era.

Siegal, Aranka. *Upon the Head of the Goat: A Childhood in Hungary 1939–44.* Farrar, 1981. Ages 12–YA. Hungary, World War II.

Skurzynski, Gloria. *Good-Bye Billy Radish.* Bradbury, 1992. Ages 10–14. Pennsylvania steel mill town, World War I era.

Snyder, Zilpha Keatley. *Cat Running.* Delacorte, 1994. Ages 9–12. California, U.S. Depression, 1933.

Taylor, Mildred. *Let the Circle Be Unbroken.* Dial, 1981. Ages 10–14. U.S. South, African Americans, 1930s.

———. *The Road to Memphis.* Dial, 1990. Ages 12–YA. U.S. South, African Americans, 1941.

———. *Roll of Thunder, Hear My Cry.* Dial, 1976. Ages 10–14. U.S. South, African Americans, 1930s.

Taylor, Theodore. *The Bomb.* Harcourt, 1995. Ages 12–YA. Hiroshima, 1944–1945.

———. *The Cay.* Doubleday, 1969. Ages 8–12. Caribbean, World War II era.

———. *Timothy of the Cay: A Prequel-Sequel.* Harcourt, 1993. Ages 11–13. Carribean, 1884, and World War II era.

Uchida, Yoshiko. *Journey to Topaz.* Illustrated by Donald Carrick. Scribner's, 1971. Ages 10–14. United States, internment of Japanese Americans, World War II.

Van Dijk, Lutz. *Damned Strong Love: The True Story of Willi G. and Stefan K.* Translated by Elizabeth D. Crawford. Holt, 1995. Ages 13–YA. Occupied Poland, homosexuality, World War II.

Vos, Ida. *Anna Is Still Here.* Translated from the Dutch by Terese Edelstein and Inez Smidt. Houghton, 1993. Ages 9–13. Holland, World War II era.

————. *Hide and Seek.* Translated from the Dutch by Terese Edelstein and Inez Smidt. Houghton, 1991. Ages 9–13. Jews, World War II.

Walters, Eric. *Caged Eagles.* Orca, 2000. Ages 11–YA. Canada, World War II, internment of Japanese Canadians.

————. *War of the Eagles.* Orca, 1998. Ages 11–YA. Canada, World War II, internment of Japanese Canadians.

Watkins, Yoko Kawashima. *So Far from the Bamboo Grove.* Lothrop, 1986. Ages 9–12. Korea, Japan, World War II.

Westall, Robert. *The Kingdom by the Sea.* Farrar, 1991. Ages 10–13. England, World War II.

## Post–World War II Era, 1945 to 1980s

Bauer, Marion Dane. *Rain of Fire.* Clarion, 1983. Ages 10–13. United States, post–World War II era.

Brooks, Martha. *Two Moons in August.* Little, 1992. Ages 12–YA. Canada, August 1959.

Conrad, Pam. *Our House: The Stories of Levittown.* Illustrated by Brian Selznick. Scholastic, 1995. Ages 9–12. Six family stories set on Long Island, each decade from 1940.

Curtis, Christopher Paul. *The Watsons Go to Birmingham—1963.* Delacorte, 1995. Ages 8–12. Flint, Michigan, to Birmingham, Alabama, Civil Rights Movement.

de Jenkins, Lyll Becerra. *The Honorable Prison.* Lodestar, 1988. Ages 12–YA. South America, 1950s.

Freeman, Suzanne. *The Cuckoo's Child.* Greenwillow, 1996. Ages 10–13. Beirut to Tennessee, 1962.

Grimes, Nikki. *Jazmin's Notebook.* Dial, 1998. Ages 11–YA. Harlem, 1960s.

Härtling, Peter. *Crutches.* Translated from the German by Elizabeth D. Crawford. Lothrop, 1988. Ages 9–14. Austria, post–World War II.

Ho, Minfong. *Rice without Rain.* Lothrop, 1988. Ages 11–14. Thailand, class struggles, 1970s.

Holt, Kimberly Willis. *My Louisiana Sky.* Holt, 1998. Ages 10–13. Small town in Louisiana in 1957.

————. *When Zachary Beaver Came to Town.* Holt, 1999. Ages 10–14. Small town in Texas in 1971, Vietnam War era.

Jiang, Ji-li. *Red Scarf Girl: A Memoir of the Cultural Revolution.* HarperCollins, 1997. Ages 12–14. China, Mao's Cultural Revolution, 1960s.

Kim, Helen. *The Long Season of Rain.* Holt, 1996. Ages 12–YA. Seoul, Korea in 1960s.

Krisher, Trudy. *Spite Fences.* Delacorte, 1994. Ages 13–YA. Georgia, race relations, 1960s.

Myers, Walter Dean. *Fallen Angels.* Scholastic, 1988. Ages 14–YA. Vietnam War.

Perera, Hilda. *Kiki: A Cuban Boy's Adventures in America.* Translated from Spanish by Warren Hampton and Hilda Gonzales. Pickering, 1992. Ages 9–12. Miami, Cuba, Florida's Seminole and Miccosukee tribes, 1960s.

Sacks, Margaret. *Beyond Safe Boundaries.* Lodestar, 1989. Ages 12–YA. South Africa, Jews, 1960s.

Talbert, Marc. *The Purple Heart.* HarperCollins, 1992. Ages 10–13. United States, Vietnam War era.

Uchida, Yoshiko. *Journey Home.* Illustrated by Charles Robinson. Atheneum, 1978. Ages 10–13. United States, Japanese Americans, post–World War II.

White, Ruth. *Memories of Summer.* Farrar, 2000. Ages 12–YA. Hills of Virginia, Michigan, 1950s.

Wolff, Virginia Euwer. *Bat 6.* Scholastic, 1998. Ages 10–YA. California, 1948, Japanese Americans, postwar adjustments.

Young, Ronder Thomas. *Learning by Heart.* Houghton, 1993. Ages 9–12. Southern United States, 1960s.

# NONFICTION: BIOGRAPHY *and* INFORMATIONAL BOOKS

## QUESTIONS AT NIGHT

*Why*
*Is the sky?*

*What starts the thunder overhead?*
*Who makes the crashing noise?*
*Are the angels falling out of bed?*
*Are they breaking all their toys?*

*Why does the sun go down so soon?*
*Why do the night-clouds crawl*
*Hungrily up to the new-laid moon*
*And swallow it, shell and all?*

*If there's a bear among the stars,*
*As all the people say,*
*Won't he jump over those pasture-bars*
*And drink up the Milky Way?*

*Does every star that happens to fall*
*Turn into a firefly?*
*Can't it ever get back to Heaven at all?*
*And why*
*Is the sky?*

—LOUIS UNTERMEYER

Children are naturally curious. Their interest in the world around them is boundless. Teachers, librarians, and parents want to nourish that curiosity with lively, intelligent answers, provocative questions, and stimulating books that provide answers and a thirst for further knowledge. Today's constantly innovative and improving works of nonfiction are an excellent source of information for children and the adults who guide their learning.

# DEFINITION AND DESCRIPTION

By now it should be understood that in children's literature there are no absolute genre definitions. For example, nonfiction for children is not limited to works containing only facts. Instead, this genre can best be defined in terms of emphasis. The content emphasis of children's nonfiction is documented fact; its primary purpose is to inform. In contrast, the content of fictional literature is largely, if not wholly, a product of the imagination, and the purpose is to entertain.

Some countries now recognize a third type of literature that has elements of both fiction and nonfiction and call it *faction*. Mogens Jansen, president of the Danish National Association of Reading Teachers, describes *faction* as " 'nonfiction' the presentation of which is mainly sustained by 'fiction elements': the well-told nonfiction which has fictional overtones, but *is* nonfictional—and absolutely correct" (Jansen, 1987, p. 16). Although North America has not designated faction as an independent genre, but considers it a part of nonfiction, adults who deal with books and children are well aware of this type of literature and its appeal to 8- to 12-year-old boys, in particular. Today a great number of books present factual information on a ribbon of narrative. Examples are *Cathedral* by David Macaulay and *My Place in Space* by Robin and Sally Hirst, illustrated by Roland Harvey with Joe Levine.

Informational books can be written on any aspect of the physical, biological, and social world, including what is known of outer space. Thus, it should come as no surprise that in most children's collections in school and public libraries well over half of the titles are nonfiction, with some estimates as high as 70 percent. In school libraries, at least, more nonfiction circulates than fiction, and informed sources say that more than half of children's books being published currently are nonfiction. Although fictional literature is better known to the general public (because of book awards and a tendency for adults to equate children's literature with stories), nonfiction is enormously popular with children as recreational reading material.

*Biography* deals with the life of an actual person of the past or present with the intent of commemorating the subject and inspiring the reader by example. Biographers report the experiences, influences, accomplishments, and legacies of their subjects. An *autobiography* is about the author's own life. *Bill Peet: An Autobiography* by Bill Peet is an example of an autobiography.

Some comment on the formats of nonfiction books is in order. Book format has to do with how information is presented on the book page, rather than with the information itself. Any topic could conceivably be presented in a number of different ways. The most common distinct formats in which informational books for children are currently being produced are as follows:

- *Nonfiction chapter book.* This format, widely used in nonfiction, features a large amount of text that is organized into chapters. Graphics and illustrations are common in the more recent nonfiction chapter books but are still less important than the text. Almost all biographies, with the exception of picture book biographies, appear in this format. Examples include *Blizzard! The Storm That Changed America* by Jim Murphy and *Columbus and the World Around Him* by Milton Meltzer.
- *Nonfiction picture book.* This format features large, uncomplicated illustrations and brief text in large typeface on oversized pages. The illustrations help to convey the information. This category includes many concept books, including ABC and counting books (discussed in Chapter 5), and picture book biographies. Examples include *The Wild Boy* by Mordecai Gerstein and *Leonardo da Vinci* by Diane Stanley.

- *Science and social science concept picture book.* Originally conceived for 4- to 8-year-olds, this book presents one or two scientific or social concepts via brief, uncomplicated text accompanied by numerous, large illustrations. It also encourages participation by including an experiment or hands-on activity. These books are now available for older children as well. *Evolution* by Joanna Cole, illustrated by Aliki, and the *Science Book* series by Neil Ardley are good examples of this type of book.
- *Photo essay.* Presentation of information in the photo essay is equally balanced between text and illustration. Excellent, information-bearing photographs, and crisp, condensed writing style are hallmarks of this nonfictional format. Photo essays are generally written for children in the intermediate grades and up. Examples include *Lincoln: A Photobiography* by Russell Freedman and *Barrio: José's Neighborhood* by George Ancona.
- *Fact books.* Presentation of information in these books is mainly through lists, charts, and tables. Examples include almanacs, books of world records, and sports trivia and statistics books. For example, see *The Guinness Book of World Records.*

## EVALUATION AND SELECTION OF NONFICTION

Criteria for evaluating children's nonfiction bear some similarity to those for evaluating fiction, since authors of both kinds of literature have stories to tell. In nonfiction, however, the story must be true. The criteria listed below will help you to distinguish the worthier books of nonfiction from the not so worthy. However, it is important to remember that not every work of nonfiction needs to meet every criterion to be worthy and that no one book can cover a topic completely. By offering children a variety of satisfactory books to be read and compared, you more than compensate for the shortcomings of a good-but-not-great book.

- Children's nonfiction must be written in a clear, direct, easily understandable style. In recent years, a tight, compressed, but conversational, writing style has come to be favored in nonfictional text. Such stylistic devices as questions and the second-person pronoun *you,* as in "Have you ever wondered how chameleons change colors?" stimulate readers' interest and involvement.
- Captions and labels must be clearly written and informative. Though brief, these pieces of text serve the vital function of explaining the significance of illustrations or of drawing the reader's attention to important or interesting details pictured.
- Facts must be accurate and current. Since today's children's book editors avoid heavy documentation, evaluators must be careful to check the resources or resource persons used by the author and listed in the introduction, reference lists, or appendix as indicators of the book's accuracy. Another reliable check is to compare the information with that found in other recently published sources on the topic.
- Nonfiction must distinguish between fact, theory, and opinion. When not clearly stated as such, theories or opinions are flagged in good nonfiction by carefully placed phrases such as "maybe," "is believed to be," or "perhaps."
- Attributing human qualities to animals, material objects, or natural forces is called *personification* and is part of the charm of works of traditional and modern fantasy. In nonfiction, however, this same device is to be avoided, because the implication is factually inaccurate. Saying in a work of

nonfiction that a horse "feels proud to carry his master" is an example of this device. A similar rhetorical device to be avoided in nonfiction is *teleology,* or giving humanlike purpose to natural phenomena. People sometimes say that nature has "donned its finery" when they are admiring springtime blossoms, and this is perfectly acceptable in our daily conversation. But to explain the forces of nature in such human terms in a work of nonfiction is unscientific.

- Works of nonfiction must be attractive to the child. An intriguing cover, impressive illustrations, and balance of text and illustrations make books look interesting to a child. Dense text that fills up each page and dull, infrequent illustrations can make a book unattractive to young readers.

- Presentation of information should be from known to unknown, general to specific, or simple to more complex to aid conceptual understanding and encourage analytical thinking. Judicious use of subheadings can make text much easier to read and comprehend. Reference aids such as tables of contents, indexes, pronunciation guides, glossaries, maps, charts, and tables also serve to make information in books easier to find and retrieve, more comprehensible, and more complete. Information presented in these ways is not only easier to understand but also provides models for students' own expository writing.

- Stereotyping must be avoided. The best nonfiction goes beyond mere avoidance of sexist or racist language and stereotyped images in text and illustrations. It also shows positive images of cultural diversity.

- Format and artistic medium should be appropriate to the content. The exactness, clarity, and precision of photography, for example, make this medium useful to authors whose purpose is to present the world as it is. Sometimes, however, a drawing is preferable to a photograph when an illustrator wishes to highlight a specific feature by omitting irrelevant details. Engineered paper or pop-up illustrations are appropriate when three dimensions are required to give an accurate sense of placement of the parts of a whole, as in human anatomy.

- Depth and complexity of subject treatment must be appropriate for the intended audience. If an explanation must be simplified to the extent that facts must be altered before a child can begin to understand, perhaps the concept or topic should be taken up when the child is older.

Selecting the best of nonfiction for children can be a challenge. With an annual North American production of over 2,000 new nonfiction titles on such divergent and complicated topics as black holes and the internal combustion engine, few individuals have time to read more than a fraction of the new titles, let alone know enough about the topics to be able to judge the technical accuracy of these books. Many teachers and librarians find the following professional review sources helpful in identifying outstanding biographies and informational books.

"Outstanding Science Trade Books for Children": An annual annotated list of notable books in the field of science coproduced by the National Science Teachers Association and the Children's Book Council (www.cbcbooks.org)

"Notable Children's Trade Books in the Field of Social Studies": An annual annotated list of notable books in the field of social studies coproduced by the National Council for the Social Studies and the Children's Book Council (www.cbcbooks.org)

*Hooray for Heroes: Books and Activities Kids Want to Share with Their Parents and Teachers* by Dennis Denenberg and Lorraine Roscoe.

For further information on these sources, see the Reference List in Appendix B.

In addition to these review sources, the Orbis Pictus Award for Outstanding Nonfiction for Children offers yet another source of good nonfiction titles. The National Council of Teachers of English (NCTE) announces at its November convention the award winner, up to five Honor Books, and other outstanding nonfiction choices published during the previous year. For a complete listing of the Orbis Pictus Award winners, see Appendix A.

## HISTORICAL OVERVIEW OF NONFICTION

The history of children's nonfiction begins in 1657 with the publication of John Amos Comenius's *Orbis Pictus (The World in Pictures)*. Not only was this the first children's picture book, but it was also a work of nonfiction. This auspicious beginning for nonfiction was cut short, however, by the Puritan Movement. For nearly two hundred years the vast majority of books published for and read by children were intended more for moralistic instruction than for information.

Although books of nonfiction continued to be written in the eighteenth and nineteenth centuries, much of the growth and development of this genre has occurred in the twentieth century. Writing in 1953 about history and biography for children, Elizabeth Nesbitt commented, "In comparison with the present, the early 1900s seem poverty-stricken in these two fields, in regard to both number of books and to significance of presentation" (Meigs, Eaton, Nesbitt, & Viguers, 1953, p. 392). The growth of public school and library systems in the United States and Canada called for more nonfiction trade books to meet the curricular demands of schools. With few exceptions, however, much of the children's nonfiction written during the first half of the twentieth century was decidedly unremarkable in quality.

Then, in 1957, the former Soviet Union launched *Sputnik,* the first artificial space satellite, and the United States was galvanized into action in an effort to catch up and win the race for space and technology. The National Defense Education Act funneled federal money into science education, and children's book publishers responded with a wave of improved science trade books on every conceivable topic. The gush of federal funding and the emphasis on science in schools lasted through most of the 1960s, during which time nonfiction continued a gradual evolution in style and format and a growing trend toward publication in series. Generous use of illustrations in nonfiction, introduced in the "picture histories" and "picture geographies" of the 1940s and 1950s, was taken to a new level in the science concept picture book, which appeared in the early 1960s (Giblin, 1988). These books, exemplified by the Let's Read and Find Out series (Crowell), successfully delivered science concepts to preschool and primary-grade audiences for the first time by using numerous, large, high-quality illustrations. Popular with children who are accustomed to watching television, this trend toward more illustrations and less text in nonfiction has continued to the present time and has resulted in the adoption (from *Life* magazine), development, and refinement of yet another format for children's nonfiction: the photo essay.

As the stature of nonfiction rose and more top-flight authors and illustrators were engaged in its production, the quality of research, writing, and art in these books improved. The inaccuracies of fictionalizing, the dullness of lengthy and stiff or overly sentimental prose, and the incidental nature of infrequent and colorless illustrations common in nonfiction through the 1950s were no longer tolerated. A lighter, yet factual, tone balanced with high-quality, informative illustrations and graphics emerged as the preferred nonfiction style of the 1980s (Elleman, 1987).

EXCELLENT  NONFICTION  FOR  READING  ALOUD

*(Books for each level vary in difficulty and should be selected with students' literary backgrounds in mind.)*

PRIMARY LEVEL                AGES 5 – 8

Borden, Louise. *A. Lincoln and Me.* Illustrated by Ted Lewin. Scholastic, 1999.

Cowley, Joy. *Red-Eyed Tree Frog.* Photographs by Nic Bishop. Scholastic, 1999.

Gerstein, Mordicai. *The Wild Boy.* Foster/Farrar, 1998.

Gray, Nigel. *A Country Far Away.* Illustrated by Philippe Dupasquier. Orchard, 1989.

Priceman, Marjorie. *How to Make an Apple Pie and See the World.* Knopf, 1994.

Provensen, Alice and Martin. *The Glorious Flight: Across the Channel with Louis Blériot.* Viking, 1983.

Robbins, Ken. *Make Me a Peanut Butter Sandwich and a Glass of Milk.* Scholastic, 1991.

INTERMEDIATE LEVEL        AGES 8 – 11

Alexander, Sally H. *Mom Can't See Me.* Photographs by George Ancona. Macmillan, 1990.

Brooks, Bruce. *Making Sense: Animal Perception and Communication.* Farrar, 1993.

Cummings, Pat. *Talking with Artists.* Bradbury, 1992. (also *Volume II,* Simon & Schuster, 1995; Volume III, Houghton, 1999.)

Fenner, Carol. *Gorilla, Gorilla.* Illustrated by Symeon Shimin. Random, 1973.

Fritz, Jean. *And Then What Happened, Paul Revere?* Illustrated by Tomie dePaola. Coward, McCann, 1973.

Giblin, James Cross. *The Amazing Life of Benjamin Franklin.* Illustrated by Michael Dooling. Scholastic, 2000.

Martin, Jacqueline Briggs. *Snowflake Bentley.* Illustrated by Mary Azarian. Houghton, 1998.

Nichol, Barbara. *Beethoven Lives Upstairs.* Illustrated by Scott Cameron. Orchard, 1994.

Peet, Bill. *Bill Peet: An Autobiography.* Houghton, 1989.

Perl, Lila. *The Great Ancestor Hunt: The Fun of Finding Out Who You Are.* Clarion, 1989.

Tsuchiya, Yukio. *Faithful Elephants.* Illustrated by Ted Lewin. Translated by Tomoko Tsuchiya Dykes. Houghton, 1988.

ADVANCED LEVEL            AGES 11 – 14

Armstrong, Jennifer. *Shipwreck at the Bottom of the World: The Extraordinary True Story of Shackleton and the Endurance.* Crown, 1998.

Bridges, Ruby and Margo Lundell. *Through My Eyes.* Scholastic, 1999.

Greenberg, Jan and Sandra Jordan. *Chuck Close, Up Close.* DK Ink, 1998.

Hamilton, Virginia. *Many Thousand Gone: African Americans from Slavery to Freedom.* Illustrated by Leo and Diane Dillon. Knopf, 1993.

Lyons, Mary E. *Letters from a Slave Girl: The Story of Harriet Jacobs.* Scribner's, 1992.

Rogasky, Barbara. *Smoke and Ashes: The Story of the Holocaust.* Holiday, 1988.

Stanley, Diane. *Leonardo da Vinci.* Morrow, 1996.

Stanley, Jerry. *Children of the Dust Bowl: The True Story of the School at Weedpatch.* Crown, 1992.

Meanwhile, children's biographies were greatly affected by the more liberal attitudes and relaxed topic restrictions that revolutionized children's fiction in the 1960s. Before this time, certain subjects (ethnic minorities, women, infamous people) and topics (the subjects' personal weaknesses, mistakes, and tragedies) were not often found in children's biographies. It was thought that subjects who were worthy of being commemorated should be placed on a pedestal. By the mid-1960s, this had changed, as Russell Freedman (1988) pointed out in his Newbery Medal acceptance speech: "The hero worship of the past has given way to a more realistic approach, which recognizes the warts and weaknesses that humanize the great" (p. 447).

Long in the literary shadow of fiction (fewer than 10 percent of the Newbery winners were nonfiction as of 1980), nonfiction finally achieved equal stature in the 1980s. Nancy Willard won a Newbery Medal for her biographical poem *A Visit to William Blake's Inn: Poems for Innocent and Experienced Travelers* (Harcourt Brace Jovanovich, 1981), and Russell Freedman won a Newbery Medal for his photo essay *Lincoln: A Photobiography* (Clarion, 1987) in 1988. In the last two decades, nine works of nonfiction have been selected as Newbery Medal winners or Honor Books, and eight works of nonfiction have been selected as Caldecott Medal winners or Honor Books.

The trend toward respect and recognition of children's nonfiction culminated in 1990 with the establishment of the Orbis Pictus Award for Outstanding Nonfiction for Children. This award program, sponsored by the National Council of Teachers of English, is for the purpose of promoting and recognizing excellence in the writing of nonfiction for children. The award itself is made annually to the author of what has been judged to be the most outstanding work of nonfiction (excluding textbooks, historical fiction, folklore, and poetry) published during the previous year. Named in honor of Comenius's book written some 300 years earlier, this award calls to mind how far children's nonfiction has come.

During the 1990s, biography and informational books for children sustained their popularity and continued to develop. They were consistently selected as Newbery and Caldecott Medalists and Honor Books (one Caldecott Medalist, two Caldecott Honor Books, and three Newbery Honor Books from 1990 to 1998). The success of the Eyewitness books, highly visual informational books featuring crisp, colorful photography and a minimum of print, influenced the genre and followed the trend of this decade toward more illustration and less print in books for children noted in Chapter 1. Recent multimedia publication (book and CD-ROM versions) of nonfictional books such as David Macaulay's *The Way Things Work* suggests an exciting future for this genre. Milestones in the development of nonfiction for children are highlighted on page 175.

## T Y P E S   O F   B I O G R A P H I E S

In adult nonfiction, biographies must be completely documented to be acceptable. In biographies for children, more latitude is allowed, and biographers use varying degrees of invention. This invention ranges from choosing what aspect of the subject the biographer wants to emphasize as the theme of the book (e.g., great energy or love of freedom) to actually inventing fictional characters and conversation.

Biographies, then, can be classified by degree of documentation, as follows:

### *Authentic Biography*

In this type of biography, all factual information is documented through eyewitness accounts, written documents, letters, diaries, and, more recently, audio and videotape recordings. Details in the lives of people who lived long ago, such as conversations, are often difficult to document, however. So, for the sake of art, biographers must use such devices as interior monologue (telling what someone probably thought or said to himself or herself based on known actions), indirect discourse (reporting the gist of

## M I L E S T O N E S

### in the Development of NONFICTION for CHILDREN

| DATE | BOOK | SIGNIFICANCE |
| --- | --- | --- |
| 1657 | *Orbis Pictus* by John Amos Comenius | First known work of nonfiction for children |
| 1683 | *New England Primer* | First concept book for American children; reflected didacticism of the Puritan era |
| 1922 | *The Story of Mankind* by Hendrik Van Loon | Won the first Newbery Medal; greatly influenced children's books with its lively style and creative approach |
| 1939 | *Abraham Lincoln* by Ingri and Edgar Parin d'Aulaire | One of the first picture book biographies for younger children. First biography to win the Caldecott Medal |
| 1940 | *Daniel Boone* by James H. Daugherty | First biography to win the Newbery Medal |
| 1948 | *The Story of the Negro* by Arne Bontemps | The first important history of the Negro |
| 1952 | *Diary of a Young Girl* by Anne Frank | Classic autobiography; helped many to understand the tragedy of the Jewish Holocaust |
| 1960 | Let's-Read-and-Find-Out series by Franklyn Branley and Roma Gans | Introduced the science concept picture book for young children |
| 1969 | *To Be a Slave* by Julius Lester | African-American nonfiction chosen as Newbery Honor Book |
| 1988 | *Lincoln: A Photobiography* by Russell Freedman | First nonfictional photo essay to win a Newbery Medal |
| 1990 | First Orbis Pictus Award for Nonfiction (*The Great Little Madison* by Jean Fritz) | Nonfiction as a genre is recognized |
| 1999 | *Snowflake Bentley* by Jacqueline Briggs Martin, illustrated by Mary Azarian | Innovative picture book biography promoted nonfiction by winning the Caldecott Medal |
| 2001 | *So You Want to Be President?* by Judith St. George, illustrated by David Small | Promoted nonfiction for younger readers by winning the Caldecott Medal |

what someone said without using quotation marks), attribution (interpretation of known actions to determine probable motives), and inference to make their stories lively and appealing and worth the children's time to read. Skillful biographers such as Jean Fritz are able to employ these devices without altering the truth or fictionalizing. Still, it is advisable to read and compare several biographies of a subject, if possible, to counteract any bias an author might have. *The Great Little Madison* by Jean Fritz is an example of an authentic biography.

### Fictionalized Biography

This type of biography is also based on careful research, but the author creates dramatic episodes from known facts by using imagined conversation. The conversation is, of course, carefully structured around the pertinent facts that are known, but the actual words are invented by the author. An example of this type of biography is *Carry On, Mr. Bowditch* by Jean Lee Latham.

## Biographical Fiction

This type of biography allows much artistic license, including invented dialogue, fictional secondary characters, and some reconstructed action. The known achievements of the biographical subjects are reported accurately, but in other respects these works are as much fiction as fact. Examples include *Anthony Burns: The Defeat and Triumph of a Fugitive Slave* by Virginia Hamilton and *Ben and Me* by Robert Lawson.

Biographies can also be classified by coverage of the subject's life. Quality in biography for young readers, as determined by accuracy of information, coverage, and writing style, will vary. In evaluating the following types of biographies, you will want to look for a balance between the need for adequate coverage and the tolerance that the target child audience has for detail.

- The *complete biography* covers the entire life of the subject from birth to death. An example is *Columbus and the World around Him* by Milton Meltzer.
- The *partial biography* covers only part of the life of the subject. Biographies for very young children will often be of this type, as will, of course, the biographies of living persons. An example is *Teammates* by Peter Golenbock, illustrated by Paul Bacon.
- The *collected biography* includes the life stories of several people in one book, organized into chapters. An example is *Indian Chiefs* by Russell Freedman.
- The *biography series* is a multivolume set of books with each book containing one separate biography. Most series of this type feature subjects with some common attribute, accomplishment, or skill, such as leadership or legendary sports ability. For example, the Women of Our Time series, published by Viking, includes biographies on such subjects as Grandma Moses, Babe Didrikson, Diana Ross, and Margaret Thatcher; and the First Biographies series by David A. Adler, published by Holiday House, written for beginning independent readers in grades 2 through 4, includes biographies on such subjects as Thomas Jefferson, Martin Luther King, and Jackie Robinson.

# TOPICS OF INFORMATIONAL BOOKS

Although nonfiction is confined to just one chapter in this book, it is by far the largest single genre in children's literature in that everything known to humankind is a conceivable topic. Organization of such an enormous variety of topics could, of course, be done in a variety of satisfactory ways, one of which is the scientific approach used here. First, the world of information is divided into the biological, the physical, the social, and the applied sciences; then the humanities are dealt with separately.

## Biological Science

Biological science deals with living organisms and the laws and phenomena that relate to any organism or group of organisms. A topic that is particularly interesting to children within this field is the human body—its anatomy, senses, nutrition, reproduction, health, handicaps, and heredity. Equally interesting to children are information books about pets and their care, breeding, and training, as well as the habits, habitats, life cycles, and migrations of wild animals. Ecology and the environment will be of interest and concern to more and more children who recognize the fragility of our global ecology and their responsibility to help protect it from destruction. Informational books can help children to understand what harms our ecology and to learn how they can participate in its protection and healing. Examples include *Oak Tree* by Gordon Morrison and *Bodies from the Bog* by James Deem.

A subtopic of biological science that deserves special attention is human anatomy and sexuality. Young children are naturally interested in their bodies, and as they grow into puberty, they become interested in sex. Experts in the field of sex education suggest that honest, straightforward answers to children's questions about their bodies, bodily functions, sex, and sexual orientation are best. Numerous books provide accurate, well-illustrated information on these topics in terms that children and young people can understand. Robie Harris's two books, *It's So Amazing! A Book about Eggs, Sperm, Birth, Babies and Families* and *It's Perfectly Normal: A Book about Changing Bodies, Growing Up, Sex, and Sexual Health,* both illustrated by Michael Emberley, are good examples.

### Physical Science

Physical science, sometimes referred to as natural science, deals primarily with nonliving materials. Rocks, landforms, oceans, the stars, and the atmosphere and its weather and seasons are all likely topics that children could learn about within the fields of geology, geography, oceanography, astronomy, and meteorology that comprise the physical sciences. Not only will children be able to satisfy their curiosity about such topics in this category as volcanoes and earthquakes, but teachers will also find the many books about the planets and our solar system helpful in presenting these topics in class. Examples include *Sand,* written by Ellen J. Prager and illustrated by Nancy Woodman, and *Blizzard! The Storm That Changed America* by Jim Murphy.

### Social Science

Social science deals with the institutions·and functioning of human society and the interpersonal relationships of individuals as members of society. Through books in this field children can learn about various forms of government, religions, different countries and their cultures, money, and transportation. Most children have a natural interest in books about careers, family relationships, and leisure activities and will appreciate finding answers to their questions without always having to ask an adult. An example is *Kids on Strike* by Susan Bartoletti.

### Applied Science

Applied science deals with the practical applications of pure science that people have devised. All machines, for example—from simple levers to super computers, from bicycles to space rockets—are part of this field, and many children are naturally interested in finding out how they work. Interest in the applied sciences can be developed in children by pointing out how their lives are affected by these applications. For example, children get sick, and medicine helps to cure them. How? Children get hungry, and food appears. What are the processes by which the food is produced, prepared, packaged, and marketed? Children like toys and buy them in stores. Who designs the toys and how are they manufactured? The answers to questions like these can be found in today's nonfictional literature. For example, see *The Way Things Work* by David Macaulay and *The Longitude Prize* by Joan Dash, illustrated by Dušan Petricic.

A specific type of book within the applied sciences—the experiment or how-to book—capitalizes on children's natural curiosity and fondness for hands-on activities. Its contents range from directions for conducting various scientific experiments to cookbooks, guides to hobbies, and directions for small construction projects, like clubhouses. For example, see *How to Make a Chemical Volcano and Other Mysterious Experiments* by Alan Kramer.

## Humanities

The humanities deal with the branches of learning that primarily have a cultural or artistic character. Of greatest interest to children and their teachers are books about the fine arts of drawing, painting, and sculpture; the performing arts of singing, dancing, making instrumental music, and acting; and handicrafts of all sorts. Since many children are artistically creative and often study dance, music, and drawing, they can be led to read about the arts and artists to learn new techniques or to draw inspiration from the experiences of others. Some might read these books to decide whether they are interested in trying to develop their artistic talents. Some books make the arts more accessible or real to children by explaining what to look for in paintings or an opera, for example, or by revealing the hard work required of an artist to achieve a spectacular performance or an intriguing work of art. Examples include *What Do Illustrators Do?* by Eileen Christelow and *i see the rhythm* by Toyomi Igus, illustrated by Michele Wood.

Today's nonfictional literature for children is able to meet the needs and interests of young readers in quality, variety, and reader appeal. With these books, children's appetites for learning can be fed while their curiosity for more information is piqued.

## REFERENCES

Elleman, Barbara. (1987). Current trends in literature for children. *Library Trends, 35*(3), 413–426.

Freedman, Russell. (1988). Newbery Medal acceptance. *The Horn Book, 64*(4), 444–451.

Giblin, James Cross. (1988). The rise and fall and rise of juvenile nonfiction, 1961–1988. *School Library Journal, 35*(2), 27–31.

Jansen, Mogens. (1987). *A little about language, words, and concepts—Or what may happen when children learn to read.* Translated by Lotte Rosbak Juhl. Dragör, Denmark: Landsforeningen af Læsepædagoger.

Meigs, C., Eaton, A. T., Nesbitt, E., & Viguers, R. H. (1953). *A critical history of children's literature.* New York: Macmillan.

Untermeyer, Louis. (1985). Questions at night. In L. Untermeyer (Selector), *Rainbow in the Sky.* San Diego: Harcourt.

## NOTABLE AUTHORS OF NONFICTION

**Aliki,** author/illustrator of informational picture books for older readers. *The King's Day; A Medieval Feast.*

**George Ancona,** illustrator/author of photoessays. *Barrio: José's Neighborhood; Charro: The Mexican Cowboy.*

**Rhoda Blumberg,** author of accounts of important explorations in U.S. history. *The Incredible Journey of Lewis and Clark; Commodore Perry in the Land of the Shogun.*

**Franklyn Branley,** originator of the science concept picture book.

**Joanna Cole,** author of a variety of informational books for beginning independent readers. Magic School Bus series.

**Ingri and Edgar Parin d'Aulaire,** authors/illustrators of several oversized picture book biographies for 5- to 7-year-olds. *Christopher Columbus; Abraham Lincoln.*

**Russell Freedman,** author of biographies of famous Americans and of informational books about U.S. history. *Lincoln: A Photobiography; Children of the Wild West.*

**Jean Fritz,** biographer of political leaders during the U.S. Revolutionary War era. *Can't You Make Them Behave, King George?; And Then What Happened, Paul Revere?*

**Gail Gibbons,** author/illustrator of numerous informational books for the 5- to 7-year-old that explain how everyday things work or get done. *The Post Office Book; Recycle: A Handbook for Kids.*

**James Cross Giblin,** author of informational books about the social implications of cultural developments and inventions. *From Hand to Mouth: Or, How We Invented Knives, Forks, and Spoons and the Tablemanners to Go with Them; When Plague Strikes: The Black Death, Smallpox, AIDS.*

**Kathryn Lasky,** author of well-regarded works of photojournalism and works concerning archaeology. *Sugaring Time; The Most Beautiful Roof in the World: Exploring the Rainforest Canopy.*

**Patricia Lauber,** author of informational books on popular topics such as volcanoes, mummies, and dinosaurs. *Volcano: The Eruption and Healing of Mt. St. Helens; Tales Mummies Tell.*

**David Macaulay,** author/illustrator of several books of faction about construction of monumental buildings and informational picture books for older readers. *Cathedral; Building Big.*

**Milton Meltzer,** author who presents the minority perspective in historical informational books. *The Black Americans: A History in Their Own Words.*

**Jim Murphy,** author of informational chapter books about events in United States history. *Across America on an Emigrant Train; The Great Fire.*

**Laurence Pringle,** author of many informational books that express concern for the environment. *Nuclear Energy: Troubled Past, Uncertain Future.*

**Seymour Simon,** author of over 100 science-related books that often contain practical activities. The Planets series; *Icebergs and Glaciers.*

**Diane Stanley,** author of picture book biographies for older readers. *Leonardo da Vinci; Joan of Arc.*

## RECOMMENDED NONFICTION BOOKS

*Ages refer to approximate reading levels. YA = young adult readers. Biography is organized by historical era as in Chapter 8.*

## BIOGRAPHY

### Civilizations of the Ancient World, 3000 B.C. to A.D. 600

Lasker, Joe. *The Great Alexander the Great.* Viking, 1983. Ages 7–9.

Lasky, Kathryn. *The Librarian Who Measured the Earth.* Illustrated by Kevin Hawkes. Little, Brown, 1994. Ages 7–10.

### Civilizations of the Medieval World, 600 to 1500

d'Aulaire, Ingri, and Edgar Parin d'Aulaire. *Columbus.* Doubleday, 1955. Ages 7–9.

Meltzer, Milton. *Columbus and the World around Him.* Watts. 1990. Ages 12–YA.

Poole, Josephine. *Joan of Arc.* Illustrated by Angela Barrett. Knopf, 1998. Ages 7–11.

Sís, Peter. *Starry Messenger.* Farrar, 1996. Ages 9–14.

Stanley, Diane. *Joan of Arc.* Morrow, 1998. Ages 11–14.

———. *Leonardo da Vinci.* Morrow, 1996. Ages 9–13.

### The Emergence of Modern Nations, 1500 to 1800

Aliki. *The King's Day: King Louis XIV of France.* Crowell, 1989. Ages 7–9.

Aronson, Marc. *Sir Walter Ralegh and the Quest for El Dorado.* Clarion, 2000. Ages 12–YA.

Bober, Natalie S. *Abigail Adams: Witness to a Revolution.* Atheneum, 1995. Ages 11–YA.

Fritz, Jean. *And Then What Happened, Paul Revere?* Illustrated by Tomie dePaola. Coward/McCann, 1973. Ages 8–10.

———. *Can't You Make Them Behave, King George?* Illustrated by Tomie dePaola. Coward/McCann, 1976. Ages 8–10.

———. *The Double Life of Pocahontas.* Illustrated by Ed Young. Putnam, 1983. Ages 8–10.

———. *The Great Little Madison.* Putnam, 1989. Ages 9–12.

———. *Traitor: The Case of Benedict Arnold.* Putnam, 1981. Ages 9–12.

———. *What's the Big Idea, Ben Franklin?* Illustrated by Margot Tomes. Coward/McCann,1978. Ages 8–10.

———. *Where Do You Think You're Going, Christopher Columbus?* Illustrated by Margot Tomes. Putnam, 1980. Ages 8–10.

———. *Where Was Patrick Henry on the 29th of May?* Illustrated by Margot Tomes. Coward/McCann, 1975. Ages 8–10.

———. *Why Don't You Get a Horse, Sam Adams?* Illustrated by Trina Schart Hyman. Coward/McCann, 1974. Ages 8–10.

———. *Will You Sign Here, John Hancock?* Illustrated by Trina Schart Hyman. Coward/McCann, 1976. Ages 8–10.

Giblin, James Cross. *The Amazing Life of Benjamin Franklin.* Illustrated by Michael Dooling. Scholastic, 2000. Ages 8–11.

———. *Thomas Jefferson: A Picture Book Biography.* Illustrated by Michael Dooling. Scholastic, 1994. Ages 8–10.

Lawson, Robert. *Ben and Me: An Astonishing Life of Benjamin Franklin by His Good Mouse Amos.* Little, Brown, 1988 (1939). Ages 7–9.

Lyons, Mary E. *Letters from a Slave Girl: The Story of Harriet Jacobs.* Scribner's, 1992. Ages 10–14.

Marrin, Albert. *The Sea King: Sir Francis Drake and His Times.* Atheneum, 1995. Ages 11–YA.

Meltzer, Milton. *George Washington and the Birth of Our Nation.* Watts, 1986. Ages 12–YA.

———. *Thomas Jefferson: The Revolutionary Aristocrat.* Watts, 1991. Ages 12–YA.

Ross, Stewart. *Shakespeare and Macbeth: The Story behind the Play.* Illustrated by Tony Karpinski. Viking, 1994. Ages 9–12.

Stanley, Diane, and Peter Vennema. *Bard of Avon: The Story of William Shakespeare.* Illustrated by Diane Stanley. Morrow, 1992. Ages 8–13.

———. *Good Queen Bess: The Story of Elizabeth I of England.* Four Winds, 1990. Ages 8–10.

## The Development of Industrial Society, 1800 to 1914

Adler, David A. *America's Champion Swimmer: Gertrude Ederle.* Illustrated by Terry Widener. Harcourt, 2000. Ages 6–10.

Blumberg, Rhoda. *Commodore Perry in the Land of the Shogun.* Lothrop, 1985. Ages 9–12.

———. *The Incredible Journey of Lewis and Clark.* Lothrop, 1987. Ages 9–12.

Borden, Louise. *A. Lincoln and Me.* Illustrated by Ted Lewin. Scholastic, 1999. Ages 5–8.

Brown, Don. *Uncommon Traveler: Mary Kingsley in Africa.* Houghton, 2000. Ages 7–10.

d'Aulaire, Ingri, and Edgar Parin d'Aulaire. *Abraham Lincoln.* Doubleday, 1939, 1957. Ages 7–9.

Fradin, Dennis B., and Judith B. Fradin. *Ida B. Wells: Mother of the Civil Rights Movement.* Clarion, 2000. Ages 10–YA.

Freedman, Russell. *Indian Chiefs.* Holiday, 1987. Ages 9–12.

———. *The Life and Death of Crazy Horse.* Holiday, 1996. Ages 9–12.

———. *Lincoln: A Photobiography.* Clarion, 1987. Ages 9–12.

———. *The Wright Brothers: How They Invented the Airplane.* Holiday, 1991. Ages 9–12.

Fritz, Jean. *Bully for You, Teddy Roosevelt!* Putnam, 1991. Ages 8–10.

———. *You Want Women to Vote, Lizzie Stanton?* Illustrated by DyAnne DiSalvo-Ryan. Putnam, 1995. Ages 8–11.

Hamilton, Virginia. *Anthony Burns: The Defeat and Triumph of a Fugitive Slave.* Knopf, 1988. Ages 11–YA.

Klausner, Janet. *Sequoyah's Gift: A Portrait of the Cherokee Leader.* Ages 9–14. HarperCollins, 1993.

Krull, Kathleen. *Lives of the Musicians: Good Times, Bad Times (and What the Neighbors Thought).* Harcourt, 1993. Ages 8–10.

———. *Lives of the Writers: Comedies, Tragedies (and What Their Neighbors Thought).* Illustrated by Kathryn Hewitt. Harcourt, 1994. Ages 8–10.

Latham, Jean Lee. *Carry On, Mr. Bowditch.* Houghton, 1955. Ages 10–12.

Lyons, Mary E. *Keeping Secrets: The Childhood Diaries of Seven Women Writers.* Holt, 1995. Ages 12–YA.

Meltzer, Milton, editor. *Frederick Douglass: In His Own Words.* Illustrated by Stephen Alcorn. Harcourt, 1995. Ages 12–14.

———. *Lincoln: In His Own Words.* Illustrated by Stephen Alcorn. Harcourt, 1993. Ages 10–14.

Marrin, Albert. *Sitting Bull and His World.* Dutton, 2000. Ages 11–YA.

Provensen, Alice, and Martin Provensen. *The Glorious Flight: Across the Channel with Louis Blériot.* Viking, 1983. Ages 5–8.

Reef, Catherine. *Walt Whitman.* Clarion, 1995. Ages 11–14.

Reich, Susanna. *Clara Schumann: Piano Virtuoso.* Clarion, 1999. Ages 10–YA.

Stanley, Diane, and Peter Vennema. *Charles Dickens: The Man Who Had Great Expectations.* Illustrated by Diane Stanley. Morrow, 1993. Ages 9–12.

Whiteley, Opal. Selected by Jane Boulton. *Only Opal.* Illustrated by Barbara Cooney. Philomel, 1994. Ages 7–10.

Wilson, Janet. *The Ingenious Mr. Peale: Painter, Patriot, and Man of Science.* Atheneum, 1996. Ages 11–14.

## World Wars of the Twentieth Century, 1914 to 1945

Adler, David A. *Lou Gehrig: The Luckiest Man.* Illustrated by Terry Widener. Harcourt, 1997. Ages 8–11.

———. *A Picture Book of Eleanor Roosevelt.* Holiday, 1991. Ages 6–8. (See others in the First Biographies series.)

Bausum, Ana. *Dragon Bones and Dinosaur Eggs: A Photobiography of Explorer Roy Chapman Andrews.* National Geographic, 2000. Ages 9–YA.

Britton-Jackson, Livia. *I Have Lived a Thousand Years: Growing Up in the Holocaust.* Simon & Schuster, 1997. Ages 12–YA.

Burleigh, Robert. *Home Run: The Story of Babe Ruth.* Illustrated by Mike Wimmer. Silver Whistle/Harcourt, 1998. Ages 7–11.

Cleary, Beverly. *A Girl from Yamhill: A Memoir.* Morrow, 1988. Ages 8–10.

Cline-Ransome, Lesa. *Satchel Paige.* Illustrated by James Ransome. Simon & Schuster, 2000. Ages 7–10.

dePaola, Tomie. *26 Fairmount Avenue.* Putnam, 1999. Ages 7–9.

Freedman, Russell. *Eleanor Roosevelt: A Life of Discovery.* Clarion, 1993. Ages 9–12.

———. *Franklin Delano Roosevelt.* Clarion, 1990. Ages 9–12.

Fritz, Jean. *China Homecoming.* Putnam, 1985. Ages 8–10.

———. *Homesick: My Own Story.* Illustrated by Margot Tomes. Putnam, 1982. Ages 8–10.

Giblin, James C. *Charles A. Lindbergh: A Human Hero.* Clarion, 1997. Ages 9–14.

Kraft, Betsy H. *Mother Jones: One Woman's Fight for Labor.* Clarion, 1995. Ages 10–14.

Lyons, Mary E. *Sorrow's Kitchen: The Life and Folklore of Zora Neale Hurston.* Scribner's, 1990. Ages 12–YA.

Martin, Jacqueline Briggs. *Snowflake Bentley.* Illustrated by Mary Azarian. Houghton, 1998. Ages 6–9.

Partridge, Elizabeth. *Restless Spirit: The Life and Work of Dorothea Lange.* Viking, 1998. Ages 11–YA.

Peet, Bill. *Bill Peet: An Autobiography.* Houghton, 1989. Ages 8–10.

Severance, John B. *Winston Churchill: Soldier, Statesman, Artist.* Clarion, 1996. Ages 10–14.

van der Rol, Ruud, and Rian Verhoeven. *Anne Frank: Beyond the Diary: A Photographic Remembrance.* Translated by Tony Langham and Plym Peters. Viking, 1993. Ages 10–YA.

Wells, Rosemary. *Mary on Horseback: Three Mountain Stories.* Illustrated by Peter McCarty. Dial, 1998. ages 7–11.

## Post–World War II Era, 1945 to 2000

Bray, Rosemary L. *Martin Luther King.* Illustrated by Malcah Zeldis. Greenwillow, 1995. Ages 7–11.

Bridges, Ruby, and Margo Lundell. *Through My Eyes.* Scholastic, 1999. Ages 9–YA.

Cleary, Beverly. *My Own Two Feet.* Morrow, 1995. Ages 8–11.

Coerr, Eleanor. *Sadako.* Illustrated by Ed Young. Putnam, 1993. Ages 8–12.

———. *Sadako and the Thousand Paper Cranes.* Illustrated by Ronald Himler. Putnam, 1977. Ages 7–10.

Filipovic, Zlata. *Zlata's Diary: A Child's Life in Sarajevo.* Viking, 1994. Ages 10–14.

Freedman, Russell. *Babe Didrikson Zaharias: The Making of a Champion.* Clarion, 1999. Ages 10–YA.

———. *Martha Graham: A Dancer's Life.* Clarion, 1998. Ages 10–YA.

Golenbock, Peter. *Teammates.* Illustrated by Paul Bacon. Harcourt, 1990. Ages 7–9.

Greenberg, Jan, and Sandra Jordan. *Chuck Close, Up Close.* DK Ink, 1998. Ages 10–14.

———. *Frank O. Gehry: Outside In.* DK Ink, 2000. Ages 9–YA.

Hearne, Betsy. *Seven Brave Women.* Illustrated by Bethanne Andersen. Greenwillow, 1997. Ages 5–9.

Lawlor, Laurie. *Shadow Catcher: The Life and Work of Edward S. Curtis.* Walker, 1994. Ages 13–YA.

Littlefield, Bill. *Champions: Stories of Ten Remarkable Athletes.* Illustrated by Bernie Fuchs. Little, Brown, 1993. Ages 11–14.

Myers, Walter Dean. *Malcolm X: By Any Means Necessary.* Scholastic, 1993. Ages 12–14.

Pinkney, Andrea Davis. *Duke Ellington: The Piano Prince and His Orchestra.* Ilustrated by Brian Pinkney. Hyperion, 1998. Ages 8–11.

Raschka, Chris. *Mysterious Thelonious.* Orchard, 1997. Ages 5–8.

Winter, Jeanette. *My Name Is Georgia: A Portrait.* Harcourt, 1998. Ages 5–8.

Women of Our Time series. Viking. Ages 9–12.

# INFORMATIONAL BOOKS

## Biological Science

Aliki. *Wild and Woolly Mammoths.* HarperCollins, 1996. Ages 5–8.

Arnold, Caroline. *On the Brink of Extinction: The California Condor.* Photos by Michael Wallace. Harcourt, 1993. Ages 9–11.

Arnosky, Jim. *All about Owls.* Scholastic, 1995. Ages 7–9.

Bash, Barbara. *Shadows of the Night: The Hidden World of the Little Brown Bat.* Sierra Club, 1993. Ages 7–12.

———. *Tree of Life: The World of the African Baobab.* Little, Brown, 1989. Ages 7–9.

Bishop Nic. *Digging for Bird Dinosaurs: An Expedition to Madagascar.* Houghton, 2000. Ages 9–YA.

———. *The Secrets of Animal Flight.* Photography by the author. Illustrated by Amy B. Wright. Houghton, 1997. Ages 8–11.

Brandenburg, Jim. Edited by Joann Bren Guernsey. *To the Top of the World: Adventures with Arctic Wolves.* Walker, 1993. Ages 9–YA.

Brenner, Barbara, and Julia Takaya. *Chibi: A True Story from Japan.* Illustrated by June Otani. Clarion, 1996. Ages 7–9.

Brooks, Bruce. *Making Sense: Animal Perception and Communication.* Farrar, 1993. Ages 8–11.

Cerullo, Mary M. *The Octopus: Phantom of the Sea.* Photography by Jeffrey L. Rotman. Cobblehill, 1997. Ages 10–14.

Cole, Henry. *Jack's Garden.* Morrow, 1995. Ages 5–9.

Cole, Joanna. *Evolution.* Illustrated by Aliki. Crowell, 1990. Ages 6–8.

———. *A Horse's Body.* Photographs by Jerome Wexler. Morrow, 1981. Ages 6–8. (Others in the series: *A Snake's Body,* 1981; *A Cat's Body,* 1982; *A Big Bird's Body,* 1983.)

———. *How You Were Born.* (rev. ed.). Photos by Margaret Miller. Morrow, 1993. Ages 5–8.

———. *The Human Body: How We Evolved.* Illustrated by Walter Gaffney-Kessel and Juan Carlos Barberis. Morrow, 1987. Ages 6–8.

———. *The Magic Schoolbus: Inside the Human Body.* Illustrated by Bruce Degen. Scholastic, 1989. Ages 7–9.

———. *My Puppy Is Born.* (rev. ed.). Photographs by Jerome Wexler. Morrow, 1991. Ages 6–8.

Cowley, Joy. *Red-Eyed Tree Frog.* Photographs by Nic Bishop. Scholastic, 1999. Ages 6–9.

Deem, James M. *Bodies from the Bog.* Houghton, 1998. Ages 9–YA.

Durell, Ann, and Jean C. George, Katherine Paterson, editors. *The Big Book for Our Planet.* Dutton, 1993. Ages 7–YA.

Ehlert, Lois. *Eating the Alphabet: Fruits and Vegetables from A–Z.* Harcourt, 1989. Ages 4–6.

Fenner, Carol. *Gorilla, Gorilla.* Illustrated by Symeon Shimin. Random, 1973. Ages 8–11.

Flackham, Margery. *And Then There Was One: The Mysteries of Extinction.* Illustrated by Pamela Johnson. Little, Brown, 1990. Ages 8–12.

George, Jean C. *Everglades.* Illustrated by Wendell Minor. HarperCollins, 1995. Ages 7–11.

Gibbons, Gail. *From Seed to Plant.* Holiday House, 1993. Ages 4–8.

————. *The Milk Makers.* Atheneum, 1985.

Gomi, Taro. *Everyone Poops.* Translated by Amanda M. Stinchecum. Kane/Miller, 1993. (See others in the *My Body Science* series: *The Gas We Pass: The Story of Farts; The Holes in Your Nose; Contemplating Your Bellybutton; All About Scabs; the Soles of Your Feet*). Ages 2–5.

Goodman, Susan E. *Bats, Bugs, and Biodiversity: Adventures in the Amazonian Rain Forest.* Photography by Michael J. Doolittle. Atheneum, 1995. Ages 9–12.

Harris, Robie H. *It's Perfectly Normal: A Book about Changing Bodies, Growing Up, Sex, and Sexual Health.* Illustrated by Michael Emberley. Candlewick, 1994. Ages 11–14.

————. *It's So Amazing! A Book about Eggs, Sperm, Birth, Babies and Families.* Illustrated by Michael Emberley. Candlewick, 1999. Ages 7–12.

Henderson, Douglas. *Dinosaur Tree.* Bradbury, 1994. Ages 6–10.

Hoyt-Goldsmith, Diane. *Buffalo Days.* Illustrated by Lawrence Migdale. Holiday, 1997. Ages 7–10.

Kitzinger, Sheila. *Being Born.* Photographs by Lennart Nilsson. Grosset, 1986. Ages 6–YA.

Lasky, Kathryn. *The Most Beautiful Roof in the World: Exploring the Rainforest Canopy.* Illustrated by Christopher G. Knight. Harcourt, 1997. Ages 8–10.

Lauber, Patricia. *Fur, Feathers, and Flippers: How Animals Live Where They Do.* Scholastic, 1994. Ages 8–12.

Lavies, Bianca. *Backyard Hunter: The Praying Mantis.* Dutton, 1990. Ages 7–9.

————. *Killer Bees.* Dutton, 1994. Ages 8–11.

Lewin, Ted, and Betsy Lewin. *Gorilla Walk.* Lothrop, 1999. Ages 9–YA.

Markle, Sandra. *Outside and Inside Snakes.* Macmillan, 1995. Ages 9–11.

Martin, James. *Hiding Out: Camouflage in the Wild.* Illustrated by Art Wolfe. Crown, 1993. Ages 8–10.

Mason, Cherie. *Wild Fox: A True Story.* Illustrated by Jo Ellen A. Stammen. Down East, 1993. Ages 7–9.

Micucci, Charles. *The Life and Times of the Honeybee.* Ticknor & Fields, 1995. Ages 7–9.

Miller, Jonathan. *The Human Body.* Designed by David Pelham. Viking, 1983. Ages 9–12.

Morrison, Gordon. *Oak Tree.* Houghton, 2000.

Patterson, Francine. *Koko's Kitten.* Photographs by Ronald H. Cohn. Scholastic, 1985. Ages 6–10.

————. *Koko's Story.* Photographs by Ronald H. Cohn. Scholastic, 1988. Ages 6–10.

Pringle, Laurence. *Vanishing Ozone: Protecting Earth from Ultraviolet Radiation.* Morrow, 1995. Ages 9–12.

## Physical Science

Branley, Franklyn. *Eclipse: Darkness in Daytime.* (rev. ed.). Illustrated by Donald Crews. Crowell, 1988. Ages 6–8.

————. *Uranus: The Seventh Planet.* Illustrated by Yvonne Buchanan. Crowell, 1989. Ages 6–8.

Cole, Joanna. *The Magic Schoolbus: Inside the Earth.* Illustrated by Bruce Degen. Scholastic, 1987. Ages 7–9.

————. *The Magic Schoolbus: Lost in the Solar System.* Illustrated by Bruce Degen. Scholastic, 1990. Ages 7–9.

Dunphy, Madeleine. *Here Is the Arctic Winter.* Illustrated by Alan J. Robinson. Hyperion, 1993. Ages 6–8.

Elkington, John, Julia Hailes, Douglas Hill, and Joel Makower. *Going Green: A Kid's Handbook to Saving the Planet.* Illustrated by Tony Ross. Puffin, 1990. Ages 8–12.

Fraser, Mary Ann. *In Search of the Grand Canyon: Down the Colorado with John Wesley Powell.* Holt, 1995. Ages 8–11.

Gibbons, Gail. *Weather Words and What They Mean.* Holiday, 1990. Ages 6–8.

Guiberson, Brenda. *Cactus Hotel.* Illustrated by Megan Lloyd. Holt, 1991. Ages 7–10.

Hirst, Robin, and Sally Hirst. *My Place in Space.* Illustrated by Roland Harvey with Joe Levine. Orchard, 1988. Ages 9–13.

Iverson, Diane. *I Celebrate Nature.* Dawn, 1993. Ages 6–9.

Krupp, E. C. *The Rainbow and You.* Illustrated by R. Krupp. HarperCollins, 2000. Ages 5–7.

Lasky, Kathryn. *Dinosaur Dig.* Illustrated by Christopher Knight. Morrow, 1990. Ages 8–10.

Lauber, Patricia. *Dinosaurs Walked Here and Other Stories Fossils Tell.* Bradbury, 1987. Ages 8–12.

———. *Volcano: The Eruption and Healing of Mount St. Helens.* Bradbury, 1986. Ages 9–12.

Murphy, Jim. *Blizzard!: The Storm That Changed America.* Scholastic, 2000. Ages 10–YA.

Prager, Ellen J. *Sand.* Illustrated by Nancy Woodman. National Geographic, 2000. Ages 4–8.

Pringle, Laurence. *Global Warming: Assessing the Greenhouse Threat.* Arcade, 1990. Ages 7–9.

Simon, Seymour. *Jupiter.* Morrow, 1985. Ages 8–10. (Others in The Planets series: *Mars,* 1987; *Saturn,* 1985; *Uranus,* 1987.)

———. *The Stars.* Morrow, 1986. Ages 8–10.

———. *Storms.* Morrow, 1989. Ages 8–10.

———. *The Sun.* Morrow, 1986. Ages 8–10.

———. *Volcanoes.* Morrow, 1988. Ages 8–10.

Skurzynski, Gloria. *Waves: The Electromagnetic Universe.* National Geographic, 1996. Ages 8–12.

Temple, Lannis, ed. *Dear World: How Children around the World Feel about Our Environment.* Random, 1993. Ages 7–12.

Tripp, Nathaniel. *Thunderstorm!* Illustrated by Juan Wijngaard. Dial, 1994. Ages 8–10.

Walker, Sally M. *Earthquakes.* Carolrhoda, 1996. Ages 9–12.

———. *Volcanoes: Earth's Inner Fire.* Carolrhoda, 1994. Ages 9–12.

Wick, Walter. *A Drop of Water: A Book of Science and Wonder.* Scholastic, 1997. Ages 8–11.

Zoehfeld, Kathleen, W. *How Mountains Are Made.* Illustrated by James G. Hale. HarperCollins, 1995. Ages 7–9.

## Social Science

Abells, Chana Byers. *The Children We Remember.* Photographs from the Archives of Yad Vashem, the Holocaust Martyrs' and Heroes' Remembrance Authority, Jerusalem, Israel. Greenwillow, 1986. Ages 12–YA.

Alexander, Sally Hobart. *Mom Can't See Me.* Photographs by George Ancona. Macmillan, 1990. Ages 4–6.

Aliki. *Communication.* Greenwillow, 1993. Ages 7–9.

———. *A Medieval Feast.* Crowell, 1983. Ages 8–10.

Ancona, George. *Barrio: José's Neighborhood.* Harcourt, 1998. Ages 8–10.

———. *Charro: The Mexican Cowboy.* Harcourt, 1999. Ages 8–10.

———. *Powwow.* Harcourt, 1993. Ages 8–10.

Anderson, Joan. *Born to the Land: An American Portrait.* Photographs by George Ancona. Harcourt, 1989. Ages 7–9.

Armstrong, Jennifer. *Shipwreck at the Bottom of the World: The Extraordinary True Story of Shackleton and the Endurance.* Crown, 1998. Ages 10–YA.

Atkin, S. Beth. *Voices from the Fields: Children of Migrant Farmworkers Tell Their Stories.* Little, Brown, 1993. Ages 8–12.

Baer, Edith. *This Is the Way We Go to School: A Book about Children around the World.* Illustrated by Steve Bjorkman. Scholastic, 1990. Ages 6–10.

Ballard, Robert D. *Exploring the Titanic.* Illustrated by Ken Marschall. Scholastic, 1988. Ages 7–9.

Bartoletti, Susan C. *Growing Up in Coal Country.* Houghton, 1996. Ages 9–11.

———. *Kids on Strike.* Houghton, 1999. Ages 11–16.

Barton, Byron. *I Want to Be an Astronaut.* Crowell, 1988. Ages 7–9.

Bash, Barbara. *In the Heart of the Village: The World of the Indian Banyan Tree.* Sierra Club, 1996. Ages 8–11.

Bial, Raymond. *Frontier Home.* Houghton, 1993. Ages 9–12.

Blumberg, Rhoda. *Commodore Perry in the Land of the Shogun.* Lothrop, 1985. Ages 9–12.

———. *Full Steam Ahead: The Race to Build a Transcontinental Railroad.* National Geographic, 1996. Ages 9–12.

————. *The Great American Gold Rush.* Bradbury, 1989. Ages 9–12.

————. *The Incredible Journey of Lewis and Clark.* Lothrop, 1987. Ages 9–12.

Burns, Khephra, and William Miles. *Black Stars in Orbit: NASA's African American Astronauts.* Harcourt, 1995. Ages 12–14.

Carrick, Carol. *Whaling Days.* Illustrated by David Frampton. Clarion, 1993. Ages 8–11.

Carter, Jimmy. *Talking Peace: A Vision for the Next Generation.* Dutton, 1993. Ages 10–14.

Chang, Ina. *A Separate Battle: Women and the Civil War.* Lodestar, 1991. Ages 10–13.

Charlip, Remy and Mary Beth. *Handtalk Birthday: A Number and Story Book in Sign Language.* Photographs by George Ancona. Four Winds, 1987. Ages 7–9.

Coleman, Penny. *Rosie the Riveter: Women Working on the Home Front in World War II.* Crown, 1995. Ages 12–14.

Ehrlich, Amy. *The Story of Hanukkah.* Illustrated by Ori Sherman. Dial, 1989. Ages 7–9.

Ellis, Veronica Freeman. *Afro-Bets First Book about Africa.* Illustrated by George Ford. Just Us Books, 1990. Ages 4–6.

Franklin, Kristine L., and Nancy McGirr, editors. *Out of the Dump: Writings and Photographs by Children from Guatemala.* Translated by Kristine L. Franklin. Lothrop, 1996. Ages 8–13.

Freedman, Russell. *An Indian Winter.* Illustrated by Karl Bodmer. Holiday, 1992. Ages 11–14.

————. *Kids at Work: Lewis Hine and the Crusade against Child Labor.* Photos by Lewis Hine. Clarion, 1994. Ages 9–12.

Fritz, Jean. *Shh! We're Writing the Constitution.* Illustrated by Tomie dePaola. Putnam, 1987. Ages 8–10.

Gerstein, Mordicai. *The Wild Boy.* Foster/Farrar, 1998. Ages 7–9.

Gibbons, Gail. *My Baseball Book.* HarperCollins, 2000 Ages 4–8.

————. *The Post Office Book: Mail and How It Moves.* HarperCollins, 1987. Ages 4–8.

————. *Recycle: A Handbook for Kids.* Little, Brown, 1996. Ages 4–8.

Giblin, James Cross. *Be Seated: A Book about Chairs.* HarperCollins, 1993. Ages 8–14.

————. *From Hand to Mouth: Or, How We Invented Knives, Forks, and Spoons and the Tablemanners to Go with Them.* Harper, 1987. Ages 6–10.

————. *When Plague Strikes: The Black Death, Smallpox, AIDS.* Illustrated by David Frampton. HarperCollins, 1995. Ages 12–YA.

Girard, Linda Walvoord. *Adoption Is for Always.* Illustrated by Judith Friedman. Albert Whitman, 1986. Ages 8–10.

Gray, Nigel. *A Country Far Away.* Illustrated by Philippe Dupasquier. Orchard, 1989. Ages 5–8.

Greenfeld, Howard. *The Hidden Children.* Ticknor & Fields, 1993. Ages 10–14.

*The Guinness Book of World Records.* Guinness Media, Inc. Published annually. Ages 7–13.

Hamilton, Virginia. *Many Thousand Gone: African Americans from Slavery to Freedom.* Illustrated by Leo and Diane Dillon. Random, 1993. Ages 10–14.

Handler, Andrew, and Susan Meschel. *Young People Speak: Surviving the Holocaust in Hungary.* Watts, 1993. Ages 10–14.

Harrison, Ted. *O Canada.* Ticknor & Fields, 1993. Ages 7–9.

Haskins, Jim. *Get on Board: The Story of the Underground Railroad.* Scholastic, 1993. Ages 10–14.

Hinojosa, Maria. *Crews: Gang Members Talk to Maria Hinojosa.* Photography by German Perez. Harcourt, 1995. Ages 14–YA.

Hoyt-Goldsmith, Diane. *Celebrating Kwanzaa.* Illustrated by Lawrence Migdale. Holiday, 1993. Ages 7–9.

————. *Day of the Dead: A Mexican-American Celebration.* Illustrated by Lawrence Migdale. Holiday, 1994. Ages 7–9.

————. *Totem Pole.* Photographs by Lawrence Migdale. Holiday, 1990. Ages 7–9.

Jenkins, Steve. *Biggest, Strongest, Fastest.* Ticknor & Fields, 1995. Ages 5–7.

————. *The Top of the World: Climbing Mount Everest.* Houghton, 1999. Ages 9–12.

————. *What Do You Do When Something Wants to Eat You?* Houghton, 1997. Ages 4–8.

Jenness, Aylette. *Families: A Celebration of Diversity, Commitment, and Love.* Houghton, 1990. Ages 8–10.

Jukes, Mavis. *It's a Girl Thing: How to Stay Healthy, Safe, and in Charge.* Illustrated by Debbie Tilley. Knopf, 1996. Ages 10–14.

Keegan, Marcia. *Pueblo Boy: Growing up in Two Worlds.* Cobblehill: Dutton, 1991. Ages 9–11.

Kenna, Kathleen. *A People Apart.* Houghton, 1995. Ages 9–11.

Kimmel, Eric. *Bar Mitzvah: A Jewish Boy's Coming of Age.* Illustrated by Erika Weihs. Viking, 1995. Ages 11–14.

Knight, Amelia Stewart. Adapted by Lillian Schlissel. *The Way West: Journal of a Pioneer Woman.* Illustrated by Michael McCurdy. Simon & Schuster, 1993. Ages 7–12.

Koralek, Jenny. *Hanukkah: The Festival of Lights.* Illustrated by Juan Wijngaard. Lothrop, 1990. Ages 7–9.

Krementz, Jill. *How It Feels to Live with a Physical Disability.* Simon & Schuster, 1992. Ages 8–14.

Kroll, Steven. *Pony Express!* Illustrated by Dan Andreason. Scholastic, 1996. Ages 6–9.

Kuklin, Susan. *Speaking Out: Teenagers Take on Sex, Race and Identity.* Putnam, 1993. Ages 12–17.

———. *What Do I Do Now?: Talking about Teenage Pregnancy.* Putnam, 1991. Ages 11–YA.

Kuskin, Karla. *The Philharmonic Gets Dressed.* Illustrated by Marc Simont. Harper, 1982. Ages 6–8.

Lawrence, Jacob. *The Great Migration: An American Story.* HarperCollins, 1993. Ages 8–12.

Leedy, Loreen. *Messages in the Mailbox: How to Write a Letter.* Holiday, 1991. Ages 7–9.

Lester, Julius. *To Be a Slave.* Dial, 1968. Ages 12–YA.

Levine, Ellen. *Freedom's Children: Young Civil Rights Activists Tell Their Own Stories.* Putnam, 1993. Ages 11–17.

Loverance, Rowena. *Ancient Greece.* Illustrated by Bill LeFever and others. Viking, 1993. Ages 10–14. (Others in the See Through History series: *Ancient Egypt; The Middle Ages; The Renaissance.*)

Macy, Sue. *A Whole New Ball Game: The Story of the All-American Girls Professional Baseball League.* Holt, 1993. Ages 10–14.

Maestro, Betsy. *The Story of Money.* Illustrated by Giulio Maestro. Clarion, 1993. Ages 7–10.

———. *The Story of the Statue of Liberty.* Illustrated by Giulio Maestro. Lothrop, 1986. Ages 9–12.

McKee, Tim. *No More Strangers Now: Young Voices from a New South Africa.* Photographs by Anne Blackshaw. DK Ink, 1998. Ages 12–YA.

McKissack, Patricia, and Fredrick McKissack. *The Civil Rights Movement in America from 1865 to the Present.* Childrens Press, 1987. Ages 9–YA.

Meltzer, Milton. *The Amazing Potato: A Story in Which the Incas, Conquistadors, Marie Antoinette, Thomas Jefferson, Wars, Famines, Immigrants, and French Fries All Play a Part.* HarperCollins, 1992. Ages 10–13.

———. *The American Revolutionaries: A History in Their Own Words 1750–1800.* Crowell, 1988. Ages 12–YA.

———. *Rescue: The Story of How Gentiles Saved Jews in the Holocaust.* Harper, 1988. Ages 12–YA.

Miller, Brandon M. *Buffalo Gals: Women of the Old West.* Lerner, 1995. Ages 9–13.

Monroe, J. *Censorship.* Macmillan, 1990. Ages 10–14.

Müller, Jörg. *The Changing City.* Atheneum, 1977. Ages 8–12.

———. *The Changing Countryside.* Atheneum, 1977. Ages 8–12.

Murphy, Jim. *Across America on an Emigrant Train.* Clarion, 1993. Ages 11–14.

———. *The Boy's War: Confederate and Union Soldiers Talk about the Civil War.* Clarion, 1990. Ages 12–YA.

———. *Gone A-Whaling: The Lure of the Sea and the Hunt for the Great Whale.* Clarion, 1998. Ages 11–YA.

———. *The Great Fire.* Scholastic, 1995. Ages 10–14.

———. *A Young Patriot: The American Revolution as Experienced by One Boy.* Clarion, 1996. Ages 10–13.

Myers, Walter Dean. *Now Is Your Time!: The African-American Struggle for Freedom.* HarperCollins, 1991. Ages 10–14.

Onyefulu, Ifeoma. *A Is for Africa.* Cobblehill, 1993. Ages 5–8.

———. *Ogbu: Sharing Life in an African Village.* Harcourt, 1996. Ages 6–10.

Perl, Lila. *The Great Ancestor Hunt: The Fun of Finding Out Who You Are.* Clarion, 1989. Ages 8–10.

Pinkney, Andrea Davis. *Seven Candles for Kwanzaa.* Illustrated by Brian Pinkney. Dial, 1993. Ages 5–9.

Priceman, Marjorie. *How to Make an Apple Pie and See the World.* Knopf, 1994. Ages 5–8.

Pringle, Laurence. *Throwing Things Away: From Middens to Resource Recovery.* Crowell, 1988. Ages 8–10.

Rhoades, Diane. *Garden Crafts for Kids: 50 Great Reasons to Get Your Hands Dirty.* Sterling, 1995. Ages 8–11.

Robbins, Ken. *Make Me a Peanut Butter Sandwich and a Glass of Milk.* Scholastic, 1991. Ages 5–8.

Rockwell, Harlow. *My Dentist.* Greenwillow, 1975. Ages 3–5.

———. *My Doctor.* Macmillan, 1973. Ages 3–5.

Roessel, Monty. *Kinaaldá: A Navajo Girl Grows Up.* Lerner, 1993. Ages 8–10.

Rogasky, Barbara. *Smoke and Ashes: The Story of the Holocaust.* Holiday, 1988. Ages 12–YA.

Rogers, Fred. *Let's Talk about It: Adoption.* Illustrated by Jim Judkis. Putnam, 1995. Ages 5–8.

Rounds, Glen. *Sod Houses on the Great Plains.* Holiday, 1995. Ages 5–8.

Scott, Elaine. *Adventure in Space: The Flight to Fix the Hubble.* Photography by Margaret Miller. Hyperion, 1995. Ages 10–14.

Stanley, Jerry. *Children of the Dust Bowl: The True Story of the School at Weedpatch.* Crown, 1992. Ages 9–13.

Tsuchiya, Yukio. *Faithful Elephants.* Illustrated by Ted Lewin. Translated by Tomoko Tsuchiya Dykes. Houghton, 1988. Ages 9–12.

Wilson, Lori Lee. *The Salem Witch Trials.* Lerner, 1997. Ages 11–YA.

Wolf, Bernard. *HIV Positive.* Dutton, 1997. Ages 9–12.

Yue, Charlotte, and David Yue. *The Wigwam and the Longhouse.* Houghton, 2000. Ages 9–YA.

## Applied Science

Aliki. *How a Book Is Made.* Crowell, 1986. Ages 6–8.

Cole, Joanna. *The Magic Schoolbus: At the Waterworks.* Illustrated by Bruce Degen. Scholastic, 1986. Ages 7–9.

Dash Joan. *The Longitude Prize.* Illustrated by Dušan Petricic. Farrar. Ages 6–YA.

DeSantis, Kenny. *A Dentist's Tools.* Photographs by Patricia A. Agre. Dodd, 1988. Ages 6–8.

———. *A Doctor's Tools.* Photographs by Patricia A. Agre. Dodd, 1985. Ages 6–8.

Gibbons, Gail. *Trains.* Holiday, 1987. Ages 5–7.

———. *Up Goes the Skyscraper!* Four Winds, 1986. Ages 5–7.

Jasperson, William. *Ice Cream.* Macmillan, 1988. Ages 8–10.

Kramer, Alan. *How to Make a Chemical Volcano and Other Mysterious Experiments.* Franklin Watts, 1989. Ages 8–10.

Kuklin, Susan. *From Head to Toe: How a Doll Is Made.* Hyperion, 1994. Ages 7–9.

Macaulay, David. *Building Big.* Houghton, 2000. Ages 12–YA.

———. *Castle.* Houghton, 1977. Ages 10–YA.

———. *Cathedral: The Story of Its Construction.* Houghton, 1973. Ages 10–YA.

———. *Ship.* Harcourt, 1993. Ages 8–12.

———. *The Way Things Work.* Houghton, 1988. Ages 10–YA. [CD-ROM version: Dorling Kindersley, 1995.]

Markle, Sandra. *Measuring Up!: Experiments, Puzzles, and Games Exploring Measurement.* Atheneum, 1995. Ages 9–12.

Maurer, Richard. *Rocket! How a Toy Launched the Space Age.* Crown, 1995. Ages 9–12.

Morris, Ann. *Bread, Bread, Bread.* Photographs by Ken Heyman. Lothrop, 1989. Ages 8–10.

## Humanities

Aliki. *William Shakespeare and the Globe.* HarperCollins, 1999. Ages 8–12.

Björk, Christina. *The Other Alice: The Story of Alice Liddell and Alice in Wonderland.* Illustrated by Inga-Karin Eriksson. R&S, 1993. Ages 8–10.

Christelow, Eileen. *What Do Illustrators Do?* Clarion, 1999. Ages 6–10.

Cummings, Pat, compiler-editor. *Talking with Artists.* Illustrated by various artists. Bradbury, 1992. Ages 8–12.

———, compiler-editor. *Talking with Artists: Volume Two.* Illustrated by various artists. Simon & Schuster, 1995. Ages 8–12.

———, compiler-editor. *Talking with Artists: Volume Three.* Houghton, 1999. Ages 8–12.

Davidson, Rosemary. *Take a Look: An Introduction to the Experience of Art.* Viking, 1994. Ages 8–12.

Hamanaka, Sheila, and Ayano Ohmi. *In Search of the Spirit: The Living National Treasures of Japan.* Morrow, 1999. Ages 10–14.

Igus, Toyomi. *i see the rhythm.* Illustrated by Michele Wood. Children's, 1998. Ages 9–14.

Kehoe, Michael. *A Book Takes Root: The Making of a Picture Book.* Carolrhoda, 1993. Ages 7–9.

Marcus, Leonard S. *A Caldecott Celebration: Six Artists Share Their Paths to the Caldecott Medal.* Walker, 1998. Ages 8–YA.

Monroe, Jean G., and Ray Williamson. *First Houses: Native American Homes and Sacred Structures.* Illustrated by Susan Carlson. Houghton, 1993. Ages 9–12.

Mühlberger, Richard. *What Makes a Van Gogh a Van Gogh?* The Metropolitan Museum of Art/Viking, 1993. (Others in this series: Bruegal, Degas, Monet, Raphael, Rembrandt.) Ages 8–12.

Nichol, Barbara. *Beethoven Lives Upstairs.* Illustrated by Scott Cameron. Orchard, 1994. Ages 8–10.

Pope, Joyce. *Kenneth Lilly's Animals: A Portfolio of Paintings.* Illustrated by Kenneth Lilly. Lothrop, 1988. Ages 8–10.

Swain, Gwenyth. *Bookworks: Making Books by Hand.* Illustrated by Jennifer Hagerman. Photography by Andy King. Carolrhoda, 1995. Ages 8–12.

Thomson, Peggy, and Barbara Moore. *The Nine-Ton Cat: Behind the Scenes at an Art Museum.* Houghton, 1997. Ages 9–14.

Ventura, Piero. *Great Painters.* Translated by Geoffrey Culverwell. Putnam, 1984. Ages 9–YA.

Welton, Jude. *Drawing: A Young Artist's Guide.* Dorling Kindersley, 1994. Ages 8–14.

# Multicultural *and* International Literature

## TABLEAU

*Locked arm in arm they cross the way,*
*The black boy and the white,*
*The golden splendor of the day,*
*The sable pride of night.*

*From lowered blinds the dark folk stare,*
*And here the fair folk talk,*
*Indignant that these two should dare*
*In unison to walk.*

*Oblivious to look and word*
*They pass, and see no wonder*
*That lightning brilliant as a sword*
*Should blaze the path of thunder.*

—COUNTEE CULLEN

This chapter is presented in two parts. The first part focuses on literature written about the major racial, religious, and language cultural groups in the United States other than the Euro-American group. The second part focuses on literature written originally for children living in other lands but also read and enjoyed by children in the United States.

According to Banks and Banks (1993), each modern nation-state has a shared core culture—a *macroculture*—and a number of *microcultures* that are part of or integrated into the macroculture to greater or lesser degrees. It must be noted that the Western European culture, although traditionally the prevailing culture in the United States, is itself a microculture and not the macroculture. Because the Bankses' schema and nomenclature are inclusive in their emphasis on the contributions of *all* citizens of a country to that country's overarching culture, we have chosen to use their terms in this chapter. We will refer to the Western European group as Euro-American.

You will have noted many references to multicultural and international books and authors throughout the previous genre chapters in discussions of trends and issues, notable author and illustrator lists, and end-of-chapter recommended booklists. In an ideal, culturally integrated world, such inclusion would be sufficient. But the groups represented in multicultural literature have, until recently, been totally absent from or misrepresented in books for children. Furthermore, neither multicultural nor international literature is well known or recognized by the educational mainstream. We have chosen to include this special focus chapter to draw attention to these two important bodies of literature.

## SECTION ONE: *Multicultural Literature*

### DEFINITION AND DESCRIPTION

*Multicultural literature* refers to trade books, regardless of genre, that have as the main character a person who is a member of a racial, religious, or language microculture other than the Euro-American one. This section of the chapter will focus on the five most populous microcultures in the United States, each of which has an established and growing body of children's literature that describes its experience. These groups are African American; Asian American (including people of Chinese, Japanese, Korean, and Vietnamese descent); Latino American (including Cuban Americans, Mexican Americans, Puerto Ricans, and others of Spanish descent); Jewish American; and Native American (a general term referring to the many tribes of American Indians).

### VALUES OF MULTICULTURAL LITERATURE FOR CHILDREN

Multicultural literature has value for all children for the following reasons:

- Children who see people like themselves represented positively in excellent multicultural literature derive self-esteem and pride in their own heritage.
- Reading multicultural literature is a way for Euro-American children (and their parents, teachers, and librarians) to learn about or to become aware of other peoples and their cultures.
- Multicultural literature shows Euro-American children not only that other groups are worthy, but also that they have something to teach others.
- Emotional involvement and vicarious experience with multicultural characters through works of literature reduce students' prejudices toward the microculture. (For more on this topic, see *Social Education,* April/May 1988.)

- Reading about issues and problems peculiar to children of a specific microculture from the perspective of story characters who themselves are members of the group may help children of that microculture to cope with the same problems themselves.

# EVALUATION AND SELECTION OF MULTICULTURAL LITERATURE

With respect to multicultural literature, your first concern as a teacher, librarian, or parent should be that well-written books of this kind are available to the children under your care. This task is often not as simple as it may at first seem. Some cultural groups in the United States are not yet well represented in children's books. Also, a wide variety of the most current and best multicultural books are not readily available everywhere. Someone, perhaps you, has to take the time and the effort to learn about, read, evaluate, and then introduce the best of this literature into a school or community. The following criteria should be considered in evaluating multicultural books:

- Multicultural literature should exhibit high literary and artistic quality, worthy themes, and appropriate reading levels for the intended audience.
- Racial and cultural stereotyping should be avoided; instead, multifaceted, well-rounded characters of the featured microculture should be found in these stories. The nature of stereotyping is that it unfairly assigns a fixed image or fixed characteristics to everyone within a group, thereby denying everyone within the group the right to any individuality or choice.
- Traditional racial, religious, and language group stereotypes that have developed over the years in the United States make clear the damage and unwarranted denigration that can result from the practice. In evaluating children's books, you will want to be alert to any generalized portrayal of African Americans as coarse-featured, musical, and poor; of Asian Americans as sly, overly diligent, and obsequious; of Hispanic Americans as lazy, holiday-minded, and impoverished; of Jewish Americans as greedy, aggressive, and penurious; and of Native Americans as savage, primitive, and warlike. Books perpetuating such stereotypes have no place in the classroom.
- Positive images of characters should be evident.
- Cultural details must be accurate. These details must be accurate when they describe subgroups *within* a microculture.
- Not only should there be books about the microcultures represented in a classroom, but there also should be books about the many other microcultures living in this country.

Variety also extends to authorship. Multicultural books written by both non-Euro-Americans and Euro-Americans should be readily available to children. In her landmark book *Shadow and Substance*, Rudine Sims (1982) established a classification system for books about African Americans that can be applied to any multicultural literature and can be helpful in evaluation and selection of these books. In the following categories we have broadened her labels and definitions to include all multicultural literature.

> *Social conscience books:* These books about microcultural groups other than Euro-American are written to help all readers know the condition of their fellow humans. Examples are *The Slave Dancer* by Paula Fox and *Iggie's House* by Judy Blume.

*Melting pot books:* These books, which feature multicultural characters, are written for all young readers on the assumption that everyone needs to be informed that children of all microcultures are exactly alike, except for the color of their skins, their language, or their religious preference. Examples include *The Snowy Day* by Ezra Jack Keats and *Jennifer, Hecate, Macbeth, William McKinley, & Me, Elizabeth* by E. L. Konigsburg.

*Culturally conscious books:* These books are written primarily (though not exclusively) by microcultural authors other than Euro-American for readers belonging to that microculture. An attempt is made to reveal the true, unique character of that microculture. Examples are *Stevie* by John Steptoe and *Roll of Thunder, Hear My Cry* by Mildred Taylor.

Having examples of all three types of multicultural books in your classroom will ensure that your students will be able to read from the perspective of both the Euro-American author and the authors of other microcultures. Students of less integrated microcultures in particular should have the experience of reading stories written about children like themselves from the perspective of someone within their microculture.

Several book selection aids focus on multicultural books. *Multicultural Literature for Children and Young Adults: A Selected Listing of Books by and about People of Color* (Kruse, Horning, & Schliesman, 1997) is a carefully selected, regularly updated, annotated listing of multicultural books of all genres produced by the University of Wisconsin, Madison's Cooperative Children's Book Center. *Native Americans in Children's Literature* (Stott, 1996) contains discussions of general stereotypes and misrepresentations of Indians but focuses on good writers and artists. *Recommended Books in Spanish for Children and Young Adults* (Schon, 2000), a guide for choosing Spanish-language books for Hispanic children, is organized by country of origin, including a large section on the United States. These books are of all genres, and some are bilingual.

Book awards for special content also can guide teachers and librarians toward high-quality multicultural books. The best known of these is the Coretta Scott King Award, founded in 1969 and, since 1979, sponsored by the American Library Association. This annual award is given to the African-American author and (since 1974) illustrator whose books published in the preceding year are judged to be the most outstanding inspirational and educational literature for children. The first Pura Belpré Awards honoring outstanding Latino authors and illustrators of children's books were bestowed in 1996. The first Asian Pacific American Award for Literature, honoring outstanding work of Asian-American authors and illustrators, was given in 2001. Awards such as these encourage the publication of more and better quality multicultural literature.

In recent years, small presses have given teachers and librarians a source of multicultural books that are particularly valuable for their distinctly multicultural (versus Euro-American) point of view. For an extensive, up-to-date list of small presses that publish multicultural books for children, go to www.education.wisc.edu/ccbc/pclist. The following publishers have focused on multicultural literature, and so their catalogs are a treasure trove for those looking for such literature.

Asian American Curriculum Project, P. O. Box 367, San Mateo, CA 94401. In addition to its own publications, this company distributes Asian-American books from other small and large presses.

Black Butterfly/Writers and Readers, Box 461, Village Station, New York, NY 10014. This company produces children's books with an Afrocentric perspective and written by African-American writers and artists.

Children's Book Press, 246 First Street, Suite 101, San Francisco, CA 94105. This company publishes folktales and contemporary stories, often bilingual, in picture book format for Native-American, Asian-American, and Latino-American children.

Cross Cultural Education Center, P.O. Box 92, Welling, OK 74471. This Cherokee-owned company produces a variety of children's literature with a distinctly Cherokee point of view.

Piñata Books/Arte Público, University of Houston, 4800 Calhoun, Houston, TX 77204. This alternative press publishes children's books with a Latino perspective.

Just Us Books, 356 Glenwood Avenue, 3rd Floor, East Orange, NJ 07017. This company produces Afrocentric books that enhance the self-esteem of African-American children.

Lee & Low Books, 95 Madison Avenue, Room 606, New York, NY 10016. This Asian-American-owned company stresses authenticity in its contemporary stories for Asian-American, Latino-American, and African-American children. Its Latino titles are also offered in Spanish.

Northland Publishing, P.O. Box 1389, Flagstaff, AZ 86002. This company produces high-quality picture books by Native-American authors and illustrators from the Southwest.

Pemmican Publications, Unit #2—1635 Burrows Avenue, Winnipeg, Canada, R2X 0T1. This company publishes excellent realistic stories about contemporary Native American children and educational books for the Métis people about Métis history and culture.

Evaluating, selecting, and then bringing multicultural literature to your classroom, though essential, are not enough to ensure that your students will actually read the books. Without adult guidance, children tend to choose books about children like themselves (Rudman, 1984), so you must also purposefully expose mainstream children to multicultural books through reading aloud, booktalking, and selecting particular titles for small group reading.

# HISTORICAL OVERVIEW OF MULTICULTURAL LITERATURE

Members of many microcultures living in the United States were long ignored as subjects for children's books. On the few occasions that representatives of these groups did appear, they did so as crudely stereotyped characters, objects of ridicule, or shadowy secondary characters. Helen Bannerman's *The Story of Little Black Sambo* (1900), Claire Bishop's *The Five Chinese Brothers* (1938), Sara Cone Bryant's *Epaminondas and His Auntie* (1907), and Hugh Lofting's *The Voyages of Dr. Dolittle* (1922) come under this category. Today, books such as these either have been rewritten to eliminate the racism or have disappeared from children's library shelves.

Although many of the Newbery Medal winners and honor books of the 1920s and 1930s were set in foreign countries, almost none had to do with multicultural groups in the United States. Laura Adams Armer's novel about Native Americans, *Waterless Mountain*, the Newbery Medal winner in 1932, was the only exception.

The 1940s offered little improvement. Although Florence Crannell Means wrote sympathetic and informative novels such as *The Moved-Outers* (1945) about American ethnic microcultures during the 1930s and 1940s, negative stereotypes, such as those of Native Americans as savages projected in Newbery Medal winners *Daniel Boone* by James Daugherty (1939) and *The Matchlock Gun* by Walter D. Edmonds (1941), were more prevalent by far.

The first harbinger of change came in 1949 when an African-American author, Arne Bontemps, won a Newbery Honor Award for his *Story of the Negro* and became the first member of a minority group to receive this honor. A more sympathetic attitude toward American microcultures, at least in literature, emerged in the 1950s, as evidenced by the positive treatment of multicultural characters in such Newbery Medal winners as *Amos Fortune, Free Man* by Elizabeth Yates (1950) and *. . . And Now Miguel* by Joseph Krumgold (1953).

The Civil Rights movement of the 1960s focused attention on the social inequities and racial injustices that prevailed in the United States. The spirit of the times resulted in two landmark publications. The first of these was *The Snowy Day* by Ezra Jack Keats (1962), the first Caldecott Medal–winning book to have an African American as the protagonist. The great popularity of this book no doubt encouraged other authors to produce books with multicultural protagonists. The second publication was a powerful article by Nancy Larrick entitled "The All-White World of Children's Books." In this article, which appeared in the September 11, 1965, issue of *Saturday Review,* Larrick reported that in nearly all U.S. children's books the African American either was omitted entirely or was scarcely mentioned (p. 63). American trade book publishers, the education system, and the public library system were called upon to fill this void.

For a time the spirit of social consciousness born in the 1960s had good results. In 1966, the Council on Interracial Books for Children was founded and helped to promote young African-American authors. In 1969 the Coretta Scott King Award was established to recognize distinguished writing in children's books by African-American authors. Also, several books with multicultural protagonists or themes were chosen as Newbery winners in the early 1970s: *Sounder* by William H. Armstrong won in 1970; *Julie of the Wolves* by Jean Craighead George won in 1973; and *The Slave Dancer* by Paula Fox won in 1974. Judging from this record, the establishment had accepted multicultural protagonists in award-winning books; but it was not until 1975 that an author of color, Virginia Hamilton, author of *M. C. Higgins, the Great,* won a Newbery Medal.

In quick succession, other African-American and Asian-American authors were recognized for their outstanding literary and artistic efforts. In 1976, Leo Dillon (in collaboration with his wife, Diane Dillon) won a Caldecott Medal for *Why Mosquitoes Buzz in People's Ears* (Aardema, 1975), and Sharon Bell Mathis and Laurence Yep received Newbery Honor Awards for *The Hundred Penny Box* and *Dragonwings,* respectively. The following year, 1977, Mildred D. Taylor, author of *Roll of Thunder, Hear My Cry,* became the second African American to win the Newbery Medal. After 1975, the prevailing opinion among U.S. children's book publishers and professional reviewers seemed to be that members of a microcultural group were the ones most able to write authoritatively about their own particular cultures and experiences. Euro-American authors were no longer as likely to win major awards for writing about minorities as they were in the early 1970s.

During the 1980s and 1990s the number of multicultural books published by large, corporate publishers increased only slightly. In response to the continuing dearth of good multicultural literature for children, a number of small, alternative presses devoted exclusively to multicultural literature have been founded. Interest in multicultural literature continues, and the number of multicultural authors and illustrators entering the field, though still very small, is increasing. The late 1990s saw some much-needed development in Latino-American literature. Bilingual books published in response to the demands of ESOL (English for Speakers of Other Languages) programs and the founding of the Américas Award and the Pura Belpré Awards contributed to this growth. The fledgling Asian Pacific American Award for Literature, given jointly by the Asian/Pacific American Librarians Association and the Chinese American Librarians Association for the first time in 2001, promises to encourage a greater output of high quality Asian-American literature for children.

Although the last several decades have seen positive changes in the status of multicultural literature in the United States, there is still a marked shortage of books of this kind. Multicultural authors and illustrators of children's books are also in short supply. In 2000, for instance, 96 of the approximately 4,500 children's books published in the United States were written or illustrated by African Americans (Horning, Kruse, & Schliesman, 2000).

A new-found public interest in family heritage that began in the 1980s in the United States began to be reflected in multicultural literature by the end of the decade. Interest in books about ethnic heritage has helped multicultural authors and illustrators to regain some of the publishing momentum of the 1970s. Awakening to the meaning and importance of one's heritage is a recurring theme in all genres of multicultural literature.

As microcultural groups intermingle, more children of mixed heritage will be born. Already this group is growing fast. Perhaps the experience of growing up with a mixed heritage will be a topic featured in the multicultural literature of the future, as in Lawrence Yep's *Child of the Owl*. Milestones in the development of multicultural literature are highlighted on page 196.

## T Y P E S   O F   M U L T I C U L T U R A L   L I T E R A T U R E

Before discussing the literature of each microculture, a general caution is in order. Each of these groups contains subgroups that differ remarkably from one another in country of origin, language, race, traditions, and present location. Teachers must be especially conscious of and sensitive to these differences and guard against presenting these groups as completely uniform or of selecting literature that does so. Gross overgeneralization is not only inaccurate but is a form of stereotyping.

Each of the following types of multicultural literature can include bilingual books, that is, books having text in two languages. Bilingual books are appearing in the United States with greater frequency each year, particularly English/Spanish books. These books, if well done, are particularly helpful to children in ESOL programs and to their teachers. Not all bilingual books have artful, or even accurate, translations, so selection should be limited to the best of those published. See the bilingual section in the Recommended Multicultural Books list at the end of this chapter.

### African-American Literature

Of all multicultural groups living in the United States, African Americans have produced the largest and most rapidly growing body of children's literature. Every genre is well represented in African-American literature, but none better than poetry. Because it is so personal, poetry portrays a culture well, as is

# M I L E S T O N E S

*in the Development of* MULTICULTURAL LITERATURE

| DATE | EVENT | SIGNIFICANCE |
|---|---|---|
| 1932 | *Waterless Mountain* by Laura Armer wins Newbery Medal | One of the few children's books about minorities in the first half of the twentieth century |
| 1946 | *The Moved-Outers* by Florence C. Means wins Newbery Honor | A departure from stereotyped depiction of minorities begins |
| 1949 | *Story of the Negro* by Arne Bontemps wins Newbery Honor | First minority author to win a Newbery Honor |
| 1950 | *Song of the Swallows* by Leo Politi wins Caldecott Medal | First picture book with a Hispanic-American protagonist to win the Caldecott Medal |
| 1963 | *The Snowy Day* by Ezra Jack Keats wins Caldecott Medal | First picture book with an African-American protagonist to win the Caldecott Medal |
| 1965 | "The All-White World of Children's Books" by Nancy Larrick published in *Saturday Review* | Called the nation's attention to the lack of multicultural literature |
| 1969 | Coretta Scott King Award founded | African-American literature and authors begin to be promoted and supported |
| 1975 | *M. C. Higgins, the Great* by Virginia Hamilton wins Newbery Medal | First book by a minority author to win the Newbery Medal |
| 1976 | *Why Mosquitoes Buzz in People's Ears* illustrated by Leo and Diane Dillon wins Caldecott Medal | First picture book illustrated by an African American to win the Caldecott Medal |
| 1990 | *Lon Po Po: A Red-Riding Hood Story from China* translated and illustrated by Ed Young wins Caldecott Medal | First picture book illustrated by a Chinese American to win the Caldecott Medal |
| 1994 | *Grandfather's Journey* written and illustrated by Allen Say wins Caldecott Medal | First picture book illustrated by a Japanese American to win the Caldecott Medal |
| 1996 | Pura Belpré Award founded | Latino literature, authors, and illustrators promoted |
| 2001 | *The Trip Back Home* by Janet S. Wong, illustrated by Bo Jia, wins first Asian Pacific American Award for Literature | Asian-American literature, authors, and illustrators promoted |

evident in the sensitive yet powerful work of poets Arnold Adoff, Gwendolyn Brooks, Nikki Giovanni, Eloise Greenfield, and Langston Hughes. For example, see *Honey, I Love and Other Love Poems* by Eloise Greenfield.

Tapping into their rich oral tradition, African Americans have contributed Anansi the Spider, Brer Rabbit, High John the Conqueror, and John Henry the Steel Drivin' Man to the list of favorite U.S. folklore characters. Even today, authors are bringing folktales to the United States from Africa. Examples include *Why Mosquitoes Buzz in People's Ears* by Verna Aardema and *The Flying Tortoise: An Igbo Tale,* by Tololwa Mollel, illustrated by Barbara Spurll.

In some cases, African Americans have reclaimed their tales by retelling (without racist elements) stories that were first written down in this country by Euro-American authors, as Julius Lester has done in his retelling of Joel Chandler Harris's *The Tales of Uncle Remus: The Adventures of Brer Rabbit.* More recent memories and family stories have begun to be written by African-American authors as modern folktales. For example, see *Mirandy and Brother Wind* by Patricia McKissack.

African Americans have told the stories of their lives in the United States through both historical and realistic fiction. The stories for older readers often include painfully harsh but accurate accounts of racial oppression, as in James Berry's slavery story *Ajeemah and His Son* or Mildred Taylor's historical fiction saga of the close-knit Logan family (*The Song of the Trees; Roll of Thunder, Hear My Cry; Let the Circle Be Unbroken;* and *The Road to Memphis*) and in Walter Dean Myers's contemporary realistic novel *Scorpions.* The characters, settings, and incidents created by these authors will be recognized by many African Americans who have lived through similar experiences; others will appreciate these stories as windows onto an understanding of today's racial situation. Teachers can see to it that such stories are balanced, however, with more positive, encouraging contemporary stories.

Recently, African-American faces have begun to appear more frequently in picture books. While these books tend to address universal topics rather than those dealing specifically with race, they can still be culturally conscious. The works of illustrators Floyd Cooper, Donald Crews, Leo and Diane Dillon, Tom Feelings, Jerry Pinkney, Brian Pinkney, and James Ransome deserve special notice. Examples include *Mufaro's Beautiful Daughters* by John Steptoe and *The Middle Passage: White Ships/Black Cargo* by Tom Feelings.

African-American nonfiction is mainly biography. In the 1960s and 1970s a large percentage of these biographical subjects were sports heroes, but more recent subjects have come from a broader spectrum of achievement. For example, see *Through My Eyes* by Ruby Bridges and Margo Lundell.

### Asian-American Literature

Asian-American children's literature is mainly represented in the United States by stories about Chinese Americans and Japanese Americans, possibly because these groups have lived as microcultures in this country longer than others such as Vietnamese Americans. A major theme in much of the fiction and nonfiction for older readers is the oppression that drove the people out of their homelands and the prejudice that they faced as newcomers in this country. A more positive theme is that of learning to appreciate one's cultural heritage while adjusting to life in the United States. Examples include *Dragonwings* and *Child of the Owl* by Laurence Yep and *In the Year of the Boar and Jackie Robinson* by Bette Bao Lord.

Traditional stories from Asia retold in English have contributed many interesting folktales and folktale variants to American and Canadian children's libraries. Characters who are generally thought of as European, such as Little Red Riding Hood and Cinderella, have their Asian counterparts. Examples are *Lon Po Po: A Red-Riding Hood Story from China* translated and illustrated by Ed Young, and *Yeh Shen: A Cinderella Story from China* by Ai-Ling Louie, illustrated by Ed Young.

Asian-American artists have brought the sophisticated style and technical artistry of the Orient to U.S. children's book illustration. Ed Young's use of screenlike panels and Allen Say's precision are especially noteworthy. Examples are *The Boy of the Three-Year Nap* by Diane Snyder, illustrated by Allen Say, and *Seven Blind Mice* by Ed Young.

The body of Asian-American children's literature is small. Nonfiction, poetry, and fantasy are almost unrepresented, with the notable exception of Rhoda Blumberg's 1986 Newbery Honor book, a work of nonfiction, *Commodore Perry in the Land of the Shogun.* The recently established Asian Pacific American Award for Literature, as well as small presses, such as Lee & Low Books, will help to improve this situation.

### Latino-American Literature

Until recently, few Latino-American children's books were published in this country. There is still an insufficient amount of high-quality literature of this kind, but recent developments hold promise for improvement in the amount and quality of Latino-American literature. The books that are available are mainly about Puerto Ricans and Mexican Americans; the works of Alma Flor Ada, George Ancona, Lulu Delacre, and Gary Soto are outstanding examples. Leo Politi's books about Mexican Americans have been popular for many years but do not describe the current Latino-American experience. More relevant examples are *Too Many Tamales* by Gary Soto, illustrated by Ed Martinez, and *The Circuit: Stories from the Life of a Migrant Child* by Francisco Jiménez.

The rise of small press publishers, such as Children's Book Press, that focus on Latino-American literature, has already resulted in more literature being written for and about this group. The trend toward marketing more Spanish-English bilingual texts in the United States also will improve the availability of Latino-American books, particularly to younger children who are learning to read. For example, see *Gathering the Sun: An Alphabet in Spanish and English* by Alma Flor Ada, illustrated by Simon Silva. The establishment in 1993 of the Américas Award for a U.S. work that authentically presents the experience of individuals in Latin America or the Caribbean or of Latinos in the United States and, in 1996, of the Pura Belpré Award honoring outstanding Latino-American children's authors and illustrators will undoubtedly promote the creation of more high-quality Latino-American literature for children.

### Jewish-American Literature

The terrible experience of the Jewish Holocaust in Europe during the 1930s and 1940s has had a tremendous influence on Jewish-American children's literature. The prejudice and cruelty that led to the Holocaust and the nightmare of the death camps themselves are recurring themes in both fiction and nonfiction for older readers. Since many Jewish people immigrated to the United States as the Nazi threat grew in Europe, much Holocaust literature has been written by eyewitnesses or by those whose relatives were victims. Examples are *The Upstairs Room* by Johanna Reiss, *Upon the Head of the Goat* by Aranka Siegal, and *Smoke and Ashes: The Story of the Holocaust* by Barbara Rogasky.

Jewish emigration from Europe during the war years brought to the United States many outstanding artists whose work has greatly influenced children's book illustration. Two subjects often presented in Jewish-American picture books are Jewish holidays and folktales. Illustrated Jewish folktale collections, particularly those by Isaac Bashevis Singer, offer excellent, witty stories and high literary quality. Examples include *Gershon's Monster: A Story for the Jewish New Year,* retold by Eric Kimmel and illustrated by Jon J. Muth and *It Could Always Be Worse* by Margot Zemach.

The Jewish-American community has produced a number of excellent authors and illustrators of children's books. Literary creativity is promoted through two book award programs: the National Jewish Book Awards and the Association of Jewish Libraries Awards.

### Native-American Literature

Almost from the moment that European explorers landed on this continent some five hundred years ago, Native Americans have suffered at the hands of Euro-Americans. Consequently, in books written from the Native-American perspective, oppression by the white population is a pervasive theme. Appreciation, celebration, and protection of nature—central tenets of Native-American cultures—are other recurrent themes in this body of literature. Examples are *Crazy Horse's Vision* by Joseph Bruchac, illustrated by S. D. Nelson, and *The Birchbark House* by Louise Erdrich.

Although much has been written *about* Native Americans, relatively little has been written *by* members of this microculture. Small press publishers specializing in literature by Native Americans may help to change this situation. Northland Press, for example, features the work of Native Americans of the southwestern United States. Native Americans who are known for their children's books include Virginia Driving Hawk Sneve for her novels, Joseph Bruchac for his retold stories, and Michael Lacapa and Shonto Begay for their illustrations. Examples are *When Thunders Spoke* by Virginia Driving Hawk Sneve and *The First Strawberries* retold by Joseph Bruchac, illustrated by Anna Vojtech.

Numerous other writers and illustrators have told and retold the folktales and history of Native Americans in picture books, historical fiction, and informational books. Paul Goble is particularly well known for his impressively illustrated retellings of the legends of the Plains Indians, as are Scott O'Dell and Canadian Jan Hudson for their award-winning works of historical fiction featuring young Native-American women. The body of nonfictional works about Native Americans is particularly rich, the works of Ann Nolan Clark, Russell Freedman, Milton Meltzer, John Bierhorst, Brent Ashabranner, and Alex Bealer being outstanding. Examples include *The Girl Who Loved Wild Horses* by Paul Goble, *Island of the Blue Dolphins* by Scott O'Dell, and *Only the Names Remain: The Cherokees and the Trail of Tears* by Alex Bealer.

## SECTION TWO: *International Literature*

## DEFINITION AND DESCRIPTION

*International literature* in the United States is defined as literary selections that were originally published for the children in a country other than the United States in a language of that country and later published in the United States. The key elements of this definition are the book's country of origin and the determination of the primary audience for the book. If a book was written and published in France for French children and then translated and published for U.S. children, it is considered an international book in the United States. Books that are classified as international literature by this definition include the following:

1.  English language books that were originally written and published in English in another country, such as Canada or Australia, then published or distributed in the United States.
2.  Translated books that were written and published in a foreign language and then translated into English and published in the United States.
3.  Foreign language books that were written and published in a foreign language in another country for children of that country and later published or distributed in the United States in the foreign language.

If a book is written and published in the United States about Australian life, then the primary audience is U.S. children, and the book is not considered international. Such books written and published in the United States about other countries are included in the lists of recommended books in the genre chapters.

Sometimes it is difficult to ascertain a book's country of origin. The publishing history page is the most reliable source of this information. (Note that in some foreign books, this publishing history is placed at the end of the book.) In any case, a careful reading will inform you of the book's original date and place of publication.

## VALUES OF INTERNATIONAL LITERATURE FOR CHILDREN

The value of international children's literature in developing an understanding of and appreciation for other cultures is undeniable. The understanding of people of other countries must be fostered early and allowed to grow throughout life.

*   Through this literature, the history, traditions, and people of other countries are brought to life.
*   By interpreting events in the everyday lives of their characters and by depicting long-term changes in the characters' lives, authors present a truer and more understandable picture of life in other countries than does the crisis-prone, single-event coverage of television and newspapers.
*   Compelling stories build students' interest in the people and places they are reading about and pave the way to a deeper understanding and appreciation of the geography and history content encountered in textbooks.
*   Literature written by natives of the country or region under study gives authenticity and an international perspective to classroom materials.
*   Today, many students in the United States speak a foreign language and have a foreign heritage. International literature reflects the cultural and language diversity often found in classrooms today. By reading international books, students can learn to respect the heritage of others and take pride in their own.
*   Through international literature, children are given an opportunity to enjoy the best-loved stories of their peers around the world. This, in turn, can help students to develop a bond of shared experience with children of other nations and can enable them to acquire cultural literacy with a global perspective.

In a study by Monson, Howe, and Greenlee (1989), two hundred U.S. children, ages 9 to 11, were asked what they would like to know about their counterparts in other countries. Their responses, categorized into nine questions, then formed the basis for a comparison of eight social studies textbooks and fifteen works of fiction appropriate for the age group about one country, Australia. It was found that both textbooks and trade books gave information about the country. The novels answered more of the children's questions, however, and were richer in detail of daily life and human emotion than the textbooks. The social studies texts gave many facts about the country, while the novels showed the implications of the facts for children's lives and helped the readers "live in" the country for a time.

# EVALUATION AND SELECTION OF INTERNATIONAL LITERATURE

International books, both chapter books and picture books, should first be judged by the standards for all good literature.

- Translated works should exhibit a good, fluent writing style that is not stilted or awkward. Some flavor of the country of origin should remain. For example, place and character names should usually remain true to the original text to foster in children a tolerance for and an appreciation of other languages and customs. Some translated books include a glossary of foreign words, meanings, and pronunciations. This permits readers to risk new and different words and sounds with no loss of confidence. Although too many words left untranslated can be annoying to the reader, a few can be enjoyable and can provoke an interest in foreign languages. The translation should not violate the tone of the book by being so idiomatic as to jar the reader. For example, a book from Czechoslovakia rings untrue if the translation of the young people's language sounds like hip American slang or street talk.

- Teachers and librarians may note in some international books differences in writing and illustrating styles. International chapter books for intermediate- and upper-grade readers lean toward introspection by the main character. Examples are 1990 Hans Christian Andersen Award winner Tormod Haugen's *Night Birds* and *Zeppelin.* Students could be alerted to the differences and could be asked to reflect on why the author may have chosen that manner of telling the story. In some cases, illustrations in international books are more abstract than is usual for U.S. picture books. Aspects of plot and theme in these books are heavily embedded in the pictorial details. For example, many layers of meaning can be unraveled with repeated readings of the story personifying the months of the year in *December's Travels,* written by Mischa Damjan and illustrated by Dušan Kállay, 1988 Hans Christian Andersen Medalist.

With the increase of internationalism in all domains of our social and cultural life, more international children's books are becoming available in the United States. A number of selection sources will prove useful and necessary in locating international children's book titles. *Bookbird: Journal of International Children's Literature,* the International Board on Books for Young People (IBBY) journal, announces recent international award-winning books and national award winners from many nations and is, therefore, an important source for current information on international books. It also features articles on international children's literature. The *USBBY Newsletter* from the United States section of IBBY highlights events of interest in the United States and other countries related to this field.

The lists of past winners of the Hans Christian Andersen Award, the Mildred L. Batchelder Award, and the British, Australian, New Zealand, and Canadian awards for children's books are excellent sources of international titles and authors. (See Appendix A.) The major children's book review sources include reviews of notable international books in their monthly review columns. (See Appendix B for lists of these journals.) *Booklist,* a review journal published by the American Library Association, has occasional summary booklists on translated books and on foreign language books.

Marianne Carus, who grew up in Nazi Germany, made a commitment when founding the children's magazine *Cricket* to include "translated stories from as many countries as possible and about as many cultures as possible" because of her belief that "the earlier in life we lay the foundation for international understanding and tolerance, the sounder will be the bridges built later and the more ready for peaceful traffic and exchange back and forth" (Carus, 1980, pp. 174–175). This outstanding magazine, a good source for short read-alouds, features U.S. and international short stories of high quality for children from ages 6 to 12. Although international children's books are published each year by many of the largest U.S. publishers, their numbers are relatively small. Many small press publishers have taken the lead in this field and in publishing multicultural books.

Four professional books that are invaluable in selecting international children's books and in learning about international children's literature have recently been published or updated:

- *Children's Books: Awards & Prizes* from the Children's Book Council (1996) is a complete listing of major book awards in other countries with an explanation of each of the awards.
- *International Companion Encyclopedia of Children's Literature,* Vol. 1, edited by Peter Hunt and Sheila G. Ray (1996), is a 923-page book featuring 28 essays on children's literature in different countries around the world.
- *Children's Books from Other Countries,* edited by Carl M. Tomlinson (1998), is a 304-page book with strategies for sharing books with children, with activities for promoting international understanding, and with an annotated bibliography of 724 international books published in the United States in English.
- *Global Perspectives in Children's Literature,* by Evelyn Freeman and Barbara Lehman (2001), is a 136-page book discussing the values of international literature for children, with chapters on current status, issues, and trends in the field. Also included is a chapter on sharing international books across the curriculum.

A few publishers have specialized in international children's books and deserve special mention here.

African Imprints Library Services, 236 Main Street, Falmouth, MA 02540. This company's catalog includes recent children's books available from twenty African nations.

Candlewick Press, 2067 Massachusetts Avenue, Cambridge, MA 02140, is the U.S. branch of Walker Publishers of London. Candlewick is responsible for bringing the works of some of the best British children's book illustrators and authors to this country.

Farrar, Straus, and Giroux, 19 Union Square West, New York, NY 10003. As a result of a translation and distribution agreement with the largest Swedish publisher of children's books, Rabén and Sjögren, this company publishes a number of translated Swedish books every year.

Henry Holt and Company, 115 West 18th Street, New York, NY 10114-0378. This publishing firm has an imprint, Edge Books, that features international young adult fiction.

Kane/Miller Book Publishers, P.O. Box 8515, La Jolla, CA 92038. This small press specializes in translated foreign children's picture books from around the world under the Cranky Nell imprint.

Lerner Publications Company/Carolrhoda Books, Inc., 241 First Avenue North, Minneapolis, MN 55401. This company publishes many multicultural and international nonfiction and fiction children's books.

North-South Books, 1133 Broadway, Suite 1016, New York, NY 10010, publishes high-quality multinational copublications and the English language editions of Michael Neugebauer Books, a Swiss publisher.

Simon & Schuster/Margaret K. McElderry Books, Macmillan Publishing Company, 866 Third Avenue, New York, NY 10022, publishes picture books and chapter books from other English-speaking countries and translated children's chapter books.

Tundra Books of Northern New York, Box 1030, Plattsburgh, NY 12901. This company specializes in Canadian and French/English bilingual books for children.

Turton and Chambers Ltd., Station Road, Woodchester Stroud, Glos GL5 5EQ, England. This firm specializes in translating into English and publishing foreign children's books for distribution in England and Australia. Books can be ordered by catalog from England.

## HISTORICAL OVERVIEW OF INTERNATIONAL LITERATURE

Much of the children's literature that was available in the United States during the seventeenth, eighteenth, nineteenth, and early twentieth centuries came from Europe. These early children's books are an important part of our cultural heritage, but we seldom think of the fact that they were originally published in other countries and many in other languages. They are so familiar to us in the United States that we consider them our children's classics, and indeed they have become so. Page 204 lists a sampling of international children's classics published from the end of the seventeenth century up to World War II.

With the rapid growth in the U.S. children's book field in the twentieth century, the flow of books from other countries became overshadowed by large numbers of U.S. publications. In addition, during World War II, little cultural exchange occurred across international borders. The end of World War II saw a change in the international mood, and two developments occurred that had far-reaching effects on the children's book field: (1) children's books in translation began to be published in unprecedented numbers (Carus, 1980), and (2) the international children's book field was established and fostered by an international organization, awards, and publishers' bookfairs of children's books.

## *Early* MILESTONES
### *in* INTERNATIONAL CHILDREN'S LITERATURE

| DATE | EVENT | SIGNIFICANCE |
| --- | --- | --- |
| 1657 | *Orbis Pictus* by John Amos Comenius | Earliest nonfiction picture book |
| 1697 | *Tales of Mother Goose* by Charles Perrault | Earliest folktales from France |
| 1719 | *Robinson Crusoe* by Daniel Defoe | Two early adult adventure books from England, |
| 1726 | *Gulliver's Travels* by Jonathan Swift | adopted by children |
| 1812 | *Nursery and Household Tales* by Jakob and Wilhelm Grimm | Traditional folktales from Germany |
| 1836 | *Fairy Tales* by Hans Christian Andersen | Early modern folktales from Denmark |
| 1846 | *Book of Nonsense* by Edward Lear | Early humorous poetry from England |
| 1865 | *Alice's Adventures in Wonderland* by Lewis Carroll | Classic English modern fantasy |
| 1880 | *Heidi* by Johanna Spyri | Early realistic story from Switzerland |
| 1881 | *The Adventures of Pinocchio* by Carlo Collodi | Modern fantasy from Italy |
| 1883 | *Treasure Island* by Robert Louis Stevenson | Adventure tale from England by a Scottish author |
| 1885 | *A Child's Garden of Verses* by Robert Louis Stevenson | Classic collection of Golden Age poems from England |
| 1894 | *The Jungle Book* by Rudyard Kipling | Animal stories set in India by an English author |
| 1901 | *The Tale of Peter Rabbit* by Beatrix Potter | Classic English picture book |
| 1906 | *The Wonderful Adventures of Nils* by Selma Lagerlöf | A fantasy trip around Sweden |
| 1908 | *The Wind in the Willows* by Kenneth Grahame | Animal fantasy from England |
| 1908 | *Anne of Green Gables* by Lucy M. Montgomery | Realistic family story from Canada |
| 1926 | *Winnie-the-Pooh* by A. A. Milne | Personified toy story from England |
| 1928 | *Bambi* by Felix Salten | Personified deer story from Germany |
| 1931 | *The Story of Babar* by Jean de Brunhoff | Personified elephant story from France |
| 1945 | *Pippi Longstocking* by Astrid Lindgren | Classic fantasy from Sweden |

The establishment of an international children's book field was advanced by Jella Lepman, who described these early developments in *A Bridge of Children's Books* (1969). Lepman, a German-born Jew who left Germany during World War II for England, returned to Germany after the war to work in the field of children's books as a way to promote international understanding and world peace. Lepman began a traveling exhibit of children's books for German children, which in 1949 was established as the International Youth Library (IYL) in Munich. The IYL is the largest collection of children's books from around the world and currently holds well over 500,000 books. In reflecting on these accomplishments, Lepman concludes in her book that "in many parts of the world children were holding books in their hands and meeting over a bridge of children's books" (p. 154).

Lepman also worked with others from many countries in establishing the International Board on Books for Young People (IBBY) in 1953. IBBY is organized by sections from member countries. The members of national sections are children's book editors, agents, librarians, publishers, educators, translators, authors, and illustrators—anyone who works in the children's book field. In 1956, IBBY founded the Hans Christian Andersen Award, an international award program that honors outstanding authors of children's literature. The first recipient of this award was Eleanor Farjeon of Great Britain. The award is given every two years, and in 1966 an award to outstanding illustrators was added. Alois Carigiet of Switzerland was the 1966 Award winner for illustrations. (See Appendix A for other Hans Christian Andersen Award winners.) IBBY holds a biennial world congress in September.

In 1963, IBBY founded *Bookbird,* an international quarterly periodical on literature for children and young people. In 1993, the publication of *Bookbird* moved to the United States. North America has thus increased its role in the affairs of IBBY in recent years. In the United States our chapter of IBBY is the United States Board on Books for Young People (USBBY), an organization that welcomes teachers, editors, librarians, and all who are interested in the international exchange of children's literature. For information on membership, publications, and conferences, contact Secretariat, USBBY, P. O. Box 8139, Newark, DE 19714-8139, or go to USBBY's Web site at www.usbby.org.

In 1967, the Biennale of Illustrations Bratislava (BIB), an international exposition of children's book illustrations, was established and takes place every other year in Bratislava, Czechoslovakia. An international jury selects prize-winning children's book illustrations for a Grand Prix, the highest award, and recognizes honor books.

In 1968, the first Mildred L. Batchelder Award was announced by the American Library Association in honor of a U.S. publisher of the most distinguished translated children's book published in the preceding year. This award is given annually to encourage the translation and publication of international books in the United States. (See Appendix A for the award list.)

An international children's bookfair is convened in Bologna, Italy, every April for children's book publishers. This forum has proved to be an important one for the international exchange of children's books—a time when publishers display their best in the interests of attracting publishers from other nations to publish the new books in their own countries. Three prizes are awarded at this fair; one is selected by a jury of children from ages 6 to 9.

The future of international children's literature depends upon our success in several arenas. First, we must encourage the development of stronger national literatures from developing nations where most literature remains at the stage of the oral tradition. We must also promote more literary exchange with nations whose literature is now growing rapidly to bring more of the world's best literature to our children's attention. Finally, we must support those organizations that can assist in these endeavors.

## INTERNATIONAL BOOKS BY WORLD REGIONS

Quite logically, the international books that are most often available in the United States have been and continue to be books from other English-speaking countries. These English language books originate in many different countries, but the largest numbers of them come from Great Britain, Australia, Canada, and New Zealand. Although the books do not require translation, they are often published in the United States with other changes: spelling, characters' names, place names, and, sometimes titles and cover illustrations. These changes are made ostensibly to increase the marketability of the books in this country and may indeed accomplish that end in some cases. Because of the shared primary language and some cultural commonalities among these nations, the literary exchange has been relatively easy. Teachers are often surprised to discover that one of their favorite authors is British, Canadian, or Australian. An example is *The Jolly Postman* by Janet and Allan Ahlberg, a book that was first published in England. However, many English language books do feature cultural attitudes and customs not typically found in the United States that warrant comparison and discussion by students. The major awards and award winners from English-speaking countries are listed in Appendix A.

*Translated books* come to the United States from around the world, but the largest numbers come from Europe. Today, many books come from Sweden, Norway, Denmark, Switzerland, the Netherlands, Germany, France, and Belgium and in considerably smaller numbers from eastern European countries, especially Czechoslovakia and the former Soviet Union. A few books come from Italy and Spain. An example from Norway is *Two Short and One Long* by Nina Aamundsen.

Translated children's literature from Asia originates mostly in Japan, but books from Korea, China, and Thailand can occasionally be found. Japan has an extremely sophisticated field of book illustrating, and many beautifully illustrated picture books are now making their way into the U.S. market. An example from Sri Lanka is *The Umbrella Thief,* by Sybil Wettasinghe.

African nations have produced little children's literature that has been exported to the United States. The reasons for this are many, but the most influential one is probably that of economics. Publishing books is expensive, especially in full color; therefore, the publishing industry is not firmly established in developing countries. An example from Ghana is *Cat in Search of a Friend* by Meshack Asare. Central and South American countries suffer from similar economic problems. Traditional literature is usually the first genre of children's literature to be published in a developing nation and, therefore, is often the only literature available to our students from those countries. Books of realistic fiction in which contemporary life in another country is portrayed are rare but worth locating. An example is Lesley Beake's *The Song of Be,* a novel set in Namibia that deals with reconciling present political realities with ancient traditions.

The difficulties of locating and translating good books from non-English-speaking countries contribute to the dearth of available titles. Certain publishing companies have been attempting to overcome this dearth of foreign literature in our country by focusing solely on foreign children's literature, whereas other publishers have made a concerted effort to increase the percentage of foreign books among their titles. These efforts are encouraging. As more librarians, teachers, and parents become interested in purchasing this body of literature, more publishers will become willing to meet the market need.

There is reason to hope that the current unrest between cultures will not always be the case. Ethnic prejudice and bias are not natural behaviors; they are learned. One of the most intriguing challenges to those who work with children is to combat the ignorance that is at the root of racial, cultural, and religious prejudice and intolerance. Children's literature, particularly the rich multicultural and international selections that are currently available, is a powerful tool in this effort, for it shows that the similarities between all people are much more fundamental than the differences.

## REFERENCES

Banks, J. A., & Banks, C. A. (1993). *Multicultural education: Issues and perspectives.* Boston: Allyn and Bacon.

Carus, M. (1980). Translation and internationalism in children's literature. *Children's Literature in Education, 11*(4), 171–179.

Children's Book Council (Ed.). (1996). *Children's books: Awards & prizes.* New York: Children's Book Council.

Cullen, C. (1998). Tableau. In *I, too sing America.* New York: Houghton.

Freeman, E., & Lehman, B. (2001). *Global perspectives in children's literature.* Needham Heights: Allyn and Bacon.

Horning, K. T., Kruse, G. M., & Schliesman, M. (2001). *CCBC Choices, 2001.* Madison: University Publications, University of Wisconsin–Madison.

Hunt, P., & Ray, S. G. (Eds.). (1996). *International companion encyclopedia of children's literature.* London: Routledge.

Kruse, G. M., Horning, K. T., & Schliesman, M. (1997). *Multicultural literature for children and young adults: A selected listing of books by and about people of color: Vol. 2. 1991–1996.* Madison, WI: Cooperative Children's Book Center and Wisconsin Department of Public Instruction.

Larrick, N. (1965). The all-white world of children's books. *Saturday Review* (September 11), 63–65, 84–85.

Lepman, J. (1969). *A bridge of children's books.* Chicago: American Library Association.

Monson, D. L., Howe, K., & Greenlee, A. (1989). Helping children develop cross-cultural understanding with children's books. *Early Child Development and Care, 48*(special issue), 3–8.

Rudman, M. (1984). *Children's literature: An issues approach* (2nd ed.). New York: Longman.

Schon, I. (2000). *Recommended books in Spanish for children and young adults.* Lanham, MD: Scarecrow.

Sims, R. (1982). *Shadow and substance: Afro-American experience in contemporary children's fiction.* Urbana, IL: NCTE.

Stott, J. (1996). *Native Americans in children's literature.* Phoenix, AZ: Oryx.

Tomlinson, C. M. (Ed.). (1998). *Children's books from other countries.* Lanham, MD: Scarecrow.

## NOTABLE AUTHORS AND ILLUSTRATORS OF MULTICULTURAL LITERATURE

### African-American

**Ashley Bryan,** collector, teller, and illustrator of African songs and folktales. *I'm Going to Sing: Black American Spirituals.*

**Leo and Diane Dillon,** illustrators of two Caldecott Medal–winning books. Leo Dillon is the first African American to win a Caldecott Medal. *Why Mosquitoes Buzz in People's Ears; Ashanti to Zulu.*

**Tom Feelings,** illustrator who uses inventive artistic techniques in books about Africans and African Americans. *Moja Means One; Soul Looks Back in Wonder.*

**Virginia Hamilton,** award-winning author whose books about African Americans include realistic fiction, mystery, fantasy, myth, and biography. *M. C. Higgins, the Great; Zeely.*

**Julius Lester,** author of nonfiction and collector and reteller of African-American folktales. *To Be a Slave.*

**Patricia McKissack,** author of modern African-American folktales and informational books. *Mirandy and Brother Wind.*

**Walter Dean Myers,** author of sometimes gritty contemporary realistic fiction about African Americans growing up. *The Scorpions; Fallen Angels.*

**Brian Pinkney,** illustrator whose swirling lines and black backgrounds in intricate scratchboard renderings create a sense of intrigue and mystery. *The Ballad of Belle Dorcas; The Faithful Friend.*

**Jerry Pinkney,** illustrator whose light-filled watercolors capture the beauty of African Americans. *The Talking Eggs.*

**James Ransome,** illustrator noted for his use of bold colors and representational style. *Aunt Flossie's Hats (and Crabcakes Later); The Creation.*

**Faith Ringgold,** author/illustrator of story quilts. *Tar Beach.*

**John Steptoe,** first African-American author/illustrator to gain fame in the United States. *Stevie; Mufaro's Beautiful Daughters.*

**Mildred Taylor,** author whose award-winning books of historical fiction chronicle the experience of growing up black in southern United States in the 1940s and 1950s. *Roll of Thunder, Hear My Cry; The Friendship.*

## Asian-American

**Allen Say,** author/illustrator whose realistic watercolors depict stories of the Japanese-American experience. *Grandfather's Journey; Tree of Cranes.*

**Yoshiko Uchida,** author of autobiographical accounts of U.S. imprisonment of Japanese-American citizens during World War II. *Journey to Topaz; Journey Home.*

**Paul Yee,** Canadian-Chinese author who writes about the Chinese Canadian experience. *Tales from Gold Mountain: Stories of the Chinese in the New World.*

**Laurence Yep,** author of historical and contemporary realistic fiction about growing up as an Asian American. *Dragonwings; Child of the Owl.*

**Ed Young,** first Asian-American illustrator to win the Caldecott Award. *Lon Po Po: A Red-Riding Hood Story from China.*

## Latino-American

**George Ancona,** Mexican-American photographer who writes about and photographs the life and culture of Mexico and Mexican Americans. *Fiesta, U.S.A.; Pablo Remembers: The Fiesta of the Day of the Dead.*

**Lulu Delacre,** collector and illustrator of songs, poems, and stories from Latin America. *Arroz con Leche: Popular Songs and Rhymes from Latin America; Vejigante/Masquerader.*

**Frané Lessac,** illustrator of Caribbean island stories and poems. *Caribbean Canvas; The Chalk Doll.*

**Gary Soto,** author of contemporary stories about the Mexican-American experience. *Trading Places; Snapshots from the Wedding.*

## Jewish-American

**Eric Kimmel,** reteller of tales, many of which are from the Jewish culture. *Hershel and the Hanukkah Goblins; The Chanukkah Guest.*

**Milton Meltzer,** author of important nonfictional works about several U.S. minorities. *Remember the Days: A Short History of the Jewish American.*

**Naomi Shihab Nye,** poet whose work celebrates the value of different cultures for everyone. *This Same Sky: A Collection of Poems from Around the World; The Tree Is Older Than You Are: Bilingual Poems and Stories from Mexico.*

## Native-American

**Brent Ashabranner,** author of nonfictional books about Native American life, past and present. *To Live in Two Worlds: American Indian Youth Today.*

**John Bierhorst,** collector of traditional literature of Native Americans and South American and Mexican Indians. *The Fire Plume: Legends of the American Indians.*

**Joseph Bruchac,** reteller of Native-American folktales and legends and biographer of famous Native Americans. *The First Strawberries; Crazy Horse's Vision.*

**Paul Goble,** reteller and illustrator of the folktales and legends of the Native Americans of the Great Plains. *The Girl Who Loved Wild Horses.*

**Scott O'Dell,** author of several works of award-winning historical fiction featuring strong female Native-American heroines. *Island of the Blue Dolphins.*

**Virginia Driving Hawk Sneve,** author of a nonfiction picture book series, poetry, and contemporary realistic fiction about Native Americans. *Dancing Teepees; When Thunders Spoke.*

## NOTABLE AUTHORS, ILLUSTRATORS, AND TRANSLATORS OF INTERNATIONAL LITERATURE

**Lena Anderson,** Swedish illustrator of the Linnea books by Christina Björk and her own Baby Bunny series.

**Mitsumasa Anno,** Japanese author/illustrator of sophisticated wordless picture books and concept books; 1984 recipient of the Hans Christian Andersen Award. *Topsy Turvies: Pictures to Stretch the Imagination; Anno's Journey.*

**Jeannie Baker,** Australian artist who uses relief collages in her illustrations. *Where the Forest Meets the Sea; Home in the Sky.*

**Graeme Base,** Australian illustrator of large, elaborate format picture books. *Animalia; The Eleventh Hour.*

**Anthea Bell,** British award-winning translator from German, Dutch, and Danish languages. Translated *Buster's World* by Bjarne Reuter and *Konrad* by Christine Nöstlinger.

**Quentin Blake,** British illustrator popular for his irreverently humorous style. *Quentin Blake's ABC; Nonstop Nonsense* by Margaret Mahy.

**Anthony Browne,** British author/illustrator whose stark surrealism reveals modern social ills. *Willy the Wimp; Gorilla.*

**Elizabeth D. Crawford,** a skillful translator of many children's books from German including *Suleiman the Elephant; Don't Say a Word; Old John;* and *Crutches,* winner of the Mildred L. Batchelder Award.

**Roald Dahl,** British author of extremely popular and wildly humorous modern fantasies. *James and the Giant Peach; Charlie and the Chocolate Factory.*

**Berlie Doherty,** British author of adolescent fiction. *Dear Nobody; Granny Was a Buffer Girl.*

**Mem Fox,** Australian author of picture storybooks often employing Australian animals. *Possum Magic; Koala Lou.*

**Bob Graham,** Australian author and illustrator of whimsical picture books. *Greetings from Sandy Beach; Rose Meets Mr. Wintergarden.*

**Peter Härtling,** German author of World War II historical fiction novels. *Crutches; Old John.*

**Monica Hughes,** Canadian author of contemporary fiction and science fiction. *The Keeper of the Isis Light; The Dream Catcher.*

**Dušan Kállay,** Czechoslovakian illustrator and winner of the Bratislava Grand Prix and the 1988 Hans Christian Andersen Award. Illustrated *December's Travels* by Mischa Damjan.

**Dennis Lee,** Canadian poet known for humorous poetry. *Alligator Pie; Garbage Delight.*

**Jean Little,** Canadian author of realistic chapter books featuring children with emotional and physical disabilities. *Mine for Keeps; Mama's Going to Buy You a Mockingbird.*

**Janet Lunn,** Canadian author of historical fantasy novels. *The Root Cellar; Shadow in Hawthorn Bay.*

**P. J. Lynch,** Irish illustrator who won the Kate Greenaway Medal for *The Christmas Miracle of Jonathan Toomey.*

**Ana Maria Machado,** Brazilian author and winner of the 2000 Hans Christian Andersen Author Award. *Nina Bonita: A Story.*

**Margaret Mahy,** New Zealand author of modern fantasies with supernatural elements. *The Haunting; The Changeover.*

**Farley Mowat,** Canadian author of animal stories. *Owls in the Family; Never Cry Wolf.*

**Jörg Müller,** Swiss illustrator and 1994 Hans Christian Andersen Award winner who unifies social conscience with experimentation in aesthetic form. *Rabbit Island.*

**A. Philippa Pearce,** British author of modern fantasies and contemporary mysteries. *Tom's Midnight Garden; The Way to Sattin Shore.*

**Philip Pullman,** British creator of *His Dark Materials* fantasies, a trilogy comprised of *The Golden Compass, The Subtle Knife,* and *The Amber Spyglass.*

**J. K. Rowling,** British author of the popular, bestselling series about Harry Potter, a child wizard. *Harry Potter and the Sorcerer's Stone.*

**Julie Vivas,** Australian illustrator of picture books. *Possum Magic; Wilfrid Gordon McDonald Partridge.*

**Patricia Wrightson,** Australian author of contemporary novels with Aboriginal folk spirits; received the Hans Christian Andersen Award in 1986. *The Nargun and the Stars; A Little Fear.*

**Lisbeth Zwerger,** Austrian illustrator and recipient of the 1990 Hans Christian Andersen Award; particularly noted for her illustrations of traditional folktales, including tales of the Brothers Grimm. *Hansel and Gretel; Little Red Cap.*

## R E C O M M E N D E D   M U L T I C U L T U R A L   B O O K S

*Ages refer to approximate interest levels.*
*YA = young adult readers.*

### African-American Literature

Aardema, Verna. *Bringing the Rain to Kapiti Plain: A Nandi Tale.* Illustrated by Beatriz Vidal. Dial, 1981. Ages 7–9. (picture book)

———. *Why Mosquitoes Buzz in People's Ears.* Illustrated by Leo and Diane Dillon. Dial, 1975. Ages 5–7. (picture book)

Adoff, Arnold. *Black Is Brown Is Tan.* Harper, 1973. Ages 8–10. (poetry)

Armstrong, William H. *Sounder.* Harper, 1969. Ages 9–12. (chapter book)

Berry, James. *Ajeemah and His Son.* HarperCollins, 1992. Ages 9–12. (chapter book)

Binch, Caroline. *Gregory Cool.* Dial, 1994. Ages 6–9. (picture book)

Blume, Judy. *Iggie's House.* Econoclad, 1999 (Simon & Schuster, 1970). Ages 9–12. (chapter book)

Bridges, Ruby. *Through My Eyes.* Scholastic, 1999. Ages 9–YA.

Bryan, Ashley. *Turtle Knows Your Name.* Atheneum, 1989. Ages 6–8. (picture book)

Cline-Ransome, Lesa. *Satchel Paige.* Illustrated by James Ransome. Simon & Schuster, 2000. Ages 7–10. (biography)

Collier, James, and Christopher Collier. *Jump Ship to Freedom.* Delacorte, 1981. Ages 9–12. (chapter book) (Others in the Arabus family saga: *War Comes to Willy Freeman,* 1983; *Who Is Carrie?,* 1984.)

Feelings, Tom. *The Middle Passage: White Ships/ Black Cargo.* Dial, 1995. Ages 9–14. (wordless picture book)

Fox, Paula. *The Slave Dancer.* Bradbury, 1973. Ages 9–12. (chapter book)

Fradin, Dennis Brindell, and Judith Bloom Fradin. *Ida B. Wells: Mother of the Civil Rights Movement.* Clarion, 2000. Ages 10–YA. (biography)

Greene, Bette. *Philip Hall Likes Me. I Reckon Maybe.* Illustrated by Charles Lilly. Dial, 1974. Ages 8–10. (chapter book)

Greenfield, Eloise. *Honey, I Love and Other Love Poems.* Viking, 1978. Ages 6–10. (poetry)

———. *Nathaniel Talking.* Illustrated by Jan Spivey Gilchrist. Black Butterfly, 1989. Ages 6–10. (picture book)

———. *Under the Sunday Tree.* Illustrated by Amos Ferguson. Harper, 1988. Ages 6–10. (poetry)

Grifalconi, Ann. *The Village of Round and Square Houses.* Little, Brown, 1986. Ages 7–9. (picture book)

Hamilton, Virginia. *Cousins.* Philomel, 1990. Ages 9–12. (Sequel: *Second Cousins.* Scholastic, 1998.) (chapter books)

———. *The House of Dies Drear.* Illustrated by Eros Keith. Macmillan, 1968. Ages 9–12. (chapter book) (See sequel: *The Mystery of Drear House,* Greenwillow, 1987.)

———. *M. C. Higgins, the Great.* Macmillan, 1974. Ages 9–12. (chapter book)

———. *Many Thousand Gone: African Americans from Slavery to Freedom.* Illustrated by Leo and Diane Dillon. Random, 1992. Ages 10–14. (chapter book)

———. *The Planet of Junior Brown.* Macmillan, 1971. Ages 12–YA. (chapter book)

Hansen, Joyce. *I Thought My Soul Would Rise and Fly: The Diary of Patsy, a Freed Girl.* Scholastic, 1997. Ages 10–13. (chapter book)

Harris, Joel Chandler. *Jump! The Adventures of Brer Rabbit.* Adapted by Van Dyke Parks. Illustrated by Barry Moser. Harcourt, 1986. Ages 7–9. (picture book) (See also *Jump Again! More Adventures of Brer Rabbit,* 1987.)

Hopkinson, Deborah. *A Band of Angels: A Story Inspired by the Jubilee Singers.* Illustrated by Raúl Colón. Atheneum, 1999. Ages 8–10. (picture book)

Howard, Elizabeth Fitzgerald. *Aunt Flossie's Hats (and Crab Cakes Later).* Illustrated by James Ransome. Clarion, 1991. Ages 6–8. (picture book)

———. *Virgie Goes to School with Us Boys.* Illustrated by E. B. Lewis. Simon & Schuster, 2000. Ages 6–9. (picture book)

Hudson, Wade, and Cheryl W. Hudson, compilers. *In Praise of Our Fathers and Our Mothers: A Black Family Treasury of Outstanding Authors and Artists.* Just Us Books, 1997. Ages 9–YA. (collected biography)

Hurmence, Belinda. *A Girl Called Boy.* Clarion, 1982. Ages 9–12. (chapter book)

Johnson, Angela. *Toning the Sweep.* Orchard, 1993. Ages 12–14. (chapter book)

Johnson, Dolores. *The Children's Book of Kwanzaa: A Guide to Celebrating the Holiday.* Atheneum, 1996. Ages 8–14. (nonfiction chapter book)

Joseph, Lynn. *A Wave in Her Pocket: Stories from Trinidad.* Illustrated by Brian Pinkney. Clarion, 1991. Ages 7–9. (collected stories)

———. *The Mermaid's Twin Sister.* Illustrated by Donna Perrone. Clarion, 1994. Ages 7–9. (collected stories)

Keats, Ezra Jack. *Goggles.* Macmillan, 1969, Ages 5–7. (picture book)

———. *Peter's Chair.* Harper, 1967. Ages 5–7. (picture book)

Lester, Julius. *From Slave Ship to Freedom Road.* Illustrated by Rod Brown. Dial, 1998. Ages 11–15. (informational)

———. *How Many Spots Does a Leopard Have?* Illustrated by David Shannon. Scholastic, 1989. Ages 7–9. (collected stories)

———. *John Henry.* Illustrated by Jerry Pinkney. Dial, 1994. Ages 7–10. (picture book)

———, reteller. *The Tales of Uncle Remus: The Adventures of Brer Rabbit.* Illustrated by Jerry Pinkney. Dial, 1987. Ages 7–9. (collected stories) (See also *More Tales of Uncle Remus: Further Adventures of Brer Rabbit, His Friends, Enemies, and Others,* 1988; *The Last Tales of Uncle Remus,* 1994.)

———. *To Be a Slave.* Dial, 1968. Ages 9–12. (chapter book)

Lyons, Mary E. *Raw Head, Bloody Bones: African-American Tales of the Supernatural.* Scribner's, 1991. Ages 8–10. (collected stories)

Mathis, Sharon Bell. *The Hundred Penny Box.* Illustrated by Leo and Diane Dillon. Viking, 1975. Ages 7–9. (chapter book)

McGill, Alice. *Molly Bannaky.* Illustrated by Chris K. Soentpiet. Houghton, 1999. Ages 7–11. (picture book)

McKissack, Patricia. *Mirandy and Brother Wind.* Illustrated by Jerry Pinkney. Knopf, 1988. Ages 7–9. (picture book)

———, and Fredrick McKissack. *Christmas in the Big House, Christmas in the Quarters.* Illustrated by John Thompson. Scholastic, 1994. Ages 8–11. (chapter book)

———. *A Long Hard Journey: The Story of the Pullman Porter.* Walker, 1989. Ages 8–10. (chapter book)

———. *Rebels against Slavery: American Slave Revolts.* Scholastic, 1996. Ages 11–YA. (nonfiction chapter book)

———. *Sojourner Truth: Ain't I a Woman?* Scholastic, 1992. Ages 12–YA. (chapter book)

Mollel, Tololwa M. *The Flying Tortoise: An Igbo Tale.* Illustrated by Barbara Spurll. Clarion, 1994. Ages 6–10.

———. *My Rows and Piles of Coins.* Illustrated by E. B. Lewis. Clarion, 1999. Ages 4–8. (picture book)

Monjo, F. N. *The Drinking Gourd.* Illustrated by Fred Brenner. Harper, 1970. Ages 6–8. (picture book)

Musgrove, Margaret. *Ashanti to Zulu: African Traditions.* Illustrated by Leo and Diane Dillon. Dial, 1976. Ages 8–10. (picture book)

Myers, Walter Dean. *Glorious Angels: A Celebration of Children.* HarperCollins, 1995. Ages 3–14. (poetry)

———. *The Glory Field.* Scholastic, 1994. Ages 11–YA. (chapter book)

———. *Malcolm X: A Fire Burning Brightly.* Illustrated by Leonard Jenkins. HarperCollins, 2000. Ages 7–11. (picture book biography)

———. *Now Is Your Time: The African-American Struggle for Freedom.* Harper, 1991. Ages 9–12. (chapter book)

―――. *Scorpions.* Harper, 1988. Ages 9–12. (chapter book)

O'Connor, Barbara. *Me and Rupert Goody.* Farrar/Frances Foster, 1999. Ages 9–12. (chapter book)

Pinkney, Andrea D. *Bill Pickett: Rodeo-Ridin' Cowboy.* Illustrated by Brian Pinkney. Harcourt, 1996. Ages 7–10. (picture book)

Ringgold, Faith. *Tar Beach.* Crown, 1991. Ages 6–8. (picture book)

Schroeder, Alan. *Minty: The Story of Young Harriet Tubman.* Illustrated by Jerry Pinkney. Dial, 1996. Ages 7–10. (picture book)

Steptoe, John. *Mufaro's Beautiful Daughters.* Lothrop, 1987. Ages 7–9. (picture book)

Taylor, Mildred. *Roll of Thunder, Hear My Cry.* Dial, 1976. (See others in the Logan family saga: *The Song of the Trees,* 1975; *Let the Circle Be Unbroken,* 1981; *The Road to Memphis,* 1990.) Ages 9–12. (chapter book)

Tillage, Leon W. *Leon's Story.* Illustrated by Susan L. Roth. Farrar, 1997. Ages 9–13. (nonfiction picture book)

Williams, Sherley Anne. *Working Cotton.* Illustrated by Carole Byard. Harcourt, 1992. Ages 7–10. (picture book)

## Asian-American Literature

Balgassi, Haemi. *Peacebound Trains.* Illustrated by Chris K. Soentpiet. Clarion, 1996. Ages 8–12. (picture book)

Blumberg, Rhoda. *Commodore Perry in the Land of the Shogun.* Lothrop, 1985. Ages 9–12. (chapter book)

―――. *Full Steam Ahead: The Race to Build a Transcontinental Railroad.* National Geographic, 1996. Ages 9–12. (nonfiction chapter book)

Cha, Dia. *Dia's Story Cloth: The Hmong People's Journey to Freedom.* Stitchery by Chue and Nhia Thao Cha. Lee & Low, 1996. Ages 8–11. (picture book)

Choi, Sook Nyul. *Year of Impossible Goodbyes.* Houghton, 1991. Ages 9–12. (chapter book)

Dooley, Norah. *Everybody Cooks Rice.* Illustrated by Peter J. Thornton. Carolrhoda, 1991. Ages 6–8. (picture book)

Kuklin, Susan. *Kodomo: Children of Japan.* Putnam, 1995. Ages 5–11. (photoessay)

Lee, Milly. *Nim and the War Effort.* Illustrated by Yangsook Choi. Farrar, 1997. Ages 7–10. (picture book)

Levine, Ellen. *A Fence Away from Freedom: Japanese Americans and World War II.* Putnam, 1995. Ages 12–YA. (nonfiction chapter book)

Lord, Bette Bao. *In the Year of the Boar and Jackie Robinson.* Illustrated by Marc Simont. Harper, 1984. Ages 7–9. (chapter book)

McKay, Lawrence, Jr. *Journey Home.* Illustrated by Dom and Keunhee Lee. Lee & Low, 1998. Ages 8–12. (picture book)

Mochizuki, Ken. *Baseball Saved Us.* Illustrated by Dom Lee. Lee and Low, 1993. Ages 7–10. (picture book)

―――. *Passage to Freedom: The Sugihara Story.* Illustrated by Dom Lee. Lee & Low, 1997. Ages 7–11. (picture book, biography)

Morimoto, Junko. *My Hiroshima.* Viking, 1990. Ages 8–10. (picture book)

Nhuong, Huynh Quang. *The Land I Lost: Adventures of a Boy in Vietnam.* Illustrated by Vo-Dinh Mai. Harper, 1982. Ages 9–12. (chapter book)

Say, Allen. *Grandfather's Journey.* Houghton, 1993. Ages 7–9. (picture book)

―――. *Lost Lake.* Houghton, 1989. Ages 7–9. (picture book)

―――. *Tea with Milk.* Lorraine/Houghton, 1999. Ages 6–9. (picture book)

Schmidt, Jeremy, and Ted Wood. *Two Lands, One Heart: An American Boy's Journey to His Mother's Vietnam.* Photography by Ted Wood. Walker, 1995. Ages 7–10. (photoessay)

Shea, Pegi Deitz. *The Whispering Cloth.* Illustrated by Anita Riggio. Stitchery by You Yang. Boyds Mills, 1995. Ages 7–11. (picture book)

Snyder, Diane. *The Boy of the Three-Year Nap.* Illustrated by Allen Say. Houghton, 1988. Ages 7–9. (picture book)

Strom, Yale. *Quilted Landscape: Conversations with Young Immigrants.* Simon & Schuster, 1996. Ages 11–14. (varied cultures)

Tompert, Ann. *Grandfather Tang's Story: A Tale with Tangrams.* Illustrated by Robert Andrew Parker. Crown, 1990. Ages 7–9. (picture book)

Tunnell, Michael O., and George W. Chilcoat. *The Children of Topaz: The Story of a Japanese-American Internment Camp, Based on a Classroom Diary.* Holiday, 1996. Ages 8–14. (nonfiction chapter book)

Uchida, Yoshiko. *The Bracelet.* Illustrated by Joanna Yardley. Philomel, 1993. Ages 8–11. (picture book)

————. *Journey to Topaz.* Scribner's, 1971. Ages 9–12. (chapter book) (See sequel: *Journey Home,* Atheneum, 1978.)

Wong, Janet S. *The Trip Back Home.* Illustrated by Bo Jia. Harcourt, 2000. Ages 7–9. (picture book)

Yee, Paul. *Tales from Gold Mountain: Stories of the Chinese in the New World.* Macmillan, 1990. Ages 8–10. (collected stories)

Yep, Laurence. *Child of the Owl.* Harper, 1977. Ages 12–YA. (chapter book)

————. *Dragon's Gate.* HarperCollins, 1993. Ages 12–YA. (chapter book)

————. *Dragonwings.* Harper, 1975. Ages 9–12. (chapter book)

Young, Ed. *Seven Blind Mice.* Philomel, 1992. Ages 6–10. (picture book)

## Latino-American Literature

Aardema, Verna. *Borreguita and the Coyote.* Illustrated by Petra Mathers. Knopf, 1991. Ages 6–8. (picture book)

Belpré, Pura. *Once in Puerto Rico.* Illustrated by Christine Price. Warne, 1973. Ages 8–10. (picture book)

Buss, Fran Leeper, with assistance of Daisy Cubias. *Journey of the Sparrows.* Lodestar, 1991. Ages 9–12. (chapter book)

Castañeda, Omar S. *Among the Volcanoes.* Lodestar, 1991. Ages 12–YA. (chapter book)

Cofer, Judith O. *An Island Like You.* Orchard, 1995. Ages 12–YA. (short stories)

Delacre, Lulu, reteller. *Golden Tales: Myths, Legends and Folktales from Latin America.* Scholastic, 1996. Ages 8–12. (anthology)

————. *Vejigante Masquerader.* Scholastic, 1993. Ages 6–10. (poetry)

Dorros, Arthur. *Abuela.* Illustrated by Elisa Kleven. Dutton, 1991. Ages 6–8. (picture book)

Gunning, Monica. *Not a Copper Penny in Me House: Poems from the Caribbean.* Illustrated by Frané Lessac. Wordsong, 1993. Ages 7–10. (poetry)

Jiménez, Francisco. *The Circuit: Stories from the Life of a Migrant Child.* Houghton, 1999 (1996). (new ed.) Ages 10–14. (short stories)

————. *La Mariposa.* Illustrated by Simón Silva. Houghton, 1998. Ages 8–11. (picture book)

Kroll, Virginia. *Butterfly Boy.* Illustrated by Gerardo Suzán. Boyds Mills, 1997. Ages 5–8. (picture book)

Krumgold, Joseph. *. . . And Now Miguel.* Illustrated by Jean Charlot. Crowell, 1953. Ages 8–10. (chapter book)

Lee, Hector V. *I Had a Hippopotamus.* Lee & Low, 1996. Ages 2–5. (picture book)

Markum, Patricia. *The Little Painter of Sabana Grande.* Macmillan, 1993. Ages 7–9. (picture book)

O'Dell, Scott. *Carlota.* Houghton, 1981. Ages 9–12. (chapter book)

Pomerantz, Charlotte. *The Chalk Doll.* Illustrated by Frané Lessac. HarperCollins, 1989. Ages 7–9. (picture book)

Soto, Gary. *Baseball in April and Other Stories.* Harcourt, 1990. Ages 9–12. (collected stories)

————. *Chato and the Party Animals.* Illustrated by Susan Guevara. Putnam, 2000. Ages 5–8. (picture book)

————. *Chato's Kitchen.* Illustrated by Susan Guevara. Putnam, 1995. Ages 5–8. (picture book)

————. *Nerdlandia, A Play.* Penguin, 1999.

————. *Snapshots from the Wedding.* Illustrated by Stephanie Garcia. Putnam, 1997. Ages 5–8. (picture book)

————. *Too Many Tamales.* Illustrated by Ed Martinez. Putnam, 1993. Ages 4–8. (picture book)

————. *Trading Places.* Harcourt, 1993. Ages 10–13. (chapter book)

Sullivan, Charles, editor. *Here Is My Kingdom: Hispanic-American Literature and Art for Young People.* Abrams, 1994. Ages 13–YA. (collected stories and poems)

Winter, Jonah. *Diego.* Illustrated by Jeanette Winter. Knopf, 1991 (bilingual, English-Spanish). Ages 7–9. (picture book)

## Bilingual Literature

Ada, Alma Flor. *Gathering the Sun: An Alphabet in Spanish and English.* English translation by Rosa Zubizarreta. Illustrated by Simón Silva. Lothrop, 1997. (poetry) English/Spanish

————. *The Lizard and the Sun/La Lagartija y el Sol.* Illustrated by Felipe Davalos. Doubleday, 1997. Ages 5–7. (picture book) English/Spanish

Afanasév, A. *Skazki: Russian Fairy Tales.* Illustrated by I. V. Bilibin. Translated by D. Martin and L. Lisitskya. Terra, 1996. (picture book) English/Russian

Alarcon, Francisco X. *Angels Ride Bikes and Other Fall Poems/Los Ángeles Andan en Bicicleta y otros poemas de otoño.* Illustrated by Christina González. Children's Book Press, 1999. Ages 6–12. (poetry) English/Spanish

————. *From the Bellybutton of the Moon and Other Summer Poems/Del Ombligo de la Luna y otros poemas de verano.* Illustrated by Christina González. Children's Book Press, 1998. Ages 6–12. (poetry) English/Spanish

————. *Laughing Tomatoes and Other Spring Poems/ Jitomates Risuenos y otros poemas de primavera.* Illustrated by Christina González. Children's Book Press, 1997. Ages 6–12. (poetry) English/Spanish

Andaldúa, Gloria. *Prietita and the Ghost Woman/Prietita y la Llorona.* Illustrated by Christina González. Children's Book Press, 1996. Ages 7–10. (picture book). English/Spanish

Bateson-Hill, Margaret. *Lao-ao of Dragon Mountain.* Illustrated by Francesca Pelizzoli. Paper cuts by Sha-liu Qu. Stewart, Tabori & Chang, 1996. Ages 4–8. (picture book) English/Chinese

Bertrand, Diane Gonzales. *Family.* Spanish translation by Julia Mercedes Castilla. Illustrated by Pauline Rodriguez Howard. Piñata Books, 1999. Ages 4–8. (picture book). English/Spanish

Brusca, Christina Maria, and Tona Wilson. *Three Friends: A Counting Book/Tres Amigos: un cuento para cuntar.* Holt, 1995. Ages 2–5. (picture book). English/Spanish

Carlson, Lori. M. *Cool Salsa: Bilingual Poems on Growing Up Latino in the United States.* Holt, 1994. Ages 10–14. (poetry) English/Spanish

————, selector. *You're On! Seven Plays in English and Spanish.* Morrow, 1999. Ages 9–15.

Corpi, Lucha. *Where Fireflies Dance/Ahi, Donde Bailan las Luciernagas.* Illustrated by Mira Reisberg. Children's Book Press, 1997. Ages 7–12. (picture book) English/Spanish

Cowcher, Helen. *Tigress.* Translated by Mei-Ling Christine Lee. Millet, 1997. Ages 5–9. (picture book). English/Vietnamese

De Sauza, J. *Brother Anansi and the Cattle Ranch/El Hermano Anansi y el Rancho de Ganado.* Illustrated by S. Von Mason. Adapted by Harriet Rohmer. Children's Book Press, 1989. Ages 6–8. (picture book) English/Spanish

Delacre, Lulu. *Arroz con Leche: Popular Songs and Rhymes from Latin America.* Scholastic, 1989. Ages 6–10. (poetry) English/Spanish

————. *Vejigante Masquerader.* Scholastic, 1993. Ages 6–10. (poetry) English/Spanish

Delgado, Maria Isabel. *Chaves's Memories/Los Recuerdos de Chave.* Illustrated by Yvonne Symank. Piñata Books, 1996. Ages 4–7. (picture book) English/Spanish

Despain, Pleasant, reteller. *The Emerald Lizard: Fifteen Latin American Tales to Tell.* Illustrated by Don Bell. Translated by Mario Lamo-Jiménez. August House, 1999. Ages 7–12. (folklore collection) English/Spanish

Ehlert, Lois. *Cuckoo: A Mexican Folktale/Cucu: Un Cuento Folklorico Mexicano.* Translated by de Aragon Andujar. Harcourt, 1997. Ages 3–8. (picture book) English/Spanish

Garza, Carmen L. *Family Pictures/Cuadros de Familia.* Edited by Harriet Rohmer. Spanish version by Rosalma Zubizarreta. Children's Book Press, 1990. Ages 5–12. (picture book) English/Spanish

————, with Harriet Rohmer. *In My Family/En Mi Familia.* Edited by David Schecter. Translated by Francisco X. Alarcón. Children's Book Press, 1996. Ages 5–12. (picture book) English/Spanish

————, as told to Harriet Rohmer. *Magic Windows: Cut-paper Art and Stories/Ventanas Magicas.* Children's Book Press, 1999. Ages 5–12. (picture book) English/Spanish

González, L. M. *The Bossy Gallito/El Gallo de Bodas.* Illustrated by Lulu Delacre. Scholastic, 1994. Ages 6–9. (picture book) English/Spanish

Gonzalez, Ralfka, and Ana Ruiz. *My First Book of Proverbs/Mi Primer Libro de Dichos.* Children's Book Press, 1995. Ages 4–8. (proverbs) English/Spanish

Han, Suzanne Crowder. *The Rabbit's Escape/Kusa Il-saenghan Tooki.* Illustrated by Yumi Heo. Holt, 1995. Ages 5–8. (picture book). English/Korean

Herrera, Juan P. *Calling the Doves/El Canto de las Palomas.* Illustrated by Elly Simmons. Children's Book Press, 1995. Ages 4–8. (picture book) English/Spanish

Ho, Minfong. *Maples in the Mist: Children's Poems from the Tang Dynasty.* Illustrated by Jean and Mou-sien Tseng. Translated by Minfong Ho. Lothrop, 1996. (poetry) English/Chinese

Holt, Daniel D. (Ed.). *Tigers, Frogs, and Rice Cakes: A Book of Korean Proverbs.* Illustrated by Lu Han Stickler. Shen's Books, 1998. (picture book) English/Korean

Keister, Douglas. *Fernando's Gift/El Regalo de Fernando.* Sierra Club, 1995. Ages 5–8. (picture book) English/Spanish

Kitsao, Jay. *McHeshi Goes to the Market* (see others in the McHeshi series). Illustrated by Wanjiku Mathenge et al. Jacaranda Designs, 1995. Ages 3–5. (picture book) English/Swahili

Lee, Jeanne. *Song of Mu Lan.* Front Street, 1995. Ages 5–8. (picture book) English/Chinese

Loya, Olga. *Magic Moments: Tales from Latin America/Momentos Magicos.* Translated by Carmen Lizardo-Rivera. August House, 1998. Ages 10–YA. (short stories) English/Spanish

Luenn, Nancy. *A Gift for Abuelita: Celebrating the Day of the Dead/Un Regalo para Abuelita: En celebración del Día de los Muertos.* Illustrated by Robert Chapman. Rising Moon, 1998. Ages 4–8. (picture book) English/Spanish

MacDonald, Margaret Read. *The Girl Who Wore Too Much: A Folktale from Thailand.* Thai text by Supaporn Vathanaprida. Illustrated by Yvonne LeBrun Davis. August House, 1998. Ages 4–8. (picture book) English/Thai

Mado, Michio. *The Magic Pocket.* Illustrated by Mitsumasa Anno. Translated by the Empress Michiko of Japan. McElderry Books, 1998. Ages 3–5. (poetry) English/Japanese

Nye, Naomi Shihab, editor. *The Tree Is Older Than You Are: A Bilingual Gathering of Poems and Stories from Mexico with Paintings by Mexican Artists.* Simon & Schuster, 1995. Ages 8–YA. (literature anthology) English/Spanish

Orozco, J. *Diez Deditos/Ten Little Fingers and Other Play Rhymes and Action Songs from Latin America.* Illustrated by Elisa Kleven. Dutton, 1997. Ages 4–7. Spanish/English

Prisilla, Maricel E. *Feliz Nochebuena, Feliz Navidad: Christmas Feasts of the Hispanic Caribbean.* Illustrated by Espinosa Ferrer. Holt, 1994. Ages 6–12. (picture book) Spanish/English

Rohmer, Harriet, O. Chow, and M. Vidaure. *The Invisible Hunters: A Legend from the Miskito Indians of Nicaragua/Los Cazadores Invisibles: Una Leyenda de los Indios Miskitos de Nicaragua.* Illustrated by J. Sam. Children's Book Press, 1987. Ages 8–10. (picture book) English/Spanish

Saenz, Benjamin Alira. *A Gift from Papa Diego/Un regalo de Papa Diego.* Illustrated by Geronimo Garcia. Cinco puntas Press, 1998. Ages 5–8. (picture book) English/Spanish

Wyndham, Robert. *Chinese Mother Goose Rhymes.* Illustrated by Ed Young. PaperStar, 1998 (originally published by World Publishing Company, 1968). English/Chinese

Zhang, Sonng Nan, reteller/illustrator. *The Ballad of Mulan/Bai Ca Moc Lau.* Translated by Nguyen Ngoc Ngan. Pan Asian Publications, 1998. Ages 5–7. (picture book). English/Vietnamese

## Jewish-American Literature

Adler, David A. *Hilde and Eli: Children of the Holocaust.* Holiday, 1994. Ages 8–10. (picture book)

————. *The Number on My Grandfather's Arm.* Illustrated by Rose Eichenbaum. UAHC Press, 1987. Ages 7–9. (picture book)

Barrie, Barbara. *Lone Star.* Delacorte, 1990. Ages 9–12. (chapter book)

Cohen, Barbara. *Molly's Pilgrim.* Illustrated by Michael Deraney. Lothrop, 1983. Ages 6–9. (picture book)

Drucker, Malka. *The Family Treasury of Jewish Holidays.* Illustrated by Nancy Patz. Little, 1994. Ages 6–YA. (chapter book)

Ehrlich, Amy. *The Story of Hanukkah.* Illustrated by Ori Sherman. Dial, 1989. Ages 6–8. (picture book)

Feder, Paula K. *The Feather-Bed Journey.* Illustrated by Stacey Schuett. Albert Whitman, 1995. Ages 5–8. (picture book)

Geras, Adèle. *My Grandmother's Stories: A Collection of Jewish Folk Tales.* Illustrated by Jael Jordan. Knopf, 1990. Ages 8–10. (collected stories)

Goldin, Barbara Diamond. *Cakes and Miracles: A Purim Tale.* Illustrated by Erika Weihs. Viking, 1991. Ages 7–9. (picture book)

———. *Just Enough Is Plenty.* Illustrated by Seymour Chwast. Viking, 1988. Ages 6–9. (picture book)

Hautzig, Esther. *The Endless Steppe: A Girl in Exile.* Crowell, 1968. Ages 9–12. (chapter book)

Kimmel, Eric, adapter. *Days of Awe: Stories for Rosh Hashanah and Yom Kippur.* Illustrated by Erika Weihs. Viking, 1991. Ages 8–10. (collected stories)

———, reteller. *Gershon's Monster: A Story for the Jewish New Year.* Illustrated by Jon J. Muth. Scholastic, 2000. Ages 6–11. (legend)

———. *Hershel and the Hanukkah Goblins.* Illustrated by Trina Schart Hyman. Holiday, 1989. Ages 7–9. (picture book)

Kuskin, Karla. *A Great Miracle Happened There: A Chanukkah Story.* Illustrated by Robert Andrew Parker. HarperCollins, 1993. Ages 7–10. (picture book)

Levitin, Sonia. *Journey to America.* Atheneum, 1970. Ages 12–YA. (chapter book) (See sequel: *Silver Days,* 1989.)

Livingston, Myra Cohn. *Poems for Jewish Holidays.* Illustrated by Lloyd Bloom. Holiday, 1986. Ages 6–10. (poetry)

Lowry, Lois. *Number the Stars.* Houghton, 1989. Ages 7–9. (chapter book)

Manushkin, Fran. *Latkes and Applesauce.* Illustrated by Robin Spowart. Scholastic, 1990. Ages 7–9. (picture book)

Meltzer, Milton. *Rescue: The Story of How Gentiles Saved Jews in the Holocaust.* Harper, 1988. Ages 9–12. (chapter book)

Newman, Lesléa. *Remember That.* Illustrated by Karen Ritz. Clarion, 1996. Ages 4–8. (picture book)

Nye, Naomi S. *This Same Sky: A Collection of Poems from Around the World.* Four Winds, 1992. Ages 7–12. (poetry)

Rael, Elsa O. *What Zeesie Saw on Delancy Street.* Illustrated by Marjorie Priceman. Simon & Schuster, 1996. Ages 5–8. (picture book)

Reiss, Johanna. *The Upstairs Room.* Crowell, 1972. Ages 9–12. (chapter book)

Rocklin, Joanne. *Strudel Stories.* Delacorte, 1999. Ages 7–12. (chapter book)

Rogasky, Barbara. *Smoke and Ashes: The Story of the Holocaust.* Holiday, 1988. Ages 12–YA. (chapter book)

Schwartz, Amy. *Mrs. Moskowitz and the Sabbath Candlesticks.* Jewish Publication Society, 1985. Ages 7–9. (picture book)

Schwartz, Lynn S. *The Four Questions.* Illustrated by Ori Sherman. Dial, 1989. (picture book)

Siegal, Aranka. *Upon the Head of the Goat: A Childhood in Hungary 1939–1944.* Farrar, 1981. (See sequel: *Grace in the Wilderness: After the Liberation, 1945–1948,* 1985.) Ages 9–12. (chapter book)

Slepian, Jan. *Risk n' Roses.* Putnam, 1990. Ages 9–11. (chapter book)

Wisniewski, David. *Golem.* Clarion, 1996. Ages 6–12. (picture book)

Yolen, Jane. *The Devil's Arithmetic.* Penguin, 1988. Ages 10–13. (chapter book)

Zemach, Margot. *It Could Always Be Worse.* Farrar, 1977. Ages 6–8. (picture book)

## Native-American Literature

Ancona, George. *Mayeros: A Yucatec Maya Family.* Lothrop, 1997. Ages 7–11. (photoessay)

Andrews, Jan. *Very Last First Time.* Illustrated by Ian Wallace. McElderry, 1986. Ages 6–8. (picture book)

Ashabranner, Brent. *To Live in Two Worlds: American Indian Youth Today.* Photographs by Paul Conklin. Dodd, 1984. Ages 9–12. (chapter book)

Baker, Olaf. *Where the Buffaloes Begin.* Illustrated by Stephen Gammell. Warne, 1981. Ages 7–9. (picture book)

Baylor, Byrd. *A God on Every Mountain Top: Stories of Southwest Indian Mountains.* Illustrated by Carol Brown. Scribner's, 1981. Ages 8–10. (collected stories)

Bealer, Alex. *Only the Names Remain: The Cherokees and the Trail of Tears.* Little, Brown, 1972. Ages 9–12. (chapter book)

Begay, Shonto. *Navajo: Visions and Voices across the Mesa.* Scholastic, 1995. Ages 12–YA. (poetry)

Benchley, Nathaniel. *Only Earth and Sky Last Forever.* Harper, 1972. Ages 11–YA. (chapter book)

Bierhorst, John, editor. *Doctor Coyote: A Native American Aesop's Fables.* Illustrated by Wendy Watson. Macmillan, 1987. Ages 7–9. (collected stories)

———, editor. *The Hungry Woman: Myths and Legends of the Aztecs.* Morrow, 1984. Ages 8–10. (collected stories)

———, editor. *The Monkey's Haircut and Other Stories Told by the Maya.* Illustrated by Robert Andrew Parker. Morrow, 1986. Ages 8–10. (collected stories)

———, translator. *Spirit Child: A Story of the Nativity.* Illustrated by Barbara Cooney. Morrow, 1984. Ages 6–8. (picture book)

Bruchac, Joseph. *The Boy Who Lived with the Bears: And Other Iroquois Stories.* HarperCollins, 1995. Ages 6–9. (collection)

———. *Crazy Horse's Vision.* Illustrated by S. D. Nelson. Lee & Low, 2000. Ages 6–10. (picture book; biography)

———. *Eagle Song.* Illustrated by Dan Andreasen. Dial, 1997. Ages 9–11. (chapter book)

———. *The First Strawberries.* Illustrated by Anna Vojtech. Dial, 1993. Ages 7–10. (picture book)

———. *Seeing the Circle.* Photographs by John Christopher Fine. Richard K. Owen, 1999. Ages 7–10. (autobiography)

Caduto, Michael, and Joseph Bruchac. *Keepers of the Earth: Native American Stories and Environmental Activities for Children.* Fulcrum, 1993. Ages 8–10. (collected stories)

Cohen, Carol. *The Mud Pony.* Illustrated by Shonto Begay. Scholastic, 1988. Ages 6–8. (picture book)

Ekoomiak, Normee. *Arctic Memories.* Holt, 1990 (Bilingual, English-Inuktitut). Ages 9–12. (picture book)

Erdrich, Louise. *The Birchbark House.* Hyperion, 1999. Ages 8–12. (historical fiction)

Freedman, Russell. *Buffalo Hunt.* Holiday, 1988. Ages 9–12. (chapter book)

———. *Indian Chiefs.* Holiday, 1987. Ages 9–12. (chapter book)

George, Jean Craighead. *Julie.* HarperCollins, 1994. Ages 10–14. (chapter book)

———. *Julie of the Wolves.* Harper, 1972. Ages 9–12. (chapter book)

———. *The Talking Earth.* Harper, 1983. Ages 9–12. (chapter book)

Goble, Paul. *Beyond the Ridge.* Bradbury, 1989. Ages 8–10. (picture book)

———. *The Girl Who Loved Wild Horses.* Bradbury, 1978. Ages 6–8. (picture book)

———. *Iktomi and the Buffalo Skull.* Orchard, 1991. Ages 7–9. (picture book) (See other Iktomi trickster tales.)

———. reteller. *The Return of the Buffaloes: A Plains Indian Story about Famine and Renewal of the Earth.* National Geographic, 1996. Ages 8–12. (picture book)

Hobbs, Will. *Bearstone.* Atheneum, 1989. Ages 11–14. (chapter book)

Hoyt-Goldsmith, Diane. *Totem Pole.* Photographs by Lawrence Migdale. Holiday, 1990. Ages 6–8. (picture book)

Hudson, Jan. *Sweetgrass.* Philomel, 1989. Ages 12–YA. (chapter book)

Hunter, Sally M. *Four Seasons of Corn: A Winnebago Tradition.* Photography by Joe Allen. Lerner, 1996. Ages 7–11. (photoessay)

Keegan, Marcia. *Pueblo Boy: Growing Up in Two Worlds.* Cobblehill, 1991. Ages 7–9. (picture book)

McDermott, Gerald. *Raven: A Trickster Tale from the Pacific Northwest.* Harcourt, 1993. Ages 7–9. (picture book)

McKissack, Patricia C. *Run Away Home.* Scholastic, 1997. Ages 10–12. (chapter book; also African American)

Miles, Miska. *Annie and the Old One.* Illustrated by Peter Parnall. Little, Brown, 1971. Ages 7–9. (picture book)

Manitonquat, adapter. *The Children of the Morning Light: Wampanoag Tales.* Illustrated by Mary Arquette. Macmillan, 1994. Ages 8–11. (collected stories)

Mowat, Farley. *Lost in the Barrens.* Illustrated by Charles Geer. McClelland and Stewart, 1984. Ages 9–12. (chapter book)

O'Dell, Scott. *Black Star, Bright Dawn.* Houghton, 1988. Ages 9–12. (chapter book)

———. *Island of the Blue Dolphins.* Houghton, 1960. Ages 9–12. (chapter book)

———. *Sing Down the Moon.* Houghton, 1970. Ages 12–YA. (chapter book)

Paulsen, Gary. *Dogsong.* Bradbury, 1988. Ages 12–YA. (chapter book)

Rappaport, Doreen. *The Flight of Red Bird: The Life of Zilkala-Sa.* Dial, 1997. Ages 11–YA. (chapter book; biography)

Rendon, Marcie R. *Powwow Summer: A Family Celebrates the Circle of Life.* Photography by Cheryl W. Bellville. Carolrhoda, 1996. Ages 7–11. (photo-essay)

Ross, Gayle. *How Turtle's Back Was Cracked: A Traditional Cherokee Tale.* Illustrated by Murv Jacob. Dial, 1995. Ages 7–9. (picture book)

Sneve, Virginia Driving Hawk, selector. *Dancing Teepees: Poems of American Indian Youth.* Illustrated by Stephen Gammell. Holiday, 1989. Ages 9–12. (poetry)

———. *The Sioux.* Illustrated by Ronald Himler. Holiday House, 1993. Ages 7–10. (picture book) (See others in the First Americans Book series)

———. *When Thunders Spoke.* Illustrated by Oren Lyons. Holiday, 1974. Ages 9–12. (chapter book)

Speare, Elizabeth George. *The Sign of the Beaver.* Houghton, 1983. Ages 8–10. (chapter book)

Steltzer, Ulli. *Building an Igloo.* Holt, 1995. Ages 7–11. (picture book)

Steptoe, John. *The Story of Jumping Mouse.* Lothrop, 1984. Ages 7–9. (picture book)

Taylor, C. J. *How We Saw the World: Nine Native Stories of the Way Things Began.* Tundra, 1993. Ages 9–12. (collected stories)

Viola, Herman J. *It Is a Good Day to Die: Indian Eyewitnesses Tell the Story of the Battle of the Little Bighorn.* Crown, 1998. Ages 11–YA. (informational)

## RECOMMENDED INTERNATIONAL BOOKS

*Ages refer to approximate interest levels. YA = young adult readers. Country of original publication is noted.*

### English Language Books

Ahlberg, Janet, and Allan Ahlberg. *Each Peach Pear Plum.* Viking, 1979. Ages 3–6. U.K.

———. *The Jolly Postman.* Little, Brown, 1986. Ages 5–8. U.K.

———. *The Jolly Christmas Postman.* Heinemann, 1991. Ages 5–8. U.K.

Allen, Pamela. *Who Sank the Boat?* Putnam, 1982. Ages 4–7. Australia.

Almond, David. *Skellig.* Delacorte, 1999. Ages 10–YA. U.K.

Anderson, Rachel. *Black Water.* Holt, 1995. Ages 10–14. Great Britain.

Andrews, Jan. *Very Last First Time.* Illustrated by Ian Wallace. Macmillan, 1986. Ages 7–10. Canadian.

Argent, Kerry, and Rod Trinca. *One Woolly Wombat.* Kane/Miller, 1985. Ages 3–6. Australia.

Armstrong, Carole. *Lives and Legends of the Saints.* Simon & Schuster, 1995. Ages 9–12. Great Britain.

Asare, Meshack. *Cat in Search of a Friend.* Kane/Miller, 1986. Ages 4–10. Ghana.

Baker, Jeannie. *The Story of Rosy Dock.* Greenwillow, 1995. Ages 5–8. Australia.

———. *Window.* Julia McRae, 1991. Ages 8–11. Australia.

———. *Where the Forest Meets the Sea.* Greenwillow, 1987. Ages 7–12. Australia.

Beake, Lesley. *The Song of Be.* Holt/Edge, 1993. Ages 12–YA. South Africa.

Breslin, Theresa. *Whispers in the Graveyard.* Heinemann, 1994. Ages 12–14. Great Britain.

Briggs, Raymond. *The Man.* Random House, 1995. Ages 9–14. Great Britain.

Brooks, Martha. *Paradise Café and Other Stories.* Little, Brown, 1988. Ages 12–YA. Canada.

————. *Traveling on into the Light: And Other Stories.* Orchard, 1994. Ages 12–YA. Canada.

Brott, Ardyth. *Jeremy's Decision.* Illustrated by Michael Martchenko. Kane/Miller, 1990. Ages 4–7. Canada.

Browne, Anthony. *Gorilla.* Knopf, 1985. Ages 6–8. U.K.

————. *Willy the Champ.* Knopf, 1986. Ages 4–8. U.K.

————. *Willy the Wizard.* Knopf, 1996. Ages 4–7. Great Britain.

————. *Zoo.* Julia McRae, 1992. Ages 6–10. U.K.

Carmody, Isobelle. *The Gathering.* Penguin, 1993. Ages 8–11. Australia.

Case, Dianne. *92 Queens Road.* Farrar, 1995. Ages 9–11. South Africa.

Casey, Maude. *Over the Water.* Holt, 1994. Ages 13–YA. Great Britain.

Catterwell, Thelma. *Sebastian Lives in a Hat.* Illustrated by Kerry Argent. Kane/Miller, 1990. Ages 2–5. Australia.

Christopher, John. *The White Mountains.* Macmillan, 1967. Ages 10–YA. U.K.

Clement-Davies, David. *Fire Bringer.* Dutton, 2000. Ages 12–YA. U.K.

Crew, Gary. *Angel's Gate.* Simon & Schuster, 1995. Ages 12–YA. Australia.

————. *First Light.* Illustrated by Peter Gouldthorpe. Gareth Stevens, 1996. Ages 8–12. Australia.

Dahl, Roald. *Matilda.* Illustrated by Quentin Blake. Viking, 1988. Ages 9–12. U.K.

Daly, Niki. *Jamela's Dress.* Farrar, 1999. Ages 4–7. South Africa.

Dickinson, Peter. *Merlin Dreams.* Delacorte, 1988. Ages 10–13. U.K.

Disher, Garry. *The Bamboo Flute.* Ticknor & Fields, 1993. Ages 10–14. Australia.

Doherty, Berlie. *Dear Nobody.* Hamish Hamilton, 1991. Ages 12–YA. U.K.

Duder, Tessa. *Alessandra: Alex in Rome.* Oxford, 1991. Ages 9–12. New Zealand.

Ellis, Sarah. *Out of the Blue.* McElderry, 1995. Ages 9–12. Canada.

Fienberg, Anna. *The Magnificient Nose and Other Marvels.* Illustrated by Kim Gamble. Little, 1992. Ages 5–8. Australia.

Fine, Anne. *Flour Babies.* Hamish Hamilton, 1992. Ages 12–YA. U.K.

————. *My War with Goggle Eyes.* Joy Street, 1989. Ages 10–YA. U.K.

Fox, Mem. *Possum Magic.* Illustrated by Julie Vivas. Abingdon, 1987. Ages 4–7. Australia.

————. *Wilfrid Gordon McDonald Partridge.* Illustrated by Julie Vivas. Kane/Miller, 1985. Ages 5–10. Australia.

Gee, Maurice. *The Fire Raiser.* Houghton, 1992. Ages 11–YA. New Zealand.

Gordon, Sheila. *Waiting for the Rain: A Novel of South Africa.* Watts, 1987. Ages 11–YA. South Africa.

Graham, Bob. *Crusher Is Coming!* Viking, 1987. Ages 7–10. Australia.

————. *Greetings from Sandy Beach.* Kane/Miller, 1992. Ages 4–8. Australia.

————. *Rose Meets Mr Wintergarden.* Viking/Penguin, 1992. Ages 6–9. Australia.

Harrison, Ted, illustrator. *O Canada.* Ticknor & Fields, 1993. Ages 7–10. Canada.

Hathorn, Elizabeth. *The Tram to Bondi Beach.* Illustrated by Julie Vivas. Kane/Miller, 1989. Ages 4–8. Australia.

Hoffman, Mary. *Amazing Grace.* Illustrated by Caroline Binch. Dial, 1991. Ages 4–9. Great Britain. (See also sequel: *Boundless Grace,* Dial, 1995.)

Houston, James. *The White Archer: An Eskimo Legend.* Harcourt, 1990. Ages 9–13. Canada.

Hughes, Monica. *The Dream Catcher.* Atheneum, 1987. Ages 10–YA. Canada.

————. *Invitation to the Game.* Simon & Schuster, 1990. Ages 12–YA. Canada.

————. *The Keeper of the Isis Light.* Nelson, 1980. Ages 11–YA. Canada.

Hughes, Shirley. *Tales of Trotter Street.* Candlewick, 1997. Ages 4–10. Great Britain.

Ibbotson, Eva. *The Secret of Platform 13.* Dutton, 1998. Ages 9–13. U.K.

————. *Which Witch?* Dutton, 1999. Ages 10–14. U.K.

Jacques, Brian. *Redwall.* Philomel, 1986. Ages 11–YA. Great Britain. (First of many books in this series.)

Jennings, Paul. *Unreal: Eight Surprising Stories.* Viking, 1991. Ages 11–14. Australia.

Johnston, Julie. *Hero of Lesser Causes.* Little, 1993. Ages 11–YA. Canada.

Kindersley, Barnabas, and Anabel Kindersley. *Children Just Like Me.* Dorling Kindersley, 1995. Ages 7–12. Great Britain.

Lee, Dennis. *Alligator Pie.* Macmillan, 1974. Ages 5–10. Canada.

———. *Jelly Belly.* Macmillan, 1983. Ages 5–10. Canada.

Lewis, C. S. *The Lion, the Witch, and the Wardrobe.* Macmillan, 1950. Ages 10–YA. U.K.

Lightburn, Ron. *Waiting for the Whales.* Illustrated by Sheryl McFarlane. Orca Books, 1991. Ages 6–8. Canada.

Little, Jean. *Mama's Going to Buy You a Mockingbird.* Viking, 1985. Ages 10–YA. Canada.

Lottridge, Celia Barker. *Ten Small Tales.* Illustrated by Joanne Fitzgerald. Groundwood, 1993. Ages 5–7. Canada.

———. *Ticket to Curlew.* Groundwood, 1992. Ages 10–13. Canada.

Lunn, Janet. *Amos' Sweater.* Illustrated by Kim LaFave. Groundwood, 1988. Ages 5–9. Canada.

———. *The Root Cellar.* Scribner's, 1983. Ages 11–YA. Canada.

———. *Shadow in Hawthorn Bay.* Scribner's, 1987. Ages 11–YA. Canada.

Mahy, Margaret. *The Blood-and-Thunder Adventure on Hurricane Peak.* McElderry, 1989. Ages 9–12. New Zealand.

———. *The Good Fortunes Gang.* Illustrated by Marion Young. Delacorte, 1993. Ages 8–11. New Zealand.

———. *The Haunting.* Atheneum, 1983. Ages 10–YA. New Zealand.

———. *The Three-Legged Cat.* Illustrated by Jonathan Allen. Viking, 1993. Ages 5–7. New Zealand.

———. *Underrunners.* Viking, 1992. Ages 10–YA. New Zealand.

Marsden, John. *Letters from the Inside.* Houghton, 1994. Ages 12–YA. Australia.

———. *So Much to Tell You.* Joy Street, 1989. Ages 12–YA. Australia.

———. *Tomorrow, When the War Began.* Houghton, 1995. Ages 12–YA. Australia.

Matas, Carol. *Lisa's War.* Scribner's, 1989. Ages 10–YA. Canada.

McKay, Hilary. *The Exiles.* Macmillan, 1992. Ages 9–12. U.K.

McKee, David. *Tusk Tusk.* Kane/Miller, 1990. Ages 5–9. U.K.

Mollel, Tololwa M. *The Orphan Boy.* Illustrated by Paul Morin. Clarion, 1991. Ages 5–8. Canada.

Montgomery, Lucy M. *Anne of Green Gables.* Bantam, 1908. Ages 9–13. Canada.

Moore, Inga. *The Truffle Hunter.* Kane/Miller, 1987. Ages 4–9. U.K.

Morpurgo, Michael. *The Wreck of the Zanzibar.* Illustrated by François Place. Viking, 1995. Ages 12–14. Great Britain.

Mowat, Farley. *Owls in the Family.* Little, Brown, 1962. Ages 8–11. Canada.

Munsch, Robert. *Pigs.* Illustrated by Michael Martchenko. Annick, 1989. Ages 5–8. Canada.

Naidoo, Beverley. *Chain of Fire.* Lippincott, 1990. Ages 11–YA. South Africa.

———. *Journey to Jo'burg.* Lippincott, 1986. Ages 10–YA. South Africa.

———. *No Turning Back: A Novel of South Africa.* HarperCollins, 1997. Ages 10–14. South Africa.

Nilsson, Eleanor. *The House Guest.* Viking, 1991. Ages 9–12. Australia.

Norton, Mary. *The Borrowers.* Harcourt, 1953. Ages 8–12. U.K.

Orr, Wendy. *Peeling the Onion.* Holiday, 1997. Ages 11–YA. Australia.

Park, Ruth. *Playing Beatie Bow.* Macmillan, 1980. Ages 10–YA. Australia.

Paterson, A. B. *Waltzing Matilda.* Illustrated by Desmond Digby. HarperCollins, 1991. Ages 4–10. Australia.

Peach, Susan, editor. *The DK Geography of the World.* Dorling Kindersley, 1996. Ages 7–14. Great Britain.

Pearce, Philippa. *Tom's Midnight Garden.* Lippincott, 1959. Ages 9–12. U.K.

Pearson, Kit. *Looking at the Moon.* Viking, 1992. Ages 10–YA. Canada.

Phipson, Joan. *Hit and Run.* Macmillan, 1986. Ages 11–YA. Australia.

Poulin, Stéphane. *Have You Seen Josephine?* Tundra, 1988. Ages 5–8. Canada.

Pullman, Philip. *Clockwork.* Illustrated by Leonid Gore. Scholastic, 1998. Ages 9–13. U.K.

_____. *The Golden Compass.* Knopf, 1996. Ages 12–YA. First of His Dark Materials trilogy. Also, *The Subtle Knife,* Knopf, 1997, and *The Amber Spyglass,* Knopf, 1999. U.K.

_____. *I Was a Rat!* Illustrated by Kevin Hawkes. Knopf, 2000. Ages 8–12. U.K.

Richler, Mordecai. *Jacob Two-Two Meets the Hooded Fang.* Bantam, 1987. Ages 5–8. Canada.

Rodda, Emily. *Pigs Might Fly.* Illustrated by Noela Young. Greenwillow, 1986. Ages 8–11. Australia.

_____. *Power and Glory.* Illustrated by Geoff Kelly. Greenwillow, 1996. Ages 5–7. Australia.

_____. *Rowan of Rin.* Ashton Scholastic, 1993. Ages 7–12. Australia.

Rowling, J. K. *Harry Potter and the Sorcerer's Stone.* Scholastic, 1998. The first in a series of quest fantasies, including *Harry Potter and the Chamber of Secrets,* 1999; *Harry Potter and the Prisoner of Azkabar,* 1999; and *Harry Potter and the Goblet of Fire,* 2000. Ages 9–13. U.K.

Ross, Christine. *Lily and the Present.* Methuen, 1992. Ages 5–8. New Zealand.

Rubinstein, Gillian. *Foxspell.* Simon & Schuster, 1996. Ages 12–14. Australia.

_____. *Galax-Arena.* Simon & Schuster, 1995. Ages 12–YA. Australia.

_____. *Space Demons.* Dial, 1986. Ages 10–14. Australia.

Service, Robert. *The Cremation of Sam McGee.* Illustrated by Ted Harrison. Greenwillow, 1986. Ages 10–YA. Canada.

_____. *The Shooting of Dan McGrew.* Illustrated by Ted Harrison. Godine, 1988. Ages 10–YA. Canada.

Sheldon, Dyan. *The Whale's Song.* Illustrated by Gary Blythe. Dial, 1990. Ages 5–8. U.K.

Southall, Ivan. *Ash Road.* Greenwillow, 1978. Ages 10–YA. Australia.

_____. *Josh.* Macmillan, 1988. Ages 12–YA. Australia.

Spence, Eleanor. *The Devil Hole.* Lothrop, 1977. Ages 10–YA. Australia. (Published in Great Britain under the title, *The October Child,* Oxford University Press in 1976.)

Sterling, Shirley. *My Name Is Seepeetra.* Groundwood, 1997. Ages 10–14. Canada.

Sutcliff, Rosemary, reteller. *Black Ships before Troy.* Illustrated by Alan Lee. Frances Lincoln, 1993. Ages 8–12. U.K.

_____. *Flame-Colored Taffeta.* Farrar, 1986. Ages 10–YA. U.K.

Swindells, Robert. *Stone Cold.* Hamish Hamilton, 1993. Ages 10–YA. U.K.

Thiele, Colin. *Fire in the Stone.* Harper, 1974. Ages 10–YA. Australia.

Thomas, Valerie. *Winnie the Witch.* Illustrated by Korky Paul. Kane/Miller, 1987. Ages 4–8. U.K.

Tomlinson, Theresa. *The Forestwife.* Orchard, 1995. Ages 10–14. Great Britain.

Trezise, Percy. *Turramulli the Giant Quinkin.* Illustrated by Dick Roughsey. Gareth Stevens, 1988. Ages 5–9. Australia.

Trinca, Rod, and Kerry Argent. *One Woolly Wombat.* Illustrated by Kerry Argent. Kane/Miller, 1982. Ages 5–7. Australia.

Trottier, Maxine. *The Tiny Kite of Eddie Wing.* Illustrated by Al Van Mil. Kane/Miller, 1996. Ages 4–9. Canada.

Valgardson, W. D. *Sarah and the People of Sand River.* Illustrated by Ian Wallace. Groundwood, 1996. Ages 8–11. Canada.

_____. *Winter Rescue.* Illustrated by Ange Zhang. McElderry Books, 1995. Ages 7–9. Canada.

Vaughn, Marcia K. *Wombat Stew.* Illustrated by Pamela Lofts. Silver Burdett, 1986. Ages 4–7. Australia.

Waddell, Martin. *Can't You Sleep, Little Bear?* Illustrated by Barbara Firth. Candlewick, 1992. Ages 3–6. Great Britain.

_____. *Farmer Duck.* Illustrated by Helen Oxenbury. Candlewick, 1992. Ages 4–6. Great Britain.

Wallace, Ian. *Chin Chiang & the Dragon's Dance.* Macmillan, 1984. Ages 4–8. Canada.

_____. *Morgan the Magnificent.* Macmillan, 1988. Ages 5–9. Canada.

Waugh, Sylvia. *Space Race.* Delacorte, 2000. Ages 9–12. U.K.

Westall, Robert. *Ghost Abbey.* Scholastic, 1989. Ages 11–YA. U.K.

_____. *The Promise.* Scholastic, 1990. Ages 12–YA. U.K.

Wild, Margaret. *The Very Best of Friends.* Illustrated by Julie Vivas. Harcourt, 1990. Ages 4–9. Australia.

Wildsmith, Brian. *Fishes.* Oxford, 1985. Ages 4–8. U.K.

Wilson, Budge. *The Leaving and Other Stories.* Philomel, 1992. Ages 12–14. Canada.

Wojciechowski, Susan. *The Christmas Miracle of Jonathan Toomey.* Illustrated by P. J. Lynch. Walker, 1995. Ages 4–9. Great Britain. Copublication with an American author and Irish illustrator.

Wrightson, Patricia. *The Nargun and the Stars.* Macmillan, 1986. Ages 9–13. Australia.

————. *A Racecourse for Andy.* Harcourt, 1968. Ages 9–12. Australia.

Wynne-Jones, Tim. *Some of the Kinder Planets.* Groundwood, 1993. Ages 10–13. Canada.

Yee, Paul. *The Curses of Third Uncle.* Illustrated by Don Besco. Lorimer, 1986. Ages 10–YA. Canada.

————. *Tales from Gold Mountain: Stories of the Chinese in the New World.* Macmillan, 1990. Ages 7–12. Canada.

Yerxa, Leo. *Last Leaf First Snowflake to Fall.* Groundwood, 1993. Ages 5–8. Canada.

## Translated Books

Aamundsen, Nina R. *Two Short and One Long.* Houghton, 1990. Ages 9–13. Norway.

Anno, Mitsumasa. *Anno's Magic Seeds.* Translated by Dowaya Publishing Co. Philomel, 1995. Ages 6–9. Japan.

———— and others. *All in a Day.* Translated from the Japanese. Putnam, 1987. Ages 3–11. Japan.

Atlan, Liliane. *The Passersby.* Translated by Rochelle Owens. Illustrated by Lisa Desimini. Holt/Edge, 1993. Ages 12–YA. France.

Barbot, Daniel. *A Bicycle for Rosaura.* Illustrated by Morella Fuenmayor. Kane/Miller, 1991. Ages 4–8. Venezuela.

Beck, Martine. *The Wedding of Brown Bear and White Bear.* Illustrated by Marie H. Henry. Translated by Aliyah Morgenstern. Little, Brown, 1990. Ages 4–8. France.

Bergman, Tamar. *Along the Track.* Translated from the Hebrew by Michael Swirsky. Houghton, 1991. Ages 10–YA. Israel.

————. *The Boy from Over There.* Translated from the Hebrew by Hillel Halkin. Houghton, 1988. Ages 12–YA. Israel.

Björk, Christina. *Linnea in Monet's Garden.* Illustrated by Lena Anderson. Translated from the Swedish by Joan Sandin. Farrar (R & S), 1987. Ages 7–11. Sweden.

————. *Linnea's Windowsill Garden.* Illustrated by Lena Anderson. Translated from the Swedish by Joan Sandin. Farrar (R & S), 1988. Ages 7–11. Sweden.

————. *The Other Alice: The Story of Alice Liddell and Alice in Wonderland.* Illustrated by Inga-Karin Eriksson. Translated from the Swedish by Joan Sandin. Farrar (R & S), 1993. Ages 10–YA. Sweden.

————. *Vendela in Venice.* Illustrated by Inga-Karin Eriksson. Translated from the Swedish by Patricia Crampton. R & S, 1999. Ages 9–12. Sweden.

Bos, Burny. *Prince Valentino.* Illustrated by Hans de Beer. North-South, 1990. Ages 5–8. Netherlands.

Bröger, Achim. *The Day Chubby Became Charles.* Illustrated by Emily Arnold McCully. Translated from the German by Renée Vera Cafiero. Lippincott, 1990. Ages 8–11. Germany.

Brunhoff, Jean de. *The Story of Babar.* Translated from the French by Merle Haas. Random, 1933. Ages 5–7. France.

Buchholz, Quint. *The Collector of Moments.* Translated from the German by Peter F. Niemeyer. Farrar, 1999. Ages 9–12. Germany.

Calders, Pere. *Brush.* Illustrated by Carme Solé Vendrell. Translated from the Spanish by Marguerite Feitlowitz. Kane/Miller, 1986. Ages 3–7. Spain.

Carmi, Daniella. *Samir and Yonatan.* Translated from the Hebrew by Yael Lotan. Scholastic, 2000. Ages 9–12. Israel.

Carrier, Roch. *The Champion.* Illustrated by Sheldon Cohen. Translated from the French by Sheila Fischman. Tundra, 1991. Ages 7–10. Canada.

————. *The Hockey Sweater.* Translated from the French by Sheila Fischman. Tundra, 1984. Canada.

Clément, Claude. *The Voice of the Wood.* Illustrated by Frédéric Clément. Translated from the French by Lenny Hort. Dial, 1989. Ages 7–11. France.

Collodi, Carlo. *The Adventures of Pinocchio.* Translated from the Italian by Marianna Mayer. Macmillan, 1981 (1881). Ages 6–9. Italy.

Damjan, Mischa. *December's Travels.* Illustrated by Dušan Kállay. Translated from the German by Anthea Bell. Dial, 1986. Ages 5–9. Germany.

de Beer, Hans. *Little Polar Bear, Take Me Home!* Translated by Rosemary Lanning. North-South, 1996. Ages 4–7. Switzerland.

de Vries, Anke. *Bruises.* Translated by Stacey Knecht. Front Street, 1995. Ages 10–14. Netherlands.

Dijk, Lutz van. *Damned Strong Love: The True Story of Willi G. and Stefan K.* Translated from the German by Elizabeth D. Crawford. Holt, 1995. Ages 14–YA. Germany.

Duquennoy, Jacques. *The Ghost's Trip to Loch Ness.* Translated by Kathryn Nanovic. Harcourt, 1996. Ages 5–7. France.

Dumas, Felipe. *A Farm.* Creative Company, 1999. Ages 7–14. France.

Escudié, René. *Paul and Sebastian.* Illustrated by Ulises Wensell. Translated from the French by Roderick Townley. Kane/Miller, 1988. Ages 4–8. France.

Frank, Anne. *Anne Frank: The Diary of a Young Girl.* Translated from the Dutch by B. M. Mooyaart. Doubleday, 1967. Netherlands.

Friedman, Carl. *Nightfather.* Translated from the Dutch by Arnold and Erica Pomerans. Persea, 1994. Ages 11–14. Netherlands.

Gaarder, Jostein. *The Solitaire Mystery.* Illustrated by Hilde Kramer. Translated by Sarah Jane Hails. Farrar, 1996. Ages 12–YA. Norway.

Gajadin, Chitra, reteller. *Amal and the Letter from the King.* Illustrated by Helen Ong. Boyds Mills, 1992. Ages 5–8. Netherlands.

Gallaz, Christophe, and Roberto Innocenti. *Rose Blanche.* Translated from the French by Martha Coventry and Richard Graglia. Creative Education, 1985. Ages 9–YA. France.

Gehrts, Barbara. *Don't Say a Word.* Translated from the German by Elizabeth D. Crawford. Macmillan, 1986. Ages 11–YA. Germany.

Gomi, Taro. *Everyone Poops.* Translated from the Japanese by Amanda Mayer Stinchecum. Kane/Miller, 1993. Ages 2–5. Japan.

———. *Summer Is Here.* Chronicle, 1989. Ages 4–6. Japan.

Grimm Brothers. *Hansel and Gretel.* Illustrated by Lisbeth Zwerger. Translated from the German by Elizabeth D. Crawford. Picture Book Studio, 1988. Ages 5–8. Germany.

Gripe, Maria. *Agnes Cecilia.* Translated from the Swedish by Rika Lesser. Harper, 1990. Ages 12–YA. Sweden.

Härtling, Peter. *Crutches.* Translated from the German by Elizabeth D. Crawford. Lothrop, 1988. Ages 11–YA. Germany.

———. *Old John.* Translated from the German by Elizabeth D. Crawford. Lothrop, 1990. Ages 10–12. Germany.

Harvard, Christian. *The Wolf: Night Howler.* Charlesbridge, 1996. Ages 7–9. France.

Haugen, Tormod. *Zeppelin.* Translated from the Norwegian by David Jacobs. Turton & Chambers, Ltd., 1991. Ages 10–14. Norway.

Heine, Helme. *Prince Bear.* McElderry, 1989. Ages 6–9. Germany.

Heuck, Sigrid. *The Hideout.* Translated from the German by Rika Lesser. Dutton, 1988. Ages 10–13. Germany.

Heymans, Annemie, and Margriet Heymans. *The Princess in the Kitchen Garden.* Translated from the Dutch by Johanna H. Prins and Johanna W. Prins. Farrar, 1993. Ages 8–10. Netherlands.

Ho, Minfong, compiler. *Maples in the Mist: Children's Poems from the Tang Dynasty.* Illustrated by Jean and Mou-sien Tseng. Translated from the Chinese by Minfong Ho. Lothrop, 1996. Ages 7–12. China.

Hoestlandt, Jo. *Star of Fear, Star of Hope.* Illustrated by Johanna Kang. Translated from the French by Mark Polizzotti. Walker, 1995. Ages 7–12. France.

Holtwijz, Ineke. *Asphalt Angels.* Front Street, 1999. Translated from the Dutch by Wanda Boeke. Ages 12–YA. The Netherlands. Story set in Rio de Janeiro.

Isami, Iksuyo. *The Fox's Egg.* Translated from the Japanese by Cathy Hirano. Carolrhoda, 1989. Ages 4–8. Japan.

Jansson, Tove. *Finn Family Moomintroll.* Translated from the Finnish by Elizabeth Portch. Farrar, 1989. Ages 6–9. Finland.

Kaldhol, Marit. *Goodbye Rune.* Illustrated by Wenche Öyen. Translated from the Norwegian. Kane/Miller, 1987. Ages 5–10. Norway.

Karvoskaia, Natacha (story told by Zidrou). *Dounia.* Translated from the French. Kane/Miller, 1995. Ages 4–7. Belgium.

Kerner, Charlotte. *Blueprint.* Translated from the German by Elizabeth D. Crawford. Lerner, 2000. Ages YA. Germany.

Kodama, Tatsuharu. *Shin's Tricycle.* Illustrated by Ando. Translated by Kazuko Hokumen-Jones. Walker, 1995. Ages 10–13. Japan.

Korschunow, Irina. *Small Fur Is Getting Bigger.* Illustrated by Reinhard Michl. Translated from the German by James Skofield. Harper, 1990. Ages 6–9. Switzerland.

Krause, Ute. *Pig Surprise.* Dial, 1989. Ages 5–8. Germany.

Kurusa. *The Streets Are Free.* Illustrated by Monica Doppert. Translated from the Spanish by Karen Englander. Annick Press, 1995 (1985). Ages 7–9. Venezuela.

Lindgren, Astrid. *Pippi Longstocking.* Illustrated by Louis S. Glanzman. Translated by Florence Lamborn. Viking, 1950. Ages 8–11. Sweden.

———. *Rasmus and the Vagabond.* Translated from the Swedish by Gerry Bothmer. Puffin, 1960. Ages 9–12. Sweden.

———. *Ronia, the Robber's Daughter.* Translated from the Swedish by Patricia Crampton. Viking, 1983. Ages 10–YA. Sweden.

Llorente, Pilar Molina. *The Apprentice.* Illustrated by Juan Ramón Alonso. Translated from the Spanish by Robin Longshaw. Farrar, 1993. Ages 11–YA. Spain.

Lobe, Mira. *Christoph Wants a Party.* Retold by Marcia Lane. Illustrated by Winfried Opgenoorth. Kane/Miller, 1995. Ages 4–6. Austria.

Lucht, Irmgard. *The Red Poppy.* Translated from the German by Frank-Jacoby Nelson. Hyperion, 1995. Ages 5–9. Germany.

Maartens, Maretha. *Paper Bird.* Translated from the Afrikaans by Madeleine van Biljon. Clarion, 1991. Ages 9–12. South Africa.

Mandelbaum, Pili. *You Be Me, I'll Be You.* Translated from the French. Kane/Miller, 1990. Ages 5–8. Belgium.

Marshak, Samuel. *The Pup Grew Up.* Illustrated by Vladimir Radunsky. Translated from the Russian by Richard Pevear. Holt, 1989. Ages 7–10. Russia.

Maruki, Toshi. *Hiroshima No Pika.* Translated from the Japanese. Lothrop, 1982. Ages 9–YA. Japan.

Müller, Jörg. *The Changing Countryside.* Atheneum, 1977. Ages 7–14. Switzerland. A dramatic wordless portfolio of eight murals showing the effects of suburban sprawl. (See also *The Changing City,* Atheneum, 1977.)

Newth, Mette. *The Abduction.* Translated from the Norwegian by Tina Nunnally and Steve Murray. Farrar, 1989. Ages 13–YA. Norway.

Nilsson, Ulf. *If You Didn't Have Me.* Illustrated by Eva Eriksson. Translated from the Swedish by George Blecher and Lone Thygesen-Blecher. McElderry, 1987. Ages 7–10. Sweden.

Nomura, Takaaki. *Grandpa's Town.* Translated from the Japanese by Amanda Mayer Stinchecum. Kane/Miller, 1991. Ages 4–8. Japan.

Orlev, Uri. *The Island on Bird Street.* Translated from the Hebrew by Hillel Halkin. Houghton, 1984. Ages 9–12. Israel.

———. *Lydia, Queen of Palestine.* Translated from the Hebrew by Hillel Halkin. Houghton, 1993. Ages 8–12.

———. *The Man from the Other Side.* Translated from the Hebrew by Hillel Halkin. Houghton, 1991. Ages 10–13. Israel.

Pausewang, Gudrun. *Fall-Out.* Translated from the German by Patricia Crampton. Viking, 1995. Ages 12–YA. Germany.

Place, François. *The Last Giants.* Translated from the French by William Rodarmor. David R. Godine, 1993. Ages 9–12. Belgium.

Popov, Nikolai. *Why?* Translated from the German. North-South, 1996. Ages 7–14. Switzerland.

Rettich, Margret. *Suleiman the Elephant.* Translated from the German by Elizabeth D. Crawford. Lothrop, 1986. Ages 6–9. Germany.

Reuter, Bjarne. *The Boys from St. Petri.* Translated from the Danish by Anthea Bell. Dutton, 1994. Ages 12–YA. Denmark.

———. *Buster's World.* Translated from the Danish by Anthea Bell. Dutton, 1989. Ages 9–12. Denmark.

———. *The Sheik of Hope Street.* Translated from the Danish by Anthea Bell. Dutton, 1991. Ages 9–12. Denmark.

Richter, Hans Peter. *Friedrich.* Translated from the German by Edite Kroll. Holt, 1970. Ages 11–YA. Germany.

Rondon, Javier. *The Absent-Minded Toad.* Illustrated by Marcela Cabrera. Translated from the Spanish by Kathryn Corbett. Kane/Miller, 1994. Ages 3–6. Venezuela.

Ruepp, Krista. *Midnight Rider.* Illustrated by Ulrike Heyne. Translated by J. Alison James. North-South, 1995. Ages 6–9. Switzerland.

Sales, Francesc. *Ibrahim.* Illustrated by Eulàlia Sariola. Translated from the Catalon by Marc Simont. Lippincott, 1989. Ages 8–12. Spain.

Schami, Rafik. *Fatima and the Dream Thief.* Illustrated by Els Cools and Oliver Streich. Translated from the German by Anthea Bell. North-South, 1996. Ages 7–9. Germany.

———. *A Hand Full of Stars.* Translated from the German by Rika Lesser. Dutton, 1990. Ages 10–YA. Germany.

Schmidt, Annie M. G. *Pink Lemonade.* Illustrated by Timothy Foley. Translated from the Dutch by Henrietta Ten Harmsel. Eerdmans, 1992 (1981). Ages 6–10. Netherlands.

Sellier, Marie. *Cézanne from A to Z.* Translated from the French by Claudia Zoe Bedrick. Peter Bedrick Books, 1996. Ages 9–YA. France.

Siekkinen, Raija. *The Curious Faun.* Illustrated by Hannu Taina. Translated from the Finnish by Tim Steffa. Carolrhoda, 1990. Ages 6–9. Finland.

———. *Mister King.* Illustrated by Hannu Taina. Translated from the Finnish by Tim Steffa. Carolrhoda, 1987. Ages 6–9. Finland.

Singer, Isaac. *Zlateh the Goat & Other Stories.* Translated from the Yiddish by Elizabeth Shub. Harper, 1984. Ages 7–10. Israel.

Solotareff, Grégoire. *Don't Call Me Little Bunny.* Translated from the French. Farrar, 1988. Ages 4–8. France.

———. *The Ogre and the Frog King.* Translated from the French. Greenwillow, 1988. Ages 4–8. France.

Spyri, Johanna. *Heidi.* Crown, 1880. Ages 9–12. Switzerland.

Stark, Ulf. *Can You Whistle, Johanna?: A Boy's Search for a Grandfather.* Illustrated by Anna Hoglund. Translated from the Swedish by Ebba Segerberg. RDR Books, 1999. Ages 6–8. Sweden.

Steiner, Jörg. *The Bear Who Wanted to Be a Bear.* Illustrated by Jörg Müller. Translated from the German. McElderry, 1977. Ages 8–12. Switzerland.

Storm, Theodor. *Little Hobbin.* Illustrated by Lisbeth Zwerger. Translated from the German by Anthea Bell. North-South, 1995. Ages 4–6. Switzerland.

Sundvall, Viveca. *Mimi and the Biscuit Factory.* Illustrated by Eva Eriksson. Translated from the Swedish by Eric Bibb. Farrar (R & S), 1989. Ages 4–7. Sweden.

———. *Santa's Winter Vacation.* Illustrated by Olof Landström. Translated from the Swedish by Kjersti Board. R & S Books, 1995. Ages 4–9. Sweden.

Tolstoy, Leo. *The Lion and the Puppy and Other Stories for Children.* Illustrated by Claus Sievert. Translated from the Russian by James Riordan. Holt, 1988. Ages 9–YA. Russia.

van der Rol, Ruud, and Rian Verhoeven. *Anne Frank, Beyond the Diary: A Photographic Remembrance.* Translated from the Dutch by Tony Longham and Plym Peters. Viking, 1993. Ages 11–YA. Netherlands.

Vincent, Gabrielle. *Ernest and Celestine.* Greenwillow, 1982. Ages 3–7. Belgium.

Vos, Ida. *Dancing on the Bridge of Avignon.* Translated by Terese Edelstein and Inez Smidt. Houghton, 1995. Ages 10–14. Netherlands.

Wettasinghe, Sybil. *The Umbrella Thief.* Kane/Miller, 1987. Ages 4–8. Sri Lanka.

Yumoto, Kazumi. *The Friends.* Translated by Cathy Hirano. Farrar, 1996. Ages 10–14. Japan.

# P LANNING *the* LITERATURE CURRICULUM

READING

*. . . We get no good*
*By being ungenerous even to a book,*
*And calculating profits . . . so much help*
*By so much reading. It is rather when*
*We gloriously forget ourselves and plunge*
*Soul-forward, headlong, into a book's profound,*
*Impassioned for its beauty and salt of truth—*
*'Tis then we get the right good from a book.*

— E LIZABETH  B ROWNING

Literature is not a regularly mandated part of the elementary school curriculum as is reading, mathematics, or social studies. Yet knowing how literature works can be valuable. Knowledge of the elements and devices of writing and illustration enriches our appreciation of an interesting story, just as knowing something of music or architecture enhances our appreciation of a beautiful song or a handsome building.

This chapter deals with long-range planning for literature instruction (short-range planning is dealt with in Chapter 12). First, the literature curriculum is defined, and ways to organize such a curriculum are presented. Ways to develop the literature curriculum are explained, followed by a discussion of how literature can be integrated into a school's reading program. The latter part of the chapter includes sections on evaluating a literature program, implementing a schoolwide literature program, and First Amendment rights of children.

# THE LITERATURE CURRICULUM

Literature is more than a collection of well-written stories and poems. Literature also has its own body of knowledge. A term that is sometimes used to label this treatment of literature is *discipline-based literature instruction.* The object of such a course of study is to teach children the mechanics of literature: the terms used to define it, its components or elements, its genres, and the craft of creating it. The terms and elements of literature are presented in Chapter 2; the genres and their characteristics are presented in Chapters 3–10.

# ORGANIZING THE LITERATURE CURRICULUM

Some teachers plan for a year-long strand of literature instruction organized variously by genre, by author or illustrator, by literary element or device, by notable books, by topic or theme, or by some combination of these. In each case, there should be goals for the course of study, specific children's trade books to be read or listened to by each child, guidelines for selection of materials, a schedule, and criteria for evaluating the course of study.

## Genre

By organizing a literature curriculum around literary genres, teachers provide a context for students to learn about the various types of literature and the characteristics of each. In the beginning, the teacher will have to direct students' attention to similarities in books of like genre—for example, the students will learn that works of historical fiction are always set in the past or that characters in folktales are two-dimensional. Soon, however, students will begin to read with more genre awareness and will enjoy finding common elements within and differences between genres.

One advantage of this plan is that students over the school year can be exposed to a wide variety of literature. Knowledge of different genres gives students useful schemata—frameworks for understanding borne of prior experience—for story types. A genre approach can work in all grade levels, given thoughtful selection of titles and delivery of literary concepts. Planning involves choosing the genres to be studied, selecting the representative children's books for each, and determining the order in which the genres will be studied.

## Author or Illustrator

The goal of a curriculum in literature organized by author or illustrator is to make students more familiar with the works and styles of selected children's book authors and illustrators. An additional goal may be knowledge of the authors' or illustrators' lives insofar as these life experiences influenced the subjects' works. The choice of authors and illustrators will naturally be guided both by students' reading interests and the teacher's desire to introduce students to important authors, illustrators, and their works. The number of works chosen to represent an author or illustrator will vary, but even when an author's books are lengthy, more than one work is recommended.

As a class experiences a sampling of the chosen author's or illustrator's work, attention will be focused on trademark stylistic elements such as unusual use of words or color or media, as well as themes, characters, character types, or settings common to these works. Later, information about the person's life can be introduced through reports, audiotaped and videotaped interviews, and even guest appearances by the author or illustrator. Many resources, including biographies and biographical reference volumes, such as *Something about the Author* (Hedblad, 2001), provide information about children's book authors and illustrators. (For more information about this resource, see Appendix B.)

Success of author and illustrator studies is not necessarily defined by wholesale student approval of the featured artists. Students must be allowed to decide whether they like a person's work or not and should be encouraged to discover why they have these feelings. Wholesale *disapproval* by students of the works of a featured author or illustrator, however, is an important form of *teacher* evaluation that should not be ignored. In such a case, the teacher's choice of author or books to be studied was not appropriate for this purpose and should be reconsidered. Students are evaluated informally through observation of their recognition of featured authors' or illustrators' works and their ability to compare literary and artistic styles of various authors and illustrators.

## Literary Element and Device

When teachers say that their teaching of literature is organized by literary element, they are usually referring to the elements of fiction (as presented in Chapter 2): plot, character, setting, theme, and style. Other elements, such as artistic styles, media, and book format, could be addressed as well. A *literary device* is "any literary technique deliberately employed to achieve a special effect" (Baldick, 1990, p. 55). Irony, symbolism, parody, and foreshadowing are examples of devices that add richness to stories.

The goal of a literature curriculum organized by literary elements and devices is to give students a better understanding of the craft of writing so that they can read more perceptively and appreciatively and possibly apply this knowledge to their own writing. Since this approach is analytical and somewhat abstract, it is more appropriate for students in the fourth grade or above.

Careful selection of children's books to accompany the investigation of each literary element or device is crucial to the success of this approach. The featured element must be prominent and must have been used by the author with extraordinary skill. In addition, the story itself must captivate young readers. Note that in this approach, books of various genres can be grouped to demonstrate the same literary element. Note also that picture books are particularly good at presenting literary elements and devices clearly and in relatively simple contexts so that they can be understood more easily. An excellent resource for selecting picture books for this use is Hall's *Using Picture Books to Teach Literary Devices,* Vols. I and II (1990, 1994).

Students' acquaintance with the literary elements and devices can go far beyond mere definition. Close reading of key passages reveals the author's craft at developing character, establishing mood, authenticating setting, or using such devices as inference, symbolism, or foreshadowing. Re-creation of these elements and devices in their own art, drama, and writing not only gives students a personal and more complete understanding of these concepts, but also gives teachers a way to evaluate their students' grasp of these concepts.

## Notable Book

Many teachers organize a literature curriculum by notable books, that is, books widely recognized for their literary excellence. Each of these books may exemplify one or more aspects of the literature curriculum that is to be taught, and so the order in which these books are read and studied determines the order in which the content of the literature study will be presented. Since the notable books are read aloud to all the students by the teacher in this approach, it is particularly important that the selections be well matched to students' general interests and abilities. A problem with this approach can be that the list of notable books does not vary from year to year, regardless of student variation from class to class. Teachers who use this approach successfully must remain flexible in their book selections so that their choices reflect students' current preferences and interests.

In this approach, the teacher reads aloud one or more chapters of the selected book each day and holds class discussions on the book in terms of its meanings and how different students perceive its meaning. Traditionally, these discussions are led by the teacher; but some instructors have found that student-led discussions in small groups, if well managed, are just as effective and have the added advantage of giving students practice in leading and contributing to serious discussions.

## Theme or Topic

Teachers who choose to organize a study of literature by theme or topic want their students generally to become aware of the power of literature to explain the human condition. Themes and topics will vary according to ages and circumstances of students. For example, primary-grade children will be interested in themes and topics having to do with school and family life. Those in the middle grades, on the other hand, will be more intrigued by themes and topics dealing with the discovery and use of inner resources to become more independent or even to survive.

Possible themes that a seventh- or eighth-grade class might explore through a year include the following:

Surviving in the Modern World
Alienation
Coping with Parents and Younger Siblings
Teenagers through History: The Same Old Problems?
Dependence and Independence
The Future World
Beneath the Skin: What Is the True Nature of Difference?

Possible themes and topics for a younger group might include these:

Families Come in All Shapes and Sizes
School Now and in the Past
Use Your Wits
The Importance of Having Good Friends
Stories from Other Countries
Old Ones and Young Ones Together
Famous People Were Children Too

In this approach, each child reads or listens to the book or books chosen by the teacher to accompany each theme. After the reading, students explore the theme through discussion, writing, drama, art, and further reading on the theme or topic. Teachers who use a whole language approach find that this method of organizing a literature curriculum works particularly well.

Themes and topics are chosen by the teacher on the basis of students' needs and interests, current events, and prior successes with previously developed thematic units. The length of time spent on any one theme or topic can vary from a school year to a day, but several weeks' duration is the norm.

Two pitfalls of thematic learning curriculum models must be avoided. The first is choosing a unit theme or topic just because a few related books are at hand. Remember: The unit theme or topic drives literature selection, not vice versa. The second pitfall is choosing literature just because it relates to the theme or topic but with no regard to its quality or appropriateness for the students. Boring books make boring thematic instructional units.

# DEVELOPING THE LITERATURE CURRICULUM

Planning for a literature curriculum involves many important practical considerations in addition to choosing the approach one takes to teaching literature. The classroom environment must be constructed, the materials collected, and the plans written.

## Designing the Classroom Environment

Much can be learned about a teacher's philosophy of learning and teaching simply by taking a look around the classroom.

The traditional classroom arrangement, with students' desks arranged in straight rows facing the teacher's desk, implies a more teacher-centered environment: The teacher is the center of attention and the main source of information. The preponderant type of discourse in this classroom is most likely a whole-class lecture, and its direction is from teacher to student. The interactive classroom arrangement, with students' desks arranged in groups so that the occupants face one another, implies a more student-centered environment. Various types of discourse seem to be encouraged here: student-to-student discussions, small group activities, and teacher-student conferences. The direction of this discourse is as much from student to student and student to teacher as it is teacher to student.

In addition to room arrangement, other aspects of a classroom reveal the nature of what goes on from day to day. What materials and resources are most apparent? What is the nature of displays and bulletin boards? What level of thinking and inquiry is indicated by the student work on display? Teachers who recognize the importance of good literature will design an attractive and comfortable classroom environment in which books are featured.

Many teachers promote literature and literature-related activities by designating a specific area of the classroom as the *library corner.* The library corner is made conducive to reading by being located as far as possible from noisy activities and by being outfitted with comfortable seating (carpeting, pillows, soft chairs) and lots of conveniently placed and easy-to-find books. The library corner houses the classroom library and can be the setting for independent silent reading, paired and small group reading, and whole-class read-aloud sessions during the day. Low shelving can serve many purposes: It provides boundaries for the corner; sound buffers; and storage for books, book circulation records, book club order forms, and audiotapes and videotapes relating to books.

The library corner is a logical place to display students' book-related writing and artwork, such as student-produced books, students' book reviews, charts showing the class's favorite books and authors, and letters to and from authors and illustrators. Walls and bulletin boards in this way become an integral part of the library corner.

Teachers with self-contained classrooms might have several centers, each devoted to a specific activity, such as acting out plays, or curricular subject, such as science or health, mathematics, and writing. By outfitting each center with appropriate books and displaying student writing and art related to their work in these areas, teachers naturally integrate the subject areas and show students the relationships between them. Another noticeable feature of the interactive classroom is the proximity and availability of books. Providing students with a rich supply of trade literature is also the result of planning.

### Building a Classroom Library Collection

Most, if not all, of the responsibility for acquiring a sufficiently large and varied collection of books in your classroom will be yours. With perseverance, it can be done. Most good classroom libraries have a permanent collection as well as a collection that comes from the school or public library and changes regularly. Beginning teachers who are willing to plan ahead with their school and public librarians can borrow enough books for adequate temporary classroom libraries while they build their own collections. Even after a large permanent collection is established, a rotating selection from the school and public library can be coordinated with specific units of study, providing depth and breadth to the unit content and to the students' learning experience.

Careful selection of titles for the classroom library makes the most of limited resources. Children's librarians can provide invaluable advice in selecting titles for a classroom library and should be consulted. If this is not an option, browsing in a well-stocked children's bookstore and consulting publishers' catalogs are alternative ways of finding out what is available. Publishers of children's books issue one or two catalogs annually in which they describe their new publications and list their previous publications that are currently available (the backlist). If your school or public librarian does not have these catalogs, publishers will supply them on request. Some teachers use catalogs to get an overview of what is available before going to a bookstore.

Your own permanent trade book collection can be built inexpensively by using several proven approaches. These include the following:

- Requesting an allocation from your principal or PTO for purchase of books
- Submitting a small grant proposal ($250–$1000) to your school district or professional organization for purchase of trade books
- Taking advantage of bonus books offered by student paperback book clubs
- Informing students' parents that you are building a collection and would like to have first refusal of any children's books that they plan to discard
- Establishing a "give a book to the classroom" policy for parents who want to celebrate their child's birthday or a holiday at school in some way
- Frequenting garage sales and library book sales, where good books can often be purchased for pennies

Most bookstores offer a 20 percent discount to teachers who use their own money to buy books to add to their classroom collections. An alternative to the bookstore is the book jobber, or wholesale dealer for many publishers. Jobbers offer even greater discounts to teachers, sometimes up to 40 percent, but it is important to remember that most jobbers do not carry small press publications. Your school librarian probably uses a jobber and can assist you in setting up a staff account with the same firm. Some of the larger firms include Baker & Taylor, Brodart, and Ingram Book Company.

With these methods and sources, classroom collections grow quickly. From the beginning, you will need to devise a coding system for your permanent collection to streamline shelving and record keeping. Many teachers find that color coding their books by genre with colored tape on the spines works well. If at all possible, students should be trained and given the responsibility for color coding, checking in and out, repairing, and reshelving books.

Remember that the whole point of building a classroom library is to promote reading, not to provide a handsome display. Inevitably, if children use their classroom library, books will be lost and damaged. Severe reprimands for losing or damaging a book may work against your ultimate goal.

## Outlining a Year-Long Literature Curriculum

Planning for the school year permits the teacher to have resources available when they are needed. In outlining for a year-long literature curriculum, several steps must be taken.

**DETERMINING THE APPROACH**   A teacher must first determine which literature curriculum to teach: genre, author/illustrator, literary element or device, notable book, or topic/theme. Another alternative is to create a hybrid literature curriculum by including aspects of several of these approaches in the plan.

**ESTABLISHING GOALS**   Goals in a literature curriculum are those aims one expects to accomplish by the end of the course of study. The term *objectives* refers to short-range aims to be accomplished day by day or week by week. Central to this part of the planning process is deciding on the literary concepts to be taught. Since goals largely determine the parameters of the course of study, they must be established early in the planning process.

Goals for a literature curriculum are established by individual teachers and sometimes by schools or school districts. Likely goals for a fifth-grade teacher who has determined to use a mixed genre/author organization to teaching literature would be these:

- Students will enjoy reading a variety of genres of literature.
- Students will be familiar with the characteristics of traditional literature, modern fantasy, historical fiction, contemporary realistic fiction, mystery, and science fiction and will be able to classify a book as belonging to one of the featured genres when reading it.
- Students will become familiar with several leading authors of each of the above genres and will be able to identify characteristics of the writing of each author.

*DETERMINING UNITS OF STUDY*   After goals have been identified and set, the next step in outlining a literature curriculum is to determine the units of study through which the literature content will be delivered. In this way, a tentative schedule can be set in order to foresee needs in terms of time and materials.

*SELECTING FOCUS BOOKS*   Each unit will require certain trade books for reading aloud by the teacher and trade books for class or small group study or independent reading. Early selection of these titles is important for several reasons. Balance in the overall book selection, for instance, is achieved much more easily in the planning stages. *Balance in book selection,* as presented in Chapter 2, means that the books selected present a diversity of characters (type, sex, age, ethnicity, place of origin), settings (urban, rural, familiar, foreign), and themes. Another advantage of early selection is being able to estimate the time necessary for each unit. Some units will take longer than others, depending on such variables as the extent of content to be covered, the length and difficulty of books to be read, and the type and complexity of planned book extension activities. A sample list of units, books, and featured authors for a fifth-grade teacher who is implementing a combined genre/author organization for teaching literature would be as follows:

---

## U N I T  1 :  T R A D I T I O N A L  L I T E R A T U R E

**M Y T H O L O G Y**

*The Gods and Goddesses of Olympus* retold and illustrated by Aliki
*Theseus and the Minotaur* adapted by Leonard Everett Fisher

**L E G E N D S**

*The Legend of King Arthur* retold by Robin Lister. Illustrated by Alan Baker
*Sir Gawain and the Loathly Lady* by Selina Hastings. Illustrated by Juan Wijngaard
*Dragonslayer: The Story of Beowulf* by Rosemary Sutcliff

**F O L K T A L E S**

*Snow White and the Seven Dwarfs* translated by Randall Jarrell. Illustrated by Nancy Ekholm Burkert
*Snow White in New York* by Fiona French

**R E A D - A L O U D**

*Sir Gawain and the Green Knight* by Selina Hastings. Illustrated by Juan Wijngaard

# UNIT 2: MODERN FANTASY

*Tuck Everlasting* by Natalie Babbitt
*A Stranger Came Ashore* by Mollie Hunter
*Konrad* by Christine Nöstlinger

READ-ALOUD

*The Lion, the Witch, and the Wardrobe* by C. S. Lewis
Featured Author: C. S. Lewis

# UNIT 3: HISTORICAL FICTION (WORLD WAR II)

*The Island on Bird Street* by Uri Orlev
*The Upstairs Room* by Johanna Reiss
*Summer of My German Soldier* by Bette Greene
*Rose Blanche* by Christophe Gallaz and Roberto Innocenti

READ-ALOUD

*Journey to Topaz* by Yoshiko Uchida
Featured Author: Yoshiko Uchida

# UNIT 4: CONTEMPORARY REALISTIC FICTION

*The Bridge to Terabithia* by Katherine Paterson
*The Friends* by Kazumi Yumoto
*Trading Places* by Gary Soto
*Monkey Island* by Paula Fox

READ-ALOUD

*Hatchet* by Gary Paulsen
Featured Author: Gary Paulsen

# UNIT 5: MYSTERY

*Peppermints in the Parlor* by Barbara Brooks Wallace
*The Mystery of Dies Drear* by Virginia Hamilton
*The Man Who Was Poe* by Avi
*The Dollhouse Murders* by Betty Ren Wright

READ-ALOUD

*Midnight Is a Place* by Joan Aiken
Featured Author: Joan Aiken

# UNIT 6: SCIENCE FICTION

*The Green Book* by Jill Paton Walsh
*The White Mountains* by John Christopher
*Collidescope* by Grace Chetwin
*The Giver* by Lois Lowry

READ-ALOUD

*A Wrinkle in Time* by Madeleine L'Engle
Featured Author: Madeleine L'Engle

An issue often discussed among children's literature instructors is the efficacy of a *literary canon* of children's literature, an official list of children's books judged by experts to be worthy of inclusion in a literature curriculum. Elementary teachers and librarians have largely rejected the idea of a literary canon mainly because its sole criterion for selection is literary excellence, with no consideration for a book's appeal or relevance to children. Moreover, teachers know that they are in the best position to select books that match their students' interests and their own planned curricula. A literary canon is rarely revised and quickly becomes dated. Being so rigid and select, it cannot reflect the varied and changing interests of a particular group of children. Although the term *literary canon* most often refers to a nationally recognized booklist, teachers should be aware that when they stick rigidly to the same set of books year after year, they are, in effect, proclaiming that their own personal literary canon of children's literature is more important than the needs and interests of the children they teach.

*SCHEDULING*   With an overview of the plan established, the teacher can begin to set dates and time allotments for each unit and for activities within units. With each year of experience, the teacher's time estimates become more accurate. At this point, it is still easy to adjust the year-long plan if it becomes obvious that too much or too little has been planned.

Planning makes it possible to integrate the literature curriculum with other areas of study. For example, the literature unit presented in Figure 11.1 could be scheduled to coincide with the U.S. history unit on World War II presented in the previous section.

### Fleshing Out the Units of Study

Thinking through, organizing, and writing down the details of daily lessons and activities are the final steps in planning for a literature curriculum. Two methods of organizing the details of units of study are to create webs and literature units.

*WEBS*   Webbing is a way of creating a visual overview of a unit of study complete with its focus, related book titles, and activities, as demonstrated in the web in Figure 11.1. Ideas for a web are generated through brainstorming. The main advantage of webbing is that the process clarifies and even suggests ties or associations between concepts, books, and activities. Webs can be organized around a theme or topic, a single book, a book genre, an author or illustrator, or a literary concept. Activities can be drawn from all skill areas—writing, reading, listening, thinking, speaking, art, crafts, drama, and music.

Information about and examples of webs are available in several resources. *Webbing with Literature: Creating Story Maps with Children's Books* by Bromley (1991) explores webbing as a way for children to respond to literature. Teachers who use webbing as a way to plan literature units will appreciate the many topics, themes, and resources suggested in *Book Links,* a journal published by the American Library Association. (For further information on these resources, see Appendix B.)

A disadvantage of webbing is that it gives no indication of the chronology of events or time allotments. Eventually, the web must be transferred to a more linear format, which is similar to the literature unit.

*LITERATURE UNITS*   The literature unit resembles an outline organized by day or by week. As with webs, units can be organized around a theme or topic, a single book, a book genre, an author or

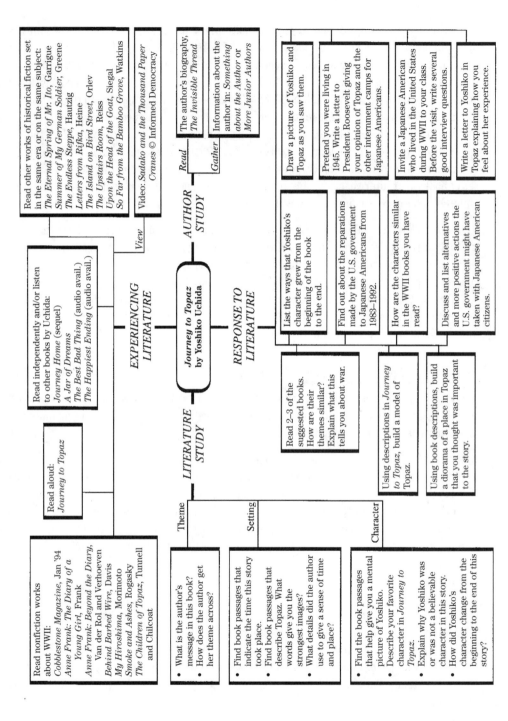

FIGURE 11.1  Literature Web

illustrator, or a literary concept or device. Specificity will vary according to the needs and experience of the teacher, but each day's plan usually includes the following components:

- *Objectives.* These are short-term aims that can conceivably be met by the end of the day or week. For example, a teacher writing a literature unit around Uchida's *Journey to Topaz* may state as an objective for the second week of his literature unit that he will read aloud Chapters 6–10 of this book. During that same week, a likely objective for his students would be that they note and share descriptions of characters' experiences in the various books of historical fiction that they are reading independently or in small groups, and that they begin to notice the attention to accuracy of details in works of historical fiction.

- *Procedures and methods.* This part of the unit tells what the teacher does, in what order, and with what materials. The procedures of the teacher conducting the *Journey to Topaz* unit may call for him to let the students choose a way to "put themselves in the shoes" of either the victims or the oppressors in the stories they are reading and to exhibit representative behavior by either group during these times. The teacher suggests some of the ways in which this might be done (dramatize a book episode, assume the persona of a book character and write a letter to the class, draw a scene as suggested in a book) and asks students to suggest other ways. Likewise, the teacher projects what materials are likely to be needed for these activities in order to have them on hand.

- *Evaluation.* Teachers must consider how they intend to evaluate each day's activities both in terms of how well they worked (a form of self-evaluation) and how well the students met the objectives.

Because units of study are several weeks long, they usually include a culminating activity that gives students an opportunity to reflect on what they have learned, review major points, and sometimes celebrate the focus of the unit in some way. Culminating activities for the *Journey to Topaz* unit might include table and bulletin board displays of books and other resources the students have read, artwork, poems, plays, letters, and stories written in response to these literary experiences, and a debate about the World War II internment issue.

An overall unit evaluation is valuable to a teacher, particularly if he or she intends to use the unit with another group of students. Revisions can make the unit even more successful in succeeding years. The unit plan should indicate how the unit will be evaluated.

Commercially developed literature units can be found. Beginning teachers may find good ideas in such resources but should avoid considering these units as complete or unalterable. Rather, you should tailor these prepared units to reflect your students' prior experiences, interests, and abilities, and your goals and objectives. Many of these commercially published units consist of little more than basal-like worksheets.

## LITERATURE   IN   THE   READING   PROGRAM

Teaching literature and teaching reading are similar in some respects: Both use similar materials— stories; both have the purpose of making meaning from texts; and both have the ultimate goal of a greater or deeper understanding of and response to the written text. Because of these similarities, literature and reading can be taught simultaneously.

A critical goal of teachers in grades K through 8 is to help students become literate—that is, to be able to read and write. Inservice and preservice teachers at the beginning of the twenty-first century will encounter two different approaches to literacy subscribed to in schools and teacher training institutions: the basal reader approach and the literature-based reading approach. Underlying the differences in these two approaches are the different learning theories upon which they are based. Your approach to literacy development will depend on your own philosophy of teaching and learning, that is, the ideas you believe in strongly enough to act on.

The philosophy you accept will affect many aspects of your teaching: the materials you choose and how you present them to your students, how you arrange your classroom furniture, the activities you engage your students in, how you behave in class, and how you encourage your students to behave. In the following discussion it is important to note the theoretical differences underlying each curriculum model in literature. You should begin to form your own philosophy of learning and literacy development.

## Literature-Based Reading

Literature-based reading is an approach to teaching reading through the exclusive use of trade books. The learning theory in which literature-based reading is grounded is that children learn by searching for meaning in the world around them, constantly forming hypotheses, testing them to determine whether they work, and subsequently accepting or rejecting them. For young children, language has meaning only when it is used in the context of *wholes* (stories, conversations, messages, etc.) and when they have sufficient prior knowledge to support the acquisition of new knowledge. Consequently, from the very beginning of literature-based reading instruction, children are presented with whole (not fragmented) language, mostly in the form of excellent stories. As they hear and see these stories, they naturally begin to form hypotheses about sound–symbol relationships, accepting those that seem to work and rejecting those that do not.

Teachers using the literature-based approach to reading will structure a classroom environment in which children are immersed in good literature. In these classrooms, children hear literature read aloud several times a day, they see good readers reading voluntarily, they discover that good books can entertain them and tell them things they want to know, and they constantly practice reading books that they themselves have chosen because they are interested in the topics.

Key elements of the literature-based reading classroom include the following:

- Daily reading aloud of good literature by the teacher
- Quantities of good trade books in the classroom (five or more books per child) selected to match specific interests and approximate reading abilities of the students in the class
- Reading experiences that stand on the merits of the literature alone (i.e., stories are not inevitably followed by exercises)
- Daily silent reading by students of books that they choose
- Daily opportunities for students to share their reactions to books orally
- Daily opportunities for students to respond to literature in a variety of ways, including writing, drama, and art
- Reading skills taught when needed and then within meaningful contexts, never in isolation
- Frequent individual student–teacher reading conferences (See the discussion of individual conferences in Chapter 12.)

Decisions about what to teach, when to teach it, and what materials to use are made by the teacher in the literature-based reading classroom. These decisions and the responsibility for materials selection and acquisition may make literature-based reading more demanding of teachers' professional judgment than other reading instruction methods; however, when it is managed well, this approach has proven to be very effective, not only in teaching students to read but also in creating a positive attitude toward reading. The stimulus of new and exciting materials and students' unique personal responses to them can make teaching less based on rote and more exciting.

The absence of a prescribed, lockstep program is one of the greatest strengths of literature-based reading, but it also makes this approach vulnerable to many abuses. The following practices have no place in the literature-based reading classroom:

- Using quantities of mediocre literature in the reading program solely on the basis of having them at hand and with no regard to their interest to students or their suitability to curricular goals
- Regularly using class sets of single trade books with a predetermined reading schedule and fill-in-the-blank worksheets (This practice is referred to as the "basalization of literature.")
- Reading works of literature by round-robin reading
- Selecting and assigning every title read by students
- Assigning book reports regularly under the guise of book response to check comprehension
- Excluding multicultural and international titles, poetry, and a balance of genres and character types from the classroom selection

There is no one right way to teach literature-based reading. The method cannot be packaged. Your best protection against bogus claims, materials, and practices is to have a complete understanding of the theory behind the practice. *Transitions* and *Invitations* by Routman (1988, 1991); *Literature-Based Reading Programs at Work,* edited by Hancock and Hill (1987); and *How to Teach Reading with Children's Books* by Veatch (1968) are a few of the excellent, practical resources available to provide this information.

Literature-based reading fits within a larger philosophy of teaching and learning called the *whole language approach.* Whole language is an entire philosophy about teaching and learning whose key tenets are materials that have meaning and relevance to students' lives, teachers who are colearners and resources rather than authoritarians, and a curriculum that is tailored by teachers to students' interests and talents. We believe that the potential for students to learn about literature is greatest in a whole language, literature-based classroom.

## Basal Reading Program Supplemented by Children's Literature

Just as children bring a variety of learning styles and needs to the task of learning, so do teachers bring a variety of teaching styles and needs to teaching. A single approach to teaching reading cannot suit all teachers or all students. The most common approach to the teaching of reading is the *basal reading approach supplemented by children's literature.*

The basal reading program has been the traditional approach to teaching reading in U.S. elementary schools for decades. According to Durkin (1987), it is "composed of a series of readers said to be written at successively more difficult levels" (p. 417). The core materials include a student reader, a teacher's manual, student workbooks, ditto masters, and tests. The strength of the basal program is that it provides teachers with an organized instructional framework upon which to build (Lapp, Flood, & Farnan, 1992). In other words, the teacher using this approach does not develop a reading program by selecting materials and planning the related activities. Basal reading programs offer teachers considerable guidance and help with the decisions and challenges involved in teaching children to read.

The learning theory upon which basal reading materials have been based for most of this century is that learning complex skills begins with mastering the simplest components of that skill before attempting the next larger components and so on until the whole skill is learned. In terms of learning to read, this means that the letters of the alphabet are learned first, followed by letter–sound patterns, words, and then sentences. Finally, when the components of reading are learned, whole works of literature, such as stories, plays, and poems, are read. As late as the beginning of the 1980s, the embodiment of this philosophy was the basal reader—with its emphasis on progressive skill and subskill mastery and its use of short and simple sentences and a controlled vocabulary. The concern with basals of the 1950s, 1960s, and 1970s was with the limitations of the story selections—specifically, the controlled vocabulary, the uninteresting plots, and the poor writing styles.

In the 1980s, U.S. publishers of basal readers made some changes in their products. These changes were made in response to two indicators: (1) criticism by teachers and teacher educators about the low literary quality and the lockstep system in basal readers and (2) the convincing literacy statistics from New Zealand (100 percent literacy), where a national literature-based reading program was begun over forty years ago. The quality of stories written specifically for the basal readers was improved. Multicultural characters began to appear in basal stories with more frequency than in the past. Most important, excerpts from high-quality trade books and some whole, albeit brief, literary works were integrated into basal readers. These changes were incorporated while retaining the skill-based instruction (particularly phonics instruction for beginning readers) that researchers regard as important to well-rounded reading programs (Anderson, Hiebert, Scott, and Wilkinson, 1985).

Even with these changes, basal readers are not designed to be a complete substitute for trade books. Even though some basal stories are good literature, not excerpted or adapted, the brevity of these selections is a problem for intermediate grades. Most students in these grades are capable of reading novel-length chapter books and should be doing so regularly in their school reading program. Students in classes where anthologies and basal readers are used exclusively are denied the all-important self-selection of reading material from a wide variety of books.

Perhaps basal readers are most effective when used in concert with a wide variety of trade books that reflect students' interests and reading abilities. In this arrangement, the basal reader provides guidance and structure to both teaching and learning, while the trade books provide the variety, opportunity for self-selection, and interest that motivates children to want to read.

Ideally, each teacher should be allowed to choose the approach to teaching reading that best suits his or her philosophy of learning and teaching style. In many school districts across the United States, however, the use of a basal approach to teach reading is mandated. Even so, many teachers in this situation have begun to move away from a slavish, "read-every-page-or-bust" attitude toward these programs. They have found ways to improve their teaching of reading by using their basal programs in innovative ways that eliminate some of the skills exercises of this approach and allow time for literature as well. Some guidelines drawn from the example of these teachers are as follows:

- Use only the best literary selections the basal offers. Substitute good trade literature for the rest.
- Let students read some of the better-written basal selections simply for enjoyment. It is the joy and wonder of reading marvelous tales or interesting information that motivate children to learn to

read, not the tests on their comprehension of these stories. Use the time saved from skill, drill, and comprehension questions for silent reading.

- Eliminate the stigma of ability grouping by forming one whole-class, heterogeneous reading group. Use the time saved from planning and conducting three or four different reading lessons to hold individual reading conferences.

- Use basal readers' phonics lessons and drills only when, in the teacher's opinion, an individual student or group of students will benefit from them. (This need is exhibited by students in their individual reading conferences and in their writing.) Children do not learn according to an imposed schedule, but only when they are ready to learn. Use the time saved from ineffective exercises to read aloud from good books or for silent reading from self-choice books.

- Avoid comprehension questions at the end of basal reading lessons that trivialize the stories or demean the students. Use the time saved to allow children to share their personal reactions to the story, to offer literary criticisms of the selection, or to respond to the story in writing, drama, or art.

- Make phonics instruction a regular but brief (10–15 minutes) part of primary-grade reading instruction. Avoid letting phonics instruction become the main attraction of reading. That role should be reserved for good stories.

## EVALUATING THE LITERATURE PROGRAM

Ongoing evaluation is part of responsible teaching, since it reveals strengths and weaknesses in instruction and indicates where revision is suggested. In today's schools, reading and mathematics skills are given the lion's share of attention in standardized evaluation programs, and all too often, no attention is paid to children's growth in literary understanding. But many teachers believe that student growth in literary understanding and appreciation is important and should be assessed. The question, then, is, How?

Well-known assessment methods include traditional paper-and-pencil testing, portfolio assessment, conferencing, and observing. Teachers have found the latter three most informative in assessing how well a literature program is meeting children's needs. Portfolio assessment and conferencing can leave information gaps, however, and do not necessarily assess the teacher's performance or the program itself. We find that observation, when carefully directed, provides a full description of the students' progress, the teacher's strengths and weaknesses, and the literature program. It is also the most efficient method of assessment, since it can be done while one is engaged in other tasks.

### Observation and Assessment of Student Learning

Evaluation of students in relation to a literature curriculum will focus mainly on the curriculum's effect on student behaviors rather than on the students' grasp of concepts. Consequently, the evaluation will be accomplished primarily by observing students rather than by testing them. An important principle to remember in planning for evaluation of teaching and learning is that evaluation must parallel the goals and objectives of the instructional plan. To look for conceptual understandings or behaviors in students when those concepts or behaviors have not been taught or encouraged is to invite failure and disappointment.

Experienced teachers often develop checklists to use in observation and assessment of various aspects of their literature programs. Also, generic checklists can be developed by teams of teachers and librarians at each grade level in a school and then may be tailored by individual teachers to fit their own specific plans.

*CHECKLIST FOR STUDENT INVOLVEMENT WITH BOOKS*   Some of the behaviors that teachers look for in their students' interaction with literature will vary by grade level and the students' development. Other behaviors will show up on checklists for all grade levels. For example, preschool or first-grade teachers would be likely to look for evidence that their students know the terms *author* and *illustrator*, use the terms correctly in their discussions of books, and recognize the work of specific authors and illustrators. Middle-grade teachers, on the other hand, would be more likely to look for evidence that students are choosing and reading novel-length stories independently. Teachers at all grade levels will be looking for evidence that their students are enjoying reading and voluntarily choosing to read. The following generic checklist gives an idea of what such an evaluation instrument might look like.

### Checklist for Student Involvement with Literature

| *Behavior* | Yes | No | *Comment* |
|---|---|---|---|
| *Reading* | | | |
| Student reads voluntarily and willingly | —— | —— | ——————— |
| Student enjoys reading | —— | —— | ——————— |
| Student reads during silent reading time | —— | —— | ——————— |
| Student reads for entertainment | —— | —— | ——————— |
| Student reads for information | —— | —— | ——————— |
| Student reads a variety of books and poems | —— | —— | ——————— |
| *Response to Literature* | | | |
| Student talks intelligently about books read or heard | —— | —— | ——————— |
| Student shares responses to books with peers | —— | —— | ——————— |
| Student is attentive during read-aloud sessions | —— | —— | ——————— |
| Student is able to discuss a book in terms of | | | |
| character | —— | —— | ——————— |
| plot | —— | —— | ——————— |
| setting | —— | —— | ——————— |
| theme | —— | —— | ——————— |
| style | —— | —— | ——————— |

## Checklist for Student Involvement with Literature    *(Continued)*

| Behavior | Yes | No | Comment |
|---|---|---|---|
| *Response to Literature (contd.)* | | | |
| Student is able to accept that different people may have different responses to the same story | —— | —— | _____ |
| Student is able to relate stories to personal experience, where applicable | —— | —— | _____ |
| *Selection of Literature* | | | |
| Student knows how to select appropriate books for independent reading | —— | —— | _____ |
| Student keeps a log of books read independently | —— | —— | _____ |
| Student is developing personal preferences in literature | —— | —— | _____ |
| Student tries new book genres | —— | —— | _____ |

*CHECKLIST FOR CLASSROOM ENVIRONMENT*    The environment of a classroom is determined mainly by what the resident teacher values in learning and teaching. These values, in turn, determine how the classroom is arranged, which materials are available, and what sorts of events and activities are regularly scheduled. The following checklist incorporates all of these features.

## Checklist for Promoting Literature through Classroom Environment

| Behavior | Yes | No | Comment |
|---|---|---|---|
| *Physical Plant* | | | |
| Desks are arranged to promote student-to-student discussion | —— | —— | _____ |
| Room arrangement provides quiet areas for reading and thinking | —— | —— | _____ |
| Reading area is well lighted | —— | —— | _____ |
| Reading area has comfortable seating | —— | —— | _____ |
| Reading area has adequate and convenient shelving for books | —— | —— | _____ |
| Reading area is well organized and orderly | —— | —— | _____ |
| Student response projects are displayed | —— | —— | _____ |

### Checklist for Promoting Literature through Classroom Environment    *(Continued)*

| *Behavior* | *Yes* | *No* | *Comment* |
|---|---|---|---|
| *Materials* | | | |
| Classroom has a trade book library | ___ | ___ | _____ |
| Classroom library is adequate in | | | |
| scope (variety of genres) | ___ | ___ | _____ |
| depth (variety of books within a genre) | ___ | ___ | _____ |
| quality (light reading for entertainment to excellent quality for study) | ___ | ___ | _____ |
| providing for varying reading abilities | ___ | ___ | _____ |
| recent books | ___ | ___ | _____ |
| multicultural and international books | ___ | ___ | _____ |
| poetry collections | ___ | ___ | _____ |
| Classroom has a temporary collection | ___ | ___ | _____ |
| Temporary collection | | | |
| addresses gaps in permanent collection | ___ | ___ | _____ |
| is exchanged regularly | ___ | ___ | _____ |
| provides for varying student interests | ___ | ___ | _____ |
| is coordinated with topics of study | ___ | ___ | _____ |
| Classroom library materials are | | | |
| easy for students to reach and reshelve | ___ | ___ | _____ |
| coded and organized logically | ___ | ___ | _____ |
| *Scheduling* | | | |
| Time is provided for self-choice reading every day | ___ | ___ | _____ |
| Time is provided for browsing and selection of books regularly | ___ | ___ | _____ |
| Time is provided for response to literature | ___ | ___ | _____ |

*CHECKLIST FOR TEACHING ACTIVITIES*    Success in making children lovers of books and reading certainly does not depend upon generous supplies of equipment or a certain physical lay-out, although these can facilitate the job. In the end, it is what the teacher does with literature that makes the biggest impression on children. Activities that make the learning experience positive and nonthreatening are generally the most successful with children. This point of view is evident in the following checklist of teaching activities.

## Checklist for Promoting Literature through Teaching Activities

| Teaching Activity | Yes | No | Comment |
|---|---|---|---|
| *Making Literature Enjoyable* | | | |
| Read aloud daily (high-quality literature) | ___ | ___ | _____ |
| Select books for read-aloud that reflect students' interests | ___ | ___ | _____ |
| represent a wide variety of genres | ___ | ___ | _____ |
| represent outstanding examples of each genre | ___ | ___ | _____ |
| Share poetry orally on a regular basis | ___ | ___ | _____ |
| Popular poets | ___ | ___ | _____ |
| NCTE Award–winning poets | ___ | ___ | _____ |
| Golden Age poets | ___ | ___ | _____ |
| Share stories through storytelling | ___ | ___ | _____ |
| *Motivating Students to Read* | | | |
| Introduce books regularly through booktalks | ___ | ___ | _____ |
| Encourage student response to literature by asking open-ended or divergent questions | ___ | ___ | _____ |
| by encouraging varied responses | ___ | ___ | _____ |
| oral response | ___ | ___ | _____ |
| written response | ___ | ___ | _____ |
| graphic response | ___ | ___ | _____ |
| Allow students to choose books for independent reading | ___ | ___ | _____ |
| Take class to school library weekly or more frequently for book browsing or selection | ___ | ___ | _____ |
| Take class to public library for a field trip | ___ | ___ | _____ |
| Invite a librarian to your class to booktalk and tell stories | ___ | ___ | _____ |
| *Modeling Reading Behaviors* | | | |
| Read during silent reading time | ___ | ___ | _____ |
| Talk enthusiastically about books read | ___ | ___ | _____ |
| Show students how to select books | ___ | ___ | _____ |

## Checklist for Promoting Literature through Teaching Activities   *(Continued)*

| *Teaching Activity* | *Yes* | *No* | *Comment* |
|---|---|---|---|
| *Showing the Relevance of Literature* | | | |
| Integrate literature across the curriculum | ___ | ___ | _____ |
| health/science | ___ | ___ | _____ |
| social studies/history | ___ | ___ | _____ |
| language arts/reading | ___ | ___ | _____ |
| mathematics | ___ | ___ | _____ |
| *Encouraging Literature Appreciation* | | | |
| Present a year-long literature curriculum | ___ | ___ | _____ |
| *Reaching beyond the Classroom* | | | |
| Send read-aloud suggestions to parents | ___ | ___ | _____ |
| Encourage parents to visit library with their children | ___ | ___ | _____ |
| Invite parents and community leaders to be guest readers for read-aloud | ___ | ___ | _____ |
| *Evaluation* | | | |
| Record student growth | | | |
| in understanding literary concepts | ___ | ___ | _____ |
| in choices of books to read | ___ | ___ | _____ |
| in attitude toward reading | ___ | ___ | _____ |

# IMPLEMENTING A SCHOOLWIDE CURRICULUM IN LITERATURE

Having a schoolwide curriculum in literature has many benefits for teachers and students and is worth pursuing. The main benefit to students is that their teachers' efforts will be coordinated from year to year. Repetition of content and titles will be avoided, and continuity will be improved. The main benefits to teachers are that ideas, expertise, and materials will be shared and planning will be facilitated by knowing what experiences with literature incoming students have had or should have.

The impetus for planning a schoolwide curriculum in literature often comes from one person or a small group of people who are committed to the idea. In your school, that person could be you. The task of developing a schoolwide literature curriculum, however, should be shared by a committee that has a representative from each grade level and the library media specialist. Having individuals on the committee who are knowledgeable about children's books is essential.

A literature curriculum committee's function is to determine what literature content will be presented at each grade level. A set of trade books appropriate for delivering the literature curriculum at each grade level can also be suggested by the committee, although the ultimate choice of books to be used in a classroom will be the individual teacher's decision. Literature curriculum committees often select and update their schoolwide read-aloud list. Such a list helps to prevent duplication of teachers' read-aloud choices at different grade levels and to assure that students hear a well-balanced selection of books over the years. Having such a list may also convince some teachers to begin a read-aloud program.

## The Library Media Center

The well-stocked, efficiently run library media center is the heart of a school, and the knowledgeable media center director has his or her finger on the pulse of each classroom. Gone are the days when the library was synonymous with dry speeches about the Dewey Decimal System and the proper way to do research reports. Lately, as literature-based reading and literature across the curriculum have gained acceptance, library media specialists and teachers have been moving toward a shared responsibility for teaching. They work as a team to provide students with the richest educational experience that their combined resources can provide. Teachers tell librarians their resource needs, and librarians help teachers by identifying and locating appropriate resources, keeping teachers updated with the newest literature and suggesting ways to present books to students. For these reasons, the librarian should be encouraged to play a key role in planning and developing a schoolwide curriculum in literature.

## Book Clubs

A marketing phenomenon of our times is the publisher-owned book club. These clubs send monthly catalogs to teachers who then distribute them to students, collect and process student book orders, and receive bonus points for each item ordered. Paperback books representing a full range of quality from award-winning books to joke books, posters, and stickers are offered at prices far below bookstore cost. Children and teachers who lack access to well-stocked libraries are especially dependent on these clubs. Another advantage of book clubs is that the selection, ownership, and reading of these books involves parents.

A national study revealed that book clubs are the major suppliers of reading matter used in literature-based language arts programs in U.S. elementary schools (Strickland & Sandmann, 1993). This study also revealed that the offerings of the major book clubs are heavy on popular, easy-reading fiction but that they also include books from all the major genres, books by major authors and illustrators from diverse cultural groups, and some books that could challenge the strongest readers. Being knowledgeable about children's literature enables you to help your students select the best book club titles. You can gently redirect children's choices from the "junk" offerings to the better books by going over the catalog with students and giving booktalks about the titles you recommend. Care should be given to verify topic and age appropriateness of any selections with which you are unfamiliar.

Teachers who participate in these clubs often use their bonus points to build their classroom book collections. With this in mind, you may want to subscribe to more than one club to have a wider choice of titles.

## Bookfairs and School Bookstores

Bookfairs and school bookstores are two ways in which schools can bring literature to children and their parents. Both entities are important in the overall development of a schoolwide literature curriculum. A bookfair is a book sale that is organized by a book vendor, such as a bookstore owner, and held in the school building for one or more days. Books are attractively displayed so that children and their parents can browse and select items for purchase. Bookfairs always call attention to literature and reading and can even be considered a reading motivator. They are especially appropriate in areas where there are no children's bookstores or well-stocked libraries.

Bookfairs send strong messages to children and their parents about a school's stance on reading and about what sorts of reading materials teachers and librarians in the school endorse. Children and parents who attend bookfairs in which joke collections, scented stickers, stamps, commercialized series books, coloring books, and posters are prominent will assume that this is what reading means to the teachers in these schools. Bookfairs in which a wide variety of good literature is prominent send an entirely different (and more defensible) message about reading to parents and children. Excellent bookfairs are the result of careful planning and active involvement in selection of books by teachers and school librarians. Book selection should not be left solely to the book vendor.

The school bookstore is a permanent part of the school. It is often a Parent–Teacher Organization project and is run by parent volunteers, but students and teachers are often enlisted or volunteer to help run the store. Most books are sold at cost, but arrangements are sometimes made for any profits to support a giveaway program in which students exchange credits for good performance in class for books.

Book selection is just as important to the school bookstore as to the school bookfair and for the same reasons. Teachers and librarians should be actively involved in selecting their bookstore stock and in advising parents on selections. Teachers who are involved in book selection can arrange for titles related to their unit themes and topics to be available in the bookstore.

## Parent Involvement

In most communities, parents and other adult members of students' families want to be involved in some way in their children's learning. In some instances parents are willing to help in classrooms on a regular basis. These people and their efforts must be integrated into the teacher's plans. In a school with an established curriculum in literature, teachers can develop a list of suggestions for using parent volunteers in the literature program. Such a list would be especially useful for new teachers. The ways in which parents can help teachers include the following:

- Listen to children read orally.
- Read aloud to small groups or individual students.
- Take children to the school library.
- Type, assemble, and bind the storybooks that children write.
- Read stories and poems on audiotapes for listening.
- Help to maintain the classroom library (code, repair, shelve, check out books).
- Fill out book club orders.

- Make book bags for carrying books back and forth from home.
- Type lists of good read-aloud books for children to take home and share with parents.

Parental involvement in literature also means getting support for the school reading program at home. Parents are almost always willing to promote their children's academic efforts at home if they are told how to do it. Many teachers give parents lists of activities that support reading, including brief, carefully worded explanations where necessary. Some typical suggestions include the following:

- Read to your child at night. (Lists of good read-alouds can be sent home regularly.)
- Listen to your child read aloud.
- Participate in shared reading with your child. (Shared reading techniques for beginning readers are explained in Chapter 12.)
- Take your child to the library to select books.
- Give books to your child as gifts. (Lists of good gift book suggestions can be sent home prior to birthdays and holidays.)

## Guest Authors and Illustrators

Professional children's authors and illustrators often visit schools to speak to children about their careers and their books. Teachers are usually instrumental in selecting, inviting, and organizing these visits. Guest authors and illustrators may be chosen on the basis of availability, but more often they are chosen because of the students' interest in their books or the relevance of their work to a topic that students are studying.

The standard procedure is to contact the marketing director or editor of the author's or artist's publishing house to determine availability and terms. Since most established children's authors and illustrators charge an honorarium and travel expenses, schools within a system often share the author and the costs.

Careful selection, previsit promotion and preparation, and scheduling can result in author or illustrator visits that are inspiring to all concerned. At the very least, planners will want to ensure that many copies of the guest's books are bought, distributed, and widely read by students for weeks before the guest arrives. As the day of the visit approaches, children can be led to think about and respond to the guest's books in many ways, to develop thought-provoking and worthwhile questions to ask the guest speaker, and to find out as much as possible about the individual. A visit from an author or illustrator can be the culminating event in an instructional unit or of an entire year-long literature curriculum. It deserves careful planning.

Many state reading associations have developed lists of children's authors and illustrators who live in state. These lists can usually be found in public libraries.

## Local Public Library

The community has no more valuable resource than its public library. Each time students, teachers, and parents seek the educational resources they need in their public libraries, the natural link between schools and public libraries is reaffirmed. Public libraries provide many services in addition to loaning books. Consider the impact of the following list of services.

- The interlibrary loan system, which gives patrons access to library holdings throughout the state, region, or nation
- Summertime reading programs for children
- Summertime bookmobile programs
- Special observances, such as National Book Week, Banned Book Week, and Hans Christian Andersen Day, which help to bring important literacy issues to the public's attention
- Story hour for young children
- Audiovisual versions of many books
- Guest appearances of authors and illustrators

Teachers can help to make the public library more effective by making students and their parents aware of the library and its programs and services.

## FIRST AMENDMENT RIGHTS OF CHILDREN

The First Amendment to the Constitution of the United States guarantees to its citizens the freedoms of religion, of speech, and of the press—collectively called "intellectual freedom." As adults, we cherish our right to choose our reading material and use it nearly every day of our lives. Elementary and middle-school social studies and civics textbooks proudly proclaim the freedom of choice that citizens of the United States have in their daily lives. But do we, as parents, teachers, and librarians, actually extend these rights to our children? Specifically,

- Do we allow children to make their own book choices, or do we make these choices or limit the reading materials made available to them?
- Do we listen to young readers' ideas about the books that they have read, or do we only ask them "comprehension" questions?
- Do we allow children to reject books that they do not like, or do we force them to read what we have chosen for them to read?
- Do we allow ourselves to be bullied by outspoken special-interest groups into taking good, but controversial, books off the library shelves, or do we stand by our convictions and book selections?
- Do we self-censor by only selecting books on "safe" topics, or do we select books on the bases of quality and age-appropriateness?

In other words, do we actually teach students, by our actions as well as by our words, about their First Amendment rights?

A study by Wollman-Bonilla (1998) of pre- and inservice teachers' ideas about acceptable and unacceptable children's books reveals a tendency toward teacher bias in book selection for children. The researcher found that teachers "commonly objected to texts that reflect gender, ethnic, race, or class experiences that differed from their own" (p. 289). This subtle form of censorship is made worse by the fact that most teachers are unaware of their own biases in text selection (Jipson & Paley, 1991; Luke, Cooke, & Luke, 1986). Wollman-Bonilla makes a strong point in favor of First Amendment rights for children when she concludes, "If we are to know how books actually affect children, we need to hear *children's* voices and understand *their* experiences before, during, and after reading" (p. 293).

## *Teaching the First Amendment*

Teaching children about their First Amendment rights is important today, because there are those who would take these rights away. Individuals, but more often organized groups from the political left and right, as well as conservative religious groups, want to assume power over what children read and learn. Their goal is to suppress anything that conflicts with their own beliefs. According to library media specialist Pat Scales (1995) "The problem is obvious. Censors want to control the minds of the young. They are fearful of the educational system because students who read learn to think. Thinkers learn to see. Those who see often question. And young people who question threaten the 'blind' and the 'nonthinkers' (p. 20).

The American Library Association's Office of Intellectual Freedom (www.ala.org/alaorg/oif/) monitors the challenges made against children's books in the United States. Most adults and children who have read the highly regarded books that often show up on the most challenged books lists find the reasons given for the challenges perplexing, if not incredible. For example, the following titles appeared on the Office of Intellectual Freedom's list of Most Frequently Challenged Children's Books for 2000:

The *Harry Potter* series by J. K. Rowling for having occult/Satanic and antifamily themes

The *Alice* series by Phyllis Reynolds Naylor for having sexual content and being unsuited to the age group

The *Scary Stories* series by Alvin Schwartz for having occult themes and violence and being unsuited to the age group

*The Giver* by Lois Lowry for being sexually explicit and having occult themes and violence.

An attempt by an individual or group to deny others access to a book is called a *challenge*. Most book challenges occur locally, and most fail. *Censorship* is the actual removal, suppression, or restricted circulation of literary, artistic, or educational materials on the grounds that they are morally or otherwise objectionable (Reichman, 2001). Censors want to make moral decisions for all others and, so doing, deny intellectual freedom not only to children, but also to those who often select books for children, such as teachers, librarians, and parents.

Often, individuals challenge books on the basis of a single word or phrase, or on hearsay, and have not read the book at all. Teachers and library media specialists have found that a written procedure is helpful for bringing order and reason into discussions with parents who want to censor school materials. Most procedures call for teachers and librarians to give would-be censors a complaint form and ask them to specify their concerns in writing. There are advantages to such a system: Both teachers and parents are given time to reflect on the issue and to control their emotions; and the would-be censor is given time to read the book in its entirety, if he or she has not done so already. Developing written procedures and complaint forms for dealing with a would-be censor are important tasks for the literature curriculum committee. Figure 11.2 presents a model form produced by the National Council of Teachers of English (NCTE) for reconsideration of a work of literature.

The American Library Association's Office for Intellectual Freedom has several publications about censorship such as Reichman's *Censorship and Selection: Issues and Answers for Schools* (2001) that provide important and helpful information to schools on this topic. (For a catalog of all ALA publications, write to ALA Publishing, 50 East Huron Street, Chicago, IL 60611 or visit the website given earlier

**FIGURE 11.2   Citizen's Request for Reconsideration of a Work**

Author _____ Paperback _____ Hardcover _____

Title _____

Publisher (if known) _____

Request initiated by _____

Telephone _____

Address _____ City _____ Zip Code _____

Complainant represents:

_____ Himself/Herself

_____ (Name Organization) _____

_____ (Identify other group) _____

1.  Have you been able to discuss this work with the teacher or librarian who ordered it or used it? _____ Yes _____ No

2.  What do you understand to be the general purpose for using this work?
    a.  Provide support for a unit in the curriculum? _____ Yes _____ No

    b.  Provide a learning experience for the reader in one kind of literature? _____ Yes _____ No
    c.  Other _____
        _____

3.  Did the general purpose for the use of the work, as described by the teacher or librarian, seem a suitable one to you? _____ Yes _____ No
    If not, please explain. _____
    _____

4.  What do you think is the general purpose of the author in this book? _____

5.  In what ways do you think a work of this nature is not suitable for the use the teacher or librarian wishes to carry out? _____
    _____

6.  Have you been able to learn what is the students' response to this work? _____ Yes _____ No

7.  What response did the students make? _____
    _____

8.  Have you been able to learn from your school library what book reviewers or other students of literature have written about this work? _____ Yes _____ No

9.  Would you like the teacher or librarian to give you a written summary of what book reviewers and other students have written about this book or film? _____ Yes _____ No

10. Do you have negative reviews of the book? _____ Yes _____ No

11. Where were they published? _____

12. Would you be willing to provide summaries of the reviews you have collected? _____ Yes _____ No

13. What would you like your library/school to do about this work?
    _____ Do not assign/lend it to my child.
    _____ Return it to the staff selection committee/department for reevaluation.
    _____ Other–Please explain
    _____

14. In its place, what work would you recommend that would convey as valuable a picture and perspective of the subject treated? _____

                    Signature _____ Date _____

*Source:* Committee on the Right to Read. (1982). *The students' right to read.* Urbana, IL: National Council of Teachers of English.

in this section). People for the American Way, an organization that provides advice and assistance in combatting school censorship, can be contacted at 2000 M St. NW, Suite 400, Washington, DC 20036.

The National Council of Teachers of English also offers a valuable document about censorship, *The Students' Right to Read* (Committee on the Right to Read, 1982), which explains the nature of censorship, the stand of those opposed to it, and ways to combat it. This document and the *Citizen's Request for Reconsideration of a Work* are available free of charge from NCTE Order Department, 1111 W. Kenyon Road, Urbana, IL 61801, or from the Internet at http://www.ncte.org/position/right.html.

In dealing with censorship attempts, teachers should let their actions be guided by two precepts: (1) A parent has the right to object to his or her child's reading or listening to a specific book, and that right should be respected; and (2) a parent does not have the right to deny everyone else the right to read or hear a book. Teachers often find that censorship problems can be solved by being flexible. For example, if a parent objects to a book that is being read aloud to his or her child, the teacher can allow that child to visit another classroom or the media center when the book is being read.

Teaching students about their First Amendment rights might begin by posting a copy of the First Amendment, having students read it, and then discussing what this amendment means to them and what its loss might mean to them. Lists of children's books that some have declared "objectionable," such as those listed previously, could be posted. Children who have read the books could discuss why they might have been found objectionable and why banning these books would violate their First Amendment rights. Children's and young adult fiction about censorship could be read and discussed. Good examples are *The Rebellious Alphabet* by Jorge Diaz, T*he Last Safe Place on Earth* by Richard Peck, *The Trials of Molly Sheldon* by Julian Thompson, and *Save Halloween!* by Stephanie Tolan. As teachers and librarians, we should do everything possible to promote the kinds of books that encourage critical thinking, inquiry, and self-expression, while maintaining respect for the views of others.

## REFERENCES

Anderson, R. C., Hiebert, E. H., Scott, J. A., & Wilkinson, I. A. (1985). *Becoming a nation of readers: The report of the commission on reading.* Champaign, IL: Center for the Study of Reading.

Baldick, C. (1990). *The concise Oxford dictionary of literary terms.* New York: Oxford University Press.

Bromley, K. D. (1991). *Webbing with literature: Creating story maps with children's books.* Boston: Allyn and Bacon.

Browning, E. B. (1902). Reading. In K. D. Wiggins and N. A. Smith, *Golden numbers.* New York: Doubleday.

Committee on the Right to Read (1982). *The students' right to read.* Urbana, IL: National Council of Teachers of English.

Durkin, D. (1987). *Teaching young children to read* (4th ed.). Boston: Allyn and Bacon.

Hall, S. (1990). *Using picture storybooks to teach literary devices: Recommended books for children and young adults.* Phoenix: Oryx.

———. (1994). *Using picture storybooks to teach literary devices: Recommended books for children and young adults* (Vol. 2). Phoenix: Oryx.

Hancock, J., & Hill, S. (1987). *Literature-based reading programs at work.* Portsmouth, NH: Heinemann.

Hedblad, A. (Ed.). (2001). *Something about the author* (Vol. 118). Detroit: Gale Research.

Jipson, J. and Paley, N. (1991) The selective tradition in children's literature: Does it exist in the elementary classroom? *English Education, 23,* 148–159.

Lapp, D., Flood, J., & Farnan, N. (1992). Basal readers and literature: A tight fit or a mismatch? In K. D. Wood & A. Moss (Eds.), *Exploring literature in the classroom: Content and methods* (pp. 33–57). Norwood, MA: Christopher-Gordon.

Luke, A., Cooke, J., & Luke, C. (1986). The selective tradition in action: Gender bias in student teachers' selections of children's literature. *English Education, 18,* 209–218.

Reichman, H. (2001). *Censorship and selection: Issues and answers for schools.* Chicago: American Library Association Editions.

Routman, R. (1988). *Transitions: From literature to literacy.* Portsmouth: Heinemann.

———. (1991). *Invitations: Changing as teachers and learners K–12.* Portsmouth: Heinemann.

Scales, P. (1995). Studying the First Amendment. *Book Links, 5*(1), 20–24.

Strickland, D., & Sandmann, A. L. (1993). Study shows teachers rely on book clubs for most K–5 literature. *The Council Chronicle: The National Council of Teachers of English, 2*(4), pp. 1, 6.

Veatch, J. (1968). *How to teach reading with children's books* (2nd ed.). New York: Richard C. Owen.

Wollman-Bonilla, J. E. (1998). Outrageous viewpoints: Teachers' criteria for rejecting works of children's literature. *Language Arts, 75*(4), 287–295.

# Developing Teaching Strategies

The teacher is the key to a well-planned, effective literature program. In the previous chapter, we addressed the long-term aspects of planning and preparing for the literature program. This chapter will focus on the strategies teachers need to carry out such a program. Having students experience and respond to literature are two major responsibilities that a teacher must assume to ensure a good literature program.

# E X P E R I E N C I N G    L I T E R A T U R E

Many teaching strategies can be used to provide students with opportunities to experience enjoyable, exciting, and thought-provoking literature. Students experience prose, poetry, fiction, and nonfiction (1) by having it read aloud to them by a skillful oral reader; (2) by reading it silently to themselves; (3) through shared reading activities with a parent, librarian, teacher, or peer; (4) through stories told to them; and (5) through other media such as audiotapes and videotapes.

## *Reading Aloud by Teachers*

Reading aloud to students is a powerful way to provide them with literary experiences; it is the centerpiece of a curriculum in literature. Beginning in their infancy and throughout their elementary school years and beyond, children should hear books read aloud. Although some teachers at the intermediate-grade level do not read aloud, this teaching strategy is just as important in the development of readers at this stage as it is in kindergarten.

Some of the more important reasons that teachers read aloud are as follows:

1. To share with students exciting and stimulating reading material that is beyond their reading ability, but well within their listening ability
2. To build background and interest in subject matter that will soon be taught in an upcoming content area unit of instruction
3. To introduce new genres of literature or new literary concepts, such as a particular element of fiction or poetry
4. To contribute to students' knowledge of their literary heritage by reading aloud the works of notable authors and illustrators, as well as the masterpieces of traditional literature
5. To assist students in developing their meaning vocabularies, their ability to comprehend connected discourse, and their ability to think critically
6. To make students aware of the delight to be found in books and poems—a delight that they can later provide to themselves through reading good books
7. To have the opportunity to share emotional, funny, exciting, and stimulating moments with students.

Three distinct aspects of the read-aloud experience need to be examined to make it as effective a teaching strategy as possible. Those aspects are (1) selecting the literature to read, (2) preparing the students for read-aloud time, and (3) reading the book aloud. Each aspect needs to be taken into consideration for a successful read-aloud experience.

*BOOK SELECTION*    No matter which book you choose to read aloud, it is essential that you first read the book to yourself. When you preread a book, you can determine whether you find the story enjoyable and worthy of children's time and whether you believe it is of an appropriate level of difficulty for your students. You also can begin to note ways in which the story lends itself to student response.

Over the course of a school year you will want to read aloud a variety of literature: poems, short, stories, picture books, and chapter books of different genres and types. You will also want to ensure that there is a balance of males and females as main characters in the books and that the main characters come from different backgrounds and settings, including multicultural and international ones.

The most recognized works in children's literature, though sometimes complex, deserve to be shared with students over the course of their elementary school years. When a book or poem is challenging for students, you need to be prepared to guide the students' understanding. Without this help, many children would never experience and enjoy some of the more difficult but worthy pieces of literature. Conversely, you will want to avoid choosing books for reading aloud that students can and will consume eagerly on their own, reserving those books for students' independent reading.

When first reading aloud to a new class, however, you will want to start with shorter and easier works, known to be popular with students, and gradually build up to longer and more challenging works as you become better acquainted with your students, their interests, and their abilities. For more discussion of students' preferences in literature, refer to Chapter 1, "Learning about Children and Their Literature," and Chapter 3, "Poetry and Plays."

*PREPARATION*   Once a selection is made, the next step is to prepare the class for read-aloud time. For students to profit from read-aloud experiences, they need to be attentive. You can prepare students for reading aloud by having them remove distractions, such as pencils and other objects, from their immediate vicinity; by having them sit quietly in the designated place for read-aloud time; and by asking them to be ready to listen. If the book has concepts that you believe will baffle your students, you may want to clarify their meaning before beginning to read.

Introduce the book by stating the title, author, and illustrator of the book, even with the smallest children. This will teach children that books are written by real people called authors and that the illustrations are made by people called illustrators. Sometimes you may want to ask the students to predict what they believe the story will be about from looking at the cover and the title; other times you may want to explain briefly why you chose this book to read to them. For example, you may say that you are going to read this book because "it's another story by one of our favorite authors, William Steig" or that "the book will tell us more about what it was like to live on the prairie in the nineteenth century." Introductions should be kept short. They serve the purpose of preparing students to be attentive to and interested in the story.

In preparing for reading aloud, some teachers set up a tape recorder so that they can record the read-aloud sessions. The tapes may be used by students who were absent and by other students who enjoy hearing repetitions of the story while following along in the book. Next, strategies for reading picture books and chapter books aloud need to be considered.

*READING PICTURE BOOKS ALOUD EFFECTIVELY*   Consider the following steps:

- Position yourself close to the class so that all students can see the pictures. Many teachers choose to have students gather on the floor (if it is carpeted) in a semicircle around the teacher, who sits in a low chair just above them. In this way the students can approach more closely than they can on chairs or at desks.
- Show the pictures as you read the book. Most teachers accomplish this by holding the book out to the side where both students and teacher can see it at the same time. If you find this method unmanageable, you can turn the book back and forth for you, and then for the students, to see each page. Some primary-grade teachers become expert at upside-down reading and can hold the book in front of them while reading it. Whatever system you use will be fine as long as students see the pictures as you read the book. Remember that in a good picture book the text and pictures are

carefully integrated to convey the story as a whole. Hearing and seeing picture books should be simultaneous.

- After the introduction, begin reading the book aloud, placing emphasis on the meaning of the story. Think of reading aloud as a type of mini–dramatic performance. Read enthusiastically and provide drama through taking on different voices for different characters, pausing for effect at exciting moments, and varying your voice in pitch (low to high), in volume (soft to loud), and in pace (slow to fast). Good oral readers often start the reading with a soft voice, of medium pace and pitch, so that as the story builds they can alter pitch, volume, and pace for special effects.

- Your body movements and facial expressions can also be used to enhance the drama of the read-aloud experience. Leaning forward during a scary, suspenseful part of a story and smiling or chuckling during a funny part can convey to the students your involvement in the story.

- Maintain eye contact with your students. Be sure you are aware of their nonverbal responses to this reading experience. Good eye contact with the students helps you to maintain class control and permits you to observe when a word of explanation may be needed.

- Read the book from beginning to end without interruptions except on an as-needed basis. Constant interruptions of the story by too many explanations or side comments interfere with the students' enjoyment of the story. On the other hand, if an illustration has a key element that needs to be observed if the listeners are to understand the story, then pointing it out when you are on that page may be worthwhile. If a child makes a spontaneous comment, you should recognize the response quickly and go on. Interruptions by the teacher should be made only to prevent confusion, misunderstanding, or longer interruptions by students.

- Some books, such as concept books and interactive books, do call for interruptions in the read-aloud process. This is particularly true for informational books.

*READING CHAPTER BOOKS ALOUD EFFECTIVELY*    Many of the same considerations discussed in reading aloud picture books also hold true with chapter book read-alouds. Of course, chapter books have few, if any, illustrations, so holding the book for students to see the pictures is not necessary. In addition, chapter books are usually read aloud over a relatively long period of time, from a few days to many weeks. Often, teachers find reading novel-length chapter books aloud challenging, and sometimes not successful.

In a qualitative study on reading aloud in grades 4 to 6, Lynch-Brown and Tomlinson (1988) found that experienced teachers include four identifiable phases in the process of reading novel-length chapter books aloud successfully:

1. *Orientation*.
   This brief, pre-book phase of the read-aloud experience includes an introduction of the author and title of the book, predictions about the story based on the title, statements by the teacher on the story setting, location of the story setting on a map, and elicitation of student knowledge of the time and place of the setting. This orientation phase is completed during the first session of the read-aloud experience; then the teacher begins reading aloud.

2. *Exposition*.
   This phase typically lasts from four to seven days. It is a period of protracted reading aloud, involving few planned extension activities. At this point, it is as though the teacher allows the book to get

its grip on the students' imaginations and does not want to break the spell of the book with any diversions. Teachers note students' nonverbal responses, such as facial expressions or restlessness, which might indicate confusion or lack of understanding, and quickly supply any clarification or information needed. In this phase, as throughout, students are given the opportunity to share their responses to the book.

The teachers view this phase as a difficult but important period for bringing the students into the story. Some teachers help their students through this period by summarizing the story events at the end of each day's reading during the first several days. Some teachers report negative student reactions to the stories during this phase until the establishment of characters, setting, and problem is supplanted by the rising action of the plot with the conflict and suspense reaching full play.

3. *Extension.*

During this phase, the teacher generally reads the middle and end of the story. Students are thoroughly engrossed in the story at this point and want the teacher to read on as quickly as possible. A characteristic of this phase is that enrichment activities are interspersed with the oral reading by the teacher. In contrast to the activities seen in the exposition phase, these activities tend to carry the students beyond the book.

4. *Completion.*

Like the orientation phase, this phase is quite brief, generally confined to one session beginning after the oral reading is finished. During this phase, the teacher encourages students to discuss their affective responses to the completed book to interpret and savor it. In this phase the teacher conducts brief activities sufficient to bring closure to the read-aloud experience without giving the flavor of a rehash.

Following are some practices that teachers have used successfully during the exposition and extension phases of chapter book read-alouds to help hook the students on the book and to keep them tuned in and involved.

- Keep a chart of the characters—their names, relationships, and roles in the story—as the characters appear. This strategy is especially helpful if the story has a large number of characters. For example, in *The Westing Game* (1978) by Ellen Raskin, the many characters of this mystery must be remembered for the plot to make sense.
- Design and display a map of the story setting to track the events of the story in sequence. In most quest fantasies this visual aid can assist students in following the characters' journey for the quest.
- Develop a time line, somewhat like a horizontal mural, on which the dates are set at intervals above the line and the story events placed below the line at the appropriate date. For historical fiction and biographies, a time line can serve as a mnemonic device for the storyline as well as for the historic events of the era. For this purpose, the dates and historic events would be noted on a third tier of the time line.

Although each teacher may handle the chapter book read-aloud situation differently, all teachers in the 1988 study took their cues from the students and from the book, letting students' verbal and nonverbal responses and the plot and setting of the book guide them in their choice of strategies.

## Silent Reading by Students

Another way for students to experience good literature is to read it to themselves. Indeed, the ultimate goal of a literature program is to turn students into readers who, of their own free will, read self-selected good literature with enjoyment, understanding, and appreciation. To assist students in becoming independent, lifelong readers, teachers in grades K–8 need to set aside time each day for students to read silently in these formative years of reading development. The amount of time for silent reading must be tailored to the reading attention spans of students. Kindergarten and first-grade students may spend only five to ten minutes reading independently, but fourth- and fifth-grade students will often read silently for up to an hour.

Many schools have instituted sustained silent reading (SSR) programs on a schoolwide basis in order to promote the reading habit in students. In these SSR programs a certain time each day is set aside for all students, teachers, librarians, coaches, principals, custodians, and office and kitchen staff to take a "reading break." The philosophy behind SSR programs is that students need to see adults who read and who place a high priority on reading. In SSR programs, students read materials of their own choosing and are not required to write book reports or give oral reports on these materials.

Whether or not you are in a school that has an SSR program, you will want to provide your students with silent reading time each day. Teachers often indicate that their students have time to read because they can read as soon as their other work is finished. This practice is not adequate in that generally the same students never finish their work and, of course, never have time to read; and these are sometimes the very students who most need encouragement to become avid readers.

Here are some tips for having successful silent reading periods.

- Have a well-stocked classroom collection of books—poetry books, plays, picture books, novels, and information books. See Chapter 11 for more information on this topic.
- Conduct booktalks regularly so that students become aware of books they may wish to read. These booktalks can be given by teachers and librarians. Many librarians keep a file of booktalks they have given and will gladly serve as resource people for teachers.
- Use other techniques to introduce books to students. For example, displaying new books attractively in the classroom and showing videos of notable authors talking about their books and craft are effective in "selling" books to children.
- Schedule the same time each day for silent reading and adhere to it. Permit no activities other than silent reading during this time. Allow enough time for students to get well into their books and to achieve some level of satisfaction from the reading.
- Insist on attentiveness to books during this time. With primary-grade students, quiet talking in pairs about books or individual lipreading aloud may be on-task behavior, but children in intermediate grades can probably read silently and should be expected to do so.
- Spend the silent reading period engrossed in books, setting yourself as an example of a reader. Be knowledgeable of and interested in the books the students are reading.
- Provide students with an opportunity to talk *voluntarily* with you or one another about their books after the silent reading period is over.

## Booktalks

A booktalk is an oral presentation by a teacher, a librarian, or a student who tells about a book to stimulate the students' interest and motivate them to read it. Booktalks are not book reports, analyses of the author's style, or the old-fashioned book report that discusses characters, setting, theme, and plot (Bodart, 1980). Booktalks have been used effectively for years by librarians who have developed this strategy into an art for the purpose of encouraging students to check out books from the library. Teachers can give booktalks on five to ten books each week from their classroom and school library collections; in this way, they can entice students to read and experience good literature.

Booktalks can be given on any book, but they are especially needed to inspire students to read chapter books. Because chapter books take longer to read and have few illustrations, students appreciate booktalks on the books' content to assist them in making wise reading choices. Booktalks can be judged a success when students read the books following the booktalks.

Some teachers who give frequent booktalks also advocate having students give booktalks to induce other students to read the suggested books. A regular feature of *Reading Rainbow,* the public television program about children's books, is children giving booktalks. One teacher taped two or three of these *Reading Rainbow* booktalks and showed them in class to help her students learn how to give good booktalks. The following are recommendations for giving a good booktalk.

- Read the book before trying to do a booktalk on it.
- Choose books that you have liked, wholly or in part, or that you think your students will enjoy. Sincere enthusiasm for a book is stimulating and infectious.
- Have the book available to show to the students as you give the booktalk. Format aspects—such as cover illustrations, length, size, and shape of the books—which also influence book choices, can be weighed by students only if they can see the book.
- Keep the booktalk brief, generally no more than two or three minutes. Do not tell too much about the book or the students will see no reason to read it. For most books, four to six sentences will suffice. At first you will want to write out your booktalks until you have a sure feel for how to give them.
- Tell the topic and something about the action in the story, but *do not tell the plot.* Feature a scene or character that the story revolves around, but do not discuss the scene that gives away the ending.
- Feature a short excerpt from the book. You can read aloud an interesting beginning of the book or a suspenseful event, but the outcome is, of course, not told.
- Compare the book with other books known to the students, suggesting that if they liked a certain book they may enjoy this one. Other times you may wish to point out that the book is by a favorite author; you may recall for the students the other titles by the author.
- Booktalk a group of books that share the same theme; in this case you will want to talk briefly about each book and how it fits with the others.

The following is an example of a short booktalk:

*The Slave Dancer* (1973) by Paula Fox. Back in the 1800s, Jessie Bollier played his fife on the docks of New Orleans for spare change from passersby. But one day he was thrown into a canvas bag and taken aboard a slave ship destined for Africa. The ship's captain wanted a fife player on board so that the black slaves who were going to be transported back from Africa would exercise and remain healthy on the return trip. Thus, Jessie, a white boy, found himself to be the first slave on board. The story of Jessie's journey and the people he met—some of them cruel and some kind—are told in this book, *The Slave Dancer,* which is based on an incident that really happened.

After you have given the booktalk, place the book back on the reading table for students to peruse and to consider for reading. Over time, you should give booktalks on a variety of books at different levels of reading difficulty, on different topics, and with male and female protagonists from many cultures. In this way, you will appeal to the wide range of interests and abilities that exist among students in a classroom.

## Storytelling

Storytelling is the oldest medium for sharing literature. Oral literature flourished for thousands of years before writing was invented and books became commonly available. When a teacher tells stories, another delightful means for children to experience literature becomes available to the class. By bringing stories to life through personal expression and interpretation, a storyteller establishes a close communication with the audience. A storyteller begins by selecting a good story. Next, she practices it until she is able to tell it with ease and then tells it to different audiences again and again.

*SELECTION OF A STORY*    Good stories take time to find. First, you must genuinely like the story. To find possible stories for telling, begin with collections of folktales and short stories. Read some of these until you find a few you especially like. Then consider these two points:

- The first stories you tell should take no longer than ten minutes. As you develop your storytelling gifts, you may want to tell longer stories.
- Good stories for telling usually have few characters (from two to five), high conflict, action that builds to a climax, and a quick conclusion that ties together all the threads of the story. Humorous elements are also worth seeking.

A good resource for teachers and students in grades 4 and above who want to tell stories more formally is Anne Pellowski's *The Storytelling Handbook: A Young People's Collection of Unusual Tales and Helpful Hints on How to Tell Them* (1995), illustrated by Martha Stoberock.

*PREPARATION FOR TELLING*    Once you have selected a story to tell, outline the story content in terms of the plot. Many storytellers note on 3" × 5" cards the title and source of the tale, the characters' names and story events, and any other information that may be helpful. These cards can then be consulted quickly just before one tells a story. A story file can be a nice resource to keep as more stories are prepared for telling. One storyteller tapes her stories and then uses them to refresh her memory for later retellings.

*PRACTICE*    Tell the story aloud to yourself again and again. Do not memorize the story, but keep in mind the characters and sequence of main story events. Each time you tell the story, it will change a bit, becoming more and more your own story as you include personal touches.

The children's imaginations and your voice and facial expressions are the foundations for good storytelling experiences. Some storytellers find props useful; others believe that props diminish the closeness between audience and storyteller. If used, props should enhance the story, not overpower or distract from it. Experiment with props to find out what works best for you. They can be simple (a hat, a stick-on mustache, or a stuffed toy) or more elaborate (a mask, a puppet, or a costume).

When puppets are used, a separate puppet is made for each character and is held by the storyteller while the character speaks. Puppets can be purchased or made by the storyteller. Another more elaborate use of props is the feltboard story—a storytelling aid some teachers especially enjoy. Pictures or objects are attached to a feltboard or display board and are moved around during the story. Cumulative stories, especially, lend themselves to feltboard presentations.

The art of storytelling can be developed with practice. Teachers who tell stories in their classrooms report that their students are appreciative listeners and soon begin telling stories themselves.

## Shared Reading

*Shared reading* is a term we use to describe a number of teaching strategies that attempt to draw on the natural literacy learning that has long occurred in book-loving homes around the world. These various strategies—shared-book experience, assisted reading, and paired reading—provide children with opportunities to experience good literature as they are learning to read. The strategies have in common a semistructured modification of the parent-child interaction with repeated readings of favorite books as the child gradually acquires an understanding of print and its relationship to our sound system or to the words we speak. A list of predictable books suitable for use in shared reading activities can be found at the end of Chapter 4, "Picture Books."

The rhythm and sound elements of poetry make it an especially useful vehicle for the teaching strategy of shared reading that is used with beginning readers. A resource for the classroom is John Ciardi's *You Read to Me, I'll Read to You* (1962), a book of poems designed for shared reading.

***SHARED-BOOK EXPERIENCE***   Don Holdaway is well known for proposing an adaptation of the home-learning experience. He proposed the shared-book experience and developed Big Books, enlarged-text books of approximately 24" × 30", to replicate a natural home-learning strategy with groups of beginning readers in school settings. A typical classroom teaching–learning sequence of shared-book experience as proposed by Holdaway (1982) can be summarized in five steps:

- *Opening activity.* Favorite poems and songs are repeated by the students and teacher while the teacher points to the text of a Big Book. Then a new poem or song is taught.
- *Review of a familiar story.* The teacher and students review a favorite story in an enlarged format. This story is used to teach skills in context. Students participate by saying the story in unison. Sometimes the story is then informally dramatized.
- *Language play.* The teacher involves the students in alphabet games, rhymes, and songs that use letter names. The purpose is to have fun with words and sounds and to avoid isolated phonic drills.
- *Presentation of a new story.* The teacher and students read aloud a new story from a Big Book. The teacher encourages students to use word-solving strategies (contextual clues and prediction) to confirm words that are new to them.

- *Output activities.* Students read independently from a wide selection of favorites, participate in art activities stemming from the new story, and compose original stories, often using structures from the new story. Sometimes, several children enjoy playing school—one acting as teacher—while they read a favorite story together. (p. 299)

This sequence encapsulates the strategy developed by Holdaway and his colleagues in New Zealand to use children's books in classrooms in a manner similar to the one used by many parents whose preschoolers readily and naturally learned to read.

*ASSISTED READING*   The natural reading approach has been adapted for various situations. For example, Hoskisson, Sherman, and Smith (1974) proposed *assisted reading* as a one-to-one strategy for use with impaired readers. In assisted reading, the child and the adult sit side by side with a book. The child reads aloud until she or he has difficulty, at which point the adult supplies the word.

*PAIRED READING*   *Paired reading* is guided practice with an adult who reads in a soft voice and invites the child to fill in words when the adult pauses and the child knows the word. Paired reading can also be enjoyed by two children of compatible personalities who read back and forth to one another.

In all of these strategies, well-chosen literature is important; the nature of the experience is companionable, not authoritative; and the child reader must see the text and hear the words simultaneously. Sometimes, the adult places a finger under each word as it is being read to draw the child's attention to the print. Selecting favorite, loved stories is essential because the success of these strategies is contingent on frequent rereadings of the same book. Although the primary purpose of these strategies is to provide a favorable situation in which children can acquire literacy, the effect of the strategies can be the promotion of a love of literature.

## Literature across the Curriculum

Students may also experience good literature in other content area classes, such as social studies, science, and health, when teachers supplement or replace textbooks with trade books for instruction. In this way, trade books can enhance the teaching of other subjects while providing students with rich literary experiences. The use of literature to teach content area subjects is not new, but it is becoming a more frequent practice in schools as teachers discover the wealth of trade books suitable for their content curricula. Many advantages accrue to content-area teachers who incorporate trade books into their teaching.

Trade books make social studies content more memorable because the stories are presented from a child's point of view. Children see the world through a narrative framework. In learning about their world, stories and narrative are more real to children than informational texts. Children are more likely to understand history if it is presented as a story with characters, settings, and events. Later, they move from an interest in the narrative to an interest in the history itself.

Trade books also permit students to read multiple perspectives on topics, which helps them develop critical thinking. Comparing historical information from various sources is a valued practice that helps students encounter differing perspectives on any particular era of history. Students may start with the textbook, then research the facts from other books, or read a work of fiction and then seek to verify to what extent the facts within the story are accurate. In addition, trade books couch political and social events in terms of the moral events related to them. Children can see how these events affected the lives of real people and can better understand the morality underlying their choices. Unlike textbook authors who must write to please all viewpoints, authors of children's literature are more likely to face controversial issues head-on.

Trade books can benefit all subjects. For example, many trade books on health and science present information in interesting ways through graphs, tables, figures, authentic photographs, and other visual presentations, coupled with a lively style of writing in the text. Comparison of information from different sources can be readily provided when students are not limited to a single source for their information. Teachers who support the whole language philosophy draw on materials of various types for their instruction. They have discovered that literature has the power to educate the mind, while enlightening the spirit and warming the heart.

## Bibliotherapy

*Bibliotherapy* is the use of selected books to help children deal with their social and emotional problems and, at the same time, to experience good literature. The practice is controversial because of the possibility of its misuse by teachers and librarians untrained in clinical psychology. The technical meaning of the term *bibliotherapy* is the use of books by professionally trained therapists in treating emotionally disturbed individuals. Most teachers and librarians are not trained as psychologists, and misguided bibliotherapy may damage students. In addition, using books to guide students' lives could become an extremely didactic practice. If books are always or often selected to correct students or to preach to them about something we want them to change in their lives, students may rebel against reading itself. This would defeat the purpose of the bibliotherapy and could result in a dislike of reading and books.

On the other hand, we know that our students benefit psychologically from reading and talking about powerful stories and the thoughts, feelings, and actions of characters in these stories. Children all face difficult situations at times; discovering that other children have faced similar problems is reassuring. Learning how others have coped successfully with problems gives children confidence that they too will be able to solve problems that may arise later in their lives.

Stories of many different genres and types may offer useful insights to students. Realistic fiction stories can help children realize that everyone faces problems in life—neighborhood bullies, siblings, social rejections. By reading about the problems others face, children can be better prepared to confront the challenges of their own lives. Through fantasy, children's imaginations are set free to explore creative solutions to life and how it may be lived. Biographies of famous people can provide students with role models and can make students realize that, by setting goals for themselves, they may achieve beyond their present life situations.

A strategy for bibliotherapy sometimes used by teachers is to read aloud a story that may have indirect application to a problem occurring in the classroom. For example, if groups of students are being cliquish and cruel to certain students on the playground, the teacher might read Eleanor Estes's *The Hundred Dresses (1944)*, the story of a girl ostracized by other girls in her class, or Brock Cole's *The Goats (1987)*, the story of a boy and a girl at camp who are singled out for rejection and mistreatment by other campers. Books like these can help students to develop understanding and empathy. Care should be taken that the situation described in the book is not so close to the real one that students will recognize it as such, because this could cause embarrassment for the ostracized students. Discussion in class of how the students think they might feel if they were similarly mistreated may help them to develop awareness and understanding of the effects of their unkind behaviors. With sensitive and caring teachers and librarians, bibliotherapy in its informal sense lends itself to a natural use of literature. Bibliotherapy in its technical sense should, however, be left to professional therapists.

### Audiotapes, Videotapes, and CD-ROM Storybooks

Many tapes are available today to bring literature to students. Recently, some well-known actors have made excellent audio recordings of favorite children's stories. Animated and iconographic videos are also readily available. *Animated videos* are cartoons or images that move; *iconographic videos* are films in which the camera moves over static illustrations. A few videos are movies based on children's books, performed by actors. Predictably, these selections vary widely in quality.

Some audiovisual media re-creations are artistically well done and deserve to be considered as another means for students to experience literature. It is generally preferable to have students read the book first and form their own images of the story. Then, after viewing the tape, students can make comparisons between the book and the tape.

Audiotapes and videotapes are usually available in school libraries, through school districts' media repositories, or from nearby public libraries. Book clubs sometimes offer audiotapes to teachers with the purchase of a certain number of books by the class.

CD-ROM multimedia storybooks, also referred to as electronic storybooks, are becoming more widely available. An advantage of electronic storybooks is that they appeal to most children and permit their independent reading to become more interactive. An electronic story can provide scaffolding for a child when no adult is available to guide reading. One disadvantage is that electronic storybooks may interfere with the child's development of print concepts; another is that the interactive options of CD-ROM storybooks may distract students from the meaning of the story (Labbo & Reinking, 2000). When one selects electronic storybooks for classroom use, one should take into consideration the quality and appropriateness of the literature itself. The best CD-ROM storybooks can add variety and interest to a classroom literature collection.

## RESPONDING TO LITERATURE

When students experience a story by listening to it, by reading it, or by viewing it, they may naturally wish to respond or express their reactions to the experience in some way. In sharing their responses with others, students profit by recapturing the experience through translating it to a new form or medium; they develop a better understanding of what they experienced by organizing and deepening their feelings and thoughts on the experience; they discover that other readers' experiences with the same book may not have been the same as theirs; and they bring closure to the experience.

Although it is important to give students opportunities to respond to books, not every book needs or merits a lengthy response. The peals of laughter and the moans of sorrow during the actual reading of the story are sometimes response enough. But with other books, students need opportunities to explore further their thoughts and feelings. Teachers can elicit student responses to literature through oral expression, written expression, and the graphic arts.

## *Oral Response*

Students love to talk, and what better to talk about than a sincerely felt, shared book experience? Rosenblatt (1978) reminds us that no two people have the same prior experiences and that it is the transaction that occurs between the text, the reader, and the present context that provokes a particular response. Teachers may generate opportunities for students to share their individual insights to literary experiences in many different ways.

*DISCUSSIONS*   Perhaps the most often used means of eliciting students' responses is through discussions. Whole-class discussion usually accompanies the reading aloud of a book to the class. In these discussions, comprehension is assumed and the discussion centers on the different ways students feel and think about the book, its characters, its events, and its outcome. Thus, to stimulate a good class discussion, a teacher will encourage students to share their individual responses to open-ended questions; the teacher will not seek supposedly right answers in order to check comprehension or recall. In a class discussion, the teacher has the pivotal role as discussion leader. The discussion tends to be a teacher-to-students, students-to-teacher format. And with a large class, only some of the students will have an opportunity to express their viewpoints.

Another format for students to discuss their responses to literature is the *literature response group.* In literature response groups, students share their responses with peers about a book they have read as a group or a book read aloud by the teacher to the whole class. One of the goals of literature response groups is to have all children learn to work with one another and to value the opinions and views of others.

Groups can be established by the desire to read the same book, by friendship, by heterogeneous assignment by the teacher, or by random assignment. Small groups are usually set up with two to six students for optimal functioning. Students who have less skill working in groups often function better in dyads or triads. The small group discussion is a student-to-student form of communication that permits students more control over the discussion and more roles to perform as group members. For example, students may assume the role of leader, recorder, arbiter, listener, or devil's advocate. The advantages of small group discussions are that students are in control, have more opportunities to express their opinions, and can become more actively involved. Unless students have been taught to work together, however, groups do not function well. Small group model discussions with the teacher as a participating member and joint planning by teacher and class before groups begin working can enable the group to set rules, goals, and time lines.

*Individual conferences* between a teacher and a student are another means of discovering students' responses to literature. Although a teacher may choose to set up conferences daily, occasional conferences in which the student comes prepared to talk about a book she has recently finished can be instructive for the teacher and motivating for the student. The conference is focused on what the student thought and felt about the book. Some teachers ask the student to read aloud a favorite part of the story and tell why it was selected. Individual conferences are from five to ten minutes long and usually end with considering the next book the student will read or the response activity the student has planned (Veatch, 1968).

Eliciting a good discussion with substantial student participation is not an easy art. First of all, it is essential to remember that comprehension of the story is assumed and that the teacher's (or group leader's) purpose is not to test the students on the meaning of the story. Beyond this, certain strategies for promoting discussions need to be considered for use in leading class discussions, in guiding literature response groups, and in interacting with students in individual conferences. Whether you, as the teacher, will be leading the discussion or guiding your students in the art of discussion leader, the questions to be posed are very important. The purpose of discussions of fiction, then, is to elicit students' responses to the work, in other words, to find out what the students think about the story and feel about the story.

*QUESTIONING*    Common sense tells us that a question that can be answered by "yes," "no," or a single word or phrase will not lead to an interactive discussion. The question, "Did you like the story?" may result in a simple "yes." "Which part of the story did you like best and what did you like about it?" is likely to elicit a more detailed response.

Divergent questions have no one right answer but a number of possible answers. They naturally provoke more discussion than convergent questions, for which only one answer is correct. Examples of each of these question types follow. They are tailored to the book *Sylvester and the Magic Pebble* (1969) by William Steig.

- "Was Sylvester turned into a rock or a lion?" ("A rock.") This question is convergent; it can be answered by a single word.
- "What did you think would happen to Sylvester after he became a rock?" ("I thought he would get rolled down the hill and the pebble would tumble on top of him and he would turn back into a donkey." "I thought he would have to be a rock forever." "I thought his dad would find the magic pebble and turn him back into a donkey.") This question is divergent; it stimulates many different answers, each of which is possible or correct. The response to this question results in more than a single word or phrase.
- "Who is the main character of the story?" ("Sylvester.") This convergent question tests the students' literal comprehension of the story and can be answered by only one word. Such a question does not provoke discussion.
- "Do you like Sylvester?" This question, though divergent, can be answered in a word. A better way to phrase this question is, "Why do you like or dislike Sylvester?" or "How do you feel about Sylvester?" The question remains divergent but now may also result in discussion.

The best ideas for questions to stimulate book discussions flow directly from your response to the particular book and why you want the students to experience the book. Usually, you will have students read works of fiction for the aesthetic experience they will have with it—enjoyment, appreciation, emotional involvement, deeper understanding of life, and so on. In this case, your questions need to permit students to talk about their experiences. Divergent questions are best suited to this goal. Your questions will tell your students what you believe is important in reading. If your questions are convergent ones about the plot, characters, and setting, then you are telling your students that reading fiction is a type of egg hunt for the particular eggs laid by this author and previously located by you. On the other hand, if you ask divergent questions that permit them to explore their individual experiences with a work of fiction, students will soon discover that you really want to understand their feelings and thoughts about books.

The purpose of reading informational books, though perhaps partially aesthetic, is usually efferent; that is, the reader's attention is centered on what should be retained as a residue after the actual reading event. Locating specific pieces of information to support an argument and comparing information from two or more sources are examples of reasons for efferent reading of literature. Convergent questions in this case would reflect that purpose and be acceptable. Questions that stimulate more than a single-word answer are still, of course, preferable. Certainly, nonfiction may be read for more than information acquisition, just as fiction may be read for more than aesthetic purposes. For example, historical fiction novels may be read aloud by teachers with a dual goal: involvement in a powerful vicarious experience and acquisition of some understandings about life during a particular era. But keeping in mind the purposes for reading will guide you in formulating good questions.

Taking notes on the interesting, provocative, funny, heart-wrenching, and problematic characters and scenes of a book is a good starting point for question development. Such questions will be specific to a book and are preferable, but formula questions can be adapted to different books and may help you in designing good questions based on specific books. Some formula questions are listed here:

- What important ideas did you find conveyed in this story?
- What made certain parts of this book so funny? Sad? Exciting? Tell which part you are thinking of and why you think it is funny (sad, exciting).
- How do you think the story should have ended, and why do you think so?
- How would you have acted if you had been (*book character*)?
- What do you think the author's main message (theme) was in this story? Explain why you agree or disagree with the message.
- Which part of the story did you like best or least? Why?
- Which character did you like best or least? Why?
- How is this story similar to other ones we have read?
- How is this story similar to (*a specific story*)? Compare the stories and tell which you liked better and why.
- Which character do you identify with? Tell why and how you identify with him or her.
- What has happened in your life that you are reminded of by this story (character, situation)?
- What would you have done in (*character*)'s predicament?
- What do you think about (*character*)?
- What would (*character*) have done if . . . ?

*FOLLOWING UP*     Another facet of leading a discussion is the follow-up question. Once a student has given an answer, take that answer and build on it with a question that asks the student to expand or carry the answer to another realm. For example, after the student has said that she expected Sylvester to remain a rock forever, you might ask her to explore how Sylvester would adjust to being a rock and whether and how his parents would adjust. In turn, asking other students to tell how and why they believe otherwise about a part of the story is a way to help students discover that each person's experience with the book may be different.

*WAITING*     What happens if no one answers the question you asked? This is not likely to happen, because students like to talk; but a good discussion leader knows the value of *waiting*. Wait long enough, and someone will finally respond. Too often, discussion leaders jump in and answer their own questions before students have had a chance to gather their thoughts on the point being raised. Some teachers find that asking students to jot notes about the book experience during and after reading gives them time to reflect on their experiences with the book and helps them to formulate their thoughts and feelings for later expression during the discussion.

*CREATIVE DRAMA*    Creative drama is informal drama that lends itself readily to the reenactment of story experiences. In discussing the features of creative drama, McCaslin (1990) urges teachers and librarians to keep the following in mind:

- The drama is based on a piece of literature.
- Dialogue is created by the actors; lines are not written or memorized.
- Improvisation is an essential element.
- Movement on "stage" by actors is an integral part of creative drama.
- Scenery and costumes are not used, although an occasional prop may assist the children's imaginations.
- Drama is a process rather than a product. It is performed not for an audience, but for the benefit of the participants. Several different dramas or different dramatic interpretations of the same piece of literature can occur simultaneously in the classroom.

Creative drama is an enjoyable and rewarding oral language activity that can be used with students at all grade levels, from kindergarten to high school. A single scene from a chapter book may be enacted, or a picture book or short story may be dramatized in its entirety. The most suitable stories to start with are relatively simple, involving two to six characters and high action. Many folktales fit this description and lend themselves to being enacted.

These are the steps to follow in guiding creative drama in the classroom:

- Once a story is selected, the students listen to it being read to them or they read it independently.
- Next, they decide whether they like the story enough to want to act it out. If so, they listen to it again or read it, paying particular attention to the characters and the story scenes in sequence.
- The students then list the characters and the scenes on the chalkboard or on chart paper.
- They cast the play by assigning parts to actors. If enough students are interested in dramatizing the same story, you may want to assign two or more casts of actors immediately. In this way, each cast of characters can observe the performances of the others and learn from them.
- Next, each cast uses the list of scenes to review the plot, ensuring that all actors recall the events. Discuss the characters at this time, too, having students describe the actions, talk, and appearance for each.
- Give the cast of characters a few minutes to decide how to handle the performance. Then run through it. The first attempt may be a bit bumpy, but by the second time, it usually goes quite smoothly.
- After completing the drama, the class or the group of students then evaluates its success. McCaslin (1990) suggests these questions:

  1.  Did they tell the story?
  2.  What did you like about the opening scene?
  3.  Did the characters show that they were excited (angry, unhappy, etc.)?
  4.  When we play it again, can you think of anything that would improve it?
  5.  Was anything important left out? (p. 174)

A useful resource book, *Making Make-Believe: Fun Props, Costumes, and Creative Play Ideas* by Mary Ann F. Kohl (1999), offers many ideas for engaging prekindergarten to fourth grade students in dramatic play. One chapter presents numerous open-ended dramatic activities related to popular children's books.

Because of its improvisational nature and simplicity of costumes and scenery, creative drama appropriately places importance on the learning and experiencing process, not on performance, and it permits drama to become a frequent means of responding to literature in the classroom. Informal performances for the principal, the class next door, and so on, give students additional opportunities for practice and provide them with an opportunity to feel proud of their efforts.

*READERS' THEATRE*   Readers' theatre is the oral presentation of literature by two or more actors, and usually a narrator, reading from a script. Children's literary response is made evident through expressive oral reading and group interpretation. This form of response is especially enjoyable for children who are able to read aloud with some fluency. Features typically associated with readers' theatre include the following:

- The readers and narrator typically remain on the "stage" throughout the production.
- Readers use little movement; instead, they suggest action with simple gestures and facial expressions.
- Chairs or stools are used for readers and narrator to sit on, and performers usually remain seated throughout the performance. Sometimes, certain readers sit with their backs to the audience to suggest that they are not in a particular scene.
- No costumes or stage settings are necessary and, at most, should be suggestive, rather than complete or literal, to permit the imaginations of the audience to have full rein. The use of sound effects may enhance the performance and give the impression of a radio play.

Scripts can be developed for readers' theatre by the teacher or by older students adapting a work of literature enjoyed by the class. Picture books readily lend themselves to adaptation, as do short stories. Some teachers have successfully adapted well-selected scenes from a favorite chapter book. (See Figure 12.1.) The qualities to seek in a promising story are natural-sounding dialogue, strong characterization, drama or humor, and a satisfactory ending. If the original work has extensive dialogue, the script writing is a very easy activity. The script begins with the title of the book being adapted, the name of the author, a list of characters, and usually an opening statement by the narrator. Following the introduction, the dialogue is written into script form, with the narrator scripted for the remaining nondialogue, narrative parts.

Scripts can also be purchased, but finding scripts that are both well written and adapted from the literature you are using in your classroom may prove difficult. In Chapter 3, "Poetry and Plays," is a list of recommended plays; some are adaptations of well-known literature and may suit your purpose. If you decide to develop readers' theatre scripts from the literature you are using, remember that developing the first script is the most difficult. Once you have created the first one, you will find out how easy the process is. Intermediate-grade students take readily to script development once they have a model to imitate. Readers' theatre can become a frequently selected response option of literature response groups.

Choice of literature to use can include virtually any literary genre—picture storybooks, novels, biographies, long poems, letters, diaries, and journals. For example, Paul Fleischman's *Bull Run* (1993), an historical novel set during the Civil War, is written as a series of episodes told by different characters at different stages of the war. At the end of the book, the author provides a list of each character's

---

<u>Scorpions</u> (adapted from Chapter 3, pp. 15-16)
by Walter Dean Myers
Harper, 1988

CHARACTERS NEEDED: 7

Narrator
Mama
Jamal
Sassy
Mr. Davidson, principal
Mrs. Rich, teacher
Christine, a student

---

Mama: Jamal, wait for Sassy so you can walk to school with her.

Jamal: I'm going to be late waiting for her.

Mama: Sassy put some vaseline on your face before you leave.

Narrator: Sassy went into the bathroom.  Jamal saw her standing in front of the sink and went to the bathroom door to watch her.  She took some Vaseline from the jar, rubbed it between her palms, and then put it on her face. She made a tight face as she smoothed it on her cheeks. and squinted her eyes as she put it on the top of her nose.  Then she turned toward Jamal and smiled.

Jamal: You think you cute or something?

Sassy: All I know is what I see in the mirror.

Narrator: Sassy walked past her brother.

Jamal: Mama, she think she cute.

Mama: She is cute.

Jamal: No she ain't.

Sassy: Tito think I'm cute.

Jamal: Tito told me you were ugly.

Sassy: No, he didn't, 'cause he told Mary I was the cutest girl in third grade.

Jamal: They must got some ugly girls in the third grade, then.

Mama: Y'all get on to school.  And don't fool around on the way.

Etc....

FIGURE 12.1   Sample Opening of a Script for Readers' Theatre entries for the use of those who wish to produce readers' theatre performances. Variations on readers' theatre can be accomplished through the addition of background music, choral poems, and brief scenes from different stories tied together by a common theme, among other options to enliven this dramatic enactment of literature.

Preparation for a readers' theatre presentation gives students a good opportunity to strengthen their oral reading abilities and to try out their expressive skills. The group typically reads through the script once or twice and then works on refining the interpretive aspects of each performer. Decisions need to be made on the arrangement of chairs and speakers for greatest visual effect. Following each presentation, an evaluation is made by the group with the goal of improving future performances.

McCaslin (1990) states that "the simplicity of production and effectiveness of result make it [readers' theatre] singularly desirable in schools with inadequate stage facilities and where rehearsal time is at a premium" (p. 263). For these same reasons, readers' theatre is extremely well suited to classroom reenactments of literary experiences. In readers' theatre, students have the opportunity to translate their experiences with a literary work to a new medium—the medium of drama—with considerable ease and pleasure.

*STORY TELLINGS AND RETELLINGS*    Children who hear good stories read aloud by teachers, librarians, and parents often recapture those happy experiences by making the stories their own through retellings. In addition, in their natural play activities during preschool years, children enjoy role-playing and making up their own stories to tell to a playmate, real or imagined. The foundation for children's storytelling comes from the children's language environment—the talk they have heard and the stories that have been read to them. As young students learn to tell and retell stories, they reinforce their concept of story and are provided with opportunities for oral language development and expansion. Children who can tell a story with a beginning, a middle, and an end have the groundwork laid for later writing activities. You will note that story tellings and retellings by children are different in purpose than storytelling by teachers, as discussed in an earlier section of this chapter. Teachers tell stories as one of many ways of sharing literature with their students.

Teachers can foster the telling and retelling of stories by structuring a classroom environment that is conducive to this activity. Setting off an area of the classroom where children can gather for quiet talk and equipping it with some props such as story puppets, feltboards with cut-out story figures, toy story characters (stuffed animals, dolls, plastic and metal figures), wordless books, and children's favorite storybooks can entice children into telling and retelling their favorite stories. Some children take the book shared by the teacher during storytime and page through it, retelling the story from the pictures; others take story puppets and re-create the story or make up an entirely new adventure with the same characters.

Tape recorders also inspire younger students to record and listen to their favorite stories, while older students find a tape recorder an incentive for developing radio shows based on favorite books. Their favorite readers' theatre performances are well suited to radio show productions.

## Written Response

Written language activities are an important means for students to respond to their experiences with literature.

*EXPRESSION OF IDEAS AND FEELINGS*   The simplest and most direct way for teachers to elicit written responses to stories is to ask students to write their ideas and feelings about a book listened to or read. Questions to stimulate written response may be formulated according to the same guidelines suggested for designing discussion questions earlier in this chapter. Divergent, open-ended questions, rather than convergent questions, will elicit students' feelings and ideas about a scene, a character, or the story as a whole, and will help students explore their personal involvement with the story.

Each student's writing ability must be considered in selecting an appropriate writing activity. Emergent writers may find it possible to write the name of their favorite character and draw a picture of that character; more able writers may be able to write a detailed character description. A notable children's author, Marion Dane Bauer, has published a book useful to young writers, *What's Your Story? A Young Person's Guide to Writing Fiction* (1992).

*LITERATURE JOURNALS AND RECORDS*   Some teachers have found a literature journal—in which students make frequent written responses to books read—a motivating tool for students. Teachers read and comment on the entries periodically, and students gain a sense of pride in their reading accomplishments.

In some cases, reactions to books by one student can be enjoyed by the rest of the class. One teacher clipped blank response sheets with columns for responses (Author, Title, Reaction) inside the front cover of books in the classroom collection. After reading the book, a student enters his or her name and writes views on the book. Other students enjoy reading the book to see whether their reaction will be the same. Some teachers have had students write 4" × 6" notecards about each book as it is read. These cards are kept on file in the library corner so that each new reader can add his or her impressions to the card.

*STORIES AS WRITING MODELS*   When children read and listen to stories, they accumulate vocabulary, sentence structures, stylistic devices, and story ideas and structures. Well-written stories and poems serve as models for children in their own writing. When an 8-year-old boy who wrote extremely well-developed, interesting stories was asked how he learned to make up such good stories, he replied, "It's really a secret, but I'll tell you if you won't tell my teacher. I don't really make up the stories. When I was little, my mother read lots of books to me; then in school my teachers read a lot more. So what I do is take a beginning from one of the stories, a middle from another, and the end from another. And then I make up a title." Children who have a rich literary background have a well-stocked storehouse of beginnings, middles, and endings to put to use in their storytelling and writing.

Modeling after different literary forms can be used to extend book experiences. Writing a story modeled after another story can be an enjoyable re-creation of the experience. In modeling, the student adapts a story form or idea into a new creation. Examples include the following:

- Students create another episode using the same characters.
- Students write a different ending to the story read.
- Students take the perspective of another character in the story and recast the story with a shift in point of view. Two examples of a change in point of view can be found in Jon Scieszka's *The*

*True Story of the 3 Little Pigs by A. Wolf* (1989), which gives the Big Bad Wolf's version, and Scieszka's *The Frog Prince Continued* (1991), which tells the shocking truth about "happily ever after."

- Students develop readers' theatre scripts, writing a story in a new form.
- Students write a prequel to a story.
- Students take a story set in the past and rewrite it with a modern-day setting. Alternatively, a character from the historical narrative can become a visitor to modern times.

*TRADITIONAL BOOK REPORTS*   Requiring students to list author, title, date, genre, setting, main characters, and a summary of the plot seldom causes students to delve more deeply into their experiences with literature. Students usually view traditional book reports as tedious busywork. Although teachers assign book reports to get students to read, students often report that they never read the books they report on, but rather read the bookflap, read a page or two at the beginning and end, and write the report. More promising ways to foster the reading habit are through a good read-aloud program, time set aside for silent reading, booktalks about lots of readily available literature, literature response groups in which students can show their excitement about stories, class discussions, and writing activities in which students' thoughts and feelings about books can be expressed.

Recently, some so-called literature response forms or worksheets have been published for use by teachers who adopt literature-based reading approaches. Be cautious in your use of these worksheets. They need to be examined carefully; some of them are little more than disguised book report forms asking for plot, setting, characters, and theme. Such comprehension assessment may be justified occasionally in the reading class, but if your interest is to elicit students' responses to literature, you should stay away from worksheets.

## Graphic Arts Response

Most students enjoy arts and crafts. Graphic design and display techniques can therefore be an enjoyable and effective way to communicate literary experiences with other students and to share book experiences with parents and visitors. *Graphic arts response* is the use of different art and graphic design and display techniques to organize, deepen, and bring closure to students' experiences with literature. These activities can be a way for students to recapture the literary experience while translating it to a new medium.

*PICTURES AND COLLAGES*   Students can make pictures and collages to illustrate a favorite story or poem. Having a variety of materials available to choose from in designing their re-creations of literature increases students' enthusiasm and creativity. Paints, colored pencils, chalk, crayons, collage materials (cloth, yarn, lace, tissue paper), colored construction paper, and magazines with pictures and printed words for cutting up and shaping into pictures can be kept readily available for use in the classroom. Teachers foster good design by asking students to think about the purpose and desired effects and by pointing out interesting visual elements in other media, especially in picture books. For example, when students observe the different ways in which illustrators frame their pictures, outline figures, and use blank space and perspective for highlighting an object, they often can replicate and adapt these techniques for their own classroom design projects.

Teachers have often overused the activity of "draw a picture of the story" by assigning it too frequently, by not planning the activity adequately, and by permitting students little or no choice of media and project. An activity that is repeated to the point of monotony becomes little more than busywork to students. Remember that it may be unnecessary to have a response activity of any kind after reading a book or that a worthy response to a book would be finding another book by the same author and reading it next.

When more active response seems warranted, however, it is important to plan worthwhile ways for students to express those responses. Providing students with a choice of projects and media and then planning collaboratively with the students on the execution of the project are the roles the teacher needs to assume. Your art specialists and school and public librarians can be of great assistance in helping you plan response activities.

*MURALS*    Murals are made from a long roll of paper mounted horizontally. The entire length of paper is usually divided into sections and often presents a chronology of the story events. Murals may feature a particular theme, such as animals from stories around the world, different kinds of homes the characters live in, personified dolls and toys from a unit on stories with personification, or various ways young story characters have overcome obstacles as they grow and mature. Groups of children decide on the theme or topic, design the segments, and allocate tasks to group members. Sometimes, students work directly on the mounted mural; other times they cut it into sections and work at tables then tape it back together for mounting. This device is well suited for literature response groups whose members collaborate in selecting, planning, and implementing the mural. The product is often dramatic and showy, offering the group members a feeling of real accomplishment.

*ROLLER MOVIES*    This technique produces a simulated movie or filmstrip of a story. The pictures are designed, frame by frame, on a long roll of paper. Once completed, each end of the paper is taped to a dowel rod or broom handle; then the paper is rolled onto the feeder rod so that the beginning frame is viewed first when the paper is unrolled. The ends of each rod are inserted into holes on the sides of a cardboard box so that the paper can be stretched from one roller to the other across the box opening and then rolled to the receiver rod to move the frames along. The box is turned on its side, television style, to face the audience, and the story unfolds as the frames are rolled onto the receiver rod. The group writes a script to go along with each frame. The need for group collaboration makes this an ideal project for literature response groups. The finished movie lends itself to story retellings.

*DIORAMAS*    A diorama is a three-dimensional display in which objects and figures are placed into a background or setting to create a scene. Dioramas are often made in classrooms by using shoeboxes set on the side, providing a framework on which to construct a setting, such as a floor, ceiling, and three walls of a room. Many materials may be used to make the figures, their background, furniture, and clothes, including modeling clay, collage materials, matchboxes, dried leaves, pine straw, and tiny dolls. Dioramas are especially well suited to individuals and pairs of students who may work alone or cooperatively in selecting and recreating in miniature an important scene from a story.

*BOOKS AND BIG BOOKS*    Children can make their own stories and poems into books for a more finished presentation of their writing efforts. There are many different ways to make books in the classroom, ranging from the simple process of stapling together students' separate pictures on a topic with an illustrated cover to the more complex task of developing books with hard covers made of cardboard with pages covered in clear or patterned adhesive paper or fabric, and then sewn together and bound for a "real book" look.

Big Books are often modeled after a favorite picture book that the class enjoyed, with the pictures drawn by students and the text printed by the teacher on 24" × 30" heavy paper or posterboard, which is then laminated, bound on metal rings, and hung on an easel. Many schools have laminators for use in these projects. Lamination is also done at many commercial copy and print shops at a moderate cost.

Making books is an activity that is most suited for individuals or pairs of students. However, a collaborative book organized around a theme or pattern can be made by a larger group in which each member contributes a story or poem. In this type of book, a table of contents with the names of each contributor offers recognition of all students while also calling students' attention to this useful part of a book. When students are first learning the steps of making books, considerable guidance from an adult is required. Parent volunteers and teacher aides can be shown how to provide this assistance. The step-by-step processes of making different types of books can be found in these sources:

- Gerry Bohning, Ann Phillips, and Sandra Bryant's *Literature on the Move: Making and Using Pop-Up and Lift-Flap Books* (1993) is a 115-page book for teachers and students, with instructions for planning, writing, drawing, and assembling pop-up books.
- Susan Purdy's *Books for You to Make* (1973) is a 96-page book that will prove useful to children and adults, gives well-illustrated, detailed instructions on how to write, design, illustrate, and bind books. Many different bindings, from simple to complex, are described and illustrated.
- Janet Stevens's *From Pictures to Words: A Book about Making a Book* (1995) is a picture book about how a book is made for students, ages 5–8.
- Charlotte Stowell's *Step-by-Step Making Books* (1994) is an easy, helpful guide for making books, appropriate for students, ages 8–12.
- Harvey Weiss's *How to Make Your Own Books* (1974) is a fine source for different types of bindings and cover ideas. In addition, many types of books (flip books, scrolls, Japanese-style books, etc.) and how to make them by hand are described and illustrated in this 72-page book.

Completed books need to be displayed for admiration and made available for reading by others. A special place in the reading corner can be reserved to exhibit student-made books.

*NEWSPAPERS AND NEWSLETTERS*   A collaborative endeavor in which students write about the books they have been reading and tell about their book-related projects can result in class newspapers and newsletters. Each issue of the paper can focus on a different topic, such as favorite authors, illustrators, story characters, and poetic forms. In some intermediate-grade classrooms, a different literature response group accepts editing responsibilities for the newsletter each month, selecting the focus, soliciting manuscripts, designing pages, and making editorial decisions. The newsletters are sent home to parents with suggestions of good books to read and new authors to check out. Since computers are generally available in schools, individuals with word processing skills can usually be found, often among the students, to produce interesting newspapers and newsletters.

*TIME LINES, MAPS, DIAGRAMS, AND CHARTS*   A type of visual figure that details a period of time covered in a story is a time line. The figure is made by drawing a line on a long strip of mural paper, then placing the dates below the line at scaled intervals. The story events are logged in above the line. This graphic aid organizes the events of the story and can permit the students to compare events from a novel of historical fiction or from a biography with actual dates from history.

Time lines can be excellent visual aids when used in conjunction with reading aloud a progressive plot chapter book. The time line is set up with the dates, then the story events are recorded after each day's reading. The time line can also serve as a reminder of what has happened thus far as a review before beginning the next chapter.

Time lines can also be useful when students are reading a variety of material on a single period of history: biographies, historical fiction novels, and photo essays on World War II, for instance. Historical events from different sources can be compared for authenticity by using parallel time lines or by adding more tiers to the same time line. Individual students may develop time lines to follow the events of an entire series of books, such as science fiction novels and quest adventure stories.

*Maps* are especially suitable for charting the settings in chapter books of many genres. They can be designed by individuals or groups of students and make interesting and helpful visual aids for telling others about books. Some chapter books in which maps are included as part of the book can be used by students as models to imitate for drawing storymaps on other books. (For example, see the endpapers of *The Nargun and the Stars* (1974) by Patricia Wrightson, *The Book of Three* (1964) by Lloyd Alexander, and *Rabbit Hill* (1944) by Robert Lawson.) Maps are also suitable for laying out the events in picture books and books with a circular journey motif in which the protagonist leaves home, encounters adversity, overcomes it, and returns home.

A *diagram* presents textual material in visual form and can be used to illustrate arrangements and relations within a story. (For example, in *Linnea in Monet's Garden* (Björk, 1987) a family tree of Monet's family is displayed.) Many information books use diagrams, and students can develop ideas for presenting information through diagrams by perusing these books. Another Linnea story, *Linnea's Windowsill Garden* (1988), has a diagram of plants and their seeds. Diagrams can also be developed to show relationships found in book series and long works, such as the Arthurian legends. Teachers and students can use diagrams to display the progression of a story, which is especially useful to help students understand unusual plot twists.

*Charts* give information in table form to show relationships, summarize information, and present facts in a capsule form. (For example, on page 8 of *Linnea's Almanac* (Björk, 1989) a chart showing species of birds and their feeding habits assists readers in the art of feeding winter birds.) When students use nonfiction books for studying content areas, they can be encouraged to consider visual means for presenting and summarizing the information gained.

*JACKDAWS*    *Jackdaws* are collections of realia or copies of realia based on a particular historical period or event; jackdaws are often available in museums for study of a period of history, and some museums lend them to teachers for use in schools. The term "jackdaw" refers to a common European bird that is related to the crow and known to collect colorful objects for its nest. Educators have borrowed the term to refer to a teaching tool that can be used to connect historical books with the real events of the times depicted through concrete objects (Devitt, 1970). For example, a teacher may put together a jackdaw based on U.S. pioneers of the 1800s, then use the jackdaw to build background knowledge to introduce the study of the historical fiction novel, *Sarah, Plain and Tall* (1985) by Patricia MacLachlan.

Jackdaws are made by collecting a wide array of related materials in their original form or in reproductions. Materials that are often collected are regional maps, photographs or models of homes, farms, machines, household furnishings, toys and dolls, kitchen tools, recipes for foods commonly eaten, newspapers and books of the era, clothing, modes of transportation, government of the time (president, congress, political parties, statehood), educational institutions, cultural artifacts such as songs, paintings, and architectural landmarks. After collection the realia are placed in a decorated box with labels and explanations attached, if desired. The jackdaw can be used as an extension activity for a book read in class as well as for building background. Many teachers enlist students in the development of jackdaws and share jackdaws with other teachers who are studying the same historical book.

*DISPLAYS AND BULLETIN BOARDS*    Displays are three-dimensional re-creations of a setting—a town, or a battle scene, for instance—placed on a large flat surface, such as a table or piece of plywood. The use of clay and cardboard for figures, papier-mâché for hills, colored construction paper for lakes and land surfaces, and so on permits students to design impressive displays from story settings. More artistically talented students can be given opportunities to excel in these design activities.

Designing and making bulletin boards provide groups of students with opportunities to demonstrate their book experiences in innovative ways. Planning bulletin boards and displays requires students to select an interesting and worthy focus or message to call attention to the display and to get the message across effectively by using only a few words.

Giving students choices of books to read and choices in the ways in which they respond to them is an essential component of a good curriculum in literature. This chapter presented a smorgasbord of ideas for having students experience literature and respond to those literary experiences.

## REFERENCES

Alexander, L. (1964). *The book of three*. New York: Holt.

Bauer, M. D. (1992). *What's your story?: A young person's guide to writing fiction*. Boston: Houghton.

Björk, C. (1989). *Linnea's almanac*. Illustrated by L. Anderson. Translated by J. Sandin. Stockholm: Rabén & Sjögren.

———. (1987). *Linnea in Monet's garden*. Illustrated by L. Anderson. Translated by J. Sandin. Stockholm: Rabén & Sjögren.

———. (1988). *Linnea's windowsill garden*. Illustrated by L. Anderson. Translated by J. Sandin. Stockholm: Rabén & Sjögren.

Bodart, J. (1980). *Booktalk!* New York: H. W. Wilson.

Bohning, G., Phillips, A. & Bryant, S. (1993). *Literature on the move: Making and using pop-up and lift-flap books*. Illustrated by S. Bryant. Englewood, CO: Libraries Unlimited.

Ciardi, J. (1962). *You read to me, I'll read to you*. Illustrated by E. Gorey. New York: Lippincott.

Cole, B. (1987). *The goats*. New York: Farrar.

Devitt, M. (Ed.). (1970). *Learning with jackdaws*. London: St. Paul's Press.

Estes, E. (1944). *The hundred dresses*. Illustrated by L. Slobodkin. New York: Harcourt.

Fatchen, M. (1988). Tailpiece. In M. Harrison and C. Stuart-Clark, Eds. *The Oxford Teasury of Children's Poems*. Oxford: Oxford University Press.

Fleischman, P. (1993). *Bull Run.* New York: Harper-Collins.

Fox, P. (1973). *The slave dancer.* New York: Bradbury.

Holdaway, D. (1982). Shared book experience: Teaching reading using favorite books. *Theory into practice, 21,* 293–300.

Hoskisson, K., Sherman, T. M., & Smith, L. L. (1974). Assisted reading and parent involvement. *The Reading Teacher, 27,* 710–714.

Kohl, M. F. (1999). *Making make-believe: Fun props, costumes, and creative play ideas.* Beltsville: Gryphon House.

Labbo, L. D., & Reinking, D. (2000). Once upon an electronic story time. *The New Advocate, 13*(1), 25–32.

Lawson, R. (1944). *Rabbit hill.* New York: Viking.

Lynch-Brown, C., & Tomlinson, C. M. (1988). *Reading aloud novel-length chapter books: A qualitative study.* Paper presented at the International Reading Association Annual Conference, Toronto.

MacLachlan, P. (1985). *Sarah, plain and tall.* New York: Harper.

McCaslin, N. (1990). *Creative drama in the classroom* (5th ed.). New York: Longman.

Myers, W. D. (1988). *Scorpions.* New York: Harper.

Pellowski, A. (1995). *The storytelling handbook: A young people's collection of unusual tales and helpful hints on how to tell them.* Illustrated by M. Stoberock. New York: Simon & Schuster.

Purdy, S. (1973). *Books for you to make.* Philadelphia: Lippincott.

Raskin, E. (1978). *The westing game.* New York: Dutton.

Rosenblatt, L. M. (1978). *The reader, the text, the poem: The transactional theory of the literary work.* Carbondale, IL: Southern Illinois University Press.

Scieszka, J. (1991). *The frog prince continued.* Illustrated by S. Johnson. New York: Viking.

———. (1989). *The true story of the three little pigs by A. Wolf.* Illustrated by L. Smith. New York: Viking.

Steig, W. (1969). *Sylvester and the magic pebble.* New York: Windmill.

Stevens, J. (1995). *From pictures to words: A book about making a book.* New York: Holiday.

Stowell, C. (1994). *Step-by-step making books.* New York: Kingfisher.

Veatch, J. (1968). *How to teach reading with children's books* (2nd ed). New York: Richard C. Owen.

Weiss, H. (1974). *How to make your own books.* New York: Crowell.

Wrightson, P. (1974). *The nargun and the stars.* New York: Atheneum.

# CHILDREN'S
# BOOK AWARDS

## THE UNITED STATES

### Caldecott Medal

*This award, sponsored by the Association for Library Service to Children Division of the American Library Association, is given to the illustrator of the most distinguished picture book for children published in the United States during the preceding year. Only U.S. residents or citizens are eligible for this award.*

1938 *Animals of the Bible, A Picture Book.* Text selected from the King James Bible by Helen Dean Fish. Illustrated by Dorothy P. Lathrop. Lippincott (Bible, ages 3–8).

HONOR BOOKS:
*Seven Simeons: A Russian Tale* by Boris Artzybasheff. Viking (Traditional, ages 6–8).
*Four and Twenty Blackbirds* compiled by Helen Dean Fish. Illustrated by Robert Lawson/Stokes. Lippincott (Traditional, ages 3–6).

1939 *Mei Li* by Thomas Handforth. Doubleday (Realism, ages 6–7).

HONOR BOOKS:
*The Forest Pool* by Laura Adams Armer. McKay/Longmans (Realism, ages 6–7).

*Wee Gillis* by Munro Leaf. Illustrated by Robert Lawson. Viking (Realism, ages 5–7).
*Snow White and the Seven Dwarfs.* Translated and illustrated by Wanda Gág. Coward-McCann (Traditional, ages 3–6).
*Barkis* by Clare Turlay Newberry. Harper (Realism, ages 3–7).
*Andy and the Lion* by James Daugherty. Viking (Fantasy, ages 3–7).

1940 *Abraham Lincoln* by Ingri d'Aulaire and Edgar Parin d'Aulaire. Doubleday (Biography, ages 6–8).

HONOR BOOKS:
*Cock-a-Doodle-Doo* by Berta and Elmer Hader. Macmillan (Animal realism, ages 3–7).
*Madeline* by Ludwig Bemelmans. Viking (Realism, ages 5–7).
*The Ageless Story* by Lauren Ford. Dodd (Bible, ages 5–8).

1941 *They Were Strong and Good* by Robert Lawson. Viking (Biography, ages 6–7).

HONOR BOOK:
*April's Kittens* by Clare Turlay Newberry. Harper (Realism, ages 3–6).

1942 *Make Way for Ducklings* by Robert McCloskey. Viking (Animal fantasy, ages 3–6).

HONOR BOOKS:

*An American ABC* by Maud and Miska Petersham. Macmillan (Alphabet, ages 3–6).

*In My Mother's House* by Ann Nolan Clark. Illustrated by Velino Herrera. Viking (Informational, ages 6–8).

*Paddle-to-the-Sea* by Holling Clancy Holling. Houghton (Informational, ages 6–8).

*Nothing at All* by Wanda Gág. Coward-McCann (Animal fantasy, ages 3–6).

1943  *The Little House* by Virginia Lee Burton. Houghton (Fantasy, ages 3–6).

HONOR BOOKS:

*Dash and Dart* by Mary and Conrad Buff. Viking (Realism, ages 3–6).

*Marshmallow* by Clare Turlay Newberry. Harper (Realism, ages 3–6).

1944  *Many Moons* by James Thurber. Illustrated by Louis Slobodkin. Harcourt (Modern folktale, ages 5–7).

HONOR BOOKS:

*Small Rain: Verses from the Bible.* Text arranged from the Bible by Jessie Orton Jones. Illustrated by Elizabeth Orton Jones. Viking (Bible, ages 3–7).

*Pierre Pigeon* by Lee Kingman. Illustrated by Arnold Edwin Bare. Houghton (Realism, ages 6–7).

*The Mighty Hunter* by Berta and Elmer Hader. Macmillan (Fantasy, ages 3–6).

*A Child's Good Night Book* by Margaret Wise Brown. Illustrated by Jean Charlot. Scott (Realism, ages 3–6).

*Good Luck Horse* by Chih-Yi Chan. Illustrated by Plato Chan. Whittlesey (Traditional, ages 6–7).

1945  *Prayer for a Child* by Rachel Field. Illustrated by Elizabeth Orton Jones. Macmillan (Realism, ages 3–6).

HONOR BOOKS:

*Mother Goose: Seventy-Seven Verses with Pictures.* Illustrated by Tasha Tudor. Walck (Traditional, ages 3–6).

*In the Forest* by Marie Hall Ets. Viking (Fantasy, ages 3–6).

*Yonie Wondernose* by Marguerite de Angeli. Doubleday (Realism, ages 6–7).

*The Christmas Anna Angel* by Ruth Sawyer. Illustrated by Kate Seredy. Viking (Modern folktale, ages 6–7).

1946  *The Rooster Crows* selected and illustrated by Maud and Miska Petersham. Macmillan (Mother Goose/Nursery rhymes, ages 3–6).

HONOR BOOKS:

*Little Lost Lamb* by Golden MacDonald. Illustrated by Leonard Weisgard. Doubleday (Realism, ages 3–6).

*Sing Mother Goose* by Opal Wheeler. Illustrated by Marjorie Torrey. Dutton (Nursery songs, ages 3–6).

*My Mother Is the Most Beautiful Woman in the World* retold by Becky Reyher. Illustrated by Ruth Gannett. Lothrop (Traditional, ages 5–7).

*You Can Write Chinese* by Kurt Wiese. Viking (Informational, ages 6–8).

1947  *The Little Island* by Golden MacDonald. Illustrated by Leonard Weisgard. Doubleday (Fantasy, ages 3–6).

HONOR BOOKS:

*Rain Drop Splash* by Alvin Tresselt. Illustrated by Leonard Weisgard. Lothrop (Informational, ages 5–7).

*Boats on the River* by Marjorie Flack. Illustrated by Jay Hyde Barnum. Viking (Informational, ages 6–7).

*Timothy Turtle* by Al Graham. Illustrated by Tony Palazzo. Viking (Animal fantasy, ages 3–6).

*Pedro, the Angel of Olvera Street* by Leo Politi. Scribner's (Realism, ages 3–6).

*Sing in Praise: A Collection of the Best Loved Hymns* by Opal Wheeler. Illustrated by Marjorie Torrey. Dutton (Informational, ages 3–8).

1948  *White Snow, Bright Snow* by Alvin Tresselt. Illustrated by Roger Duvoisin. Lothrop (Realism, ages 3–6).

HONOR BOOKS:

*Stone Soup: An Old Tale* by Marcia Brown. Scribner's (Traditional, ages 6–8).

*McElligot's Pool* by Dr. Seuss (pseudonym of Theodor Geisel). Random (Fantasy, ages 3–6).

*Bambino the Clown* by George Schreiber. Viking (Realism, ages 5–7).

*Roger and the Fox* by Lavinia Davis. Illustrated by Hildegard Woodward. Doubleday (Realism, ages 5–7).

*Song of Robin Hood* edited by Anne Malcolmson. Illustrated by Virginia Lee Burton. Houghton (Traditional, ages 9–YA).

1949  *The Big Snow* by Berta and Elmer Hader. Macmillan (Animal realism, ages 3–6).

HONOR BOOKS:

*Blueberries for Sal* by Robert McCloskey. Viking (Realism, ages 3–6).

*All Around Town* by Phyllis McGinley. Illustrated by Helen Stone. Lippincott (Alphabet, ages 3–6).

*Juanita* by Leo Politi. Scribner's (Realism, ages 3–6).

*Fish in the Air* by Kurt Wiese. Viking (Fantasy, ages 5–7).

1950 *Song of the Swallows* by Leo Politi. Scribner's (Realism, ages 3–6).

HONOR BOOKS:

*America's Ethan Allen* by Stewart Holbrook. Illustrated by Lynd Ward. Houghton (Biography, ages 6–8).

*The Wild Birthday Cake* by Lavinia R. Davis. Illustrated by Hildegard Woodward. Doubleday (Realism, ages 5–6).

*The Happy Day* by Ruth Krauss. Illustrated by Marc Simont. Harper (Animal fantasy, ages 3–6).

*Henry-Fisherman* by Marcia Brown. Scribner's (Realism, ages 5–7).

*Bartholomew and the Oobleck* by Dr. Seuss (pseudonym of Theodor Geisel). Random (Modern folktale, ages 5–7).

1951 *The Egg Tree* by Katherine Milhous. Scribner's (Realism, ages 3–6).

HONOR BOOKS:

*Dick Whittington and His Cat.* Translated and illustrated by Marcia Brown. Scribner's (Traditional, ages 6–8).

*The Two Reds* by Will (pseudonym of William Lipkind). Illustrated by Nicolas (pseudonym of Nicolas Mordvinoff). Harcourt (Fantasy, ages 3–6).

*If I Ran the Zoo* by Dr. Seuss (pseudonym of Theodor Geisel). Random (Fantasy, ages 3–6).

*T-Bone, the Baby-Sitter* by Clare Turlay Newberry. Harper (Realism, ages 3–6).

*The Most Wonderful Doll in the World* by Phyllis McGinley. Illustrated by Helen Stone. Lippincott (Realism, ages 6–7).

1952 *Finders Keepers* by Will (pseudonym of William Lipkind). Illustrated by Nicolas (pseudonym of Nicolas Mordvinoff). Harcourt (Modern folktale, ages 3–6).

HONOR BOOKS:

*Mr. T. W. Anthony Woo* by Marie Hall Ets. Viking (Modern folktale, ages 3–6).

*Skipper John's Cook* by Marcia Brown. Scribner's (Realism, ages 5–7).

*All Falling Down* by Gene Zion. Illustrated by Margaret Bloy Graham. Harper (Informational, ages 3–6).

*Bear Party* by William Pène du Bois. Viking (Animal fantasy, ages 3–7).

*Feather Mountain* by Elizabeth Olds. Houghton (Modern folktale, ages 5–7).

1953 *The Biggest Bear* by Lynd Ward. Houghton (Realism, ages 3–7).

HONOR BOOKS:

*Puss in Boots.* Translated and illustrated by Marcia Brown. Scribner's (Traditional, ages 5–7).

*One Morning in Maine* by Robert McCloskey. Viking (Realism, ages 5–7).

*Ape in a Cape: An Alphabet of Odd Animals* by Fritz Eichenberg. Harcourt (Alphabet, ages 3–6).

*The Storm Book* by Charlotte Zolotow. Illustrated by Margaret Bloy Graham. Harper (Informational, ages 3–6).

*Five Little Monkeys* by Juliet Kepes. Houghton (Animal fantasy, ages 3–6).

1954 *Madeline's Rescue* by Ludwig Bemelmans. Viking (Realism, ages 3–6).

HONOR BOOKS:

*Journey Cake, Ho!* by Ruth Sawyer. Illustrated by Robert McCloskey. Viking (Traditional, ages 5–7).

*When Will the World Be Mine?* by Miriam Schlein. Illustrated by Jean Charlot. Scott (Animal fantasy, ages 3–6).

*The Steadfast Tin Soldier* by Hans Christian Andersen. Translated by M. R. James. Illustrated by Marcia Brown. Scribner's (Modern folktale, ages 5–7).

*A Very Special House* by Ruth Krauss. Illustrated by Maurice Sendak. Harper (Fantasy, ages 3–6).

*Green Eyes* by Abe Birnbaum. Capitol (Animal fantasy, ages 3–6).

1955 *Cinderella, or the Little Glass Slipper* by Charles Perrault. Translated and illustrated by Marcia Brown. Scribner's (Traditional, ages 3–7).

HONOR BOOKS:

*Book of Nursery and Mother Goose Rhymes* compiled and illustrated by Marguerite de Angeli. Doubleday (Nursery rhymes, ages 3–6).

*Wheel on the Chimney* by Margaret Wise Brown. Illustrated by Tibor Gergely. Lippincott (Realism, ages 6–7).

*The Thanksgiving Story* by Alice Dalgliesh. Illustrated by Helen Sewell. Scribner's (Historical fiction [United States, 1700s], ages 5–7).

1956 *Frog Went A-Courtin'* retold by John Langstaff. Illustrated by Feodor Rojankovsky. Harcourt (Traditional, ages 3–7).

HONOR BOOKS:

*Play with Me* by Marie Hall Ets. Viking (Realism, ages 3–6).

*Crow Boy* by Taro Yashima. Viking (Realism, ages 5–7).

1957 *A Tree Is Nice* by Janice May Udry. Illustrated by
Marc Simont. Harper (Informational, ages 3–7).

HONOR BOOKS:

*Mr. Penny's Race Horse* by Marie Hall Ets. Viking
(Animal fantasy, ages 5–7).

*1 Is One* by Tasha Tudor. Walck. (Counting, ages
3–6).

*Anatole* by Eve Titus. Illustrated by Paul Galdone.
McGraw (Animal fantasy, ages 5–7).

*Gillespie and the Guards* by Benjamin Elkin. Illustrated by James Daugherty. Viking (Realism, ages
5–7).

*Lion* by William Pène du Bois. Viking (Animal fantasy, ages 5–7).

1958 *Time of Wonder* by Robert McCloskey. Viking
(Realism, ages 6–8).

HONOR BOOKS:

*Fly High, Fly Low* by Don Freeman. Viking (Animal
fantasy, ages 3–6).

*Anatole and the Cat* by Eve Titus. Illustrated by Paul
Galdone. McGraw (Animal fantasy, ages 3–6).

1959 *Chanticleer and the Fox* by Chaucer. Adapted
and illustrated by Barbara Cooney. Crowell (Traditional, ages 5–7).

HONOR BOOKS:

*The House That Jack Built ("La Maison Que
Jacques a Bâtie"): A Picture Book in Two Languages*
by Antonio Frasconi. Harcourt (Informational, ages
5–8).

*What Do You Say, Dear? A Book of Manners for All
Occasions* by Sesyle Joslin. Illustrated by Maurice
Sendak. Scott (Fantasy, ages 3–6).

*Umbrella* by Taro Yashima. Viking (Realism, ages
3–6).

1960 *Nine Days to Christmas* by Marie Hall Ets and
Aurora Labastida. Illustrated by Marie Hall Ets.
Viking (Realism, ages 3–7).

HONOR BOOKS:

*Houses from the Sea* by Alice E. Goudey. Illustrated
by Adrienne Adams. Scribner's (Informational, ages
5–7).

*The Moon Jumpers* by Janice May Udry. Illustrated
by Maurice Sendak. Harper (Realism, ages 3–6).

1961 *Baboushka and the Three Kings* by Ruth Robbins. Illustrated by Nicolas Sidjakov. Parnassus
(Traditional, ages 5–7).

HONOR BOOK:

*Inch by Inch* by Leo Lionni. Obolensky (Animal fantasy, ages 3–6).

1962 *Once a Mouse* retold by Marcia Brown. Scribner's (Traditional, ages 5–7).

HONOR BOOKS:

*The Fox Went Out on a Chilly Night: An Old Song* by
Peter Spier. Doubleday (Traditional, ages 3–6).

*Little Bear's Visit* by Else Minarik. Illustrated by
Maurice Sendak. Harper (Animal fantasy, ages 3–7).

*The Day We Saw the Sun Come Up* by Alice Goudey.
Illustrated by Adrienne Adams. Scribner's (Informational, ages 5–7).

1963 *The Snowy Day* by Ezra Jack Keats. Viking (Realism, ages 3–6).

HONOR BOOKS:

*The Sun Is a Golden Earring* by Natalia Belting. Illustrated by Bernarda Bryson. Holt (Modern folktale,
ages 7–10).

*Mr. Rabbit and the Lovely Present* by Charlotte Zolotow. Illustrated by Maurice Sendak. Harper (Animal
fantasy, ages 3–6).

1964 *Where the Wild Things Are* by Maurice Sendak.
Harper (Fantasy, ages 3–7).

HONOR BOOKS:

*Swimmy* by Leo Lionni. Pantheon (Animal fantasy,
ages 5–7).

*All in the Morning Early* by Sorche Nic Leodhas
(pseudonym of Leclaire Alger). Illustrated by Evaline Ness. Holt (Traditional, ages 3–6).

*Mother Goose and Nursery Rhymes* by Philip Reed.
Atheneum (Traditional, ages 3–6).

1965 *May I Bring a Friend?* by Beatrice Schenk de
Regniers. Illustrated by Beni Montresor.
Atheneum (Fantasy, ages 5–7).

HONOR BOOKS:

*Rain Makes Applesauce* by Julian Scheer. Illustrated
by Marvin Bileck. Holiday (Fantasy, ages 5–7).

*The Wave* by Margaret Hodges. Illustrated by Blair
Lent. Houghton (Traditional, ages 6–9).

*A Pocketful of Cricket* by Rebecca Caudill. Illustrated
by Evaline Ness. Holt (Realism, ages 5–7).

1966 *Always Room for One More* by Sorche Nic Leodhas (pseudonym of Leclaire Alger). Illustrated by
Nonny Hogrogian. Holt (Traditional, ages 3–6).

HONOR BOOKS:

*Hide and Seek Fog* by Alvin Tresselt. Illustrated by
Roger Duvoisin. Lothrop (Realism, ages 5–7).

*Just Me* by Marie Hall Ets. Viking (Realism, ages
3–5).

*Tom Tit Tot* adapted by Joseph Jacobs. Illustrated by
Evaline Ness. Scribner's (Traditional, ages 5–7).

1967 *Sam, Bangs and Moonshine* by Evaline Ness. Holt (Realism, ages 6–8).

HONOR BOOK:

*One Wide River to Cross* adapted by Barbara Emberley. Illustrated by Ed Emberley. Prentice Hall (Bible, ages 3–6).

1968 *Drummer Hoff* adapted by Barbara Emberley. Illustrated by Ed Emberley. Prentice Hall (Traditional, ages 3–6).

HONOR BOOKS:

*Frederick* by Leo Lionni. Pantheon (Animal fantasy, ages 5–7).

*Seashore Story* by Taro Yashima. Viking (Realism, ages 6–8).

*The Emperor and the Kite* by Jane Yolen. Illustrated by Ed Young. World (Modern folktale, ages 5–7).

1969 *The Fool of the World and the Flying Ship: A Russian Tale* by Authur Ransome. Illustrated by Uri Shulevitz. Farrar (Traditional, ages 6–8).

HONOR BOOK:

*Why the Sun and the Moon Live in the Sky: An African Folktale* by Elphinstone Dayrell. Illustrated by Blair Lent. Houghton (Traditional, ages 6–8).

1970 *Sylvester and the Magic Pebble* by William Steig. Windmill (Animal fantasy, ages 5–7).

HONOR BOOKS:

*Goggles!* by Ezra Jack Keats. Macmillan (Realism, ages 3–6).

*Alexander and the Wind-Up Mouse* by Leo Lionni. Pantheon (Animal fantasy, ages 3–6).

*Pop Corn and Ma Goodness* by Edna Mitchell Preston. Illustrated by Robert Andrew Parker. Viking (Modern folktale, ages 5–7).

*Thy Friend, Obadiah* by Brinton Turkle. Viking (Historical fiction [New England, 1700s], ages 3–7).

*The Judge: An Untrue Tale* by Harve Zemach. Illustrated by Margot Zemach. Farrar (Modern folktale, ages 5–7).

1971 *A Story, A Story: An African Tale* by Gail E. Haley. Atheneum (Traditional, ages 5–7).

HONOR BOOKS:

*The Angry Moon* retold by William Sleator. Illustrated by Blair Lent. Atlantic/Little, Brown (Traditional, ages 6–8).

*Frog and Toad Are Friends* by Arnold Lobel. Harper (Animal fantasy, ages 3–7).

*In the Night Kitchen* by Maurice Sendak. Harper (Fantasy, ages 5–7).

1972 *One Fine Day* by Nonny Hogrogian. Macmillan (Traditional, ages 5–7).

HONOR BOOKS:

*If All the Seas Were One Sea* by Janina Domanska. Macmillan (Traditional, ages 3–6).

*Moja Means One: Swahili Counting Book* by Muriel Feelings. Illustrated by Tom Feelings. Dial (Counting, ages 5–8).

*Hildilid's Night* by Cheli Duran Ryan. Illustrated by Arnold Lobel. Macmillan (Modern folktale, ages 3–6).

1973 *The Funny Little Woman* retold by Arlene Mosel. Illustrated by Blair Lent. Dutton (Traditional, ages 5–7).

HONOR BOOKS:

*Hosie's Alphabet* by Hosea Baskin, Tobias Baskin, and Lisa Baskin. Illustrated by Leonard Baskin. Viking (Alphabet, ages 6–9).

*When Clay Sings* by Byrd Baylor. Illustrated by Tom Bahti. Scribner's (Informational, ages 6–8).

*Snow-White and the Seven Dwarfs* by the Brothers Grimm. Translated by Randall Jarrell. Illustrated by Nancy Ekholm Burkert. Farrar (Traditional, ages 3–7).

*Anansi the Spider: A Tale from the Ashanti* adapted and illustrated by Gerald McDermott. Holt (Traditional, ages 6–8).

1974 *Duffy and the Devil* retold by Harve Zemach. Illustrated by Margot Zemach. Farrar (Traditional, ages 6–8).

HONOR BOOKS:

*Three Jovial Huntsmen* adapted and illustrated by Susan Jeffers. Bradbury (Traditional, ages 3–6).

*Cathedral: The Story of Its Construction* by David Macaulay. Houghton (Informational, ages 8–YA).

1975 *Arrow to the Sun* adapted and illustrated by Gerald McDermott. Viking (Traditional, ages 7–9).

HONOR BOOK:

*Jambo Means Hello: Swahili Alphabet Book* by Muriel Feelings. Illustrated by Tom Feelings. Dial (Alphabet, ages 6–8).

1976 *Why Mosquitoes Buzz in People's Ears* retold by Verna Aardema. Illustrated by Leo and Diane Dillon. Dial (Traditional, ages 6–8).

HONOR BOOKS:

*The Desert Is Theirs* by Byrd Baylor. Illustrated by Peter Parnall. Scribner's (Informational, ages 6–8).

*Strega Nona* retold and illustrated by Tomie de Paola. Prentice Hall (Traditional, ages 5–8).

1977 *Ashanti to Zulu: African Traditions* by Margaret Musgrove. Illustrated by Leo and Diane Dillon. Dial (Informational, ages 7–11).

HONOR BOOKS:

*The Amazing Bone* by William Steig. Farrar (Fantasy, ages 6–8).

*The Contest* by Nonny Hogrogian. Greenwillow (Traditional, ages 6–8).

*Fish for Supper* by M. B. Goffstein. Dial (Realism, ages 3–6).

*The Golem: A Jewish Legend* retold and illustrated by Beverly Brodsky McDermott. Lippincott (Traditional, ages 6–9).

*Hawk, I'm Your Brother* by Byrd Baylor. Illustrated by Peter Parnall. Scribner's (Realism, ages 7–9).

1978 *Noah's Ark* by Peter Spier. Doubleday (Bible/Wordless, ages 3–7).

HONOR BOOKS:

*Castle* by David Macaulay. Houghton (Informational, ages 8–YA).

*It Could Always Be Worse* retold by Margot Zemach. Farrar (Traditional, ages 5–7).

1979 *The Girl Who Loved Wild Horses* by Paul Goble. Bradbury (Traditional, ages 6–8).

HONOR BOOKS:

*Freight Train* by Donald Crews. Greenwillow (Concept, ages 3–6).

*The Way to Start a Day* by Byrd Baylor. Illustrated by Peter Parnall. Scribner's (Informational, ages 6–9).

1980 *Ox-Cart Man* by Donald Hall. Illustrated by Barbara Cooney. Viking (Historical fiction [New England, 1800s], ages 5–8).

HONOR BOOKS:

*Ben's Trumpet* by Rachel Isadora. Greenwillow (Realism, ages 5–7).

*The Treasure* by Uri Shulevitz. Farrar (Traditional, ages 6–8).

*The Garden of Abdul Gasazi* by Chris Van Allsburg. Houghton (Fantasy, ages 6–8).

1981 *Fables* by Arnold Lobel. Harper (Animal fantasy, ages 3–6).

HONOR BOOKS:

*The Bremen-Town Musicians* retold and illustrated by Ilse Plume. Doubleday (Traditional, ages 5–7).

*The Grey Lady and the Strawberry Snatcher* by Molly Bang. Four Winds (Fantasy/wordless, ages 6–8).

*Mice Twice* by Joseph Low. Atheneum (Animal fantasy, ages 3–6).

*Truck* by Donald Crews. Greenwillow (Concept, ages 3–6).

1982 *Jumanji* by Chris Van Allsburg. Houghton (Fantasy, ages 6–8).

HONOR BOOKS:

*A Visit to William Blake's Inn: Poems for Innocent and Experienced Travelers* by Nancy Willard. Illustrated by Alice and Martin Provensen. Harcourt (Biography/Poetry, ages 7–10).

*Where the Buffaloes Begin* by Olaf Baker. Illustrated by Stephen Gammell. Warne (Traditional, ages 7–10).

*On Market Street* by Arnold Lobel. Illustrated by Anita Lobel. Greenwillow (Alphabet, ages 4–6).

*Outside Over There* by Maurice Sendak. Harper (Fantasy, ages 7–10).

1983 *Shadow* by Blaise Cendrars. Translated and illustrated by Marcia Brown. Scribner's (Traditional, ages 8–11).

HONOR BOOKS:

*When I Was Young in the Mountains* by Cynthia Rylant. Illustrated by Diane Goode. Dutton (Realism, ages 7–9).

*A Chair for My Mother* by Vera B. Williams. Greenwillow (Realism, ages 6–8).

1984 *The Glorious Flight: Across the Channel with Louis Blériot* by Alice and Martin Provensen. Viking (Historical fiction [France, 1909], ages 7–10).

HONOR BOOKS:

*Ten, Nine, Eight* by Molly Bang. Greenwillow (Counting, ages 3–6).

*Little Red Riding Hood* by the Brothers Grimm. Retold and illustrated by Trina Schart Hyman. Holiday (Traditional, ages 5–8).

1985 *Saint George and the Dragon* adapted by Margaret Hodges. Illustrated by Trina Schart Hyman. Little, Brown (Traditional, ages 9–12).

HONOR BOOKS:

*Hansel and Gretel* adapted by Rika Lesser. Illustrated by Paul O. Zelinksy. Dodd (Traditional, ages 6–8).

*The Story of Jumping Mouse* retold and illustrated by John Steptoe. Lothrop (Traditional, ages 7–10).

*Have You Seen My Duckling?* by Nancy Tafuri. Greenwillow (Animal fantasy, ages 4–6).

1986 *The Polar Express* by Chris Van Allsburg. Houghton (Fantasy, ages 5–9).

HONOR BOOKS:

*The Relatives Came* by Cynthia Rylant. Illustrated by Stephen Gammell. Bradbury (Realism, ages 6–9).

*King Bidgood's in the Bathtub* by Audrey Wood. Illustrated by Don Wood. Harcourt (Fantasy, ages 5–8).

1987  *Hey, Al* by Arthur Yorinks. Illustrated by Richard Egielski. Farrar (Fantasy, ages 7–10).

HONOR BOOKS:

*The Village of Round and Square Houses* by Ann Grifalconi. Little, Brown (Traditional, ages 7–9).

*Alphabatics* by Suse MacDonald. Bradbury (Alphabet, ages 4–6).

*Rumpelstiltskin* by the Brothers Grimm. Retold and illustrated by Paul O. Zelinsky. Dutton (Traditional, ages 6–9).

1988  *Owl Moon* by Jane Yolen. Illustrated by John Schoenherr. Philomel (Realism, ages 5–8).

HONOR BOOK:

*Mufaro's Beautiful Daughters* retold by John Steptoe. Lothrop (Traditional, ages 6–9).

1989  *Song and Dance Man* by Karen Ackerman. Illustrated by Stephen Gammell. Knopf (Realism, ages 7–10).

HONOR BOOKS:

*Free Fall* by David Wiesner. Lothrop (Fantasy/Wordless, ages 7–10).

*Goldilocks and the Three Bears* retold and illustrated by James Marshall. Dial (Modern Folktale, ages 5–8).

*Mirandy and Brother Wind* by Patricia McKissack. Illustrated by Jerry Pinkney. Knopf (Traditional, ages 7–9).

*The Boy of the Three-Year Nap* by Diane Snyder. Illustrated by Allen Say. Houghton (Traditional, ages 7–10).

1990  *Lon Po Po: A Red-Riding Hood Story from China* translated and illustrated by Ed Young. Philomel (Traditional, ages 5–8).

HONOR BOOKS:

*Hershel and the Hanukkah Goblins* by Eric Kimmel. Illustrated by Trina Schart Hyman. Holiday (Modern folktale, ages 7–10).

*The Talking Eggs* adapted by Robert D. San Souci. Illustrated by Jerry Pinkney. Dial (Traditional, ages 6–9).

*Bill Peet: An Autobiography* by Bill Peet. Houghton (Biography, ages 7–10).

*Color Zoo* by Lois Ehlert. Lippincott (Concept, ages 3–6).

1991  *Black and White* by David Macaulay. Houghton (Mystery, ages 8–12).

HONOR BOOKS:

*Puss'n Boots* by Charles Perrault. Illustrated by Fred Marcellino. Farrar (Traditional, ages 5–7).

*"More, More, More." Said the Baby: 3 Love Stories* by Vera Williams. Greenwillow (Realism, ages 3–5).

1992  *Tuesday* by David Wiesner. Clarion (Fantasy/Wordless, ages 7–10).

HONOR BOOK:

*Tar Beach* by Faith Ringgold. Crown (Multicultural [African-American], ages 6–9).

1993  *Mirette on the High Wire* by Emily Arnold McCully. Putnam (Realism, ages 7–9).

HONOR BOOKS:

*Seven Blind Mice* by Ed Young. Philomel (Modern folktale, ages 6–10).

*The Stinky Cheese Man and Other Fairly Stupid Tales* by Jon Scieszka and Lane Smith. Illustrated by Lane Smith. Viking (Modern folktale, ages 7–11).

*Working Cotton* by Sherley Anne Williams. Illustrated by Carole Byard. Harcourt (Realism [African-American], ages 7–9).

1994  *Grandfather's Journey* by Allen Say. Houghton (Biography, ages 7–9).

HONOR BOOKS:

*Peppe the Lamplighter* by Elisa Bartone. Illustrated by Ted Lewin. Lothrop (Realism, ages 7–9).

*In the Small, Small Pond* by Denise Fleming. Holt (Pattern, ages 5–7).

*Owen* by Kevin Henkes. Greenwillow (Animal fantasy, ages 5–7).

*Raven: A Trickster Tale from the Pacific Northwest* by Gerald McDermott. Harcourt (Traditional [Native-American], ages 7–9).

*Yo! Yes?* by Chris Raschka. Orchard (Realism/Multicultural, ages 5–7).

1995  *Smoky Night* by Eve Bunting. Illustrated by David Diaz. Harcourt (Realism/Multicultural, ages 6–8).

HONOR BOOKS:

*Swamp Angel* by Anne Isaacs. Illustrated by Paul O. Zelinsky. Dutton (Modern folktale, ages 6–9).

*John Henry* by Julius Lester. Illustrated by Jerry Pinkney. Dial (Traditional, ages 6–9).

*Time Flies* by Eric Rohmann. Crown (Wordless, ages 6–9).

1996  *Officer Buckle and Gloria* by Peggy Rathman. Putnam (Animal fantasy, ages 5–7).

HONOR BOOKS:

*Alphabet City* by Stephen T. Johnson. Viking (Concept, ages 7–9).

*The Faithful Friend* by Robert D. San Souci. Illustrated by Brian Pinkney. Simon & Schuster (Traditional, ages 10–14).

*Tops & Bottoms* by Janet Stevens. Harcourt (Traditional, ages 6–8).

*Zin! Zin! Zin! A Violin* by Lloyd Moss. Illustrated by Marjorie Priceman. Simon & Schuster (Concept, ages 5–7).

1997 *Golem* by David Wisniewski. Clarion (Traditional, ages 6–12).

HONOR BOOKS:

*Hush! A Thai Lullaby* by Minfong Ho. Illustrated by Holly Meade. Orchard (Poetry, ages 2–6).
*The Graphic Alphabet* by David Pelletier. Orchard (ABC/Art, ages 7–10).
*The Paperboy* by Dav Pilkey. Orchard (Picture storybook, ages 8–10).
*Starry Messenger* by Peter Sís. Farrar (Biography, ages 9–14).

1998 *Rapunzel* by Paul O. Zelinsky. Dutton (Traditional, ages 7–10).

HONOR BOOKS:

*The Gardener* by Sarah Stewart. Illustrated by David Small. Farrar (Picture storybook, ages 7–10).
*Harlem* by Walter Dean Myers. Illustrated by Christopher Myers. Scholastic (Poetry, ages 10–14).
*There Was an Old Lady Who Swallowed a Fly* by Simms Taback. Viking (Folk poem/Engineered, ages 5–7).

1999 *Snowflake Bentley* by Jacqueline Briggs Martin. Illustrated by Mary Azarian. Houghton (Biography, ages 8–12).

HONOR BOOKS:

*Duke Ellington: The Piano Prince and His Orchestra* by Andrea Davis Pinkney. Illustrated by Brian Pinkney. Hyperion (Biography, ages 8–10).
*No, David!* by David Shannon. Scholastic. (Realism/Pattern, ages 3–5).
*Snow* by Uri Shulevitz. Farrar (Realism, ages 4–6).
*Tibet through the Red Box* by Peter Sís. Farrar (Realism, ages 7–9).

2000 *Joseph Had a Little Overcoat* by Simms Taback. Viking (Traditional fantasy/ Pattern, ages 4–7).

HONOR BOOKS:

*When Sophie Gets Angry—Really, Really Angry* by Molly Bang. Scholastic (Realism, ages 4–6).
*A Child's Calendar* by John Updike. Illustrated by Trina Schart Hyman. Holiday House (Poetry, ages 5–9).
*The Ugly Duckling* adapted and illustrated by Jerry Pinkney. Morrow (Modern folktale, ages 4–7).
*Sector 7* by David Weisner. Clarion (Modern fantasy/Wordless, ages 5–9).

2001 *So You Want to Be President?* by Judith St. George. Illustrated by David Small. Philomel (Informational, ages 7–10).

HONOR BOOKS:

*Casey at the Bat: A Ballad of the Republic Sung in the Year 1888* by Ernest L. Thayer. Illustrated by Christopher Bing. Handprint (Poetry, ages 7–12).
*Click, Clack, Moo: Cows That Type* by Doreen Cronin. Illustrated by Betsy Lewin. Simon & Schuster (Animal fantasy, ages 6–9).
*Olivia* by Ian Falconer. Atheneum (Animal fantasy, ages 4–8).

## Newbery Medal

*This award, sponsored by the Association for Library Service to Children Division of the American Library Association, is given to the author of the most distinguished contribution to children's literature published during the preceding year. Only U.S. citizens or residents are eligible for this award.*

1922 *The Story of Mankind* by Hendrik Willem Van Loon. Liveright (Informational, ages 12–YA).

HONOR BOOKS:

*The Great Quest* by Charles Boardman Hawes. Little, Brown (Historical fiction [New England, 1826], ages 11–YA).
*Cedric the Forester* by Bernard G. Marshall. Appleton (Historical fiction [England, 1200s], ages 11–YA).
*The Old Tobacco Shop* by William Bowen. Macmillan (Fantasy, ages 9–12).
*The Golden Fleece and the Heroes Who Lived before Achilles* by Padraic Colum. Macmillan (Traditional fantasy, ages 9–13).
*Windy Hill* by Cornelia Meigs. Macmillan (Realism, ages 9–12).

1923 *The Voyages of Doctor Dolittle* by Hugh Lofting. Lippincott (Fantasy, ages 8–12).

(No record of the runners-up.)

1924 *The Dark Frigate* by Charles Boardman Hawes. Little, Brown (Historical fiction [England, 1600s], ages 10–YA).

(No record of the runners-up.)

1925 *Tales from Silver Lands* by Charles J. Finger. Illustrated by Paul Honoré. Doubleday (Traditional fantasy, ages 9–YA).

HONOR BOOKS:

*Nicholas* by Anne Carroll Moore. Putnam (Fantasy [Little people], ages 8–11).
*Dream Coach* by Anne and Dillwyn Parrish. Macmillan (Fantasy, ages 7–11).

1926 *Shen of the Sea* by Arthur Bowie Chrisman. Illustrated by Else Hasselriis. Dutton (Fantasy [Literary tales], ages 9–12).

HONOR BOOK:

*The Voyagers* by Padraic Colum. Macmillan (Traditional fantasy/Informational, ages 10–12).

1927 *Smoky, the Cowhorse* by Will James. Scribner's (Animal realism, ages 9–12).

(No record of the runners-up.)

1928 *Gay-Neck, The Story of a Pigeon* by Dhan Gopal Mukerji. Illustrated by Boris Artzybasheff. Dutton (Animal realism, ages 9–YA).

HONOR BOOKS:

*The Wonder Smith and His Son* by Ella Young. McKay/Longmans (Traditional fantasy [Ireland], ages 10–YA).

*Downright Dencey* by Caroline Dale Snedeker. Doubleday (Historical fiction [New England, 1812], ages 9–13).

1929 *The Trumpeter of Krakow* by Eric P. Kelly. Illustrated by Angela Pruszynska. Macmillan (Historical Fiction [Poland, 1400s], ages 11–YA).

HONOR BOOKS:

*The Pigtail of Ah Lee Ben Loo* by John Bennett. McKay/Longmans (Fantasy/Poetry, ages 8–13).

*Millions of Cats* by Wanda Gág. Coward-McCann (Picture book; Fantasy, ages 5–7).

*The Boy Who Was* by Grace T. Hallock. Dutton (Historical fiction [Italy through 3,000 years], ages 10–YA).

*Clearing Weather* by Cornelia Meigs. Little, Brown (Historical fiction [USA, 1787], ages 11–YA).

*The Runaway Papoose* by Grace P. Moon. Doubleday (Realism/Multicultural, ages 8–11).

*Tod of the Fens* by Eleanor Whitney. Macmillan (Historical fiction [England 1400s], ages 11–YA).

1930 *Hitty: Her First Hundred Years* by Rachel Field. Illustrated by Dorothy P. Lathrop. Macmillan (Historical fantasy, ages 9–13).

HONOR BOOKS:

*The Tangle-Coated Horse and Other Tales: Episodes from the Fionn Saga* by Ella Young. Illustrated by Vera Brock. Longmans (Traditional, ages 10–13).

*Vaino: A Boy of New Finland* by Julia Davis Adams. Illustrated by Lempi Ostman. Dutton (Historical fiction [Finland, 1920s], ages 11–YA).

*Pran of Albania* by Elizabeth C. Miller. Doubleday (Realism, ages 11–YA).

*The Jumping-Off Place* by Marian Hurd McNeely. McKay/Longmans (Realism, ages 10–YA).

*A Daughter of the Seine* by Jeanette Eaton. Harper (Biography, ages 12–YA).

*Little Blacknose* by Hildegarde Hoyt Swift. Illustrated by Lynd Ward. Harcourt (Fantasy, ages 8–11).

1931 *The Cat Who Went to Heaven* by Elizabeth Coatsworth. Illustrated by Lynd Ward. Macmillan (Fantasy, ages 10–13).

HONOR BOOKS:

*Floating Island* by Anne Parrish. Harper (Fantasy, ages 8–11).

*The Dark Star of Itza* by Alida Malkus. Harcourt (Historical fiction [Mayan Empire], ages 11–YA).

*Queer Person* by Ralph Hubbard. Doubleday (Historical fiction/Multicultural [Native-American], ages 9–13).

*Mountains Are Free* by Julia Davis Adams. Dutton (Historical fiction [Switzerland], ages 11–YA).

*Spice and the Devil's Cave* by Agnes D. Hewes. Knopf (Historical fiction [Portugal, 1400s], ages 11–YA).

*Meggy McIntosh* by Elizabeth Janet Gray. Doubleday (Historical fiction [Scotland, USA, 1775], ages 10–YA).

*Garram the Hunter: A Boy of the Hill Tribes* by Herbert Best. Illustrated by Allena Best (Erick Berry). Doubleday (Realism [Africa], ages 9–13).

*Ood-Le-Uk, the Wanderer* by Alice Lide and Margaret Johansen. Illustrated by Raymond Lufkin. Little, Brown (Realism [Alaska], ages 11–14).

1932 *Waterless Mountain* by Laura Adams Armer. Illustrated by Sidney Armer and Laura Adams Armer. McKay/Longmans (Realism/Multicultural [Native-American], ages 9–13).

HONOR BOOKS:

*The Fairy Circus* by Dorothy Lathrop. Macmillan (Fantasy, ages 6–9).

*Calico Bush* by Rachel Field. Macmillan (Historical fiction, [USA, 1743], ages 9–13).

*Boy of the South Seas* by Eunice Tietjens. Coward-McCann (Realism, ages 9–12).

*Out of the Flame* by Eloise Lownsbery. McKay/Longmans (Historical fiction [France, 1500s], ages 10–YA).

*Jane's Island* by Marjorie Hill Alee. Houghton (Realism, ages 9–13).

*The Truce of the Wolf and Other Tales of Old Italy* by Mary Gould Davis. Harcourt (Traditional fantasy, ages 8–13).

1933 *Young Fu of the Upper Yangtze* by Elizabeth Foreman Lewis. Illustrated by Kurt Wiese. Holt (Realism, ages 10–YA).

HONOR BOOKS:

*Swift Rivers* by Cornelia Meigs. Little, Brown (Historical fiction [USA, 1835], ages 10–13).

*The Railroad to Freedom* by Hildegarde Swift. Harcourt (Biography, ages 10–YA).

*Children of the Soil* by Nora Burglon. Doubleday (Realism, ages 9–12).

1934 *Invincible Louisa: The Story of the Author of "Little Women"* by Cornelia Meigs. Little, Brown (Biography, ages 10–12).

HONOR BOOKS:

*The Forgotten Daughter* by Caroline Dale Snedeker. Doubleday (Historical fiction [Italy, second century B.C.], ages 11–YA).

*Swords of Steel* by Elsie Singmaster. Houghton (Historical fiction [USA, 1859], ages 11–YA).

*ABC Bunny* by Wanda Gág. Coward-McCann (Picture book. Fantasy/Alphabet, ages 3–7).

*Winged Girl of Knossos* by Erik Berry. Appleton (Historical fiction [Ancient Greece], ages 10–YA).

*New Land* by Sarah L. Schmidt. McBride (Realism, ages 10–YA).

*The Apprentice of Florence* by Anne Kyle. Houghton (Historical fiction [Italy, 1400s], ages 11–YA).

*The Big Tree of Bunlahy: Stories of My Own Countryside* by Padraic Colum. Illustrated by Jack Yeats. Macmillan (Fantasy, ages 8–YA).

*Glory of the Seas* by Agnes D. Hewes. Illustrated by N. C. Wyeth. Knopf (Historical fiction [USA, 1850s], ages 11–YA).

1935 *Dobry* by Monica Shannon. Illustrated by Atanas Katchamakoff. Viking (Realism, ages 9–11).

HONOR BOOKS:

*The Pageant of Chinese History* by Elizabeth Seeger. McKay/Longmans (Informational, ages 11–YA).

*Davy Crockett* by Constance Rourke. Harcourt (Biography, ages 12–YA).

*A Day on Skates: The Story of a Dutch Picnic* by Hilda Van Stockum. Harper (Realism, ages 6–8).

1936 *Caddie Woodlawn* by Carol Ryrie Brink. Illustrated by Kate Seredy. Macmillan (Historical fiction [USA, 1860s], ages 9–12).

HONOR BOOKS:

*Honk: The Moose* by Phil Strong. Illustrated by Kurt Wiese. Dodd (Realism, ages 7–11).

*The Good Master* by Kate Seredy. Viking (Realism, ages 9–11).

*Young Walter Scott* by Elizabeth Janet Gray. Viking (Biography, ages 11–YA).

*All Sail Set* by Armstrong Sperry. Winston (Historical fiction [United States, 1851], ages 10–13).

1937 *Roller Skates* by Ruth Sawyer. Illustrated by Valenti Angelo. Viking (Realism, ages 8–10).

HONOR BOOKS:

*Phoebe Fairchild: Her Book* by Lois Lenski. Lippincott (Historical fiction [New England, 1830s], ages 9–12).

*Whistler's Van* by Idwal Jones. Viking (Realism, ages 9–13).

*The Golden Basket* by Ludwig Bemelmans. Viking (Realism, ages 6–9).

*Winterbound* by Margery Bianco. Viking (Realism, ages 11–YA).

*Audubon* by Constance Rourke. Harcourt (Biography, ages 11–YA).

*The Codfish Musket* by Agnes D. Hewes. Doubleday (Historical fiction [USA, 1780s], ages 11–YA).

1938 *The White Stag* by Kate Seredy. Viking (Traditional, ages 10–YA).

HONOR BOOKS:

*Bright Island* by Mabel L. Robinson. Random (Realism, ages 11–YA).

*Pecos Bill* by James Cloyd Bowman. Little, Brown (Traditional, ages 9–YA).

*On the Banks of Plum Creek* by Laura Ingalls Wilder. Harper (Historical fiction [USA, 1870s], ages 8–11).

1939 *Thimble Summer* by Elizabeth Enright. Holt (Realism, ages 8–11).

HONOR BOOKS:

*Leader by Destiny: George Washington, Man and Patriot* by Jeanette Eaton. Harcourt (Biography, ages 11–YA).

*Penn* by Elizabeth Janet Gray. Viking (Biography, ages 11–YA).

*Nino* by Valenti Angelo. Viking (Realism, ages 9–11).

*"Hello, the Boat!"* by Phyllis Crawford. Holt (Historical fiction [USA, 1817], ages 9–13).

*Mr. Popper's Penguins* by Richard and Florence Atwater. Little, Brown (Animal fantasy, ages 7–11).

1940 *Daniel Boone* by James H. Daugherty. Viking (Biography, ages 10–YA).

HONOR BOOKS:

*The Singing Tree* by Kate Seredy. Viking (Historical fiction [Eastern Europe, 1910s], ages 9–12).

*Runner of the Mountain Tops* by Mabel L. Robinson. Random (Biography, ages 11–YA).

*By the Shores of Silver Lake* by Laura Ingalls Wilder. Harper (Historical fiction [USA, 1880s], ages 8–10).

*Boy with a Pack* by Stephen W. Meader. Harcourt (Historical fiction [USA, 1837], ages 9–13).

1941 *Call It Courage* by Armstrong Sperry. Macmillan (Realism, ages 9–12).

HONOR BOOKS:

*Blue Willow* by Doris Gates. Viking (Historical fiction [USA, 1930s], ages 8–11).

*Young Mac of Fort Vancouver* by Mary Jane Carr. Crowell (Historical fiction [Canada, early 1800s], ages 10–YA).

*The Long Winter* by Laura Ingalls Wilder. Harper (Historical fiction [USA, 1880s], ages 9–13).

*Nansen* by Anna Gertrude Hall. Viking (Biography, ages 11–YA).

1942 *The Matchlock Gun* by Walter D. Edmonds. Illustrated by Paul Lantz. Dodd (Historical fiction [Colonial America, 1757], ages 8–11).

HONOR BOOKS:

*Little Town on the Prairie* by Laura Ingalls Wilder. Harper (Historical fiction [USA, 1881], ages 8–10).

*George Washington's World* by Genevieve Foster. Scribner's (Informational/Biography, ages 10–YA).

*Indian Captive: The Story of Mary Jemison* by Lois Lenski. Lippincott (Historical fiction [USA, 1750s], ages 9–11).

*Down Ryton Water* by Eva Roe Gaggin. Illustrated by Elmer Hader. Viking (Historical fiction [England, Netherlands, 1600s], ages 12–YA).

1943 *Adam of the Road* by Elizabeth Janet Gray. Illustrated by Robert Lawson. Viking (Historical fiction [England, 1290s], ages 9–12).

HONOR BOOKS:

*The Middle Moffat* by Eleanor Estes. Harcourt (Realism, ages 8–10).

*"Have You Seen Tom Thumb?"* by Mabel Leigh Hunt. Lippincott (Biography, ages 10-YA).

1944 *Johnny Tremain* by Esther Forbes. Illustrated by Lynd Ward. Houghton (Historical fiction [Boston, 1770s], ages 12–YA).

HONOR BOOKS:

*These Happy Golden Years* by Laura Ingalls Wilder. Harper (Historical fiction [USA, 1880s], ages 8–10).

*Fog Magic* by Julia L. Sauer. Viking (Modern fantasy, ages 9–12).

*Rufus M.* by Eleanor Estes. Harcourt (Realism, ages 8–10).

*Mountain Born* by Elizabeth Yates. Coward-McCann (Animal realism, ages 9–11).

1945 *Rabbit Hill* by Robert Lawson. Viking (Animal fantasy, ages 7–9).

HONOR BOOKS:

*The Hundred Dresses* by Eleanor Estes. Harcourt (Realism, ages 7–9).

*The Silver Pencil* by Alice Dalgliesh. Scribner's (Realism, ages 10–YA).

*Abraham Lincoln's World* by Genevieve Foster. Scribner's (Informational/Biography, ages 10–YA).

*Lone Journey: The Life of Roger Williams* by Jeanette Eaton. Illustrated by Woodi Ishmael. Harcourt (Biography, ages 13–YA).

1946 *Strawberry Girl* by Lois Lenski. Lippincott (Historical fiction [Florida, early 1900s], ages 8–10).

HONOR BOOKS:

*Justin Morgan Had a Horse* by Marguerite Henry. Follett (Animal Realism, ages 8–10).

*The Moved-Outers* by Florence Crannell Means. Houghton (Multicultural, ages 10–12).

*Bhimsa, the Dancing Bear* by Christine Weston. Scribner's (Realism, ages 8–10).

*New Found World* by Katherine B. Shippen. Viking (Informational, ages 10–YA).

1947 *Miss Hickory* by Carolyn Sherwin Bailey. Illustrated by Ruth Gannett. Viking (Fantasy/Toys and dolls, ages 7–9).

HONOR BOOKS:

*The Wonderful Year* by Nancy Barnes. Messner (Realism, ages 9–12).

*The Big Tree* by Mary and Conrad Buff. Viking (Informational, ages 9–13).

*The Heavenly Tenants* by William Maxwell. Harper (Fantasy, ages 10–YA).

*The Avion My Uncle Flew* by Cyrus Fisher. Appleton (Realism, ages 10–13).

*The Hidden Treasure of Glaston* by Eleanore M. Jewett. Viking (Historical fiction [England, 1172], ages 10–13).

1948 *The Twenty-One Balloons* by William Pène du Bois. Lothrop (Fantasy, ages 9–11).

HONOR BOOKS:

*Pancakes-Paris* by Claire Huchet Bishop. Viking (Realism, ages 8–11).

*Li Lun, Lad of Courage* by Carolyn Treffinger. Abingdon (Realism, ages 9–12).

*The Quaint and Curious Quest of Johnny Longfoot, The Shoe-King's Son* by Catherine Besterman. Bobbs-Merrill (Traditional, ages 8–10).

*The Cow-Tail Switch, And Other West African Stories* by Harold Courlander and George Herzog. Holt (Traditional, ages 8–13).

*Misty of Chincoteague* by Marguerite Henry. Illustrated by Wesley Dennis. Rand (Animal realism [horse], ages 9–12).

1949 *King of the Wind* by Marguerite Henry. Illustrated by Wesley Dennis. Rand (Historical fiction [Morocco, Europe, 1700s], ages 9–12).

HONOR BOOKS:
*Seabird* by Holling Clancy Holling. Houghton (Informational, ages 9–12).
*Daughter of the Mountains* by Louise Rankin. Viking (Realism, ages 9–11).
*My Father's Dragon* by Ruth S. Gannett. Random (Fantasy, ages 6–9).
*Story of the Negro* by Arna Bontemps. Knopf (Informational, ages 10–YA).

1950 *The Door in the Wall* by Marguerite de Angeli. Doubleday (Historical fiction [England, 1300s], ages 9–11).

HONOR BOOKS:
*Tree of Freedom* by Rebecca Caudill. Viking (Historical fiction [USA, 1780s], ages 10–12).
*The Blue Cat of Castle Town* by Catherine Coblentz. McKay/Longmans (Traditional, ages 9–YA).
*Kildee House* by Rutherford Montgomery. Doubleday (Realism, ages 8–12).
*George Washington* by Genevieve Foster. Scribner's (Biography, ages 8–11).
*Song of the Pines* by Walter and Marion Havighurst. Holt (Historical fiction [USA, 1850s], ages YA).

1951 *Amos Fortune, Free Man* by Elizabeth Yates. Illustrated by Nora Unwin. Dutton (Biography, ages 9–11).

HONOR BOOKS:
*Better Known as Johnny Appleseed* by Mabel Leigh Hunt. Lippincott (Biography, ages 11–YA).
*Gandhi, Fighter without a Sword* by Jeanette Eaton. Morrow (Biography, ages 11–YA).
*Abraham Lincoln, Friend of the People* by Clara I. Judson. Follett (Biography, ages 9–13).
*The Story of Appleby Capple* by Anne Parrish. Harper (Fantasy, ages 6–8).

1952 *Ginger Pye* by Eleanor Estes. Harcourt (Realism, ages 8–10).

HONOR BOOKS:
*Americans before Columbus* by Elizabeth Chesley Baity. Viking (Informational, ages 10–YA).
*Minn of the Mississippi* by Holling Clancy Holling. Houghton (Informational, ages 7–9).
*The Defender* by Nicholas Kalashnikoff. Scribner's (Realism, ages 9–13).
*The Light at Tern Rock* by Julia L. Sauer. Viking (Realism, ages 7–9).
*The Apple and the Arrow* by Mary and Conrad Buff. Houghton (Biography, ages 8–10).

1953 *Secret of the Andes* by Ann Nolan Clark. Illustrated by Jean Charlot. Viking (Realism/Multicultural [Native-American], ages 11–13).

HONOR BOOKS:
*Charlotte's Web* by E. B. White. Harper (Animal fantasy, ages 7–9).
*Moccasin Trail* by Eloise J. McGraw. Coward-McCann (Historical fiction [USA, 1830s], ages 11–YA).
*Red Sails to Capri* by Ann Weil. Viking (Historical fiction [Italy, 1826], ages 9–11).
*The Bears on Hemlock Mountain* by Alice Dalgliesh. Scribner's (Historical fiction [USA, 1800s], ages 6–9).
*Birthdays of Freedom* (Vol. 1), by Genevieve Foster. Scribner's (Informational/Biography, ages 10–13).

1954 *And Now Miguel* by Joseph Krumgold. Illustrated by Jean Charlot. Crowell (Historical fiction [New Mexico, 1940s], ages 9–12).

HONOR BOOKS:
*All Alone* by Claire Huchet Bishop. Viking (Realism, ages 8–11).
*Shadrach* by Meindert DeJong. Harper (Animal realism, ages 8–10).
*Hurry Home, Candy* by Meindert DeJong. Harper (Animal realism, ages 8–10).
*Theodore Roosevelt, Fighting Patriot* by Clara I. Judson. Follett (Biography, ages 9–11).
*Magic Maize* by Mary and Conrad Buff. Houghton (Realism, ages 8–11).

1955 *The Wheel on the School* by Meindert DeJong. Illustrated by Maurice Sendak. Harper (Realism, ages 8–11).

HONOR BOOKS:
*The Courage of Sarah Noble* by Alice Dalgliesh. Scribner's (Historical fiction [USA, 1707], ages 8–10).
*Banner in the Sky* by James Ramsey Ullman. Lippincott (Historical fiction [Europe, 1860s], ages 10–YA).

1956 *Carry On, Mr. Bowditch* by Jean Lee Latham. Houghton (Biography, ages 10–13).

HONOR BOOKS:
*The Golden Name Day* by Jennie D. Lindquist. Harper (Realism, ages 8–11).
*The Secret River* by Marjorie Kinnan Rawlings. Scribner's (Fantasy, ages 6–9).
*Men, Microscopes and Living Things* by Katherine B. Shippen. Viking (Informational, ages 10–YA).

1957  *Miracles on Maple Hill* by Virginia Sorensen. Illustrated by Beth and Joe Krush. Harcourt (Realism, ages 8–10).

HONOR BOOKS:

*Old Yeller* by Fred Gipson. Harper (Animal realism, ages 9–12).

*The House of Sixty Fathers* by Meindert DeJong. Harper (Historical fiction [China, 1940s], ages 9–13).

*Mr. Justice Holmes* by Clara I. Judson. Follett (Biography, ages 9–13).

*The Corn Grows Ripe* by Dorothy Rhoads. Viking (Realism, ages 9–11).

*The Black Fox of Lorne* by Marguerite de Angeli. Doubleday (Historical fiction [Scotland, tenth century], ages 9–12).

1958  *Rifles for Watie* by Harold Keith. Illustrated by Peter Burchard. Crowell (Historical fiction, [USA, 1860s], ages 10–YA).

HONOR BOOKS:

*The Horsecatcher* by Mari Sandoz. Westminster (Realism, ages 11–YA).

*Gone-Away Lake* by Elizabeth Enright. Harcourt (Realism, ages 8–11).

*The Great Wheel* by Robert Lawson. Viking (Historical fiction [USA, 1890s], ages 9–12).

*Tom Paine, Freedom's Apostle* by Leo Gurko. Crowell (Biography, ages 11–YA).

1959  *The Witch of Blackbird Pond* by Elizabeth George Speare. Houghton (Historical fiction [USA, 1680s], ages 12–YA).

HONOR BOOKS:

*The Family under the Bridge* by Natalie S. Carlson. Harper (Realism, ages 8–10).

*Along Came a Dog* by Meindert DeJong. Harper (Animal realism, ages 9–YA).

*Chucaro: Wild Pony of the Pampa* by Francis Kalnay. Harcourt (Animal realism, ages 9–13).

*The Perilous Road* by William O. Steele. Harcourt (Historical fiction [USA, 1860s], ages 9–13).

1960  *Onion John* by Joseph Krumgold. Illustrated by Symeon Shimin. Crowell (Realism, ages 9–12).

HONOR BOOKS:

*My Side of the Mountain* by Jean George. Dutton (Realism, ages 10–12).

*America Is Born* by Gerald Johnson. Morrow (Informational, ages 9–13).

*The Gammage Cup* by Carol Kendall. Harcourt (Fantasy [little people], ages 9–12).

1961  *Island of the Blue Dolphins* by Scott O'Dell. Houghton (Historical fiction [USA, 1800s]/Multicultural [Native-American], ages 9–13).

HONOR BOOKS:

*America Moves Forward* by Gerald Johnson. Morrow (Informational, ages 9–13).

*Old Ramon* by Jack Schaefer. Houghton (Realism, ages 10–YA).

*The Cricket in Times Square* by George Selden. Farrar (Animal fantasy, ages 7–9).

1962  *The Bronze Bow* by Elizabeth George Speare. Houghton (Historical fiction [Jerusalem, 1st century A.D.], ages 12–YA).

HONOR BOOKS:

*Frontier Living* by Edwin Tunis. World (Informational, ages 10–YA).

*The Golden Goblet* by Eloise J. McGraw. Coward (Historical fiction [Ancient Egypt], ages 10–YA).

*Belling the Tiger* by Mary Stolz. Harper (Fantasy, ages 7–9).

1963  *A Wrinkle in Time* by Madeleine L'Engle. Farrar (Fantasy [science fiction], ages 9–12).

HONOR BOOKS:

*Thistle and Thyme* by Sorche Nic Leodhas (pseudonym of Leclaire Alger). Holt (Traditional fantasy, ages 7–11).

*Men of Athens* by Olivia Coolidge. Houghton (Biography, ages 11–YA).

1964  *It's Like This, Cat* by Emily Cheney Neville. Harper (Realism, ages 10–YA).

HONOR BOOKS:

*Rascal* by Sterling North. Dutton (Animal realism, ages 9–11).

*The Loner* by Esther Wier. McKay/Longmans (Realism, ages 9–13).

1965  *Shadow of a Bull* by Maia Wojciechowska. Atheneum (Realism, ages 10–12).

HONOR BOOK:

*Across Five Aprils* by Irene Hunt. Follett (Historical fiction [USA, 1860s], ages 10–13).

1966  *I, Juan de Pareja* by Elizabeth Borten de Treviño. Farrar (Biography, ages 10–12).

HONOR BOOKS:

*The Black Cauldron* by Lloyd Alexander. Holt (Fantasy [quest], ages 10–12).

*The Animal Family* by Randall Jarrell. Pantheon (Fantasy, ages 10–13).

*The Noonday Friends* by Mary Stolz. Harper (Realism, ages 9–11).

1967 *Up a Road Slowly* by Irene Hunt. Follett (Realism, ages 10–YA).

HONOR BOOKS:

*The King's Fifth* by Scott O'Dell. Houghton (Historical fiction [Spain, 1500s], ages 10–12).
*Zlateh the Goat and Other Stories* by Isaac Bashevis Singer. Harper (Fantasy, ages 8–11).
*The Jazz Man* by Mary H. Weik. Atheneum (Realism, ages 9–12).

1968 *From the Mixed-up Files of Mrs. Basil E. Frankweiler* by E. L. Konigsburg. Atheneum (Realism, ages 10–12).

HONOR BOOKS:

*Jennifer, Hecate, Macbeth, William McKinley, and Me, Elizabeth* by E. L. Konigsburg. Atheneum (Realism, ages 9–11).
*The Black Pearl* by Scott O'Dell. Houghton (Realism, ages 9–11).
*The Fearsome Inn* by Isaac Bashevis Singer. Scribner's (Fantasy, ages 10–YA).
*The Egypt Game* by Zilpha Keatley Snyder. Atheneum (Realism, ages 9–11).

1969 *The High King* by Lloyd Alexander. Holt (Fantasy [quest], ages 10–12).

HONOR BOOKS:

*To Be a Slave* by Julius Lester. Dial (Informational, ages 11–YA).
*When Shlemiel Went to Warsaw and Other Stories* by Isaac Bashevis Singer. Farrar (Fantasy, ages 9–YA).

1970 *Sounder* by William H. Armstrong. Harper (Historical fiction [Southern USA, early twentieth century], ages 10–13).

HONOR BOOKS:

*Our Eddie* by Sulamith Ish-Kishor. Pantheon (Realism, ages 11–YA).
*The Many Ways of Seeing: An Introduction to the Pleasure of Art* by Janet Gaylord Moore. World (Informational, ages 10–YA).
*Journey Outside* by Mary Q. Steele. Viking (Fantasy, ages 10–13).

1971 *The Summer of the Swans* by Betsy Byars. Viking (Realism, ages 10–13).

HONOR BOOKS:

*Kneeknock Rise* by Natalie Babbitt. Farrar (Fantasy, ages 9–13).
*Enchantress from the Stars* by Sylvia Louise Engdahl. Atheneum (Fantasy [science fiction], ages 11–YA).
*Sing Down the Moon* by Scott O'Dell. Houghton (Historical fiction [USA, 1860s], ages 12–YA).

1972 *Mrs. Frisby and the Rats of NIMH* by Robert C. O'Brien. Atheneum (Animal fantasy, ages 10–12).

HONOR BOOKS:

*Incident at Hawk's Hill* by Allan W. Eckert. Little, Brown (Historical fiction [Canada, 1870]/Animal realism, ages 10–12).
*The Planet of Junior Brown* by Virginia Hamilton. Macmillan (Realism, ages 11–YA).
*The Tombs of Atuan* by Ursula K. LeGuin. Atheneum (Fantasy [quest], ages 10–YA).
*Annie and the Old One* by Miska Miles. Little, Brown. (Picture book; Realism/Multicultural [Native-American], ages 8–10).
*The Headless Cupid* by Zilpha Keatley Snyder. Atheneum (Realism [mystery], ages 10–12).

1973 *Julie of the Wolves* by Jean Craighead George. Harper (Realism/Multicultural [Native-American], ages 10–13).

HONOR BOOKS:

*Frog and Toad Together* by Arnold Lobel. Harper (Picture book; Animal fantasy, ages 3–7).
*The Upstairs Room* by Johanna Reiss. Crowell (Historical fiction [Holland, 1940s], ages 9–13).
*The Witches of Worm* by Zilpha Keatley Snyder. Atheneum (Realism, ages 10–12).

1974 *The Slave Dancer* by Paula Fox. Bradbury (Historical fiction [USA, Africa, 1840s], ages 10–13).

HONOR BOOK:

*The Dark Is Rising* by Susan Cooper. Atheneum/McElderry (Fantasy [quest], ages 11–YA).

1975 *M. C. Higgins, the Great* by Virginia Hamilton. Macmillan (Realism/Multicultural [African-American], ages 10–13).

HONOR BOOKS:

*Figgs & Phantoms* by Ellen Raskin. Dutton (Realism, ages 10–13).
*My Brother Sam Is Dead* by James Lincoln Collier and Christopher Collier. Four Winds (Historical fiction [Colonial America, 1700s], ages 10–YA).
*The Perilous Gard* by Elizabeth Marie Pope. Houghton (Historical fiction [England, 1558], ages 12–YA).
*Philip Hall Likes Me. I Reckon Maybe* by Bette Greene. Dial (Realism/Multicultural [African-American], ages 9–11).

1976 *The Grey King* by Susan Cooper. Atheneum/McElderry (Fantasy [quest], ages 11–YA).

HONOR BOOKS:

*The Hundred Penny Box* by Sharon Bell Mathis. Viking (Realism/Multicultural [African-American], ages 8–11).

*Dragonwings* by Laurence Yep. Harper (Historical fiction [San Francisco, 1903–1909]/Multicultural [Chinese-American], ages 10–13).

1977 *Roll of Thunder, Hear My Cry* by Mildred D. Taylor. Dial (Historical fiction [Mississippi, 1934]/ Multicultural [African-American], ages 9–13).

HONOR BOOKS:

*Abel's Island* by William Steig. Farrar (Animal fantasy, ages 8–10).

*A String in the Harp* by Nancy Bond. Atheneum/ McElderry (Fantasy, ages 11–13).

1978 *The Bridge to Terabithia* by Katherine Paterson. Crowell (Realism, ages 9–11).

HONOR BOOKS:

*Anpao: An American Indian Odyssey* by Jamake Highwater. Lippincott (Traditional fantasy/Multicultural [Native American], ages 10–12).

*Ramona and Her Father* by Beverly Cleary. Morrow (Realism, ages 7–9).

1979 *The Westing Game* by Ellen Raskin. Dutton (Realism [mystery], ages 10–12).

HONOR BOOK:

*The Great Gilly Hopkins* by Katherine Paterson. Crowell (Realism, ages 9–12).

1980 *A Gathering of Days: A New England Girl's Journal, 1830–32* by Joan Blos. Scribner's (Historical fiction [New England, 1830s], ages 11–YA).

HONOR BOOK:

*The Road from Home: The Story of an Armenian Girl* by David Kherdian. Greenwillow (Historical fiction [Turkey, Greece, 1907–24], ages 11–YA).

1981 *Jacob Have I Loved* by Katherine Paterson. Crowell (Historical fiction [USA, 1940s], ages 12–YA).

HONOR BOOKS:

*The Fledgling* by Jane Langton. Harper (Fantasy, ages 9–11).

*A Ring of Endless Light* by Madeleine L'Engle. Farrar (Fantasy [science fiction], ages 10–12).

1982 *A Visit to William Blake's Inn: Poems for Innocent and Experienced Travelers* by Nancy Willard. Illustrated by Alice and Martin Provensen. Harcourt (Picture book/Poetry, ages 9–11).

HONOR BOOKS:

*Ramona Quimby, Age 8* by Beverly Cleary. Morrow (Realism, ages 7–9).

*Upon the Head of the Goat: A Childhood in Hungary, 1939–1944* by Aranka Siegal. Farrar (Historical fiction, ages 10–13).

1983 *Dicey's Song* by Cynthia Voigt. Atheneum (Realism, ages 9–12).

HONOR BOOKS:

*The Blue Sword* by Robin McKinley. Greenwillow (Fantasy [quest], ages 12–YA).

*Doctor De Soto* by William Steig. Farrar (Picture book/Animal fantasy, ages 5–8).

*Graven Images* by Paul Fleischman. Harper (Fantasy, ages 10–12).

*Homesick: My Own Story* by Jean Fritz. Putnam (Biography, ages 9–11).

*Sweet Whispers, Brother Rush* by Virginia Hamilton. Philomel (Fantasy/Multicultural [African-American], ages 12–YA).

1984 *Dear Mr. Henshaw* by Beverly Cleary. Morrow (Realism, ages 8–10).

HONOR BOOKS:

*The Sign of the Beaver* by Elizabeth George Speare. Houghton (Historical fiction [Colonial America], ages 9–11).

*A Solitary Blue* by Cynthia Voigt. Atheneum (Realism, ages 11–13).

*Sugaring Time* by Kathryn Lasky. Photographs by Christopher Knight. Macmillan (Informational, ages 9–13).

*The Wish Giver* by Bill Brittain. Harper (Fantasy, ages 9–12).

1985 *The Hero and the Crown* by Robin McKinley. Greenwillow (Fantasy [quest], ages 12–YA).

HONOR BOOKS:

*Like Jake and Me* by Mavis Jukes. Illustrated by Lloyd Bloom. Knopf (Picture book; Realism, ages 7–9).

*The Moves Make the Man* by Bruce Brooks. Harper (Realism/Multicultural [African-American], ages 11–YA).

*One-Eyed Cat* by Paula Fox. Bradbury (Realism, ages 9–12).

1986 *Sarah, Plain and Tall* by Patricia MacLachlan. Harper (Historical fiction [U.S. western frontier, 1800s], ages 8–10).

HONOR BOOKS:

*Commodore Perry in the Land of the Shogun* by Rhoda Blumberg. Lothrop (Informational, ages 9–13).

*Dogsong* by Gary Paulsen. Bradbury (Realism/Multicultural [Native-American], ages 10–13).

1987    *The Whipping Boy* by Sid Fleischman. Green-willow (Historical fiction [Medieval England], ages 9–11).

HONOR BOOKS:

*On My Honor* by Marion Dane Bauer. Clarion (Realism, ages 8–11).

*Volcano: The Eruption and Healing of Mount St. Helens* by Patricia Lauber. Bradbury (Informational, ages 8–13).

*A Fine White Dust* by Cynthia Rylant. Bradbury (Realism, ages 10–12).

1988    *Lincoln: A Photobiography* by Russell Freedman. Clarion (Biography, ages 8–12).

HONOR BOOKS:

*After the Rain* by Norma Fox Mazer. Morrow (Realism, ages 12–YA).

*Hatchet* by Gary Paulsen. Bradbury (Realism, ages 9–13).

1989    *Joyful Noise: Poems for Two Voices* by Paul Fleischman. Harper (Poetry, ages 9–YA).

HONOR BOOKS:

*In the Beginning: Creation Stories from around the World* by Virginia Hamilton. Harcourt (Traditional fantasy, ages 9–YA).

*Scorpions* by Walter Dean Myers. Harper (Realism/Multicultural [African-American, Hispanic-American], ages 10–13).

1990    *Number the Stars* by Lois Lowry. Houghton (Historical fiction [Denmark, 1940s], ages 8–10).

HONOR BOOKS:

*Afternoon of the Elves* by Janet Taylor Lisle. Orchard (Realism, ages 10–13).

*Shabanu, Daughter of the Wind* by Suzanne Fisher Staples. Knopf (Realism, ages 12–YA).

*The Winter Room* by Gary Paulsen. Orchard (Realism, ages 10–13).

1991    *Maniac Magee* by Jerry Spinelli. Little, Brown (Realism, ages 9–13).

HONOR BOOK:

*The True Confessions of Charlotte Doyle* by Avi. Orchard (Historical fiction [England, USA, 1830], ages 10–13).

1992    *Shiloh* by Phyllis Reynolds Naylor. Atheneum (Animal realism, ages 8–10).

HONOR BOOKS:

*Nothing but the Truth* by Avi. Orchard (Realism, ages 10–14).

*The Wright Brothers: How They Invented the Airplane* by Russell Freedman. Holiday (Informational/Biography, ages 9–12).

1993    *Missing May* by Cynthia Rylant. Orchard (Realism, ages 10–13).

HONOR BOOKS:

*The Dark-Thirty: Southern Tales of the Supernatural* by Patricia McKissack. Knopf (Modern fantasy/Ghost stories [African-American], ages 8–12).

*Somewhere in the Darkness* by Walter Dean Myers. Scholastic (Realism [African-American], ages 11–14).

*What Hearts* by Bruce Brooks. HarperCollins (Realism, ages 11–14).

1994    *The Giver* by Lois Lowry. Houghton (Modern fantasy, ages 10–12).

HONOR BOOKS:

*Crazy Lady* by Jane Leslie Conly. HarperCollins (Realism, ages 10–12).

*Dragon's Gate* by Laurence Yep. HarperCollins (Historical fiction [China, USA West, 1860s], ages 12–14).

*Eleanor Roosevelt: A Life of Discovery* by Russell Freedman. Clarion (Biography, ages 10–14).

1995    *Walk Two Moons* by Sharon Creech. HarperCollins (Realism [Native-American], ages 11–14).

HONOR BOOKS:

*Catherine, Called Birdy* by Karen Cushman. Clarion (Historical fiction, [England, 1200s] ages 10–14).

*The Ear, the Eye and the Arm* by Nancy Farmer. Orchard (Modern fantasy, ages 10–13).

1996    *The Midwife's Apprentice* by Karen Cushman. Clarion (Historical fiction [England, 1200s], ages 10–14).

HONOR BOOKS:

*The Great Fire* by Jim Murphy. Scholastic (Informational, ages 9–13).

*The Watsons Go to Birmingham—1963* by Christopher Paul Curtis. Delacorte (Historical fiction [U.S. South, 1960s; African-American], ages 10–14).

*What Jamie Saw* by Carolyn Coman. Front Street (Realistic, ages 10–14).

*Yolanda's Genius* by Carol Fenner. McElderry (Realistic/Multicultural [African-American], ages 10–14).

1997    *The View from Saturday* by E. L. Konigsburg. Atheneum (Realistic, ages 9–12).

HONOR BOOKS:

*A Girl Named Disaster* by Nancy Farmer. Orchard (Realistic/Multicultural [Black African], ages 12–14).

*The Moorchild* by Eloise McGraw. McElderry/Simon & Schuster (Modern fantasy, ages 9–12).

*The Thief* by Megan Whalen Turner. Greenwillow (Modern fantasy, ages 12–YA).

*Belle Prater's Boy* by Ruth White. Farrar (Realistic, ages 10–12).

1998 *Out of the Dust* by Karen Hesse. Scholastic (Historical fiction [USA, 1920–1934], ages 14–YA).
HONOR BOOKS:
*Lily's Crossing* by Patricia Reilly Giff. Delacorte (Historical fiction [United States, 1944], ages 9–11).
*Ella Enchanted* by Gail Carson Levine. HarperCollins (Modern fantasy, ages 9–12).
*Wringer* by Jerry Spinelli. HarperCollins (Realism, ages 9–12).

1999 *Holes* by Louis Sachar. Farrar (Realism, ages 10–13).
HONOR BOOK:
*A Long Way from Chicago* by Richard Peck. Dial (Realism, ages 9–12).

2000 *Bud, Not Buddy* by Christopher Paul Curtis. Delacorte (Multicultural [African-American], ages 9–12).
HONOR BOOKS:
*Getting Near to Baby* by Audrey Couloumbis. Putnam (Realism, ages 10–12).
*26 Fairmount Avenue* by Tomie dePaola. Putnam (Biography, ages 7–9).
*Our Only May Amelia* by Jennifer L. Holm. HarperCollins (Historical fiction [United States, 1899], ages 10–14).

2001 *A Year Down Yonder* by Richard Peck. Dial (Realism, ages 10–14).
HONOR BOOKS:
*Because of Winn Dixie* by Kate DiCamillo. Candlewick (Animal realism, ages 8–12).
*Hope Was Here* by Joan Bauer. Putnam (Realism, ages 12–14).
*Joey Pigza Loses Control* by Jack Gantos. Farrar (Realism, ages 9–12).
*The Wanderer* by Sharon Creech. HarperCollins (Realism, ages 12–14).

## Boston Globe— Horn Book Awards

*These awards, sponsored by* **The Boston Globe** *and* **The Horn Book Magazine**, *are given to an author for outstanding fiction or poetry for children, to an illustrator for outstanding illustration in a children's book, and, since 1976, to an author for outstanding nonfiction for children.*

1967 TEXT: *The Little Fishes* by Erik Christian Haugaard. Houghton.
ILLUSTRATION: *London Bridge Is Falling Down* by Peter Spier. Doubleday.

1968 TEXT: *The Spring Rider* by John Lawson. Crowell.
ILLUSTRATION: *Tikki Tikki Tembo* by Arlene Mosel. Illustrated by Blair Lent. Holt.

1969 TEXT: *A Wizard of Earthsea* by Ursula K. Le Guin. Houghton.
ILLUSTRATION: *The Adventures of Paddy Pork* by John S. Goodall. Harcourt.

1970 TEXT: *The Intruder* by John Rowe Townsend. Lippincott.
ILLUSTRATION: *Hi, Cat!* by Ezra Jack Keats. Macmillan.

1971 TEXT: *A Room Made of Windows* by Eleanor Cameron. Atlantic/Little.
ILLUSTRATION: *If I Built a Village* by Kazue Mizumura. Crowell.

1972 TEXT: *Tristan and Iseult* by Rosemary Sutcliff. Dutton.
ILLUSTRATION: *Mr. Gumpy's Outing* by John Burningham. Holt.

1973 TEXT: *The Dark Is Rising* by Susan Cooper. Atheneum/McElderry.
ILLUSTRATION: *King Stork* by Trina Schart Hyman. Little, Brown.

1974 TEXT: *M. C. Higgins, the Great* by Virginia Hamilton. Macmillan.
ILLUSTRATION: *Jambo Means Hello* by Muriel Feelings. Illustrated by Tom Feelings. Dial.

1975 TEXT: *Transport 7–41-R* by T. Degens. Viking.
ILLUSTRATION: *Anno's Alphabet* by Mitsumasa Anno. Crowell.

1976 FICTION: *Unleaving* by Jill Paton Walsh, Farrar.
NONFICTION: *Voyaging to Cathay: Americans in the China Trade* by Alfred Tamarin and Shirley Glubok. Viking.
ILLUSTRATION: *Thirteen* by Remy Charlip and Jerry Joyner. Parents.

1977 FICTION: *Child of the Owl* by Laurence Yep. Harper.
NONFICTION: *Chance, Luck and Destiny* by Peter Dickinson. Atlantic/Little, Brown.
ILLUSTRATION: *Granfa' Grig Had a Pig and Other Rhymes* by Wallace Tripp. Little, Brown.

1978  FICTION: *The Westing Game* by Ellen Raskin. Dutton.

NONFICTION: *Mischling, Second Degree: My Childhood in Nazi Germany* by Ilse Koehn. Greenwillow.

ILLUSTRATION: *Anno's Journey* by Mitsumasa Anno. Philomel.

1979  FICTION: *Humbug Mountain* by Sid Fleischman. Atlantic/Little, Brown.

NONFICTION: *The Road from Home: The Story of an Armenian Girl* by David Kherdian. Greenwillow.

ILLUSTRATION: *The Snowman* by Raymond Briggs. Random.

1980  FICTION: *Conrad's War* by Andrew Davies. Crown.

NONFICTION: *Building: The Fight against Gravity* by Mario Salvadori. Atheneum/McElderry.

ILLUSTRATION: *The Garden of Abdul Gasazi* by Chris Van Allsburg. Houghton.

1981  FICTION: *The Leaving* by Lynn Hall. Scribner's.

NONFICTION: *The Weaver's Gift* by Kathryn Lasky. Warne.

ILLUSTRATION: *Outside over There* by Maurice Sendak. Harper.

1982  FICTION: *Playing Beatie Bow* by Ruth Park. Atheneum.

NONFICTION: *Upon the Head of the Goat: A Childhood in Hungary, 1939–1944* by Aranka Siegal. Farrar.

ILLUSTRATION: *A Visit to William Blake's Inn: Poems for Innocent and Experienced Travelers* by Nancy Willard. Illustrated by Alice and Martin Provensen. Harcourt.

1983  FICTION: *Sweet Whispers, Brother Rush* by Virginia Hamilton. Philomel.

NONFICTION: *Behind Barbed Wire: The Imprisonment of Japanese Americans during World War II.* by Daniel S. Davis. Dutton.

ILLUSTRATION: *A Chair for My Mother* by Vera B. Williams. Greenwillow.

1984  FICTION: *A Little Fear* by Patricia Wrightson. McElderry/Atheneum.

NONFICTION: *The Double Life of Pocahontas* by Jean Fritz. Putnam.

ILLUSTRATION: *Jonah and the Great Fish* retold and illustrated by Warwick Hutton. McElderry/Atheneum.

1985  FICTION: *The Moves Make the Man* by Bruce Brooks. Harper.

NONFICTION: *Commodore Perry in the Land of the Shogun* by Rhoda Blumberg. Lothrop.

ILLUSTRATION: *Mama Don't Allow* by Thatcher Hurd. Harper.

1986  FICTION: *In Summer Light* by Zibby Oneal. Viking Kestrel.

NONFICTION: *Auks, Rocks, and the Odd Dinosaur* by Peggy Thomson. Crowell.

ILLUSTRATION: *The Paper Crane* by Molly Bang. Greenwillow.

1987  FICTION: *Rabble Starkey* by Lois Lowry. Houghton.

NONFICTION: *Pilgrims of Plimoth* by Marcia Sewall. Atheneum.

ILLUSTRATION: *Mufaro's Beautiful Daughters* by John Steptoe. Lothrop.

1988  FICTION: *The Friendship* by Mildred Taylor. Dial.

NONFICTION: *Anthony Burns: The Defeat and Triumph of a Fugitive Slave* by Virginia Hamilton. Knopf.

ILLUSTRATION: *The Boy of the Three-Year Nap* by Diane Snyder. Illustrated by Allen Say. Houghton.

1989  FICTION: *The Village by the Sea* by Paula Fox. Orchard.

NONFICTION: *The Way Things Work* by David Macaulay. Houghton.

ILLUSTRATION: *Shy Charles* by Rosemary Wells. Dial.

1990  FICTION: *Maniac Magee* by Jerry Spinelli. Little, Brown.

NONFICTION: *The Great Little Madison* by Jean Fritz. Putnam.

ILLUSTRATION: *Lon Po Po: A Red-Riding Hood Story from China* retold and illustrated by Ed Young. Philomel.

1991 FICTION: *The True Confessions of Charlotte Doyle* by Avi. Orchard.

NONFICTION: *Appalachia: The Voices of Sleeping Birds* by Cynthia Rylant. Illustrated by Barry Moser. Harcourt.

ILLUSTRATION: *The Tale of the Mandarin Ducks* retold by Katherine Paterson. Illustrated by Leo and Diane Dillon. Lodestar.

1992 FICTION: *Missing May* by Cynthia Rylant, Orchard.

NONFICTION: *Talking with Artists* by Pat Cummings, Bradbury.

ILLUSTRATION: *Seven Blind Mice* by Ed Young, Philomel.

1993 FICTION: *Ajeemah and His Son* by James Berry, Harper.

NONFICTION: *Sojourner Truth: Ain't I a Woman?* by Patricia and Fredrick McKissack, Scholastic.

ILLUSTRATION: *The Fortune-Tellers* by Lloyd Alexander. Illustrated by Trina Schart Hyman, Dutton.

1994 FICTION: *Scooter* by Vera B. Williams, Greenwillow.

NONFICTION: *Eleanor Roosevelt: A Life of Discovery* by Russell Freedman, Clarion.

ILLUSTRATION: *Grandfather's Journey* by Allen Say, Houghton.

1995 FICTION: *Some of the Kinder Planets* by Tim Wynne-Jones, Orchard.

NONFICTION: *Abigail Adams: Witness to a Revolution* by Natalie S. Bober. Atheneum.

ILLUSTRATION: *John Henry* retold by Julius Lester. Illustrated by Jerry Pinkney. Dial.

1996 FICTION: *Poppy* by Avi. Illustrated by Brian Floca. Orchard.

NONFICTION: *Orphan Train Rider: One Boy's True Story* by Andrea Warren. Houghton.

ILLUSTRATION: *In the Rain with Baby Duck* by Amy Hest. Illustrated by Jill Barton. Candlewick.

1997 FICTION: *The Friends* by Kazumi Yumoto. Farrar.

NONFICTION: *A Drop of Water: A Book of Science and Wonder* by Walter Wick. Scholastic.

ILLUSTRATION: *The Adventures of Sparrow Boy* by Brian Pinkney. Simon & Schuster.

1998 FICTION: *The Circuit: Stories from the Life of a Migrant Child* by Francisco Jiménez. University of New Mexico Press.

NONFICTION: *Leon's Story* by Leon Walter Tillage. Illustrated by Susan L. Roth. Farrar.

ILLUSTRATION: *And If the Moon Could Talk* by Kate Banks. Illustrated by Georg Hallensleben. Farrar.

1999 FICTION: *Holes* by Louis Sachar. Farrar.

NONFICTION: *The Top of the World: Climbing Mount Everest* by Steve Jenkins. Houghton.

ILLUSTRATION: *Red-Eyed Tree Frog* by Joy Cowley. Illustrated with photographs by Nic Bishop. Scholastic.

2000 FICTION: *The Folk Keeper* by Franny Billingsley. Atheneum.

NONFICTION: *Sir Walter Ralegh and the Quest for El Dorado* by Marc Aronson. Clarion.

ILLUSTRATION: *Henry Hikes to Fitchburg* by D. B. Johnson. Houghton.

## National Book Award for Young People's Literature

*This award, sponsored by the National Book Foundation, is presented annually to recognize what is judged to be the outstanding contribution to children's literature, in terms of literary merit, published during the previous year. The award committee considers books of all genres written for children and young adults by U.S. writers. The award, which was added to the U.S. National Book Awards in 1996, carries a $10,000 cash prize.*

1996 *Parrot in the Oven: Mi Vida* by Victor Martinez. HarperCollins.

1997 *Dancing on the Edge* by Han Nolan. Harcourt.

1998 *Holes* by Louis Sachar. Farrar.

1999 *When Zachary Beaver Came to Town* by Kimberley Willis Holt. Holt.

2000 *Homeless Bird* by Gloria Whelan. HarperCollins.

## GREAT BRITAIN

### Kate Greenaway Medal

*This award, sponsored by the British Library Association, is given to the illustrator of the most distinguished work in illustration in a children's book first published in the United Kingdom during the preceding year.*

1957  *Tim All Alone* by Edward Ardizzone. Oxford.

1958  *Mrs. Easter and the Storks* by V. H. Drummond. Faber.

1959  No award

1960  *Kashtanka and a Bundle of Ballads* by William Stobbs. Oxford.

1961  *Old Winkle and the Seagulls* by Elizabeth Rose. Illustrated by Gerald Rose. Faber.

1962  *Mrs. Cockle's Cat* by Philippa Pearce. Illustrated by Anthony Maitland. Kestrel.

1963  *Brian Wildsmith's ABC* by Brian Wildsmith. Oxford.

1964  *Borka* by John Burningham. Jonathan Cape.

1965  *Shakespeare's Theatre* by C. W. Hodges. Oxford.

1966  *Three Poor Tailors* by Victor Ambrus. Hamilton.

1967  *Mother Goose Treasury* by Raymond Briggs. Hamilton.

1968  *Charlie, Charlotte & the Golden Canary* by Charles Keeping. Oxford.

1969  *Dictionary of Chivalry* by Grant Uden. Illustrated by Pauline Baynes. Kestrel.

1970  *The Quangle-Wangle's Hat* by Edward Lear. Illustrated by Helen Oxenbury. Heinemann.
*Dragon of an Ordinary Family* by Margaret Mahy. Illustrated by Helen Oxenbury. Heinemann.

1971  *Mr. Gumpy's Outing* by John Burningham. Jonathan Cape.

1972  *The Kingdom under the Sea* by Jan Piénkowski. Jonathan Cape.

1973  *The Woodcutter's Duck* by Krystyna Turska. Hamilton.

1974  *Father Christmas* by Raymond Briggs. Hamilton.

1975  *The Wind Blew* by Pat Hutchins. Bodley Head.

1976  *Horses in Battle* by Victor Ambrus. Oxford. *Mishka* by Victor Ambrus. Oxford.

1977  *The Post Office Cat* by Gail E. Haley. Bodley Head.

1978  *Dogger* by Shirley Hughes. Bodley Head.

1979  *Each Peach Pear Plum* by Janet and Allan Ahlberg. Kestrel.

1980  *The Haunted House* by Jan Piénkowski. Heinemann.

1981  *Mr. Magnolia* by Quentin Blake. Jonathan Cape.

1982  *The Highwayman* by Alfred Noyes. Illustrated by Charles Keeping. Oxford.

1983  *Long Neck and Thunder Foot.* Kestrel; and *Sleeping Beauty and Other Favorite Fairy Tales.* Gollancz. Both illustrated by Michael Foreman.

1984  *Gorilla* by Anthony Browne. Julia MacRae Books.

1985  *Hiawatha's Childhood* by Errol LeCain. Faber.

1986  *Sir Gawain and the Loathly Lady* by Selina Hastings. Illustrated by Juan Wijngaard. Walker.

1987  *Snow White in New York* by Fiona French. Oxford.

1988  *Crafty Chameleon* by Mwenye Hadithi. Illustrated by Adrienne Kennaway. Hodder & Stoughton.

1989  *Can't You Sleep, Little Bear?* by Martin Waddell. Illustrated by Barbara Firth. Walker.

1990  *War Boy: A Country Childhood* by Michael Foreman. Arcade.

1991  *The Whale's Song* by Dyan Sheldon. Illustrated by Gary Blythe. Dial.

1992 *The Jolly Christmas Postman* by Janet and Allan Ahlberg. Heinemann.

1993 *Zoo* by Anthony Browne. Julia MacRae.

1994 *Black Ships before Troy* retold by Rosemary Sutcliff. Illustrated by Alan Lee. Frances Lincoln.

1995 *Way Home* by Libby Hathorn. Illustrated by Gregory Rogers. Random House.

1996 *The Christmas Miracle of Jonathon Toomey* by Susan Wojciechowski. Illustrated by P. J. Lynch. Walker.

1997 *The Baby Who Wouldn't Go to Bed* by Helen Cooper. Doubleday.

1998 *When Jessie Came Across the Sea* by Amy Hest. Illustrated by P. J. Lynch. Candlewick.

1999 *Pumpkin Soup* by Helen Cooper. Farrar.

2000 *Alice's Adventures in Wonderland* by Lewis Carroll. Illustrated by Helen Oxenbury. Walker.

## Carnegie Medal

*This award, sponsored by the British Library Association, is given to the author of the most outstanding children's book first published in English in the United Kingdom during the preceding year.*

1937 *Pigeon Post* by Arthur Ransome. Cape.

1938 *The Family from One End Street* by Eve Garnett. Muller.

1939 *The Circus Is Coming* by Noel Streatfield. Dent.

1940 *Radium Woman* by Eleanor Doorly. Heinemann.

1941 *Visitors from London* by Kitty Barne. Dent.

1942 *We Couldn't Leave Dinah* by Mary Treadgold. Penguin.

1943 *The Little Grey Men* by B. B. Eyre & Spottiswoode.

1944 No award

1945 *The Wind on the Moon* by Eric Linklater. Macmillan.

1946 No award

1947 *The Little White Horse* by Elizabeth Goudge. Brockhampton Press.

1948 *Collected Stories for Children* by Walter de la Mare. Faber.

1949 *Sea Change* by Richard Armstrong. Dent.

1950 *The Story of Your Home* by Agnes Allen. Transatlantic.

1951 *The Lark on the Wing* by Elfrida Vipont Foulds. Oxford.

1952 *The Wool-Pack* by Cynthia Harnett. Methuen.

1953 *The Borrowers* by Mary Norton. Dent.

1954 *A Valley Grows Up* by Edward Osmond. Oxford.

1955 *Knight Crusader* by Ronald Welch. Oxford.

1956 *The Little Bookroom* by Eleanor Farjeon. Oxford.

1957 *The Last Battle* by C. S. Lewis. Bodley Head.

1958 *A Grass Rope* by William Mayne. Oxford.

1959 *Tom's Midnight Garden* by Philippa Pearce. Oxford.

1960 *The Lantern Bearers* by Rosemary Sutcliff. Oxford.

1961 *The Making of Man* by I. W. Cornwall. Phoenix.

1962 *A Stranger at Green Knowe* by Lucy Boston. Faber.

1963 *The Twelve and the Genii* by Pauline Clarke. Faber.

1964 *Time of Trial* by Hester Burton. Oxford.

1965 *Nordy Banks* by Sheena Porter. Oxford.

1966 *The Grange at High Force* by Philip Turner. Oxford.

1967 No award

1968 *The Owl Service* by Alan Garner. Collins.

1969 *The Moon in the Cloud* by Rosemary Harris. Faber.

1970  *The Edge of the Cloud* by K. M. Peyton. Oxford.

1971  *The God beneath the Sea* by Leon Garfield and Edward Blishen. Kestrel.

1972  *Josh* by Ivan Southall. Angus and Robertson.

1973  *Watership Down* by Richard Adams. Rex Collings.

1974  *The Ghost of Thomas Kempe* by Penelope Lively. Heinemann.

1975  *The Stronghold* by Mollie Hunter. Hamilton.

1976  *The Machine-Gunners* by Robert Westall. Macmillan.

1977  *Thunder and Lightnings* by Jan Mark. Kestrel.

1978  *The Turbulent Term of Tyke Tiler* by Gene Kemp. Faber.

1979  *The Exeter Blitz* by David Rees. Hamish Hamilton.

1980  *Tulku* by Peter Dickinson. Dutton.

1981  *City of Gold* by Peter Dickinson. Gollancz.

1982  *The Scarecrows* by Robert Westall. Chatto and Windus.

1983  *The Haunting* by Margaret Mahy. Dent.

1984  *Handles* by Jan Mark. Kestrel.

1985  *The Changeover* by Margaret Mahy. Dent.

1986  *Storm* by Kevin Crossley-Holland. Heinemann.

1987  *Granny Was a Buffer Girl* by Berlie Doherty. Methuen.

1988  *The Ghost Drum* by Susan Price. Faber.

1989  *Pack of Lies* by Geraldine McCaughrean. Oxford.

1990  *My War with Goggle-Eyes* by Anne Fine. Joy Street.

1991  *Wolf* by Gillian Cross. Oxford.

1992  *Dear Nobody* by Berlie Doherty. Hamish Hamilton.

1993  *Flour Babies* by Anne Fine. Hamish Hamilton.

1994  *Stone Cold* by Robert Swindells. Hamish Hamilton.

1995  *Whispers in the Graveyard* by Theresa Bresling. Methuen.

1996  *Dark Materials: Book 1, Northern Lights* by Philip Pullman. Scholastic.

1997  *Junk* by Melvin Burgess. Andersen.

1998  *River Boy* by Tim Bowler. Oxford.

1999  *Skellig* by David Almond. Delacorte.

2000  *Postcards from No Man's Land* by Aidan Chambers. Bodley Head.

# CANADA

## *Amelia Frances Howard-Gibbon Medal*

*This award, sponsored by the Canadian Library Association, is given to an illustrator for the most distinguished illustrations in a children's book published in Canada during the preceding year. Only Canadian citizens are eligible for this award.*

1971  *The Wind Has Wings* edited by Mary Alice Downie and Barbara Robertson. Illustrated by Elizabeth Cleaver. Oxford.

1972  *A Child in Prison Camp* by Shizuye Takashima. Tundra.

1973  *Au-délà du Soleil/Beyond the Sun* by Jacques de Roussan. Tundra.

1974  *A Prairie Boy's Winter* by William Kurelek. Tundra.

1975  *The Sleighs of My Childhood/Les Traîneaux de Mon Enfance* by Carlo Italiano. Tundra.

1976  *A Prairie Boy's Summer* by William Kurelek. Tundra.

1977  *Down by Jim Long's Stage: Rhymes for Children and Young Fish* by Al Pittman. Illustrated by Pam Hall. Breakwater.

1978  *The Loon's Necklace* by William Toye. Illustrated by Elizabeth Cleaver. Oxford.

1979  *A Salmon for Simon* by Betty Waterton. Illustrated by Ann Blades. Douglas & McIntyre.

1980  *The Twelve Dancing Princesses* retold by Janet Lunn. Illustrated by László Gál. Methuen.

1981  *The Trouble with Princesses* by Christie Harris. Illustrated by Douglas Tait. McClelland & Stewart.

1982  *Ytek and the Arctic Orchid: An Inuit Legend* by Garnet Hewitt. Illustrated by Heather Woodall. Douglas & McIntyre.

1983  *Chester's Barn* by Lindee Climo. Tundra.

1984  *Zoom at Sea* by Tim Wynne-Jones. Illustrated by Ken Nutt. Douglas & McIntyre.

1985  *Chin Chiang and the Dragon's Dance* by Ian Wallace. Groundwood.

1986  *Zoom Away* by Tim Wynne-Jones. Illustrated by Ken Nutt. Douglas & McIntyre.

1987  *Moonbeam on a Cat's Ear* by Marie-Louise Gay. Stoddart.

1988  *Rainy Day Magic* by Marie-Louise Gay. Hodder & Stoughton.

1989  *Amos's Sweater* by Janet Lunn. Illustrated by Kim LaFave. Douglas & McIntyre.

1990  *Til All the Stars Have Fallen: Canadian Poems for Children* selected by David Booth. Illustrated by Kady MacDonald Denton. Kids Can Press.

1991  *The Orphan Boy* by Tololwa M. Mollel. Illustrated by Paul Morin. Oxford.

1992  *Waiting for the Whales* by Ron Lightburn. Illustrated by Sheryl McFarlane. Orca Books.

1993  *The Dragon's Pearl* by Julie Lawson. Illustrated by Paul Morin. Oxford.

1994  *Last Leaf First Snowflake to Fall* by Leo Yerxa. Groundwood.

1995  *Gifts* by Jo Ellen Bogart. Illustrated by Barbara Reid. Scholastic Canada.

1996  *Just like New* by Ainslie Manson. Illustrated by Karen Reczuch. Groundwood.

1997  *Ghost Train* by Paul Yee. Illustrated by Harvey Chan. Groundwood/Douglas & MacIntyre.

1998  *The Party* by Barbara Reid. Scholastic.

1999  *A Child's Treasury of Nursery Rhymes* by Kady M. Denton. Kingfisher.

2000  *The Dragon New Year: A Chinese Legend* by Dave Bouchard. Illustrated by Zhong-Yang Huang. Peachtree.

## Canadian Children's Book of the Year Award

*This award, sponsored by the Canadian Library Association, is given to the author of a children's book of outstanding literary merit. Since 1954, an equivalent award has been presented to the author of a children's book published in French. Only Canadian citizens are eligible for these awards.*

1947  *Starbuck Valley Winter* by Roderick Haig-Brown. Collins.

1948  *Kristli's Trees* by Mabel Dunham. Hale.

1949  No award

1950  *Franklin of the Arctic* by Richard S. Lambert. McClelland & Stewart.

1951  No award

1952  *The Sun Horse* by Catherine Anthony Clark. Macmillan of Canada.

1953  No award

1954  No English award
      *Le Vénérable Francois de Montmorency-Laval* by Émile S. J. Gervais. Comité des Fondateurs de l'Église Canadienne.

1955  No award

1956  *Train for Tiger Lily* by Louise Riley, Macmillan of Canada.
No French award

1957  *Glooskap's Country* by Cyrus Macmillan. Oxford.
No French award

1958  *Lost in the Barrens* by Farley Mowat. Little.
*Le Chevalier du Roi* by Beatrice Clément. Atelier.

1959  *The Dangerous Cove* by John F. Hayes. Copp Clark.
*Un Drôle de Petit Cheval* by Hélène Flamme. Leméac.

1960  *The Golden Phoenix* by Marius Barbeau and Michael Hornyansky. Walck/Oxford.
*L'Été Enchanté* by Paule Daveluy. Atelier.

1961  *The St. Lawrence* by William Toye. Oxford.
*Plantes Vagabondes* by Marcelle Gauvreau. Centre de Psychologie et de Pédagogie.

1962  No English award
*Les Îles du Roi Maha Maha II* by Claude Aubry. Pélican.

1963  *The Incredible Journey* by Sheila Burnford. Little, Brown.
*Drôle D'Automne* by Paul Daveluy. Pélican.

1964  *The Whale People* by Roderick Haig-Brown. Collins.
*Férie* by Cécile Chabot. Beauchemin.

1965  *Tales of Nanabozho* by Dorothy Reid. Oxford.
*Le Loup de Nöel* by Claude Aubry. Centre de Psychologie et de Pédagogie.

1966  *Tiktá Liktak* by James Houston. Kestrel/Longmans.
*Le Chêne des Tempêtes* by Andrée Mallet-Hobden. Fides.
*The Double Knights* by James McNeal. Walck.
*Le Wapiti* by Monique Corriveau. Jeunesse.

1967  *Raven's Cry* by Christie Harris. McClelland & Stewart.
No French award

1968  *The White Archer* by James Houston. Academic/Kestrel.

*Légendes Indiennes du Canada* by Claude Mélancon. Editions du Jour.

1969  *And Tomorrow the Stars* by Kay Hill. Dodd.
No French award

1970  *Sally Go Round the Sun* by Edith Fowke. McClelland & Stewart.
*La Merveilleuse Histoire de la Naissance* by Lionel Gendron. Les Editions de l'Homme.

1971  *Cartier Discovers the St. Lawrence* by William Toye. Oxford.
*La Surprise de Dame Chenille* by Henriette Major. Centre de Psychologie et de Pédagogie.

1972  *Mary of Mile 18* by Ann Blades. Tundra.
No French award

1973  *The Marrow of the World* by Ruth Nichols. Macmillan.
*Le Petit Sapin Qui a Poussé sur une Étoile* by Simone Bussières. Laurentiennes.

1974  *The Miraculous Hind* by Elizabeth Cleaver. Holt.
No French award

1975  *Alligator Pie* by Dennis Lee. Macmillan.
No French award

1976  *Jacob Two-Two Meets the Hooded Fang* by Mordecai Richler. McClelland & Stewart.
No French award

1977  *Mouse Woman and the Vanished Princesses* by Christie Harris. McClelland & Stewart.
No French award

1978  *Garbage Delight* by Dennis Lee. Macmillan.
No French award

1979  *Hold Fast* by Kevin Major. Clarke, Irwin.
No French award

1980  *River Runners: A Tale of Hardship and Bravery* by James Houston. McClelland & Stewart.
No French award

1981  *The Violin Maker's Gift* by Donn Kushner. Macmillan.
No French award

1982  *The Root Cellar* by Janet Lunn. Dennys.
No French award

1983  *Up to Low* by Brian Doyle. Douglas & McIntyre.
No French award

1984  *Sweetgrass* by Jan Hudson. Tree Frog Press.
No French award

1985  *Mama's Going to Buy You a Mockingbird* by Jean Little. Penguin.
No French award

1986  *Julie* by Cora Taylor. Western.
No French award

1987  *Shadow in Hawthorn Bay* by Janet Lunn. Dennys.
No French award

1988  *A Handful of Time* by Kit Pearson. Penguin.
No French award

1989  *Easy Avenue* by Brian Doyle. Groundwood.
No French award

1990  *The Sky Is Falling* by Kit Pearson. Penguin.
No French award

1991  *Redwork* by Michael Bedard. Dennys.
No French award

1992  *Eating between the Lines* by Kevin Major. Doubleday.
No French award

1993  *Ticket to Curlew* by Celia Barker Lottridge. Groundwood.
No French award

1994  *Some of the Kinder Planets* by Tim Wynne-Jones. Groundwood.
No French award

1995  *Summer of the Mad Monk* by Cora Taylor. Douglas & MacIntyre.

1996  *The Tiny Kite of Eddie Wing* by Maxine Trottier. Stoddart.

1997  *Uncle Ronald* by Brian Doyle. Groundwood/Douglas & MacIntyre.

1998  *Silverwing* by Kenneth Oppel. HarperCollins.

1999  *Stephen Fair* by Tim Wynne-Jones. DK Ink.

2000  *Sunwing* by Kenneth Oppel. HarperCollins.


## AUSTRALIA

### Australian Children's Books of the Year Awards

*The Australian Children's Book Council sponsors three awards for excellence in children's books: the Picture Book of the Year Award; the Children's Book of the Year for Younger Readers (for books that bridge the gap between picture books and longer novels); and the Children's Book of the Year for Older Readers.*

### Australian Picture Book of the Year Award

1956  *Wish and the Magic Nut* by Peggy Barnard. Illustrated by Shelia Hawkins. Sands.

1957  No award

1958  *Piccaninny Walkabout* by Axel Poignant. Angus & Robertson.

1959–1964  No awards

1965  *Hugo's Zoo* by Elizabeth MacIntyre. Angus & Robertson.

1966–1968  No awards

1969  *Sly Old Wardrobe* by Ivan Southall. Illustrated by Ted Greenwood. Cheshire.

1970  No award

1971  *Waltzing Matilda* by A. B. Paterson. Illustrated by Desmond Digby.

1972–1973  No awards

1974  *The Bunyip of Berkeley's Creek* by Jenny Wagner. Illustrated by Ron Brooks. Kestrel.

1975 *The Man from Ironbark* by A. B. Paterson. Illustrated by Quentin Hole. Collins.

1976 *The Rainbow Serpent* by Dick Roughsey. Collins.

1977 *ABC of Monsters* by Deborah Niland. Hodder & Stoughton.

1978 *John Brown, Rose and the Midnight Cat* by Jenny Wagner. Illustrated by Ron Brooks. Kestrel.

1979 *The Quinkins* written and illustrated by Percy Trezise and Dick Roughsey. Collins.

1980 *One Dragon's Dream* by Peter Pavey. Nelson.

1981 No award

1982 *Sunshine* by Jan Ormerod. Kestrel.

1983 *Who Sank the Boat?* by Pamela Allen. Nelson.

1984 *Bertie and the Bear* by Pamela Allen, Nelson.

1985 No award
    Highly commended: *The Inch Boy* by Junko Morimoto. Collins.

1986 *Felix and Alexander* written and illustrated by Terry Denton. Oxford.

1987 *Kojuro and the Bears* adapted by Helen Smith. Illustrated by Junko Morimoto. Collins.

1988 *Crusher Is Coming!* by Bob Graham. Lothian.

1989 *Drac and the Gremlins* by Allan Baillie. Illustrated by Jane Tanner. Viking/Kestrel.
    *The Eleventh Hour* by Graeme Base. Viking/Kestrel.

1990 *The Very Best of Friends* by Margaret Wild. Illustrated by Julie Vivas. Margaret Hamilton.

1991 *Greetings from Sandy Beach* by Bob Graham. Lothian.

1992 *Window* by Jeannie Baker. Julia MacRae.

1993 *Rose Meets Mr Wintergarden* by Bob Graham. Viking/Penguin.

1994 *First Light* by Gary Crew. Illustrated by Peter Gouldthorpe. Lothian.

1995 *The Watertower* by Gary Crew. Illustrated by Steven Woolman. Era.

1996 *The Hunt* by Narelle Oliver. Lothian.

1997 *Not a Nibble* by Elizabeth Honey. Allen & Unwin.

1998 *The Two Bullies* by Junko Morimoto. Translated by Isao Morimoto. Crown.

1999 *The Rabbits* by John Marsden. Illustrated by Shaun Tan. Lothian.

2000 *Jenny Angel* by Margaret Wild. Illustrated by Anne Spudvilas. Penguin.

*Australian Children's Book of the Year for Younger Readers Award*

1982 *Rummage* by Cristobel Mattingley. Illustrated by Patricia Mullins. Angus & Robertson.

1983 *Thing* by Robin Klein. Illustrated by Allison Lester. Oxford.

1984 *Bernice Knows Best* by Max Dann. Illustrated by Ann James. Oxford.

1985 *Something Special* by Emily Rodda. Illustrated by Noela Young. Angus & Robertson.

1986 *Arkwright* by Mary Steele. Hyland House.

1987 *Pigs Might Fly* by Emily Rodda. Illustrated by Noela Young. Angus & Robertson.

1988 *My Place* by Nadia Wheatley and Donna Rawlins. Collins Dove.

1989 *The Best-Kept Secret* by Emily Rodda. Angus & Robertson.

1990 *Pigs and Honey* by Jeanie Adams. Omnibus.

1991 *Finders Keepers* by Emily Rodda. Omnibus.

1992 *The Magnificent Nose and Other Marvels* by Anna Fienberg. Illustrated by Kim Gamble. Allen and Unwin.

1993 *The Bamboo Flute* by Garry Disher. Collins/Angus & Robertson.

1994 *Rowan of Rin* by Emily Rodda. Omnibus.

1995 *Ark in the Park* by Wendy Orr. HarperCollins.

1996 *Swashbuckler* by James Moloney. University of Queensland Press.

1997 *Hannah Plus One* by Libby Gleeson. Illustrated by Ann James. Penguin.

1998 *Someone Like Me* by Elaine Forrestal. Penguin.

1999 *My Girragundji* by Meme McDonald and Boori Pryor. Illustrated by Meme McDonald. Allen & Unwin

2000 *Hitler's Daughter* by Jackie French. Harper-Collins.

## Australian Children's Book of the Year for Older Readers Award

1946 *Karrawingi, the Emu* by Leslie Rees. Sands.

1947 No award

1948 *Shackleton's Argonauts* by Frank Hurley. Angus & Robertson.

1949 *Whalers of the Midnight Sun* by Alan Villiers. Angus & Robertson.

1950 No award

1951 *Verity of Sydney Town* by Ruth Williams. Angus & Robertson.

1952 *The Australia Book* by Eve Pownall. Sands.

1953 *Aircraft of Today and Tomorrow* by J. H. and W. D. Martin. Angus & Robertson.
*Good Luck to the Rider* by Joan Phipson. Angus & Robertson.

1954 *Australian Legendary* by K. L. Parker. Angus & Robertson.

1955 *The First Walkabout* by H. A. Lindsay and N. B. Tindale. Kestrel.

1956 *The Crooked Snake* by Patricia Wrightson. Angus & Robertson.

1957 *The Boomerang Book of Legendary Tales* by Enid Moodie-Heddle. Kestrel.

1958 *Tiger in the Bush* by Nan Chauncy. Oxford.

1959 *Devil's Hill* by Nan Chauncy. Oxford.
*Sea Menace* by John Gunn. Constable.

1960 *All the Proud Tribesmen* by Kylie Tennant. Macmillan.

1961 *Tangara* by Nan Chauncy. Oxford.

1962 *The Racketty Street Gang* by H. L. Evers. Hodder & Stoughton.
*Rafferty Rides a Winner* by Joan Woodbery. Parrish.

1963 *The Family Conspiracy* by Joan Phipson. Angus & Robertson.

1964 *The Green Laurel* by Eleanor Spence. Oxford.

1965 *Pastures of the Blue Crane* by Hesba F. Brinsmead. Oxford.

1966 *Ash Road* by Ivan Southall. Angus & Robertson.

1967 *The Min Min* by Mavis Thorpe Clark. Landsdowne.

1968 *To the Wild Sky* by Ivan Southall. Angus & Robertson.

1969 *When Jays Fly to Barbmo* by Margaret Balderson. Oxford.

1970 *Uhu* by Annette Macarther-Onslow. Ure Smith.

1971 *Bread and Honey* by Ivan Southall. Angus & Robertson.

1972 *Longtime Passing* by Hesba F. Brinsmead. Angus & Robertson.

1973 *Family at the Lookout* by Noreen Shelly. Oxford.

1974 *The Nargun and the Stars* by Patricia Wrightson. Hutchinson.

1975 No award

1976 *Fly West* by Ivan Southall. Angus & Robertson.

1977 *The October Child* by Eleanor Spence. Oxford.

1978 *The Ice Is Coming* by Patricia Wrightson. Hutchinson.

1979  *The Plum-Rain Scroll* by Ruth Manley. Hodder & Stoughton.

1980  *Displaced Person* by Lee Harding. Hyland House.

1981  *Playing Beatie Bow* by Ruth Park. Nelson.

1982  *The Valley Between* by Colin Thiele. Rigby.

1983  *Master of the Grove* by Victor Kelleher. Penguin.

1984  *A Little Fear* by Patricia Wrightson. Hutchinson.

1985  *The True Story of Lilli Stubeck* by James Aldridge. Hyland House.

1986  *The Green Wind* by Thurley Fowler. Rigby.

1987  *All We Know* by Simon French. Angus & Robertson.

1988  *So Much to Tell You* by John Marsden. Walter McVitty Books.

1989  *Beyond the Labyrinth* by Gillian Rubinstein. Hyland House.

1990  *Came Back to Show You I Could Fly* by Robin Klein. Viking/Kestrel.

1991  *Strange Objects* by Gary Crew. Heinemann Australia.

1992  *The House Guest* by Eleanor Nilsson. Viking.

1993  *Looking for Alibrandi* by Melina Marchetta. Penguin.

1994  *The Gathering* by Isobelle Carmody. Penguin. *Angel's Gate* by Gary Crew. Heinemann.

1995  *Foxspell* by Gillian Rubinstein. Hyland House.

1996  *Pagan's Vows* by Catherine Jinks. Omnibus.

1997  *A Bridge to Wiseman's Cove* by James Moloney. University of Queensland Press.

1998  *Eye to Eye* by Catherine Jinks. Penguin.

1999  *Deadly, Unna?* by Phillip Gwynne. Penguin.

2000  *48 Shades of Brown* by Nick Earls. Penguin.

## NEW ZEALAND

### Russell Clark Award for Illustrations

*This award is given to an illustrator for the most distinguished illustrations for a children's book published in New Zealand the previous year. Only citizens or residents of New Zealand are eligible for this award.*

1978  *The House of the People* by Ron L. Bacon. Illustrated by Robert F. Jahnke. Collins.

1979  *Kim* by Bruce Treloar. Collins.

1980–1981  No awards

1982  *Mrs. McGinty and the Bizarre Plant* by Gavin Bishop. Oxford.

1983  No award

1984  *The Tree Witches* by Gwenda Turner. Penguin.

1985  *The Duck in the Gun* by Joy Cowley. Illustrated by Robyn Belton. Shortland.

1986  *A Lion in the Night* by Pamela Allen. Hamilton.

1987  *Taniwha* by Patricia Grace. Illustrated by Robyn Kahukiwa. Viking/Kestrel.

1988  *The Magpies* by Denis Glover. Illustrated by Dick Frizzell.

1989  *Joseph's Boat* by Caroline Macdonald. Illustrated by Chris Gaskin. Hodder & Stoughton.

1990  *A Walk to the Beach* by Chris Gaskin.

1991  *Arthur and the Dragon* by David Elliot. Steck-Vaughn.

1992  *One Lonely Kakapo* by Sandra Morris. Hodder & Stoughton.

1993  *Lily and the Present* by Christine Ross. Methuen.

1994  *The Trolley* by Patricia Grace. Illustrated by Kerry Gemmill. Viking.

1995  *Kotuku: The Flight of the White Heron* by Philip Temple. Illustrated by Chris Gaskin. Hodder.

1996 *The Cheese Trap* by Joy Cowley. Illustrated by Linda McClelland. Scholastic.

1997 *George's Monster* by Amanda Jackson. Illustrated by Murray Grimsdale. Learning Media.

1998 *Emily's Wonderful Pie* by Jane Cornish. Illustrated by Sue Hitchcock-Pratt. Scholastic.

1999 No award

2000 No award

## Esther Glen Award

*This award is given to an author for the most distinguished contribution to New Zealand children's literature during the previous year. Only New Zealand citizens or residents are eligible.*

1945 *The Book of Wiremu* by Stella Morice. Angus & Robertson.

1946 No award

1947 *Myths and Legends of Maoriland* by A. W. Reed. Reed.

1948–1949 No awards

1950 *The Adventures of Nimble, Rumble and Tumble* by Joan Smith. Paul's Book Arcade.

1951–1958 No awards

1959 *Falter Tom and the Water Boy* by Maurice Duggan. Paul's Book Arcade.

1960–1963 No awards

1964 *The Story of a Little Boy* by Leslie C. Powell. Paul's Book Arcade.

1965–1969 No awards

1970 *A Lion in the Meadow* by Margaret Mahy. Dent.

1971–1972 No awards

1973 *The First Margaret Mahy Story Book* by Margaret Mahy. Dent.

1974 No award

1975 *My Cat Likes to Hide in Boxes* by Eve Sutton and Lynley Dodd. Hamish Hamilton.

1976–1977 No awards

1978 *The Lighthouse Keeper's Lunch* by Ronda Armitage. Deutsch.

1979 *Take the Long Path* by Joan de Hamel. Lutterworth.

1980 No award

1981 *The Year of the Yelvertons* by Katherine O'Brien. Oxford.

1982 *The Haunting* by Margaret Mahy. Dent.

1983 *Jacky Nobody* by Anne de Roo. Methuen.

1984 *Elephant Rock* by Caroline Macdonald. Hodder.

1985 *The Changeover* by Margaret Mahy. Dent.

1986 *Motherstone* by Maurice Gee. Oxford.

1987 No award

1988 *Alex* by Tessa Duder. Oxford.

1989 *The Mangrove Summer* by Jack Lazenby. Oxford.

1990 *Alex in Winter* by Tessa Duder. Oxford.

1991 *Agnes the Sheep* by William Taylor. Scholastic.

1992 *Alessandra: Alex in Rome* by Tessa Duder. Oxford.

1993 *Underrunners* by Margaret Mahy. Hamish Hamilton.

1994 *Sasscat to Win* by Paula Boock. McIndle.

1995 *The Fat Man* by Maurice Gee. Viking.

1996 *Crossroads* by Janice Marriot. Reed.

1997 *Sanctuary* by Kate De Goldi. Penguin.

1998 *Fat, Four-Eyed and Useless* by David Hill. Scholastic.

1999 No award

2000 No award

## AWARDS FOR A BODY OF WORK

### *Hans Christian Andersen Award*

*This international award, sponsored by the International Board on Books for Young People, is given every two years to a living author and, since 1966, to a living illustrator whose complete works have made important international contributions to children's literature.*

1956  Eleanor Farjeon (Great Britain)

1958  Astrid Lindgren (Sweden)

1960  Erich Kästner (Germany)

1962  Meindert DeJong (USA)

1964  René Guillot (France)

1966  AUTHOR: Tove Jansson (Finland)
ILLUSTRATOR: Alois Carigiet (Switzerland)

1968  AUTHORS: James Krüss (Germany) and José Maria Sanchez-Silva (Spain)
ILLUSTRATOR: Jirí Trnka (Czechoslovakia)

1970  AUTHOR: Gianni Rodari (Italy)
ILLUSTRATOR: Maurice Sendak (USA)

1972  AUTHOR: Scott O'Dell (USA)
ILLUSTRATOR: Ib Spang Olsen (Denmark)

1974  AUTHOR: Maria Gripe (Sweden)
ILLUSTRATOR: Farshid Mesghali (Iran)

1976  AUTHOR: Cecil Bödker (Denmark)
ILLUSTRATOR: Tatjana Mawrina (USSR)

1978  AUTHOR: Paula Fox (USA)
ILLUSTRATOR: Otto S. Svend (Denmark)

1980  AUTHOR: Bohumil Riha (Czechoslovakia)
ILLUSTRATOR: Suekichi Akaba (Japan)

1982  AUTHOR: Lygia Bojunga Nunes (Brazil)
ILLUSTRATOR: Zbigniew Rychlicki (Poland)

1984  AUTHOR: Christine Nöstlinger (Austria)
ILLUSTRATOR: Mitsumasa Anno (Japan)

1986  AUTHOR: Patricia Wrightson (Australia)
ILLUSTRATOR: Robert Ingpen (Australia)

1988  AUTHOR: Annie M. G. Schmidt (Netherlands)
ILLUSTRATOR: Dušan Kállay (Czechoslovakia)

1990  AUTHOR: Tormod Haugen (Norway)
ILLUSTRATOR: Lisbeth Zwerger (Austria)

1992  AUTHOR: Virginia Hamilton (USA)
ILLUSTRATOR: Květa Pacovská (Czechoslovakia)

1994  AUTHOR: Michio Mado (Japan)
ILLUSTRATOR: Jörg Müller (Switzerland)

1996  AUTHOR: Uri Orlev (Israel)
ILLUSTRATOR: Klaus Ensikat (Germany)

1998  AUTHOR: Katherine Paterson (USA)
ILLUSTRATOR: Tomi Ungerer (France)

2000  AUTHOR: Ana Maria Machado (Brazil)
ILLUSTRATOR: Anthony Browne (United Kingdom)

### *Laura Ingalls Wilder Award*

*This award, sponsored by the Association for Library Service to Children of the American Library Association, is given to a U.S. author or illustrator whose body of work has made a lasting contribution to children's literature. Awarded every five years until 1980, the award is now given every three years.*

1954  Laura Ingalls Wilder

1960  Clara Ingram Judson

1965  Ruth Sawyer

1970  E. B. White

1975  Beverly Cleary

1980  Theodore S. Geisel (Dr. Seuss)

1983  Maurice Sendak

1986  Jean Fritz

1989  Elizabeth George Speare

1992  Marcia Brown

1995  Virginia Hamilton

1998  Russell Freedman

2001  Milton Meltzer

## NCTE Excellence in Poetry for Children Award

*For the list of award winners, see Chapter 3, page 43.*

## AWARDS FOR SPECIFIC GENRES OR GROUPS

### Mildred L. Batchelder Award

*This award, sponsored by the ALA's Association for Library Service to Children, is given to the American publisher of a children's book considered to be the most outstanding of those books originally published in a country other than the United States in a language other than English and subsequently translated and published in the United States during the previous year.*

1968  *The Little Man* by Erich Kästner. Translated from German by James Kirkup. Illustrated by Rick Schreiter. Knopf.

1969  *Don't Take Teddy* by Babbis Friis-Baastad. Translated from Norwegian by Lise Sömme McKinnon. Scribner's.

1970  *Wildcat under Glass* by Alki Zei. Translated from Greek by Edward Fenton. Holt.

1971  *In the Land of Ur: The Discovery of Ancient Mesopotamia* by Hans Baumann. Translated from German by Stella Humphries. Illustrated by Hans Peter Renner. Pantheon.

1972  *Friedrich* by Hans Peter Richter. Translated from German by Edite Kroll. Holt.

1973  *Pulga* by Siny Rose Van Iterson. Translated from Dutch by Alexander and Alison Gode. Morrow.

1974  *Petros' War* by Alki Zei. Translated from Greek by Edward Fenton, Dutton.

1975  *An Old Tale Carved Out of Stone* by Aleksandr M. Linevski. Translated from Russian by Maria Polushkin. Crown.

1976  *The Cat and Mouse Who Shared a House* written and illustrated by Ruth Hürlimann. Translated from German by Anthea Bell. Walck.

1977  *The Leopard* by Cecil Bödker. Translated from Danish by Gunnar Poulsen. Atheneum.

1978  No award

1979  *Konrad* by Christine Nöstlinger. Translated from German (Austrian) by Anthea Bell. Illustrated by Carol Nicklaus. Watts.

*Rabbit Island* by Jörg Steiner. Translated from German (Swiss) by Ann Conrad Lammers. Illustrated by Jörg Müller. Harcourt.

1980  *The Sound of Dragon's Feet* by Alki Zei. Translated from Greek by Edward Fenton. Dutton.

1981  *The Winter When Time Was Frozen* by Els Pelgrom. Translated from Dutch by Raphael and Maryka Rudnik. Morrow.

1982  *The Battle Horse* by Harry Kullman. Translated from Swedish by George Blecher and Lone Thygesen-Blecher. Bradbury.

1983  *Hiroshima No Pika* written and illustrated by Toshi Maruki. Translated from Japanese through Kurita-Bando Literary Agency. Lothrop.

1984  *Ronia, the Robber's Daughter* by Astrid Lindgren. Translated from Swedish by Patricia Crampton. Viking.

1985  *The Island on Bird Street* by Uri Orlev. Translated from Hebrew by Hillel Halkin. Houghton.

1986  *Rose Blanche* by Christophe Gallaz and Roberto Innocenti. Translated from French by Martha Coventry and Richard Graglia. Illustrated by Roberto Innocenti. Creative Education.

1987  *No Hero for the Kaiser* by Rudolf Frank. Translated from German by Patricia Crampton. Illustrated by Klaus Steffens. Lothrop.

1988 *If You Didn't Have Me* by Ulf Nilsson. Translated from Swedish by Lone Thygesen-Blecher and George Blecher. Illustrated by Eva Eriksson. McElderry.

1989 *Crutches* by Peter Härtling. Translated from German by Elizabeth D. Crawford. Lothrop.

1990 *Buster's World* by Bjarne Reuter. Translated from Danish by Anthea Bell. Dutton.

1991 *A Hand Full of Stars* by Rafik Schami. Translated from German by Rika Lesser. Dutton.
HONOR BOOK:
*Two Short and One Long* by Nina Ring Aamundsen. Translated from Norwegian by the author. Houghton.

1992 *The Man from the Other Side* by Uri Orlev. Translated from Hebrew by Hillel Halkin. Houghton.

1993 No award

1994 *The Apprentice* by Pilar Molina Llorente. Illustrated by Juan Ramón Alonso. Translated from Spanish by Robin Longshaw. Farrar.
HONOR BOOKS:
*Anne Frank, Beyond the Diary: A Photographic Remembrance* by Ruud van der Rol and Rian Verhoeven. Translated from Dutch by Tony Langham and Plym Peters. Viking.
*The Princess in the Kitchen Garden* by Annemie and Margriet Heymans. Translated from Dutch by Johanna H. Prins and Johanna W. Prins. Farrar.

1995 *The Boys from St. Petri* by Bjarne Reuter. Translated from Danish by Anthea Bell. Dutton.

1996 *The Lady with the Hat* by Uri Orlev. Translated from Hebrew by Hillel Halkin. Houghton.

1997 *The Friends* by Kazumi Yumoto. Translated from Japanese by Cathy Hirano. Farrar.

1998 *The Robber and Me* by Joseph Holub. Translated from German by Elizabeth D. Crawford. Holt.

1999 *Thanks to My Mother* by Schoschana Rabinovici. Translated from German by James Skofield. Dial.

2000 *The Baboon King* by Anton Quintana. Translated from Dutch by John Nieuwenhuizen. Walker.

2001 *Samir and Yonatan* by Daniella Carmi. Translated from Hebrew by Yael Lotan. Levine/Scholastic.

## Coretta Scott King Awards

*These awards, founded to commemorate the late Dr. Martin Luther King, Jr., and his wife, Coretta Scott King, for their work in promoting peace and world brotherhood, are given to an African-American author and, since 1974, an African-American illustrator whose children's books, published during the preceding year, made outstanding inspirational and educational contributions to literature for children and young people. The awards are sponsored by the Social Responsibilities Round Table of the American Library Association.*

1970 *Martin Luther King, Jr.: Man of Peace* by Lillie Patterson. Garrard.

1971 *Black Troubador: Langston Hughes* by Charlemae Rollins. Rand.

1972 *17 Black Artists* by Elton C. Fax. Dodd.

1973 *I Never Had It Made* by Jackie Robinson as told to Alfred Duckett. Putnam.

1974 AUTHOR: *Ray Charles* by Sharon Bell Mathis. Crowell.
ILLUSTRATOR: The same title, illustrated by George Ford.

1975 AUTHOR: *The Legend of Africana* by Dorothy Robinson. Johnson.
ILLUSTRATOR: The same title, illustrated by Herbert Temple.

1976 AUTHOR: *Duey's Tale* by Pearl Bailey. Harcourt.
ILLUSTRATOR: No award

1977 AUTHOR: *The Story of Stevie Wonder* by James Haskins. Lothrop.
ILLUSTRATOR: No award

1978 AUTHOR: *Africa Dream* by Eloise Greenfield. Day/Crowell.
ILLUSTRATOR: The same title, illustrated by Carole Bayard.

1979 AUTHOR: *Escape to Freedom* by Ossie Davis. Viking.

ILLUSTRATOR: *Something on My Mind* by Nikki Grimes. Illustrated by Tom Feelings. Dial.

1980 AUTHOR: *The Young Landlords* by Walter Dean Myers. Viking.

ILLUSTRATOR: *Cornrows* by Camille Yarbrough. Illustrated by Carole Bayard. Coward.

1981 AUTHOR: *This Life* by Sidney Poitier. Knopf.

ILLUSTRATOR: *Beat the Story-Drum, Pum-Pum* by Ashley Bryan. Atheneum.

1982 AUTHOR: *Let the Circle Be Unbroken* by Mildred D. Taylor. Dial.

ILLUSTRATOR: *Mother Crocodile: An Uncle Amadou Tale from Senegal* adapted by Rosa Guy. Illustrated by John Steptoe. Delacorte.

1983 AUTHOR: *Sweet Whispers, Brother Rush* by Virginia Hamilton. Philomel.

ILLUSTRATOR: *Black Child* by Peter Magabane. Knopf.

1984 AUTHOR: *Everett Anderson's Good-Bye* by Lucille Clifton. Holt.

ILLUSTRATOR: *My Mama Needs Me* by Mildred Pitts Walter. Illustrated by Pat Cummings. Lothrop.

1985 AUTHOR: *Motown and Didi* by Walter Dean Myers. Viking.

ILLUSTRATOR: No award

1986 AUTHOR: *The People Could Fly: American Black Folktales* by Virginia Hamilton. Knopf.

ILLUSTRATOR: *Patchwork Quilt* by Valerie Flournoy. Illustrated by Jerry Pinkney.

1987 AUTHOR: *Justin and the Best Biscuits in the World* by Mildred Pitts Walter. Lothrop.

ILLUSTRATOR: *Half Moon and One Whole Star* by Crescent Dragonwagon. Illustrated by Jerry Pinkney. Macmillan.

1988 AUTHOR: *The Friendship* by Mildred D. Taylor. Illustrated by Max Ginsburg. Dial.

ILLUSTRATOR: *Mufaro's Beautiful Daughters: An African Tale* retold and illustrated by John Steptoe. Lothrop.

1989 AUTHOR: *Fallen Angels* by Walter Dean Myers. Scholastic.

ILLUSTRATOR: *Mirandy and Brother Wind* by Patricia McKissack. Illustrated by Jerry Pinkney. Knopf.

1990 AUTHOR: *A Long Hard Journey* by Patricia C. and Fredrick L. McKissack. Walker.

ILLUSTRATOR: *Nathaniel Talking* by Eloise Greenfield. Illustrated by Jan Spivey Gilchrist. Black Butterfly Press.

1991 AUTHOR: *The Road to Memphis* by Mildred D. Taylor. Dial.

ILLUSTRATOR: *Aïda* retold by Leontyne Price. Illustrated by Leo and Diane Dillon. Harcourt.

1992 AUTHOR: *Now Is Your Time! The African-American Struggle for Freedom* by Walter Dean Myers. HarperCollins.

ILLUSTRATOR: *Tar Beach* by Faith Ringgold. Crown.

1993 AUTHOR: *The Dark-Thirty: Southern Tales of the Supernatural* by Patricia McKissack. Knopf.

ILLUSTRATOR: *Origins of Life on Earth: An African Creation Myth* by David A. Anderson. Illustrated by Kathleen Atkins Smith. Sight Productions.

1994 AUTHOR: *Toning the Sweep* by Angela Johnson. Orchard.

ILLUSTRATOR: *Soul Looks Back in Wonder* compiled and illustrated by Tom Feelings. Dial.

1995 AUTHOR: *Christmas in the Big House, Christmas in the Quarters* by Patricia C. McKissack and Fredrick L. McKissack. Illustrated by John Thompson. Scholastic.

ILLUSTRATOR: *The Creation* by James Weldon Johnson. Illustrated by James E. Ransome. Holiday.

1996 AUTHOR: *Her Stories: African American Folktales, Fairy Tales, and True Tales* by Virginia Hamilton. Illustrated by Leo and Diane Dillon. Blue Sky.

ILLUSTRATOR: *The Middle Passage: White Ships Black Cargo* by Tom Feelings. Dial.

1997    AUTHOR: *Slam!* by Walter Dean Myers. Scholastic.

ILLUSTRATOR: *Minty: A Story of Young Harriet Tubman* by Alan Schroeder. Illustrated by Jerry Pinkney. Dial.

1998    AUTHOR: *Forged by Fire* by Sharon M. Draper. Atheneum.

ILLUSTRATOR: *In Daddy's Arms I Am Tall: African Americans Celebrating Fathers* by Javaka Steptoe. Lee & Low.

1999    AUTHOR: *Heaven* by Angela Johnson. Simon & Schuster.

ILLUSTRATOR: *i see the rhythm* by Toyomi Igus. Illustrated by Michele Wood. Children's Book Press.

2000    AUTHOR: *Bud, Not Buddy* by Christopher Paul Curtis. Delacorte.

ILLUSTRATOR: *In the Time of the Drums* retold by Kim L. Siegelson. Illustrated by Brian Pinkney. Hyperion.

2001    AUTHOR: *Miracle Boys* by Jacqueline Woodson. Putnam.

ILLUSTRATOR: *Uptown* by Bryan Collier. Holt.

## Pura Belpré Award

*The Pura Belpré Award honors Latino writers and illustrators whose work best portrays, affirms, and celebrates the Latino cultural experience in a work of literature for youth. This biennial award is sponsored by the Association for Library Service to Children and the National Association to Promote Library Service to the Spanish Speaking.*

1996    AUTHOR: *An Island Like You: Stories of the Barrio* by Judith Ortiz Cofer. Orchard.

ILLUSTRATOR: *Chato's Kitchen* by Gary Soto. Illustrated by Susan Guevara. Putnam.

1998    AUTHOR: *Parrot in the Oven: Mi Vida* by Victor Martinez. HarperCollins.

ILLUSTRATOR: *Snapshots from the Wedding* by Gary Soto. Illustrated by Stephanie Garcia. Putnam.

2000    AUTHOR: *Under the Royal Palms: A Childhood in Cuba* by Alma Flor Ada. Atheneum.

ILLUSTRATOR: *Magic Windows: Cut-Paper Art and Stories* by Carmen Lomas Garza. Children's Book Press.

## Distinguished Play Award

*This award, sponsored by the American Alliance of Theatre and Education, honors the playwright(s) and the publisher of the work voted as the best play for young people published during the past calendar year (January to December). Starting in 1989, two categories were instituted: Category A—Plays primarily for upper and secondary school age audiences; Category B—Plays primarily for elementary and middle school age audiences. Beginning in 1998 Category C was established for adaptations.*

1983    *My Days as a Youngling, John Jacob Niles: The Early Years,* a musical adapted for the stage and scripted by Nancy Niles Sexton, Vaughn McBride, Martha Harrison Jones; songs by John Niles; published by Anchorage Press.

1984    *Nightingale* by John Urquhart and Rita Grossberg, published by Anchorage Press.

1985    *A Play Called Noah's Flood* by Suzan Zeder, published by Anchorage Press.

1986    *Doors* by Suzan Zeder, published by Anchorage Press.

1987    *Mother Hicks* by Suzan Zeder, published by Anchorage Press.

1988    *Babies Having Babies* by Kathryn Montgomery and Jeffrey Auerbach, published by Baker's Plays.

1989    Category A: *A Separate Peace* by Nancy Pahl Gilsenan, published by Dramatic Publishing Company.

Category B: *Becca* by Wendy Kesselman, published by Anchorage Press.

1990    Category A: *The Man-Child* by Arnold Rabin, published by Baker's Plays.

Category B: *The Chicago Gypsies* by Virginia Glasgow Koste, published by Dramatic Publishing Company.

Category B: *Aalmauria: The Voyage of the Dragonfly* by Max Bush, published by Anchorage Press.

1991 Category A: *In the Middle of Grand Central Station* by Nancy Pahl Gilsenan, published by Dramatic Publishing Company.

Category A: *Jungalbook* by Edward Mast, published by Anchorage Press.

Category B: *Monkey Magic: Chinese Story Theatre* by Aurand Harris, published by Anchorage Press.

1992 Category A: *The Secret Garden* by Pamela Sterling, published by Dramatic Publishing Company.

Category B: *Amber Waves* by James Still, published by Samuel French, Inc.

1993 Category A: *This Is Not a Pipe Dream* by Barry Kornhauser, published by Anchorage Press.

Category B: *The Pinballs* by Aurand Harris, published by Anchorage Press.

1994 Category A: *Song for the Navigator* by Michael Cowell, published by Dramatic Publishing Company.

Category B: *A Woman Called Truth* by Sandra Fenichel Asher, published by Dramatic Publishing Company.

1995 Category A: *T-Money & Wolf* by Kevin Willmott and Ric Averill, published by Dramatic Publishing Company.

Category A: *Scars and Stripes* by Thomas Cadwaleder Jones, published by Encore Publishing Company.

Category B: *Ramona Quimby* by Len Jenkins, published by Dramatic Publishing Company.

1996 Category A: *Angel in the Night* by Joanna Halpert Kraus, published by Dramatic Publishing Company.

Category B: *The Prince and the Pauper* adapted for the stage by Aurand Harris, published by Anchorage Press.

1997 Category A: *The Less than Human Club* by Timothy Mason, published by Smith Kraus, Inc.

Category B: No award

1998 Category A: *Selkie* by Laurie Brooks, published by Anchorage Press.

Category B: *The Yellow Boat* by David Saar, published by Anchorage Press.

Category C: *Bambi: A Life in the Woods* by James DeVita, published by Anchorage Press.

1999 Category A: *North Star* by Gloria Bond Clunie, published by Dramatic Publishing Company.

Category B: *Still Life with Iris* by Steve Dietz, published by Dramatic Publishing Company.

Category C: *Journey of the Sparrows* by Meryl Friedman, published by Dramatic Publishing Company.

2000 Category A: *And Then They Came for Me* by James Still, published by Dramatic Publishing Company.

Category A: *The Taste of Sunrise* by Suzan Zeder, published by Anchorage Press.

Category B: *The Wolf Child* by Edward Mast, published by Anchorage Press.

Category C: No award

### Edgar Allan Poe Award (Mystery)— Best Juvenile Novel Category

*This award, sponsored by the Mystery Writers of America, is given to the author of the best mystery of the year written for young readers.*

1961 *The Mystery of the Haunted Pool* by Phyllis A. Whitney. Westminster.

1962 *The Phantom of Walkaway Hill* by Edward Fenton. Doubleday.

1963 *Cutlass Island* by Scott Corbett. Atlantic/Little.

1964 *The Mystery of the Hidden Hand* by Phyllis A. Whitney. Westminster.

1965 *The Mystery at Crane's Landing* by Marcella Thum. Dodd.

1966 *The Mystery of 22 East* by Leon Ware. Westminster.

1967 *Sinbad and Me* by Kin Platt. Chilton.

1968 *Signpost of Terror* by Gretchen Sprague. Dodd.

1969 *The House of Dies Drear* by Virginia Hamilton. Macmillan.

1970 *Danger at Black Dyke* by Winifred Finlay. Phillips.

1971 *The Intruder* by John Rowe Townsend. Lippincott.

1972 *Night Fall* by Joan Aiken. Holt.

1973 *Deathwatch* by Robb White. Doubleday.

1974 *The Long Black Coat* by Jay Bennett. Delacorte.

1975 *The Dangling Witness* by Jay Bennett. Delacorte.

1976 *Z for Zachariah* by Robert C. O'Brien. Atheneum.

1977 *Are You in the House Alone?* by Richard Peck. Viking.

1978 *A Really Weird Summer* by Eloise Jarvis McGraw. Atheneum.

1979 *Alone in Wolf Hollow* by Dana Brookins. Clarion.

1980 *The Kidnapping of Christina Lattimore* by Joan Lowery Nixon. Harcourt.

1981 *The Seance* by Joan Lowery Nixon. Harcourt.

1982 *Taking Terri Mueller* by Norma Fox Mazer. Avon.

1983 *The Murder of Hound Dog Bates* by Robbie Branscum. Viking.

1984 *The Callender Papers* by Cynthia Voigt. Atheneum.

1985 *Night Cry* by Phyllis Reynolds Naylor. Atheneum.

1986 *The Sandman's Eyes* by Patricia Windsor. Delacorte.

1987 *Other Side of Dark* by Joan Lowery Nixon. Delacorte.

1988 *Lucy Forever and Miss Rosetree, Shrinks* by Susan Shreve. Holt.

1989 *Megan's Island* by Willo Davis Roberts. Atheneum.

1990 No award

1991 *Stonewords* by Pam Conrad. Harper.

1992 *Wanted . . . Mud Blossom* by Betsy Byars. Delacorte.

1993 *Coffin in a Case* by Eve Bunting. HarperCollins.

1994 *The Twin in the Tavern* by Barbara Brooks Wallace. Atheneum.

1995 *The Absolutely True Story . . . How I Visited Yellowstone Park with the Terrible Rupes* by Willo Davis Roberts. Atheneum.

1996 *Looking for Jamie Bridger* by Nancy Springer. Dial.

1997 *The Clearing* by Dorothy R. Miller. Atheneum.

1998 *Sparrows in the Gallery* by Barbara Brooks Wallace. Atheneum.

1999 *Sammy Keyes and the Hotel Thief* by Wendelin Van Draanen. Knopf.

2000 *The Night Flyers* by Elizabeth McDavid Jones. Pleasant Company.

### Scott O'Dell Award for Historical Fiction

*This award, donated by the author Scott O'Dell and administered by Zena Sutherland, is given to the author of a distinguished work of historical fiction for children or young adults set in the New World and published in English by a U.S. publisher.*

1984 *The Sign of the Beaver* by Elizabeth George Speare. Houghton.

1985 *The Fighting Ground* by Avi (Wortis). Harper.

1986 *Sarah, Plain and Tall* by Patricia MacLachlan. Harper.

1987 *Streams to the River, River to the Sea: A Novel of Sacagawea* by Scott O'Dell. Houghton.

1988 *Charley Skedaddle* by Patricia Beatty. Morrow.

1989 *The Honorable Prison* by Lyll Becerra de Jenkins. Lodestar.

1990 *Shades of Gray* by Carolyn Reeder. Macmillan.

1991  *A Time of Troubles* by Pieter van Raven. Scribner's.

1992  *Stepping on the Cracks* by Mary Downing Hahn. Clarion.

1993  *Morning Girl* by Michael Dorris. Hyperion.

1994  *Bull Run* by Paul Fleischman. HarperCollins.

1995  *Under the Blood-Red Sun* by Graham Salisbury. Delacorte

1996  *The Bomb* by Theodore Taylor. Harcourt Brace.

1997  *Jip: His Story* by Katherine Paterson. Dutton.

1998  *Out of the Dust* by Karen Hesse. Scholastic.

1999  *Forty Acres and Maybe a Mule* by Harriette Gillem Robinet. Atheneum.

2000  *Two Suns in the Sky* by Miriam Bat-Ami. Front Street/Cricket.

2001  *The Art of Keeping Cool* by Janet Taylor Lisle. Atheneum.

## Orbis Pictus Award

*This award, sponsored by NCTE's Committee on Using Nonfiction in the Elementary Language Arts Classroom, is given to an author in recognition of excellence in writing of nonfiction for children published in the United States in the preceding year.*

1990  *The Great Little Madison* by Jean Fritz. Putnam.

1991  *Franklin Delano Roosevelt* by Russell Freedman. Clarion.

1992  *Flight: The Journey of Charles Lindbergh* by Robert Burleigh. Illustrated by Mike Wimmer. Philomel.

1993  *Children of the Dustbowl: The True Story of the School at Weedpatch Camp* by Jerry Stanley. Random.

1994  *Across America on an Emigrant Train* by Jim Murphy. Clarion.

1995  *Safari beneath the Sea* by Diane Swanson. Photographs by the Royal British Columbia Museum. Sierra Club.

1996  *The Great Fire* by Jim Murphy. Scholastic.

1997  *Leonardo da Vinci* by Diane Stanley. Morrow.

1998  *An Extraordinary Life: The Story of a Monarch Butterfly* by Laurence Pringle. Illustrated by Bob Marstall. Orchard.

1999  *Shipwreck at the Bottom of the World: The Extraordinary True Story of Schackleton and the Endurance* by Jennifer Armstrong. Crown.

2000  *Through My Eyes* by Ruby Bridges and Margo Lundell. Scholastic.

2001  *Hurry Freedom: African Americans in Gold Rush California* by Jerry Stanley. Crown.

## Phoenix Award

*This award, sponsored by the Children's Literature Association, is given to the author of a book first published 20 years earlier. The book must have been originally published in English and cannot have been the recipient of a major children's book award.*

1985  *Mark of the Horse Lord* by Rosemary Sutcliff. Walck.

1986  *Queenie Peavy* by Robert Burch. Viking.

1987  *Smith* by Leon Garfield. Constable.

1988  *The Rider and His Horse* by Eric Christian Haugaard. Houghton.

1989  *The Night Watchmen* by Helen Cresswell. Macmillan.

1990  *Enchantress from the Stars* by Sylvia Louise Engdahl. Macmillan.

1991  *A Long Way from Verona* by Jane Gardam. Macmillan.

1992  *A Sound of Chariots* by Mollie Hunter. Harper.

1993  *Carrie's War* by Nina Bawden. Puffin.

1994  *Of Nightingales That Weep* by Katherine Paterson. Harper.

1995  *Dragonwings* by Laurence Yep. Harper.

1996  *The Stone Book* by Alan Garner. Philomel. (Others in The Stone Quartet: *Granny Reardun* [1978], *The Aimer Gate* [1979], *Tom Fobble's Day* [1979])

1997  *I Am the Cheese* by Robert Cormier. Random.

1998  *A Chance Child* by Jill Paton Walsh. Avon.

1999  *Throwing Shadows* by E. L. Konigsburg. Collier.

2000  *The Keeper of the Isis Light* by Monica Hughes. Atheneum.

2001  *Seventh Raven* by Peter Dickinson. Penguin.

## OTHER NOTABLE BOOK EXHIBITIONS AND AWARDS

### Biennale of Illustrations Bratislava

*This biannual international exposition of books was begun in 1967 and is held in Bratislava, Slovak Republic. A Grand Prix and five honor book awards are given to children's books for excellence in illustration.*

### American Institute of Graphic Arts Book Show

*This annual book show features approximately 100 books, both children's and adult, selected for excellence in design and manufacture. Lists of books selected each year can be found in AIGA Graphic Design USA (Watson-Guptil).*

### New York Times Best Illustrated Children's Books of the Year

*Sponsored by **The New York Times**, this list of 10 books appears annually in the **Times**. A three-member panel of experts chooses the books.*

### International Reading Association Children's Book Award

*Sponsored by the Institute for Reading Research and administered by the International Reading Association, this international award is given annually to an author for a first or second book that shows unusual promise in the children's book field.*

### International Board on Books for Young People Honor List

*Sponsored by the International Board on Books for Young People (IBBY), this biennial list is composed of three books (one for text, one for illustration, and one for translation) from each IBBY National Section to represent the best in children's literature published in that country in the past two years.*

*The books selected are recommended as suitable for publication worldwide.*

### State Children's Choice Award Programs

*Nearly all states have a children's choice book award program. Usually, a ballot of about twenty-five titles is generated from children's or teachers' nominations. Children from all over the state then vote for their favorite title. For information about your state children's choice award program, contact your state library association.*

# PROFESSIONAL RESOURCES

## Books

Bamford, R. A., & Kristo, J. V. (1998). *Making facts come alive: Choosing quality nonfiction literature K–8.* Norwood, MA: Christopher-Gordon.

*This practical guide helps users to find and integrate nonfiction titles across the curriculum.*

Bany-Winters, L. (1997). *On stage: Theater games and activities for kids.* Chicago: Chicago Review Press.

*An assortment of theater games are divided among improvisations, creating characters, puppetry, costumes, suggestions for monologues, scenes, and plays for grades 1–6.*

Barchers, S. I. (2000). *Multicultural folktales: Readers' theatre for elementary students.* Englewood, NJ: Libraries Unlimited, 2000.

*Barchers provides practical advice on how to get kids reading and performing stories. The book includes 40 scripts with reading level indicated.*

Bauer, C. F. (1997). *Leading kids to books through puppets.* Chicago: American Library Association.

*Bauer links readers to a wide variety of literature through puppets. She also explains how to make and use different types of puppets.*

Bohning, G., Phillips, A., & Bryant, S. H. (1993). *Literature on the move: Making and using pop-up and lift-flap books.* Englewood, CO: Libraries Unlimited.

*Directions are provided for making eight basic types of engineered (movable) pages with variations for each.*

Cart, M. (1995). *What's so funny? Wit and humor in American children's literature.* New York: HarperCollins.

*An enjoyable study of selected children's books, characters, and authors, and their humor.*

Chatton, B. (1993). *Using poetry across the curriculum: A whole language approach.* Phoenix, AZ: Oryx Press.

*Ways to integrate poetry into all subject areas.*

Cullinan, B. E., Scala, M. C., & Schroder, V. C. with A. K. Lovett (1995). *Three voices: An invitation to poetry across the curriculum.* York, ME: Stenhouse.

*Teaching strategies with sample vignettes for integrating poetry into the curriculum.*

Day, F. A. (1997). *Latina and Latino voices in literature for children and teenagers.* Portsmouth, NH: Heinemann.

*Day explains bias and how to recognize it in books for young people. She also highlights authors and illustrators and describes their works.*

Egoff, S., Stubbs, G., Ashley, R., & Sutton, W. (Eds.). (1996). *Only connect: Readings on children's literature* (3rd ed.). New York: Oxford Press.

*Essays.*

Freeman, E., & Lehman, B. (2001). *Global perspectives in children's literature.* Needham Heights, MA: Allyn and Bacon.

*This book reviews the status, value, historical context, and contemporary trends in international children's literature.*

Glover, M. K. (1999). *A garden of poets: Poetry writing in the elementary classroom.* Urbana, IL: National Council of Teachers of English.

*Glover offers ideas on creating an atmosphere conducive to poetry writing. Includes bibliographies on music for inspiring writing and on bilingual poetry books.*

Greene, E., & Baker, A. (1996). *Storytelling: Art and technique.* New Providence, NJ: R. R. Bowker.

*An update of this successful guide on storytelling includes a chapter on telling stories to young adults.*

Hall, S. (1990, 1994). *Using picture storybooks to teach literary devices: Recommended books for children and young adults* (Vol. 1 & 2). Phoenix, AZ: Oryx Press.

*How picture books can be used to teach complex literary devices.*

Hancock, J., & Hill, S. (Eds.). (1997). *Literature-based reading programs at work.* Portsmouth, NH: Heinemann.

*This book from Australia suggests solutions to the possible problems encountered when teachers implement a literature-based reading program.*

Hansen, J. (2001). (2nd ed.) *When writers read.* Portsmouth, NH: Heinemann.

*Teachers and researchers working together in an elementary school discovered the principles to encourage children to develop helpful reading strategies.*

Harris, V. J. (Ed.). (1997). *Using multiethnic literature in the K–8 classroom.* Norwood, MA: Christopher-Gordon.

*Essays on important issues concerning the field of multiethnic children's literature and bibliographies of books about different ethnic groups.*

Hickman, J., Cullinan, B. E., & Hepler, S. (Eds.). (1994). *Children's literature in the classroom: Extending Charlotte's web.* Norwood, MA: Christopher-Gordon Publishers.

*Essays.*

Hopkins, L. B. (1998). *Pass the poetry, please!* New York: HarperCollins.

*This revised classic introduces favorite works by contemporary poets and is a must for teachers who wish to encourage students to appreciate poetry.*

Horning, K. T. (1997). *From cover to cover: Evaluating and reviewing children's books.* New York: HarperCollins.

*A handbook on evaluating children's books with recommendations for specific genres.*

Janeczko, P. B. (1999). *How to write poetry.* New York: Scholastic.

*Poet Janeczko guides would-be poets through the writing process.*

Janeczko, P. B., & Bobak, C. (1994). *Poetry from A to Z: A guide for young writers.* New York: Bradbury Press.

*Poets talk about their writing; also many suggestions for middle-graders who would like to try writing poetry.*

Johnson, N. J., Schlick, K. L., & Hill, B. B. (Eds.). (1995). *Literature circles and response.* Norwood, MA: Christopher-Gordon.

*The editors advise on how to establish literature circles and how to elicit responses to literature from students.*

Koch, K. (1999). *Wishes, lies, and dreams: Teaching children to write poetry.* New York: HarperPerennial.

*Koch describes working with inner-city children who had never done much writing of any kind and encouraging them to express themselves by writing down their feelings.*

————. (1973/1990). *Rose, where did you get that red? Teaching great poetry to children.* New York: Vintage.

*Koch explains his approach to exposing children to adult poetry by providing samples of the lessons he used.*

Lamme, L. L., Krogh, S. L., & Yachmetz, K. A. (1992). *Literature-based moral education: Children's books & activities for teaching values, responsibility, & good judgment in the elementary school.* Phoenix, AZ: Oryx Press.

*Books for teaching children about such things as responsibility, respect for others, sharing, truthfulness, and solving conflicts peacefully.*

Marantz, S. S., & Marantz, K. A. (1995). *The art of children's picture books: A selective reference guide.* (2nd ed.). New York: Garland.

*A work of history and criticism of children's picture books presents an indepth study of the art within picture books.*

McClure, A. A., Harrison, P., & Reed, S. (1990). *Sunrises and songs: Reading and writing poetry in an elementary classroom.* Portsmouth, NH: Heinemann.

*Describes how two teachers guided their fifth- and sixth-grade students into writing and reading poetry over a period of a year.*

Moss, J. F. (1994). *Using literature in the middle grades: A thematic approach.* Norwood, MA: Christopher-Gordon.

*Moss explains how she integrates content matter and language arts by setting up literature units around a topic, genre, literary theme, or narrative element.*

Pellowski, A. (1990). *The world of storytelling: A practical guide to the origins, development, and applications of storytelling* (expanded and revised edition). New York: H. W. Wilson.

*Comprehensive information about the oral tradition and the history of storytelling as well as a list of storytelling festivals held around the world.*

————. (1995). *The storytelling handbook.* New York: Simon & Schuster.

*This indispensable guide to the art of storytelling discusses how to tell stories and includes stories from around the world to use for successful storytelling.*

Raphael, T. E., & Au, K. H. (Eds.). (1998). *Literature-based instruction: Reshaping the curriculum.* Norwood, MA: Christopher-Gordon.

*Theories of literature-based instruction and where and how it fits into the curriculum are discussed by various noted teacher-researchers and teacher educators.*

Ray, K. W. (2000). *Wondrous words: Writers and writing in the elementary classroom.* Urbana, IL: National Council of Teachers of English.

*Ray uses examples of student writing to show how students learn to write from reading such authors as Gary Paulsen and Cynthia Rylant.*

Robb, L. (1994). *Whole language, whole learners: Creating a literature-centered classroom.* New York: Morrow.

*Robb offers sound advice about whole language and literature-based teaching for primary-, intermediate-, and middle-school grades.*

Routman, R. (1991, 1994). *Invitations: Changing as teachers and learners K–12.* Portsmouth, NH: Heinemann.

*In her second book, Routman provides additional assistance to teachers committed to improving the way they teach.*

Rudman, M. K. (1995). *Children's literature: An issues approach* (3rd ed.). White Plains, NY: Longman.

*Criteria for evaluating children's books dealing with issues affecting our society today, such as siblings, adoption, divorce, sexuality, aging, and death, as well as annotations describing recommended books for children.*

Short, K. G. (Ed.). (1995). *Research and professional resources in children's literature: Piecing a patchwork quilt.* Newark, DE: International Reading Association.

*An annotated bibliography of studies and professional resources on children's literature.*

Trelease, J. (2001). *The read-aloud handbook* (4th ed.). New York: Putnam Penguin.

*Trelease annotates three hundred of his favorite read-alouds, giving the listening level of each. Many of the annotations include suggestions of other books by the same author.*

Zipes, J. D. (2000). *Sticks and stones: The troublesome success of children's literature from Slovenly Peter to Harry Potter.* New York: Routledge.

*In this series of essays Zipes comments on the field of children's literature and its too frequent homogeneity.*


*Books about the History of Children's Literature*

Bingham, J., & Scholt, G. (1980). *Fifteen centuries of children's literature: An annotated chronology of British and American works in historical context.* Westport, CT: Greenwood.

Davis, D. (1981). *Theatre for young people.* New York: Beaufort.

Gillespie, M. C. (1970). *History and trends: Literature for children.* Dubuque, IA: Brown.

Hunt, P. (1995). *Children's literature: An illustrated history.* Oxford: Oxford University Press.

Hunt, P., & Ray, S. G. (1996). *International companion encyclopedia of children's literature.* London: Routledge.

Marshall, M. R. (1988). *An introduction to the world of children's books: Books about the history of children's literature* (2nd ed.). Aldershot, England: Gower.

McCaslin, N. (1971). *Theatre for children in the United States.* Norman: University of Oklahoma Press.

Murray, G. S. (1998). *American children's literature and the construction of childhood.* New York: Twayne.

Smith, E. S. (1980). In M. Hodges & S. Steinfirst (Eds.). *The history of children's literature* (rev. ed.). Chicago: ALA.


*Journal Articles*

Byrnes, D. A. (1988). "Children and prejudice." *Social Education, 52,* 267–271.

*Specific activities and strategies for teachers to use to reduce children's prejudices.*

Cohen, D. H. (1968). "The effect of literature on vocabulary and reading achievement." *Elementary English, 45,* 209–213, 217.

*This landmark study demonstrates that spending classroom time reading aloud to second-graders from low socioeconomic backgrounds results in significant increases in vocabulary, word knowledge, and reading comprehension.*

DeFord, D. E. (1981). "Literacy: Reading, writing, and other essentials." *Language Arts, 58,* 652–658.

*Different approaches to reading and writing in first-grade classrooms were studied. Analysis of the children's writing indicated that the writing of the children in the whole language classroom reflected familiarity with a greater variety of literary forms, such as stories, poetry, and newspaper reports.*

Durkin, D. (1961). "Children who read before grade one." *The Reading Teacher, 14,* 163–166.

*Children identified in this study had learned to read before they started first grade, and the author found that they all had been read to regularly at home, some since the age of 2. This was one of the first studies to recognize this important correlation.*

Eldredge, J. L., & Butterfield, D. (1986). "Alternatives to traditional reading instruction." *The Reading Teacher, 40,* 32–37.

*This research found more significant gains in achievement and attitudes toward reading in second-grade classrooms where literature was part of the reading instruction program than in those classrooms relying on basal instruction.*

Elleman, B. (1998). To market to market: A look at children's book publishing. *School Library Journal, 44*(4), 44–45.

*Elleman examines the impact of marketing on the publication of children's books.*

Flood, J., & Lapp, D. (1994). "Teacher book clubs: Establishing literature discussion groups for teachers." *The Reading Teacher, 47,* 574–576.

*When teachers participate in book club discussions on a regular basis and become aware of their own literacy processing, they also develop a greater understanding of teaching and learning.*

Goodman, K. S. (1986). "Basal readers: A call for action." *Language Arts, 63,* 358–363.

*Goodman points to an ever-widening gap between the methods employed in basal readers and the latest theory and research in reading instruction.*

———. (1988). "Look what they've done to Judy Blume!: The 'basalization' of children's literature." *The New Advocate, 1,* 29–41.

*Goodman suggests that we should offer authentic children's literature rather than adaptations that have been rewritten under the mistaken notion that they can be made easier to read by controlling vocabulary.*

Hearne, B. (1998). Perennial picture books: Seeded by the oral tradition. *Journal of Youth Services in Libraries, 12*(1), 26–33.

*The article makes a strong statement about what makes a successful picture book and lists the 50 most enduring ones of the 20th century.*

Holdaway, D. (1982). "Shared book experience: Teaching reading using favorite books." *Theory into Practice, 21,* 293–300.

*The rationale and research behind the "shared-book experience," a form of natural literacy learning that has become widely used in classroom literature programs in both New Zealand and the United States.*

Huck, C. S. (1982). "I give you the end of a golden string." *Theory into Practice, 21,* 315–321.

*Huck cites research that firmly supports her plea for making children's literature the central part of programs for helping children learn to read.*

International Relations Committees, ALSC and YALSA. (2001). Bilingual books for children. *Journal of Youth Services in Libraries, 14*(2), 32–37.

*Fifty-one 1998–2000 children's bilingual books, in 13 languages are recommended.*

Jalongo, M. R., & Creany, A. D. (1991). "Censorship in children's literature: What every educator should know." *Childhood Education, 67*(3), 143–148.

*The authors explain the complex distinctions between censorship, selection, and self-censorship and provide suggestions about how educators can be prepared to handle censorship controversies.*

Kutiper, K., & Wilson, P. (1993). "Updating poetry preferences: A look at the poetry children really like." *The Reading Teacher, 47,* 28–35.

*The authors recommend classroom experiences that will broaden their students' appreciation for a diverse array of poetry.*

Larrick, N. (1965). "The all-white world of children's books." *Saturday Review of Literature, 11,* 63–65, 84–85.

*This landmark article describes a study Larrick made of children's books published between 1962 and 1964 in which she found very little mention of people of color in the texts or illustrations and described some of the negative stereotypes that were prevalent in the early 1960s.*

Lynch-Brown, C., & Tomlinson, C. M. (1998). Children's literature past and present. Is there a future? *Peabody Journal of Education, 73*(4).

*An overview of the field of children's literature in the twentieth century including current trends and recommendations for the future.*

McKean, B. (2000–2001). Speak the speech, I pray you! Preparing to read aloud dramatically. *The Reading Teacher, 54*(4), 358–360.

Menon, M. B. & Mirabito, J. (1999). "Ya' mean all we hafta do is read?" *The Reading Teacher, 53*(3), 190–196.

*A flexible book club program as implemented in fourth and sixth grade classrooms.*

Smolkin, L. B. (1995). The literature of the theatre and aesthetic response: Welcoming plays into the world of children's literature. *The New Advocate, 8*(2), 109–123.

*A study on children's responses to plays as literary texts.*

Traw, R. (1998). Literature-based programs can work!: Large scale assessment of two school districts. *The New Advocate, 11*(2), 135–151.

*A report on two large-scale literature-based reading programs found to be successful as measured on standardized tests and teacher survey data.*

Tunnell, M. O., & Jacobs, J. S. (1989). "Using 'real' books: Research findings on literature-based reading instruction." *The Reading Teacher, 42,* 470–477.

*Tunnell and Jacobs looked at a number of studies that directly compared literature-based reading programs with basal instruction and at research reports on the reading growth of children in whole language classrooms where real literature was prevalent.*

## Journals and Periodicals

**Bookbird: Journal of International Children's Literature.** Published quarterly by IBBY, the International Board on Books for Young People, Nonnenweg 12 Postfach, CH-4003 Basel, Switzerland. For subscriptions write to Bookbird, P. O. Box 807, Highland Park, IL 60035–0807, USA.

*This journal includes articles, authors' and illustrators' portraits, reports and announcements, and reviews of children's books and professional literature of international interest.*

**Book Links: Connecting Books, Libraries, and Classrooms.** A bimonthly magazine published by Booklist Publications, an imprint of the American Library Association, 50 E. Huron St., Chicago, IL 60611.

*This magazine publishes articles with suggestions for exploring a particular theme through literature. Descriptions of books, strategies for stimulating classroom discussion about them, and activities for student involvement are among the offerings.*

**Children's Literature in Education: An International Quarterly.** Published by Human Sciences Press, Inc., 233 Spring Street, New York, NY 10013–1578.

*This journal includes interviews with authors and illustrators, accounts of classroom practice involving literature or the reading process, and commentary on social issues as reflected in books.*

**The Dragon Lode.** The Journal of the Children's Literature and Reading Special Interest Group of the International Reading Association is published three times a year for members. IRA members may join this interest group by obtaining the name and address of its current Membership Chair from IRA, 800 Barksdale Road, P. O. Box 8139, Newark, DE 19714–8139.

*This journal publishes articles about children's literature and the teaching of it, classroom ideas, and book reviews of books published internationally as well as in the United States.*

**Journal of Children's Literature.** Journal of the Children's Literature Assembly of the National Council of Teachers of English, published and sent to CLA members twice a year. NCTE members may join the Children's Literature Assembly by obtaining the name and address of the current Membership Chair of CLA. Write to NCTE, 111 Kenyon Road, Urbana, IL 61801.

*This journal solicits and publishes manuscripts regarding any aspect of children's literature, as well as reviews of children's books and professional resources.*

**JOYS, Journal of Youth Services in Libraries.** Quarterly journal of the Association for Library Service to Children and the Young Adult Library Services Association, divisions of the American Library Association, 50 Huron St., Chicago, IL 60611.

*This journal informs librarians who work with children and/or young adults about current practices. Teachers as well as librarians will find the thorough reviews of professional resources helpful.*

**Language Arts.** Published monthly, September through April, by the National Council of Teachers of English, for its members. For membership information, write NCTE, 1111 Kenyon Road, Urbana, IL 61801–1096.

*This journal publishes themed issues on topics relating to the content and teaching of language arts. Regular features include author profiles, annotations of children's books, and commentaries on trends in the field.*

**The New Advocate for Those Involved with Young People and Their Literature.** Published quarterly since 1988 by Christopher-Gordon Publishers, 480 Washington Street, Norwood, MA 02062.

*This journal contains articles on using children's literature in the classroom. Reviews of children's books and literature resources for teachers appear in each issue.*

**The Reading Teacher.** A journal of the International Reading Association, published monthly eight times during the school year. For information on joining the IRA and subscribing to its journals, write to IRA, 800 Barksdale Road, P.O. Box 8139, Newark, DE 19714–8139.

*This journal contains articles that reflect current theory, research, and practice regarding the teaching of reading. Regular columns deal with evaluation of children's trade books and professional resources.*

**The United States Board on Books for Young People, Inc. (USBBY) Newsletter.** Published twice a year by the U.S. section of the International Board on Books for Young People (IBBY). To join USBBY and receive the newsletter, write to USBBY Secretariat, c/o International Reading Association, P.O. Box 8139, Newark, DE 19714-8139.

*This newsletter includes news and articles concerning national and international activities related to children's literature. It also includes reviews of international children's books.*

## Information on Authors and Illustrators

*Children's literature review: Excerpts from reviews, criticism, and commentary on books for children and young people, 1–43* (1976–1997). Detroit: Gale Research.

*This reference provides information about authors and illustrators, often in their own words, as well as excerpts from reviews of their work. Each volume contains a cumulative index to authors and titles.*

Copeland, J. S., & Copeland, V. L. (1995). *Speaking of poets 2: More interviews with poets who write for children and young adults.* Urbana, IL: National Council of Teachers of English.

*This resource includes 20 interviews with both newer poets and well established poets, such as Paul Janeczko and Lucille Clifton.*

*Junior Book of Authors* (1951). *More junior authors* (1963), and the *Third, fourth, fifth, sixth, seventh, and eighth book of junior authors and illustrators.* (1972–2000). New York: H. W. Wilson.

*This reference includes biographical sketches of authors and illustrators written for young people.*

Silvey, A. (Ed.). (1995). *Children's books and their creators.* New York: Houghton.

*This reference volume focuses on twentieth-century books and contains more than eight hundred entries including biographical sketches of authors and illustrators.*

*Something about the author: Facts and pictures about authors and illustrators of books for young people, 1–119* (1971–2001). Detroit: Gale Research.

*This series includes comprehensive information about authors and illustrators, written for young people.*

## Bibliographies: Annual Lists

"CCBC Choices."

*An annual spring annotated booklist, published by and for the members of the Friends of the CCBC, Inc. (Cooperative Children's Book Center). For information about CCBC publications and/or membership in the Friends, send a self-addressed stamped envelope to Friends of the CCBC, P. O. Box 5288, Madison, WI 53705–0288.*

"Children's Choices."

*This yearly list of newly published books, chosen by young readers themselves, appears each October in* **The Reading Teacher** *as a project of the International Reading Association/Children's Book Council Joint Committee.*

"Notable Children's Books."

*This annual American Library Association list appears in the March issue of* **School Library Journal** *and also in the March 15th issue of* **Booklist.**

"Notable Children's Books in the Language Arts (K-8)."

> *This annual list of outstanding trade books for enhancing language awareness among students in grades K-8 appears in each October issue of* **Language Arts.**

"Notable Children's Trade Books in the Field of Social Studies."

> *This list appears in the April/May issue of* **Social Education.**

"Outstanding Science Trade Books for Children."

> *This list appears in the March issue of* **Science and Children.**

"Teachers' Choices."

> *This yearly list includes books recommended by teachers. It appears each November in* **The Reading Teacher.**

"Young Adults' Choices."

> *The books on this annual list were selected by readers in middle, junior high, and senior high schools. It appears in the November issue of* **Journal of Adolescent and Adult Literacy.**

## Bibliographies

Adamson, L. G. (1997). *Literature connections to American history, K–6: Resources to enhance and entice.* Englewood, NJ: Libraries Unlimited.

> *An annotated bibliography of materials divided by format includes age ranges, descriptive synopses, and awards received. It also includes an excellent subject index and author, illustrator, and title indices.*

———. (1998). *American historical fiction: An annotated guide to novels for adults and young adults published since 1985.* Phoenix, AZ: Oryx.

> *Adamson provides readers with plot summaries of well-written historical fiction.*

*The black experience in children's books.* (1999). New York: New York Public Library.

> *This periodically revised pamphlet briefly annotates folklore, fiction, and nonfiction written for children from preschool to age 12 that portrays African-American life.*

Cerullo, M. M. (1997). *Reading the environment: Children's literature in the science curriculum.* Portsmouth, NH: Heinemann.

> *Cerullo provides criteria for selecting science books and then provides a bibliography of recommended fiction and nonfiction about earth science, oceans, weather, seasons, and movement of water.*

*Children's book review index.* (1975–2000). Detroit: Gale Research.

> *This annual work indexes the reviews appearing in two hundred periodicals. This work compiles citations appearing in* **Book Review Index,** *which locates reviews of books written for children and young adults.*

*Children's books: Awards & prizes.* (1996). Children's Book Council (Compiler-Ed.). New York: The Children's Book Council, Inc.

> *Major domestic and international children's book awards and prizes are identified in this frequently revised book.*

*Children's books in print.* (Published annually). New Providence, NJ: R. R. Bowker.

> *This is an index of juvenile titles that are listed in publishers' catalogs as "in print," but it does not always include books from smaller publishing companies. This work includes a separate listing of addresses of publishers.*

*The children's catalog* (17th ed, supplement). (2000). J. Yaakov (Ed.). New York: H. W. Wilson.

> *Part 1 lists books and magazines recommended for preschool children through sixth-graders, as well as useful professional resources. Part 2 helps the user locate entries through one alphabetical, comprehensive key that includes author, title, subject, and analytical listings.*

Day, F. A. (2000). *Lesbian and gay voices: An annotated guide to literature for children and young adults.* Westport, CT: Greenwood.

> *This thorough guide provides detailed, critical annotations for more than 275 recommended books.*

Denenberg, D. & Roscoe, L. (1994). *Hooray for heroes!: Books and activities kids want to share with their parents and teachers.* Metuchen, NJ: Scarecrow Press.

> *A bibliography of biographies for children and related activities that will be a useful tool for teachers.*

*The elementary school library collection: A guide to books and other media* (22nd ed.). (2000). Williamsport, PA: Brodart.

*In addition to books and periodicals, this work also recommends all kinds of nonprint media and resources for teachers and parents. Entries provide critically descriptive annotations as well as such information as priority for acquisition and estimates of reading level and interest level.*

Fredericks, A. D. (1999). *Science adventures with children's literature: A thematic approach.* Illustrated by A. A. Stoner. Englewood, NJ: Libraries Unlimited.

*This idea book features thematic resource lists of more than 400 trade books with activities.*

Friedler, A. B. (1997). *Guide to the 400 best children's and adults' multicultural books about lesbian and gay people.* Newton Centre, MA: Lift Every Voice.

*An annotated list of books for children and adults about gays and lesbians.*

Gunning, T. G. (1998). *Best books for beginning readers.* Needham Heights, MA: Allyn and Bacon.

———. (2000). *Best books for building literacy for elementary school children.* Needham Heights, MA: Allyn and Bacon.

*Gunning provides explanations of reading levels and useful lists of recommended books by reading levels for beginning and transitional readers.*

Kaczmarski, K. (1998). *Exploring math with books kids love.* Golden, CO: Fulcrum.

*This book with a bibliography integrates math and literature for grades 4–8.*

Krey, D. (1998). *Children's literature in the social studies: Teaching to the standards.* Washington, DC: National Council for the Social Studies.

*Krey identifies excellent children's books published between 1990 and 1997 that can be used for teaching each of 10 social studies themes at different levels.*

Kruse, G. M., Horning, K. T., & Schliesman, M. (1997). *Multicultural literature for children and young adults: A selected listing of books by and about people of color* (4th ed.). Madison, WI: Wisconsin Department of Public Instruction.

*This reference annotates recently published multicultural books recommended for their high quality.*

Lewis, V., & Mayes, W. M. (1998) *Valerie and Walter's best books for children.* New York: Avon.

*A guide for parents, educators, and librarians that lists and annotates more than 2,000 children's books. Readable reviews with information about reading and listening levels.*

Lima, C. W., & Lima, J. A. (2001). *A to zoo: Subject access to children's picture books* (6th ed.). New York: R. R. Bowker.

*This index indicates the subject matter of 14,000 picture books for children with access through author, illustrator, and title, as well as 800 subjects.*

Muse, D. (Ed.). (1998). *The New Press guide to multicultural resources for young readers.* New York: New Press.

*Features more than 1,000 reviews of books that deal with diverse ethnic and racial groups as well as disabled persons and gay and lesbian communities.*

NCTE bibliography series (National Council of Teachers of English):

*Adventuring with books: A booklist for pre-K–grade 6* (12th ed.). (2000). Urbana, IL: NCTE.

*Kaleidoscope: A multicultural booklist for grades K–8.* (2nd ed.) (1997). Urbana, IL: NCTE.

*Your reading: An annotated booklist for junior high and middle-school students* (10th ed.). (1995). Urbana, IL: NCTE.

*All of these books include annotated listings of fiction and nonfiction books recommended for children and young people in the grades specified in each title.*

*The Newbery and Caldecott Awards: A guide to the medal and honor books.* (1999). Chicago: American Library Association.

*This annual guide includes annotations on each of the award winners and honor books, as well as information concerning the criteria on which the awards are based.*

Oaks, H. (Ed.). (1996). *Outstanding plays for young audiences: International bibliography,* vol. 5. Seattle, WA: United States Center for the International Association of Theatre for Children and Young People.

Phelan, C. (1996). *Science books for young people.* Chicago: American Library Association.

*An annotated bibliography of 500 of the best science books published from 1990 to 1995.*

Roberts, P. L. (1997). *Taking humor seriously in children's literature: Literature-based mini-units and humorous books for children.* Lanham, MD: Scarecrow.

*Roberts outlines types of humor and describes curriculum units based on popular children's books. A good annotated bibliography that includes more than 500 titles.*

Schon, I. (2000). *Books in Spanish for children and young adults: An annotated guide* (1996–1999). Metuchen, NJ: Scarecrow Press.

*Periodic volumes each cover a three-year period. These are selection guides for books in Spanish written by Hispanic authors for children, preschool through high school. The list is comprehensive and includes some negative reviews because not all of the included books are recommended.*

Slaight, C., & Esty, J. (Eds.). (1997). *The Smith and Kraus play index for young actors.* North Stratford, NH: Smith and Kraus.

*A play index of over 500 plays for elementary, middle, and high school students includes ordering information. Each play is described in detail with the number of cast members, and time and place of setting.*

Slapin, B., & Seale, D. (1999). *Through Indian eyes: The native experience in books for children* (4th ed.). Los Angeles: American Indian Studies Center, UCLA.

*An annotated bibliography with critical reviews of children's books about Native Americans.*

Stoll, D. R. (Ed.). (1997). *Magazines for kids and teens.* Newark, DE: International Reading Association.

*Describes 249 magazines geared toward children from ages 2 to 17. Information concerning circulation, cost, and frequency of publication is included, as well as indexes of age levels, subjects, and whether the magazine publishes readers' writing.*

*Subject guide to children's books in print* (Published annually). New York: R. R. Bowker.

*This comprehensive reference provides a subject approach to children's books in print. A directory of publishers and distributors is included.*

Susag, D. M. (1998). *Roots and branches: A resource of Native American literature—Themes, lessons, and bibliographies.* Urbana, IL: National Council of Teachers of English.

*Susag examines the historical and literary contexts of Native American literature. Also provides lessons, activities, and detailed, annotated bibliographies.*

Tomlinson, C. M. (Ed.). (1998). *Children's books from other countries.* Lanham, MD: Scarecrow Press.

*This complete guide to international children's literature with an annotated bibliography of 724 children's books also provides suggestions on sharing international books with children.*

Van Orden, P. (2000). *Selecting books for the elementary school library media center: A complete guide.* New York: Neal-Schuman.

*An essential tool for new school libraries and useful for most libraries in balancing collections.*

## Review Journals

*Booklist.* Published twice monthly September through June and monthly in July and August by American Library Association, 50 E. Huron St., Chicago, IL 60611.

*This journal reviews current print and nonprint materials for children and adults that are worthy of consideration for purchase by small and medium-sized public libraries and school media centers.*

*The Bulletin of the Center for Children's Books.* Published monthly except August by the University of Illinois Press, 1325 S. Oak, Champaign, IL 61820.

*This publication reviews current children's books, with adverse as well as favorable reviews, assigning a recommendation code to each. An age or grade level is given to each book, and annotations include information on curricular use, developmental values, and literary merit.*

*Children's Book News.* Quarterly newsletter published by the Canadian Children's Book Center, 35 Spadina Road, Toronto, Ontario M5R 2S9.

*This newsletter features articles and reviews; it lists all children's books published in Canada. Subscribers also receive* **Our Choice: Your Annual Guide to Canada's Best Children's Books,** *which contains brief reviews of the three hundred best Canadian children's books of the year.*

*Children's Book and Play Review.* Published five times a year by Brigham Young University, Marsha D. Broadway, Managing Editor, Children's Book and Play Review, Harold B. Lee Library, Brigham Young University, Provo, UT 84602

*This journal reviews children's books and plays and includes three or four feature articles about plays in each volume.*

*The Horn Book Guide to Children's and Young Adult Books.* Published twice a year in March and September by the Horn Book, Inc., 11 Beacon Street, Suite 1000, Boston, MA 02108.

**The Horn Book Guide** *contains brief reviews of all hardcover children's trade books published in the United States during the previous six months.*

*The Horn Book Magazine.* Published six times a year by the Horn Book, Inc., 11 Beacon Street, Suite 1000, Boston, MA 02108.

*This magazine includes detailed reviews of children's books deemed the best in children's literature by the editorial staff. It also contains articles about literature and interviews with authors. The Newbery and Caldecott acceptance speeches are features in the July/August issue.*

*School Library Journal: The Magazine of Children's, Young Adult, and School Librarians.* A Cahners/R. R. Bowker Publication, published monthly. For subscription information, write to School Library Journal, P.O. Box 1978, Marion, OH 43305–1978.

*This journal prints both negative and positive reviews of most children's books published. It also includes articles of interest to school librarians.*

## PROFESSIONAL ORGANIZATIONS

American Alliance of Theatre and Education. (AATE). c/o Arizona State University, Theatre Department, P.O. Box 872002, Tempe, AZ 85287–2002.

American Library Association. 50 E. Huron Street, Chicago, IL 60611. Special Divisions: Association for Library Service to Children, Young Adult Library Services Association.

Association of Childhood Education International, 11501 Georgia Avenue, Suite 315, Wheaton, MD 20902–2443.

Children's Book Council. 568 Broadway, Suite 404, New York, NY 10012.

Children's Literature Association. 210 Education Department, Purdue University, West Lafayette, IN 47907.

International Reading Association. 800 Barksdale Road, P.O. Box 8139, Newark, DE 19714–8139. Special Interest Group: Children's Literature and Reading.

National Council of Teachers of English. 1111 W. Kenyon Road, Urbana, IL 61801–1096. Special Interest Group: Children's Literature Assembly.

United States Board on Books for Young People. USBBY Secretariat, International Reading Association, P.O. Box 8139, Newark, DE 19714–8139.

United States Center for the International Association of Theatre for Children and Young People. (ASSITEJ/USA). 742 2nd Avenue S., Nashville, TN 37210–2006.

## WEB SITES

Association for Library Service to Children (ALSC)
Site: http://www.ala.org/alsc/

*Includes the Newbery and Caldecott home pages. New awards are announced on this site.*

Carol Hurst's Children's Literature Site:
http://www.carolhurst.com/

*Provides a collection of book reviews, curriculum ideas, themes, and professional topics for teachers.*

The Children's Book Council (CBC) Site:
http://www.cbcbooks.org/

*This nonprofit association of children's book publishers offers book-related literacy materials for children. Also provides information an National Children's Book Week.*

Cooperative Children's Book Center Site:
http://www.soemadison.wisc.edu/ccbc/

*Learn about the University of Wisconsin's CCBC collections, upcoming events, and publications.*

Kay Vandergrift's Special Interest Page:
http://www.scils.rutgers.edu/special/kay/kayhp2.html

*A large site with information about children's and young adult literature that includes many links.*

*Booklist* site: http:/www.ala.org/booklist/

*Includes selected reviews, articles, and cumulative index of the review journal* **Booklist** *from the American Library Association.*

# CHILDREN'S MAGAZINES

*The following list includes some of the most popular children's magazines available to young people today. A more complete list of children's magazines may be found in D. R. Stoll, Ed. (1997),* **Magazines for Kids and Teens** *(International Reading Association). The following list is organized by subject of primary emphasis.*

## Drama

***Plays, the Drama Magazine for Young People.*** Scripts for plays, skits, puppet shows, and round-the-table readings (a type of readers' theatre). 8–10 scripts per issue. Ages 6–17. 7 issues/year. Order from: Plays, Inc., Kalmbach Publishing Co., 21027 Crossroads Circle, Waukesha, WI 53187. Web site: www.playsmag.com

## Geography

***World Newsmap of the Week/Headline Focus.*** News summaries, maps, background information, graphics, and teaching suggestions. Ages 10–17. Weekly. Order from: Weekly Reader Corp., 3001 Cindel Drive, Delran, NJ 08370.

## Health

***Child Life.*** Articles, fiction, activities with an emphasis on nutrition and safety. Ages 9–11. 8 issues/year. Similar magazines for different age groups by the same publisher include ***Humpty Dumpty's Magazine*** (ages 4–6), ***Children's Playmate Magazine*** (ages 6–8), ***Jack and Jill*** (ages 7–10), and ***Children's Digest*** (preteen). Order from: (Magazine title), P. O. Box 7133, Red Oak, IA 51591–0133.

## History

***Calliope.*** Articles, stories, time lines, maps, and authentic photos to generate an interest in world history. Themed issues. Ages 8–15. 9 issues/year. Order from: Cobblestone Publishing, Inc., 30 Grove Street, Suite C, Peterborough, NH 03458.

***Cobblestone.*** Articles about U.S. history. Themed issues. Ages 9–15. 9 issues/year. Order from: Cobblestone Publishing, Inc., 30 Grove Street, Suite C, Peterborough, NH 03458.

*Footsteps.* Themed issues incorporate art, poetry, literature, and information about historical and cultural sites related to African-American history. Ages 9–14. 5 issues/year. Order from: Cobblestone Publishing, Inc., 30 Grove Street, Suite C, Peterborough, NH 03458. Web site: www.cobblestonepub.com/pages/footmain.htm

## Language

*Bonjour.* Topics of interest to 13- to 15-year-olds in French. Information and cultural details of French-speaking countries. 6 issues/year.

*Das Rad.* Topics of interest to 13- to 16-year-olds in German. Information and cultural details of German-speaking countries. 6 issues/year.

*¿Qué Tal?* Topics of interest to 11- to 16-year-olds in Spanish. Information and cultural details of Spanish-speaking countries. 6 issues/year. Order all language magazines from: (Magazine title), Scholastic, Inc., 2931 E. McCarty Street, P. O. Box 3710, Jefferson City, MO 65102–3710. Web site for this and all Scholastic magazines: http://teacher.scholastic.com/products/classmags

## Language Arts

*Merlyn's Pen: The National Magazine of Student Writing.* Fiction, nonfiction, and poetry by students in grades 6–9. Ages 12–15. 4 issues/year. Order from: Merlyn's Pen, Inc. P. O. Box 910, East Greenwich, RI 02818.

*Scholastic Scope.* Plays, short stories, reading lists, writing exercises, and skill builders. Ages 12–17. 18 issues/year. Order from: Scholastic, Inc., 2931 E. McCarty Street, P. O. Box 3710, Jefferson City, MO 65102.

*Scholastic Story Works.* Focuses on development of basic reading and writing skills. Ages 8–11. 7 issues/year. Order from: Scholastic, Inc., 2931 E. McCarty Street, P. O. Box 3710, Jefferson City, MO 65102.

*Stone Soup: The Magazine by Young Writers and Artists.* Stories, poems, book reviews, and art by children through age 13. Ages 6–13. 5 issues/year. Order from: Stone Soup, Children's Art Foundation, P. O. Box 83, Santa Cruz, CA 95063.

*Writing!* Articles, advice, exercises for writing improvement, interviews with successful authors. Ages 12–17. 7 issues/year. Order from: Writing!, Weekly Reader Corp., 3001 Cindel Drive, Delran, NJ 08370.

## Literature

*Cricket.* Fiction, nonfiction, book reviews, activities. Features international literature. Ages 9–14. 12 issues/year. Order from: P. O. Box 7436, Red Oak, IA 51591–0436. Web site for this and all Cricket magazines: www.cricketmag.com

*Lady Bug.* Fiction, poems, songs, and games. Ages 2–6. 12 issues/year. Order from: P. O. Box 7436, Red Oak, IA 51591–0436.

*Spider.* Fiction, poems, songs, and games for the beginning reader. Ages 6–9. 12 issues/year. Order from: P. O. Box 7436, Red Oak, IA 51591–0436.

## Math

*Scholastic Dynamath.* Humorously formatted word problems, computation, and test preparation. Ages 10–12. 8 issues/year. Order from: Scholastic, Inc., 2931 E. McCarty Street, P. O. Box 3710, Jefferson City, MO 65102–3710.

*Scholastic Math Magazine.* Math problems, computation, statistics, consumer math, real-life applications, career math, critical reasoning. Ages 12–14. 14 issues/year. Order from: Scholastic, Inc., 2931 E. McCarty Street, P. O. Box 3710, Jefferson City, MO 65102–3710.

## Nature

*National Geographic World.* Nonfiction articles and nature photography. Promotes geographic awareness. Ages 8–14. 12 issues/year. Order from: National Geographic World, P. O. Box 2330, Washington, DC 20013–2330. Web site: www.nationalgeographic.com/world

*Ranger Rick.* Fiction and nonfiction, photoessays, jokes, riddles, crafts, plays, and poetry promoting the appreciation of nature. Superlative nature photography. Ages 6–12. 12 issues/year. Order from: Ranger Rick, National Wildlife Federation, 8925 Leesburg Pike, Vienna, VA 22184–0001. Web site: www.nwf.org/rangerrick

*Your Big Backyard.* Animal and nature stories and photography for the preschooler. Ages 3–6. 12 issues/year. Order from: Your Big Backyard, National Wildlife Federation, 8925 Leesburg Pike, Vienna, VA 22184–0001. Web site: www.nwf.org/yourbigbackyard

## Recreation

*Boys' Life.* News, nature, sports, history, fiction, science, comics, Scouting, colorful graphics, and photos. Published by the Boy Scouts of America. Ages 7–18. 12 issues/year. Order from: Subscription Service, 1325 Walnut Hill Lane, P. O. Box 152079, Irving, TX 75015–2079.

*Highlights for Children.* General-interest magazine offering fiction and nonfiction, crafts, poetry, and thinking features. Ages 2–12. 11 issues/year. Order from: Highlights, P. O. Box 269, Columbus, OH 43272–0002.

*New Moon: The Magazine for Girls and Their Dreams.* An international magazine by and about girls. Builds healthy resistance to gender inequities. Ages 8–14. 6 issues/year. Order from: New Moon, P.O. Box 3587, Duluth, MN 55803–3587. Web site: www.newmooncatalog.com

## Science

*Click.* Stories, concept pieces, photography, and posters featuring science for the very young. Ages 3–7. 6 issues/year. Order from Click, Box 7499, Red Oak, IA 51591–2499.

*Current Science.* News in science, health, and technology; science activities, U.S. national science projects, science mystery photos, and kids in the news. Ages 12–15. 14 issues/year. Order from: Weekly Reader Corp., 3001 Cindel Drive, Delran, NJ 08370.

*Dragonfly.* Themed issues in this inquiry-driven magazine include articles, poetry, autobiographies, natural history essays, humor, artwork, and other creative expressions by children and research scientists. Bimonthly. Order from: Project Dragonfly, Miami University, Oxford, OH 45056.

*Odyssey.* Articles and illustrations on astronomy, space exploration, and technology. Ages 8–14. 9 issues/year. Order from: Cobblestone Publishing, Inc., 30 Grove Street, Suite C, Peterborough, NH 03458.

*Scienceland.* Nurtures scientific thinking about nature and physical science through content reading. Ages 5–10. 4 issues/year. Order from: Scienceland, 501 Fifth Avenue, Suite 2108, New York, NY 10017–6107.

*Science World.* Articles, experiments, and news to supplement the science curriculum. Ages 12–16. 14 issues/year. Order from: Science World, Scholastic, Inc., 2931 E. McCarty Street, P. O. Box 3710, Jefferson City, MO 65102–9957.

*SuperScience* (Red Edition). Science concepts, critical thinking, and reasoning through hands-on activities and experiments. Themed issues. Ages 6–8. 8 issues/year. Order from: SuperScience "Red," Scholastic, Inc., 2931 E. McCarty Street, Jefferson City, MO 65101–3710.

*SuperScience* (Blue Edition). Same general format as Red Edition. Ages 9–11. 6 issues/year. Order from: SuperScience "Blue," Scholastic, Inc., 2931 E. McCarty Street, Jefferson City, MO 65101–3710.

*3–2–1 Contact.* Articles on animals, nature, psychology, and sociology; information on math and computers; puzzles, games, and experiments. Ages 8–12. 10 issues/year. Order from: 3–2–1 Contact, P. O. Box 51177, Boulder, CO 80322–1177.

## Social Studies

**Faces.** Articles and activities exploring human diversity. Features lifestyles, beliefs, and customs throughout the world. Ages 8–14. 9 issues/year. Order from: Faces, Cobblestone Publishing, Inc., 30 Grove Street, Suite C, Peterborough, NH 03458.

**Junior Scholastic.** Features U.S. and world history, current events, world cultures, map skills, and geography. Ages 11–14. 18 issues/year. Order from: Scholastic, Inc., 2931 E. McCarty Street, P. O. Box 3710, Jefferson City, MO 6510–9957.

**Muse.** Articles, photoessays, biographies, experiments, cartoons, and jokes. Ages 6–14. 6 issues/year. Joint publication of Cricket Magazine Group and Smithsonian Magazine. Order from Muse, Box 7468, Red Oak, IA 51591–2499.

**Skipping Stones: A Multicultural Children's Magazine.** Articles by, about, and for children about world cultures and cooperation. Multilingual. Ages 7–16. 5 issues/year. Order from: Skipping Stones, Box 3939, Eugene, OR 97403–0939. Web site: www.efn.org/~skipping

# SHORT STORY COLLECTIONS

*Ages refer to approximate interest levels.*
*YA = young adult readers.*

Ahlberg, Allan. *The Better Brown Stories.* Illustrated by Fritz Wagner. Viking, 1996. Ages 10–13.

Aiken, Joan. *Give Yourself a Fright: Thirteen Tales of the Supernatural.* Delacorte, 1989. Ages 11–YA.

———. *Past Eight O'Clock: Goodnight Stories.* Viking, 1987. Ages 8–11.

Alcock, Vivien. *Ghostly Companions: A Feast of Chilling Tales.* Delacorte, 1984. Ages 10–14.

Asher, Sandy, editor. *But That's Another Story: Favorite Authors Introduce Popular Genres.* Walker, 1996. Ages 10–13. Each story a specific genre with author explanation.

Atkin, S. Beth. *Voices from the Streets: Young Former Gang Members Tell Their Stories.* Little, Brown, 1996. Ages 13–YA.

Babbitt, Natalie. *The Devil's Other Storybook.* Farrar, 1987. Ages 9–12.

Bierhorst, John. *The Deetkatoo: Native American Stories about Little People.* Morrow, 1998. Ages 9–12.

Brooke, William J. *A Telling of the Tales: Five Stories.* Harper, 1990. Ages 9–12.

Brooks, Martha. *Paradise Café and Other Stories.* Little, Brown, 1990. Ages 12–YA.

Carlson, Lori M., & Cynthia Ventura, editors. *American Eyes: New Asian-American Short Stories for Young Adults.* Holt, 1994. Ages 13–YA.

———. *Where Angels Glide at Dawn: New Stories from Latin America.* Lippincott, 1990. Ages 10–14.

Carlstrom, Nancy White. *Light: Stories of a Small Kindness.* Illustrated by Desimini. Little, Brown, 1990. Ages 9–12.

Cart, Michael, compiler. *Tomorrowland: Ten Stories about the Future.* Scholastic, 1999. Ages 11–YA.

Carus, Marianne, editor. *That's Ghosts for You.* Front Street, 2000. Ages 9–12.

Cofer, Judith Ortiz. *An Island Like You: Short Stories of the Barrio.* Orchard, 1995. Ages 12–YA.

Coville, Bruce, editor. *Herds of Thunder, Manes of Gold: A Collection of Horse Stories and Poems.* Illustrated by Ted Lewin. Doubleday, 1990. Ages 9–YA.

Coville, Bruce. *Older Than Ever.* Harcourt, 1999. Ages 10–14.

Crutcher, Chris. *Athletic Shorts.* Greenwillow, 1991. Ages 12–YA.

Datlow, Ellen, and Terri Windling, editors. *A Wolf at the Door and Other Retold Fairy Tales.* Simon & Schuster, 2000. Ages 10–YA.

Dickinson, Peter. *The Lion Tamer's Daughter: And Other Stories.* Delacorte, 1997. Ages 10–YA.

Doyle, Malachy. *Tales from Old Ireland.* Barefoot Books, 2000. Ages 8–12.

Drimmer, Frederick. *Born Different: The Amazing Stories of Some Very Special People.* Atheneum, 1988. Ages 11–14.

Duncan, Lois, editor. *On the Edge: Stories at the Brink.* Simon & Schuster, 2000. Ages 10–YA.

Durell, Ann, & Marilyn Sachs. *The Big Book for Peace.* Dutton, 1990. Ages 9–12.

Fleischman, Paul. *Seedfolks.* HarperCollins, 1997. Thirteen loosely connected vignettes. Ages 9–14.

Gallo, Donald R., editor. *Ultimate Sports: Sports Stories by Outstanding Writers for Young Adults.* Delacorte, 1995. Ages 13–YA.

Galloway, Priscilla. *Truly Grim Tales.* Delacorte, 1995. Ages 12–YA. Eight folktales retold from different points of view.

Gantos, Jack. *Jack's New Power: Stories from a Caribbean Year.* Farrar, 1995. Ages 11–YA.

Haas, Jessie. *The Sixth Sense and Other Stories.* Greenwillow, 1988. Ages 9–12.

Holt, David, and Bill Mooney, editors. *More Ready-to-Tell Tales from Around the World.* August House, 2000. Ages 9–YA.

Hurwitz, Johanna, editor. *Birthday Surprises: Ten Great Stories to Unwrap.* Morrow, 1995. Ages 9–12.

Jiménez, Francisco. *The Circuit: Stories from the Life of a Migrant Child.* University of New Mexico, 1996. Ages 12–14.

Johnson, Angela. *Gone from Home: Short Takes.* DK Ink, 1998. Ages 12–YA.

Joseph, Lynn. *A Wave in Her Pocket: Stories from Trinidad.* Illustrated by Brian Pinkney. Clarion, 1991. Ages 8–10.

Konigsburg, E. L. *Throwing Shadows.* Peter Smith, 1994 (1979). Ages 10–14. Won the Phoenix Award in 1999.

Larsen, Jean Russell, reteller. *The Fish Bride and Other Gypsy Tales.* Illustrated by Michael Larson. Linnet, 2000. Ages 9–13.

Leary, Una, reteller. *Irish Fairy Tales and Legends.* Rinehart, 1997. Ages 8–11.

Little, Jean. *Hey World, Here I Am!* HarperCollins, 1989. Ages 12–YA.

Lunge-Larsen, Lise, reteller. *The Troll with No Heart in His Body: And Other Tales of Trolls from Norway.* Illustrated by Betsy Bowen. Houghton, 1999. Ages 7–9.

Mama, Raouf, reteller. *The Barefoot Book of Tropical Tales.* Illustrated by Deirdre Hyde. Barefoot Books, 2000. Ages 7–11.

Mazer, Harry, editor. *Twelve Shots: Outstanding Short Stories about Guns.* Delacorte, 1997. Ages 13–YA. Impact of guns on the main characters.

McKee, Tim. *No More Strangers Now: Young Voices from a New South Africa.* Illustrated by Anne Blackshaw. DK Ink, 1998. Ages 10–YA.

Miller, Brandon Marie. *Buffalo Gals: Women of the Old West.* Lerner, 1995. Ages 9–13. Stories of women pioneers in the 1830s to 1890s.

Myers, Walter Dean. *145th Street Stories.* Delacorte, 2000. Ages 11–YA.

Nixon, Joan Lowry. *Ghost Town: Seven Ghostly Stories.* Delacorte, 2000. Ages 10–YA.

Park, Ruth. *Things in Corners.* Viking, 1991. Ages 11–13.

Pearce, Philippa. *Who's Afraid? And Other Strange Stories.* Greenwillow, 1987. Ages 9–12.

Rappaport, Doreen. *Escape from Slavery: Five Journeys to Freedom.* Illustrated by Charles Lilly. HarperCollins, 1991. Ages 11–13.

Rochman, Hazel, editor. *Somehow Tenderness Survives: Stories of Southern Africa.* HarperCollins, 1988. Ages 12–YA.

———, & Darlene Z. McCampbell, editors. *Leaving Home.* HarperCollins, 1997. Ages 11–YA.

Rocklin, Joanne. *Strudel Stories.* Delacorte, 1999. Ages 8–11.

Rylant, Cynthia. *A Couple of Kooks and Other Stories.* Watts, 1990. Ages 12–YA.

———. *Every Living Thing.* Bradbury, 1985. Ages 10–14. Effect of animals on the lives of the main characters.

San Souci, Robert D. *Short and Shivery: Thirty Chilling Tales.* Illustrated by Katherine Coville. Doubleday, 1987. Ages 9–12.

———, reteller. *A Terrifying Taste of Short and Shivery: Thirty Creepy Tales.* Illustrated by Lenny Wooden. Delacorte, 1998. Ages 10–14..

Segel, Elizabeth, editor. *Short Takes: A Short Story Collection for Young Readers.* Lothrop, 1986. Ages 8–11.

Silvey, Anita, editor. *Help Wanted: Short Stories about Young People Working.* Little, Brown, 1997. Ages 12–YA.

Soto, Gary. *Baseball in April, and Other Stories.* Harcourt, 1990. Ages 10–14.

———. *Petty Crimes.* Harcourt, 1998. Ages 10–YA.

Taylor, Theodore. *Rogue Wave: And Other Red-Blooded Sea Stories.* Harcourt, 1996. Ages 10–YA.

Testa, Maria. *Dancing Pink Flamingos and Other Stories.* Lerner, 1995. Ages 14–YA.

Thomas, Joyce Carol, editor. *A Gathering of Flowers: Stories about Being Young in America.* Harper, 1990. Ages 10–13.

Thomas, Rob. *Doing Time: Notes from the Undergrad.* Simon & Schuster, 1997. Ages 13–YA. Ten vignettes on volunteer work.

Turner, Megan Whelan. *Instead of Three Wishes.* Greenwillow, 1995. Ages 8–12.

Vande Velde, Vivian. *Curses, Inc.: And Other Stories.* Harcourt, 1997. Ages 11–YA.

———. *The Rumplestiltskin Problem.* Houghton, 2000. Ages 10–YA.

———. *Tales from the Brothers Grimm and the Sisters Weird.* Harcourt, 1995. Ages 9–13. Retelling of traditional folktales.

Van Laan, Nancy. *With a Whoop and a Holler: A Bushel of Lore from Way Down South.* Atheneum, 1998. Ages 9–12.

Wilson, Budge. *The Dandelion Garden.* Philomel, 1995. Ages 13–YA.

———. *The Leaving.* Philomel, 1992. Ages 13–YA.

Wyeth, Sharon D. *Vampire Bugs: Stories Conjured from the Past.* Illustrated by Curtis E. James. Delacorte, 1995. Ages 8–13.

Wynne-Jones, Tim. *The Book of Changes.* Orchard, 1995. Ages 11–14.

———. *Lord of the Fries and Other Stories.* DK Ink, 1999. Ages 10–13.

———. *Some of the Kinder Planets.* Orchard, 1995. Ages 9–13.

Yee, Paul. *Tales from Gold Mountain: Stories of the Chinese in the New World.* Macmillan, 1989. Ages 9–12.

Yolen, Jane. *The Faery Flag: Stories and Poems of Fantasy and the Supernatural.* Orchard, 1989. Ages 10–14.

———, and Martin H. Greenberg, editors. *Things That Go Bump in the Night: A Collection of Original Stories.* Harper, 1989. Ages 10–14.

———, Martin H. Greenberg, & Charles G. Waugh, editors. *Dragons and Dreams: A Collection of New Fantasy and Science Fiction Stories.* Harper, 1986. Ages 9–12.

———, editors. *Spaceships & Spells: A Collection of New Fantasy and Science Fiction Stories.* Harper, 1987. Ages 10–13.

# TRANSITIONAL BOOKS

*These books are generally suitable for ages 6–9.*

Baker, Barbara. *Digby and Kate and the Beautiful Day.* Dutton, 1998.

Banks, Kate. *Howie Bowles, Secret Agent.* Illustrated by Isaac Millman. Farrar, 1999.

Brown, Marc T. (creator), and Stephen Krensky. *Arthur and the Big Blow-up.* Illustrated by Marc Brown. Little Brown, 2000. (Representative of others in the lengthy Arthur Chapter Book series: *Arthur and the Perfect Big Brother; Francine, the Superstar.*)

Bulla, Clyde Robert. *Shoeshine Girl.* Illustrated by Jim Burke. Crowell, 1994 (1975).

Byars, Betsy. *Beans on the Roof.* Illustrated by Melodye Rosales. Delacorte, 1990 (1988).

Cameron, Ann. *Stories Julian Tells.* Illustrated by Ann Strugnell. Knopf, 1989 (1984). (Others in this series: *More Stories Julian Tells; Julian's Glorious Summer; Julian, Dream Doctor; Julian, Secret Agent,* all published by Random House.)

dePaola, Tomie. *26 Fairmount Avenue.* Putnam, 1999.

Fowler, Susi Gregg. *Albertina, the Animals, and Me.* Illustrated by Jim Fowler. Greenwillow, 2000.

————. *Albertina the Practically Perfect.* Illustrated by Jim Fowler. Greenwillow, 1998.

Greene, Stephanie. *Owen Foote, Frontiersman.* Illustrated by Martha Weston. Clarion, 1999.

Jukes, Mavis. *Blackberries in the Dark.* Illustrated by Thomas B. Allen. Random House, 1994 (originally published by Knopf, 1985).

Korschunow, Irina. *Adam Draws Himself a Dragon.* Translated from German by James Skofield. Illustrated by Mary Rahn. Harper, 1987.

Lewis, Maggy. *Morgy Makes His Move.* Illustrated by Michael Chesworth. Houghton, 1999.

Marshall, James. *Rats on the Roof and Other Stories.* Dial, 1991.

McDonough, Yona Zeldis. *The Dollhouse Magic.* Illustrated by Diane Palmisciano. Holt, 2000.

Parish, Peggy. *Amelia Bedelia.* Illustrated by Lynn Sweat. Econo-Clad, 1999 (originally published by Greenwillow, 1985). (Others in this series: *Amelia Bedelia Helps Out; Amelia Bedelia Goes Camping; Amelia Bedelia and the Baby; Amelia Bedelia's Family Album.*)

Peck, Robert Newton. *Soup.* Knopf, 1998 (1974). (Others in this series: *Soup for President; Soup in the Saddle; Soup's Goat; Soup on Ice; Soup's Hoop-Yearling.*)

Rodowsky, Colby. *Not My Dog.* Illustrated by Thomas F. Yezerski. Farrar, 1999.

Sachar, Louis. *Marvin Redpost: A Flying Birthday Cake?* Illustrated by Amy Wummer. Random House, 1999. (Another in this series: *Marvin Redpost: A Magic Crystal?*)

Scieszka, Jon. *Knights of the Kitchen Table.* Illustrated by Lane Smith. Viking, 1991. (Also in *The Time Warp Trio* series: *The Not-So-Jolly Roger.*)

Sobol, Donald J. *Encyclopedia Brown: Boy Detective.* Illustrated by Leonard Shortall, Bantam, 1985 (originally published by Scholastic, 1968). (Others in this series: *Encyclopedia Brown Tracks Them Down; Encyclopedia Brown and the Case of the Secret Pitch; Encyclopedia Brown and the Case of the Mysterious Handprints; Encyclopedia Brown and the Case of the Midnight Visitor; Encyclopedia Brown Sets the Pace; Encyclopedia Brown Solves Them All.*)

Stolz, Mary. *The Bully of Barkham Street.* Illustrated by Leonard Shortall. HarperTrophy, 1985. (1963).

———. *A Dog on Barkham Street.* Illustrated by Leonard Shortall. HarperTrophy, 1985 (1960).

These pages constitute a continuation of the copyright page.

Front End Page: "A Story Is a Doorway," by Richard Peck. Copyright by Richard Peck. Reprinted by permission of the author.

Page 1: "Books Fall Open." From *One at a Time* by David McCord. Copyright 1965, 1966 by David McCord. By permission of Little, Brown and Company.

Page 37: "Poetry," by Eleanor Farjeon. From *Eleanor Farjeon's Poems for Children*. Copyright © 1951 by Eleanor Farjeon. Reprinted by permission of Harold Ober Associates, Incorporated.

Pages 40–41: "Song for a Blue Roadster," by Rachel Field. From *Poems* by Rachel Field (Macmillan, NY, 1957). Reprinted with permission of Simon & Schuster Books for Young Readers, an imprint of Simon & Schuster Children's Publishing Division.

Page 41: "Slowly." From *The Wondering Moon*. Published by William Heinemann Ltd. Copyright © The Estate of James Reeves, 1950.

Page 46: "Giraffes." From *Triptich* by Sy Kahn. By permission of the author.

Page 47: "The Broken Legg'd Man." From *The Things I Want: Poems for Two Children* by John Mackey Shaw. Copyright 1967 by the John M. Shaw Collection, Florida State University Library. Reprinted with permission.

Page 49: "Small Bird, Forgive Me." From *More Cricket Songs*, Japanese haiku translated by Harry Behn. Copyright © 1971 by Harry Behn. Reprinted by permission of Marian Reiner.

Page 49: "Last Day of School." From *Cold Stars and Fireflies: Poems of the Four Seasons* by Barbara Juster Esbensen. Copyright © 1984 by Barbara Juster Esbensen. Used by permission of Harper-Collins publishers.

Page 72: "My Book!" from *Somebody Catch My Homework*. Text copyright © 1993 by David L. Harrison. Published by Wordsong, Boyds Mills Press, Inc. Reprinted by permission.

Page 97: "Listen!" by Walter de la Mare. From *The Complete Poems of Walter de la Mare*. Reprinted by permission of the Literary Trustees of Walter de la Mare and the Society of Authors as their representative.

Page 114: "Ladder to the Sky." Text copyright © 1987 by Sheree Fitch. From *Toes in My Nose* by Sheree Fitch. Published by Boyds Mills Press, Inc. Reprinted by permission.

Page 131: "Listening to Grownups Quarreling." From the *Marriage Wig and Other Poems*. Copyright © 1968 and renewed 1998 by Ruth Whitman. Reprinted by permission of Harcourt Brace & Company.

Page 151: "Ancestors" by Grey Cohoe. From *Whispering Wind* by Terry Allen. Copyright © 1972 by the Institute of American Indian Arts. Used by permission of Doubleday, a division of Random House, Inc.

Page 168: "Questions at Night." From *Rainbow in the Sky*. Copyright 1935 and renewed 1963 by Louis Untermeyer. Reprinted by permission of Harcourt Brace & Company.

# S UBJECT INDEX

*Page numbers for figures and tables are followed by f and t, respectively.*